AA

THE
RESTAURANT
GUIDE
2019

D1099217

Image credits:
The Automobile Association wishes to thank the following photographers and organisations for their assistance in the preparation of this book.

Abbreviations for the picture credits are as follows – (t) top; (b) bottom; (l) left; (r) right; (c) centre; (AA) AA World Travel Library.

11tl Courtesy of Sorrel, Dorking; 11tr Courtesy of Sabor, London W1; 11bl Courtesy of The Newport Restaurant, Newport-on-Tay; 11br Courtesy of Machine House, Wrexham; 12 Courtesy of Claude Bosi at Bibendum; 14 Courtesy of Margot, London WC2; 18 Courtesy of The Brasserie, Milton Keynes College.

Every effort has been made to trace the copyright holders, and we apologise in advance for any unintentional omissions or errors. We would be pleased to apply any corrections in a following edition of this publication.

Photographs in the gazetteer are provided by the establishments.

This book was compiled by the AA Lifestyle Guides team and D & N Publishing, Baydon, Wiltshire.

Restaurant descriptions were contributed by Jackie Bates, Phil Bryant, Mike Pedley, Allen Stidwill, Mark Taylor, Andrew Turvil and Stuart Walton.

AA Lifestyle Guides would like to thank Carly Bristow, Geoff Chapman, Liz Haynes, Lin Hutton, David Popey, Jacqui Savage and Katharine Stockermans for their help in the preparation of this guide.

Cover design by Austin Taylor.

Printed in the UK by Bell & Bain.

ISBN: 978-0-7495-7984-5

A05604

Visit www.theaa.com/restaurants

Contents

Welcome to the
AA Restaurant Guide 2019

The AA Restaurant Guide has come a long way since its first edition in 1992. That year, the Rosette system was revised from 3 to 5 Rosette levels, which has been used ever since, and awarded to thousands of restaurants up and down the UK.

It's been a busy year for the AA inspectorate, making anonymous visits to hundreds of establishments and setting high standards of culinary excellence. See pages 6–7 for more details on how the food is assessed and the Rosettes awarded. At the time of publication, there are 17 five-Rosette, 45 four-Rosette and 225 three-Rosette restaurants, which form the Top Ten Percent as listed on pages 8–10. There are over 1,800 1 and 2-Rosette venues across the UK – they're all here in the guide.

Award winners

Our award winners are chosen as best in class by our Hospitality Awards panel. The RESTAURANTS OF THE YEAR for each of the home nations and London represent both established and up-and-coming places to eat that are sure to be stars of the future (see page 11). Likewise, the winner of our FOOD SERVICE AWARD (page 14) is a champion of that all-important connection with the most crucial aspect of a restaurant – the diners.

The AA CHEFS' CHEF OF THE YEAR is both a star in his field and with an international career that has led to him taking the reins and injecting new life into Bibendum. Read more on pages 12–13.

The AA WINE AWARDS (see pages 16–17) singles out three restaurants that our inspectors feel have shown a real passion for and knowledge of wine. This year's trio were chosen from around 950 wine list submissions. We've also highlighted over 260 notable wine lists throughout the guide – so look out for ⚑ NOTABLE WINE LIST.

It's not just the established and experienced venues that are celebrated by the AA. This year sees the third annual AA COLLEGE RESTAURANT OF THE YEAR award (see page 18), which is designed to mirror the main Rosette award process by highlighting the best catering college teams.

Things can change

The transient nature of the hospitality industry means that chefs move around all the time, and restaurants may change ownership. As any change at the multi-Rosette level requires a new inspection to verify their award, some of these restaurants appear in the guide with their Rosette level suspended at the time of going to press. Our inspections are ongoing throughout the year, however, so once their award is confirmed it will be published at www.theaa.com/restaurants where you can also read articles about recommended restaurants and get the latest news on AA award-winning venues.

Using the guide

A few handy tips to help you get the most out of using the AA Restaurant Guide. We send an annual questionnaire to restaurants and the information we provide is based on their responses.

1 Order
Restaurants are listed in country and county order, then by town and then alphabetically within the town. There is an index by restaurant name at the back of the guide.

2 AA Rosette award
Restaurants can be awarded from 1 to 5 Rosettes (see pages 6–7). 'Rosettes suspended' indicates that an award of 3 Rosettes or above was suspended shortly before going to press.

3 Food style
A summary of the main cuisine type(s). V indicates a vegetarian menu. Restaurants with some vegetarian dishes available are indicated under Notes. The description may provide further information about the food style.

4 Notable wine list
The symbol indicates a wine list chosen as notable by an AA panel (see pages 16–17).

5 Chef
The name of the chef(s) is as up-to-date as possible at the time of going to press, but changes in personnel often occur, and may affect both the style and quality of the restaurant.

6 Seats
Number of seats in the restaurant and private dining room.

7 Open/Closed
We note if a restaurant is open all year. Otherwise, we list a period or periods when a venue is closed. Check in advance via a venue's website for daily opening times.

8 Prices
We list minimum prices for Starter (S), Main (M) and Dessert (D) based on details provided by the restaurant. Service charges are not included here and may vary depending on the size of the party. Most restaurants will have some form of service charge.

9 Parking
Number of spaces for on-site parking or nearby parking.

10 Notes
Additional information regarding the availability of vegetarian dishes and their policy towards children. We recommend that you phone in advance to ensure that the establishment you have chosen has appropriate facilities.

1.——— NEWBURY
Donnington Valley Hotel & Spa
2.——— ⊛⊛ MODERN BRITISH **V** NOTABLE WINE LIST ——— 3–4.
01635 551199 | Old Oxford Road, Donnington,
RG14 3AG
www.donningtonvalley.co.uk
A likeable, informal sort of place, not least the Wine Press restaurant: a light-filled, raftered room on two levels. There's much to like on the menu too, with lots of modern takes on conventional British fare, such as a scrumptious Old Spot pig terrine.

5.——— **Chef** Darren Booker-Wilson **Seats** 120, Private dining 130 **Open** All year **Prices from** S £6.95, M £17, D £7.50 **Parking** 150 **Notes** Children welcome ——— 6–10.

5

How the AA assesses for Rosette awards

First introduced in 1956, the AA's Rosette award scheme was the first nationwide scheme for assessing the quality of food served by restaurants and hotels. It has been a 5-tier system since 1992.

A consistent approach

The Rosette scheme is an award, not a classification, and although there is necessarily an element of subjectivity when it comes to assessing taste, we aim for a consistent approach throughout the UK. Our awards are made solely on the basis of a meal visit or visits by one or more of our hotel and restaurant inspectors, who have an unrivalled breadth and depth of experience in assessing quality. Essentially it's a snapshot, whereby the entire meal including ancillary items (when served) are assessed. Of all the restaurants across the UK, approximately 10% are of a standard which is worthy of 1 Rosette and above.

What makes a restaurant worthy of a Rosette award?

For AA inspectors, the top and bottom line is the food. The taste of a dish is what counts, and whether it successfully delivers to the diner the promise of the menu. A restaurant is only as good as its worst meal. Although presentation and competent service should be appropriate to the style of the restaurant and the quality of the food, they cannot affect the Rosette assessment as such, either up or down. The summaries opposite indicate what our inspectors look for, but are intended only as guidelines. The AA is constantly reviewing its award criteria, and competition usually results in an all-round improvement in standards, so it becomes increasingly difficult for restaurants to reach an award level.

The next level

Receiving a Rosette is a huge achievement and something not to be underestimated. We are often asked by chefs and proprietors: "What is the difference between 1 and 5 Rosettes and how can I get to the next level?" We answer that it's how well a chef manages to apply advanced technique while retaining maximum flavour, and assuming an appropriate quality of source ingredients.

While we endeavour to work with the industry and promote great cooking across the UK, it is of paramount importance for chefs to always serve their market first. We recommend they don't chase awards, but see them as something to celebrate when they come along. Where, however, the winning of Rosettes is an aspiration, the simple guidelines, shown opposite, may help. Experiencing AA food tastings, enhanced food tastings or signing up to one of the AA Rosette Academies can also give further insight and guidance, but these are separate from the awards process and do not influence any assessments.

◉ One Rosette

These restaurants will be achieving standards that standout in their local area, featuring:
- food prepared with care, understanding and skill
- good quality ingredients

The same expectations apply to hotel restaurants where guests should be able to eat in with confidence and a sense of anticipation. *Around 45% of restaurants/hotels in this guide have one Rosette.*

◉◉ Two Rosettes

The best local restaurants, which aim for and achieve:
- higher standards
- better consistency
- greater precision is apparent in the cooking
- obvious attention to the selection of quality ingredients

Around 45% of restaurants/hotels in this guide have two Rosettes.

◉◉◉ Three Rosettes

These are outstanding restaurants that achieve standards that demand national recognition well beyond their local area. The cooking will be underpinned by:
- the selection and sympathetic treatment of the highest quality ingredients
- timing, seasoning and the judgment of flavour combinations will be consistently excellent

These virtues will tend to be supported by other elements such as intuitive service and a well-chosen wine list. *Around 10% of the restaurants/hotels in this guide have three Rosettes and above.*

◉◉◉◉ Four Rosettes

Among the top restaurants in the UK where the cooking demands national recognition. These restaurants will exhibit:
- intense ambition
- a passion for excellence
- superb technical skills
- remarkable consistency
- an appreciation of culinary traditions combined with a passionate desire for further exploration and improvement

45 restaurants in this guide have four Rosettes.

◉◉◉◉◉ Five Rosettes

The pinnacle, where the cooking compares with the best in the world. These restaurants will have:
- highly individual voices
- exhibit breathtaking culinary skills and set the standards to which others aspire, yet few achieve

17 restaurants in this guide have five Rosettes.

Announcements of awards

One and two Rosettes are awarded at the time of inspection. Three and four Rosette awards are announced twice during the year, but never at the time of inspection. Five Rosettes are awarded just once a year and never at the time of inspection.

The top ten percent

All the 3, 4 and 5 Rosette restaurants together comprise the top ten percent of restaurants in this guide – they're listed on pages 8–10.

Suspension of multi-Rosettes (3, 4, 5 Rosettes)

When a chef holds 3, 4 or 5 Rosettes and moves from one establishment to another, the award is suspended at that establishment and does not follow the chef automatically. We recommend that when a change of chef occurs, establishments let us know as soon as possible in order for us to schedule inspections.

The top ten percent

ENGLAND

BERKSHIRE
The Fat Duck, Bray

BRISTOL
Casamia Restaurant, Bristol

CAMBRIDGESHIRE
Midsummer House Restaurant, Cambridge

CUMBRIA
L'Enclume, Cartmel

LANCASHIRE
Moor Hall Restaurant with Rooms, Ormskirk

LONDON
Claude Bosi at Bibendum, SW3
Core by Clare Smyth, W11
Hélène Darroze at The Connaught, W1
Marcus, SW1
Pollen Street Social, W1
Restaurant Story, SE1
Sketch (Lecture Room & Library), W1

NOTTINGHAMSHIRE
Restaurant Sat Bains with Rooms, Nottingham

OXFORDSHIRE
Belmond Le Manoir aux Quat'Saisons, Great Milton

CHANNEL ISLANDS

JERSEY
Bohemia Restaurant, St Helier

SCOTLAND

EDINBURGH
The Kitchin, Edinburgh

WALES

CEREDIGION
Ynyshir, Eglwys Fach

ENGLAND

BERKSHIRE
The Waterside Inn, Bray

BUCKINGHAMSHIRE
The Hand & Flowers, Marlow

CHESHIRE
Simon Radley at The Chester Grosvenor, Chester

CORNWALL & ISLES OF SCILLY
Driftwood, Portscatho
Paul Ainsworth at No. 6, Padstow
Restaurant Nathan Outlaw, Port Isaac

CUMBRIA
Forest Side, Grasmere

COUNTY DURHAM
The Orangery, Darlington

GLOUCESTERSHIRE
Le Champignon Sauvage, Cheltenham

GREATER MANCHESTER
Adam Reid at The French, Manchester

LANCASHIRE
Northcote, Langho

LINCOLNSHIRE
Winteringham Fields, Winteringham

LONDON
Alain Ducasse at The Dorchester, W1
Alyn Williams at The Westbury, W1
Dinner by Heston Blumenthal, SW1
The Five Fields, SW3
Le Gavroche Restaurant, W1
The Greenhouse, W1
The Ledbury, W11
Murano, W11

Restaurant Gordon Ramsay, SW3
Seven Park Place by William Drabble, SW1
Texture Restaurant, W11

MERSEYSIDE
Fraiche, Oxton

NORFOLK
Morston Hall, Blakeney

OXFORDSHIRE
Orwells, Henley-on-Thames

RUTLAND
Hambleton Hall, Oakham

SURREY
Matt Worswick at The Latymer, Bagshot
Stovell's, Chobham
The Tudor Room, Egham

TYNE & WEAR
House of Tides, Newcastle upon Tyne

WEST MIDLANDS
Hampton Manor, Solihull

YORKSHIRE, NORTH
The Black Swan at Oldstead, Oldstead
The Burlington Restaurant, Bolton Abbey

YORKSHIRE, WEST
The Man Behind The Curtain, Leeds

CHANNEL ISLANDS

JERSEY
Tassili, St Helier

SCOTLAND

EDINBURGH
Number One, The Balmoral
Restaurant Martin Wishart
21212

PERTH & KINROSS
Andrew Fairlie at Gleneagles, Auchterarder

WALES

ISLE OF ANGLESEY
Sosban & The Old Butcher's Restaurant, Menai Bridge

MONMOUTHSHIRE
The Whitebrook, Whitebrook

VALE OF GLAMORGAN
Restaurant James Sommerin, Penarth

REPUBLIC OF IRELAND

DUBLIN
Restaurant Patrick Guilbaud

COUNTY WATERFORD
The House Restaurant, Ardmore

ENGLAND

BEDFORDSHIRE
Paris House Restaurant, Woburn

BERKSHIRE
The Crown, Burchett's Green
The Hind's Head, Bray
L'Ortolan, Shinfield
Restaurant Coworth Park, Ascot
The Royal Oak Paley Street, Maidenhead
The Vineyard, Newbury
The Woodspeen – Restaurant and Cookery School, Newbury

BUCKINGHAMSHIRE
André Garrett at Cliveden, Taplow
The Artichoke, Amersham
The Coach, Marlow
Humphry's at Stoke Park, Stoke Poges

CHESHIRE
1851 Restaurant at Peckforton Castle, Peckforton

CORNWALL & ISLES OF SCILLY
Hell Bay, Bryher
Hotel Tresanton, St Mawes
Kota Kai, Porthleven
Merchants Manor, Falmouth
The Seafood Restaurant, Padstow

CUMBRIA
Hrishi at Gilpin Hotel & Lake House, Windermere
Lake Road Kitchen, Ambleside
Rogan & Company Restaurant, Cartmel
The Samling, Windermere

DERBYSHIRE
Fischer's Baslow Hall, Baslow
The Peacock at Rowsley, Rowsley

DEVON
Boringdon Hall Hotel, Plymouth
The Coach House by Michael Caines, Kentisbury
The Elephant Restaurant, Torquay
Gidleigh Park, Chagford
Great Western, Moretonhampstead
The Old Inn, Drewsteignton

DORSET
Summer Lodge Country House Hotel, Restaurant & Spa, Evershot

GLOUCESTERSHIRE
Buckland Manor, Buckland
The Feathered Nest Country Inn, Nether Westcote
The Greenway Hotel and Spa, Cheltenham

Jackrabbit Restaurant, Chipping Camden
Lumière, Cheltenham
The Slaughters Manor House, Lower Slaughter

HAMPSHIRE
Avenue Restaurant at Lainston House Hotel, Winchester
Cambium, Brockenhurst
The Elderflower Restaurant, Lymington
Hartnett Holder & Co, Lyndhurst
JSW, Petersfield
The Montagu Arms Hotel, Beaulieu
36 on the Quay, Emsworth

HERTFORDSHIRE
Colette's at The Grove, Chandler's Cross
THOMPSON St Albans, St Albans

KENT
ABode Canterbury, Canterbury
Thackeray's, Royal Tunbridge Wells
The West House Restaurant with Rooms, Biddenden

LANCASHIRE
The Freemasons at Wiswell, Whalley
Hipping Hall, Cowan Bridge

LINCOLNSHIRE
Harry's Place, Grantham

LONDON
Ametsa with Arzak Instruction, SW1
Anglo, EC1
A. Wong, SW1
Bingham, Richmond upon Thames
Céleste at The Lanesborough, SW1
Chapter One, Bromley
Chez Bruce, SW17
City Social, EC2
Clos Maggiore, WC2
The Clove Club, EC1
Club Gascon, EC1

Corrigan's Mayfair, W1
CUT at 45 Park Lane, W1
La Dame de Pic, EC3
Elystan Street, SW3
Fera at Claridge's, W1
Frog by Adam Handling, WC2
The Frog Restaurant, E1
Galvin at Windows Restaurant & Bar, W1
Galvin La Chapelle, E1
Gauthier Soho, W1
The Gilbert Scott, NW1
The Glasshouse, Kew
The Goring, SW1
Hakkasan Mayfair, W1
Hedone, W4
Kitchen Table, W1
Kitchen W8, W8
L'Atelier de Joël Robuchon, WC2
La Belle Époque, Heathrow Airport
Little Social, W1
Locanda Locatelli, W1
Medlar Restaurant, SW10
Merchants Tavern, EC2
Mere, W1
Min Jiang, W8
The Ninth, W1
Odette's, NW1
Orrery, W1
Outlaw's at The Capital, SW3
The Peninsula Restaurant, SE10
Pidgin, E8
Pied à Terre, W1
Portland, W1
The Ritz Restaurant, W1
Rivea London, SW7
The River Café, W6
Roganic, W1
Roka Charlotte Street, W1
Roka Mayfair, W1
Roux at Parliament Square, SW1
Sketch (The Gallery), W1
Social Eating House, W1
Sosharu, EC1
The Square, W1
Trinity Restaurant, SW4
Umu, W1
Wild Honey, W1

NORFOLK
Benedicts, Norwich
The Neptune Restaurant with Rooms, Hunstanton
Roger Hickman's Restaurant, Norwich
Titchwell Manor Hotel, Titchwell

NORTHAMPTONSHIRE
Rushton Hall Hotel and Spa, Kettering

OXFORDSHIRE
The Oxford Kitchen, Oxford
Restaurant 56, Faringdon
The Wild Rabbit, Kingham
Shaun Dickens at The Boathouse, Henley-on-Thames

SHROPSHIRE
Old Downton Lodge, Ludlow

SOMERSET
The Bath Priory Hotel, Restaurant & Spa, Bath
Castle Bow Restaurant, Taunton
Dan Moon at the Gainsborough Restaurant, Bath
The Dower House Restaurant, Bath
Little Barwick House, Yeovil
The Mount Somerset Hotel & Spa, Taunton
The Olive Tree at the Queensberry Hotel, Bath

STAFFORDSHIRE
Swinfen Hall Hotel, Lichfield

SUFFOLK
Tuddenham Mill, Newmarket

SURREY
The Clock House, Ripley
Sorrel, Dorking

SUSSEX, EAST
The Little Fish Market, Brighton

SUSSEX, WEST
AG's Restaurant at
Alexander House
Hotel, Turners Hill
Amberley Castle,
Amberley
Gravetye Manor Hotel,
West Hoathly
Langshott Manor,
Gatwick Airport
The Lickfold Inn, Lickfold
The Pass Restaurant,
Lower Beeding
Restaurant Tristan,
Horsham

WARWICKSHIRE
The Dining Room at
Mallory Court Hotel,
Royal Leamington
Spa
Salt, Stratford-upon-Avon

WEST MIDLANDS
Adam's, Birmingham
Carters of Moseley,
Birmingham
Purnell's, Birmingham
Simpsons, Birmingham

WILTSHIRE
The Bybrook at The
Manor House, an
Exclusive Hotel & Golf
Club, Castle Combe
The Dining Room,
Malmesbury
The Harrow at Little
Bedwyn, Little
Bedwyn
Red Lion Freehouse,
Pewsey
Restaurant Hywel Jones
by Lucknam Park,
Colerne

WORCESTERSHIRE
Brockencote Hall
Country House Hotel,
Chaddesley Corbett
Dormy House Hotel,
Broadway

YORKSHIRE, NORTH
Black Swan Hotel,
Helmsley

The Coach House,
Middleton Tyas
The Grand Hotel & Spa,
York, York
The Hare Inn, Scawton
Horto Restaurant,
Harrogate
The Park Restaurant,
York
Yorebridge House,
Bainbridge

YORKSHIRE, SOUTH
Jöro Restaurant,
Sheffield

YORKSHIRE, WEST
Box Tree, Ilkley

CHANNEL ISLANDS

JERSEY
Château la Chaire, Rozel
Longueville Manor Hotel,
St Saviour
Ocean Restaurant at
The Atlantic Hotel, St
Brelade
Restaurant Sirocco@The
Royal Yacht, St Helier
Samphire, St Helier

SCOTLAND

ABERDEENSHIRE
Douneside House,
Tarland

ANGUS
Gordon's, Inverkeilor

ARGYLL & BUTE
Airds Hotel and
Restaurant, Port
Appin
Inver Restaurant,
Strachur

SOUTH AYRSHIRE
Glenapp Castle,
Ballantrae
Lochgreen House Hotel,
Troon

**DUMFRIES &
GALLOWAY**
Knockinaam Lodge,
Portpatrick

EDINBURGH
Castle Terrace
Restaurant
The Pompadour by
Galvin
Restaurant Mark
Greenaway
Timberyard

FIFE
The Cellar, Anstruther
The Peat Inn, Peat Inn
Road Hole Restaurant,
St Andrews
Rocca Restaurant, St
Andrews

GLASGOW
Cail Bruich
The Gannet

HIGHLAND
The Cross, Kingussie
Inverlochy Castle Hotel,
Fort William
Kilcamb Lodge, Strontian
The Torridon, Torridon

PERTH & KINROSS
Fonab Castle Hotel &
Spa, Pitlochry

SOUTH LANARKSHIRE
Crossbasket Castle,
Blantyre

STIRLING
Cromlix and Chez Roux,
Dunblane
Roman Camp Country
House Hotel,
Callander

SCOTTISH ISLANDS

ISLE OF SKYE
Kinloch Lodge, Isleornsay
The Three Chimneys &
The House Over-By,
Colbost
Ullinish Country Lodge,
Struan

WALES

CONWY
Bodysgallen Hall and
Spa, Llandudno

GWYNEDD
Pále Hall Hotel &
Restaurant, Bala

MONMOUTHSHIRE
The Walnut Tree Inn,
Abergavenny

PEMBROKESHIRE
The Fernery, Narberth

POWYS
Llangoed Hall, Llyswen

NORTHERN IRELAND

COUNTY ANTRIM
Galgorm Resort & Spa,
Ballymena

BELFAST
Deanes EIPIC
OX

COUNTY FERMANAGH
Lough Erne Resort,
Enniskillen

REPUBLIC OF
IRELAND

COUNTY CLARE
Gregans Castle,
Ballyvaughan

COUNTY KILKENNY
The Lady Helen
Restaurant,
Thomastown

Restaurants of the Year 2018–19

Potential Restaurants of the Year are nominated by our team of full-time inspectors based on their routine visits. We are looking for somewhere that is exceptional in its chosen area of the market. While the Rosette awards are based on the quality of the food alone, the Restaurants of the Year awards take into account all aspects of the dining experience.

England winner
SORREL, DORKING, SURREY
See page 300

London winner
SABOR, LONDON W1
See page 221

Scotland winner
THE NEWPORT RESTAURANT,
NEWPORT-ON-TAY, FIFE
See page 386

Wales winner
MACHINE HOUSE RESTAURANT,
ROSSETT, WREXHAM
See page 438

AA Chefs' Chef of the Year 2018–19

CLAUDE BOSI

Born in Lyon, the food capital of France, Claude Bosi has cooking in his DNA. His career got off to a flying start in the family bistro before he spread his wings to build on his innate talent during stints at the venerable Léon de Lyon and a series of top-drawer French kitchens, including L'Arpège with Alain Passard and a stint with French super-chef Alain Ducasse in Paris. The UK's burgeoning gastronomic renaissance lured Bosi across the Channel in 1997 to work as sous-chef at Overton Grange in Shropshire, going on to lead the charge in establishing sleepy Ludlow as a foodie hotspot when he opened Hibiscus in 2000. Now soundly lauded by his peers as a Premier League culinary star, the lure of the capital led Bosi to follow his big-city dreams and move Hibiscus to London in 2008, continually evolving a unique cooking style that allies the finest produce with immensely skilled classical technique in elegantly understated dishes. In October 2016 he closed the curtains on Hibiscus to start a new chapter with his name above the door at Bibendum in 2017. And for the UK's lucky diners there's now the prospect of a chef at the top of his game injecting a new lease of life into one of London's most gorgeous dining rooms.

PREVIOUS WINNERS

RAYMOND BLANC OBE
Belmond Le Manoir aux Quat' Saisons,
    Great Milton, Oxfordshire

HESTON BLUMENTHAL
The Fat Duck, Bray, Berkshire
Hinds Head, Bray, Berkshire
Dinner by Heston Blumenthal,
    London SW1
The Crown at Bray, Berkshire

MICHAEL CAINES
The Coach House by Michael Caines, Kentisbury,
    Devon

DANIEL CLIFFORD
Midsummer House, Cambridge, Cambridgeshire

ANDREW FAIRLIE
Andrew Fairlie at Gleneagles,
    Auchterarder, Perth & Kinross

CHRIS AND JEFF GALVIN
Galvin La Chapelle, London E1

SHAUN HILL
Walnut Tree Inn, Abergavenny,
    Monmouthshire

PHILIP HOWARD
Elystan Street, London SW3

TOM KERRIDGE
The Hand and Flowers, Marlow, Buckinghamshire
The Coach, Marlow, Buckinghamshire

PIERRE KOFFMANN

JEAN-CHRISTOPHE NOVELLI

NATHAN OUTLAW
Restaurant Nathan Outlaw,
    Port Isaac, Cornwall
Outlaw's Fish Kitchen,
    Port Isaac, Cornwall
Outlaw's at The Capital,
    London SW3

GORDON RAMSAY
Restaurant Gordon Ramsay,
    London SW3

SIMON ROGAN
L'Enclume, Cartmel, Cumbria

GERMAIN SCHWAB

RICK STEIN
The Seafood Restaurant,
    Padstow, Cornwall
Rick Stein at Sandbanks,
    Sandbanks, Dorset

KEVIN VINER

MARCUS WAREING
Marcus, The Berkeley,
    London SW1

MARCO PIERRE WHITE

JOHN T WILLIAMS
The Ritz Restaurant, London W1

MARTIN WISHART
Restaurant Martin Wishart, Edinburgh

AA Food Service Award 2018–19

Introduced in 2013, this award recognises restaurants that deliver excellent standards of service and hospitality. The teams at these restaurants demonstrate technical service skills, and their food and beverage knowledge is of the highest standard.

MARGOT, LONDON WC2

The wow factor of a stellar chef who has all the flair and technical skill in the world become lost if the service team aren't up to scratch. Margot co-owners, Paulo de Tarso and Nicolas Jaouën knew this and made sure that service took centre stage when its doors opened in 2016. And when it comes to top-drawer service, they have form: with career paths taking in stints at Scott's, Alain Ducasse, Bar Boulud and The Wolseley, the service ethos is clearly evident in the DNA of this restaurant. Both are deeply passionate about the guest experience being both personal and memorable, and the attention to detail that the Margot service team deliver is truly impressive.

The Margot experience has been thought through carefully to project a slick and classy image, and the service team back this up 100% – all are professional, well-drilled and looking the part in sharp black suits and ties, or in long cream aprons. From the sincere welcome, the operation runs like a well-oiled machine – the team are both natural and engaging in equal measure. A true sign of service excellence is that it just flows and happens at all the right moments, present when you need it and subtly in the background when you don't.

Read about Margot on page 241

TWIRL

The new hand-decorated TWIRL series captures the colours of the tropics...

MAKE SURE IT'S RAK

RAK
PORCELAIN

RAK Porcelain Europe S.A. • Nick Salman • T 07952 348495 • nsalman@rakporcelaineurope.com • www.rakporcelain.eu

AA Wine Awards 2018–19

The annual AA Wine Awards, sponsored by Matthew Clark Wines, attracted a huge response from our AA recognised restaurants with over 950 wine lists submitted for judging. Three national winners were chosen.

Wales and Overall winner
PARK HOUSE RESTAURANT, CARDIFF
See page 413

Scotland
TIMBERYARD, EDINBURGH
See pages 384–385

England
THE HARROW AT LITTLE BEDWYN,
LITTLE BEDWYN
See pages 332–333

All the restaurants in this year's guide were invited to submit their wine lists. From these the panel selected a shortlist of over 200 establishments who are highlighted in the guide with the Notable Wine List symbol ⚱ NOTABLE WINE LIST.

The shortlisted establishments were asked to choose wines from their list (within a budget of £80 per bottle) to accompany a menu designed by last year's winner Gareth Ward of Ynyshir.

The final judging panel included Nick Zalinski, Business Director, Matthew Clark Wines (our sponsor) and Simon Numphud, Managing Director, AA Hotel Services. The judges' comments are shown opposite.

What makes a wine list notable?
We are looking for high-quality wines, with diversity across grapes and/or countries and style, and the best individual growers and vintages. The list should be well presented, clear and easy to navigate. To reflect the demand of diners, there should be a good choice of varied wines available by the glass.

Things that disappoint the judges are spelling errors on the lists, wines under incorrect regions or styles, split vintages (which are still far too common), lazy purchasing (all wines from a country from just one grower or negociant) and confusing wine list layouts. Sadly, many restaurants still do not pay much attention to wine, resulting in ill-considered lists.

To reach the final shortlist, we look for a real passion for wine, which should come across to the customer; a fair pricing policy (depending on the style of the restaurant); interesting coverage (not necessarily a large list), which might include areas of specialism, perhaps a particular wine area; and sherries or larger formats such as magnums.

The AA Wine Awards are sponsored by:

Matthew Clark, Whitchurch Lane, Bristol, BS14 0JZ
tel: 01275 891400
email: enquiries@matthewclark.co.uk
web: www.matthewclark.co.uk

PARK HOUSE RESTAURANT, CARDIFF – the winning wine selection:

MENU	WINE SELECTION
Canapés – Crispy Duck Leg – Black Bean Glaze – Sesame (deep-fried duck leg, brushed in black bean and soy glaze, garnished with toasted sesame and spring onion)	Aperitif: 2013 'The Trouble with Dreams' Brut, Sugrue Pierre, Sussex, England
Starter – Miso Onion Soup – Tofu – Croûtons – Sea Vegetables – Dashi Stock (puréed onions blended with miso, pickled shallots, croûtons and diced tofu, onion oil, pickled sea vegetables with a dashi stock poured over the top)	2013 Lorcher Schlossberg, Riesling, Spaetlese, Eva Fricke, Rheingau, Germany
Fish course – Mackerel – Sweet & Sour (sashimi-style mackerel, fermented pineapple, sweet and sour ketchup, beansprouts and micro coriander finished with a mackerel soy and charcoal oil)	2012 Farrago Chardonnay, Kooyong, Mornington Peninsula, Australia
Meat course – Salt Wagyu Rib – Shiitake – Seaweed (salted Wagyu beef rib finished on the BBQ, shiitake mushroom ketchup, pickled seaweed, dehydrated shiitakes, deep-fried puffed wild rice and a beef soy)	2006 Gattinara, Vallana, Gattinara, DOCG, Piedmont, Italy
Cheese course – Tunworth – Bianchetto Truffle – Sour Crumpet (warmed aged Tunworth cheese, placed on a crumpet made with the sourdough levain with a truffle and maple syrup blend spooned on top)	NV Taittinger Nocturne Champagne, Champagne, France
Pudding course – Tiramisú (classic tiramisú flavours – coffee, mascarpone and bitter chocolate sprayed with cremovo)	Digestif: 1995 Vin Santo del Chianti Classico, Fontodi, Tuscany, Italy

Judges' notes

PARK HOUSE RESTAURANT

A stunning list that is both accessible and easy to navigate. It allows customers to indulge and explore in great depth a particular style or just to go for something more specific. The favourites section was very helpful. Real care and sense of attention to detail is evident throughout this list, from the clean layout and presentation through to its personal tasting notes. Affordable too, with sensible mark-ups that encourage you to be adventurous in your wine selections. There is a clear passion and keenness to share expertise with this list. It has bags of character which typifies the stunning magnum selection. Sparkling and champagne sections are also given equal attention.

TIMBERYARD

The Timberyard list is a brave one, that sets out to challenge and excite away from the main stream convention of most wine lists. It is deliberately quirky and obscure in equal measure and exclusively features European wines. It seeks out new and less established growers with a focus on natural wines from small artisan producers. Hence the list is packed full of interest and for most customers will offer wine choices that are both new and unknown.

THE HARROW AT LITTLE BEDWYN

An amazing curated list that has continued to evolve since it was first created back in 1998. It has so many strengths that it comes as no surprise that settling on what to order is the greatest challenge guests will have with this list. Every page is filled with quality selections, great depth in vintages and superb tasting notes. It offers stunning value throughout, making the list a standout feature in its own right.

AA College Restaurant of the Year 2018–19

Now in its third successful year, the AA College Restaurant of the Year celebrates the very best of future talent. Open exclusively to all People 1st Accredited colleges, each holding an AA college Rosette for culinary excellence, at either the Award or Highly commended levels, many of these colleges are People 1st centres of excellence. This year's entrants had to produce an advertising video to highlight their college restaurant to the prospective guests, a marketing analysis and plans for the future. Judging took place at the Principal Hotel London, where the teams not only faced an industry panel of judges but also benefited from an inspirational talk from AA-award winning restaurateur Marcus Wareing. After a tough judging day and plenty of debate, the three finalists were agreed upon by our panel of industry experts.

Winner
THE BRASSERIE – MILTON KEYNES COLLEGE

Runners up
TREVENSON RESTAURANT – CORNWALL COLLEGE (CAMBORNE)
PARCS RESTAURANT – PETERBOROUGH COLLEGE

ENGLAND

BEDFORDSHIRE

▶ BEDFORDSHIRE

BOLNHURST
The Plough at Bolnhurst
◉ MODERN BRITISH
01234 376274 | Kimbolton Road, MK44 2EX
www.bolnhurst.com
The restaurant is a striking contrast to the pub – the airy extension features lofty oak-beamed ceilings while full-length windows flood the room with light. Top-quality produce is transformed into big-flavoured modern dishes on daily changing menus.
Chef Martin Lee **Seats** 96, Private dining 32 **Closed** 27 December to 14 January **Parking** 30 **Notes** Vegetarian dishes, Children welcome

FLITWICK
Hallmark Hotel Flitwick Manor
◉◉ MODERN, TRADITIONAL
01525 712242 | Church Road, MK45 1AE
www.hallmarkhotels.co.uk
A Georgian house in its own wooded parkland, classic British dishes with modern European influence are the stock-in-trade at Flitwick. Making a strong impact are a starter of braised pig's cheek scattered with dried grapefruit and crumbled walnuts, alongside silky parsnip purée.
Chef Simon Harris **Seats** 30, Private dining 60 **Open** All year **Prices from** S £8, M £18 **Parking** 75 **Notes** Vegetarian dishes, Children welcome

HENLOW
The Crown
◉ MODERN BRITISH
01462 812433 | 2 High Street, SG16 6BS
www.crownpub.co.uk
The busy pub on the main road through the village functions as a quintessential rural hostelry, full of enthusiastic local custom in both bar and dining room. Despite modernisation it retains its pub ethos, and boasts a young, classically trained chef.
Chef Will Ingarfill **Seats** 80, Private dining 24 **Closed** 25–26 December **Parking** 60 **Notes** Vegetarian dishes, Children welcome

LUTON
Adam's Brasserie at Luton Hoo
◉ MODERN BRITISH ▮NOTABLE WINE LIST
01582 734437 | Luton Hoo Hotel, Golf & Spa, The Mansion House, LU1 3TQ
www.lutonhoo.com
The extensive Luton Hoo Estate, with its golf course and magnificent gardens, is home to this spa hotel. Adam's Brasserie is found in the former stables, where high ceilings and large windows give a sense of space, and the menu is a roster of feel-good dishes.
Chef Chris Mouyiassi **Seats** 90, Private dining 290 **Open** All year **Parking** 100 **Notes** Vegetarian dishes, Children welcome

Wernher Restaurant at Luton Hoo Hotel, Golf & Spa
◉◉ MODERN EUROPEAN
01582 734437 | The Mansion House, LU1 3TQ
www.lutonhoo.co.uk
When only the full stately-home extravaganza will do – the sort of place where the chaps are required to sport jacket and tie at dinner – the magnificent Wernher in Luton Hoo is hard to top, with its marble panelling, ornate chandeliers and opulent fabrics.
Chef William Dimartino **Seats** 80, Private dining 290 **Closed** 1st 2 weeks in January (Monday to Thursday all day, Friday and Saturday lunch) **Parking** 316 **Notes** Vegetarian dishes, Children welcome

WOBURN
Paris House Restaurant
◉◉◉ MODERN BRITISH **V**
See pages 22–23

The Woburn Hotel
◉◉ MODERN BRITISH, FRENCH
01525 290441 | George Street, MK17 9PX
www.thewoburnhotel.co.uk
The cooking at the beautifully refurbished Olivier's Restaurant is rooted in the great French traditions but it is very much of the present, so roast cod fillet, for instance, is served with brandade and chorizo and bean cassoulet. Combinations in dishes intrigue without seeming wacky.
Chef Olivier Bertho **Seats** 40, Private dining 90 **Open** All year **Prices from** S £5.50, M £13.95, D £7.25 **Parking** 80 **Notes** Vegetarian dishes, Children welcome

WYBOSTON
The Waterfront Restaurant at Wyboston Lakes
◉ TRADITIONAL BRITISH, EUROPEAN
0333 700 7667 | Great North Road, MK44 3BA
www.thewaterfronthotel.co.uk
The Waterfront Restaurant offers a relaxed and modern brasserie-style dining experience with views over the south lake. The breads are home made and served with tapenade as well as oil and balsamic vinegar. For dessert, tuck into tiramisu with Madagascan vanilla cream and biscotti.
Chef Sumit Chakrabarty **Seats** 90, Private dining 70 **Closed** 25–26 December **Prices from** S £6.95, M £12.95, D £5.95 **Parking** 200 **Notes** Vegetarian dishes, Children welcome

▶ BERKSHIRE

ASCOT

The Barn at Coworth
◉◉ BRITISH
01344 756784 | Blacknest Road, SL5 7SE
www.coworthpark.com

There's a fine-dining restaurant at this lavish country hotel, plus this converted barn where you can tuck into classy brasserie-style food. It looks great with its open-to-view kitchen, unbuttoned vibe and cheerful service team sporting orange polo tops, and there's a fabulous terrace, too.

Chef Tom Hankey **Seats** 75 **Open** All year
Prices from S £10, M £19, D £12 **Parking** 100
Notes Children welcome

Bluebells Restaurant & Garden Bar
◉◉ MODERN EUROPEAN
01344 622722 | Shrubbs Hill, London Road, Sunningdale, SL5 0LE
www.bluebells-restaurant.co.uk

Bluebells stands out from the crowd with its sleek modern looks and upbeat, buzzy ambience. The kitchen works a modern British groove, allowing that old stager, chicken liver parfait, to get a kick from red Muscadet wine jelly, quince chutney, poached pear and toasted hazelnuts.

Chef Tamas Baranyai **Seats** 90, Private dining 14
Closed 25–26 December, 1–11 January and Bank holidays **Parking** 100 **Notes** Vegetarian dishes, Children welcome

Restaurant Coworth Park
◉◉◉ MODERN BRITISH V ⦚NOTABLE WINE LIST⦙
01344 876600 | London Road, SL5 7SE
www.coworthpark.com

Handy for the racing or for a day out at Windsor, Coworth Park looms above its slab of rural Berkshire in shimmering wedding-cake white. A Georgian mansion house on the grander than average scale, it's surrounded by meadows full of wildflowers and ancient woodland, and has a bevy of amenities to offer, from deep tissue massages to polo. It also has a very pretty dining room with a design of oak foliage in glass and a view over the rose terrace. Here, a discreetly modernised take on country-house cooking is offered, with a seven-course taster and Best of British menus supplementing the main carte. The last deals in the likes of a very grand caviar tart with white crabmeat, yuzu and cucumber to start, ahead of steamed turbot in champagne sauce with truffled cauliflower, or perfectly tender short rib of 60-day salt-aged beef with its bone marrow, spinach and onions for main. Finish with vanilla mousse, served with pineapple, lime and coconut, or perhaps a serving of Lincolnshire's Cote Hill Blue cheese with fruitcake and pear.

Chef Adam Smith **Seats** 66, Private dining 16 **Open** All year **Prices from** S £16, M £43, D £16 **Parking** 100
Notes No children under 8 years

BAGNOR

The Blackbird – Restaurant & Public House
◉◉ CLASSIC EUROPEAN
01635 40005 | A34, RG20 8AQ
www.theblackbird.co.uk

A family-run pub that plays Sixties to Eighties music all day. Not only that, but the interior resembles a front room from a bygone age, with a fretwork-fronted wireless, commemorative mugs, and table doilies. Dishes on the imaginative menu, however, are bang up to date.

Chef Dominic Robinson **Seats** 38 **Closed** 25–26 December, 1st January and 1st week in January
Prices from S £10, M £18, D £8 **Parking** 15
Notes Vegetarian dishes, Children welcome

BRAY

Caldesi in Campagna
◉◉ TRADITIONAL ITALIAN
01628 788500 | Old Mill Lane, SL6 2BG
www.caldesi.com

Here, in an immaculate house on the edge of Bray, expect classic Italian stuff made with (mostly) British ingredients. Among antipasti, deep-fried courgette flowers are filled with ricotta and basil, and to finish, traditional desserts might include Sicilian lemon tart.

Chef Gregorio Piazza **Seats** 50, Private dining 12
Closed Christmas for approximately 5 days **Parking** 8
Notes Vegetarian dishes, Children welcome

The Crown
◉◉ TRADITIONAL BRITISH
01628 621936 | High Street, SL6 2AH
www.thecrownatbray.com

Devotees of the British pub know the Crown is safe in Heston Blumenthal's hands. His third address in the village, this 16th-century inn offers real ales, a well-constructed wine list and a menu that owes much to pub traditions while honouring the Blumenthal name.

Chef Matt Larcombe **Seats** 50 **Open** All year
Prices from S £7.95, M £15.95 **Parking** 37
Notes Vegetarian dishes, Children welcome

BEDFORDSHIRE

WOBURN
Paris House Restaurant

◉◉◉ MODERN BRITISH **V**

01525 290692 | London Road, Woburn Park, MK17 9QP

www.parishouse.co.uk

Striking setting for dynamic contemporary cooking

Paris House makes a powerful first impression on new arrivals. The Duke of Bedford's Woburn Estate is a pretty impressive back yard for a start, and once you're through a grand gateway, the drive across the deer park makes for a stately approach. When the house comes into view, it's as pretty as a picture, a handsome Tudor black-and-white box with ornately decorated facade. Or so it seems. For Paris House isn't Tudor, it was built as part of the 1878 International Exhibition in Paris to represent the architectural styles of 28 nations. The French did such a good job that the Duke of Bedford saw this representation of an English Tudor house, loved, it, bought it, and reassembled it on his estate.

That's the backstory, and charming though it is, this story of Paris House is about the here and now. Phil and Claire Fanning run the place with passion and have developed it into one of the region's most compelling dining addresses. If the house is a historical curiosity, the interior has bags of style, with modern chandeliers, sleek contemporary

furniture, and artworks which include a wall of seasonally changing food-related works that are for sale.

The seasons loom large in Phil's cooking as well, which is full of invention and pin-sharp execution. Delivered via menus headed by Roman numerals which indicate the number of courses, choose between the VI lunch, VIII and X course tasting menus, and, the exception to the rule, the fourteen course CT menu (Chef's Table). European and Asian influences combine on the menus, with modern cooking techniques used to great effect, and the integrity of the superb produce maintained at all times. The professional service adds to the sense of anticipation.

An opening salvo might be halibut with the well-judged intervention of rhubarb, fennel and saffron, followed by the alluring aroma of truffle in a course of potato gnocchi with parmesan and black winter truffle. A mantou steamed bun shows an understanding of Asian techniques, with tender duck and hoisin sauce, while another winning flavour combination is venison with black pudding, adzuki beans and cranberries. Fit in the artisan cheese course if you can. Among sweet courses, 'Parma Violet' is as pretty as a picture, with pistachio, cherry and mascarpone. The top-drawer wine list is arranged by style, with wine flights designed to maximise the impact of each course.

Chef Phil Fanning, Ben Hyman **Seats** 37, Private dining 12 **Closed** Christmas **Parking** 24 **Notes** Children welcome

BERKSHIRE

BRAY continued

The Fat Duck

◉◉◉◉◉ MODERN BRITISH **V** ♦ NOTABLE WINE LIST

01628 580333 | High Street, SL6 2AQ

www.thefatduck.co.uk

To understand this restaurant, it is necessary to go back to the heroic days of traditional haute cuisine in the grand hotels to come across examples of refined cooking – and indeed of a celebrity chef – having attained such a pitch of mythology. We mean it in both senses of the term. Heston Blumenthal's The Fat Duck, and its ubiquitously telegenic proprietor himself, have entered the latter-day pantheon of culinary legend but are often misunderstood. On the latter side, many have come to believe that the cooking here is all something of an elaborate jape, for the TV starstruck generation who choose to dine by reputation alone. Nothing could be further from the truth: The Fat Duck is so much more – and with the new booking system it's much easier to access. Reservations are opened 4 months in advance, so if dates are flexible you're likely to find a spot.

Upon entering, disciples who descend upon the dining room are regaled with a culinary performance that, with awe-inspiring consistency, transcends the known limits from most other kitchens. Yes, the food is highly conceptualised. Dishes arrive on sandy beaches accompanied by gigantic seashells or perched on great white cushions floating in mid-air. There is humour of course, but only the kind that comes with a level of personalised service rarely found in 5-rosette venues. What the presentations might obscure, it should be admitted, is the unimpeachable quality of their prime ingredients and creations. If Blumenthal has spoken of wanting to create the sense of thrilled anticipation one had as a child when the family set out on a summer holiday, that joy is tangible in the intensity of the flavours as much as in the entertaining menu concept that it generates. The glass box of oceanic wonders with its shellfish foam and 'sand' of miso oil, tapioca and panko crumbs would be remarkable in itself, even without the iPod earbud that pours a soundtrack of crashing waves into your emotional memory bank evoking a very personal nostalgic moment. There are dishes during Heston's holiday journey menu that take inspiration from an old school table d'hote when he presents the most artful concept of all; serving a duck à l'orange that is poignantly intense, the meat so treasurably tender and flavourful, transporting us back to a moment in time. That's ultimately what great cooking is about: when all the theatrical ingenuity makes sense and has purpose delivering flavour, emotion and craftsmanship; something the Fat Duck is incomparably good at.

Chef Heston Blumenthal **Seats** 42 **Closed** 2 weeks at Christmas **Notes** Children welcome

The Hind's Head

◉◉◉ BRITISH ♦ NOTABLE WINE LIST

01628 626151 | High Street, SL6 2AB

www.hindsheadbray.com

The nearby Fat Duck's culinary pyrotechnics aren't for everyone's tastes or budget, so for a glimpse of that Blumenthal wizardry consider what was once Bray's village boozer, where Heston offers traditional true-Brit cooking in tune with the building's 15th-century heritage. After a thorough refurb in 2017 the place is split between a clubby lounge bar upstairs with eccentric hunting-lodge touches in its funky decor, while the deal in the main ground-floor restaurant is either a carte, a five-course taster or a budget-friendly set-lunch menu, all offering well-crafted versions of robust British dishes. Layers of clear flavours are the key to a modern take on Waldorf salad, wherein beautifully caramelised scallops are highlighted by celery gel and flowers, pickled and candied walnuts, sea vegetables and dill oil. Technically astute, sure-footed cooking produces spring on a plate in a delightful main course of chicken and Alsace bacon with grilled lettuce, broad beans, pea purée and mint oil. Pudding is so simple but so good: zingy lemon tart is a pastry-skills masterclass, helped along by racy raspberry and verbena sorbet.

Chef Peter Gray **Seats** 82, Private dining 18 **Closed** 25 December **Prices from** S £5, M £20, D £8.95 **Parking** 40 **Notes** Vegetarian dishes, Children welcome

The Riverside Brasserie

◉ MODERN EUROPEAN

01628 780553 | Bray Marina, Monkey Island Lane, SL6 2EB

www.riversidebrasserie.co.uk

Tucked away beside the Thames in Bray Marina, this waterside restaurant oozes understated class and an easygoing ambience. Full-length glass doors mean the river views are still there whether you dine inside or alfresco on the decked area, while chefs turn out unfussy brasserie food.

Chef Ben Spatharakis **Seats** 36 **Parking** 30 **Notes** Vegetarian dishes, Children welcome

The Waterside Inn

◉◉◉◉ FRENCH ♦ NOTABLE WINE LIST

01628 620691 | Ferry Road, SL6 2AT

www.waterside-inn.co.uk

Long before Bray became gastronomy central, a pair of French brothers who had made a name for themselves in London (Le Gavroche, anyone?) set up shop in this old English pub on the banks of the River Thames; we are, of course, talking about the Roux family, and heading for 50 years later it is Alain, son of Michel, who ensures the place remains a benchmark experience for anyone who wants to get acquainted with supremely refined French cooking. The dining room looks the part, all crisp linen, green silk banquettes and gleaming crystal and silverware, but it's the view opening onto the riverside terrace that lifts the spirits at any time of year. That sense of being somewhere special is reinforced by world-class service – take a bow, Diego Masciaga. Alain Roux still cooks some of the traditional dishes of his father's day – witness game pâté wrapped in pastry and rich with truffles and foie gras – but there is also modernity and innovation throughout the bilingual menu – the Chinese cabbage and lime and vodka sauce, for example, that accompanies poached halibut, or you might go for a classic cocotte of oxtail and beef cheek braised in Beaujolais wine with button onions, mushrooms and smoked bacon lardons. Alain is a master pâtissier, so expect exquisite desserts such as ethereal banana soufflé flavoured with orange and Valrhona's sublime Caramélia chocolate. Needless to say, The Waterside is not a cheap date, particularly if you delve into the eye-watering depths of the remarkable wine list.

Chef Alain Roux **Seats** 75, Private dining 8 **Closed** 26 December to 31 January **Prices from** S £41, M £53.50, D £32 **Parking** 20 **Notes** Vegetarian dishes, No children under 9 years

BURCHETT'S GREEN
The Crown
◉◉◉ MODERN
01628 824079 | Burchett's Green SL5 6QZ
www.thecrownburchettsgreen.com
The 19th-century pub is a cut above your average village watering hole, its original features offset by understated country-chic furnishings, slate floors and bare tables laid with fresh flowers and classy tableware. At the beating heart of the enterprise is chef-patron Simon Bonwick who clearly has an ongoing love affair with French gastronomical ways and an intuitive grasp of how ingredients work together. This is sharp, precise cooking with intense flavours that leave a big smile on your face. Menu descriptions seriously underplay what arrives on the plate, as in a multi-layered starter of falafel with harissa-spiced grains atop a wafer-thin croûte, all highlighted by pomegranate, reduced balsamic and parmesan crisp. Main-course turbot Lyonnaise delivers precision-timed fish of exceptional quality served with crisp onions, tiger prawns, celeriac, beetroot, broccoli and spinach, all cooked spot-on, plus silky mashed potato and a punchy jus. Classic skills are on display in a dessert that packs a dark

chocolate 'cigar' with coffee mousse and sets it alongside hazelnut praline, pear and rum and raisin ice cream.

Chef Simon Bonwick **Closed** Monday and Tuesday **Notes** No children under 12

CHIEVELEY
Crab & Boar
◉◉ MODERN EUROPEAN
01635 247550 | Wantage Road, RG20 8UE
www.crabandboar.com
The Crab & Boar has had a stylish refurb: walls in the interconnecting rooms are decorated in muted tones, with exposed beams, while bare wooden tables are smartly set and chairs are a mixed bag, all presenting a refined ambience.

Chef Vincenzo Raffone **Seats** 120, Private dining 14 **Open** All year **Prices from** S £9, M £14, D £6 **Parking** 80 **Notes** Vegetarian dishes, Children welcome

COOKHAM
The White Oak
◉◉ MODERN BRITISH
01628 523043 | The Pound, SL6 9QE
www.thewhiteoak.co.uk
The team behind the White Oak reopened it in 2008 as a modern dining pub. Set in Stanley Spencer's beloved Cookham, it has splashy contemporary artwork, bare tables and generous washes of natural light from a skylight and patio doors.

Chef Graham Kirk **Seats** 80, Private dining 12 **Open** All year **Parking** 32 **Notes** Vegetarian dishes, Children welcome

FRILSHAM
The Pot Kiln
◉◉ BRITISH, EUROPEAN
01635 201366 | RG18 0XX
www.potkiln.org
This rural red-brick country inn is worth tracking down for its proper pubby vibe and unpretentious approach to modern British cooking. The owners source their produce with care, but what makes the Pot Kiln stand out from the herd is its passion for game.

Chef Shaun Cheyney **Seats** 48 **Closed** 25 December **Parking** 70 **Notes** Vegetarian dishes, Children welcome

BERKSHIRE

HUNGERFORD
Littlecote House Hotel
◉◉ MODERN EUROPEAN
01488 682509 | Chilton Foliat, RG17 0SU
www.warnerleisurehotels.co.uk
Littlecote has history: there's the remains of a Roman settlement in the grounds, and Cromwell's soldiers were billeted here in the Civil War. In Oliver's Bistro, fast-forward to the 21st century: the kitchen turns out resolutely up-to-date, creative ideas, supported by a globetrotting wine list.
Chef Philip O'Hagan **Seats** 40, Private dining 8 **Open** All year **Prices from** S £6.50, M £16.50, D £7 **Parking** 200 **Notes** Vegetarian dishes, No children

HURLEY
Hurley House
◉◉ MODERN BRITISH
01628 568500 | Henley Road, SL6 5LH
www.hurleyhouse.co.uk
In the village of Hurley and close to Marlow and Henley-on-Thames, the candlelit restaurant at Hurley House has a refined feel with green leather banquettes, tan leather chairs and linen napkins on the unclothed tables. It all adds up to create a mood of informality.
Chef Michael Chapman **Seats** Private dining 28 **Open** All year **Prices from** S £8, M £17, D £8 **Parking** 65 **Notes** Vegetarian dishes, Children welcome

MAIDENHEAD
Fredrick's Hotel and Spa
◉◉ MODERN BRITISH, FRENCH
01628 581000 | Shoppenhangers Road, SL6 2PZ
www.fredricks-hotel.co.uk
Under new ownership, the kitchen team continue to produce assiduously researched contemporary cooking. Take the starters: home-smoked salmon tian comes with potato galette and dill pickle, and pork is put to good use in rillettes and crackling salad with pickled apple.
Chef Charlie Murray **Seats** 60, Private dining 120 **Open** All year **Parking** 80 **Notes** Vegetarian dishes, Children welcome

The Royal Oak Paley Street
◉◉◉ MODERN BRITISH ⚑NOTABLE WINE LIST
See opposite.

NEWBURY
Donnington Valley Hotel & Spa
◉◉ MODERN BRITISH V ⚑NOTABLE WINE LIST
01635 551199 | Old Oxford Road, Donnington, RG14 3AG
www.donningtonvalley.co.uk
A likeable, informal sort of place, not least the Wine Press restaurant: a light-filled, raftered room on two levels. There's much to like on the menu too, with lots of modern takes on conventional British fare, such as a scrumptious Old Spot pig terrine.
Chef Darren Booker-Wilson **Seats** 120, Private dining 130 **Open** All year **Prices from** S £6.95, M £17, D £7.50 **Parking** 150 **Notes** Children welcome

The Vineyard
◉◉◉ MODERN BRITISH V ⚑NOTABLE WINE LIST
01635 528770 | Stockcross, RG20 8JU
www.the-vineyard.co.uk
Spoiler alert: no wine is made at The Vineyard, but they do have a world-class cellar that runs to a staggering 30,000 bottles by way of compensation. The vinous theme of this opulent, contemporary country house is apparent as soon as you're through the door, with a glass floor above the wine vault. Style-magazine rooms, chic public areas and a glossy spa are what to expect, while Robby Jenks's classy, intelligent cooking provides ample justification to explore that stupendous cellar. In an elegant split-level dining room, where a sweeping staircase sports a grapevine-style balustrade and striking artworks , the show opens with lobster ravioli, its richness cut with citrus bisque, grapefruit, pickled ginger and basil. A highly worked, razor-sharp main course brings slow-cooked chicken with liver parfait, a riff on broccoli including lustrous purée and charred stems, and pungent kimchi. At the end, a stimulating beurre noisette parfait is partnered with blueberries, nasturtium leaf, and lemon purée and espuma. Expert sommeliers guide the way through that astonishing cellar, starting with around 100 available by the glass.
Chef Robby Jenks **Seats** 86, Private dining 140 **Open** All year **Parking** 100 **Notes** Children welcome

The Woodspeen – Restaurant and Cookery School
◉◉◉ MODERN BRITISH
01635 265070 | Lambourn Road, RG20 8BN
www.thewoodspeen.com
Once a country boozer that had fallen on hard times, The Woodspeen is now a destination restaurant with a swanky cookery school just across the road. The building has been reworked from top to toe and expanded with an impressive glass-fronted, double

continued on page 28

MAIDENHEAD

The Royal Oak Paley Street

◉◉◉ MODERN BRITISH 🍾 NOTABLE WINE LIST

01628 620541 | Paley Street, Littlefield Green, SL6 3JN

www.theroyaloakpaleystreet.com

Contemporary British cooking chez Parkinson

In the safe hands of the Parkinson family (co-owned by Sir Michael and son Nick), the Oak has been reborn as a dining pub of our times where it's much more 'pre-meal aperitifs than pints' these days. New head chef Leon Smith (with Craig Johnston – *MasterChef: The Professionals* 2017 champion – as sous chef) continues the Oak's kitchen ethos, built around prime seasonal ingredients, simplicity and bold flavour, while looking smart on the plate too. On-trend 'snacks' (think chorizo muffins) pave the way, while starters like wood pigeon with caramelised chicory, walnuts and port illustrate the bold style. Roasted cod with a garlic crumb might follow, teamed with salsify, sea vegetables and a red wine sauce, while classy desserts, perhaps poached Yorkshire rhubarb with whipped custard and orange cake, show form to the end. Service is on-cue yet unstuffy, while the serious wine list reinforces the more-restaurant-than-pub status.

Chef Leon Smith **Seats** 80, Private dining 20 **Open** All year **Prices from** S £7, M £18, D £8 **Parking** 70 **Notes** Vegetarian dishes, Children welcome

BERKSHIRE

volume extension that has a touch of contemporary Scandi-chic about it. But it takes more than a fancy makeover to establish a foothold on the ever-competitive gastro scene, and the pull here is chef-patron John Campbell's highly skilled modern British cooking supported by his naturally engaging staff. Impressive technique and clever food combinations are there from the off – roasted scallops with pork cheek, their assertive flavours highlighted with mulled wine pears and thyme and shallot purée. Next comes venison, a juicy pavé and faggot matched with bacon choucroute, mustard potato, Swiss chard and blackberry jus, or perhaps roasted cod with salsify, braised onion and potted shrimps. Desserts are a high point, judging by a finale that riffs on the banana and custard theme, deftly accessorised with salted caramel sauce and crystallised peanuts – think posh Snickers bar, and you're there.

Chef John Campbell **Seats** 70, Private dining 12 **Closed** 26 December **Prices from** S £11, M £18, D £9 **Parking** 30 **Notes** Vegetarian dishes, Children welcome

READING
Caprice Restaurant
◉◉ MODERN BRITISH, INDIAN
0118 944 0444 | Holiday Inn Reading M4 Jct 10, Wharfedale Road, Winnersh Triangle, RG41 5TS
www.hireadinghotel.com

Floor-to-ceiling windows overlooking the plaza form one side of the split-level Caprice dining room in the Holiday Inn at junction 10 of the M4. It's an expansive, light-filled space with a relaxed feel, where the modern British cooking has clear, well-balanced flavours in abundance.

Chef Leon Sharp **Seats** 120, Private dining 40 **Open** All year **Prices from** S £9.25, M £24.50, D £7.50 **Parking** 132 **Notes** Vegetarian dishes, Children welcome

See advertisement opposite

Chez Mal Brasserie
◉ MODERN EUROPEAN, INTERNATIONAL
0118 956 2300 | Malmaison Reading, Great Western House, 18–20 Station Road, RG1 1JX
www.malmaison.com

By all accounts the world's oldest railway hotel, the early Victorian property is a real charmer. Its historic past is recognised in some decorative touches, and the overall finish is glamorous and stylish.

Chef Jan Chmelicek **Seats** 64, Private dining 22 **Open** All year **Notes** Vegetarian dishes, Children welcome

Forbury's Restaurant
◉ FRENCH, MEDITERRANEAN ▮ NOTABLE WINE LIST
0118 957 4044 | RG1 3BB
www.forburys.com

Cross the small terrace to enter the smart, warm and inviting interior of Forbury's, boasting floor-to-ceiling windows, white-clothed tables, mirror-reflected spotlights in the ceiling, and approachable, friendly staff. The forward-thinking kitchen stamps its own distinctive style on essentially French-oriented dishes.

Chef Davy Bonte **Open** All year **Parking** 20 **Notes** Vegetarian dishes, Children welcome

The French Horn
◉◉ TRADITIONAL FRENCH, BRITISH **V**
0118 969 2204 | Sonning, RG4 6TN
www.thefrenchhorn.co.uk

The riverside setting is a treat, with the dining room opening on to a terrace, at the family-run French Horn, which is full of old-school charm with slick and well-managed service. The menu looks across the Channel for its inspiration, with a classically based repertoire.

Chef Josiane Diaga **Seats** 70, Private dining 24 **Closed** 1–4 January **Parking** 40 **Notes** Children welcome

Millennium Madejski Hotel Reading
◉◉ BRITISH, INTERNATIONAL **V**
0118 925 3500 | Madejski Stadium, RG2 0FL
www.millenniumhotels.co.uk

The Madejski Stadium, base of Reading Football Club, shares an ultra-modern complex with this swishly smart hotel. There's a champagne bar on entry, while Cilantro is the fine-dining restaurant, its refined feel defined by a display of wines, neatly clothed tables and sharp service.

Chef Denzil Newton **Seats** 55, Private dining 20 **Closed** 25 December, 1 January and Bank holidays **Parking** 100 **Notes** No children under 12 years

SHINFIELD
L'Ortolan
◉◉◉ MODERN FRENCH **V** ▮ NOTABLE WINE LIST
0118 988 8500 | Church Lane, RG2 9BY
www.lortolan.com

A sophisticated high-end operation, L'Ortolan is a name synonymous with modern British gastronomy since the 1980s, with big-hitting names like Nico Ladenis, John Burton-Race and Alan Murchison all gracing its kitchen. Now, rising-star chef Tom Clarke

continued on page 30

28

2 AA Rosette
Caprice Restaurant & Terrace -
Holiday Inn Reading M4 Jct10

The stylish 2 AA Rosette Caprice Restaurant & Terrace at the Holiday Inn Reading M4 Jct10 is the epitome of fine dining, offering modern British cuisine and authentic Asian specialties.

Guests are spoilt for choice, with a seasonal à la carte menu featuring the finest local ingredients, and a set menu from £24.95. You really must leave space for the exceptional desserts. There are even pâtissiers who prepare an array of tempting treats - well worth the extra calories. For something more informal, try the stunning Monty's Lounge Bar, with resident pianist, serving authentic Indian specialties. The Afternoon High Teas are also highly recommended.

The Hotel offers a range of great features including the Esprit Wellness & Spa with 9m Pool, Sauna, Steam Room & large Gym, and the 'Academy', the ideal venue for hosting Meetings & Conferences, Weddings and Christmas Parties.

SHINFIELD continued

brings renewed prestige and sparkle with his take on vibrant contemporary cooking, raising the bar at the smart, country-house style restaurant (once a vicarage) in Reading's hinterland close to the M4. Underpinned by classical French grounding, Tom's highly detailed and technically savvy, adventurous cooking is honed from a larder of seasonal ingredients and delivered with flavour and gusto via jour, carte and gourmand or surprise tasting menus. Intricate presentation is to the fore, with pretty plates spun with surprise elements; take 'melting' torched mackerel with horseradish and beetroot to open proceedings, its intelligently balanced marriage of textures, colours and flavours hitting top marks. Mains ambition doesn't falter either; perhaps succulent glazed duck breast accompanied by apricot and lavender, or ocean-fresh pan-fried sea bream served with basil gnocchi and bouillabaisse. Equally smart desserts, like orange and yuzu tart with pickled butternut squash and buttermilk ice cream continue the high-energy delivery. Wines give France and Italy prime time, while the rest of Europe and the New World have a voice, but with a softer accent. Staff are as smartly turned out as the modern furnishings, and are expectedly professional and informed. A dinky chef's table in the kitchen, relaxing bar and private dining rooms round-off a polished act.

Chef Tom Clarke **Seats** 58, Private dining 22 **Closed** 2 weeks Christmas to New Year **Parking** 30 **Notes** No children under 3 years

THATCHAM
The Bunk Inn
@ @ MODERN BRITISH, FRENCH
01635 200400 | Curridge, RG18 9DS
www.thebunkinn.co.uk

A short canter from Newbury Racecourse, this convivial inn is still very much the village hub where locals prop up the bar by the open fire with a glass of ale and a packet of crisps, but its confident modern cooking also attracts foodies.

Chef Lewis Spreadbury **Seats** 50, Private dining 22 **Open** All year **Parking** 50 **Notes** Vegetarian dishes, Children welcome

WHITE WALTHAM
The Beehive
@ @ BRITISH
01628 822877 | Waltham Road, SL6 3SH
www.thebeehivewhitewaltham.com

With the cricket ground opposite, The Beehive is the epitome of the English village pub. A bar menu, daily changing lunch and dinner menus, and a specials board reveal season-driven, modern British dishes known for their gimmick-free, 'less is more' simplicity.

Chef Dominic Chapman **Seats** 75 **Closed** 25–26 December **Prices from** S £6.95, M £15.95, D £5.95 **Parking** 40 **Notes** Vegetarian dishes, Children welcome

WINDSOR
The Brasserie at Sir Christopher Wren
@ MODERN EUROPEAN
01753 442400 | Thames Street, SL4 1PX
www.sirchristopherwren.co.uk

At this Thames-side hotel consisting of several buildings clustered around a cobbled street, the menu is an appealingly varied slate of contemporary ideas. Starters take in scallops complemented by spicy tomato salsa and a balsamic reduction, or duo of duck terrine (foie gras and leg).

Chef Darran Kimber **Seats** 120, Private dining 100 **Open** All year **Prices from** S £6.95, M £12.50, D £7.50 **Parking** 14 **Notes** Vegetarian dishes, Children welcome

The Dining Room Restaurant
@ @ MODERN BRITISH V
01753 609988 | The Oakley Court, Windsor Road, Water Oakley, SL4 5UR
www.oakleycourt.co.uk

With turrets, gables and 37 acres of well-tended grounds, Oakley Court is a prime example of a Victorian Gothic castle. The half-panelled dining room, with its crisply clothed tables and formal service, is the place to head for creative modern British cooking.

Chef Coalin Finn **Seats** 96 **Closed** Christmas and New Year **Parking** 200 **Notes** Children welcome

The Greene Oak
@ MODERN BRITISH
01753 864294 | Oakley Green, SL4 5UW
www.thegreeneoak.co.uk

Very much a dining pub, The Greene Oak is a charming old place with bright, homely decor and cheerful staff who keep it all ticking along nicely. The kitchen makes good use of local seasonal ingredients, focusing on gently contemporary British- and European-inspired ideas.

Chef Graeme Terrell **Seats** 85 **Open** All year **Prices from** S £7, M £12.50, D £6.50 **Notes** Vegetarian dishes, Children welcome

WOKINGHAM
Miltons Restaurant
◉◉ EUROPEAN, INTERNATIONAL **V**
0118 989 5100 | Cantley House Hotel, Milton Road, RG40 1JY
www.miltonsrestaurant.co.uk

The Cantley House Hotel is a 17th-century barn, with a split-level dining space done in a rustic-chic manner, and modern brasserie food is the name of the game. Duck and bacon ballotine with seared foie gras and apple rösti is a well-conceived and well-executed starter.

Chef Jack Crocker **Seats** 60, Private dining 34 **Open** All year **Parking** 70 **Notes** Children welcome

▶ BRISTOL

BRISTOL
Adelina Yard
◉◉ MODERN BRITISH
0117 911 2112 | Queen Quay, Welsh Back, BS1 4SL
www.adelinayard.com

Owner-chef couple Jamie Randall and Olivia Barry have made quite an impact on the local scene since opening this stylish restaurant at the end of 2015. Located on the water's edge in the city's revitalised harbourside area, the open-plan kitchen provides an informal setting.

Chef Jamie Randall, Olivia Barry **Seats** 35 **Closed** 23 December to 8 January, 3 April and 21 July **Prices from** S £10, M £19, D £8 **Notes** Vegetarian dishes, Children welcome

Berwick Lodge
◉◉ MODERN BRITISH
0117 958 1590 | Berwick Drive, Henbury, BS10 7TD
www.berwicklodge.co.uk

The Victorian gent who built this manor house back in the 1890s picked a good spot, surrounded by 18 acres of gardens and woodland. The smart boutique restaurant, Hattua, is the perfect setting for creative modern dishes which look as good as they taste.

Chef Istvan Ullman **Seats** 80, Private dining 16 **Open** All year **Prices from** S £8.95, M £13.95 **Parking** 100 **Notes** Vegetarian dishes, Children welcome

The Bird in Hand
◉ MODERN BRITISH
01275 395222 | Weston Road, Long Ashton, BS41 9LA
www.bird-in-hand.co.uk

This tastefully renovated inn, a short drive from Bristol, strikes the correct balance between its various roles. If you're in search of a pint of local real ale, it fits the bill

as the village pub but scores highly as an informal destination dining venue.

Chef Felix Rayment **Seats** 30 **Open** All year **Prices from** S £7.50, M £16, D £6 **Notes** Vegetarian dishes, Children welcome

The Brasserie – Mercure Bristol North The Grange
◉ BRITISH, INTERNATIONAL
01454 777333 | Northwoods, Winterbourne, BS36 1RP
www.mercurebristol.co.uk

A lick of Farrow & Ball paint and some bold artworks have created an appealing contemporary space, but it's still a warm and comfortable setting, even with a bit of glamour about it. The kitchen's populist brasserie-style menu offers broad appeal.

Chef Ross McCarthy **Seats** 54, Private dining 12 **Open** All year **Prices from** S £6, M £14, D £6 **Parking** 150 **Notes** Vegetarian dishes, Children welcome

Casamia Restaurant
◉◉◉◉ MODERN BRITISH **V** NOTABLE WINE LIST
0117 959 2884 | The General, Lower Guinea Street, BS1 6SY
www.casamiarestaurant.co.uk

The location in a former hospital is the first singular statement that Peter Sanchez-Iglesias' Bristol high-flier makes, and it won't be the last. Pass through the monumental stone archway into a sleek, subtly monochrome interior with linen-clad tables and a tiled floor, the walls hung with arboreal pictures that are rotated by season, the better to orient city-dwellers to nature's rhythms. There is an open kitchen, in which a battalion of chefs works in fiercely concentrated calm to produce a succession of tasting menu dishes – four at lunch, seven at dinner – that are breathtakingly ingenious in their novelty and well-nigh flawless in execution. Dishes are brought to the table by chefs themselves, for true interaction with diners, since the menus themselves give next to nothing away, when 'salad / Beetroot / Duck / Rhubarb' might be the order of the day. Bookending it are the 'snacks' and 'sweets' that make modern dining out sound a little like midnight feasts in the dorm. That salad might be an assemblage of vinaigretted vegetables with tremulous sheep's-milk mousse and carrot jam, before a risotto simmered in beetroot juice, with yogurt sorbet and pickled fennel creating temperature and texture contrasts, arrives. A bowl of powerfully concentrated duck broth is copiously stocked with oyster mushroom, apple, mooli and a poached quail's egg, with a haunting note of lemon thyme running through it, while star billing goes to the honey-glazed duck itself, cooked with recourse to the ladling of hot oil à la Peking, the protean accompaniments – celeriac, fermented lentils, chia seeds in ponzu, mustard greens with chilli, baby lychee, and pak choi with orange – all pulling their respective weight. A first dessert of passionfruit and mini-meringues is deepened with intense tarragon mousse, and then an apple composition incorporating a chocolate-striped sorbet, rich apple mousse, pink peppercorns and a waft of bay orchestrates its various themes in full harmony. Wine pairings are chosen with the requisite attention to the complex detail of each dish. Casamia operates a non-refundable ticketing system, under which menu bookings must be paid in advance, with drinks and service charge added on the day.

Chef Peter Sanchez-Iglesias **Seats** 28 **Closed** Christmas, New Year and bank holidays **Notes** Children welcome

Glass Boat Restaurant
◉◉ MODERN FRENCH
0117 929 0704 | Welsh Back, BS1 4SB
www.glassboat.co.uk

This converted 1920s barge has been moored in the heart of Bristol's Harbourside area since 1986. It's a handsome and appealing restaurant with walnut floors, a beautiful marble bar and lovely river views and the menu offers modern French bistro fare with plenty of imagination.

Chef Jake Platt **Seats** 120, Private dining 40 **Closed** 24–26 December **Prices from** S £4, M £16, D £4 **Notes** Vegetarian dishes, Children welcome

Henbury Lodge Hotel
◉ MODERN
0117 950 2615 | Station Road, Henbury, BS10 7QQ
www.henburyhotel.com

A handsome Palladian villa close to Cribbs Causeway, on the outskirts of Bristol, Henbury Lodge is well positioned just a mile from junction 17 of the M5. With stripped wood floors and twinkling chandelier, Blaise Restaurant is a contemporary setting for modern British cooking interspersed with old favourites.

Chef Grant Spencer **Seats** 22 **Open** All year **Parking** 20 **Notes** Vegetarian dishes, Children welcome

Hotel du Vin Bristol
◉ FRENCH, BRITISH
0117 925 5577 | The Sugar House, Narrow Lewins Mead, BS1 2NU
www.hotelduvin.com

In a former sugar warehouse close to the waterfront, the casual French-inspired bistro at the Bristol HdV is a buzzy and easy-going venue. Factor in the world-class wine list, and you've got a compelling package. The bilingual menu deals in classic stuff.

Chef Marcus Lang **Seats** 85, Private dining 72 **Open** All year **Parking** 8 **Notes** Vegetarian dishes, Children welcome

The Ivy Clifton Brasserie
◉ BRITISH
0117 203 4555 | 42–44 Caledonia Place, BS8 4DN
www.theivycliftonbrasserie.com

Set in the heart of Clifton, just moments from the famous suspension bridge, this former bank has been tastefully converted into a must-visit restaurant in this area. Taking inspiration from her London big sister, it is a great casual dining all-day concept.

Chef Sean Burbidge **Seats** 130, Private dining 16 **Open** All year

The Ox
◉ MODERN BRITISH
0117 922 1001 | The Basement, 43 Corn Street, BS1 1HT
www.theoxbristol.com

Head down to the basement – a one-time bank vault – and you'll find a restaurant that the old boys of yesteryear would have admired, with its oak panels, ox blood leather seats and murals. They'd have appreciated the red-blooded menu too.

Chef Todd Francis **Seats** 80 **Closed** Christmas **Notes** Vegetarian dishes, Children welcome

Paco Tapas
◉◉ ANDALUSIAN TAPAS
0117 925 7021 | 3A Lower Guinea Street, BS1 6SY
www.pacotapas.co.uk

Located directly on the docks at Bristol harbourside, this bustling tapas bar offers authentic dishes from the owners' Andalusian home. Much of the produce comes directly from the region while daily specials are added by way of fresh fish and seafood delivered daily from Cornwall.

Chef Peter Sanchez-Iglesias **Seats** 28 **Closed** 24–26 December and 1 January **Notes** Vegetarian dishes, Children welcome

The Pump House
◉◉ MODERN BRITISH
0117 927 2229 | Merchants Road, Hotwells, BS8 4PZ
www.the-pumphouse.com

A hydraulic pumping station down on the waterside is the venue for a buzzy gastro pub and restaurant with a mezzanine seating area. The kitchen champions local produce, including foraged materials, and everything from bread to chutneys is made in-house.

Chef Toby Gritten, Nick Fenlon **Seats** 50 **Closed** 25 December **Prices from** S £6.50, M £15.50, D £6 **Parking** 20 **Notes** Vegetarian dishes, Children welcome

riverstation
◉ MODERN EUROPEAN
0117 914 4434 | The Grove, BS1 4RB
www.riverstation.co.uk

This lively venue is glazed from top to bottom to make the most of its harbourside location, both from the ground-floor café-bar and the industrial-chic first-floor restaurant. Inspiration is drawn from far and wide to create bright, up-to-date dishes rooted in good culinary sense.

Chef Alex Parsons **Seats** 120, Private dining 30 **Closed** 24–26 December **Notes** Vegetarian dishes, Children welcome

Root
◉ SMALL PLATES
0117 930 0260 | Unit 9, Cargo 1, Gaol Ferry Steps, BS1 6WP
www.eatdrinkbristolfashion.co.uk

Originating at the Queen Square Festival, Root is the restaurant venture of Eat Drink Bristol Fashion, and is stationed on the historic dockside at Wapping Wharf. In a vibrant, chattery atmosphere, with seating around the bar overlooking the kitchen, a menu of small sharing plates encompasses globally influenced cooking with plenty of attitude.

Chef Rob Howell **Seats** 30 **Closed** 25–26 December **Prices from** S £4 D £4 **Notes** Children welcome

Second Floor Restaurant
◉◉ MODERN BRITISH V ♦ NOTABLE WINE LIST
0117 916 8898 | Harvey Nichols, 27 Philadelphia Street, Quakers Friars, BS1 3BZ
www.harveynichols.com

Overlooking the old Quakers Friars Dominican friary in the heart of Cabot Circus shopping quarter, this gold and beige-hued second-floor dining room is a supremely relaxing place. The kitchen turns out a menu of lively modern British European food. There are interesting wines on offer.

Chef Louise McCrimmon **Seats** 60, Private dining 10 **Closed** 25 December, 1 January and Easter Sunday **Prices from** S £7.50, M £22, D £6.50 **Notes** Vegetarian dishes, Children welcome

The Spiny Lobster
◉ MEDITERRANEAN, SEAFOOD
0117 973 7384 | 128 Whiteladies Road, Clifton, BS8 2RS
www.thespinylobster.co.uk

Mitch Tonks' seafood brasserie and fish market maintains a rigorous commitment to freshness and simplicity, using fish and shellfish mostly landed by the Brixham boats. The dining room sports linen-clothed tables, staff are friendly, and top-class materials slapped onto a charcoal-burning Josper grill can't be beaten.

Chef Neil Roach, Charlie Hearn **Seats** 45 **Closed** 25 December and 1 January **Prices from** S £6.50, M £15, D £5 **Notes** Vegetarian dishes, Children welcome

Wilks Restaurant
◉◉ MODERN BRITISH, CLASSICAL FRENCH
0117 973 7999 | 1–3 Chandos Road, Redland, BS6 6PG
www.wilksrestaurant.co.uk

The sober seaweed-green frontage in the Redland district conceals a bright white interior adorned with the works of local studio and street artists. A versatile culinary output stretches to tasting menus of five and seven courses, with many memorable highs, including the top-drawer meats.

Chef James Wilkins **Open** All year **Notes** No children

▶ BUCKINGHAMSHIRE

AMERSHAM
The Artichoke
◉◉◉ MODERN EUROPEAN V ♦ NOTABLE WINE LIST
01494 726611 | 9 Market Square, Old Amersham, HP7 0DF
www.artichokerestaurant.co.uk

Laurie and Jacqueline Gear's effortlessly stylish restaurant can be found in an understated 16th-century building on Amersham's market square. Elegant, contemporary interior design mixes seamlessly with the beams and wooden floorboards – pale walls, cream leather button-backed banquettes, unclothed tables, and a view of the kitchen pass from one of the dining rooms. The service is polished and professional from smartly dressed staff who know their stuff. Laurie spent time at Copenhagen's Noma, inspiring not only the slightly Scandi feel of the decor, but also the direction of the cooking. Choose from the tasting menu, carte or the set-price lunch menu. You can expect brilliantly conceived, complex dishes, along the lines of roasted salsify with chervil emulsion, truffle, mushrooms, puffed wild rice and rye bread, or smoked haddock tartare with Royal Russet apple, radish and horseradish ice cream to begin, followed by saddle of Wooburn Common venison with smoked celeriac purée and blue cheese crumble. Desserts might include a stunning mandarin rice pudding soufflé with white chocolate and cardamom mousse and fresh mandarin – well worth the 15-minute wait. Breads are really excellent, so don't miss out.

Chef Laurie Gear, Ben Jenkins **Seats** 48, Private dining 16 **Closed** 2 weeks at Christmas, 1 week April (from Easter Sunday), 2 weeks in August/September **Prices from** S £13.50, M £24, D £6.50 **Notes** No children under 8 years at dinner

BUCKINGHAMSHIRE

Gilbey's Restaurant
◉◉ MODERN BRITISH
01494 727242 | 1 Market Square, HP7 0DF
www.gilbeygroup.com
Low ceilings, wood flooring and cheerful art on sky-blue walls create an ambience of stylish, intimate rusticity at this former grammar school, while friendly staff contribute to the congenial atmosphere. The kitchen makes a virtue of simplicity, working an intelligent vein of modern British ideas.
Chef Adam Whitlock **Seats** 50, Private dining 12 **Closed** 23–28 December **Prices from** S £7.95, M £17.95, D £7.95 **Notes** Vegetarian dishes, Children welcome

Hawkyns
◉◉ MODERN BRITISH INDIAN
01494 721541 | The Crown, 16 High Street, HP7 0DH
www.hawkynsrestaurant.co.uk
Set within The Crown Inn, a Tudor-style building, Hawkyns is run by the celebrated Indian chef Atul Kochhar. Set against a backdrop of original wooden beams, stripped floorboards and brick fireplaces, the scrubbed farmhouse-style tables and mismatched chairs add an informal pub feel.
Chef Atul Kochhar **Seats** 60, Private dining 40 **Open** All year **Parking** 35 **Notes** Vegetarian dishes, Children welcome

AYLESBURY
The Chequers Inn
◉ MODERN BRITISH
01296 613298 | 35 Church Lane, Weston Turville, HP22 5SJ
www.thechequerswt.co.uk
Dating from the 16th century, The Chequers Inn ticks all the 'quintessential inn' boxes with its open fireplace, venerable beams and polished flagstone and timber floors. The kitchen turns out a strong please-all roster of inventive modern gastro pub dishes.
Chef Jamie Maserati, Dritan Lani **Seats** 60, Private dining 32 **Open** All year **Prices from** S £7, M £15.50, D £5.50 **Parking** 30 **Notes** Vegetarian dishes, No children under 6 years

Hartwell House Hotel, Restaurant & Spa
◉◉ MODERN BRITISH ▪ NOTABLE WINE LIST
01296 747444 | Lower Hartwell, HP17 8NR
www.hartwell-house.com
Within 90 acres of parkland in the Vale of Aylesbury, Hartwell House is a majestic property with enough pomp to have served as home to an exiled claimant to the French throne (Louis XVIII, no less). Seafood normally crops up among well-constructed starters.
Chef Daniel Richardson **Seats** 56, Private dining 36 **Open** All year **Prices from** S £11, M £40, D £11 **Parking** 50 **Notes** Vegetarian dishes, No children under 6 years

BEACONSFIELD
Crazy Bear Beaconsfield
◉ BRITISH, INTERNATIONAL
01494 673086 | 75 Wycombe End, Old Town, HP9 1LX
www.crazybeargroup.co.uk
The word 'restraint' was not in the designers' brief when they converted this 15th-century coaching inn into a flamboyant, English-themed restaurant. It's a high-energy place, with a menu covering classics, chargrilled meats and some lively modern global ideas. The set-up has its own farm shop.
Chef Martin Gallon **Seats** 75, Private dining 22 **Open** All year **Parking** 20 **Notes** Vegetarian dishes, Children welcome

The Jolly Cricketers
◉ MODERN BRITISH
01494 676308 | 24 Chalfont Road, Seer Green, HP9 2YG
www.thejollycricketers.co.uk
The Jolly Cricketers ticks all the boxes with its cosy, low-ceilinged bar, cricket-themed pictures, congenial atmosphere (four-legged friends welcome too), real ales and a sensibly concise menu of crowd-pleasing modern dishes. Devilled Cornish crab with melba toast gets things off to a flying start.
Chef Matt Lyons **Seats** 36, Private dining 22 **Closed** 25–26 December **Prices from** S £6, M £14, D £6 **Parking** 10 **Notes** Vegetarian dishes, Children welcome

BRILL
The Pointer
◉◉ MODERN BRITISH
01844 238339 | 27 Church Street, HP18 9RT
www.thepointerbrill.co.uk
The Pointer's roots extend deep into its local community. As well as being a welcoming pub in the picturesque village of Brill near Aylesbury, it also encompasses a working organic farm and kitchen garden, and an adjacent butcher's shop for take-outs of its pedigree meats.
Chef James Graham **Seats** 30 **Closed** 1 week January **Prices from** S £8, M £19, D £7 **Parking** 5 **Notes** Vegetarian dishes, Children welcome

BUCKINGHAMSHIRE

BUCKINGHAM
Duke's Restaurant & Bar
◉ MODERN BRITISH
01280 822444 | Villiers Hotel, 3 Castle Street, MK18 1BS
www.villiers-hotel.co.uk

The Villiers has a smartly kitted-out restaurant overlooking a courtyard and the kitchen concentrates on tried-and-tested dishes but more innovative dishes are just as well handled, such as slow-cooked breast of lamb with piperade, goats' curd, aubergine, polenta and pine nuts.

Chef Paul Stopps **Seats** 70, Private dining 150 **Open** All year **Prices from** S £5, M £15, D £7 **Parking** 52 **Notes** Vegetarian dishes, Children welcome

BURNHAM
Burnham Beeches Hotel
◉◉ MODERN BRITISH, EUROPEAN
01628 429955 | Grove Road, SL1 8DP
www.corushotels.com/burnham

Close to Windsor, this extended Georgian manor house is set in 10 acres of attractive grounds. The oak-panelled Gray's restaurant is a formal affair with white linen and views of the pretty garden. The gently contemporary dishes are based on classical themes and techniques.

Chef Nenad Bibic **Seats** 70, Private dining 120 **Open** All year **Parking** 150 **Notes** Vegetarian dishes, Children welcome

CUBLINGTON
The Unicorn
◉ MODERN, TRADITIONAL BRITISH
01296 681261 | 12 High Street, LU7 0LQ
www.theunicornpub.co.uk

This 17th-century inn serves the community. It has a shop, opens for coffee mornings and afternoon teas on Friday and Saturday and serves bar snacks all day. Interesting ways with seafood can be seen in crab cakes with mango salsa, pea shoots and beurre blanc.

Chef Christopher George **Seats** 60, Private dining 30 **Open** All year **Prices from** S £5, M £10, D £6 **Notes** Vegetarian dishes, Children welcome

GERRARDS CROSS
The Bull Hotel
◉ MODERN BRITISH
01753 885995 | Oxford Road, SL9 7PA
www.sarova.com

The old Bull started life in 1688, serving travellers on the road between London and Oxford, and is now a swish four-star hotel. Its Beeches restaurant has a smart contemporary look and a Mediterranean-accented menu but puddings can be as Brit as Cox's apple tart.

Chef Siddarth Kapoor **Seats** 110, Private dining 150 **Open** All year **Parking** 100 **Notes** Vegetarian dishes, Children welcome

GREAT MISSENDEN
Nags Head Inn & Restaurant
◉ BRITISH, FRENCH
01494 862200 | London Road, HP16 0DG
www.nagsheadbucks.com

Only a 10-minute stroll from the enchantments of the Roald Dahl Museum, the family-run Nags Head is a 15th-century country inn by the River Misbourne. Lightly modernised inside, it makes a relaxed, welcoming setting for creatively fashioned cooking, and dishes with the populist touch.

Chef Claude Paillet, Tom Bell **Seats** 60 **Closed** 25 December **Prices from** S £6.45, M £13.95, D £4.95 **Parking** 50 **Notes** Vegetarian dishes, Children welcome

LONG CRENDON
The Angel Restaurant
◉ MODERN EUROPEAN, MEDITERRANEAN V
01844 208268 | 47 Bicester Road, HP18 9EE
www.angelrestaurant.co.uk

A one-time coaching inn dating from the 16th century, the Angel retains plenty of period charm, though it's more restaurant with rooms than country pub these days. There's a cosy bar for a pre-dinner drink, dining areas filled with original features, and a smart conservatory.

Chef Trevor Bosch **Seats** 75, Private dining 14 **Closed** 25 December **Parking** 30 **Notes** Children welcome

MARLOW
The Coach
◉◉◉ FRENCH, BRITISH
3 West Street, SL7 2LS
www.thecoachmarlow.co.uk

The Coach is a cosy, pubby sort of venue dominated by the L-shaped bar, with elbow-to-elbow tables, and an open kitchen where chefs are part of the buzzy dynamic, pitching in to help chatty staff whisk dishes out to the tables. Head chef Tom De Keyser turns out tapas-sized plates with the same DNA as the garlanded Hand & Flowers, Tom Kerridge's mothership up the road – deeply satisfying, big on flavour and glowing with technical finesse. Divided between 'meat' and 'no meat' dishes, the menu reads like a roster of big-hearted modern pub fodder – crispy pig's head with celeriac remoulade and spiced date sauce, perhaps, or a terrine of duck leg, heart and gizzard with prune and Armagnac ketchup. From the 'no meat' side might come potted crab with cucumber chutney and smoked paprika butter. For pudding, tonka bean pannacotta could arrive with mango, honeycomb and ginger wine jelly. The Coach doesn't take bookings, and with the Kerridge name sure to draw in the crowds, make sure to turn up nice and early with fingers firmly crossed.

Chef Tom De Keyser, Tom Kerridge **Seats** 40 **Closed** 25–26 December **Prices from** S £6.50, M £7.50, D £7.50 **Notes** Vegetarian dishes, Children welcome

Danesfield House Hotel & Spa
◉◉ MODERN BRITISH
01628 891010 | Henley Road, SL7 2EY
www.danesfieldhouse.co.uk

Danesfield House is nothing short of magnificent: a 1901 white mansion with a castellated roof in beautifully maintained grounds. The cooking comes out of the contemporary British mould. The odd luxury appears but the kitchen generally takes a down-to-earth approach.

Chef Billy Reid **Seats** 84, Private dining 14 **Open** All year **Parking** 100 **Notes** Vegetarian dishes, Children welcome

Glaze Restaurant
◉ MODERN BRITISH AND INDIAN
01628 496800 | Crowne Plaza Marlow, Field House Lane, SL7 1GJ
www.cpmarlow.co.uk/dine

The flagship restaurant of the Crowne Plaza Hotel, Glaze is a light-filled, stylish modern space, with full-drop windows enjoying views over the lake in the grounds from raspberry-coloured banquette seating. Seasonally changing menus of brasserie cooking keep up with the times in every sense.

Chef Lee Clarke **Seats** 150, Private dining 300 **Open** All year **Prices from** S £5.50, M £16.50, D £7.50 **Parking** 300 **Notes** Vegetarian dishes, Children welcome

See advertisement opposite

The Hand & Flowers
◉◉◉◉ FRENCH, BRITISH **V**
01628 482277 | 126 West Street, SL7 2BP
www.thehandandflowers.co.uk

Tom Kerridge remains a popular TV presence, most recently seen advocating a rational and enjoyable approach to dieting after the Christmas blowout. It's a career that speaks not just of a commitment to culinary excellence, though there is that too of course, but of thinking about cooking in ways that are neither excessively precious nor alienating in their technicality. What Kerridge is about, above all, is food that people want to eat, rather than baffling peculiarities they feel they ought to try. The nerve-centre remains the whitewashed country pub with its hanging baskets (plus its private dining space, The Shed, just up the road), where an atmosphere of endearing bonhomie prevails amid the bare tables and half-boarded walls. Marlow regulars doubtless appreciate the fact that the kitchen prides itself as much on producing a matchless roast beef and Yorkshire pudding for Sundays, as it does on working creative transformations on familiar ingredients. Slices of warm malt loaf accompany chunky pork and mushroom terrine dressed with Branston pickle, while the British attachment to Indian food produces accoutrements of lamb keema, dhal purée and lime pickle for a salt-baked carrot tart. At main, you might opt for the 'fish du jour' with butter-roasted cauliflower and caviar beurre blanc, but it's undoubtedly with pedigree meats that the principal emphasis rests. Cotswold venison with a game and bacon pie, Stiltoned parsnips and date purée vies for attention with duck breast on oat crumble and blood orange. It's all pretty substantial, but don't even think of resisting the signature chocolate and ale cake with salt caramel muscovado ice cream.

Chef Tom Kerridge **Seats** 54, Private dining 9 **Closed** 24–26 December **Prices from** S £11.50, M £29.50, D £13.50 **Parking** 20 **Notes** Children welcome

The Riverside Restaurant
◉◉ MODERN BRITISH
01628 484444 | Macdonald Compleat Angler, Marlow Bridge, SL7 1RG
www.macdonaldhotels.co.uk/compleatangler

There's a magnificent view of the Thames from the Riverside's conservatory dining room, while the service team, slick and professional, ensure there's nothing to detract from the occasion, be it a summer lunch or wintertime dinner. Tables on the outdoor terrace are a treat in warm weather.

Chef Michael Lloyd **Seats** 90, Private dining 100 **Open** All year **Parking** 100 **Notes** Vegetarian dishes, Children welcome

Glaze Restaurant at Crowne Plaza Marlow

Experience superb food and fine wine in Crowne Plaza Marlow's stylish Glaze Restaurant, awarded an AA Rosette for culinary excellence.

Glaze Restaurant offers contemporary, eclectic cuisine in a great atmosphere, with floor-to-ceiling windows providing stunning and uninterrupted views over the landscaped grounds and lake.

Choose from the creative seasonal modern British à la carte menu or the new authentic Indian menu. The splendid Afternoon Teas are also highly recommended.

Whether you are looking to enjoy an intimate meal for two or simply meet a few friends for cocktails on the lawns, we've got the perfect environment for you!

BUCKINGHAMSHIRE

MARLOW continued

Sindhu by Atul Kochhar
◉◉ MODERN INDIAN **V**
01628 405405 | Macdonald Compleat Angler, Marlow Bridge, SL7 1RG
www.sindhurestaurant.co.uk
This is Macdonald Hotels' second restaurant within its Compleat Angler on the River Thames by Marlow Weir. Atul is an acclaimed chef, renowned for his modern Indian cuisine and passion for sustainable fishing. Desserts work well and bhapi doi, rose yogurt cheesecake, is no exception.
Chef Prabhu Ganapati **Seats** 58 **Closed** 25 December **Prices from** S £11, M £17, D £7 **Parking** 100 **Notes** Children welcome

The Vanilla Pod
◉◉ BRITISH, FRENCH **V** ♨ NOTABLE WINE LIST
01628 898101 | 31 West Street, SL7 2LS
www.thevanillapod.co.uk
The culinary bar is set high in this stretch of the Thames Valley stockbroker belt, and The Vanilla Pod delivers a sure-footed take on modern British cooking, its roots clearly in the French classics. The setting is a handsome townhouse where TS Eliot once lived.
Chef Michael Macdonald **Seats** 28, Private dining 8 **Closed** 23 December to 10 January, Easter weekend, 28 May to 6 June, 27 August to 5 September **Notes** Children welcome

MEDMENHAM
The Dog and Badger
◉ BRITISH, EUROPEAN
01491 579944 | Henley Road, SL7 2HE
www.thedogandbadger.com
A short walk from the River Thames in the picturesque village of Medmenham, The Dog and Badger is also close to Henley-on-Thames and Marlow. A Grade II listed building with an abundance of original features, the kitchen adopts a 'please all' approach.
Chef Sam Walton **Open** All year **Notes** Children welcome

STOKE POGES
Humphry's at Stoke Park
◉◉◉ MODERN BRITISH
See pages 40–41

TAPLOW
André Garrett at Cliveden
◉◉◉ BRITISH, FRENCH **V** ♨ NOTABLE WINE LIST
01628 668561 | Cliveden Estate, SL6 0JF
www.clivedenhouse.co.uk
Dripping with a history of high society scandal and lording it over a whopping 376-acres of National Trust estate, Cliveden belongs unquestionably in the premier league of England's stately homes. The dining experience is pretty special too, in an impeccably elegant, swagged and chandeliered restaurant with shimmering views over parterre gardens to the Thames. André Garrett's dazzling cooking is more than a match for this luxurious setting, his pin-sharp technique deftly dovetailing French classics with inventive British modernism. The results are served up via a carte or an eight-course taster, plus a weekday lunchtime market menu that, while not exactly a bargain, represents great value considering the high-flying setting. Opening the show, Orkney scallops arrive in a picturesque medley with flower-like slices of radish, neatly aromatized with lemon and herb oil. Next up, braised shoulder of locally stalked venison is offset with watercress, chestnut, and pickled blackberries adding a balancing fruity note. Dessert also seduces with a classic idea – a masterclass Bramley apple soufflé – raised to another level by the gently aromatic note of bayleaf ice cream.
Chef André Garrett **Seats** 78, Private dining 60 **Open** All year **Prices from** S £15, M £21 **Parking** 60 **Notes** Children welcome

Berry's Restaurant and Terrace
◉ CLASSIC BRITISH
01628 670056 | Taplow House Hotel, Berry Hill, SL6 0DA
www.taplowhouse.com
The original Elizabethan manor was destroyed by fire, so today's house is a handsome piece of Georgian architecture instead, with suitably formal public rooms. The elegant Berry's Restaurant looks over the six acres of landscaped grounds, with huge French doors opening onto the terrace.
Chef Calvin Mallows **Seats** Private dining 86 **Open** All year **Parking** 40 **Notes** Vegetarian dishes, Children welcome

WADDESDON
The Five Arrows
◉◉ MODERN BRITISH
01296 651727 | High Street, HP18 0JE
www.waddesdon.org.uk
Part of the Rothschild estate, this small Victorian hotel stands at the gates of Waddesdon Manor but has none of the airs and graces of the grand French

château-style stately home. The relaxed restaurant sports a smart, contemporary look with wine-related prints on the walls.

Chef Karl Penny **Seats** 60, Private dining 30 **Open** All year **Parking** 30 **Notes** Vegetarian dishes, Children welcome

WOOBURN
Chequers Inn
◉◉ BRITISH, FRENCH
01628 529575 | Kiln Lane, Wooburn Common, HP10 0JQ
www.chequers-inn.com

A former 17th-century coaching inn, there's no denying that the Chequers has moved with the times. The Anglo-French cooking in its newly extended chic restaurant delivers compelling flavour combinations. Desserts are creative: try blueberry cheesecake with confit lemon and crème fraîche sorbet.

Chef Pascal Lemoine **Seats** 60, Private dining 60 **Open** All year **Parking** 50 **Notes** Vegetarian dishes, Children welcome

▶ CAMBRIDGESHIRE
BALSHAM
The Black Bull Inn
◉ MODERN BRITISH
01223 893844 | 27 High Street, CB21 4DJ
www.blackbull-balsham.co.uk

Topped by a mop of thatch and with a fabulous garden and terrace, Balsham's village hostelry has its own-brewed real ale on tap and a choice of eating spaces from the tucked-away nooks around the bar to a barn with a lofty vaulted ceiling.

Chef Andrew Price **Seats** 60, Private dining 60 **Open** All year **Prices from** S £5.50, M £10, D £6 **Parking** 20 **Notes** Vegetarian dishes, Children welcome

BARTLOW
The Three Hills
◉◉ MODERN BRITISH
01223 890500 | Dean Road, CB21 4PW
www.thethreehills.co.uk

The Three Hills is a charming 17th-century, Grade II listed pub with a lovely garden leading down to a river. A collection of wicker bulls' heads on the dining room's white clapboard-style walls are a sign this is a restaurant that reflects its rural location.

Chef Keith Deeks **Seats** Private dining 34 **Open** All year **Prices from** S £6, M £15, D £6.50 **Notes** Vegetarian dishes, Children welcome

CAMBRIDGE
Hotel du Vin Cambridge
◉ FRENCH BISTRO
01223 227330 | 15–19 Trumpington Street, CB2 1QA
www.hotelduvin.com

Hotel du Vin's Cambridge outpost is all reclaimed wooden floors, banquettes, unclothed wooden tables, candlelight, an open-to-view kitchen and references to wine all around. The place is normally humming, and well-drilled staff deliver authentic, well-executed bistro staples. Good-quality rustic bread is part of the package.

Chef Gareth Davies **Seats** 82, Private dining 32 **Open** All year **Notes** Vegetarian dishes, Children welcome

Hotel Felix
◉◉ MODERN MEDITERRANEAN
01223 277977 | Whitehouse Lane, Huntingdon Road, CB3 0LX
www.hotelfelix.co.uk

Combining elegant period features with the contemporary, this Victorian mansion is now home to a sleek boutique hotel. The Graffiti restaurant sports abstract modern art and the food is as vibrant as the decor, mixing modern British with plenty of sunny Mediterranean flavours.

Chef Edward Barker **Seats** 45, Private dining 60 **Open** All year **Prices from** S £7, M £17.50, D £5.75 **Parking** 90 **Notes** Vegetarian dishes, Children welcome

Midsummer House Restaurant
◉◉◉◉◉ MODERN BRITISH V ⬩NOTABLE WINE LIST
See pages 42–43

See advertisement on page 44

Quy Mill Hotel & Spa, Cambridge
◉◉ MODERN EUROPEAN, BRITISH, FRENCH
01223 293383 | Church Road, Stow-Cum-Quy, CB25 9AF
www.cambridgequymill.co.uk

Situated in the miller's house, and overlooking the waterwheel and mill race, the refurbished Mill House restaurant makes the most of this feature, while putting on a distinctly contemporary country inn look. By night it's an intimate place with open fires, candlelight, and cool jazz.

Chef Gavin Murphy **Seats** 48, Private dining 80 **Closed** 25 December **Prices from** S £8, M £18, D £8.50 **Parking** 90 **Notes** Vegetarian dishes, Children welcome

Cambridge continues on page 42

STOKE POGES

Humphry's at Stoke Park

◉◉◉ MODERN BRITISH

01753 717171 | Park Road, SL2 4PG

www.humphrysrestaurant.co.uk

Innovative cooking amid Georgian magnificence

If all you know of Stoke Poges is exhausted by its contiguity to Slough, think again. In the Edwardian decade, it saw the establishment of England's first ever country club and hotel, in the palatial form of Stoke Park. Aldous Huxley references Stoke in Brave New World as the location of a much-visited golf course, and a sprawling championship green surrounds a mansion that boasts celebrity credentials in abundance. James Wyatt, architect to George III, designed the house itself, with its magnificent balustraded frontage and soaring cupola, while the grounds were subject to a do-over, starting in 1791, by Humphry Repton, working with the grain of the 'Capability' Brown original. It's Repton, of course, who is acknowledged in the restaurant name, and a more fitting space could scarcely be imagined. Full-drop windows, a marble fireplace and a light gold colour scheme over a deep-pile, pink-hued carpet are enhanced by the utmost professionalism of the service approach.

This is a potentially humbling context for any chef to step into, but in Chris Wheeler, Stoke Park has a confident and inspired practitioner. What is refreshing about the menus is

that there is no sense of taking the most obvious route, layering old-fashioned luxuries on a tried-and-tested foundation. Many of the dishes are imbued with the same innovative spirit that characterises modern British cooking in much less opulent surroundings than these. Yes, there are oysters to start, but offered in three contrasting treatments: dressed in lime, ginger and soy; tempura-battered with pickled cucumber and topped with chorizo foam, matched with the juicy freshness of early strawberries. The terrine of ham hock and foie gras may seem more mainstream, but its accompaniments of salt-baked pineapple and chilli-boosted pineapple chutney lift it into another dimension.

Main courses are built on impeccable prime materials, treated both with respect and with inventive energy. A stupendous game dish offers succulent pheasant with hay-baked celeriac and pear, in a jus sweetened with blackberry liqueur, while halibut is gently sautéed and teamed with miso-glazed octopus, kohlrabi and parmesan gnocchi. The Brookfield Farm beef fillet remains a reference dish, with its shallot purée, bone marrow crumb and glossy red wine jus. Similarly, variations of sablé Breton, salty buttery biscuit layered with brûlée cream, served perhaps with clotted cream ice cream, are the basis of a signature dessert.

Chef Chris Wheeler **Seats** 50, Private dining 146 **Closed** 24–26 December, 1st week in January **Prices from** S £11.50, M £27.50, D £11.50 **Parking** 400 **Notes** Vegetarian dishes, No children under 12 years at dinner

CAMBRIDGE
Midsummer House Restaurant
◉◉◉◉◉ MODERN BRITISH V ⬩ NOTABLE WINE LIST

01223 369299 | Midsummer Common, CB4 1HA
www.midsummerhouse.co.uk

Beautiful, confident cooking in an elegant Victorian villa

Daniel Clifford's elegant, sophisticated modern British continues to go from strength to strength as he celebrates 20 years at Midsummer House. A comfortable Victorian villa, certainly not overly grand, but comfortable and confident, it stands with its back to the Cam, and looking out on the grazing cows of Midsummer Common from the front. It's a destination restaurant in the best sense of the phrase, with everything in place to ensure your journey, whether local or from much further afield, is not just worthwhile but truly memorable. The sunny conservatory dining room has been described as the perfect combination of formal and informal, smart in slate and charcoal, with starched white linen and a calm, friendly atmosphere. A window to the kitchen lets you see behind the scenes, where Clifford, along with head chef Mark Abbott and their dedicated team, are busy constructing precise, thoughtful dishes.

If you go for lunch there's a five-course tasting menu, (full vegetarian and pescatarian menus are available too, and vegan options), while at dinner there are eight courses. The

somewhat terse menu descriptions belie the complexity of the dishes, where every ingredient has been carefully considered, and you can be assured that every last detail has been given the attention it deserves. Not just delicious but beautiful to look at, this is eating elevated to its highest level. Seasonal flavours are spot on, and a winter meal might begin with a mouthful or two of velvety smooth pumpkin velouté, topped with a barley cracker and cubes of sherry jelly, before moving on to a perfectly balanced offering of braised pork knuckle with raclette, potato and morteaux sausage.

The scallop with apple is something of a signature dish, never off the menu, and you might follow that with game; partridge, perhaps, or quail, before monkfish arrives, paired with spiced aubergine, black quinoa, and burnt lemon purée. Grouse with pink fir apple, mushrooms and Savoy is richly satisfying, and the sorbet that follows, perhaps crème fraîche, with pear and pickled elderberries, a refreshing and unusual contrast. For dessert, the coriander white chocolate dome with coconut and mango and snowy jasmine rice is a delicate, exotic finale. If you've the appetite, the cheese trolley is a truly magnificent example.

Chef Daniel Clifford **Seats** 45, Private dining 16 **Closed** 2 weeks Christmas to New Year **Prices from** S £29, M £49, D £22 **Notes** No children

See advertisement on page 44

MIDSUMMER HOUSE

Midsummer House is located in the heart of historic Cambridge. This Victorian Villa encapsulates Daniel Clifford's vision for culinary perfection and is home to some seriously stylish food.

Daniel Clifford's quest for culinary perfection has taken the restaurant to another level over the past 13 years; his cooking has a modern-focus which is underpinned by classical French technique offering seriously sophisticated food with dishes arriving dressed to thrill.

Upstairs there is a private dining room, and a sophisticated bar and terrace for alfresco drinks with river views. Our private dining room is the perfect location for small weddings, lavish birthday celebrations, simple family gatherings or corporate entertaining.

Midsummer Common, Cambridge CB4 1HA

Tel: 01223 369299 • **Fax:** 01223 302672

Website: www.midsummerhouse.co.uk

Email: reservations@midsummerhouse.co.uk

CAMBRIDGE continued

Restaurant 22
◉ MODERN BRITISH
01223 351880 | 22 Chesterton Road, CB4 3AX
www.restaurant22.co.uk

The converted Victorian townhouse near Jesus Green conceals a discreetly elegant and comfortable dining room in shades of fawn, brown and beige. The monthly changing set-price menu consists of three courses and a sorbet, and the cooking is distinguished by a lack of unnecessary frill and flounce.

Chef Sam Carter **Seats** 26, Private dining 14 **Closed** 25 December, New Year **Prices from** S £6.50, M £15.50, D £6.50 **Notes** Vegetarian dishes, No children under 10 years

Restaurant Alimentum
Rosettes suspended MODERN EUROPEAN ◗ NOTABLE WINE LIST
See pages 46–47

ELLINGTON
The Mermaid
◉ FUSION, EUROPEAN, ASIAN **V**
01480 891106 | High Street, PE28 0AB
www.themermaidellington.co.uk

A charming 14th-century inn with ancient beams, stone floors and exposed brickwork, The Mermaid occupies an idyllic spot in this Cambridgeshire village. Just two minutes from the A14, the large garden offers spectacular views of the local church and welcoming log fires in the winter.

Chef Nicholas Marriott **Seats** 38, Private dining 12 **Closed** 25 December and 1st week in January **Prices from** S £4.50, M £18.50, D £4.50 **Notes** Children welcome

ELY
The Anchor Inn
◉ MODERN BRITISH **V**
01353 778537 | Bury Lane, Sutton Gault, Sutton, CB6 2BD
www.anchor-inn-restaurant.co.uk

Right out in the sticks, The Anchor was built more than 360 years ago for workers digging the canals that drained the Fens. The heritage of the building looms large when you get inside and the contemporary British food is the star attraction.

Chef Maciej Bilewski **Seats** 60 **Closed** 25–26 December **Parking** 10 **Notes** Children welcome

The Dining Room
◉ MODERN BRITISH **V**
01353 887777 | Poets House, 40–44 St Mary's Street, CB7 4EY
www.poetshouse.uk.com

The Dining Room restaurant at Poets House in the centre of Ely offers a good selection of seasonal dishes using fresh and locally sourced ingredients. The smart dining space is beautifully decorated in shades of grey right down to the softly padded chairs.

Chef Daniel Perjesi **Seats** 40, Private dining 20 **Open** All year **Notes** Children welcome

FORDHAM
The White Pheasant
◉◉ BRITISH, EUROPEAN
01638 720414 | 21 Market Street, CB7 5LQ
www.whitepheasant.com

The White Pheasant is a modern foodie pub with simply decorated interior, log fires and plain wood tables, but chef-proprietor Calvin Holland's cooking sets it a cut above the average. The kitchen sources the very best materials from local producers.

Chef Calvin Holland **Seats** 50 **Open** All year **Prices from** S £6.95, M £14.50, D £6.95 **Parking** 25 **Notes** Vegetarian dishes, Children welcome

HINXTON
The Red Lion Inn
◉ MODERN BRITISH
01799 530601 | 32 High Street, CB10 1QY
www.redlionhinxton.co.uk

With its timeless rustic cosiness, the timbered Tudor Red Lion's bar is a great spot for classic pub grub, but seekers of contemporary British cuisine head for the airy, oak-raftered restaurant, where there's an eclectic carte pitched just right for the kitchen's ambitions.

Chef Jiri Wolker **Seats** 60 **Open** All year **Parking** 43 **Notes** Vegetarian dishes, Children welcome

HUNTINGDON
The Abbot's Elm
◉ MODERN EUROPEAN
01487 773773 | Abbots Ripton, PE28 2PA
www.theabbotselm.co.uk

The interior of this 17th-century inn has a contemporary sheen while retaining its soul, with a lounge bar serving real ales and a cosy snug as well as a smart restaurant. Expect classy pub classics in the bar, while the restaurant ups the ante.

Chef Julia Abbey **Seats** 54 **Closed** 2 weeks January **Prices from** S £5.50, M £9.50, D £6.95 **Parking** 50 **Notes** Vegetarian dishes, Children welcome

CAMBRIDGESHIRE

CAMBRIDGE
Restaurant Alimentum
Rosettes suspended MODERN EUROPEAN 🍷 NOTABLE WINE LIST
01223 413000 | 152–154 Hills Road, CB2 8PB
www.restaurantalimentum.co.uk

Cooking of complex impact in a gastronomic boomtown

As we went to press, the Rosette award for this establishment was suspended due to a change of chef. Reassessment will take place in due course. The present-day dining scene in the old university city has for some time now been having a moment that bears all the signs of turning into a golden age. Some of the most innovative and original cooking is going on at Alimentum, a contemporary-styled venue not far from Homerton College that's all burnished hard surfaces, from the glossy flooring to the small unclothed tables. Fishtank windows allow that all-important view on the kitchen action, while full-length glazing looks out on the bustle of Hills Road. The first Sunday of the month is consecrated alternately to a Supper Club and Wine Club, the latter overseen by Alimentum's resident wine wizard Maxwell Allwood, and there is even a home catering service, but it's at the regular lunch and dinner sessions that the culinary sparks really start to fly.

The kitchen likes to try the very latest in culinary technique, with slow cooking a particular speciality, coaxing the tender succulence out of fine prime materials without

sacrificing any of their inherent flavour. The seven-course tasting menu, with optional wine pairing, sourced from the main carte, is clearly the most ambitious route to take, and showcases the imaginative approach to building taste and texture. Its two principal dishes on the winter offering might be stone bass and langoustine with cauliflower, goats' cheese and Pedro Ximénez, followed by beef sirloin and cheek aged for all of 80 days in a classically earthy medium of morels and red wine.

On the main carte, starters might involve an appealing pairing of roast scallop and smoked eel with pistachio and apple, or a duo of lamb neck and cockles in rhubarb vinegar and black garlic, before duck breast follows on, given its traditional sweetenings with carrot and maple syrup, but balanced out by the respectively sharper notes of pink grapefruit and Sichuan peppercorns. A discerningly stocked cheeseboard intervenes as a sore temptation before desserts refer back to olden days for Battenburg made with apricot and Amaretto, a Black Forest lineup of dark chocolate and cherry, satisfyingly boozed up with cherry beer as well as Kirsch. The impressive wine list is a labour of love, equally confident in both classics and new-wave thinking. Glass selections, boosted by a slate of Coravin-served fine wines, are particularly well chosen with the complex impact of the cooking in mind.

Chef Samira Effa **Seats** 62, Private dining 30 **Closed** 24–30 December and Bank holidays **Notes** Vegetarian dishes, Children welcome

CAMBRIDGESHIRE

HUNTINGDON continued

The Old Bridge Hotel
MODERN BRITISH NOTABLE WINE LIST
01480 424300 | 1 High Street, PE29 3TQ
www.huntsbridge.com

Once a bank, this 18th-century townhouse is now a boutique hotel with a popular restaurant. Although the kitchen occasionally looks to the Far East for inspiration, the modern style is more influenced by British and Mediterranean flavours.

Chef Jack Woolner **Seats** 80, Private dining 60
Open All year **Prices from** S £6.95, M £16.95, D £6.95
Parking 60 **Notes** Vegetarian dishes, Children welcome

KEYSTON
Pheasant Inn
MODERN BRITISH, EUROPEAN NOTABLE WINE LIST
01832 710241 | Loop Road, PE28 0RE
www.thepheasant-keyston.co.uk

Every inch the classic thatched village inn, the Pheasant flaunts its centuries-old pedigree, with simple furniture, welcoming open fires and oak beams. For over 50 years the place has been known for fine food — way before anyone added the gastro prefix to pub.

Chef Simon Cadge **Seats** 80, Private dining 30
Closed 2–15 January **Prices from** S £6.50,
M £11.95, D £5.95 **Parking** 40 **Notes** Vegetarian dishes, Children welcome

MELBOURN
Sheene Mill
MODERN, TRADITIONAL BRITISH
01763 261393 | 39 Station Road, SG8 6DX
www.sheenemill.com

The 16th-century mill house no longer works the River Mel, but the waterway and pond are reminders of its former life. Now, there are glorious gardens, a spa and stylish bedrooms, while the restaurant is watched over by an engaging service team.

Chef Neil Scott **Seats** 120, Private dining 60
Open All year **Parking** 50 **Notes** Vegetarian dishes, Children welcome

See advertisement below

PETERBOROUGH
Bull Hotel
MODERN EUROPEAN, BRITISH
01733 561364 | Westgate, PE1 1RB
www.peelhotels.co.uk

From the outside, this 17th-century former coaching inn displays its period credentials but there's a contemporary swagger once you get inside, not least

in the brasserie-style restaurant out back. With cream-painted brickwork and darkwood tables, the vibe is informal and cheerful.

Chef Chris Newman **Seats** 80, Private dining 200 **Open** All year **Prices from** S £5.25, M £15.50, D £5.95 **Parking** 100 **Notes** Vegetarian dishes, Children welcome

ST NEOTS
The George Hotel & Brasserie
◉◉ MODERN BRITISH
01480 812300 | High Street, Buckden, PE19 5XA
www.thegeorgebuckden.com

The Furbank family brought this old coaching inn back to life in 2003 by creating a cool and contemporary venue and respecting the integrity of the old building. The menu delivers feel-good flavours based on quality ingredients (including some they grow themselves).

Chef Benaissa El Akil **Seats** 60, Private dining 30 **Open** All year **Parking** 25 **Notes** Vegetarian dishes, Children welcome

STILTON
Bell Inn Hotel
◉◉ MODERN BRITISH V
01733 241066 | Great North Road, PE7 3RA
www.thebellstilton.co.uk

This coaching inn in a charming village may date from 1642 but its kitchen turns out bright ideas in the contemporary mode. Pulled pork and apple terrine with piccalilli and a deep-fried egg offers a good balance of flavours, and presentation is a forte.

Chef Jerzy Michalak **Seats** 60, Private dining 20 **Closed** 25 December, Bank holidays **Prices from** S £5.90, M £14.50, D £6.60 **Parking** 30 **Notes** Children welcome

WHITTLESFORD
The Red Lion at Whittlesford Bridge
◉ MODERN, TRADITIONAL BRITISH
01223 832047 | Station Road, CB22 4NL
www.redlionwhittlesfordbridge.com

Just off the M11 outside Cambridge, the Red Lion can trace its history back to the early Edwards, as is evidenced by its low-slung timbered facade and beamed interiors. Winter warmth radiates from the brick fireplaces, and staff are a model of friendly efficiency.

Chef Keith Deeks **Seats** 70, Private dining 120 **Open** All year **Parking** 80 **Notes** Vegetarian dishes, Children welcome

WISBECH
Crown Lodge Hotel
◉ MODERN, TRADITIONAL
01945 773391 | Downham Road, Outwell, PE14 8SE
www.thecrownlodgehotel.co.uk

A modern hotel kitted out to host conferences and meetings, Crown Lodge is a useful local resource. The flexible approach to dining means you can go for simple things like fish and chips or a burger, but there's also a more ambitious carte.

Chef Jamie Symons **Seats** 40, Private dining 100 **Closed** 25–26 December and 1 January **Parking** 50 **Notes** Vegetarian dishes, Children welcome

▶ CHESHIRE
ALDERLEY EDGE
Alderley Edge Hotel
◉◉ MODERN, CLASSIC BRITISH V
01625 583033 | Macclesfield Road, SK9 7BJ
www.alderleyedgehotel.com

The wealthy industrialist who built this hilltop Victorian Gothic pile certainly bagged pole position for its views over lush grounds, gardens and the surrounding countryside. The kitchen doesn't stint on top-class ingredients and its modern British dishes are well rehearsed and delivered.

Chef Sean Sutton **Seats** 80, Private dining 120 **Open** All year **Prices from** S £6.50, M £13.50, D £6.50 **Parking** 82 **Notes** Children welcome

BROXTON
Carden Park Hotel, Golf Resort & Spa
◉ MODERN BRITISH V
01829 731000 | Carden Park, CH3 9DQ
www.cardenpark.co.uk

Carden Park is a lavishly scaled country estate not far from Chester. If you look hard, you'll see its Jacobean core, but the views from the formal gardens to the Welsh mountains beyond are enough to be going on with.

Chef Graham Tinsley MBE **Seats** 300, Private dining 80 **Open** All year **Prices from** S £7, M £13, D £6.50 **Parking** 500 **Notes** Children welcome

BURWARDSLEY
The Pheasant Inn
◉ BRITISH, EUROPEAN
01829 770434 | Higher Burwardsley, CH3 9PF
www.thepheasantinn.co.uk

The Pheasant's wide-ranging menu features a healthy showing of local produce and pleases both traditionalists seeking pub classics done well (home-made pies and gravy, or beer-battered haddock and chunky chips with mushy peas and tartare sauce, say) or those looking for more contemporary ideas.

Chef Matt Leech **Seats** 120 **Open** All year **Prices from** S £4.50, M £12.25, D £6.95 **Parking** 60 **Notes** Vegetarian dishes, Children welcome

CHESTER
Brasserie ABode
◉◉ MODERN CLASSIC FRENCH **V**
01244 405820 | Grosvenor Road, CH1 2DJ
www.abodechester.co.uk/brasserie-abode/brasserie

The Cheshire outpost of the ABode hotel group occupies a shiny modern rotunda overlooking Chester racecourse. Its restaurant is on the fifth floor, with stellar views over the castle and lush countryside. There's a contemporary finish, with stylish fixtures and rather glam light fittings.

Chef Matthew Lloyd **Seats** 90, Private dining 16 **Open** All year **Prices from** S £5.50, M £9.99, D £5.50 **Parking** 36 **Notes** Children welcome

La Brasserie at The Chester Grosvenor & Spa
◉◉ MODERN EUROPEAN **V**
01244 324024 | Eastgate, CH1 1LT
www.chestergrosvenor.co.uk

La Brasserie offers commendable support to its superstar sibling the Simon Radley restaurant. With all the swagger of an authentique Parisian outfit, it has black-leather banquettes, shimmering brass and a giant hand-painted skylight, plus a menu that builds confidently on classic ideas.

Chef Simon Radley, Gareth Jones **Seats** 80 **Closed** 25 December **Prices from** S £7.95, M £19.95, D £6.95 **Notes** Vegetarian dishes, Children welcome

Chef's Table
◉◉ MODERN BRITISH
01244 403040 | Music Hall Passage, CH1 2EU
www.chefstablechester.co.uk

At the end of a narrow alley between a dress shop and a coffee house, Chef's Table is the place for an all-day brunch, maybe an Isle of Man crab sandwich, a roast lamb rump salad or a Hebridean black pudding tattie scone.

Chef Liam McKay **Seats** 26 **Closed** Christmas and New Year **Prices from** S £5.95, M £14.95, D £5.50 **Notes** Vegetarian dishes, Children welcome

Grosvenor Pulford Hotel & Spa
◉ MEDITERRANEAN, EUROPEAN
01244 570560 | Wrexham Road, Pulford, CH4 9DG
www.grosvenorpulfordhotel.co.uk

The sprawling red-brick hotel has a swish spa, luxe bedrooms, and pretty gardens, but the main dining option of Ciro's Brasserie stands out with its classical theme recalling ancient Rome via arches, murals and stucco paintwork. It's the setting for a broadly Mediterranean-inspired menu.

Chef Richard Pierce **Seats** 120, Private dining 200 **Open** All year **Parking** 200 **Notes** Vegetarian dishes, Children welcome

Hallmark Hotel Chester The Queen
◉ BRITISH
01244 305000 | City Road, CH1 3AH
www.hallmarkhotels.co.uk/hotels/The-Queen-Chester

This Victorian railway hotel has been given an eye-popping makeover, with much use of loudly patterned fabrics. There are three restaurants, the principal one being a sleek space with kitchen views. The style is brasserie, with quality ingredients treated with respect in vigorously flavoured dishes.

Chef Alan Davies **Seats** 54, Private dining 16 **Open** All year **Parking** 153 **Notes** Vegetarian dishes, No children under 8 years

Restaurant 1539
◉ MODERN BRITISH
01244 304611 | Chester Race Company Limited, The Racecourse, CH1 2LY
www.restaurant1539.co.uk

Part of the Chester racecourse complex, 1539 was given a cool half-million's worth of upgrade in 2014. The full-drop windows of the restaurant are still a major feature, and if your heart isn't given to equestrianism, swivel round for an ambient view into the kitchen.

Chef Ian Penn **Seats** 160, Private dining 60 **Open** All year **Parking** 60 **Notes** Vegetarian dishes, Children welcome

Simon Radley at The Chester Grosvenor
◉◉◉◉ MODERN FRENCH **V** ⚑ NOTABLE WINE LIST
01244 324024 | Eastgate, CH1 1LT
www.chestergrosvenor.co.uk

The hotel has a prime spot within the ancient Roman walls of the city, next to the historic Eastgate Clock, and with its Simon Radley restaurant, The Chester Grosvenor is the undoubted epicentre of the city's culinary activity. The opulent dining room is rich with shades of gold and cream, with plush chairs to sink into, and a smart and well organised team on hand to service your needs. The dress code is smart, but this is the 21st century, and the mood is suitably buoyant. The fixed-price menu and eight-course tasting menus (vegetarians get their own bespoke version) offer up Mr Radley's creative take on contemporary British and

European cookery, with superlative ingredients and flavour combinations that are nearly always compelling. Take a combination of beautifully caramelised scallops and tender suckling pig, with wild nettles and gooseberries adding layers of sharp and sweet, or another seafood-meat combination, with braised turbot and chicken wings, wee dumplings and blackened artichokes. A lobster and fennel roll is the star of a halibut main course (with poached mussels and saffron sauce), while two might share Edge's beef sirloin, smoked on Douglas Fir needles. There's just as much skill and modern pizzazz in desserts such as the en coque – a chocolate and apple combination that is something to behold. The wine list is an epic journey into some of the world's best vintages.

Chef Simon Radley, Ray Booker **Seats** 45, Private dining 14 **Closed** 25 December **Notes** No children under 12 years

The Sticky Walnut
⊛⊛ MODERN EUROPEAN
01244 400400 | 11 Charles Street, CH2 3AZ
www.stickywalnut.com

The Sticky Walnut is spread over two floors, with chunky wooden tables, blackboards and an open kitchen. With cracking desserts like a deconstructed lime cheesecake with pecan butter biscuits and chocolate sorbet, this is a kitchen that delivers real impact.

Chef Luke Richardson **Seats** 50 **Closed** 25–26 December **Notes** Vegetarian dishes, Children welcome

CONGLETON
Pecks
⊛ MODERN BRITISH
01260 275161 | Newcastle Road, Moreton, CW12 4SB
www.pecksrest.co.uk

Hiding behind hedges on the A34, Pecks is decorated in soothing variations of cream and white, its principal dining area adorned with a whopping chandelier and a wall of celebrity photographs. A multi-course taster called Dinner at Eight is teeming with innovative dash all through.

Chef Les Wassall **Seats** 105, Private dining 30 **Closed** 25–30 December **Prices from** S £7.50, M £12, D £7.95 **Parking** 30 **Notes** Vegetarian dishes, Children welcome

See advertisement below

CHESHIRE

CREWE
Crewe Hall
⊛ MODERN EUROPEAN
01270 253333 | Weston Road, CW1 6UZ
www.qhotels.co.uk

Jacobean Crewe Hall is reminiscent of a grand stately home with magnificent interiors, but there's nothing stuffy about it, and that especially goes for the Brasserie, housed in a modern wing of the building, with its open-plan layout and buzzy atmosphere.

Chef Dave Ashton **Seats** 120 **Open** All year
Prices from S £5, M £13, D £5.50 **Parking** 500
Notes Vegetarian dishes, Children welcome

KNUTSFORD
Cottons Hotel & Spa
⊛ MEDITERRANEAN
01565 650333 | Manchester Road, WA16 0SU
www.thwaites.co.uk/cottons-hotel-knutsford

A large, modern hotel at the edge of town, Cottons' menu is an appealing Mediterranean brasserie-style package. Try the hand-stretched, stone-baked pizza for main and perhaps something a little more English like sticky toffee pudding for dessert.

Chef Adrian Sedden **Seats** 80, Private dining 30
Open All year **Prices from** S £6.95, M £114.95, D £4.50
Parking 120 **Notes** Vegetarian dishes, Children welcome

Mere Court Hotel & Conference Centre
⊛ MODERN MEDITERRANEAN
01565 831000 | Warrington Road, Mere, WA16 0RW
www.merecourt.co.uk

Mere Court hotel has bags of appeal. Dating from the turn of the 20th century, this imposing Arts and Crafts house has plenty of period swagger. The oak-panelled Arboretum Restaurant is an elegant spot with lake views, and is the setting for upbeat European-inspired cooking.

Chef Mike Malbon **Seats** 40, Private dining 150
Open All year **Parking** 150 **Notes** Vegetarian dishes, Children welcome

The Mere Golf Resort & Spa
⊛⊛ INTERNATIONAL
01565 830155 | Chester Road, Mere, WA16 6LJ
www.themereresort.co.uk

The Mere is a must for Cheshire's fairways fans, plus it's a good location for accomplished brasserie dining in the open-plan Browns. Expect relatively formal service and food that makes some good modern statements.

Chef Mark Fletcher **Seats** 76, Private dining 60
Open All year **Parking** 400 **Notes** Vegetarian dishes, Children welcome

LYMM
The Church Green British Grill
⊛⊛ MODERN BRITISH
01925 752068 | Higher Lane, WA13 0AP
www.thechurchgreen.co.uk

Chef-patron Aiden Byrne will be a familiar face to *MasterChef* fans, and known to anyone who's eaten recently at some of London's premier addresses. The focus is on traditional British grill cooking, with excellent prime materials.

Chef Aiden Byrne **Seats** 50 **Closed** 25 December
Prices from S £6, M £17.50, D £6 **Parking** 25
Notes Vegetarian dishes, Children welcome

MOTTRAM ST ANDREW
Mottram Hall
⊛ MODERN BRITISH
01625 828135 | Wilmslow Road, SK10 4QT
www.qhotels.co.uk/mottramhall

A dapper 18th-century pile, Mottram Hall's attractions stretch as far as golf, pampering in the spa, and modern country-house dining in the classy Carrington Grill. The food keeps step with the times and is well prepared from high-quality raw materials.

Chef Colin Gannon **Seats** 90, Private dining 14
Open All year **Parking** 300 **Notes** Children welcome

NANTWICH
Rookery Hall Hotel & Spa
⊛⊛ MODERN BRITISH
01270 610016 | Main Road, Worleston, CW5 6DQ
www.handpickedhotels.co.uk/rookeryhall

Rookery Hall was built in 1816 by a Jamaican sugar plantation owner whose wealth is evident in the sumptuous interior. Sound technique and accuracy are hallmarks. Try breast of Yorkshire grouse with creamed potato, bread purée, cabbage and bacon fricassée, watercress cream and wood sorrel.

Chef Matthew Jencitis **Seats** 90, Private dining 160
Closed 31 December **Prices from** S £12, M £32, D £10
Parking 100 **Notes** Vegetarian dishes, Children welcome

PECKFORTON
1851 Restaurant at Peckforton Castle
⊛⊛⊛ MODERN BRITISH V
01829 260930 | Stone House Lane, CW6 9TN
www.peckfortoncastle.co.uk

Built straight out of the imagination of a wealthy Victorian gent, this mightily imposing building replete with turrets and crenellations still does justice to the lofty ambition of its originator. It's 21st-century incarnation as a hotel and wedding venue features pampering treatments, events, luxe bedrooms and a host of outdoor activities on hand. The 1851 Restaurant has made the hotel a dining destination, too. The slick and stylish dining room matches the modern thinking in the kitchen, with its sparkling glassware and cutlery and a shimmering wall of wine bottles as you enter. Chef Jason Hodnett has a knack for coaxing out the max from flavours – in a starter of hand-dived scallops partnered with shellfish-packed ravioli and roast leek consommé or in a main course showcasing wood pigeon, the tender roast breast matched with a confit leg bonbon, beetroot in various colours and textures, sweetcorn granola and purée and the tart balancing note of blueberry. Another virtuoso workout of flavours and textures closes the show – English strawberries playing the lead role in parfait and consommé form, together with milk sorbet, lavender and sweet herbs.

Chef Jason Hodnett **Seats** 65, Private dining 160 **Open** All year **Parking** 300 **Notes** Children welcome

PUDDINGTON
Macdonald Craxton Wood Hotel
@ MODERN BRITISH **V**
0151 347 4000 | Parkgate Road, Ledsham, CH66 9PB
www.macdonaldhotels.co.uk/craxtonwood

Set in 27 acres of peaceful woodland, this grand-looking hotel near Chester is stylish and relaxed. Muted colours and dining chairs in striped fabric add an elegance to the restaurant, where the Josper grill comes into its own for main-course meats.

Chef Matthew Jencitis **Seats** 100, Private dining 12 **Open** All year **Parking** 300 **Notes** Children welcome

SANDIWAY
Nunsmere Hall Hotel
@@ BRITISH, EUROPEAN
01606 889100 | Tarporley Road, Oakmere, CW8 2ES
www.nunsmere.co.uk

A delightful country house with its own lake. Start with a drink in the Captain's Bar, then glide in state to a berth in the Crystal dining room, where pictures of polo players adorn the walls. The cooking keeps things firmly anchored in European tradition.

Chef Alex Rees **Seats** 60, Private dining 120 **Open** All year **Prices from** S £10, M £22, D £10 **Parking** 120 **Notes** Vegetarian dishes, Children welcome

TARPORLEY
Macdonald Portal Hotel Golf & Spa
@ MODERN
01829 734100 | Cobblers Cross Lane, CW6 0DJ
www.macdonaldhotels.co.uk/the portal

The Portal restaurant has panoramic views of its golf courses and the Cheshire countryside. Comfortable leather banquette seating and unclothed tables make for an unfussy look – the cooking likewise with classic steaks and grills supporting forays into a modern style.

Chef Mark Burke **Seats** 100, Private dining 45 **Open** All year **Prices from** S £7, M £13, D £6 **Parking** 200 **Notes** Vegetarian dishes, Children welcome

WARMINGHAM
The Bear's Paw
@ MODERN EUROPEAN, BRITISH
01270 526317 | School Lane, CW11 3QN
www.thebearspaw.co.uk

A Victorian pub given a modern makeover inside, with lots of light wood, and library shelves in the dining room. Local farmers supply the kitchen with quality North Western produce, with cheeses and ice creams also sourced from within a tight radius.

Chef Scott Cunningham **Seats** 150 **Open** All year **Prices from** S £5.50, M £13.95, D £6.25 **Parking** 75 **Notes** Vegetarian dishes, Children welcome

WARRINGTON
The Park Royal
@ MODERN BRITISH
01925 730706 | Stretton Road, Stretton, WA4 4NS
www.qhotels.co.uk

The opulent country hotel at Stretton began life more humbly in late Georgian times as the vicarage for nearby St Matthew's, but has grown in grandeur with the years. Its expansive restaurant, Topiary in the Park, takes its name from the sculpted greenery on view.

Chef Dave Ashton **Open** All year **Parking** 400 **Notes** Vegetarian dishes, Children welcome

WILMSLOW
The Stanneylands
@@ BRITISH
01625 525225 | Stanneylands Road, SK9 4EY
www.stanneylands.co.uk

Despite being over the county border in Cheshire, Wilmslow has long been a gentrified refuge from nearby Manchester and the airport. This stylish country hotel delivers a gently modern repertoire, ideal for those seeking an escape from urban bustle.

Chef Robert Egginton **Seats** 60, Private dining 120 **Open** All year **Parking** 110 **Notes** Vegetarian dishes, Children welcome

▶ CORNWALL & ISLES OF SCILLY

BODMIN
Trehellas House Hotel & Restaurant
◉ TRADITIONAL
01208 72700 | Washaway, PL30 3AD
www.trehellashouse.co.uk

Trehellas House is a modern country hotel, its rooms spread between an inn and coach house. Its beamed, slate-flagged dining room makes a homely setting for bright Cornish cooking mixing innovation and tradition. Proximity to Camel Valley makes that vineyard's benchmark fizz the obvious aperitif.

Chef Simon Woon **Seats** 40 **Open** All year
Prices from S £6, M £13, D £7 **Parking** 30
Notes Vegetarian dishes, Children welcome

BOSCASTLE
The Wellington Hotel
◉◉ MODERN BRITISH, FRENCH
01840 250202 | The Harbour, PL35 0AQ
www.wellingtonhotelboscastle.com

There's a traditional bar with real ales and blackboard menus and a charming restaurant with chandeliers at this 16th-century coaching inn with a castellated tower. The kitchen sources its materials from within the county and serves bright, modern ideas with their roots in the classics.

Chef Kit Davis **Seats** 35, Private dining 30 **Open** All year **Parking** 15 **Notes** Vegetarian dishes, Children welcome

BRYHER (THE ISLES OF SCILLY)
Hell Bay
◉◉◉ MODERN BRITISH **V**
01720 422947 | TR23 0PR
www.hellbay.co.uk

Not nearly as alarming as it sounds, Hell Bay is actually an idyllic secluded cove embraced by benign gorse-laden hillocks. Reached by ferry from St Mary's or Tresco, tiny Bryher is small enough to get around on foot, and the unassuming white hotel the perfect spot to set off from. There is much to love in its Cornish art-filled rooms and sea views, while on the food front Richard Kearsley's assured, confident cooking is a

major draw. You're in the right place when it comes to fish and seafood, whether it's halibut gravad lax with gribiche sauce, fennel and potato crisp, or mains such as wild sea bass, pan-roasted and partnered with a harmonious broth of saffron, mussels and herbs. And there are thoroughbred meats too, with West Country venison making its way across the waves for a signature dish of the haunch in chocolate jus with turnip gratin and red cabbage. The bar stays equally high for dessert: perhaps a tour de force of chocolate mousse brownie, frozen peanut butter mousse, caramel popcorn, chocolate ganache and peanut brittle.

Chef Richard Kearsley **Seats** 70, Private dining 12
Closed 14 October to 16 March **Parking** 5
Notes Children welcome

CALLINGTON
Langmans Restaurant
◉◉ MODERN BRITISH
01579 384933 | 3 Church Street, PL17 7RE
www.langmansrestaurant.co.uk

This restaurant offers finely crafted regional food in an unassuming venue between the moorlands of Bodmin and Dart. A digestive pause will do nicely before Cornish and West Country cheeses appear, prior to two desserts. A chocolate version of the B52 cocktail shot might precede crumble.

Chef Anton Buttery **Seats** 24 **Open** All year
Notes Vegetarian dishes, No children

FALMOUTH
The Greenbank Hotel
◉◉ MODERN BRITISH
01326 312440 | Harbourside, TR11 2SR
www.greenbank-hotel.co.uk

The house that became the Greenbank Hotel has occupied this spot since 1640, and in 2015 its restaurant received a top-to-toe facelift. A new head chef delivers a roster of classics and modern dishes with Cornish produce as a starting point.

Chef Nick Hodges **Seats** 80, Private dining 16
Open All year **Prices from** S £6, M £11, D £6
Parking 60 **Notes** Vegetarian dishes, Children welcome

Merchants Manor
@@@ MODERN BRITISH
01326 312734 | 1 Weston Manor, TR11 4AJ
www.merchantsmanor.com

Falmouth isn't short of spa hotels, but there is a pleasingly historic air to the Merchants Manor, a white-fronted house on a hill, built in 1913 for a local brewing family. Bright interiors create a fresh feeling, and the Rastella dining room is done in white linen with vintage candles and designer flatware. Regionally sourced materials are the mainstay, many of them finding their way on to the wood-fired grill, and there's a clear seam of creativity to the menus. Hazelnut-crumbed duck confit with rhubarb poached in grenadine offers succulence and depth of flavour, or there could be Newlyn mackerel with apple and cucumber, as a prelude to locally landed fish of the day with celery in beurre noisette, or Trewithick lamb loin and shoulder, teamed with crab, sea vegetables and garlic purée. Steaks from the grill are abidingly popular, served with ale-pickled mushrooms, onion rings and salsa verde. Finish with Milk and Honey, an assemblage of milk sorbet, Cornish honey, lemon posset and white chocolate, or with cinnamon-spiced pear in mulled wine with cocoa nibs.

Chef Hylton Espey **Seats** 64 **Open** All year
Notes Vegetarian dishes, Children welcome

Oliver's Eatery
@@ MODERN, TRADITIONAL BRITISH
01326 218138 | 33 High Street, TR11 2AD
www.oliversfalmouth.com

When the ingredients are either foraged or fresh from Falmouth harbour, you're off to a flying start at this relaxed and unassuming high-street venue run by a husband-and-wife team. The kitchen makes everything from scratch. The place is booked well in advance.

Chef Ken Symons **Seats** 28 **Closed** 10 December to 8 January and Bank holidays **Notes** Vegetarian dishes

The Pendennis Restaurant
@@ MODERN BRITISH
01326 313042 | The Royal Duchy Hotel,
Cliff Road, TR11 4NX
www.royalduchy.com

With palm trees framing splendid sea views across the bay from its alfresco terrace, the Royal Duchy Hotel certainly has a glorious setting. It's a fitting backdrop for confident, gently contemporary cooking. Simple intuitive combinations are the style.

Chef John Mijatovic **Seats** 100, Private dining 24
Open All year **Parking** 40 **Notes** Vegetarian dishes, Children welcome

See advertisement below

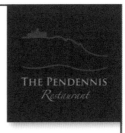

Penmorvah Manor

◉ MODERN BRITISH

01326 250277 | Budock Water, TR11 5ED

www.penmorvah.co.uk

The stone-built manor house has stood in its six acres of wooded gardens near Falmouth since 1872. The atmosphere is white-linened gentility, the culinary style is modern brasserie, with well turned-out dishes making an impact on both eye and palate.

Chef Mark Firth **Seats** 60, Private dining 60 **Open** All year **Prices from** S £5.50, M £14.95, D £4.50 **Parking** 100 **Notes** Vegetarian dishes, Children welcome

St Michael's Hotel and Spa

◉◉ MODERN MEDITERRANEAN, BRITISH

01326 312707 | Gyllyngvase Beach, Seafront, TR11 4NB

www.stmichaelshotel.co.uk

There's a stylishly upmarket vibe at this seaside hotel with its hip-looking bar and nautically themed restaurant. The kitchen buys materials solely from local producers, and its passion for cooking is palpable. Try the peanut butter parfait with moreish chocolate sorbet and chunks of banana.

Chef Stuart Shaw **Seats** 80, Private dining 25 **Open** All year **Prices from** S £7.50, M £16.95, D £6.95 **Parking** 30 **Notes** Vegetarian dishes, Children welcome

FOWEY
Fowey Hall

◉◉ BRITISH

01726 833866 | Hanson Drive, PL23 1ET

www.foweyhallhotel.co.uk

Writer Kenneth Grahame was a regular visitor to this grand Victorian pile overlooking Fowey Estuary – it was the inspiration behind Toad Hall in *The Wind in The Willows*. The wood-panelled restaurant showcases the unpretentious food, made with the best ingredients sourced from the region.

Chef James Parkinson **Seats** 36, Private dining 20 **Open** All year **Prices from** S £8, M £16, D £8 **Parking** 36 **Notes** Vegetarian dishes, No children under 8 years

GOLANT
Cormorant Hotel & Restaurant

◉◉ MODERN EUROPEAN

01726 833426 | PL23 1LL

www.cormoranthotel.co.uk

The Cormorant occupies a roost above the estuary, as a seat on the sunny terrace confirms. A pastel-hued dining room is the setting for Mediterranean-style cooking with Cornish produce is in evidence throughout. At dessert, go Caribbean with pineapple Tatin and coconut ice cream.

Chef Dane Watkins **Seats** 30 **Open** All year **Prices from** S £7, M £14, D £5 **Parking** 20 **Notes** Vegetarian dishes, No children under 12 years at dinner

HAYLE
Rosewarne Manor

◉◉ MODERN BRITISH

01209 610414 | 20 Gwinear Road, TR27 5JQ

www.rosewarnemanor.co.uk

Family-run, this striking 1920s building near Hayle beach has all the trappings of the small country manor house. A large sitting area leads on to the rear restaurant with views of the hotel's lovely gardens. Modern British cooking is delivered with confidence and the prime local ingredients shine.

Chef Phil Thomas **Seats** 36, Private dining 12 **Closed** 1st 2 weeks of May **Prices from** S £7, M £18, D £7 **Parking** 50 **Notes** Vegetarian dishes, Children welcome

HELSTON
New Yard Restaurant

◉◉ BRITISH

01326 221595 | Trelowarren Estate, Mawgan, TR12 6AF

www.newyardrestaurant.co.uk

On Cornwall's stunning Lizard peninsula, the New Yard Restaurant is at the heart of the historic Trelowarren Estate. Occupying the former stable yard, the distinctive interior sports a chequered floor, arched windows and bare wooden tables, while the open-plan kitchen produces punchy, seasonal cooking.

Chef Jeffery Robinson **Seats** 50, Private dining 20 **Closed** January **Prices from** S £7.95, M £14.95, D £6.95 **Parking** 20 **Notes** Vegetarian dishes, Children welcome

HIGHER TOWN (THE ISLES OF SCILLY)
Cloudesley Shovell Restaurant

◉◉ MODERN SEASONAL, SEAFOOD

01720 422368 | Karma St Martin's Hotel TR25 0QW

www.karmastmartins.com

The Karma St Martin's hotel restaurant is named after former Admiral of the Fleet who lost 22 ships off the Scilly coast in a 1707 naval disaster. The seasonally changing menu includes several 'true' catches of the day with whole crab and lobster a speciality. Alfresco dining is available in the summer months.

Chef Mike Potts **Open** All year **Notes** Children welcome

LOOE
Trelaske Hotel & Restaurant
◉◉ MODERN BRITISH
01503 262159 | Polperro Road, PL13 2JS
www.trelaske.co.uk

In a rural location between Looe and Polperro, this small hotel is surrounded by four acres of grounds. Dishes are intelligently composed to allow flavours to sparkle. Kick things off with the starter of crabmeat with pink grapefruit and rösti.

Chef Ross Lewin **Seats** 40 **Closed** November to March **Parking** 60 **Notes** Vegetarian dishes, No children under 5 years

LOSTWITHIEL
Asquiths Restaurant
◉◉ MODERN BRITISH
01208 871714 | 19 North Street, PL22 0EF
www.asquithsrestaurant.co.uk

Its black-and-white decor, smartly set tables and elegant staff create positive impressions of this restaurant opposite the church, where food is taken seriously. Confit duck and beetroot pastilla is teamed with silky pomegranate molasses and couscous, for example.

Chef Graham Cuthbertson **Seats** 28, Private dining 10 **Closed** Christmas and January **Prices from** S £6, M £14, D £7 **Notes** Vegetarian dishes, Children welcome

MAWGAN PORTH
The Scarlet Hotel
◉◉ MODERN EUROPEAN ♦NOTABLE WINE LIST
01637 861800 | Tredragon Road, TR8 4DQ
www.scarlethotel.co.uk

The Scarlet has impeccable eco credentials, but first and foremost it's about hedonistic pleasures – wining, dining and serious pampering. The kitchen team focuses on the West Country. Dessert of white chocolate mousse is surrounded by honeycomb shell, joined by pistachio cake and griottine cherries.

Chef Tom Hunter, Mike Francis **Seats** 70, Private dining 20 **Closed** 2–27 January **Prices from** S £7.50, M £12, D £6.50 **Parking** 37 **Notes** Vegetarian dishes, No children

MAWNAN SMITH
Budock Vean Hotel
◉ MODERN BRITISH V
01326 250288 | TR11 5LG
www.budockvean.co.uk/food

Cornwall's climate helped create the 65 acres of sub-tropical gardens that surround Budock Vean, but it is the owners' vision that made an organically managed landscape of woodlands, gardens and golf course. In the elegant restaurant, Cornish produce is treated with simplicity and respect.

Chef Darren Kelly **Seats** 100, Private dining 40 **Closed** 3 weeks in January **Parking** 100 **Notes** Children welcome

Meudon Hotel
◉ MODERN CLASSIC V
01326 250541 | TR11 5HT
www.meudon.co.uk

Bream Cove Restaurant presents an inviting space amid coastal gardens overlooking Falmouth Bay. The order of the day is modern cooking with a nod to classic cuisine, offering a true flavour of Cornwall and a sound helping of local wines.

Chef Chris Carr **Seats** 75 **Closed** 28 December to January **Prices from** S £6, M £15, D £6 **Parking** 40 **Notes** Children welcome

MEVAGISSEY
Trevalsa Court Hotel
◉◉ MODERN BRITISH
01726 842460 | School Hill, Polstreth, PL26 6TH
www.trevalsa-hotel.co.uk

Situated on a clifftop, there is a real sub-tropical feel to this handsome granite and slate house. When the sun shines, a table on the terrace with views across Mevagissey Bay is worth its weight in gold, but the view is special from inside, too.

Chef Adam Cawood **Seats** 26 **Closed** December to January **Parking** 20 **Notes** Vegetarian dishes, Children welcome

MULLION
Mullion Cove Hotel
◉◉ MODERN BRITISH
01326 240328 | TR12 7EP
www.mullion-cove.co.uk

This solidly built white property on the Lizard Peninsula sits on the clifftop, giving uninterrupted sea and coast views. The kitchen is committed to local suppliers, with day boats providing seafood but an international element is evident in some dishes.

Chef Paul Stephens **Seats** 60, Private dining 20 **Open** All year **Parking** 45 **Notes** Vegetarian dishes, No children under 7 years

CORNWALL & ISLES OF SCILLY

The Restaurant at the Polurrian Bay Hotel
◉◉ MODERN BRITISH
01326 240421 | TR12 7EN
www.polurrianhotel.com

This one-time Victorian railway hotel has been reworked in smart contemporary style. From its perch on the cliffs of the Lizard Peninsula, the rather grand restaurant presents those wild coastal views as a backdrop to inventive modern cooking based on tip-top ingredients from local producers.

Chef Wesley Wheeler **Seats** 60, Private dining 25 **Open** All year **Prices from** S £7, M £19, D £7 **Parking** 35 **Notes** Vegetarian dishes, Children welcome

NEWQUAY
Samphire
◉◉ MODERN BRITISH
01637 872211 | Fistral Beach, TR7 1EW
www.headlandhotel.co.uk

You'll likely find yourself distracted by the incredible views from the Headland's elegant dining room when you should be perusing the menu – you might even spot dolphins out in the bay. Inside it's smart and sharp – crisp linens, formal service.

Chef Christopher Archambault **Seats** 150, Private dining 100 **Open** All year **Prices from** S £10, M £14, D £8 **Parking** 100 **Notes** Vegetarian dishes, Children welcome

Silks Bistro and Champagne Bar
◉ MEDITERRANEAN SEAFOOD
01637 839048 | Atlantic Hotel, Dane Road, TR7 1EN
www.atlantichotelnewquay.co.uk

Although it was built in 1892 this is no gloomy Victorian haunt. Silks is bright and modern, with zebra-patterned bar stools, and sunburst-styled café chairs at linen-swathed tables. In the evenings, candlelight softens the scene. Save room for feel-good puddings.

Chef Gavin Hill **Seats** 100, Private dining 24 **Open** All year **Prices from** S £3.95, M £12.95, D £4.50 **Notes** Vegetarian dishes, Children welcome

The Terrace
◉ CLASSIC BRITISH
01637 872211 | The Headland Hotel and Spa, TR7 1EW
www.headlandhotel.co.uk

Located just steps from the famous sands of Fistral Beach, the Terrace restaurant has floor to ceiling glass, wooden floors, and a laid-back beach vibe. The short bistro-style menu presents such starters as garlic prawns and harissa dip, or Cornish mussels.

Chef Tony Ward, Chris Archambault **Seats** 50 **Open** All year **Prices from** S £7, M £12, D £6 **Parking** 100 **Notes** Vegetarian dishes, Children welcome

PADSTOW
Paul Ainsworth at No. 6
◉◉◉◉ MODERN BRITISH **V** 🍷 NOTABLE WINE LIST
See pages 60–61

Rojano's in the Square
◉ ITALIAN, MEDITERRANEAN
01841 532796 | 9 Mill Square, PL28 8AE
www.paul-ainsworth.co.uk/rojanos

This vibrant restaurant brings a pleasing Mediterranean warmth to the local foodie scene. A few tables out front and a heated first-floor balcony keep alfresco-dining die-hards happy, while the kitchen takes its cue from Italian cuisine and Cornish ingredients in a crowd-pleasing roster of sourdough pizzas, classic pasta dishes and daily blackboard specials.

Chef Paul Dodd, Jack Clements **Seats** 72 **Closed** 3 weeks in January **Notes** Vegetarian dishes, Children welcome

St Petroc's Bistro
◉ MEDITERRANEAN, FRENCH **V**
01841 532700 | 4 New Street, PL28 8EA
www.rickstein.com

The bistro is an informal and relaxing sort of place, with simple tables and chairs on worn wooden floorboards, modern paintings on plain white walls, and professional service from attentive staff. There's a cosy bar and a pleasant lounge for pre-dinner drinks.

Chef Mark O'Hagan **Seats** 54, Private dining 14 **Closed** 25–26 December **Prices from** S £5.95, M £15.95, D £6.95 **Notes** Vegetarian dishes, Children welcome

The Seafood Restaurant
◉◉◉ INTERNATIONAL SEAFOOD **V** 🍷 NOTABLE WINE LIST
01841 532700 | Riverside, PL28 8BY
www.rickstein.com

Padstow's rather different these days from the little fishing village of Rick Stein's youth, with great places to eat a dime a dozen, but this is the granddaddy of them all and still top of everyone's list – so book well ahead for the busy season. There's a sunny conservatory at the front, a roof terrace, views of the harbour, and a bright, friendly, informal air – seaside colours, comfortable seating, and an eclectic selection of modern art. Once you're in, sit at the bar with a drink and watch them plating up starters and you'll soon be keen to get cracking – literally, if you go for one of the magnificent fruits de mer platters. Otherwise you could begin with fresh-as-a-daisy Cornish crab with wakame, cucumber and dashi salad – sweet and vibrant flavours given a kick by wasabi mayonnaise – before moving on to a fillet of chargrilled seabass, perhaps – accurately timed, succulent fish complemented by a tomato and vanilla vinaigrette. Raspberry soufflé with pistachio ice cream is the perfect finale – excellently executed, beautiful to look at, and delicious.

Chef Stephane Delourme **Seats** 120 **Closed** 25–26 December **Prices from** S £10.50, M £20, D £8.90 **Notes** No children under 3 years

Treglos Hotel

◉◉ MODERN BRITISH **V**

01841 520727 | Constantine Bay, PL28 8JH

www.tregloshotel.com

A family-run hotel overlooking Constantine Bay near Padstow, this was converted from a Victorian house in the 1930s. Wallis Simpson stayed here before the abdication, and the smart interiors certainly look fitting for the glitterati. Menus take a modern approach.

Chef David Koeman **Seats** 80 **Closed** 30 November to 10 February **Parking** 40 **Notes** No children under 3

PENZANCE
The Bay@Hotel Penzance

◉◉ MODERN SEAFOOD

01736 366890 | Britons Hill, TR18 3AE

www.thebaypenzance.co.uk

The Bay sources its materials from the West Country, with fresh fish and shellfish hauled in from Cornish ports to appear in mains such as roast cod fillet with squid and vegetable compôte and seaweed salsa, or grilled brill with brown shrimps, tomato and samphire.

Chef Ben Reeve **Seats** 60, Private dining 12 **Closed** 1st 2 weeks in January **Prices from** S £6.50, M £15, D £7.25 **Parking** 11 **Notes** Vegetarian dishes, Children welcome

Ben's Cornish Kitchen

◉◉ MODERN BRITISH

01736 719200 | West End, Marazion, TR17 0EL

www.benscornishkitchen.com

Seagulls wheel about the thriving little village of Marazion, just outside Penzance, in a coastal scene that may strike a chord with followers of *Doc Martin*. Tropical elements add up to an irresistible dessert of coconut pannacotta with dried pineapple, lime-macerated mango, and spiced caramel.

Chef Ben Prior **Seats** 35, Private dining 20 **Open** All year **Notes** Vegetarian dishes, Children welcome

Harris's Restaurant

◉ BRITISH, FRENCH

01736 364408 | 46 New Street, TR18 2LZ

www.harrissrestaurant.co.uk

The Harris family have run their appealing restaurant on a cobbled side street in the town centre for over 30

years, offering professionally prepared and freshly cooked quality produce (local meats, seafood from Newlyn, for instance), with the kitchen taking an unshowy line.

Chef Roger Harris **Seats** 40, Private dining 20 **Closed** 3 weeks winter, 25–26 December, 1 January **Prices from** S £8.95, M £17.95, D £7.50 **Notes** Vegetarian dishes, No children under 5 years

The Tolcarne Inn

◉ SEAFOOD

01736 363074 | Newlyn, TR18 5PR

www.tolcarneinn.talktalk.net

Only the high sea wall separates The Tolcarne Inn from the crashing waves on the other side, adding considerable charm to this traditional pub next to Newlyn's fish market. Close links with local fishermen mean the day's catch dictates what appears on the chalkboard menu.

Chef Ben Tunnicliffe

POLPERRO
Talland Bay Hotel

◉◉ INTERNATIONAL

01503 272667 | Porthallow, PL13 2JB

www.tallandbayhotel.co.uk

Close to the pretty Cornish towns of Looe and Fowey, the dining room offers lovely views over the gardens and across the bay. Arty knick-knacks add an eclectic touch to the place's boutique charm and there are similar contemporary twists to the classic cookery.

Chef Nick Hawke **Seats** 40, Private dining 24 **Open** All year **Prices from** S £9, M £23, D £9 **Parking** 23 **Notes** Vegetarian dishes, Children welcome

PORT GAVERNE
Pilchards

◉ MODERN BRITISH

01208 880244 | Port Gaverne Hotel PL29 3SQ

www.portgavernehotel.co.uk

The Port Gaverne is a traditional inn, set in a tiny cove on Cornwall's dramatic north coast, just five minutes' walk from Port Isaac. Pilchards is their café, slap-bang on the beach. It's relaxed and friendly, offering excellent snacky dishes as well as larger plates.

Chef James Lean **Seats** 40 **Closed** January to Easter **Prices from** S £6.50, M £8.50, D £5.50 **Notes** Vegetarian dishes, Children welcome

PORT GAVERNE continues on page 62

PADSTOW
Paul Ainsworth at No. 6

◎◎◎◎ MODERN BRITISH V ⟨NOTABLE WINE LIST⟩

01841 532093 | 6 Middle Street, PL28 8AP

www.paul-ainsworth.co.uk

Technically innovative food in the bustling town centre

Padstow is certainly not short of custom, especially in the season when the narrow streets are thronged with the curious, keen to see one of the destination locales in gastronomic Cornwall. Paul Ainsworth's place is tucked away in the town centre, though only seconds from the harbour front, and is possessed of its own special appeal. The twin windows of the whitewashed frontage look into the compact front rooms of a Georgian townhouse, but dining goes on over two storeys, the neutral decor of the upper rooms offset by bold artworks, while the black-and-white tiled floors and stolid dressers laden with bottles of wine establish a homely atmosphere below.

Ainsworth's culinary vision, facilitated here by John Walton, has always been drawn to the creative sharp end of the modern British spectrum. There are technical peculiarities galore, and presentational innovations in abundance too – dishes arrive on boards and blocks, in grass-lined boxes and little pans, with sauces in transparent teapots for self-serving. While much press comment has been excited lately about this tendency, at

No 6 it works to enhance the novelty and delight of dishes, rather than as a distraction technique. Prime materials here are of the finest and freshest, from the locally landed fish to the thoroughbred meats such as Tamworth pork and Tamar Valley hogget to the never less than splendid cheeses. Remodelled classic dishes are powerfully persuasive, as in the version of quiche lorraine made with smoked haddock, but new-fangled combinations are sensational too, perhaps a pig's head fritter with smoked eel, Cox's Orange Pippin and roast onion. At main, that hogget is accompanied by a fricassée of the creamy sweetbreads, with a relish of red garlic ketchup to provide lift-off, while Dartmoor fallow deer comes in a very meaty array with a serving of pâté in crackling and January king cabbage roasted in duck fat. Fish of the day is typically teamed with white crabmeat for a true taste of the Cornish waters, offset with leek royale and shellfish gravy. Mellow Barkham Blue is the star cheese, served with a little apple pie for sweet contrast, but the ingeniously conceived desserts are equally hard to pass up. Expect Michel Cluizel 100% chocolate with olive oil sponge, sheep's-milk cheesecake on puff pastry, or a revolutionary trifle made with tea-soaked prunes and saffron. The set lunch menu offers exemplary value, perhaps centring on a serving of grass-fed beef short rib with cauliflower cheese in red wine sauce.

Chef Paul Ainsworth, John Walton **Seats** 46, Private dining 8 **Closed** 24–26 December, 13 January to 6 February **Prices from** S £14, M £32, D £12 **Notes** No children under 4 years

CORNWALL & ISLES OF SCILLY

PORT GAVERNE continued

Port Gaverne

◉◉ MODERN BRITISH, SEAFOOD **V**

01208 880244 | PL29 3SQ

www.portgavernehotel.co.uk

Tucked away in a hidden cove, a hilly but short stroll from Port Isaac, this whitewashed village inn with its hanging baskets and outdoor tables is pretty as a picture, the slate-floored bar giving way to a pair of interlinked dining rooms. The traditionally based cooking is inventive.

Chef James Lean **Seats** 80, Private dining 16 **Open** All year **Parking** 12 **Notes** Children welcome

See advertisement opposite

PORTHLEVEN

Kota Kai

◉ ASIAN

01326 574411 | Celtic House, The Shipyard, TR13 9JY

www.kotakai.co.uk

On the upper floor of Celtic House, Kota Kai is blessed with unbeatable views over the inner harbour of Porthleven, Britain's southernmost port. The menu, with its Asian bias, also rewards close attention, listing, for example, bao bun with hoisin sauce, kimchi, spring onions and peanuts.

Chef Jude Kereama **Notes** Children welcome

Kota Restaurant with Rooms

◉◉◉ BRITISH, PACIFIC RIM, SEAFOOD

01326 562407 | Harbour Head, TR13 9JA

www.kotarestaurant.co.uk

Situated on the harbour head by Porthleven's shingle beach and the bay, Kota is a streamlined operation, centred on a tiled dining room under an old beamed ceiling. Jude Kereama hails from New Zealand and brings the Asian-influenced approach of the southern hemisphere to bear on dishes such as Porthilly oysters with cucumber and rice wine granita in spring onion and smoked ponzu dressing, while salmon tartare is wasabied up and garnished with marinated keta caviar, avocado and a sesame tuile. 'Rockpool' is the signature main, an omnium gatherum of marine goodies in dashi broth, but there are also meat dishes such as five-spiced duck breast in teriyaki orange glaze with carrots, turnips and winter greens, while for vegetarians it may be pumpkin and quinoa pithivier with shiitakes and spinach. A fine balance of sweet and savoury is offered in a tart of wine-poached pear with Cropwell Bishop blue cheese ice cream and walnuts.

Chef Jude Kereama **Seats** 40 **Closed** January **Prices from** S £3, M £14.95, D £7.50 **Notes** Vegetarian dishes, Children welcome

PORT ISAAC

Outlaw's Fish Kitchen

◉◉ MODERN BRITISH, SEAFOOD

01208 881183 | 1 Middle Street, PL29 3RH

www.nathan-outlaw.com

Nathan Outlaw is a big fish in Cornwall with a number of restaurants across the county (plus one in London), the pick of which is Restaurant Nathan Outlaw itself. The Fish Kitchen is a rustic little place right on the harbour, with sea views.

Chef Tim Barnes, Max Allen **Seats** 25 **Closed** Christmas and January **Notes** Vegetarian dishes, Children welcome

Restaurant Nathan Outlaw

◉◉◉◉ MODERN BRITISH, SEAFOOD **V** ♦ NOTABLE WINE LIST

01208 880896 | 6 New Road, PL29 3SB

www.nathan-outlaw.com

When it comes to seafood cookery, Nathan Outlaw is the big fish these days, with a TV career, a host of cookery books, and restaurants in Cornwall, London and Dubai. At the top end of the village of Port Isaac, with inspiring sea views, you'll find the flagship restaurant, where admirers come to sample the food on which his reputation has been built. The first-floor dining room is an intimate space with Cornish artworks and an understated, natural finish, while downstairs the kitchen bar provides a few ringside seats to the culinary action. A six-course tasting menu is the way to go for lunch and dinner, with a wine flight if you want to leave all the decisions in their hands (and you're in safe hands). Things get off the mark with cured brill, with the harmonious partnership of peas and mint, before pickled herring arrives with cucumber and seaweed. The seafood is spectacularly fresh, sustainable, and hailing from these parts, and the technical proficiency of the kitchen team maximises the flavours on show. Salt-cod with cuttlefish, red wine and peppers may recall holidays in the Med, while lemon sole is as fresh as a daisy, with tartare hollandaise. Desserts are no afterthought, given the same level of precision and invention; malted orange profiteroles, say, with a top-notch chocolate sauce. The wine list includes a host of fizz options by the glass, including English and Japanese selections, with the rest of impressive the list arranged by style.

Chef Nathan Outlaw **Seats** 30 **Closed** Christmas and January **Notes** No children under 10 years

PORTLOE
The Lugger
◉◉ EUROPEAN
01872 501322 | TR2 5RD
www.luggerhotel.com

Dating from the 16th century, now a luxury hotel, The Lugger overlooks the sea and tiny harbour of a picturesque village on the Roseland Peninsula, with a terrace outside the smart, spacious restaurant for summer dining. Local ingredients are the kitchen's linchpin, particularly seafood.

Chef James Brougham **Seats** 45 **Open** All year **Parking** 25 **Notes** Vegetarian dishes, Children welcome

PORTSCATHO
Driftwood
◉◉◉◉ MODERN EUROPEAN
See opposite

REDRUTH
Penventon Park Restaurant
◉◉ MODERN BRITISH
01209 203000 | West End, TR15 1TE
www.penventon.co.uk

Set within a Georgian mansion run by the same family for over 45 years, the restaurant at Penventon Park juxtaposes original features with contemporary artwork and lighting. The food is just as eclectic, with Asian influences and a wood-charcoal oven.

Chef Keith Brooksbank **Open** All year **Parking** 100 **Notes** Children welcome

ST AGNES
Rose-in-Vale Country House Hotel
◉◉ MODERN BRITISH
01872 552202 | Mithian, TR5 0QD
www.roseinvalehotel.co.uk

At this gorgeous creeper-clad Georgian manor house on the north Cornish coast, the refurbished Valley Restaurant has a clean-lined contemporary look. Main courses draw on local fish landed at St Agnes but there may also be a two-way serving of local duck.

Chef Tom Bennetts **Closed** 4 January to 1 February **Notes** Vegetarian dishes, No children

ST AUSTELL
Boscundle Manor
◉◉ MODERN BRITISH V
01726 813557 | Boscundle, PL25 3RL
www.boscundlemanor.co.uk

Set in five acres of grounds, this 18th-century manor offers spa treatments and indoor pool. The smart restaurant is a draw in its own right. The candlelit dining room is intimate, and everything is made in-house, from bread to ice cream.

Chef Jenny Reed **Seats** 24, Private dining 14 **Open** All year **Notes** Children welcome

Carlyon Bay Hotel
◉ MODERN, TRADITIONAL BRITISH V
01726 812304 | Sea Road, Carlyon Bay, PL25 3RD
www.carlyonbay.com

Perched on a clifftop, this large hotel, spa and golf course is an imposing presence above the bay. The huge windows allow maximum exposure to the rugged Cornish coast views. The kitchen keeps it simple and relies on the quality and provenance of its ingredients.

Chef Paul Leaky **Open** All year **Notes** Children welcome

The Cornwall Hotel, Spa & Estate
◉ MODERN BRITISH V
01726 874050 | Pentewan Road, Tregorrick, PL26 7AB
www.thecornwall.com

The Arboretum Restaurant in the old White House part of the hotel is a classy, contemporary space done out in a fashionably muted palette. The menu here treads an uncomplicated modern path, keeping step with the seasons and making good use of regional ingredients.

Chef Andrew Dudley **Seats** 40, Private dining 16 **Open** All year **Parking** 100 **Notes** Children welcome

ST IVES
Carbis Bay Hotel
◉◉ INTERNATIONAL
01736 795311 | Carbis Bay, TR26 2NP
www.carbisbayhotel.co.uk

The family that run the hotel also own the sandy beach that is only 90 seconds away, and the view over sand and sea is breathtaking. The Sands Restaurant with its glorious sea views and contemporary finish has plenty of seafood up for grabs.

Chef Andrew Houghton **Seats** 150, Private dining 40 **Open** All year **Prices from** S £9.50, M £17.95, D £7.50 **Parking** 100 **Notes** Vegetarian dishes, Children welcome

The Garrack
◉ MODERN
01736 796199 | Burthallan Lane, TR26 3AA
www.thegarrack.co.uk

The restaurant offers sea views over St Ives and has a stylish contemporary look. Pan-fried scallops with crispy-coated black pudding, silky celeriac purée and roast pepper emulsion is a starter of vibrant, well-defined flavours, and global cuisines add variety.

Chef Tom Avery, Mark Forster **Seats** 52 **Open** All year **Prices from** S £5.50, M £15.95, D £5.95 **Parking** 20 **Notes** Vegetarian dishes, Children welcome

PORTSCATHO
Driftwood
◉◉◉◉ MODERN EUROPEAN
01872 580644 | Rosevine, TR2 5EW
www.driftwoodhotel.co.uk

Technically innovative cooking on the coastal path

The hotel stands in seven of its own acres, with a woodland path winding down to the private beach and cove on Gerrans Bay, a restorative location near a slip of a village on the South West Coast Path. The restaurant is bright and airy, a fitting context for Chris Eden's technically innovative and exciting food. Local materials feature, with expressive seafood dishes a particular strength. Start with crisped sea bass in beurre noisette bisque with saffroned kohlrabi, and then proceed to roast monkfish with samphire and textures of artichoke in thyme-laced roasting juices. If you're on a meatier roll, it could be red-leg partridge with honeynut squash and pickled plum to begin, followed by tender lamb loin with honey-glazed aubergine, olives, feta, pine nuts and vine leaves. The house dessert is 'thunder and lightning tart', a clotted cream custard with a crushed almond base.

Chef Christopher Eden **Seats** 34 **Closed** early December to early February **Parking** 20
Notes Vegetarian dishes, No children under 6 years

ST IVES continued

Porthminster Beach Restaurant
◉◉ MODERN MEDITERRANEAN, PACIFIC RIM **V**
01736 795352 | TR26 2EB
www.porthminstercafe.co.uk

Slap bang on stunning Porthminster Beach, this landmark white building occupies an enviable position. Whether you dine in the restaurant or on the terrace, the sea views are breathtaking. Vibrant pan-Asian dishes dominate the menu, which uses the best local seafood available.

Chef Mick Smith **Seats** 120, Private dining 60 **Closed** 25 December **Prices from** S £4, M £10, D £6.50 **Notes** Children welcome

Porthminster Kitchen
◉ INTERNATIONAL, PACIFIC RIM
01736 799874 | Wharf Road, TR26 1LG
www.porthminster.kitchen

A companion venue to the Porthminster Beach Restaurant just along the bay, the Kitchen also enjoys a bracing seaside location. Slick, stylish decor resists the indignity of seashells, and the menus deal in populist global cuisine with a Cornish accent.

Chef Michael Smith, Paul Olliver **Seats** 50 **Open** All year **Prices from** S £3.50, M £9, D £6.50 **Notes** Vegetarian dishes, Children welcome

The Queens
◉ MODERN BRITISH
01736 796468 | 2 High Street, TR26 1RR
www.queenshotelstives.com

Behind the flower-planted frontage of this pub it's all quite trendy and modern while retaining a traditional feel, so all comers are happy, as they are with the appealingly interesting cooking. Ideas for the dishes are plucked from a variety of sources.

Chef Chris Richards **Seats** 70 **Closed** 25 December **Notes** Vegetarian dishes, Children welcome

ST MAWES
Hotel Tresanton
◉◉◉ BRITISH, MEDITERRANEAN
01326 270055 | 27 Lower Castle Road, TR2 5DR
www.tresanton.com

A stunning cliffside location is the setting for this collection of cottages, transformed by Olga Polizzi into a supremely elegant and understated hotel. Superb views of the Cornish coast and laidback nautical chic contribute to an atmosphere of refined luxury. The calm, airy restaurant, with its mosaic tiled floor and shell-like lighting is classy, with simple table settings and engaging, responsive staff. If you're here in

daylight it will be hard to drag yourself away from the views. The cooking matches the environment with a pleasing simplicity; the uncluttered dishes have a refreshing Mediterranean influence. Kick off with a couple of Porthilly oysters, or salt cod croquettes with sauce vierge – a very simple, confident dish, reassuring in its accuracy. Monkfish with piperade and black olives, or Launceston lamb with heritage carrots, beetroot and sauté potatoes, are satisfying main courses, and you can finish with burnt English custard with raspberries and a poppy seed tuile, or keep it simple with strawberries, clotted cream and ice cream sundae.

Chef Paul Wadham **Seats** 60, Private dining 50 **Open** All year **Prices from** S £8, M £24, D £8 **Parking** 30 **Notes** Vegetarian dishes, No children under 6 years at dinner

ST MELLION
St Mellion International Resort
◉◉ MODERN INTERNATIONAL
01579 351351 | PL12 6SD
www.st-mellion.co.uk

St Mellion's culinary focus is the An Boesti restaurant, a spacious room with a striking colour scheme of black and white. Try the beef Wellington or loin of lamb with rhubarb, garlic confit and potatoes mashed with rosemary.

Chef Mark Brankin **Seats** 60 **Closed** Christmas and New Year **Parking** 750 **Notes** Vegetarian dishes, No children under 4 years

TRESCO (THE ISLES OF SCILLY)
New Inn
◉ MODERN, TRADITIONAL
01720 422849 | TR24 0QQ
www.tresco.co.uk

The friendly and welcoming New Inn sits beside the water, right at the heart of this small community, where guests and islanders mix happily. The fine dining here is based around island produce (everything else has to be brought in by sea, don't forget).

Chef James Jones **Seats** 80, Private dining 50 **Open** All year **Prices from** S £7, M £13, D £7 **Notes** Vegetarian dishes, Children welcome

Ruin Beach Café
◉◉ MODERN MEDITERRANEAN
01720 424849 | TR24 0PU
www.tresco.co.uk/eating-on-tresco/ruin-cafe

This former smugglers' cottage boasts stunning views of the Scilly Isles. A contemporary space with bare wooden tables and cutlery laid out on crisp tea towels, the food has similarly clean lines. Excellent island ingredients and classic cooking techniques makes for strong flavour definitions.

Chef James Jones **Seats** 65 **Closed** Winter **Prices from** S £8, M £14, D £7 **Notes** Vegetarian dishes, Children welcome

TRURO
The Alverton Hotel
⊚⊚ MODERN BRITISH, EUROPEAN
01872 276633 | Tregolls Road, TR1 1ZQ
www.thealverton.co.uk

Dating from 1830, The Alverton is an impressive building designed by the same chap as Truro Cathedral. There is plenty of period charm and a contemporary sheen to the upmarket brasserie. The menu takes a modern European path with a good representation of Cornish ingredients.

Chef Simon George **Seats** 60, Private dining 120 **Open** All year **Prices from** S £6, M £12, D £6 **Parking** 100 **Notes** Vegetarian dishes, Children welcome

Hooked Restaurant & Bar
⊚ MODERN BRITISH, SEAFOOD
01872 274700 | Tabernacle Street, TR1 2EJ
www.hookedrestaurantandbar.co.uk

Tucked away down a quiet street just off the city centre, there's a lively buzz about this smart brasserie. Uncovered tables, exposed brickwork and high ceilings with a sail loft feel add a seaside vibe, as do fish shoal lampshades. Seafood is the leading suit.

Chef Robert Duncan **Seats** 36, Private dining 24 **Open** All year **Prices from** S £2.95, M £12.95, D £4.95 **Notes** Vegetarian dishes, Children welcome

Mannings Hotel
⊚⊚ MODERN, PACIFIC RIM
01872 270345 | Lemon Street, TR1 2QB
www.manningshotels.co.uk

Mannings is a classic-looking solid-stone building – Grade II listed no less – but within it is all slick modernity and contemporary attitude. The restaurant has its own entrance, and an interior design spec that includes moody black-and-white photos, stainless steel, and trendy light fittings.

Chef Joseph Brimson **Seats** 69 **Closed** 25–26 December **Notes** Vegetarian dishes, Children welcome

Tabb's Restaurant
⊚⊚ MODERN BRITISH
01872 262110 | 85 Kenwyn Street, TR1 3BZ
www.tabbs.co.uk

The recently refurbished Tabb's occupies a white corner building that looks for all the world like a private dwelling. The kitchen's a busy place, producing everything in-house. Puddings run to tonka bean pannacotta with strawberry sorbet given a kick of black pepper.

Chef Nigel Tabb **Seats** 28 **Closed** 25 December, 1 January and 1 week January **Prices from** S £7.25, M £15.75, D £7.50 **Notes** Vegetarian dishes, Children welcome

VERYAN
The Quarterdeck at The Nare
⊚⊚ TRADITIONAL BRITISH ⚴ NOTABLE WINE LIST
01872 500000 | Carne Beach, TR2 5PF
www.quarterdeckrestaurant.co.uk

The Quarterdeck is a shipshape, yachtie-themed setting of polished teak, gingham seats and square rails. The kitchen produces modern dishes bursting with bold flavours and local fish and shellfish are a strong point too, perhaps a luxurious duo of pan-fried turbot and lobster medallion

Chef Nick Lawrie, Brett Cambourne-Paynter **Seats** 60 **Closed** 25 December **Prices from** S £7, M £17, D £6 **Parking** 60 **Notes** Vegetarian dishes, Children welcome

WATERGATE BAY
Fifteen Cornwall
⊚ MODERN ITALIAN V
01637 861000 | On The Beach, TR8 4AA
www.fifteencornwall.co.uk

Floor-to-ceiling windows show off the ever-changing sea views from this large, contemporary space, but it's just as smart and welcoming after sunset. Jamie Oliver's guiding principle remains the same – to give young people a solid grounding in skills and experience.

Chef Adam Banks **Seats** 120, Private dining 10 **Open** All year **Prices from** S £12, M £19, D £8 **Notes** Children welcome

▶ CUMBRIA

AMBLESIDE
Lake Road Kitchen
⊚⊚⊚ NORTHERN EUROPEAN V
015394 22012 | Lake Road, LA22 0AD
www.lakeroadkitchen.co.uk

Nordic sensibilities are a clear driver behind this foodie beacon just off Ambleside's main street, from the stark simplicity of its Scandi-style pine plank walls and bare tables to chef-patron James Cross's fervour for pickling, foraging and fermenting, as well as sourcing pedigree Lakeland meat and fine northern European seafood. The five- and eight-course menus change daily, and the self-styled 'cold climate cooking' brings on some remarkable combinations of taste and texture. A revelatory summer meal might open with a celeriac taco, involving remoulade, pastrami tongue, cured egg yolk and nasturtium, segueing in a carefully considered progression to Arctic king crab matched with Sungold tomatoes, fresh cheese and nasturtium. Along the way, there may be Cumbrian milk-fed veal with a hyper-seasonal stew of summer legumes, or a superb piece of monkfish, steamed simply and boosted with chicken dripping and herbs. To finish, excellent pastry work is a hallmark of ideas such as a buckwheat tart of lemon verbena and alpine strawberries. Home-baked breads include an exemplary sourdough with crunchy dark crust, served with hand-churned whey butter.

Chef James Cross **Seats** 21 **Open** All year **Notes** No children under 12 years

The Old Stamp House Restaurant
◉◉ MODERN BRITISH **V**
015394 32775 | Church Street, LA22 0BU
www.oldstamphouse.com

It's not widely known that William Wordsworth was Cumbria's 'Distributor of Stamps' back in the 19th century, and this is where he plied his trade. The organic and foraged ingredients on show make this a thoroughly modern sort of restaurant.

Chef Ryan Blackburn **Seats** 30, Private dining 8 **Closed** Christmas **Prices from** S £8, M £24, D £8.50 **Notes** Children welcome

Rothay Manor Hotel & Fine Dining
◉◉ MODERN BRITISH **V**
01539 433605 | Rothay Bridge, LA22 0EH
www.rothaymanor.co.uk

A great example of a traditional Lake District country-house hotel, whitewashed Rothay Manor stands in attractive landscaped gardens a short walk from bustling Ambleside. A Liverpool shipping merchant built it in 1823 and many Regency features are still much in evidence.

Chef Daniel McGeorge **Seats** 40, Private dining 20 **Closed** 2–20 January **Parking** 25 **Notes** Children welcome

APPLEBY-IN-WESTMORLAND
Appleby Manor Hotel & Garden Spa
◉ MODERN BRITISH **V**
017683 51571 | Roman Road, CA16 6JB
www.applebymanor.co.uk

The outlook over Appleby Castle and the Eden Valley is a pastoral treat, and this Victorian sandstone house was put up by someone with an eye for a view. The 1871 Bistro delivers breezy feel-good dishes while the main restaurant takes a more refined approach.

Chef Chris Thompson **Seats** 100, Private dining 20 **Closed** 24–26 December **Parking** 60 **Notes** Children welcome

ASKHAM
Allium at Askham Hall
◉◉ CONTEMPORARY BRITISH
01931 712350 | CA10 2PF
www.askhamhall.co.uk

Perched on the edge of the Lake District, surrounded by splendid Cumbrian countryside, this Grade I listed building can be traced back to the 14th century. The chefs work in harmony with the produce grown in the kitchen gardens and the farms within the estate.

Chef Richard Swale **Seats** 40, Private dining 18 **Closed** Christmas, 3 January to mid February (excluding groups) **Notes** Vegetarian dishes, No children under 10 years

BARROW-IN-FURNESS
Abbey House Hotel & Gardens
◉ TRADITIONAL BRITISH, FRENCH
01229 838282 | Abbey Road, LA13 0PA
www.abbeyhousehotel.com

This grand red-brick house in 14 acres of countryside is home to the charming and gently contemporary Oscar's restaurant. There's nothing stuffy about the place, with a relaxed (but professional) approach all round. The kitchen turns out modern dishes based on good regional produce.

Chef James Lowery **Seats** 100, Private dining 24 **Open** All year **Parking** 200 **Notes** Vegetarian dishes, Children welcome

BASSENTHWAITE
Lake View Restaurant
◉◉ BRITISH, FRENCH **V**
017687 76551 | Armathwaite Hall CA12 4RE
www.armathwaite-hall.com

Standing in 400 acres of grounds bordering Bassenthwaite, Armathwaite Hall has rich fabrics and acres of oak panelling. The Lake View Restaurant is a high-ceilinged room in rich golds and reds with formally laid tables. The kitchen steers a course to keep traditionalists and modernists happy.

Chef Kevin Dowling **Seats** 80 **Open** All year **Parking** 100 **Notes** Children welcome

The Pheasant
◉◉ MODERN BRITISH
017687 76234 | CA13 9YE
www.the-pheasant.co.uk

Dating from the 17th century, this long, low-slung building has a charming, atmospheric bar and a beamed bistro as well as the more formal Fell Restaurant. The kitchen relies on local sources for its ingredients and keeps a finger on the contemporary pulse.

Chef Malcolm Ennis **Seats** 45, Private dining 18 **Closed** 25 December **Parking** 40 **Notes** Vegetarian dishes, No children

Ravenstone Lodge Country House Hotel
BRITISH
01768 776629 | CA12 4QG
www.ravenstonelodge.co.uk

Enjoying an enviable position near Bassenthwaite Lake, this country-house hotel has plenty going on, including a bar and bistro in the former stables. The Coach House restaurant is smartly turned out and the team in the kitchen uses quality regional ingredients.

Chef James Cooper **Seats** 26 **Open** All year **Prices from** S £5, M £15, D £5 **Parking** 15 **Notes** Vegetarian dishes, No children under 8 years

BORROWDALE
Borrowdale Gates Hotel
BRITISH, FRENCH V
017687 77204 | CA12 5UQ
www.borrowdale-gates.com

In an area of the Borrowdale Valley hailed by Wainwright as one of the most picturesque in the Lake District, this classic Lakeland country house is set in the heart of prime walking territory. The kitchen has ramped up its efforts since the hotel's refurbishment.

Chef Christopher Standhaven **Seats** 50 **Closed** Christmas, New Year and January **Parking** 25 **Notes** Children welcome

Borrowdale Hotel
MODERN BRITISH V
017687 77224 | CA12 5UY
www.lakedistricthotels.net/borrowdalehotel

This handsome Victorian hotel has been in business since 1866 and still has the old room bells in reception. Gently made over for the modern world, the place marries contemporary good looks with original features, a formula which works equally well in the restaurant.

Chef Robert Weston **Open** All year **Prices from** S £6.95, M £14.95, D £7.95 **Notes** Children welcome

Hazel Bank Country House
BRITISH
017687 77248 | Rosthwaite, CA12 5XB
www.hazelbankhotel.co.uk

This classic stone-built Lakeland house sits amid four acres in the village of Rosthwaite in the gorgeous

Borrowdale Valley. The drill is a daily changing four-course menu, with a cheeseboard as optional extra. Save room for featherlight chocolate brownie, Belgian truffle and white chocolate ice cream.

Chef David Jackson **Seats** 20 **Closed** December to January **Parking** 12 **Notes** Vegetarian dishes, No children

Leathes Head Hotel
BRITISH
017687 77247 | CA12 5UY
www.leatheshead.co.uk

The Leathes Head is tucked away in the heart of the beautiful Borrowdale Valley, and their chef shows real passion for locally grown and reared produce in daily changing menus. Local Herdwick hogget is showcased in a main course involving cutlets, roasted shoulder and kidney.

Chef Noel Breaks **Seats** 30 **Closed** mid November to mid February **Parking** 15 **Notes** Vegetarian dishes, No children under 9 years

Lodore Falls Hotel
MODERN BRITISH V
017687 77285 | CA12 5UX
www.lakedistricthotels.net/lodorefalls

The Lodore Falls Hotel has enjoyed a magnificent setting on the shores of Derwentwater for over 200 years. The Lake View Restaurant, stylishly done out with modern furnishings and pristine white tablecloths, is the setting for equally stylish and thoughtfully constructed contemporary menus.

Chef Shane Hamilton **Seats** 140, Private dining 30 **Open** All year **Parking** 90 **Notes** Children welcome

BOWNESS-ON-WINDERMERE
Belsfield Restaurant
MODERN, INTERNATIONAL
015394 42448 | Laura Ashley The Belsfield, Kendal Road, LA23 3EL
www.lauraashleyhotels.com/thebelsfield

This lovingly restored Windermere hotel is set in six acres of landscaped gardens. As you might expect from a hotel owned by the Laura Ashley brand, it's tastefully furnished, forming an elegant setting for a menu that fuses British dishes with inspiration from further afield.

Chef Chris Lee **Seats** 70, Private dining 60 **Open** All year **Parking** 60 **Notes** Vegetarian dishes, Children welcome

CUMBRIA

The Ryebeck
◉ ◉ MODERN BRITISH
015394 88195 | Lyth Valley Road, LA23 3JP
www.ryebeck.com
Formerly known as Fayrer Garden, The Ryebeck is an appealingly isolated country house overlooking the shining expanse of Windermere. The informal conservatory dining room serves up a delicious view and a modern British menu that shows off the technical skills of the team in the kitchen.

Chef Cameron Smith **Seats** 52 **Open** All year **Prices from** S £6.50, M £13.50, D £6.50 **Parking** 40 **Notes** Vegetarian dishes, Children welcome

BRAITHWAITE
The Cottage in the Wood
Rosettes suspended MODERN BRITISH **V**
017687 78409 | Whinlatter Pass, CA12 5TW
www.thecottageinthewood.co.uk
The Rosette award for this establishment has been suspended due to a change of chef and reassessment will take place in due course. Located at the top of the Whinlatter Pass, deep in the Lake District National Park, this restaurant with rooms in a building that dates partly from the 17th century and is surrounded by forest; from the terrace and front half of the dining room there are wonderful views down the valley. The bare wood tables with round slate place mats prove the perfect foil for very pretty dishes, inspired by Cumbria's wonderful produce. There's a six-course tasting menu that takes you on a culinary journey through the woods and along the coastline of this stunningly beautiful region, or if time is an issue you could just opt for the well-balanced set-price menu.

Chef Richard Collingwood **Seats** 40 **Closed** January **Parking** 16 **Notes** No children under 10 years at dinner

CARLISLE
Crown Hotel
◉ MODERN BRITISH
01228 561888 | Station Road, Wetheral, CA4 8ES
www.crownhotelwetheral.co.uk
The Georgian hotel is in a picturesque village a few miles out of Carlisle, close to Hadrian's Wall. Its Conservatory Restaurant overlooks the landscaped gardens, and has a striking raftered ceiling and red quarry floor tiles. The kitchen favours a largely modern British approach.

Chef Deborah Templeton-Jadron **Seats** 80, Private dining 120 **Open** All year **Parking** 70 **Notes** Vegetarian dishes, Children welcome

CARTMEL
Aynsome Manor Hotel
◉ MODERN, TRADITIONAL BRITISH
015395 36653 | LA11 6HH
www.aynsomemanorhotel.co.uk
A charming small country-house hotel in the untouched Vale of Cartmel with views south to the Norman priory, meadows and woods. The cooking shows accurate timings, judiciously considered combinations and clear flavours on short, daily changing menus, with seasonal vegetables served separately.

Chef Gordon Topp **Seats** 28 **Closed** 25–26 December and 2–28 January **Parking** 20 **Notes** Vegetarian dishes, No children under 5 years

L'Enclume
◉ ◉ ◉ ◉ ◉ MODERN BRITISH **V** ⓦ NOTABLE WINE LIST
See pages 72–73

See advertisement opposite

Rogan & Company Restaurant
◉ ◉ ◉ MODERN BRITISH
015395 35917 | The Square, LA11 6QD
www.roganandcompany.co.uk
The understudy to L'Enclume sits cheek by jowl with its elder sibling in tranquil Cartmel, with a trickle of a river running alongside it. Behind the stone facade, a modern space has been fashioned, with zinc-topped tables under the gnarled old beams and a happy buzz of contented custom. The Rogan signature style of modernist treatments of gold-standard Cumbrian produce, some of it sourced from the proprietor's own farm in the surrounding valley, is capably expressed in menus that showcase a broad range of technique. Start with cured mackerel and an oyster, a bracing dish set alight with the contrasting sharpnesses of pickled vegetables and wasabi, before turning to a main such as roast venison loin with smoked beetroot and chicory, or the Rogan farm's pork loin in its own broth with spiced cannellini beans. Cauliflower dressed in Red Leicester, or confit new potatoes with garlic and thyme, are a cut above the side-dish norm, and things conclude with the apparent tautology of a caramelised caramel tart, offset with shiso vinegar and ice cream made with yogurt.

Chef Simon Rogan **Seats** 40, Private dining 10 **Closed** 1st week January **Prices from** S £10, M £18, D £8 **Notes** Vegetarian dishes, Children welcome

CLIFTON
George and Dragon
◉ BRITISH **V**
01768 865381 | CA10 2ER
www.georgeanddragonclifton.co.uk

Comfy sofas and little alcoves all characterise this popular inn, meticulously renovated by owner Charles Lowther, on his historic family estate. His ancestor Lord Lonsdale helped found the AA, which adopted yellow, his favourite colour, as its trademark. British cooking relies on the estate for pedigree Shorthorn beef, and pork from rare-breed stock, while game and most fish is also pretty local.

Chef Gareth Webster **Seats** 126 **Closed** 26 December **Notes** Vegetarian dishes, Children welcome

COCKERMOUTH
The Trout Hotel
◉ INTERNATIONAL, CLASSIC **V**
01900 823591 | Crown Street, CA13 0EJ
www.trouthotel.co.uk

After suffering two floods in six years, The Trout has benefited from a full refurbishment including Herdwick wool-carpeted floors in keeping with its idyllic Lake District location in the lovely market town of Cockermouth. Elegant glass chandeliers and ornate marble fireplaces add a classy touch.

Chef Alex Hartley **Seats** 56, Private dining 56 **Open** All year **Prices from** S £5, M £16, D £5.80 **Parking** 40 **Notes** Children welcome

CROSTHWAITE
The Punchbowl Inn at Crosthwaite
◉◉ MODERN BRITISH **V**
015395 68237 | Lyth Valley, LA8 8HR
www.the-punchbowl.co.uk

A small country house in the Lyth Valley, The Punchbowl is one of Lakeland's homelier places, run with great civility by the hands-on team. A slate-topped bar and modern rustic furniture give the place a fresh look, and the menu shows plenty of fashion-conscious technique.

Chef Arthur Bridgeman Quin **Seats** 50, Private dining 16 **Open** All year **Prices from** S £5.50, M £14.95, D £7.95 **Parking** 40 **Notes** Children welcome

CARTMEL
L'Enclume

◎◎◎◎◎ MODERN BRITISH V 🍷NOTABLE WINE LIST
015395 36362 | Cavendish St, LA11 6PZ
www.lenclume.co.uk

State-of-the-art contemporary cooking at the forge

If Cartmel was once about little else than a trip to the famous Priory and a slab of mint cake from one of the souvenir shops, there's a bit more to it these days. Upmarket cafés and places to buy artisanal cheese have multiplied around the dual focal points of Simon Rogan's two restaurants, Rogan & Company and the flagship L'Enclume. Hewn out of what was once a blacksmith's forge in days that seem as distant as a George Eliot novel now, the Anvil (for so it translates) retains a spare but elegant look within, the cream-washed roughcast stone walls and slender beams still bearing witness to the age of the building. Staff are fully conversant with the kitchen's output, explaining and guiding you through the complex, multi-layered production that constitutes a visit here. To call it a destination restaurant is like saying that Cumbria has lakes.

What you get is state-of-the-art contemporary cooking, with the emphasis on natural, often raw ingredients that are allowed to speak for themselves within the dazzling artistry on show in every dish. The familiar opener of Maran egg with hazelnut cream and leek

fondue is an astonishment that never fails, and might appear alongside a tartlet of scallop roe and gooseberry with bracing scallop tartare. Umami is the predominant note in a dish of fathoms-deep beef broth with bone marrow custard and grilled kale, and then fish arrives in the shape of turbot braised in ham fat, underlined with a thin layer of pork back fat and pieces of crackling in a shell-based bisque. The meat main might well be the fabled Goosnargh duck with cherries and smoked beetroot, a study in reds and pinks that produces deep bass-notes of resonant flavour.

More sparkling fireworks are produced in the concluding dessert parade, which may encompass sheep's curd, rosehip and buckwheat with a drift of hyssop snow, figleaf ice cream with fig syrup, crumbled hazelnuts and meadowsweet, and the signature Anvil confection, a gold-sprayed caramel custard with two apple varieties and a juglet of pine juice. The lunch offering is a shorter digest of the above, and yet still manages to work in all the culinary magic of the evening sessions, perhaps centring on venison loin with accompanying croquette and beeswax-cooked pear. Comprehensive packages that include overnight stays are the kind of whole hog that it's worth going for that once-in-a-lifetime experience.

Chef Simon Rogan, Paul Burgalieres **Seats** 50, Private dining 6 **Closed** 25–26 December, 2–16 January **Parking** 7 **Notes** No children under 6 years at lunch, 12 years at dinner

See advertisement on page 71

ELTERWATER
Stove at Langdale Hotel & Spa

⊛ MODERN BRITISH

015394 37302 | The Langdale Estate, LA22 9JD
www.langdale.co.uk

The gastronomic action at this smart Lakeland resort is in Stove dining room, a contemporary space with an open kitchen with a wood-fired oven, and a mezzanine with valley views. The kitchen produces good fare that hits the comfort food brief.

Chef Scott Barge **Seats** 100 **Open** All year **Parking** 50 **Notes** Vegetarian dishes, Children welcome

GLENRIDDING
Inn on the Lake

⊛⊛ MODERN EUROPEAN V

017684 82444 | Lake Ullswater, CA11 0PE
www.lakedistricthotels.net

In 15 acres of grounds surrounding Ullswater, this hotel's main culinary action takes place in its Lake View Restaurant, the elegant dining room decorated with shades of lilac and fawn. The kitchen makes good use of regional ingredients to produce dishes of modernity and creativity.

Chef James Watt **Seats** 100, Private dining 40 **Open** All year **Parking** 100 **Notes** Children welcome

GRANGE-OVER-SANDS
Clare House

⊛ MODERN BRITISH

015395 33026 | Park Road, LA11 7HQ
www.clarehousehotel.co.uk

The Read family has owned this traditional hotel with secluded gardens overlooking Morecambe Bay since the 1960s, and their passionate care is evident. In the two-roomed dining area, well-spaced tables are attended by smartly turned-out, long-serving staff.

Chef Andrew Read, Mark Johnston, Adrian Fenton **Seats** 36 **Closed** mid December to end March **Parking** 16 **Notes** Vegetarian dishes, Children welcome

GRASMERE
The Daffodil Hotel & Spa

⊛ MODERN BRITISH

015394 63550 | Keswick Road, LA22 9PR
www.daffodilhotel.com

Made of local stone and with a prime spot by Grasmere, The Daffodil enjoys a fine Lakeland vista, and sensibly the restaurant is up on the first floor to make the best of it. The contemporary finish within extends to the restaurant.

Chef Graham Harrower **Seats** Private dining 200 **Open** All year **Prices from** S £6.95, M £14.95, D £7 **Parking** 70 **Notes** Vegetarian dishes, Children welcome

The Dining Room

⊛⊛ MODERN BRITISH

015394 35217 | Oak Bank Hotel, Broadgate, LA22 9TA
www.lakedistricthotel.co.uk

With pretty gardens running down to the River Rothay, the Victorian Oak Bank Hotel has plenty of charm. The comfortable and refined Dining Room restaurant is the setting for some ambitious, creative food and the kitchen clearly has an eye for presentation and enticing combinations.

Chef Matt Clarke **Seats** 30 **Closed** 16–26 December, 6–25 January **Prices from** S £7.50, M £16, D £7.50 **Parking** 14 **Notes** Vegetarian dishes, No children under 10 years

Forest Side

⊛⊛⊛⊛ MODERN BRITISH V ◆ NOTABLE WINE LIST

015394 35250 | Keswick Road, LA22 9RN
www.theforestside.com

In the 1840s the new-fangled railway reached what was then known as the 'District of the Lakes', much to the exasperation of the Wordsworths, and brought not just excursioners but relocators into the area, prompting a modest building boom. Among its products was the present stone building, so named for its position in the shelter of a stretch of wooded hillside, now sensitively reborn as an appealing country hotel. An expansive dining room staffed with smart, knowledgeable personnel looks out on to the Lakeland setting, which takes on vital importance in Kevin Tickle's regionally inspired, exciting culinary style. There are foragings and gatherings aplenty, as well as prime materials such as Cumbrian rare breed pork, which might form the centrepiece of the multi-course taster, accompanied by smoked potato custard, damsons, and what the menu summarises as 'garden shenanigans'. Technique is key to the surprise element in every dish, from chanterelles cooked in bone marrow with corned brisket, anointed in mushroom broth, to the scorched pear with malt, birch sap and a shot of staggeringly intense ginger beer. Those haunting herbal notes lend fragrance to many dishes, including savory-scented lemon sole and dill-fronded cod and oyster, while autumnal fruits are celebrated in a dessert of salted wild plum with apple and sloes. The vegetarian menu is a tour de force in itself, building up to a principal serving of smoked squash with hen of the woods and vitamin C-laden scurvy grass. Accompanying it all is an inspired collection of biodynamic and natural wines.

Chef Kevin Tickle **Seats** 50, Private dining 12 **Open** All year **Parking** 44 **Notes** No children under 8 years

Rothay Garden Hotel
◉◉ MODERN BRITISH **V**
01539 435334 | Broadgate, LA22 9RJ
www.rothaygarden.com

On the edge of Grasmere, this refurbished Victorian hotel sits in riverside gardens, with the panoramic sweep of the Lakeland fells as background. In the Garden Restaurant, try Lakeland lamb, served as roast rump and shepherd's pie with carrot purée, parsnip and potato rösti, green beans and rosemary jus.

Chef Andrew Burton, Adrian Kneeshaw **Seats** 60 **Open** All year **Parking** 38 **Notes** No children

The Wordsworth Hotel & Spa
◉ MODERN BRITISH
015394 35592 | Stock Lane, LA22 9SW
www.thewordsworthhotel.co.uk

Set in two acres of riverside gardens with breathtaking Grasmere views, this was once the hunting lodge for the Earl of Cadogan. These days, this plush hotel offers cutting-edge cooking in the Signature Restaurant, with atmospheric lighting and an airy conservatory.

Chef Jaid Smallman **Seats** 65, Private dining 18 **Open** All year **Parking** 50 **Notes** Vegetarian dishes, No children under 5 years

See advertisement below

HAWKSHEAD
The Queen's Head Inn & Restaurant
◉ BRITISH
01539 436271 | Main Street, LA22 0NS
www.queensheadhawkshead.co.uk

The black-and-white timbered facade of this classic Lakeland inn has been well rooted into Hawkshead life since the 17th century. Inside, there's a lively buzz and the timeless charm of head-skimming oak beams, panelled walls and wood and flagstone floors.

Chef Kevin Hodge **Seats** 62 **Closed** 25 December **Notes** Vegetarian dishes, Children welcome

The Sun Inn
◉ TRADITIONAL BRITISH
015394 36236 | Main Street, LA22 0NT
www.suninn.co.uk

This listed 17th-century coaching inn, at the heart of the charming village of Hawkshead, is always popular with locals and visitors alike. Inside, low ceilings, open stonework and wooden floors hark back to former times. The kitchen sends out well considered and generous dishes.

Chef Vincent Mulama, Edijs Medveds **Seats** 30 **Open** All year **Prices from** S £4.50, M £12.50, D £7.50 **Notes** Vegetarian dishes, Children welcome

IRTHINGTON
The Golden Fleece
@ MODERN BRITISH
01228 573686 | Rule Holme, CA6 4NF
www.thegoldenfleececumbria.co.uk

Refurbishment has transformed this white two-storey inn into the eye-catching combination of bar and restaurant with rooms it is today. The menu neatly encapsulates both pub elements and more refined offerings. Dessert might be burnt Cambridge cream (a precursor of crème brûlée) with berry compôte.

Chef Robert Cowan **Seats** 70, Private dining 30 **Closed** 25–26 December and 1–8 January **Parking** 100 **Notes** Vegetarian dishes, Children welcome

KENDAL
The Castle Dairy Restaurant
@@ CONTEMPORARY BRITISH **V**
01539 733946 | 26 Wildman St, LA9 6EN
www.castledairy.co.uk

Dating from the 16th century, Kendal's oldest inhabited building makes a classy setting for some well-tuned modern cooking. The place survived Storm Desmond in 2015 and is back with a new look throughout its warren of low-beamed rooms, all slate floors, fires and modern art.

Chef Chris O'Callaghan **Seats** 32, Private dining 4 **Closed** 23 December to 24 January; 5–18 August **Parking** 3 **Notes** No children under 6 years

Castle Green Hotel in Kendal
@@ MODERN BRITISH
01539 734000 | Castle Green Lane, LA9 6RG
www.castlegreen.co.uk

The Greenhouse restaurant at this charming country house, now a spa hotel, benefits from great natural daylight shining through large windows that showcase panoramic views over the fells. Innovative cooking is the order of the day, putting fine Cumbrian produce to good use.

Chef Justin Woods (Executive chef), Martin Cartwright (Head chef) **Seats** 80, Private dining 250 **Open** All year **Parking** 200 **Notes** Vegetarian dishes, Children welcome

KESWICK
Brossen Steakhouse
@@ MODERN BRITISH
01768 773333 | Inn on the Square, Main Street, CA12 5JF
www.innonthesquare.co.uk/brossen

The Inn on the Square is a revamped hotel with a contemporary edge and a restaurant that is all about prime protein cooked over coals. The dining room is a light, bright and casual space, with a view into the kitchen.

Chef Daniel Lansley **Seats** 64, Private dining 40 **Open** All year **Notes** Vegetarian dishes, Children welcome

KIRKBY LONSDALE
Pheasant Inn
@ MODERN BRITISH
015242 71230 | Casterton, LA6 2RX
www.pheasantinn.co.uk

An 18th-century coaching inn with a proper bar complete with real ales and snug. Grab a table by the fire in the bar, or head through to the slightly more refined restaurant – the menu is the same throughout. Expect dishes that reflect the easy-going pub setting but don't lack ambition.

Chef Duncan Wilson **Seats** 40 **Closed** 25–26 December **Parking** 32 **Notes** Vegetarian dishes, Children welcome

Sun Inn Restaurant
@@ MODERN BRITISH **V**
015242 71965 | 6 Market Street, LA6 2AU
www.sun-inn.info

Anyone with foodie inclinations should visit the white-painted 17th-century Sun Inn, a proper pub with log fires and real ales in the convivial bar, and a smart contemporary dining room. The reliable kitchen conjures up full-flavoured dishes using local produce.

Chef Joe Robinson **Seats** 40 **Open** All year **Prices from** S £7.95, M £14.95, D £7 **Notes** Children welcome

KIRKBY STEPHEN
The Inn at Brough
@ MODERN BRITISH
01768 341252 | Main Street, Brough, CA17 4AY
www.theinnatbrough.co.uk

A thorough makeover has added a chic, contemporary look to this 18th-century former coaching inn on Brough high street, and the kitchen toes that up-to-date line with switched-on modern ideas. A penchant for local and regional supplies drives the menu.

Chef Rob Keefe **Seats** 42, Private dining 16 **Open** All year **Parking** 20 **Notes** Vegetarian dishes, Children welcome

LEVENS
The Villa Levens
@@ MODERN AND TRADITIONAL **V**
01539 980980 | Brettargh Holt, LA8 8EA
www.thevillalevens.co.uk

An imposing Victorian family home that spent many years as a convent before being converted into the smart hotel it is now, The Villa Levens occupies a peaceful spot in the South Lakes. The intimate dining room offers plenty of original features.

Chef Bryan Parsons **Seats** 35, Private dining 25 **Open** All year **Prices from** S £6.50, M £13.95, D £7.50 **Parking** 130 **Notes** Children welcome

LUPTON
Plough Inn
◉ MODERN BRITISH
015395 67700 | Cow Brow, LA6 1PJ
www.theploughatlupton.co.uk

The Plough sports a clean-lined contemporary look without sacrificing the best of its pubby character. It's a classy act with leather sofas, a Brathay slate-topped bar and real fires. Comforting modern takes on classic dishes prevail.

Chef Robert Stacey **Seats** 120, Private dining 8 **Open** All year **Prices from** S £5.50, M £11.95, D £3.95 **Parking** 40 **Notes** Vegetarian dishes, Children welcome

NEAR SAWREY
Ees Wyke Country House
◉ MODERN BRITISH
015394 36393 | LA22 0JZ
www.eeswyke.co.uk

Beatrix Potter spent her holidays in this white Georgian house. These days, on a scale small enough to unite guests, a four-course dinner menu is served at a single start time. A pair of choices is offered at most stages.

Chef Richard Lee **Seats** 16 **Open** All year **Parking** 12 **Notes** Vegetarian dishes, No children

NEWBY BRIDGE
Lakeside Hotel Lake Windermere
◉◉ MODERN BRITISH **V**
015395 30001 | Lakeside, LA12 8AT
www.lakesidehotel.co.uk

Surrounded by wooded slopes on the southern shore of Lake Windermere, the hotel began as a coaching inn, and is now a substantial building, with a lakeside terrace, spa and pool and a brasserie named after John Ruskin.

Chef Richard Booth **Seats** 70, Private dining 30 **Closed** 23 December to 16 January **Prices from** S £8, M £24, D £8 **Parking** 200 **Notes** Children welcome

PENRITH
Devonshire Restaurant
◉◉ CONTEMPORARY BRITISH
01768 862696 | Devonshire Street, CA11 7SU
www.lakedistricthotels.net/georgehotel

Penrith's 300-year-old George Hotel is a local institution and full of charm and friendly hospitality.

The Devonshire Restaurant is the heart of the operation, stylishly brought up to date. The food, too, is contemporary but with a firm basis in traditional techniques.

Chef Kyle Philips **Seats** 28 **Open** All year

FYR
◉ BRITISH
01768 868111 | North Lakes Hotel & Spa, Ullswater Road, CA11 8QT
www.northlakeshotel.co.uk

Next to Wetheriggs Country Park, this Thwaites-owned hotel occupies an enviable position in Penrith at the edge of the Lake District. FYR restaurant features an impressive bespoke open fire grill at the heart of the restaurant where guests can experience the theatre of live cooking.

Chef Douglas Hargreaves **Open** All year

Stoneybeck Inn
◉ TRADITIONAL BRITISH
01768 862369 | Bowscar, CA11 8RP
www.stoneybeckinn.co.uk

In a stunning location with views over the Cumbrian Fells, yet handily close to the M6, Stoneybeck is a much extended traditional-looking inn. It's opened up and contemporary on the inside, with well turned-out, efficient staff and a kitchen producing updated versions of classic dishes.

Chef Steven Ratcliffe, Marcus Turnbull **Seats** 50, Private dining 130 **Closed** 26 December **Prices from** S £4.95, M £10.95, D £5.95 **Parking** 70 **Notes** Vegetarian dishes, Children welcome

POOLEY BRIDGE
1863 Bar Bistro Rooms
◉ MODERN EUROPEAN
017684 86334 | High Street, CA10 2NH
www.1863ullswater.co.uk

This charming detached house occupies an enviable position within the Lake District National Park. With its blue leather banquettes, abundance of mirrors, and framed maps, the contemporary dining room lives up to its bistro billing, while the modern European menu is brimming with prime ingredients.

Chef Phil Corrie **Open** All year **Parking** 9 **Notes** No children under 10 years at dinner from 7.30pm

CUMBRIA

RAVENGLASS
The Pennington Hotel
🏵 BRITISH

0845 450 6445 | CA18 1SD
www.penningtonhotels.com

The venerable black-and-white hotel wears its age on its sleeve, having started out as a coaching inn in the Tudor era. Culinary modernism is the order of the day in the light, relaxing dining room where seafood is imaginatively handled.

Chef Helen Todd **Seats** 36 **Open** All year **Parking** 20 **Notes** Vegetarian dishes, Children welcome

RAVENSTONEDALE
The Black Swan
🏵🏵 MODERN BRITISH V

015396 23204 | CA17 4NG
www.blackswanhotel.com

Ravenstonedale is a pretty conservation village, and this handsome Victorian inn has friendly bars and tranquil riverside gardens. There are two handsome restaurants, equally cosy and welcoming, where you can enjoy the seasonally changing menus. There are pub classics, too, if you fancy fish and chips.

Chef Scott Fairweather **Seats** 90, Private dining 14 **Open** All year **Prices from** S £6, M £12, D £6 **Parking** 20 **Notes** Children welcome

ROSTHWAITE
Scafell Hotel
🏵 MODERN BRITISH

017687 77208 | CA12 5XB
www.scafell.co.uk

Surrounded by peaks and the lush greenery of the Borrowdale Valley, the Scafell Hotel is ideal for those seeking time in the great outdoors. The Riverside Bar and lounge bar offer informal dining, with the main restaurant a more formal option.

Chef Rob Henshaw **Seats** 65 **Open** All year **Parking** 100 **Notes** Vegetarian dishes, Children welcome

ULVERSTON
Virginia House
🏵🏵 MODERN BRITISH V

01229 584844 | 24 Queen Street, LA12 7AF
www.virginiahouseulverston.co.uk

A boutique restaurant with rooms in pretty Ulverston, south of the Lake District, Virginia House's amenities include an on-trend gin parlour with over 100 brands, a feature you might have kept quiet about in centuries past. A smart dining room is the setting for innovative British cooking.

Chef Craig Sherrington **Seats** 34 **Closed** 2 weeks January **Notes** No children under 12 years at dinner

WATERMILLOCK
Macdonald Leeming House
🏵 MODERN BRITISH

01768 486674 | CA11 0JJ
www.macdonald-hotels.co.uk

Macdonald Leeming House is an impressive-looking property boasting direct access to Ullswater. For full-on Lakeland dining, head for the elegant Regency Restaurant, where floor-to-ceiling windows give views to the lake and fells and dishes served are well executed and attractively presented.

Chef Gary Fothersgill **Seats** 60, Private dining 24 **Open** All year **Parking** 50 **Notes** Vegetarian dishes, Children welcome

WINDERMERE
Beech Hill Hotel & Spa
🏵 MODERN BRITISH V

015394 42137 | Newby Bridge Road, LA23 3LR
www.beechhillhotel.co.uk

After canapés and pre-dinner drinks you can soak up the dramatic views over Lake Windermere to the fells beyond from Burlington's Restaurant. The menu is altogether more wide-ranging than that usually found in such environments, adding its own spin on dishes with a French grounding.

Chef Lukasz Zebryk **Seats** 130, Private dining 90 **Parking** 60 **Notes** Children welcome

Briery Wood Country House Hotel
🏵 MODERN BRITISH V

015394 33316 | Ambleside Road, Ecclerigg, LA23 1ES
www.lakedistrictcountryhotels.co.uk

Set in seven acres of grounds, Briery Wood is a charming, white-painted property, dating to the late 19th century. It's a cosy, relaxing place with an informal atmosphere. In the dining room you'll find attentive staff serving modern country-house style cooking.

Chef Miguel De La Porta **Seats** 40, Private dining 10 **Open** All year **Parking** 25 **Notes** Children welcome

Cedar Manor Hotel & Restaurant
🏵 MODERN BRITISH

015394 43192 | Ambleside Road, LA23 1AX
www.cedarmanor.co.uk

Built of grey stone in 1854, the manor occupies a peaceful spot in attractive gardens, complete with eponymous cedar, on the outskirts of Windermere. It's a small hotel with an elegant restaurant and well-trained staff. Seasonality leads the kitchen, which turns out modern country-house dishes.

Chef Roger Pergl-Wilson **Seats** 22, Private dining 10 **Closed** Christmas and 2–19 January **Parking** 12 **Notes** Vegetarian dishes, No children

WINDERMERE
Holbeck Ghyll Country House Hotel

Rosettes suspended MODERN BRITISH **V**

01539 432375 | Holbeck Lane, LA23 1LU

www.holbeckghyll.com

Contemporary cooking overlooking Windermere

The Rosette award for this establishment has been suspended at the time of going to press due to a change of chef. Reassessment will take place in due course. Holbeck Ghyll began life as a Victorian hunting lodge. Passing through successive stages of private ownership, it embarked on its career as a hotel in the 1970s, gradually acquiring the accretions of contemporary luxury style. Dining goes on in an austerely panelled room, where the window seats are literally that, rather than freestanding chairs, for those with their backs to the view. Having your back to the view is not the luckiest option, as the sweeping panorama over the lake, with Coniston Old Man brooding in the background, is one of the magnetic attractions of Holbeck. Then again, for those who are single-mindedly focused on the food and its production, a chef's table for up to 10 diners is a trendy option.

Seats 50, Private dining 20 **Closed** 1st 2 weeks January **Parking** 50 **Notes** No children under 8 years

CUMBRIA

WINDERMERE
Hrishi at Gilpin Hotel & Lake House
◉◉◉ MODERN BRITISH, ASIAN INFLUENCES **V**
015394 88818 | Crook Road, LA23 3NE
www.thegilpin.co.uk

Modern European food with Asian influences in Lakeland tranquillity

An Edwardian house in 22 acres of tranquil gardens and woodland near Windermere, Gilpin has been run by the Cunliffes for over 40 years. It is the very essence of a tranquil and luxurious retreat, the feel-good factor boosted further still by the Lake House which lies a short drive away in its own 100 acres, and offers six more gorgeous bedrooms, a lakeside vista and spa complex. There's gastronomic magic afoot too (see also Gilpin Spice with 2 AA Rosettes), in a lavish dining room that goes by the nickname of its head chef Hrishikesh Desai, whose glittering career has taken him from a high-flying apprenticeship in France to a stint at California's legendary French Laundry and a victorious appearance on the BBC's *Chefs on Trial*. Desai breaks the crusty country-house dining mould at Gilpin, bringing a genuine feeling of individuality and excitement to the menus, mingling notes from his own Asian heritage into contemporary European cooking to dynamic effect.

Attention-grabbing openers might feature the freshest of Lochalsh scallops, thinly sliced and cured céviche-style with lemon, thyme and Cornish salt, and matched with a dazzling

array of supporting elements – set cauliflower cream, rapeseed oil and curry mayonnaise and pink grapefruit granita. Otherwise, you might start with a more substantial composition of slow-poached loin of Cumbrian veal, the sweetbreads glazed and wrapped in pancetta and pointed up with mustard cream, celeriac textures, pickled mushrooms and milk foam. Main courses too are handled with the same mixture of inventiveness and respect for tradition, as typified in a dish that takes slow-roasted belly of salt-aged pork as a focal point then adds in a raviolo of pulled braised rib meat, Goan-inspired fermented white cabbage 'foogath' and Chinese five spice sauce, while locally reared Herdwick lamb might appear as roast loin and 24-hour-cooked shoulder with Moroccan-style baby aubergine, crispy potato cake, buttered carrots and lamb jus. Sure, there is plenty going on in these dishes, but nothing is done for novelty's sake, and it all hangs together in harmonious balance – a fish dish involving brined and poached turbot fillet with a sesame seed, red chilli and toasted pine nut crust served with steamed mussels, truffled white onion marmalade, tapioca crisp and saffron foam being a case in point. Dessert might be dark chocolate délice with lime leaf pannacotta, strawberries done three ways, verjus jelly and lemon balm, or banana soufflé with coffee and orange sauce and bourbon vanilla ice cream.

Chef Hrishikesh Desai **Seats** 50, Private dining 20 **Open** All year **Parking** 40 **Notes** No children under 7 years

CUMBRIA

WINDERMERE continued

Cragwood Country House Hotel
◉ BRITISH, FRENCH
01539 488177 | Ambleside Road, LA23 1LQ
www.lakedistrictcountryhotels.com
Built in 1910 from stone quarried in its own 21 acres of grounds, Cragwood has views over Lake Windermere and bags of country-house charm. The two dining rooms have lovely views and smart furnishings. Things get rolling with three canapés and five types of bread.
Chef Calvin Harrison **Seats** 40, Private dining 20
Open All year **Parking** 50 **Notes** Vegetarian dishes, Children welcome

Gilpin Spice
◉◉ PAN ASIAN **V**
015394 88818 | Gilpin Hotel & Lake House, Crook Road, LA23 3NE
www.thegilpin.co.uk/eat-and-drink/gilpinspice
Annexed of the main Gilpin Hotel building with its own entrance, this restaurant is a stunner – divided into three sections, each decorated differently in bright colours. There is an open kitchen with high, comfortable bar-stool seating directly facing the chefs at work. The pan-Asian menu is designed to offer lots of taster dishes rather than the traditional starter–main–dessert options; taster menus for two are available too.
Chef Hrishikesh Desai **Seats** 50 and Private dining
Closed 25 December **Prices from** S £8, M £12, D £7
Parking 40 **Notes** Vegetarian dishes, Children welcome

Holbeck Ghyll Country House Hotel
Rosettes suspended MODERN BRITISH **V**
See page 79

Hrishi at Gilpin Hotel & Lake House
◉◉◉ MODERN BRITISH, ASIAN INFLUENCES **V**
See pages 80–81

Langdale Chase
◉◉ BRITISH
015394 32201 | Ambleside Road, LA23 1LW
www.langdalechase.co.uk
This impressive Victorian building was 'the first residence in Windermere to have electricity installed' and it still boasts a fabulous late 19th-century interior, full of period details. Six acres of grounds lead down to the lake, and the terraces and reception rooms enjoy wonderful views.
Chef Daniel Hopkins **Open** All year

Lindeth Howe Country House Hotel & Restaurant
◉◉ CLASSIC FRENCH **V**
015394 45759 | Lindeth Drive, Longtail Hill, LA23 3JF
www.lindeth-howe.co.uk
Beatrix Potter not only lived in this classic country house on a hillside overlooking Windermere and the mountains, but wrote some of her tales here. The word 'hillside' undersells what are in fact six acres of sweeping gardens, worth exploring before eating.
Chef Chris Davies **Seats** 70, Private dining 35 **Open** All year **Prices from** S £9.50, M £24.95, D £8.75
Parking 50 **Notes** No children under 7 years

Linthwaite House Hotel & Restaurant
Rosettes suspended ITALIAN
015394 88600 | Crook Road, LA23 3JA
www.linthwaite.com
The Rosette award for this establishment has been suspended due to a change of chef and reassessment will take place in due course. In a county hardly short of lovely country-house hotels, Linthwaite has plenty of distinctive appeal. This large white house sits on a rise overlooking Lake Windermere and has immaculate gardens and soothing views. At the time of going to press the hotel and restaurant areas were undergoing refurbishment, but when it opens later in 2018, the new Stella restaurant will be offering Italian cuisine based on locally sourced and organic produce that highlights the Cumbrian region.
Chef Marcus Hall **Seats** 64, Private dining 16
Closed Christmas and New Year (excluding residents)
Parking 40 **Notes** Vegetarian dishes, No children under 7 years at dinner

Macdonald Old England Hotel & Spa
◉ TRADITIONAL BRITISH, EUROPEAN
015394 87890 | 23 Church Street, Bowness, LA23 3DF
www.macdonaldhotels.co.uk
On the shore of England's largest lake, this Windermere hotel offers superb views across the water towards the fells, particularly through the restaurant's floor-to-ceiling windows and terrace. The menu has broad appeal, from steaks cooked on the grill, through to some gently contemporary dishes.
Chef Michael Cole **Seats** 120, Private dining 14
Open All year **Parking** 100 **Notes** Vegetarian dishes, Children welcome

Merewood Country House Hotel
◉◉ MODERN BRITISH **V**
015394 46484 | Ambleside Road, Ecclerigg, LA23 1LH
www.lakedistrictcountryhotels.co.uk/merewood-hotel
Built in 1812 from stone quarried in the hotel's grounds, Merewood is perfectly positioned to make

the best of the views over Lake Windermere. There are 20 acres of woodland and gardens, and this Lakeland country house is equally on the money on the inside.

Chef Carl Semple **Seats** 40, Private dining 32
Open All year **Prices from** S £4.95, M £15.95, D £7.95
Parking 60 **Notes** Children welcome

Miller Howe Hotel
@@ MODERN BRITISH **V** NOTABLE WINE LIST
015394 42536 | Rayrigg Road, LA23 1EY
www.millerhowe.com

Miller Howe has become the yardstick by which other country-house hotels are judged. 'Modern British with a twist' is the self-described cooking style. Menus are impressive, with home-grown and wild produce in evidence, while presentation is precise and colourful throughout.

Chef Liam Lang **Seats** 80, Private dining 30 **Open** All year **Parking** 40 **Notes** Children welcome

Porto
@ MODERN BRITISH, EUROPEAN
015394 48242 | 3 Ash Street, Bowness, LA23 3EB
www.porto-restaurant.co.uk

Now refurbished, Porto is situated in the heart of Bowness, just a short stroll from Lake Windermere itself. Whether it's the comfortable dining room or an alfresco meal on the heated roof terrace or in the garden, the eclectic food blends Asian and European influences.

Chef Slav Miskiewicz **Seats** 68, Private dining 50
Closed 24–26 December, 2nd week January to 1st week February **Prices from** S £5, M £13, D £7
Notes Vegetarian dishes, Children welcome

The Samling
@@@ MODERN BRITISH **V** NOTABLE WINE LIST
015394 31922 | Ambleside Road, LA23 1LR
www.thesamlinghotel.co.uk

The country around Windermere is pretty spectacular from whichever angle you look at it, but The Samling has a particularly enviable prospect, its contemporary dining room of Lakeland slate and full-length glass offering dioramic views of the hotel gardens and the mirror-like expanse of water. Peter Howarth is a practitioner of the modern British culinary arts, devising complex dishes with many elements that nonetheless retain their interplay of clear flavours, the multi-course tasting menus – Seasonal or the longer Signature – delivering plenty of delight and surprise. First up might be thinly sliced torched sea trout with asparagus, Charentais melon and oscietra in dashi, before duck roasted in five-spice and sloe gin makes an intermediate appearance. Superb Anjou pigeon

comes pastrami-style with coleslaw wrapped in a cabbage leaf, dressed in Emmenthal, mustard and dill. John Dory and mussels gain depth from a punchy bouillabaisse and Barolo reduction, but the star of the show is Cumbrian lamb with St George's mushrooms, wild garlic and Yukon Gold fondant. The pick of desserts is a refashioned carrot cake, complete with pralined walnuts, raisins and milk sorbet.

Chef Peter Howarth **Seats** 40, Private dining 8
Open All year **Parking** 40 **Notes** Children welcome

Storrs Hall Hotel
@@ MODERN BRITISH **V**
015394 47111 | Storrs Park, LA23 3LG
www.storrshall.com

Within 17 acres of grounds on the shore of Lake Windermere, this Georgian villa provides a quintessential Lakeland country house setting. Overlooking the lawns and glorious scenery, the elegant restaurant makes for a relaxed backdrop to the modern cooking. The kitchen displays a sound skill-set.

Chef Paul Nicholson **Seats** 82, Private dining 40
Open All year **Parking** 50 **Notes** Children welcome

The Wild Boar Inn, Grill & Smokehouse
@ TRADITIONAL BRITISH
015394 45225 | Crook, LA23 3NF
www.thewildboarinn.co.uk

The white-painted Wild Boar is a classic inn with a host of stylish bedrooms, a smart bar, and a restaurant with an open kitchen at its heart. They even have an on-site microbrewery. The dining area has oak beams and darkwood tables.

Chef Miroslav Likus **Seats** 100, Private dining 22
Open All year **Prices from** S £3.75, M £16, D £3.50
Parking 30 **Notes** Vegetarian dishes, Children welcome

▶ DERBYSHIRE

BAKEWELL
Piedaniel's
@ TRADITIONAL FRENCH, EUROPEAN
01629 812687 | Bath Street, DE45 1BX
www.piedaniels-restaurant.com

Run with great personal warmth and charm by a husband-and-wife team who keep the town supplied with reliable bistro cooking. Main courses nail their colours to the mast while hearty prime cuts while fish gets a look-in too.

Chef E Piedaniel **Seats** 50, Private dining 16
Closed Christmas and New Year, 2 weeks January, 2 weeks August **Notes** Vegetarian dishes, Children welcome

DERBYSHIRE

BASLOW
Cavendish Hotel
◉◉ MODERN BRITISH **V**
01246 582311 | Church Lane, DE45 1SP
www.cavendish-hotel.net
The Cavendish is a stone-built hotel acquired in 1830, where dining consists of modern classics such as seared scallops with black pudding and pea purée, roast pigeon breast with couscous, and loin and haunch of venison with celeriac and beetroot in chocolate jus.
Chef Alan Hill **Seats** 50, Private dining 18 **Open** All year **Parking** 40 **Notes** Children welcome

Fischer's Baslow Hall
◉◉◉ MODERN EUROPEAN **V**
See pages 86–87

BEELEY
The Devonshire Arms at Beeley
◉ MODERN BRITISH
01629 733259 | Devonshire Square, DE4 2NR
www.devonshirebeeley.co.uk
A night in one of the guest rooms would allow you to say you'd stayed at Chatsworth, sort of, as this stone-built village inn is situated in the heart of the estate. Expect cask-conditioned ales and a terrific wine list, and some contemporary pub food.
Chef Ian Smith **Seats** 60, Private dining 14 **Open** All year **Parking** 30 **Notes** Vegetarian dishes, Children welcome

BRADWELL
The Samuel Fox Country Inn
◉◉ MODERN BRITISH
01433 621562 | Stretfield Road, S33 9JT
www.samuelfox.co.uk
A stone-built inn near the Pennine Way named after the Victorian steel magnate who invented the folding ribbed umbrella. Breads of the day, variously flavoured with treacle or with Henderson's relish and onion, make an encouraging prelude to tasty starters.
Chef James Duckett **Seats** 40 **Closed** 2–27 January **Parking** 15 **Notes** Vegetarian dishes, Children welcome

BUXTON
Best Western Lee Wood Hotel
◉ BRITISH, EUROPEAN
01298 23002 | The Park, SK17 6TQ
www.leewoodhotel.co.uk
Refurbished style exudes from every pore of Lee Wood, a Georgian grey-stone manor house in the Peak District. Modern brasserie cooking is served in an expansive conservatory room with fronds of hanging foliage overhead and refreshing views of the grounds all about.
Chef Steven Thornley **Seats** 150, Private dining 10 **Open** All year **Prices from** S £5.95, M £14.95, D £6.50 **Parking** 40 **Notes** Vegetarian dishes, Children welcome

CHESTERFIELD
Casa Hotel
◉◉ MODERN BRITISH, MEDITERRANEAN
01246 245990 | Lockoford Lane, S41 7JB
www.casahotels.co.uk
Casa's Cocina restaurant is an über-chic space with darkwood, white chairs and floor-to-ceiling windows. The menu has a selection of salads and tapas running from a board of Spanish charcuterie to a croquette of hake, cheese and chives with tartare dressing.
Chef Andrew Wilson **Seats** 100, Private dining 200 **Closed** 1 January, Bank Holiday Mondays **Parking** 200 **Notes** Vegetarian dishes, Children welcome

Peak Edge Hotel at the Red Lion
◉◉ MODERN BRITISH **V**
01246 566142 | Darley Road, Stone Edge, S45 0LW
www.peakedgehotel.co.uk
A new-build stone edifice on the border of the Peak District National Park, the family-owned hotel is handy for Chatsworth and Haddon Hall. Next door is the Red Lion, a Georgian coaching inn that is home to the hotel's bar and bistro.
Chef Eddie Kilty **Seats** 80 **Open** All year **Notes** Children welcome

CLOWNE
Van Dyk
◉ MODERN BRITISH
01246 387386 | Worksop Road, S43 4TD
www.vandykcountryhotel.co.uk
The white-fronted Van Dyk stands on the A619 not far from Chesterfield. Amid the surrounding ruggedness, it looks a little like a sugar-frosting confection, which only adds to its idiosyncratic character. There's a hint of old-school formality about the Bowden dining room.
Chef Richard Dean **Seats** 89, Private dining 14 **Open** All year **Prices from** S £8.95, M £16.95, D £7.95 **Parking** 120 **Notes** Vegetarian dishes, Children welcome

DARLEY ABBEY
Darleys Restaurant
◉◉ MODERN BRITISH **V**
01332 364987 | Haslams Lane, DE22 1DZ
www.darleys.com
This converted silk mill by the River Derwent is the setting for some bright, modern cooking making really

excellent use of regional produce. The shady terrace makes the most of the riverside location, a great backdrop for the thoroughly contemporary menus. Desserts demonstrate real creativity.

Chef Jonathan Hobson **Seats** 70 **Closed** Bank holidays and 1st 2 weeks January **Prices from** S £8.25, M £22.75, D £8.75 **Parking** 9 **Notes** Children welcome

DERBY
Masa Restaurant
◉ MODERN EUROPEAN **V**
01332 203345 | The Old Chapel, Brook Street, DE1 3PF
www.masarestaurantwinebar.com

This stylish contemporary restaurant occupies the gallery of an old chapel, with a lounge bar, and the lawned front garden and rear patio available for outdoor imbibing. The restaurant deals in brasserie-style dishes via a sensibly concise carte and terrific value set menu.

Chef Matt Gabbitas **Seats** 120 **Open** All year **Prices from** S £6, M £14, D £6 **Notes** Children welcome

ELLASTONE
The Duncombe Arms
◉◉ MODERN BRITISH
01335 324275 | Main Road, DE6 2GZ
www.duncombearms.co.uk

In the picturesque village of Ellastone on the Staffordshire–Derbyshire border, this attractive whitewashed country inn close to Alton Towers makes for an enjoyable pitstop for a pint but the modern food with intelligent flavours ensures visitors stay for much longer.

Chef Stuart Langdell **Seats** 75, Private dining 12 **Open** All year **Prices from** S £7, M £16, D £7 **Parking** 20 **Notes** Vegetarian dishes, Children welcome

FROGGATT
The Chequers Inn
◉◉ TRADITIONAL BRITISH
01433 630231 | S32 3ZJ
www.chequers-froggatt.com

The Tindalls' country inn in the Hope Valley charms, with a warm colour scheme, wooden pub-style furniture and a fireplace creating a relaxing atmosphere. The menu deftly steers between stalwarts and more modern offerings. You might try lavender pannacotta with blackberry sorbet, blackberry gel and honeycomb.

Chef Lee Vintin **Seats** 90 **Closed** 25 December **Prices from** S £7, M £15, D £6.50 **Parking** 50 **Notes** Vegetarian dishes, Children welcome

GRINDLEFORD
The Maynard
◉◉ MODERN BRITISH
01433 630321 | Main Road, S32 2HE
www.themaynard.co.uk

If Grindleford sounds like the made-up location of a Miss Marple mystery, The Maynard suits it to perfection, its stone-built majesty rising out of Derwent Valley. Sautéed breast of wood pigeon might open, with braised baby leeks and puréed butter beans in a port reduction.

Chef Mark Vernon **Seats** 50, Private dining 120 **Closed** 25 December and 1 January **Parking** 60 **Notes** Vegetarian dishes, Children welcome

HARTINGTON
Biggin Hall Hotel
◉ MODERN BRITISH
01298 84451 | Biggin-by-Hartington, SK17 0DH
www.bigginhall.co.uk

Seventeenth century, 1,000ft up in the Peak District National Park – what's not to like? Plus oak beams, stone walls, flagstones and great views. Always cosy, the restaurant is full of character, with daily changing menus that acknowledge vegetarian tastes.

Chef Mark Wilton **Open** All year **Notes** Vegetarian dishes

HATHERSAGE
The Plough Inn
◉ MODERN EUROPEAN
01433 650319 | Leadmill Bridge, S32 1BA
www.theploughinn-hathersage.co.uk

Set in nine acres of grounds that slope gently to the River Derwent, the stone-built 16th-century Plough is welcoming and friendly. The courtyard's the place to be in summer, and the dining room is always smartly turned out, as is the cooking.

Chef Robert Navarro **Seats** 40, Private dining 24 **Closed** 25 December **Prices from** S £6, M £18, D £6 **Parking** 40 **Notes** Vegetarian dishes, Children welcome

HIGHAM
Santo's Higham Farm Hotel
◉ MODERN INTERNATIONAL
01773 833812 | Main Road, DE55 6EH
www.santoshighamfarm.co.uk

With the rolling Amber Valley all about, this rural retreat in a prime slice of Derbyshire walking country has been fashioned from an old farmstead. Menus mobilise plenty of pedigree local produce and Italian influences are never distant.

Chef Raymond Moody **Seats** 50, Private dining 34 **Open** All year **Prices from** S £5, M £11, D £6 **Parking** 100 **Notes** Vegetarian dishes, Children welcome

DERBYSHIRE

BASLOW
Fischer's Baslow Hall
◉◉◉ MODERN EUROPEAN V
01246 583259 | Calver Road, DE45 1RR
www.fischers-baslowhall.co.uk

Versatile modern cooking in a country retreat

Baslow was built just as the heroic era of architectural pastiche was drawing to a close, an Edwardian take on a Caroline manor house of solid stone construction with mullioned windows, trim gables, globe-topped gateposts, and formally laid gardens including an ornamental pond. Bounded by box and yew hedges, the grounds have been beautifully restored, and with foliage creeping over the facade of the house itself, the proper feeling of gracious country living is established. In its early years, it was owned by the Ferranti family, who electrified it to the extent of floodlighting the tennis courts, but under the ownership of the Fischers since the 1980s, it has become one of northern England's destination country retreats. When it comes to the business of dining, the cons are mod enough these days to include a kitchen bench for watching the chefs going about their tasks, but for those who value a more relaxed old-school approach, the modestly proportioned dining room with its pink and gold striped wallpaper and views over the gardens on two sides is run with the utmost courtesy and professional aplomb.

Served on hand-crafted tableware of Derbyshire and Yorkshire pottery, Rupert Rowley's cooking has obvious roots in the French classical repertoire but is overlaid with a versatile range of modern technique, underlined by a resourcefulness in the art of combining and a true understanding of flavour. Seasonally evolving tasting menus are the eye-catching aspect of the business, but there is an impressive wealth of choice on the three-course carte. South Asian notes have been a recent feature, producing openers of tandoori-roasted quail with mango and lime, or a sautéed brill fillet with spiced lentils, spinach and an onion bhaji. Main courses offer plenty of pedigree meat – Glenarm shorthorn sirloin, Creedy Carver duck, local pork jowl – in presentations that bring out their best. That duck could be paired with Yorkshire rhubarb in a sauce of Monbazillac sweet wine, while the beef dish is as Gallic as can be, with snails and pommes Anna, all perfumed with garlic and parsley. Fish might be sea bass in Italian guise with fennel, artichoke, parmesan and lemon. Finish with prune, Armagnac and jasmine parfait, served with honeycomb and brioche.

The Lunch for Less deal is an irresistible proposition – perhaps truffled mushroom risotto, saddle and shoulder of miso-glazed Cumbrian hogget with peppers and bok choi, and rhubarb fool with matching sorbet.

Chef Rupert Rowley **Seats** 74, Private dining 38 **Closed** 25–26 and 31 December
Parking 20 **Notes** No children under 8 years in the main dining room

DERBYSHIRE

HOPE
Losehill House Hotel & Spa
◉◉ MODERN BRITISH V
01433 621219 | Lose Hill Lane, Edale Road, S33 6AF
www.losehillhouse.co.uk
The Orangery Restaurant in this secluded spot in the Peak District National Park offers stunning views from a light-filled, comfortable room with a contemporary look. The kitchen has a modern, creative style, adding novel and intriguing elements to many dishes.
Chef Joshua Hilton **Seats** 50, Private dining 30
Open All year **Parking** 25 **Notes** Children welcome

MATLOCK
Stones Restaurant
◉◉ MODERN BRITISH V
01629 56061 | 1 Dale Road, DE4 3LT
www.stones-restaurant.co.uk
Stones may be an intimate basement venue, but it has the best of both worlds on fine days, thanks to a stylish conservatory and tiled sun terrace perched above the Derwent. The decor is a mix of subtle earthy tones, to match a Mediterranean-inflected menu.
Chef Kevin Stone **Seats** 44, Private dining 16 **Closed** 25 December to 5 January **Notes** Children welcome

MELBOURNE
Amalfi White
◉◉ MODERN BRITISH
01332 694890 | 50 Derby Road, DE73 8FE
www.amalfiwhite.com
With a terraced garden plus a children's play area, this stylish brasserie has all the attributes needed to make a family-friendly venue all year round. Inside, there's a contemporary space in greys and silvers with a mixture of artwork in the softly lit dining room.
Chef Matthew Clayton **Seats** 64, Private dining 14
Closed 25–26 December and 1 January
Prices from S £7, M £25.75, D £6.75 **Notes** Vegetarian dishes, No children under 8 years after 7.30pm

The Bay Tree
◉ MODERN BRITISH, NEW WORLD V
01332 863358 | 4 Potter Street, DE73 8HW
www.baytreerestaurant.com
Set across different levels, the building was once home to several shops but beyond its stone facade is a contemporary restaurant with clean lines, decorated in very sophisticated shades of muted grey and beige. Menus are thoughtfully constructed, and feature complex but elegant dishes.
Chef Rex Howell **Seats** 60 **Closed** Christmas, 1 January and Bank holidays **Prices from** S £9.95, M £22, D £7.95 **Notes** Children welcome

Harpur's of Melbourne
◉◉ MODERN FRENCH
01332 862134 | 2 Derby Road, DE73 8FE
www.harpursofmelbourne.co.uk
The inn evolved in the 19th century from a pair of Georgian houses in this lovely market town. These days, it puts on all sort of special occasions, and there's plenty going on in the smart first-floor restaurant. Pub classics are the backbone.
Chef Lee Emerson **Seats** 75 **Open** All year
Prices from S £5.95, M £12.95, D £4 **Parking** 25
Notes Vegetarian dishes, Children welcome

MORLEY
The Morley Hayes Hotel
◉◉ MODERN BRITISH
01332 780480 | Main Road, DE7 6DG
www.morleyhayes.com
Morley Hayes has been a dynamic hotel since the 1980s, and with its golf complex, conference facilities and wedding venue, it has most bases covered. The kitchen offers a roster of unpretentious modern dishes, with influences from around the globe adding vibrancy and colour.
Chef Nigel Stuart **Seats** 106, Private dining 24
Closed 27 December and 1 January **Parking** 250
Notes Vegetarian dishes, Children welcome

QUARNDON
Kedleston Country House
◉ BRITISH
01332 477222 | Kedleston Road, Kedleston, DE22 5JD
www.thekedleston.co.uk
Located on the outskirts of Derby, this handsome Georgian property makes good use of produce from the Kedleston Estate. Vegetables and herbs from the hotel's kitchen garden and meat from local farmers appear on the seasonal menus, which change weekly.
Chef Adam Keelinge **Open** All year

REPTON
The Boot Inn
◉◉ MODERN BRITISH
01283 346047 | 12 Boot Hill, DE65 6FT
www.thebootatrepton.co.uk
Five miles from the National Brewery Centre, you would expect beer to be a strong draw, especially in a refurbished 17th-century coaching inn. A range of evocatively named ales from its microbrewery is a plank of The Boot's huge popularity.
Chef Rob Taylor **Seats** 65 **Open** All year
Prices from S £6.95, M £14.95, D £6.95 **Parking** 9
Notes Vegetarian dishes, Children welcome

THE PEACOCK AT ROWSLEY

The Peacock at Rowsley is a cosy, chic boutique hotel, originally a manor house in the heart of the Peak District National Park and very close to Haddon Hall and Chatsworth House. Perfect for a countryside break with comfortable bedrooms including four posters and one of the best hotel suites in the region. Our award winning restaurant serves a delicious fine dining menu, crafted by Head Chef Dan Smith. Dan worked with notable chefs such as Tom Aikens before joining The Peacock. The atmospheric bar with open fire is a very convivial place to meet for lunch, dinner or just a drink – with its own menu of freshly cooked seasonal food. Treat yourself to a drink from the extensive cocktail menu. Sunday lunch at The Peacock is a local favourite. The hotel is famed for is excellent fly fishing on the Derbyshire Wye and river Derwent.

For further information or to make a booking please call **01629 733518** or email **reception@thepeacockatrowsley.com**. The Peacock at Rowsley, Derbyshire DE4 2EB,

ROWSLEY
The Peacock at Rowsley
◉◉◉ MODERN BRITISH V
01629 733518 | Bakewell Road, DE4 2EB
www.thepeacockatrowsley.com

Technically nimble, creative cooking in an aristocratic manor

The Peacock is weathered Derbyshire stone manor house of the late 17th century that became a hotel at about the time Queen Victoria got the top job, so it has a comforting sense of deep roots in the village. The delightful riverside grounds are worth a wander, while keen anglers might join the in-house club and cast a fly into the nearby Wye and Derwent rivers. The old-world dependability of the original building overlaid with 21st-century sensibilities is a winning combination because the makeover enhances the charms of the original without ripping out its soul or overwhelming the place with overblown flourishes. It's a tasteful job. While the bar has the feel of a village inn, with its low ceiling, venerable timber columns and stone walls, the dining room goes for a contemporary country-chic look, with lime-green and plum-coloured walls offset by modern fringed light fixtures and old oil portraits forming the backdrop for dinner.

Having served time with Tom Aikens in London, Dan Smith produces a technically nimble rendition of creative British cooking, looking to nearby estates for organically

reared meats, as well as the Peacock's own kitchen gardens, for the bedrock of his dynamic modern output. Whether you go for the à la carte or multi-course taster, things set off on a hearty note: pig's head croquettes might be served alongside local ham, with celeriac purée and the heady note of truffle helping things along; otherwise, a rustic soup of Jersey Royals and Lincolnshire cheese boosted by bacon, nettle and hazelnut pesto brings flavours of emphatic precision.

Main courses turn up the volume, building layers of flavour from pedigree prime materials – local lamb cutlet, say, with onion, broad beans, goats' curd and boulangère potatoes, or Goosnargh chicken partnered with wild garlic, leeks, morels and a little pie of the leg meat. If you're in the mood for fish, there may be a happy duo of hake and squid, supported by a Japanese-inspired array of radish, edamame beans, shimeji mushrooms and sea-fresh squid broth delivering deep satisfaction. The kitchen's technical dexterity extends to impressive desserts, when spikes of sweetness and acidity combine in the likes of white chocolate crème brûlée, its luxuriant creaminess pointed up with kalamansi lime and strawberries, or a zingy assemblage of rhubarb, fromage frais, mandarin sorbet and pistachio delivering the final hit.

Chef Dan Smith **Seats** 56, Private dining 14 **Open** All year **Prices from** S £7.45, M £24, D £7.45 **Parking** 25 **Notes** No children under 10 years Friday and Saturday

See advertisement on page 89

ROWSLEY
The Peacock at Rowsley
🏵🏵🏵 MODERN BRITISH **V**
See pages 90–91

See advertisement on page 89

SANDIACRE
La Rock
🏵🏵 MODERN BRITISH
0115 939 9833 | 4 Bridge Street, NG10 5QT
www.larockrestaurant.co.uk
Hidden away down a side street in Sandiacre, La Rock's sophisticated and contemporary interior has exposed brick walls, wooden floors, solid oak tables with granite centres and sparkling glassware, and there's a glass-roofed lounge area with inviting comfy sofas; soft music plays in the background.
Chef Nick Gillespie **Seats** 40 **Closed** 12–20 March, 4–12 June, 10–18 September, 2 weeks after 23 December **Prices from** S £8.50, M £19, D £8 **Notes** Vegetarian dishes, No children under 10 years

THORPE
The Izaak Walton Hotel
🏵🏵 MODERN, TRADITIONAL
01335 350981 | Dovedale, DE6 2AY
www.izaakwaltonhotel.com
This creeper-clad country house has glorious views over the Dovedale Valley and the Derbyshire peaks. Decorated in rich hues of red and gold, the elegant Haddon Restaurant favours a traditional candlelight-and-linen look, in contrast to the up-to-date and creative menu.
Chef Simon Harrison **Seats** 120, Private dining 40 **Open** All year **Parking** 50 **Notes** Vegetarian dishes, Children welcome

TIDESWELL
The Merchant's Yard
🏵🏵 CONTEMPORARY, CLASSIC
01298 872442 | St Joan's Road, SK17 8NY
www.themerchantsyard.com
The Merchant's Yard is in the centre of the Peak District in the village of Tideswell. The restaurant is found tucked away in a traditional stone building. Set on two levels, the atmosphere is one of relaxed dining with local produce given a global treatment.
Chef Carl Riley **Seats** 80, Private dining 24 **Open** All year **Prices from** S £5.50, M £13.95, D £4.95 **Notes** Vegetarian dishes, Children welcome

▶ DEVON

ASHBURTON
The Old Library Restaurant
🏵 MODERN BRITISH
01364 652896 | North Street, TQ13 7QH
www.theoldlibraryrestaurant.co.uk
Housed at the back of the Ashburton library, facing the car park, Joe Suttie and Amy Mitchell's place is a valuable local resource. Happy locals crowd the chunky tables, overseen by a busy kitchen counter, for a short, punchy menu that changes every six weeks or so.
Chef Amy Mitchell, Joe Suttie **Seats** 22 **Closed** 23 December to 16 January **Prices from** S £6.50, M £16.50, D £7 **Notes** Vegetarian dishes, Children welcome

AXMINSTER
Fairwater Head Hotel
🏵 MODERN BRITISH, FRENCH
01297 678349 | Hawkchurch, EX13 5TX
www.fairwaterheadhotel.co.uk
Just five miles from Axminster, Fairwater Head enjoys panoramic views over the Axe Valley and stands amidst three acres of manicured lawns. The appealing stone building covered in climbing foliage has a relaxed rural ambience. Flawless Devon produce is worked into modern classics.
Chef Tony Golder **Seats** 60, Private dining 18 **Closed** January **Prices from** S £6, M £14, D £6.50 **Parking** 40 **Notes** Vegetarian dishes, Children welcome

Tytherleigh Arms
🏵 MODERN BRITISH
01460 220214 | Tytherleigh, EX13 7BE
www.tytherleigharms.com
This family-run 16th-century coaching inn on the borders of Devon, Dorset and Somerset creates a welcoming atmosphere with its beamed ceilings, wooden floors, and a wood-burner ablaze in the winter months. Local produce drives the menus here, and the well-conceived dishes are prepared with sensitivity.
Chef Nick Topham **Seats** 60, Private dining 37 **Closed** 2nd and 3rd weeks of January **Parking** 36 **Notes** Vegetarian dishes, No children under 5 years

BAMPTON
The Swan
◉◉ MODERN BRITISH
01398 332248 | Station Road, EX16 9NG
www.theswan.co

The Swan is a smart country pub – warm colours, lots of oak, a few sofas, soft lighting – with a convivial atmosphere. The bar is the heart of the operation, but it's easy to see why the whole place can be full of diners.

Chef Paul Berry, Tom Lugg **Seats** 60, Private dining 20 **Closed** 25 December **Notes** Vegetarian dishes, Children welcome

BEESANDS
The Cricket Inn
◉ MODERN SEAFOOD
01548 580215 | TQ7 2EN
www.thecricketinn.com

Smack on the seafront overlooking the shingle beach, with stunning views across Start Bay, The Cricket enjoys an unrivalled location and retains every ounce of its identity as a former fisherman's pub. Blackboard menus advertise what has been freshly drawn from the bay.

Chef Scott Heath **Seats** 65, Private dining 40 **Closed** 25 December, January **Prices from** S £5.50, M £12.50, D £6.50 **Parking** 30 **Notes** Vegetarian dishes, Children welcome

BIDEFORD
The Pig on the Hill
◉◉ FRENCH, ENGLISH V
01237 459222 | Pusehill, EX39 5AH
www.pigonthehillwestwardho.co.uk

Created in a converted cowshed, The Pig on the Hill is a country pub together with a modern restaurant that's reminiscent of an American-style diner – black-and-white chequered floor, bare wooden tables, large windows creating an airy atmosphere and informal yet professional service.

Chef Greg Martin **Seats** Private dining 20 **Closed** 25 December **Parking** 40 **Notes** Children welcome

BIGBURY-ON-SEA
The Oyster Shack
◉ SEAFOOD
01548 810876 | Stakes Hill, TQ7 4BE
www.oystershack.co.uk

A warm-hearted place with a casual atmosphere, where a friendly greeting gets everything off on the right foot. Super-fresh seafood is the name of the game, and it's all the better if you sit outside under the sail-like awning. Giant blackboards reveal what's on offer.

Chef Andy Richardson **Seats** 60 **Closed** 25 December and 2–31 January **Parking** 25 **Notes** Vegetarian dishes, Children welcome

BRIXHAM
Quayside Hotel
◉ MODERN BRITISH
01803 855751 | 41–49 King Street, TQ5 9TJ
www.quaysidehotel.co.uk

The restaurant at the Quayside Hotel majors in seafood and what reaches the menu depends on the catch. They know how to treat this prime product with respect. It takes place in a candlelit dining room with harbour views and a refreshing lack of pretence.

Chef Philip Winsor **Seats** 40, Private dining 18 **Open** All year **Prices from** S £5.60, M £12.50, D £5.75 **Parking** 30 **Notes** Vegetarian dishes, No children under 5 years

BURRINGTON
Northcote Manor
◉◉ MODERN BRITISH V
01769 560501 | EX37 9LZ
www.northcotemanor.co.uk

Set in 20 acres of lush Devon countryside, the 18th-century stone manor trades these days as a classy country-house hotel with an impressive restaurant. There's a reassuringly traditional feel, and fine West Country ingredients lead the charge on an enticing menu in the modern country-house mould.

Chef Richie Herkes **Seats** 34, Private dining 50 **Open** All year **Parking** 30 **Notes** Children welcome
See advertisement on page 94

CHAGFORD
Gidleigh Park
◉◉◉ MODERN CLASSIC V 🍷 NOTABLE WINE LIST
01647 432367 | TQ13 8HH
www.gidleigh.co.uk

Sitting in lordly isolation on its bluff above the Teign Valley, Gidleigh nonetheless manages not to feel overly grandiloquent. It still feels like the house it was designed as in the 1920s, albeit one accoutred with oak panelling, fine furnishings and bevies of utterly professional staff. Its trio of adjacent dining rooms is now the preserve of chef Chris Simpson, formerly with Nathan Outlaw in Cornwall, and he has made an instant splash with cooking that has an elegant, sharply delineated style, with carefully articulated flavours and subtle interplay of textures. Veal sweetbread in sourdough crumb with pickled mushrooms works its uncluttered magic as a first course and could be followed by lightly cooked Cornish turbot with broad beans and leeks in a concentrated sauce of celeriac. Otherwise, it may be

CHAGFORD continued

lemon sole with brown shrimps and kohlrabi, and then Creedy Carver duck breast with chicory and onion tart, beetroot and kale. Great pastry-work also shows up in a silky chocolate tart with salted pistachios, offset with gentle yogurt sorbet. The seven-course tasting menu offers a comprehensive tour of the territory.

Chef Chris Simpson **Seats** 45, Private dining 22 **Open** All year **Parking** 45 **Notes** No children under 8 years at lunch and dinner

Mill End Hotel

MODERN BRITISH

01647 432282 | Dartmoor National Park, TQ13 8JN
www.millendhotel.com

The River Teign flows past this pretty white-painted hotel, where a Devon cream tea is just the ticket, with a lush pastoral backdrop. There's an air of genteel formality in the restaurant with its linen-clad tables, while the kitchen's output is modern, seasonal, and well-presented.

Chef Darren Knockton **Seats** 50 **Open** All year **Prices from** S £8, M £14.50, D £7.50 **Parking** 30 **Notes** Vegetarian dishes, Children welcome

CHITTLEHAMHOLT

Highbullen Hotel, Golf & Country Club

MODERN BRITISH **V**

01769 540561 | Highbullen Hotel EX37 9HD
www.highbullen.co.uk

The Devon View Restaurant doesn't disappoint when it comes to the promised vista, and that is indeed the rolling Devon countryside you can see through the bank of windows. The restaurant makes this golfing and spa hotel a useful stopover.

Chef Stephen Walker **Seats** 60, Private dining 25 **Open** All year **Prices from** S £12.50, M £24.50, D £12.50 **Parking** 150 **Notes** Vegetarian dishes, Children welcome

CREDITON

The Lamb Inn

MODERN BRITISH

01363 773676 | The Square, Sandford, EX17 4LW
www.lambinnsandford.co.uk

A 16th-century former coaching house with open fires, low ceilings and a pretty, sheltered garden on three levels, this lovely village pub is unpretentious and welcoming. The accomplished cooking makes good use of quality, local produce, the seasonal menu changing daily. Leave room for comforting desserts.

Chef Andy Bennett **Seats** 48, Private dining 15 **Closed** 25 December **Prices from** S £5.25, M £13.95, D £5.95 **Notes** Vegetarian dishes, Children welcome

DARTMOUTH

The Dart Marina Hotel

MODERN BRITISH **V**

01803 832580 | Sandquay Road, TQ6 9PH
www.dartmarina.com

The hotel is a contemporary paradise with neutral colour tones, tasteful and trendy furniture and a swish spa, and it's also home to the River Restaurant. Views of the river are guaranteed through floor-to-ceiling windows, while the menu features regional produce.

Chef Peter Alcroft **Seats** 86 **Closed** 23–26 and 30–31 December **Parking** 100 **Notes** Children welcome

The Grill Room

BRITISH, SEAFOOD

01803 833033 | Royal Castle Hotel, 11 The Quay, TQ6 9PS
www.royalcastle.co.uk

With the River Dart in sight, it's refreshing to see an emphasis on locally caught, fresh fish in the first-floor dining room of this 17th-century quayside hotel, while die-hard carnivores will find no fault with the prime slabs of British beef and Devon lamb on offer.

Chef Ankur Biswas **Seats** 60, Private dining 70 **Open** All year **Prices from** S £8, M £15, D £7 **Notes** Vegetarian dishes, Children welcome

The Seahorse

MEDITERRANEAN, SEAFOOD **V**

01803 835147 | 5 South Embankment, TQ6 9BH
www.seahorserestaurant.co.uk

Located in the bustling strip along the Dart waterfront, this is an inviting evening venue, while big windows let in the Devon light on summer days. Local seafood, as you might imagine, features widely on the menus, but there's plenty for non-fish fans as well.

Chef Mat Prowse, Mitch Tonks **Seats** 40, Private dining 14 **Closed** 25 December and 1 January **Prices from** S £10, M £18, D £5 **Notes** Children welcome

DODDISCOMBSLEIGH

The Nobody Inn

MODERN BRITISH

01647 252394 | EX6 7PS
www.nobodyinn.co.uk

This characterful 17th-century inn has a good local reputation, built upon its stylish food, excellent local cheeses, hefty wine list and a 240-long list of whiskeys. Reached via winding lanes, inside it has blackened beams, mismatched tables, and walls adorned with plenty of visual interest.

Chef Mike Pooley **Seats** 80, Private dining 24 **Closed** 1 January **Parking** 30 **Notes** Vegetarian dishes, Children welcome

DEVON

DREWSTEIGNTON

The Old Inn

◎◎◎ INTERNATIONAL

01647 281276 | EX6 6QR

www.old-inn.co.uk

Despite the narrow roads that lead into it on either side, Drewsteignton was once a major staging-post on the coach route from Exeter to Okehampton. A slip of a Dartmoor village to the modern eye, it boasts Duncan Walker's white-fronted 17th-century inn, the transformation of which into a contemporary restaurant with rooms has made the place a destination. In a homely, low-ceilinged ambience with striking modern artworks, a menu of assured, classically based cooking offers a wealth of enticement within its modest compass of four choices per course. European notes could be as inimitably French as grilled sole fillets with morels and Madeira, followed by Dexter beef pot-au-feu, but influences from further afield result in a pairing of spiced pork belly and seared scallops to start, with sesame-dressed pak choi. Quality shines forth from a fillet of halibut crusted in lemon and parsley, served with braised celery. Traditionally conceived desserts punch above their weight as in their textbook tarte Tatin, or a billowing apricot soufflé with vanilla ice cream. A compact wine list is impeccably chosen and complements the heartening simplicity of the approach.

Chef Duncan Walker **Seats** 16, Private dining 10 **Closed** 3 weeks in January **Notes** No children under 12 years

ERMINGTON

Plantation House

◎◎ MODERN BRITISH V

01548 831100 | Totnes Road, PL21 9NS

www.plantationhousehotel.co.uk

This elegant boutique hotel exudes character, with stunning garden views, bucket chairs in twisted wicker at solid darkwood tables, and attractive soft furnishings in both dining rooms. After a swig of truffled wild garlic and nettle soup, it's on to shellfish in a Thai broth.

Chef Richard Hendey, John Raines **Seats** 28, Private dining 16 **Open** All year **Parking** 30 **Notes** Children welcome

EXMOUTH

Lympstone Manor

Rosettes suspended MODERN BRITISH V

01395 202040 | Courtlands Lane, EX8 3NZ

www.lympstonemanor.co.uk

A late new entry into the guide, our inspectors have not completed the inspection process at the time of going to print. Not far south of Exeter, down along the eastern flank of the Exe estuary, Lympstone Manor is a creamy-white Georgian mansion with views to spare. Gently undulating land sweeps down to the river, with Lyme Bay in the distance, and the hotel grounds themselves will soon be home to a vineyard producing sparkling wine. A trio of adjacent dining rooms capitalises on the serene prospect in three strikingly different decorative rigs, but the service tone is the same throughout, friendly and engaging. These surroundings might have been made to measure for Michael Caines, who returns to the first rank of Devon cooking.

Chef Michael Caines MBE, Dan Gambles **Seats** 60 **Open** All year

Saveur

◎◎ MODERN EUROPEAN

01395 269459 | 9 Tower Street, EX8 1NT

www.saveursrestaurant.com

Hidden down a quiet pedestrianised street behind the church, this neighbourhood restaurant ticks all the right boxes when it comes to cosiness, informality and fine cooking. Meaning 'flavour', Saveur celebrates local seafood from Lyme Bay and Brixham as well as other, equally local produce.

Chef Nigel Wright **Seats** 30 **Closed** 3 weeks January **Prices from** S £6.50, M £14.50, D £6.50 **Notes** Vegetarian dishes, Children welcome

HAYTOR VALE

Rock Inn

◎◎ MODERN BRITISH, EUROPEAN

01364 661305 | TQ13 9XP

www.rock-inn.co.uk

The rustic Rock Inn's pre-Victorian air provides a welcoming backdrop to the modern European culinary style on show in its candlelit dining room. A crisp-coated duck Scotch egg with chilli jam and salad leaves is listed among the well-executed starters.

Chef Josh Trolley, Sophie Collier **Seats** 75, Private dining 20 **Closed** 25–26 December **Parking** 25 **Notes** Vegetarian dishes, Children welcome

HONITON

The Deer Park Country House Hotel

◎◎ MODERN BRITISH V

01404 41266 | Weston, EX14 3PG

www.deerpark.co.uk

This 18th-century Georgian mansion set in 80 acres of glorious grounds is a quintessentially English set-up brought into the 21st century with a sprinkle of boutique style and great food served in an elegant dining room to seal the deal.

Chef Hadleigh Barrett **Seats** 45, Private dining 30 **Open** All year **Parking** 60 **Notes** Children welcome

The Holt Bar & Restaurant
◉ MODERN BRITISH
01404 47707 | 178 High Street, EX14 1LA
www.theholt-honiton.com

The Holt's main dining area is upstairs: open-plan, with a wooden floor, simple decor, candlelight, and pleasant, efficient service. Food is a serious commitment here and standards are consistently high, with the menu a happy blend of the traditional and more à la mode.

Chef Angus McCaig, Billy Emmett **Seats** 50 **Closed** 25–26 December **Notes** Vegetarian dishes, Children welcome

THE PIG at Combe
◉◉ SEASONAL BRITISH ⚑ NOTABLE WINE LIST
01404 540400 | Giltisham, EX14 3AD
www.thepighotel.com/at-combe

Set in a honeyed stone Elizabethan mansion in 3,500 acres, THE PIG at Combe is part of a mini-chain of deliciously relaxed bolt-holes for 21st-century sybarites. Any hint of starchy country-house formality is banished here, so dining is an informal affair in a rustic-chic setting.

Chef Daniel Gavriilidis **Seats** 75, Private dining 22 **Open** All year **Prices from** S £6.50, M £14, D £7.50 **Parking** 57 **Notes** Vegetarian dishes, Children welcome

ILFRACOMBE
The Quay Restaurant
◉ BRITISH, EUROPEAN
01271 868090 | 11 The Quay, EX34 9EQ
www.11thequay.co.uk

Perched on the harbour front of this coastal town, the Quay has a strong sense of identity. Adorned with original artworks by Damien Hirst at his more docile, the Atlantic Room with its vaulted ceiling is a bright and breezy setting for internationally inspired brasserie classics.

Chef Seb Davidson **Seats** 45, Private dining 26 **Closed** 24–26 December and 2 weeks in January **Prices from** S £6, M £15, D £6.50 **Notes** Vegetarian dishes, Children welcome

Sandy Cove Hotel
◉◉ MODERN BRITISH
01271 882243 | Old Coast Road, Combe Martin Bay, Berrynarbor, EX34 9SR
www.sandycove-hotel.co.uk

With stunning views of both the bay and the wild landscape of Exmoor, Sandy Cove Hotel offers the best of both worlds. Positioned to maximise the vista with large windows (and a terrace when the weather allows), the restaurant offers a hypnotic view.

Chef Neil Gilson **Seats** 150, Private dining 30 **Open** All year **Parking** 50 **Notes** Vegetarian dishes, Children welcome

ILSINGTON
Ilsington Country House Hotel
◉◉ MODERN EUROPEAN
01364 661452 | Ilsington Village, TQ13 9RR
www.ilsington.co.uk

A substantial white property, Ilsington's diverse menu includes some divertingly appealing dishes. Accompaniments complement the main ingredients without swamping them, seen in main courses of roast chicken with a maple and mustard gel, pommes Anna, pea purée, mushrooms, confit tomato and smoked beetroot.

Chef Mike O'Donnell **Seats** 75, Private dining 60 **Closed** 2–12 January **Parking** 60 **Notes** Vegetarian dishes, Children welcome

KENTISBURY
The Coach House by Michael Caines
◉◉◉ MODERN BRITISH V
01271 882295 | Kentisbury Grange, EX31 4NL
www.kentisburygrange.com

On the fringes of Exmoor National Park, just a short, pretty drive to the north coast, Kentisbury Grange is a former Victorian manor lovingly morphed into classy boutique hotel. The old manor's coach house was not forgotten in the transition and has been turned into a stunning restaurant, and with its kitchen under the guidance of Michael Caines, it's quite the dining destination. The impressive space is contemporarily rustic, with a stylish bar on the first floor and tables outside for when the mercury has risen in north Devon. Regional ingredients get a good outing on menus that show intelligent flavour combinations in the modern British manner. A first course squab pigeon comes with beetroot tartare and preserved blueberries, while crab ravioli has spikes of lemongrass and ginger, and a full-flavoured crab bisque. Among main courses, Cornish sea bass stars with hay-roasted Jerusalem artichokes and a hit of truffles, and slow-cooked pork tenderloin arrives with white pudding purée. Apple and blackcurrant soufflé with Granny Smith apple sorbet is a fine, fruity finale.

Chef James Mason **Seats** 54, Private dining 16 **Open** All year **Parking** 70 **Notes** Children welcome

DEVON

KINGSBRIDGE
Buckland-Tout-Saints
◉◉◉ MODERN BRITISH **V**
01548 853055 | Goveton, TQ7 2DS
www.tout-saints.co.uk

Set in four acres of stunning grounds in the South Hams, this handsome William and Mary-era manor house provides a classy country-house package. The interior is packed with period details such as wood panelling and grand fireplaces, not least in the Queen Anne Restaurant.

Chef Ted Ruewell **Seats** 40, Private dining 40 **Open** All year **Prices from** S £9.50, M £24, D £9.50 **Parking** 40 **Notes** Children welcome

KNOWSTONE
The Masons Arms
◉◉ MODERN BRITISH
01398 341231 | EX36 4RY
www.masonsarmsdevon.co.uk

In the idyllic village of Knowstone, this thatched 13th-century country inn is set deep in the lush countryside on the Devon and Somerset border. Chef-patron Mark Dodson once cooked under Michel Roux at Bray, which might explain the flair and precision evident in the kitchen.

Chef Mark Dodson, Jamie Coleman **Seats** 28 **Closed** 1st week in January, February half term and 1 week August Bank holiday **Prices from** S £9.50, M £25.50, D £8.75 **Parking** 10 **Notes** Vegetarian dishes, No children under 5 years at dinner

LIFTON
Arundell Arms
◉◉ MODERN BRITISH **V**
01566 784666 | Fore Street, PL16 0AA
www.arundellarms.com

What looks like a rural pub on the outside is an elevated country hotel within, with lavish traditional furnishings and a large dining room. The kitchen offers a traditionally based Anglo-French repertoire founded on quality materials. There's a gentle richness to the impact of dishes.

Chef Steven Pidgeon **Seats** 70, Private dining 24 **Open** All year **Parking** 70 **Notes** Children welcome

LYNMOUTH
Rising Sun
◉◉ BRITISH, FRENCH
01598 753223 | Harbourside, EX35 6EG
www.risingsunlynmouth.co.uk

The Rising Sun rocks with good vibrations with its bar plus an atmospheric oak-panelled dining room. The food strikes a balance between hearty generosity and contemporary combinations, with plenty of seafood dishes. Start with seared king scallops with cauliflower cream and crisp pancetta.

Chef Matthew Rutter **Seats** 22 **Closed** Christmas **Notes** Vegetarian dishes, No children under 7 years

MORETONHAMPSTEAD
Great Western
◉◉◉ MODERN BRITISH **V** ⚲ NOTABLE WINE LIST
01647 445000 | Bovey Castle, Dartmoor National Park, North Bovey, TQ13 8RE
www.boveycastle.com

Built in 1890 by stationery supremo WH Smith, Bovey Castle was reinvented as a 'golfing hotel' by the Great Western Railway company back in 1930, an association acknowledged in its top dining venue, the Great Western restaurant. It's a grand old pile, big, bold, and glamorous, with the requisite spa and golf course to keep 21st-century sybarites busy until dinner. The Great Western is an equally plush space, suitably romantic with art deco lines. Local lad Mark Budd leads the kitchen team, and his fondness for regional ingredients from land and sea looms large in good-looking contemporary dishes that reveal well-honed technical skills and sound classical roots – perhaps ballotine of rabbit and serrano ham with butternut squash and parsley risotto to open the show. First-rate fish is always a good call – monkfish, say, poached bourguignon-style in red wine with smoked bacon, parsley and wild mushrooms – while meatier fare could be Devon pork and perry with crushed turnips, wood sorrel, and potato and pear terrine. Finish in style with warm plum soufflé with Garibaldi biscuits and buttermilk ice cream.

Chef Mark Budd **Seats** 120, Private dining 32 **Open** All year **Parking** 100 **Notes** Children welcome

Smith's Brasserie
◉ MODERN BRITISH **V**
01647 445000 | Bovey Castle, Dartmoor National Park, North Bovey, TQ13 8RE
www.boveycastle.com

Set in 275 acres of stunning countryside in the heart of Dartmoor National Park, Bovey Castle boasts a spa and 18-hole championship golf course. Smith's Brasserie is the more informal of the hotel's two restaurants and offers a relaxed dining experience with broad appeal.

Chef Ivan Dobrinin **Open** All year **Prices from** S £6, M £14.50, D £8 **Notes** Children welcome

PLYMOUTH

Artillery Tower Restaurant

◉ MODERN BRITISH

01752 257610 | Firestone Bay, Durnford Street,
PL1 3QR

www.artillerytower.co.uk

A 16th-century circular gunnery tower on Plymouth waterfront, be sure to grip the handrail tight as you climb the spiral staircase. Arched windows that once served as gun emplacements in three-foot walls surround the dining space, where simple modern bistro food is the drill.

Chef Peter Constable **Seats** 26, Private dining 16
Closed Christmas and New Year **Parking** 20
Notes Vegetarian dishes, Children welcome

Barbican Kitchen

◉ MODERN, INTERNATIONAL

01752 604448 | Plymouth Gin Distillery, 60 Southside Street, PL1 2LQ

www.barbicankitchen.com

The Plymouth Gin distillery is home to the Tanner brothers' vibrant restaurant, and entering past the huge vats gives a reminder of the esteemed history of the building. The Barbican Kitchen packs a visual punch with its bold colours and contemporary prints.

Chef Martyn Compton, Christopher and James Tanner
Seats 100, Private dining 22 **Closed** 25–26 and 31 December **Prices from** S £5.50, M £13.95, D £5.95
Notes Vegetarian dishes, Children welcome

Best Western Duke of Cornwall Hotel

◉◉ MODERN BRITISH, EUROPEAN

01752 275850 | Millbay Road, PL1 3LG

www.thedukeofcornwall.co.uk

A Plymouth landmark for the past 150 years, you certainly can't miss the Duke of Cornwall hotel with its imposing Gothic exterior and Corinthian-style pillars. The kitchen works a modern European repertoire with a decent showing of West Country ingredients.

Chef Nicholas Reed **Seats** 80, Private dining 30
Closed 26–31 December **Parking** 40 **Notes** Vegetarian dishes, Children welcome

Boringdon Hall Hotel

◉◉◉ MODERN FRENCH

01752 344455 | Boringdon Hill, Plympton, PL7 4DP

www.boringdonhall.co.uk

Boringdon was gifted as a deconsecrated priory during Henry VIII's Dissolution to one of his favoured courtiers, the Earl of Southampton, who in turn sold it on to the Grey family that produced England's nine-day queen. Dripping with historical stories, the Tudor manor is beautifully preserved. Its dining room occupies a gallery overlooking the Great Hall with its moulded plaster coat of arms, where Scott Paton is fully up to the task of matching the grand surroundings – no mean feat. The five-course taster offers a middle way between the carte and the longer seven-act performance, embracing Vulscombe goats' cheese with pickled beetroot, elderflower and gingerbread, liver parfait in truffled sherry dressing, John Dory with ham hock, leeks and apple on smoked hollandaise, and a fish or meat choice for main, the latter perhaps venison with ceps, Crown Prince squash and winter greens. It all finishes on a climactic note with intense raspberry mousse, jelly and sorbet with pistachio cream. Vegetarian and vegan menus, the latter incorporating soy-glazed tofu with carrot, tarragon and sesame, demonstrate admirable versatility.

Chef Scott Paton **Seats** 40, Private dining 26
Open All year

The Greedy Goose

◉◉ MODERN BRITISH

01752 252001 | Prysten House, Finewell Street,
PL1 2AE

www.thegreedygoose.co.uk

Tucked away in the oldest part of Plymouth, ancient beams bear witness to this building's antiquity. The up-to-date cooking is built on fresh seasonal West Country produce, while local boats supply goodies such as plaice, mussels, seaweed and sea spinach.

Chef Ben Palmer **Seats** 50, Private dining 30
Closed 24 December to 1st Tuesday in January
Prices from S £6, M £14, D £6 **Notes** Vegetarian dishes, No children under 4 years

Langdon Court Hotel & Restaurant

◉◉ TRADITIONAL BRITISH, FRENCH V

01752 862358 | Adams Lane, Down Thomas, PL9 0DY
www.langdoncourt.com

A 16th-century manor house in the beautiful South Hams, Langdon Court has played host to royal personages and their consorts since the days of Henry VIII and Catherine Parr. A country-house hotel since 1960, local farms and Devon fishermen supply the kitchen.

Chef Edward Nagy **Seats** 36, Private dining 92
Open All year **Parking** 60 **Notes** Children welcome

DEVON

Rock Salt Café and Brasserie
◉◉ MODERN BRITISH V
01752 225522 | 31 Stonehouse Street, PL1 3PE
www.rocksaltcafe.co.uk
The sign outside says 'good, honest food' and that's certainly what this place is all about. Open all day, all week, the easy-going seaside vibe strikes a relaxed pose but takes the food seriously. There's attention to detail whether it's breakfast, lunch or dinner.
Chef David Jenkins, Joe Turner Seats 60, Private dining 25 Closed 24–26 December
Prices from S £5.95, M £12.95, D £6.50
Notes Vegetarian dishes, Children welcome

The Wildflower Restaurant
◉ CLASSIC BRITISH
01822 852245 | Moorland Garden Hotel, Yelverton, PL20 6DA
www.moorlandgardenhotel.co.uk
The Moorland Garden Hotel's colourful and smart restaurant has views over the pristine garden to wild Dartmoor beyond, with floor-to-ceiling windows and its own terrace to make the best of the setting.
Chef Jake Westlake Seats 70 Open All year
Prices from S £5.95, M £12.95, D £5.95 Parking 120
Notes Vegetarian dishes, Children welcome

PLYMPTON
Treby Arms
◉◉ MODERN BRITISH
01752 837363 | Sparkwell, PL7 5DD
www.thetrebyarms.co.uk
Stake your claim early and be rewarded with energetic modern cookery of a high order at the Treby Arms. Why not let yourself be tempted by torched loin of native pig and glazed cheek with lovage emulsion, celery root and leaf.
Chef Fletcher Andrews Seats 60 Closed 25–26 December and 1 January Prices from S £6, M £14, D £7 Parking 14 Notes Vegetarian dishes, Children welcome

ROCKBEARE
The Jack In The Green Inn
◉◉ MODERN BRITISH V
01404 822240 | EX5 2EE
www.jackinthegreen.uk.com
This family-friendly roadside pub has gained a well-deserved reputation. With its low-beamed rooms and a wood-burning stove, the smart interior creates a contemporary atmosphere and innovative menus offer smart, thoughtful dishes with punchy flavours.
Chef Matthew Mason Seats 80, Private dining 60
Closed 25 December to 5 January Parking 120
Notes Children welcome

SALCOMBE
The Jetty
◉ MODERN, INTERNATIONAL V ♦ NOTABLE WINE LIST
01548 844444 | Salcombe Harbour Hotel, Cliff Road, TQ8 8JH
www.salcombe-harbour-hotel.co.uk
There are fabulous views over the estuary from The Jetty's prime position within the Salcombe Harbour Hotel. The hotel's spa facilities, and even a private cinema, offer many distractions, but time is never better spent than when sitting in the smart, contemporary restaurant.
Chef Jamie Gulliford Seats 100 Open All year
Prices from S £7.50, M £17, D £7.50 Parking 10
Notes Children welcome

Soar Mill Cove Hotel
◉◉ MODERN BRITISH
01548 561566 | Soar Mill Cove, Marlborough, TQ7 3DS
www.soarmillcove.co.uk
This family-run hotel is in a lovely location, with the cove below and uninterrupted sea views. The kitchen has its roots in the classical techniques with a modern spin. Thus, sautéed scallops are partnered by melting crab thermidor and sautéed leeks. Presentation is a strength.
Chef I Macdonald Seats 60 Closed January
Prices from S £8, M £12, D £8 Parking 25
Notes Vegetarian dishes, Children welcome

South Sands Hotel
◉◉ MODERN BRITISH
01548 845900 | Bolt Head, TQ8 8LL
www.southsands.com
The beachside location and terrace are out of this world, and a breezy, New England-style decor adds to the feeling of a summer idyll in South Sands' light-filled restaurant. The kitchen hauls in some prime Devon ingredients as the backbone of an unchallenging menu.
Chef Allister Bishop Open All year Notes Vegetarian dishes, Children welcome

SAUNTON
Saunton Sands Hotel
◉◉ TRADITIONAL, MODERN BRITISH
01271 890212 | EX33 1LQ
www.sauntonsands.com
The location alone is a draw at this long white art deco hotel overlooking a three-mile stretch of unspoiled sandy beach. Watch the sun set from the terrace or

soak up the maritime views from the stylish restaurant with original 1930s chandeliers.

Chef Mathias Oberg **Seats** 200, Private dining 60 **Open** All year **Parking** 140 **Notes** Vegetarian dishes, Children welcome

SIDMOUTH
Hotel Riviera
◉◉ MODERN BRITISH
01395 515201 | The Esplanade, EX10 8AY
www.hotelriviera.co.uk

The name may suggest Cannes or Las Vegas, but the spotless bow-fronted Riviera is a prime example of Devon's own seaside grandeur. Terrace tables make the most of the summer weather, and a menu of gently modernised British cooking caters for most tastes.

Chef Martin Osedo **Seats** 85, Private dining 65 **Open** All year **Prices from** S £10.50, M £16, D £6.50 **Parking** 26 **Notes** Vegetarian dishes, Children welcome

The Salty Monk
◉◉ MODERN BRITISH ⬛ NOTABLE WINE LIST
01395 513174 | Church Street, Sidford, EX10 9QP
www.saltymonk.com

The name is not a reference to a seafaring friar, but rather to the building's 16th-century role as a store for the salt the monks traded at Exeter Cathedral. The Garden Room restaurant makes a smart yet understated backdrop for unpretentious cooking.

Chef Annette and Andy Witheridge **Seats** 30 **Closed** 1 week in November, January **Prices from** S £6.50, M £14, D £6.50 **Parking** 20 **Notes** Vegetarian dishes, Children welcome

The Victoria Hotel
◉ TRADITIONAL
01395 512651 | The Esplanade, EX10 8RY
www.victoriahotel.co.uk

The setting at the end of the town's impressive Georgian esplanade is alluring, with the expansive bay offered up in all its shimmering glory. From the doorman to the pianist, The Victoria oozes old-world charm and what appears on the plate is generally classically minded.

Chef Stuart White **Seats** 120, Private dining 30 **Open** All year **Notes** Children welcome

SOUTH ZEAL
Oxenham Arms
◉ CLASSIC BRITISH
01837 840244 | EX20 2JT
www.theoxenhamarms.com

Set in deepest Dartmoor country, the historic Oxenham Arms is still the hub of village life. The place began in the 12th century as a monastery but contemporary touches blend seamlessly with an ambience of gnarled beams, whitewashed stone walls and stone mullioned windows.

Chef **Seats** 60, Private dining 32 **Open** All year **Prices from** S £5.25, M £9.50, D £4.50 **Parking** 7 **Notes** Vegetarian dishes, Children welcome

STRETE
The Laughing Monk
◉ MODERN BRITISH
01803 770639 | Totnes Road, TQ6 0RN
www.thelaughingmonkdevon.co.uk

The South West Coast Path runs practically outside the front door of this converted school, and Slapton and Blackpool Sands are a mere mile off. Inside is an airy space and cheery atmosphere, and a kitchen making use of Devon's resources.

Chef Ben Handley **Seats** 60 **Closed** Christmas and January **Parking** 4 **Notes** Vegetarian dishes, Children welcome

TAVISTOCK
Bedford Hotel
◉ BRITISH
01822 613221 | 1 Plymouth Road, PL19 8BB
www.bedford-hotel.co.uk

Despite the castellated walls, this imposing Gothic building has always been about hospitality, and there is no lack of character or charm in the restaurant, with its moulded ceilings and panelled walls. The kitchen takes a more contemporary position, but a reassuringly gentle one.

Chef Mike Palmer **Seats** 55, Private dining 30 **Closed** 24–26 December **Parking** 48 **Notes** Vegetarian dishes, Children welcome

The Horn of Plenty
◉◉ MODERN BRITISH V
01822 832528 | Gulworthy, PL19 8JD
www.thehornofplenty.co.uk

The Horn sits on the Devon-Cornwall border, a stone-built manor house that's a picture of serenity. The place is run with reassuring warmth and confidence. Local produce is used to its best and West Country cheeses come with pickles and jellies.

Chef Ashley Wright **Seats** 40, Private dining 16 **Open** All year **Parking** 25 **Notes** Children welcome

THURLESTONE
Thurlestone Hotel
◉◉ BRITISH **V**
01548 560382 | TQ7 3NN
www.thurlestone.co.uk
The view across the golf course and sub-tropical gardens to the sea is a cracker, making The Trevilder restaurant a star attraction. The menu, including the daily changing 'Market Dishes', makes good use of the region's produce in dishes that have classical foundations.
Chef Hugh Miller **Seats** 150, Private dining 150 **Closed** 2 weeks January **Parking** 120 **Notes** Children welcome

The Village Inn
◉ MODERN BRITISH
01548 563525 | TQ7 3NN
www.thurlestone.co.uk
Among the original building materials of the 16th-century Village Inn are timbers from ships of the Spanish Armada wrecked off the Devon coast. It's all been sensitively spruced up, with plenty of light wood, a log burner, and an outdoor dining space by the pool.
Chef Rene Muller **Seats** Private dining 31 **Open** All year **Prices from** S £6, M £11, D £7 **Parking** 60 **Notes** Vegetarian dishes, Children welcome

TORQUAY
Cary Arms
◉ BRITISH, SEAFOOD
01803 327110 | Babbacombe Beach, TQ1 3LX
www.caryarms.co.uk
On a glorious summer's day, the terraced gardens leading to the water's edge are an unforgettable place to eat, but the whitewashed Cary Arms does have more than its fair share of good things: a beamed bar with stone walls and dreamy views.
Chef Ben Kingdon **Open** All year

The Elephant Restaurant
◉◉◉ MODERN BRITISH
01803 200044 | 3–4 Beacon Terrace, TQ1 2BH
www.elephantrestaurant.co.uk
Positioned on a rising side-street just off the Torquay marina, Simon Hulstone's destination venue has kept the Devon resort firmly on the gastronomic map of the south-west for over a decade now. It's a daylight-filled, split-level space that takes on a softly lit intimate ambience in the evenings, when an infectious buzz hovers over the amply proportioned tables. The produce of The Elephant's own farm makes its way into virtually every dish on the menu, from a slow-cooked bantam egg in sweet onion consommé with gruyère and lemon thyme, to mains such as cod fillet with parsnip purée and lardo Ibérico in spring onion butter, or the succulent roast Southdown lamb with Savoy cabbage, Roscoff onion and black garlic. Medlar jelly and green tomato chutney then provide the sweet and sour notes to a plate of artisan south-west cheeses, for those not intent on going full-spectrum indulgence with bitter chocolate fondant tart, brown butter ice cream and malt cookie crumbs. Loose-leaf teas make a refreshing alternative to yet another espresso: they include lemon and ginger, and South Africa's organic rooibos tea.
Chef Simon Hulstone **Seats** 75 **Closed** 1st 2 weeks in January **Prices from** S £8, M £16.50, D £7.50 **Notes** Vegetarian dishes, Children welcome

The Imperial Hotel
◉ MODERN BRITISH
01803 294301 | Park Hill Road, TQ1 2DG
www.theimperialtorquay.co.uk
The Imperial's Victorian founders couldn't have chosen a better spot for their hotel, whose clifftop position has wide-ranging views over the bay and Channel. The kitchen chooses its ingredients diligently, making good use of fish and local produce, and turns out well-considered, carefully timed dishes.
Chef Zibi Klapsia **Seats** 170, Private dining 350 **Open** All year **Parking** 110 **Notes** Vegetarian dishes, Children welcome

Orestone Manor
◉◉ MODERN, EUROPEAN **V**
01803 328098 | Rockhouse Lane, Maidencombe, TQ1 4SX
www.orestonemanor.com
This handsome Georgian manor house occupies landscaped grounds over Lyme Bay. The main restaurant is a traditional space with wooden floors and linen-swathed tables – a suitable setting for the kitchen's ambitious à la carte menus. Classic French-accented technique delivers refined dishes.
Chef Neil and Catherine D'Allen, Daryll Sharpe **Seats** 55 **Closed** 3–30 January **Prices from** S £6.50, M £19.50, D £6.50 **Parking** 38 **Notes** Children welcome

Seasons
◉ MODERN BRITISH
01803 226366 | Belgrave Sands Hotel & Spa, Belgrave Road, TQ2 5HF
www.belgravesands.com
Set in the Belgrave Sands Hotel, just a stone's throw from the seafront, Seasons restaurant is a bright, comfortable space, with unclothed, dark wood tables and live music in the evenings. Contemporary British

cooking features on the six-course menu, with particular attention paid to seasonality.

Chef Stephen Sanders **Seats** 90 **Open** All year **Parking** 50 **Notes** Vegetarian dishes, Children welcome

TOTNES
The Riverford Field Kitchen
◉ MODERN BRITISH, ORGANIC
01803 762074 | Riverford, TQ11 0JU
www.riverford.co.uk

Wash Farm is the hub of the Riverford brand, delivering organically grown fruit and veg across the land. Hunker down here at communal tables for hearty organic food, a fixed deal of whatever is on-the-money that day, always teeming with superlative vegetable and salad accompaniments.

Chef James Dodd **Seats** 72 **Closed** 24–26 December and Monday to Tuesday in January and February **Parking** 30 **Notes** Vegetarian dishes, Children welcome

TWO BRIDGES
Two Bridges Hotel
◉◉ MODERN BRITISH **V**
01822 892300 | PL20 6SW
www.twobridges.co.uk

In a building of obvious venerability, with a prettily appointed dining room named Tors, a gentle style of British modernism is practised. Try the goats' cheese tortellini in tomato consommé, or cheek, loin and belly of local pork in maple syrup with broccoli and walnuts.

Chef Mike Palmer **Seats** 85, Private dining 20 **Open** All year **Parking** 150 **Notes** Children welcome

WOOLACOMBE
Doyles Restaurant
◉ MODERN BRITISH
01271 870388 | South Street, EX34 7BN
www.woolacombe-bay-hotel.co.uk

Overlooking Woolacombe Bay, this stylish hotel is set in six acres of landscaped grounds and is a six-minute walk from the beach. No surprise that the menu in the elegant Doyle's restaurant puts such emphasis on local meat and fresh fish from the Devon coast.

Chef Eduard Grecu **Seats** 80, Private dining 40 **Closed** 2 January to mid February **Prices from** S £6, M £13, D £6.50 **Notes** Vegetarian dishes, Children welcome

Watersmeet Hotel
◉◉ TRADITIONAL BRITISH, EUROPEAN
01271 870333 | Mortehoe, EX34 7EB
www.watersmeethotel.co.uk

This sparkling-white meringue of a building stands above the bay at Mortehoe, with views across to

Lundy. An enterprising fixed-price menu may lead you from smoked pigeon breast with game sausage, to a serving of Exmoor sirloin with a dinky steak-and-tongue pudding and truffled mash.

Chef John Prince **Seats** 56, Private dining 18 **Open** All year **Parking** 40 **Notes** Vegetarian dishes, No children under 8 years

▶ DORSET

BEAMINSTER
Brassica Restaurant
◉ MODERN EUROPEAN
01308 538100 | 4 The Square, DT8 3AS
www.brassicarestaurant.co.uk

On the main square, Brassica occupies a Grade II listed property overlooking the hubbub (or what passes for hubbub) of this small market town. Chef-director Cass Titcombe draws on a wealth of experience to deliver a daily changing menu of local ingredients and broader European ideas.

Chef Cass Titcombe **Seats** 40 **Closed** Christmas **Prices from** S £7, M £14, D £6 **Notes** Vegetarian dishes, Children welcome

BOURNEMOUTH
Best Western Plus The Connaught Hotel
◉◉ MODERN BRITISH
01202 298020 | 30 West Hill Road, West Cliff, BH2 5PH
www.theconnaught.co.uk

With sandy beaches stretching below, the grand old Connaught rules the roost on Bournemouth's West Cliff. The Blakes restaurant overlooks the hotel's gardens, where candlelit outdoor tables are popular on summer evenings. Inside, the lightly formal tone makes an agreeable ambience for traditionally based British dishes.

Chef Ben Nicol **Seats** 80, Private dining 16 **Open** All year **Parking** 66 **Notes** Vegetarian dishes, Children welcome

The Crab at Bournemouth
◉◉ SEAFOOD
01202 203601 | Exeter Road, BH2 5AJ
www.crabatbournemouth.com

The epitome of a seafront venue, the Crab is part of the white-fronted Park Central Hotel, but functions as a restaurant in its own right, smartly done out in sandy hues. An array of fresh fish and shellfish is on the menu.

Chef Anthony Brand **Seats** 80 **Open** All year **Prices from** S £6.50, M £15.95, D £5.95 **Notes** Vegetarian dishes, Children welcome

Cumberland Hotel

⊚⊚ TRADITIONAL BRITISH

01202 290722 | 27 East Overcliffe Drive, BH1 3AF

www.cumberlandbournemouth.co.uk

High up on Bournemouth's East Cliff, this art deco hotel boasts all the monochrome touches of that decadent period. Not that the cooking in the hotel's elegant Ventana Grand Café restaurant is stuck in the 1930s – the food is modern British to the core.

Chef Robert Feuillet **Open** All year

The Green House

⊚⊚ MODERN BRITISH

01202 498900 | 4 Grove Road, BH1 3AX

www.thegreenhousehotel.co.uk

The Green House is a striking-looking, centrally located property converted and run on sustainable principles. There are beehives on the roof, and the Arbor (Latin for 'tree' to further underline its green credentials) Restaurant deals in only organic, Fairtrade and farm-assured, mostly local produce.

Chef Andrew Hilton **Seats** 38, Private dining 70 **Open** All year **Parking** 30 **Notes** Vegetarian dishes, Children welcome

Hermitage Hotel

⊚ TRADITIONAL BRITISH

01202 557363 | Exeter Road, BH2 5AH

www.hermitage-hotel.co.uk

Hardy's Restaurant at the Hermitage, opposite the beach, is a large, traditionally styled room. The interesting menus serve local and sustainable ingredients and offer variety aplenty, as they must with residents eating here perhaps every evening.

Chef Iain McBride **Seats** 120, Private dining 50 **Open** All year **Prices from** S £7.95, M £17.95, D £6.95 **Parking** 60 **Notes** Vegetarian dishes, Children welcome

No 34 at The Orchid Hotel

⊚ EUROPEAN

01202 551600 | 34 Gervis Road, BH1 3DH

www.orchidhotel.co.uk

Close to the beach, No 34 is the flagship restaurant at The Orchid, a contemporary and secluded hotel in Bournemouth's lovely Eastcliff area. Now refurbished, the kitchen cuts no corners when it comes to premium ingredients, much of it sourced from the region. Watch out for the inventive desserts.

Chef Jean Gysemans **Seats** 40 **Open** All year

Roots

⊚⊚ MODERN EUROPEAN **V**

01202 430005 | 141 Belle Vue Road, BH6 3EN

www.restaurantroots.co.uk

The food here is simple, confident and effective. Service is charming, passionate and knowledgeable, and a key part of the experience. Monthly changing tasting menus, either 5- or 7-course, feature well-executed dishes with punchy flavours.

Chef Jan Bretschneider **Seats** 20 **Closed** 23 December to beginning of January **Notes** Children welcome

WestBeach

⊚ MODERN BRITISH, SEAFOOD

01202 587785 | Pier Approach, BH2 5AA

www.west-beach.co.uk

For a fish restaurant, the setting is unbeatable: it's smack on the beach, with a sunny terrace above the waves. The full-length glass frontage opens up the views, flooding light into the restaurant, a bright, modern space of stripped-out, beachcomber-chic pastel shades and bleached wood.

Chef Marcin Pacholarz **Seats** 75 **Closed** 25 December **Prices from** S £7.75, M £14.95, D £6.25 **Notes** Vegetarian dishes, Children welcome

See advertisement opposite

BRIDPORT

Riverside Restaurant

⊚ SEAFOOD, INTERNATIONAL

01308 422011 | West Bay, DT6 4EZ

www.riverside-restaurant.com

Run by the same family for over 50 years, the tradition of serving pearly fresh fish and seafood from the day's catch, with views over the sea, lives on. The cooking keeps things as simple as the prime materials require, with occasional forays into the modern cookbook.

Chef A Shaw, N Larcombe **Seats** 90, Private dining 30 **Closed** 10 February to November **Prices from** S £5.50, M £17.95, D £4.95 **Notes** Vegetarian dishes, Children welcome

CHRISTCHURCH

Captain's Club Hotel & Spa

⊚⊚ MODERN EUROPEAN

01202 475111 | Wick Ferry, Wick Lane, BH23 1HU

www.captainsclubhotel.com

A glass-fronted boutique hotel by the River Stour, where the kitchen serves up modern brasserie fare, fully in keeping with the attractive surroundings. Veggie possibilities include an Indian-spiced cauliflower risotto with coconut and coriander, and the desserts include some crowd-pleasers.

WESTBEACH

The stunning location, situated just metres from the beach and Bournemouth Pier, makes WestBeach a beautiful place for any occasion.

**Pier Approach
Bournemouth,
Dorset BH2 5AA**

01202 587785

west-beach.co.uk

Chef Andrew Gault **Seats** 100, Private dining 120 **Open** All year **Prices from** S £7, M £17, D £7 **Parking** 41 **Notes** Vegetarian dishes, Children welcome

The Jetty
◉◉ MODERN BRITISH **V**
01202 400950 | 95 Mudeford, BH23 3NT
www.thejetty.co.uk

A dashing contemporary construction of glass and wood, The Jetty's culinary output is headed up by Alex Aitken. Provenance is everything here. In fine weather, grab a table on the terrace if you can, although floor-to-ceiling windows provide glorious views over Mudeford Quay.

Chef Alex Aitken **Seats** 70 **Open** All year **Prices from** S £8.95, M £19.50, D £7.50 **Parking** 40 **Notes** Children welcome

The Lord Bute & Restaurant
◉◉ BRITISH, MEDITERRANEAN
01425 278884 | 179–181 Lymington Road, Highcliffe on Sea, BH23 4JS
www.lordbute.co.uk

Once the entrance lodge to Highcliffe Castle, this eye-catching boutique hotel is superbly placed for access to the golden beaches and blustery clifftops of the Dorset coast. Modern within, the classical dining room boasts an orangery extension and well-drilled service to boot.

Chef Kevin Brown **Seats** 95 **Open** All year **Parking** 50 **Notes** Vegetarian dishes, Children welcome

Upper Deck Bar & Restaurant
◉ MODERN BRITISH **V**
01202 400954 | 95 Mudeford, BH23 3NT
www.christchurch-harbour-hotel.co.uk/upper-deck

Good views over the water are guaranteed, as is a fine showing of regional produce. The Upper Deck is pretty swanky, featuring a sleek, contemporary bar and an upmarket seasidey vibe, or there's the recently extended terrace. The cooking takes a modern British route through contemporary tastes and, given the setting, plenty of locally-landed fish.

Chef Alex Aitken **Seats** 95, Private dining 20 **Open** All year **Parking** 100 **Notes** Children welcome

DORSET

CORFE CASTLE
Mortons House Hotel
◉◉ MODERN BRITISH
01929 480988 | 49 East Street, BH20 5EE
www.mortonshouse.co.uk

Mortons is a beautifully maintained Elizabethan manor of the 1590s on the Isle of Purbeck, within sight of Corfe Castle. An openness to East Asian tastes might see you an open a meal with a teriyaki-sesame dressing to seared salmon seasoned with Dorset's own wasabi.

Chef Ed Firth **Seats** 60, Private dining 22 **Open** All year **Prices from** S £6.75, M £13, D £6.75 **Parking** 40 **Notes** Vegetarian dishes, No children under 5 years

EVERSHOT
The Acorn Inn
◉ BRITISH
01935 83228 | 28 Fore Street, DT2 0JW
www.acorn-inn.co.uk

Plumb in the middle of Thomas Hardy's favourite stretch of England, the 16th-century coaching inn makes an appearance in *Tess of the d'Urbervilles* as the Sow and Acorn. The chocolate fondant has an unctuous oozy filling, accompanied by brilliantly intense salted caramel ice cream.

Chef Robert Ndungu **Seats** 45, Private dining 35 **Open** All year **Prices from** S £6, M £12, D £7 **Parking** 20 **Notes** Vegetarian dishes, Children welcome

George Albert Hotel
◉ MODERN BRITISH
01935 483430 | Wardon Hill, DT2 9PW
www.georgealberthotel.co.uk

The George Albert opened its doors in 2010, but despite its relative newness, monogrammed carpets and starched table linen bring a traditional feel to Kings Restaurant. On the menu, main courses bring all their components together in well-balanced harmony.

Chef Andy Pike **Seats** 40, Private dining 200 **Open** All year **Parking** 200 **Notes** Vegetarian dishes, Children welcome

Summer Lodge Country House Hotel, Restaurant & Spa
◉◉◉ MODERN BRITISH ♨ NOTABLE WINE LIST
01935 482000 | Fore Street, DT2 0JR
www.summerlodgehotel.com

Starting life as a dower house in the Georgian era, Summer Lodge had another layer added in 1893 when its resident Earl commissioned local architect (and sometime novelist) Thomas Hardy to draw up the plans. It stands in a neat four acres next to an extensive deer park, and is decorated throughout in impeccable country-house elegance. A riot of pinks and purples illuminates the dining room, with tables got up in ceremonial ribbon like wedding presents, which makes a suitably dramatic setting for Steven Titman's exploratory modern cooking. The evening carte offers a wealth of inspired choice, in a range that spans Lyme Bay scallop céviched in lime and chilli with coriander gel and watermelon, to main courses built on pedigree prime materials, as witness an easternised Creedy Carver duck breast with shiitakes and a stir-fry of bok choi and cashews, or gilthead bream with braised fennel and Kalamata olives. For the grand finale, there could be a giant pineapple-centred macaron of coconut and Malibu, or white chocolate bavarois with basil gel and pink grapefruit sorbet.

Chef Steven Titman **Seats** 60, Private dining 20 **Closed** 3–24 January **Prices from** S £14, M £24, D £12 **Parking** 60 **Notes** Vegetarian dishes, Children welcome

FARNHAM
The Museum Inn
◉◉ MODERN, TRADITIONAL BRITISH
01725 516261 | DT11 8DE
www.museuminn.co.uk

Victorian archaeologist General Augustus Pitt-Rivers was responsible for the Oxford museum collection that bears his name, and for extending the partly thatched Museum Inn. While there is a solid pub foundation to proceedings, there are also excursions over the Channel.

Chef Neil Molyneux **Seats** 69, Private dining 40 **Open** All year **Prices from** S £5.95, M £13.95, D £6.50 **Parking** 14 **Notes** Vegetarian dishes, Children welcome

MAIDEN NEWTON
Le Petit Canard
◉ MODERN BRITISH, FRENCH
01300 320536 | Dorchester Road, DT2 0BE
www.le-petit-canard.co.uk

A former coaching inn, this homely place has been run with passion and charm by Gerry and Cathy Craig for more than 15 years. The linen-covered tables are topped with flowers and candles, with wooden beams and exposed stonework adding to its appeal.

Chef Gerry Craig **Seats** 28 **Closed** 2 weeks January, 1 week June and September **Notes** Vegetarian dishes, No children under 12 years

See advertisement opposite

POOLE

Harbour Heights Hotel
◉◉ BRITISH, FRENCH
01202 707272 | 73 Haven Road, Sandbanks, BH13 7LW
www.fjbhotels.co.uk

The teak-decked alfresco terrace of this 1920s art deco beauty offers views across Poole harbour but the glossy Harbar Bistro is an equally inviting prospect. Do check out the fresh fish counter, laden with the day's catch from Poole Quay.

Chef Loic Gratadoux **Seats** 90, Private dining 120 **Open** All year **Prices from** S £6.50, M £19.50, D £6.50 **Parking** 50 **Notes** Vegetarian dishes, Children welcome

Hotel du Vin Poole
◉ MODERN BRITISH, FRENCH
01202 785578 | Mansion House, Thames Street, BH15 1JN
www.hotelduvin.com

Hotel du Vin's Poole outpost is a bit of a landmark just off the quayside, a creeper-covered Georgian mansion. As expected, the kitchen deals in crowd-pleasing brasserie staples from over the Channel, all cooked just so. Start perhaps with escargots in garlic and herb butter.

Chef Lee Coote **Seats** 85, Private dining 48 **Open** All year **Parking** 8 **Notes** Vegetarian dishes, Children welcome

The Point Restaurant
◉◉ MODERN BRITISH
01202 707333 | Haven Hotel, 161 Banks Road, Sandbanks, BH13 7QL
www.fjbhotels.co.uk/haven

At the southern end of Sandbanks, The Point brasserie is as close as you will get to dining on a cruise ship without leaving dry land. The kitchen buys the best regional produce but doesn't confine itself to the fruits of the sea.

Chef Jason Hornbuckle **Seats** 80, Private dining 156 **Open** All year **Parking** 90 **Notes** Vegetarian dishes, Children welcome

Rick Stein Sandbanks
◉ SEAFOOD **V** 🍷 NOTABLE WINE LIST
01202 283280 | 10–14 Banks Road, BH13 7QB
www.rickstein.com

The globetrotting Mr Stein has picked a promising spot in well-heeled Sandbanks for another outpost of his empire. The food bears the Stein imprint, nothing too elaborate, just light-touch treatment to let the quality of the produce strut its stuff.

Chef Pete Murt **Seats** 200 **Closed** 25 December **Prices from** S £5.95, M £16.95, D £6.95 **Notes** No children under 3 years at dinner (not permitted in upper restaurant)

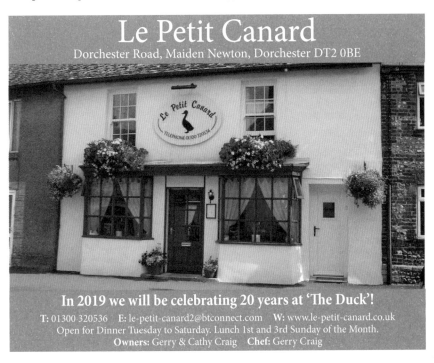

Le Petit Canard
Dorchester Road, Maiden Newton, Dorchester DT2 0BE

In 2019 we will be celebrating 20 years at 'The Duck'!
T: 01300 320536   E: le-petit-canard2@btconnect.com   W: www.le-petit-canard.co.uk
Open for Dinner Tuesday to Saturday. Lunch 1st and 3rd Sunday of the Month.
Owners: Gerry & Cathy Craig   **Chef:** Gerry Craig

DORSET

SHAFTESBURY
La Fleur de Lys Restaurant with Rooms
◉◉ MODERN FRENCH
01747 853717 | Bleke Street, SP7 8AW
www.lafleurdelys.co.uk
Smartly linened-up tables are the order in the dining room of this creeper-covered restaurant with rooms. Lemon-yellow and exposed stone walls produce a relaxing atmosphere, and fixed-price menus, built on a core of modern French notions, offer a variety of choices.
Chef D Shepherd, M Preston **Seats** 45, Private dining 12 **Closed** 3 weeks January **Prices from** S £8, M £19, D £8 **Parking** 10 **Notes** Vegetarian dishes, Children welcome

SHERBORNE
Eastbury Hotel
◉◉ MODERN BRITISH **V**
01935 813131 | Long Street, DT9 3BY
www.theeastburyhotel.co.uk
The Eastbury offers a hint of country-estate living, with much of the kitchen's raw material coming from its own garden and beehives. Despite the utterly English surroundings, the menu looks all over the world for inspiration, producing clever, complex dishes with a contemporary twist.
Chef Matthew Street **Seats** 40, Private dining 40 **Open** All year **Parking** 20 **Notes** Children welcome

The Green
◉◉ MODERN EUROPEAN
01935 813821 | 3 The Green, DT9 3HY
www.greenrestaurant.co.uk
The Green, a charming Grade II listed building in the centre of picturesque Sherborne, sets its sights on locally and ethically sourced raw materials. Quality ingredients are evident throughout, and menus are thoughtfully constructed, offering contemporary dishes with classic roots, inspired by the seasons.
Chef Alexander and Sasha Matkevich **Seats** 40, Private dining 24 **Closed** 25–26 December **Prices from** S £6.50, M £16.50, D £6 **Notes** Vegetarian dishes, Children welcome

The Kings Arms
◉ MODERN BRITISH
01963 220281 | Charlton Herethorne, DT9 4NL
www.thekingsarms.co.uk
First licensed in the Regency era, Sarah and Tony Lethbridge have given this stone-built inn a thoroughly modern makeover, though not to the detriment of its original charm. Sarah heads up the kitchen, capitalising on West Country produce, as well as drying and curing meats.

Chef Sarah Lethbridge, Wayne Greenfield **Seats** 120, Private dining 70 **Closed** 25 December **Prices from** S £6, M £12, D £7.50 **Parking** 30 **Notes** Vegetarian dishes, Children welcome

The Rose and Crown Inn, Trent
◉◉ MODERN BRITISH
01935 850776 | Trent, DT9 4SL
www.theroseandcrowntrent.co.uk
Located on the Ernest Cook Trust estate that surrounds Trent, the inn has a lounge with a large, log-surrounded open fire and comfortable leather sofa; the main bar looks out over fields, and from the restaurant you can see the valley of the Trent Brook.
Chef Mike Rust **Open** All year **Notes** Children welcome

STUDLAND
THE PIG on the Beach
◉◉ MODERN BRITISH ▌NOTABLE WINE LIST
01929 450288 | The Manor House, Manor Road, BH19 3AU
www.thepighotel.com
Part of a mini chain of quirky boutique hotels, this little piggy overlooks sandy Studland Bay. Fruit, veg and herbs are plucked from the walled kitchen garden, a coop of chickens and quails supplies eggs, and fish and seafood is locally landed.
Chef Andy Wright **Seats** 70, Private dining 12 **Open** All year **Prices from** S £3.95, M £16, D £5.50 **Parking** 30 **Notes** Vegetarian dishes, Children welcome

WEST BEXINGTON
The Club House
◉ SEAFOOD
01308 898302 | Beach Road, DT2 9DF
www.theclubhousewestbexington.co.uk
A 1930s bungalow overlooking the Jurassic Coast, The Club House has the air of somewhere you might expect to pay a membership fee to enter. What it offers instead is a seafood-rich menu of energetic modern cooking, changing daily according to the catch.
Chef Charlie Soole **Seats** 50, Private dining 12 **Closed** 24–26 December **Prices from** S £7.50, M £15, D £6.50 **Parking** 7 **Notes** Vegetarian dishes, No children

WEYMOUTH
Moonfleet Manor Hotel
◉ MEDITERRANEAN
01305 786948 | Fleet Road, DT3 4ED
www.moonfleetmanorhotel.co.uk
The village of Fleet played a central role in J. Meade Falkner's smuggling yarn, *Moonfleet* (1898), and the sparkling-white Georgian hotel, which gazes out

over Chesil Beach, is the jewel in its crown. Inside is all squashy sofas and crackling fires, with bracing sea views.

Chef Stephen Wilson, Tony Smith **Seats** Private dining 45

WIMBORNE MINSTER
Les Bouviers Restaurant with Rooms
◉◉ MEDITERRANEAN, FRENCH
01202 889555 | Arrowsmith Road, Canford Magna, BH21 3BD
www.lesbouviers.co.uk

A modern house in over five acres of land complete with stream and lake is the setting for this restaurant done out in shades of claret and gold, with contemporary artwork on the walls. Cheese soufflé with watercress and horseradish sauce is a signature starter.

Chef James and Kate Coward **Seats** 50, Private dining 120 **Open** All year **Parking** 50 **Notes** Vegetarian dishes, Children welcome

WYKE REGIS
Crab House Café
◉ BRITISH, SEAFOOD
01305 788867 | Ferrymans Way, Portland Road, DT4 9YU
www.crabhousecafe.co.uk

Situated in a spruced up wooden hut overlooking Chesil Beach, the Crab House Café has natural charms aplenty. Simplicity and freshness is the name of the game, with oysters coming from their own beds and everything sourced from within a 40-mile radius.

Chef Nigel Bloxham, William Smith **Seats** 40 **Closed** mid December to January **Prices from** S £7.50, M £18.90, D £6.95 **Parking** 40 **Notes** Vegetarian dishes, Children welcome

▶ COUNTY DURHAM
BARNARD CASTLE
The Morritt Country House Hotel & Spa
◉◉ MODERN FRENCH
01833 627232 | Greta Bridge, DL12 9SE
www.themorritt.co.uk

The arrival of transport by mail coach in the 18th century saw this former farm develop into an overnight stop for travellers between London and Carlisle. Charles Dickens probably stayed here in 1839, hence the fine-dining restaurant is named after him. Start with an amuse-bouche.

Chef Alex Wood **Seats** 60, Private dining 50 **Open** All year **Parking** 30 **Notes** Vegetarian dishes, Children welcome

BILLINGHAM
Wynyard Hall Hotel
◉◉ MODERN BRITISH
01740 644811 | Wynyard, TS22 5NF
www.wynyandhall.co.uk

Built to impress, this vast Victorian pile sits in 150 acres of grounds with its own lake. Inside, marble, mahogany and stained-glass combine in a display of jaw-dropping opulence, a style that continues in the Wellington Restaurant, where the menu offers elegant, classical dishes.

Chef Errol Defeo **Seats** 80, Private dining 30 **Open** All year **Prices from** S £7.50, M £17.50, D £6.50 **Parking** 200 **Notes** Vegetarian dishes, Children welcome

DARLINGTON
Headlam Hall
◉ MODERN BRITISH, FRENCH
01325 730238 | Headlam, Gainford, DL2 3HA
www.headlamhall.co.uk

Refurbished in 2016, this handsome house dates from the beginning of the 17th century and retains plenty of period charm including its walled garden. The restaurant offers diners a series of settings that take in an elegant panelled dining room and the more contemporary orangery.

Chef Derek Thomson **Seats** 70, Private dining 30 **Closed** 25–26 December **Parking** 80 **Notes** Vegetarian dishes, Children welcome

The Orangery
◉◉◉◉ MODERN BRITISH V ♦ NOTABLE WINE LIST
01325 729999 | Rockliffe Hall, Rockliffe Park, Hurworth-on-Tees, DL2 2DU
www.rockliffehall.com

Guests are spoilt for leisure pursuits at this impressive Georgian country mansion, from indulgence in the luxurious spa to tackling its 18-hole championship golf course, and a trio of restaurants. Cream of the crop is The Orangery, where gilded wrought-iron columns soar upwards to a glass roof in a romantic gothic-inspired space, and a large wall of windows opens up sweeping views across the gardens and the action on the fairways. It's an exceedingly pleasant place to linger. And linger you must, for Richard Allen's contemporary 10-course tasting menus, in omnivore, veggie, pescatarian versions, are a delight in conception and delivery. The local and seasonal boxes are ticked by produce from polytunnels and the walled garden, plus foraged ingredients from Rockliffe's 365-acre estate, and the workmanship is first class whether in a dish of langoustine and crab with bergamot, harissa, creamy bisque and sea purslane, or a punchy pork ragout offset by pickled carrot and mushroom. Imaginative juxtapositions of flavour, texture and temperature might include a luxuriant duo of smoked eel and duck liver parfait with the balancing acidity of rhubarb vinegar, or pigeon partnered by quince, dhal and an aromatic honey and cumin jus. Imaginative meat-free options could see flame-grilled celeriac matched with chard, dry-roasted hazelnuts and dill, or smoked artichoke pointed up with beer vinegar and sour cream. At the end come intriguing ideas involving the likes of pistachio and pear with the contrastingly bitter note of matcha, or perhaps sea buckthorn macaron ramped up with miso and butterscotch.

Chef Richard Allen **Seats** 60, Private dining 20 **Open** All year **Parking** 300 **Notes** Children welcome

DURHAM
Fusion Restaurant
PAN ASIAN, THAI **V**
0191 386 5282 | Ramside Hall Hotel Golf & Spa, Carrville, DH1 1TD
www.ramsidehallhotel.co.uk

Surrounded by 350 acres of grounds including two 18-hole championship golf courses at Ramside Hall, the restaurant at the hotel's spa serves South East Asian-inspired food throughout the day. Overlooking the spa's thermal suite, the Oriental-styled restaurant combines the dishes of Thailand, Japan and China.

Chef Watcharin Dechbamrung **Seats** 100, Private dining 64 **Open** All year **Parking** 600 **Notes** Children welcome

Honest Lawyer Hotel
MODERN BRITISH
0191 378 3780 | Croxdale Bridge, Croxdale, DH1 3SP
www.honestlawyerhotel.com

A modern hotel with a bright and welcoming restaurant and a policy of sourcing produce from within 20 miles. Start with baked scallops with pancetta lardons and leeks in a creamy fish sauce, accompanied by a brioche topped with parmesan and herbs.

Chef Harry Bailie **Seats** 45, Private dining 60 **Open** All year **Parking** 150 **Notes** Vegetarian dishes, Children welcome

The Rib Room
INTERNATIONAL **V**
0191 386 5282 | Ramside Hall Hotel Golf & Spa, Carrville, DH1 1TD
www.ramsidehallhotel.co.uk

Sprawling outwards from a largely Victorian house, 2015 saw the opening of a glossy spa and health club at Ramside. Culinary options run from straightforward carvery dishes to the menu in the brasserie-style Rib Room, a temple to slabs of locally reared 28-day aged beef.

Chef Jim Hall **Open** All year **Notes** Children welcome

ROMALDKIRK
The Rose & Crown
MODERN BRITISH, INTERNATIONAL
01833 650213 | DL12 9EB
www.rose-and-crown.co.uk

In a tiny village with a Saxon church and original stocks, this 18th-century inn is steeped in tradition. Eat in the bar with its oak settles, antique chairs and crackling log fire, or the candlelit oak-panelled dining room, where menus are built on local produce.

Chef David McBride **Seats** 24 **Closed** 23–27 December **Parking** 25 **Notes** Vegetarian dishes, No children under 7 years at dinner

SEAHAM
Seaham Hall – The Dining Room
MODERN BRITISH NOTABLE WINE LIST
0191 516 1400 | Seaham Hall Hotel, Lord Byron's Walk, SR7 7AG
www.seaham-hall.co.uk

These days a state-of-the-art spa hotel, the late-18th-century Seaham Hall offers a brace of stimulating eating options. The Dining Room is a swish contemporary space with a glossy sheen, delivering a crowd-pleasing menu aiming unashamedly at the hearts of carnivores, although well-sourced fish provides meat-free alternatives.

Chef Damian Broom **Seats** 40, Private dining 100 **Prices from** S £7, M £16, D £7 **Parking** 120 **Notes** Vegetarian dishes, Children welcome

▶ ESSEX
BRAINTREE
The Chophouse Braintree
ENGLISH
01376 345615 | 34 New Street, CM7 1ES
www.thechophousebraintree.co.uk

Previously a home for 'wayward women' and a haberdashery, this old inn is relaxed and informal, with a choice of dining areas and attentive service throughout. Where possible, ingredients are sourced from within a 30-mile radius and the modern British food is underpinned by classic techniques.

Chef Richard Cutting and Stefan Clyde (Sous Chef) **Seats** 58, Private dining 12 **Open** All year **Prices from** S £7.50, M £16.95, D £6.95 **Notes** Vegetarian dishes, Children welcome

BRENTWOOD
Marygreen Manor Hotel
◉◉ MODERN EUROPEAN **V**
01277 225252 | London Road, CM14 4NR
www.marygreenmanor.co.uk

Dating from the early 16th century, when it was built by a courtier of Catherine of Aragon, the manor is a perfect example of a half-timbered building, the restaurant an impressive room with a profusion of wall and ceiling timbers and carved stanchions.

Chef Majid Bourote **Seats** 80, Private dining 85 **Open** All year **Prices from** S £7.50, M £23.50, D £7.50 **Parking** 100 **Notes** Children welcome

CHELMSFORD
Samphire Restaurant
◉ MODERN EUROPEAN
01245 455700 | 29 Rainsford Road, CM1 2PZ
www.countyhotelchelmsford.co.uk

The County Hotel has a cheery modern style, as typified in the Samphire Restaurant, where oak floors and leather seats in summery pastel hues of mustard, mint and tangerine add colour to the neutral contemporary decor. Uncomplicated modern European cooking is the kitchen's stock-in-trade.

Chef Roy Ortega **Seats** 64, Private dining 135 **Open** All year **Parking** 60 **Notes** Vegetarian dishes, Children welcome

COGGESHALL
Ranfield's Brasserie
◉◉ MODERN BRITISH **V**
01376 561453 | 4–6 Stoneham Street, CO6 1TT
www.ranfieldsbrasserie.co.uk

A fixture of the local dining scene for almost 30 years, its setting may be a 16th-century timbered house but there's nothing old about the approach. The mood is laid-back and cosmopolitan, and the decor akin to an eclectic art gallery with antique linen-clothed tables.

Chef John Ranfield **Seats** 80 **Open** All year **Notes** Children welcome

COLCHESTER
Church Street Tavern
◉◉ MODERN BRITISH **V**
01206 564325 | 3 Church Street, CO1 1NF
www.churchstreettavern.co.uk

Just off the main shopping mayhem, the handsome Victorian former bank building has been repurposed as a trendy bar and first-floor restaurant full of light and artwork. Bare tables, banquettes and wood floors fit the smart-casual mood, and the seasonal menu is full of up-to-date ideas.

Chef Ewan Naylon **Seats** 75, Private dining 18 **Closed** 25–26 December, 1–7 January **Prices from** S £5.50, M £12.50, D £6 **Notes** Children welcome

Cloisters
◉ MODERN BRITISH
01206 575913 | High Street, CO1 1UG
www.greyfriarscolchester.co.uk

Cloisters restaurant is in the 20th-century part of GreyFriars Hotel, once a Franciscan monastery. Parquet floored with an art deco feel, it's known for modern European dishes with a British touch. Proving irresistible, perhaps, might be a starter of oysters from Mersea Island nine miles away.

Chef Liam Keating **Seats** 65, Private dining 25 **Open** All year **Prices from** S £7.45, M £14.50, D £6.25 **Parking** 38 **Notes** Vegetarian dishes, Children welcome

Stoke by Nayland Hotel, Golf & Spa
◉◉ MODERN BRITISH
01206 262836 | Keepers Lane, Leavenheath, CO6 4PZ
www.stokebynayland.com

This purpose-built hotel complex comes complete with spa, high-tech gym, two championship-level golf courses and The Lakes Restaurant, a bright and airy room with panoramic views. The enterprising kitchen sends out ambitious dishes. For dessert, try a palate-challenging doughnut stuffed with sticky toffee bacon.

Chef Alan Paton **Seats** 100, Private dining 60 **Open** All year **Parking** 350 **Notes** Vegetarian dishes, Children welcome

DEDHAM
milsoms
◉ MODERN BRITISH
01206 322795 | Stratford Road, CO7 6HN
www.milsomhotels.com

This old creeper-covered house offers a little piece of boutique glamour in a pretty Essex village. The bar and brasserie strike a contemporary pose. The menu sticks to the modern and offers everything from posh lunchtime sandwiches to steaks and burgers cooked on the grill.

Chef Sarah Norman, Ben Rush **Seats** 80, Private dining 30 **Open** All year **Prices from** S £6.50, M £13.50, D £7 **Parking** 80 **Notes** Vegetarian dishes, Children welcome

ESSEX

The Sun Inn
◉◉ MODERN ITALIAN ♨ NOTABLE WINE LIST
01206 323351 | High Street, CO7 6DF
www.thesuninndedham.com

The Sun is a 15th-century village inn with open fires, doughty timbers and panelling. Its culinary leanings are distinctly Mediterranean, with the kitchen turning fresh produce and quality Italian ingredients such as cured meats, cheeses and oils into uncomplicated, well-executed dishes.

Chef Jack Levine **Seats** 70 **Closed** 25–26 December, 3–4 January **Prices from** S £5.50, M £12.50, D £5.50 **Parking** 15 **Notes** Vegetarian dishes, Children welcome

Le Talbooth
◉◉ MODERN BRITISH V ♨ NOTABLE WINE LIST
01206 323150 | Stratford Road, CO7 6HN
www.milsomhotels.com/letalbooth

In a former toll house by the River Stour dating from Tudor times, the Milsom family have run this East Anglian stalwart for over half a century. Inside, the look is slick and contemporary, and the kitchen stays abreast of culinary trends.

Chef Andrew Hirst, Ian Rhodes **Seats** 80, Private dining 34 **Open** All year **Prices from** S £13, M £28, D £9.75 **Parking** 50 **Notes** Children welcome

GREAT TOTHAM
The Bull & Willow Room at Great Totham
◉◉ MODERN, TRADITIONAL BRITISH
01621 893385 | 2 Maldon Road, CM9 8NH
www.thebullatgreattotham.co.uk

This 16th-century village inn has an uncommonly posh eating area, the Willow Room, where the kitchen produces a repertoire of modern dishes. Opt for a pub classic such as Atlantic prawn cocktail or goats' cheese mousse and endive salad to start.

Chef Sam Baxter **Seats** 75, Private dining 20 **Open** All year **Parking** 80 **Notes** Vegetarian dishes, Children welcome

GREAT YELDHAM
The White Hart
◉◉ BRITISH, EUROPEAN
01787 237250 | Poole Street, CO9 4HJ
www.whitehartyeldham.com

Dating back to the Tudor era, this is a classic timbered country inn set in extensive grounds. Crisp white napery and quality tableware confer distinctive class on the dining room, where salt marsh lamb is stuffed with haggis alongside a pink noisette and a kidney.

Chef Wu Zhenjang, K White **Seats** 44, Private dining 200 **Closed** 25 December evening **Parking** 50 **Notes** Vegetarian dishes, Children welcome

HARWICH
The Pier at Harwich
◉◉ MODERN BRITISH, SEAFOOD V
01255 241212 | The Quay, CO12 3HH
www.milsomhotels.com

Right on the quayside, the Pier provides super-fresh seafood and, following an extensive redevelopment, you can dine in the first-floor brasserie and take the air in the balcony seating. It's a tough choice between chargrilled Dedham Vale steaks and Harwich crab.

Chef John Goff, Stephen Robson **Seats** 80, Private dining 24 **Open** All year **Prices from** S £7, M £14.50, D £7.50 **Parking** 12 **Notes** Children welcome

HOCKLEY
The Anchor Riverside Pub and Restaurant
◉ MODERN BRITISH V
01702 230777 | Ferry Road, Hullbridge, SS5 6ND
www.theanchorhullbridge.co.uk

Shortly before the road ends at the River Crouch is this thoroughly modern gastro pub where, if the weather's kind, you can sit outside in the extensive gardens with something light. Otherwise, head for the restaurant, designed for lingering over a decent three-course meal.

Chef Daniel Watkins **Seats** 160 **Closed** 25 December **Parking** 50 **Notes** Children welcome

HOWE STREET
Galvin Green Man
◉◉ MODERN BRITISH V
01245 408820 | Main Road, CM3 1BG
www.galvingreenman.com

Dating back to the 13th century, this rural inn is run by Essex-born chef brothers, Chris and Jeff Galvin. With the River Chelmer running through the beer garden it's a welcoming place for a pint and the glass-roofed dining room pulls in foodies from all over.

Chef Daniel Lee **Seats** 104, Private dining 40 **Open** All year **Prices from** S £5.50, M £12.50, D £5 **Parking** 60 **Notes** Vegetarian dishes, Children welcome

MANNINGTREE
The Mistley Thorn
◉◉ MODERN BRITISH, SEAFOOD
01206 392821 | High Street, Mistley, CO11 1HE
www.mistleythorn.co.uk

A gem of a place in an old coaching inn a short stroll from the harbour, the Georgian details remain in the restaurant, and neutral colours keep it contemporary. Look for the specials menu offering the catch of the day.

Chef Sherri Singleton, Karl Burnside **Seats** 75, Private dining 28 **Closed** 25 December **Prices from** S £5.95, M £12.95, D £5.95 **Parking** 7 **Notes** Vegetarian dishes, Children welcome

THE HOOP

1 High Street, Stock, Essex, CM4 9BD   01277 871137
www.thehoopstock.co.uk
email:thehoopstock@yahoo.co.uk

A traditional 15th century, oak beamed free house,
located in the pretty village of Stock, offering gastro
food and award winning real ales. In addition, our fine
dining restaurant offer an a la carte menu and boutique
wine list. Enjoy our large beer garden and beer festival
held over the spring bank holiday each year.

ORSETT
The Garden Brasserie
@ MODERN BRITISH

01375 891402 | Prince Charles Avenue, RM16 3HS
www.orsetthall.co.uk

The 17th-century Orsett Hall was rebuilt, phoenix like, following a fire a decade ago. Its floral-inspired Garden Brasserie is beautiful, with super views of the landscaped grounds, or if you just want a snack, Café Sartoria awaits.

Chef Robert Pearce **Open** All year **Notes** Vegetarian dishes

SOUTHEND-ON-SEA
Holiday Inn Southend
@ TRADITIONAL BRITISH

01702 543001 | 77 Eastwoodbury Crescent, SS2 6XG
www.hisouthend.com/dining/1935-rooftop-restaurant-bar

Calling all plane spotting foodies: both of your interests can be indulged in one fell swoop at the fifth-floor 1935 Restaurant overlooking the aviation action at Southend Airport. Naturally enough, soundproofing is of the highest order, and there's a real sense of occasion.

Chef Michael Walker **Seats** 82, Private dining 14 **Open** All year **Prices from** S £4.50, M £10.95, D £4.50 **Parking** 226 **Notes** Vegetarian dishes, Children welcome

The Roslin Beach Hotel
@ BRITISH

01702 586375 | Thorpe Esplanade, Thorpe Bay, SS1 3BG
www.roslinhotel.com

If you do like to be beside the seaside, The Roslin Beach Hotel has a sea-facing terrace, plus indoor space shielded by glass, so it is beach ready whatever the weather. The tables are dressed up in white linen and there's a buzzy ambience.

Chef Wayne Hawkins **Seats** 70, Private dining 30 **Open** All year **Parking** 57 **Notes** Vegetarian dishes, Children welcome

STOCK
Ellis's Restaurant
@ MODERN BRITISH

01277 829990 | Greenwoods Hotel & Spa, Stock Road, CM4 9BE
www.greenwoodshotel.co.uk

An appealing 17th-century, Grade II listed building set in expansive landscaped gardens, Greenwoods Hotel is just a few minutes from Billericay town centre. Named after the manor house's previous owner, the hotel's contemporary Ellis's Restaurant offers a pleasing array of innovative, fuss-free dishes.

Chef Daniel Holland Robinson **Seats** 64, Private dining 20 **Closed** 26 December, 1 January **Prices from** S £7, M £21, D £7 **Parking** 100 **Notes** Vegetarian dishes, Children welcome

The Hoop
@ MODERN BRITISH

01277 841137 | High Street, CM4 9BD
www.thehoop.co.uk

An amalgam of three weavers' cottages that became an alehouse 450 years ago, at ground level The Hoop is a classic beamed pub, while upstairs a raftered dining room offers smartly linened tables and a confident, crowd-pleasing menu that spans both the traditional and modern.

Chef Phil Utz **Seats** 40 **Closed** Beer festival week and 1st week in January **Prices from** S £5.95, M £14.95, D £3 **Notes** Vegetarian dishes, Children welcome

See advertisement on page 113

THORPE-LE-SOKEN
Harry's Bar & Restaurant
@ MODERN BRITISH

01255 860250 | High Street, CO16 0EA
www.harrysbarandrestaurant.co.uk

It may be a long way from the original Harry's Bar in Venice but this Essex village namesake offers a similarly relaxed and stylish brasserie ambience. The seasonally changing menu combines modern British dishes with more global influences. Wines cover the world's best regions.

Chef Ricky Latter **Seats** 55 **Open** All year **Parking** 16 **Notes** Vegetarian dishes, Children welcome

▶ GLOUCESTERSHIRE

ALMONDSBURY
Aztec Hotel & Spa
@ MODERN BRITISH

01454 201090 | Aztec West, BS32 4TS
www.aztechotelbristol.com

This restaurant occupies a contemporary space with a high-vaulted ceiling, rustic stone fireplace, polished wooden floors, leather seating and bold modern abstract art. The menu takes a broad sweep through global culinary culture, with British 28-day aged beef cooked on the chargrill a speciality.

Chef Marc Payne **Seats** 100, Private dining 30 **Prices from** S £5, M £12.95, D £6.95 **Parking** 200 **Notes** Vegetarian dishes, Children welcome

ALVESTON
Alveston House Hotel
◉ MODERN EUROPEAN
01454 415050 | Davids Lane, BS35 2LA
www.alvestonhousehotel.co.uk
This Georgian hotel set within walled gardens with a restaurant to one side is well worth the short drive out from Bristol. Gardens with an ornamental lily pond are a pleasant drinking spot, and inside the place is done in calming pastel shades.
Chef Tony Krajcir **Seats** 75, Private dining 40 **Open** All year **Prices from** S £5.75, M £15.75, D £6.50 **Parking** 60 **Notes** Vegetarian dishes, Children welcome

ARLINGHAM
The Old Passage Inn
◉◉ SEAFOOD, MODERN BRITISH
01452 740547 | Passage Road, GL2 7JR
www.theoldpassage.com
On the bank of the River Severn, The Old Passage is a white-painted restaurant with rooms. The kitchen's focus is on seafood, with choices like wild turbot fillet counterbalanced by oxtail, served with braised pak choi, celeriac purée and girolles.
Chef Jon Lane **Seats** 50, Private dining 12 **Closed** 25–26 December **Prices from** S £10.50, M £19.50, D £5.25 **Parking** 40 **Notes** Vegetarian dishes, No children aged 10 years and under at lunch

BUCKLAND
Buckland Manor
◉◉◉ BRITISH ◖NOTABLE WINE LIST
01386 852626 | WR12 7LY
www.bucklandmanor.co.uk
At some indeterminate point, the village of Buckland melds into the 10-acre corner in which the old manor stands, next to the village church. It's a delightful Cotswold location for a country house that exudes a sense of history from its every pore. White wood-panelled walls interspersed with mullioned windows overlooking the gardens and the hills beyond are the setting for Will Guthrie's finely crafted modern cooking, which is lent extra fragrance by the products of the manor's own herb garden. First up might be a duo of seared scallop and chicken oyster in red curry sauce with puffed saffron rice, an ingenious textural composition, or ashed Bosworth goats' cheese dressed in balsamic and candied walnuts. Main course treatments work with the grain of their prime materials, adding a gingery jus and puréed butternut to duck breast, or salmon and shrimp ravioli and a shellfish bisque to a fine cut of hake. For dessert, an intense orange marmalade soufflé is accompanied by brown bread ice cream, and the dark chocolate délice with mandarin parfait and confit orange lacks nothing in sophistication.

Chef Will Guthrie **Seats** 40, Private dining 14 **Open** All year **Parking** 20 **Notes** Vegetarian dishes, No children under 8 years

CHELTENHAM
Le Champignon Sauvage
◉◉◉◉ MODERN FRENCH
01242 573449 | 24–28 Suffolk Road, GL50 2AQ
www.lechampignonsauvage.co.uk
Having breasted the billows of restaurant fashion since the 1980s, the Champignon has now sailed serenely into its fourth decade of operations, a remarkable testament to the tenacity and dedication of David and Helen Everitt-Matthias, the more so since the place has stayed in the upper echelons of British gastronomy throughout that period and has achieved its longevity without the need for attention-grabbing culinary stunts. Indeed, the place itself seems to blend in with the row of shops it rubs shoulders with, and the interior prospect of blond wood and dove-grey, with striking artworks and the quality mise-en-place of each trimly linened table, creates a civilised, discreet feel. David's cooking, for all its appropriation of modern ingredients and techniques, maintains a tap-root in classical French cuisine, as may be seen in an opener of loin, rillettes and parfait of rabbit with heritage carrots and carrot and Muscat jelly, perhaps succeeded by opalescent sea bass in oyster emulsion with celeriac remoulade, or loin and sweetbreads of outstanding Shurdington lamb, accompanied by baby onions, lettuce and peas in a burdock-scented jus. Where things get more avant-garde, they do so with point and precision, as when a scallop is partnered with milk-crumbed salsify, cured pork jowl and leek purée in onion dashi broth. Desserts might also try out Asian seasonings, for mango with Thai-spiced cream and green curry sorbet, or construct layers of counterpointing flavours, as for the long-running bergamot parfait with orange jelly and liquorice cream. A highly distinguished wine list completes the picture.
Chef David Everitt-Matthias **Seats** 40 **Closed** 10 days Christmas, 3 weeks June **Notes** Children welcome

The Curry Corner Est.1977
◉◉ BANGLADESHI, INDIAN
01242 528449 | 133 Fairview Road, GL52 2EX
www.thecurrycorner.com
This restaurant occupies a white Georgian townhouse on the edge of Cheltenham's main shopping area. It has a chic, contemporary look, featuring ruby-red wall coverings offset by carvings. Bangladeshi home cooking is the theme, with spices flown in from India, Morocco and Turkey.
Chef Shamsul & Monrusha Krori **Seats** 50 **Closed** 25 December **Notes** Vegetarian dishes, Children welcome

GLOUCESTERSHIRE

The Greenway Hotel & Spa

◉◉◉ MODERN BRITISH, FRENCH **V**
01242 862352 | Shurdington, GL51 4UG
www.thegreenwayhotelandspa.com

Lurking in Shurdington, on the verdant outskirts of leafy Cheltenham, the Greenway is an Elizabethan manor house of Cotswold stone, its facade half-hidden in clambering ivy, the tock of the long-case clock marking the passage of time in the entrance hall. Up-to-the-minute spa facilities are always a draw, while the Garden Restaurant is named after its soothing view, with a majestic stone fireplace and venerable oak panelling adding lustre. Marcus McGuinness is a model modern-day practitioner, overseeing a thriving kitchen garden, engaging in forays into the countryside to gather wild provender, and sourcing thoroughbred prime materials, before turning it all into elegant, eye-catching dishes of striking character. Start with a Chinese-influenced broth of char siu pork and langoustine with langoustine tartare and pickled cucumber, before turning to Hereford beef fillet and oxtail croustillant with classical Rossini garniture, or maybe poached and roast brill with spiced bread, walnuts and pear. Meticulously selected cheeses are a worthwhile extra to a dessert such as bergamot lemon curd with pine nut brittle and clove ice cream, or rhubarb savarin with matching sorbet.

Chef Marcus McGuinness **Seats** 60, Private dining 22 **Open** All year **Notes** Children welcome

Hotel du Vin Cheltenham

◉ FRENCH, EUROPEAN
01242 588450 | Parabola Road, GL50 3AQ
www.hotelduvin.com

The restaurant at the Cheltenham branch of this popular hotel chain follows the usual bistro look of wooden floor, unclothed tables, banquettes and a wine-related theme of empty bottles, prints and memorabilia. The menu goes along the expected bistro route.

Chef Paul Mottram **Seats** 120, Private dining 32 **Open** All year **Prices from** S £6.50, M £12.50, D £5.95 **Parking** 23 **Notes** Vegetarian dishes, Children welcome

Lumière

◉◉◉ MODERN BRITISH **V**
01242 222200 | Clarence Parade, GL50 3PA
www.lumiere.cc

The Howes' elegant venue lies a little way off the arboreal Promenade for which Cheltenham is famous, and looks the very image of a modern dining room. Its soothing combination of cream and aubergine tones, and the capable hand of Helen Howe on the front-of-

house tiller, makes for a supremely relaxing experience, the better to highlight Jon's accomplished culinary wizardry. Every technical flourish of the latter-day kitchen is on show in the all-encompassing tasting menu, which begins with appetisers such as pork scratchings with burnt apple and fennel pollen, and a cornet of Stinking Bishop with savoury granola. Not that those taking fewer courses are in any way short-changed, when a starter of Brixham pollock with shrimps, Jerusalem artichoke and chorizo could be followed by Cotswold fallow deer and cavolo nero with an assertive partnership of chocolate and Stilton. By the time you're on to a dessert of Valrhona Guanaja with passionfruit, pineapple, mango and popcorn, the tasters could well be just hitting their mid-meal tequila shot with salt and lime. Don't overlook the cheeses, a fine selection served with truffle honey.

Chef Jon Howe **Seats** 25 **Closed** 2 weeks in winter and 2 weeks in summer **Notes** No children under 8 years

Monty's Brasserie

◉◉ MODERN BRITISH **V**
01242 227678 | George Hotel, 41 St Georges Road, GL50 3DZ
www.montysbraz.co.uk

Situated in the heart of Cheltenham, this modern brasserie is part of the Grade II-listed George Hotel, built in the Georgian era. Friendly, uniformed staff add to the cheerful atmosphere. The kitchen takes sound seasonal ingredients, adding a degree of complication to dishes without pushing.

Chef Clemente Zamora **Seats** 40, Private dining 32 **Closed** 25–26 December **Parking** 30 **Notes** Children welcome

The Restaurant at Ellenborough Park

Rosettes suspended MODERN BRITISH ◖NOTABLE WINE LIST
01242 545454 | Southam Road, GL52 3NH
www.ellenboroughpark.com

The Rosette award for this establishment has been suspended due to a change of chef and reassessment will take place in due course. Although the original house had been pottering along unexceptionally since the 1530s, Ellenborough really hit its stride when the first Earl of that ilk, erstwhile governor general of British India, moved himself and his wife into it 300 years later. The place itself is a sumptuous beauty in Cotswold honey, looking a little like an Oxford college, with a high-glitz panelled dining room.

Chef David Williams **Seats** 60, Private dining 20 **Open** All year **Parking** 130 **Notes** Vegetarian dishes, Children welcome

THE WHARF HOUSE

RESTAURANT WITH ROOMS

9 course Tasting Menu £52

á la carte menu also available

Available Tues-Sat 12-4pm and 5.30 onwards

Afternoon Tea £17.50

drinks and coffees
light bite Terrace Menu

Available Tues-Sat 12-4pm and 5.30 onwards

Mon & Sun 12-2pm

01452 332 900

www.thewharfhouse.co.uk

Over, Gloucester, GL2 8DB

info@thewharfhouse.co.uk

Directions: Turn off the A40
at traffic lights 250 yds west
of Over Roundabout (junction
A40/A417). GR SO 816197

AA
Gold Star Award
★★★★
Restaurant with Rooms

AA Awarded
Rosette
Restaurant

Green
Tourism
GOLD

CHIPPING CAMPDEN

Fig

◉◉ MODERN ITALIAN, MEDITERRANEAN **V**

01386 840330 | Cotswold House Hotel & Spa, Upper High Street, The Square, GL55 6AN

www.bespokehotels.com/cotswoldhouse

A handsome Regency building in the middle of Chipping Campden, Fig is the more formal of the two dining options at Cotswold House Hotel. The kitchen stays abreast of contemporary trends and prime ingredients are given a global twist.

Chef Pasquale Russo **Seats** 40, Private dining 30 **Open** All year **Parking** 28 **Notes** Children welcome

Jackrabbit Restaurant

◉◉◉ MODERN BRITISH **V**

01386 840256 | The Kings Hotel, The Square, High Street, GL55 6AW

www.kingscampden.co.uk

A classic Georgian townhouse built in honey-hued Cotswold stone right on Chipping Campden's square, The Kings is a glossy boutique bolt-hole these days. Inside, the place wears the look of a smartly casual modern operation – that's to say unclothed antique tables, a flagged floor, a log fire, artworks and moody lighting in the beamed Jackrabbit Restaurant. The up-to-date approach carries through to what appears on the plate: headed up by Greg Newman, the kitchen cleverly combines flavour, texture and visual appeal in well-judged modern food built on splendid seasonal ingredients. An attention-grabbing starter allies splendid Salcombe crab with a Caesar salad-style medley bringing the crunch of radish, baby gem lettuce, parmesan crisps and croûtons, and buttermilk dressing. Main course teams black Ibérico pork neck and belly with miso-glazed cauliflower, Cotswold cider, golden raisins and spring onion, while pan-roasted halibut might enjoy the salty punch of clam and coco bean cassoulet, caviar and coastal herbs. To finish, a play on the Snickers bar theme brings a glorious confection of chocolate-glazed peanut butter parfait, salted toffee and milk ice cream.

Chef Greg Newman **Seats** 45, Private dining 20 **Open** All year **Parking** 12 **Notes** Children welcome

The Seagrave Arms

◉◉ MODERN BRITISH

01386 840192 | Friday Street, GL55 6QH

www.seagravearms.com

Stone-built and four-square, the 400-year-old Seagrave is a Cotswolds inn of considerable character. Strong classic undertones are discernible beneath the modern British cooking style. A good selection of wines by the glass includes a sparkling white from Nyetimber's South Downs vineyard.

Chef Iain Hobbs, Laura Harper **Seats** 30 **Open** All year **Parking** 11 **Notes** Vegetarian dishes, Children welcome

Three Ways House

◉ MODERN BRITISH

01386 438429 | Chapel Lane, Mickleton, GL55 6SB

www.threewayshousehotel.com

This Cotswold-stone building dates back to 1870, but it was made world-famous in the 1980s with the formation of the Pudding Club. The food is big-hearted British stuff, although the kitchen team isn't afraid to look further afield for inspiration.

Chef Dan Foxall **Seats** 80, Private dining 70 **Open** All year **Parking** 37 **Notes** Vegetarian dishes, Children welcome

CIRENCESTER

Barnsley House

◉◉ MODERN EUROPEAN

01285 740000 | GL7 5EE

www.barnsleyhouse.com

The restaurant at 17th-century Barnsley House is named the Potager, after the ornamental and vegetable garden designed in the 1950s by Rosemary Verey, which it overlooks. Perfectly cooked lamb sweetbreads in a noteworthy jus are served with no more than morels and garden chard.

Chef Francesco Volgo **Seats** 40, Private dining 14 **Open** All year **Parking** 25 **Notes** Vegetarian dishes, No children under 14 years at dinner

Jesse's Bistro

◉◉ MODERN BRITISH

01285 641497 | 14 Blackjack Street, GL7 2AA

www.jessesbistro.co.uk

Tucked into a brick-paved back alley in the town centre, the bistro has an old beamed interior and a British menu that makes excursions to the Mediterranean and East Asia. First up might be Serrano ham with salami, figs and pine nuts in sherry dressing.

Chef David Witnall **Seats** 55, Private dining 12 **Open** All year **Prices from** S £6.50, M £17.50, D £7 **Notes** Vegetarian dishes, Children welcome

CLEARWELL

Tudor Farmhouse Hotel & Restaurant

◉◉ MODERN BRITISH **V** ◗ NOTABLE WINE LIST

01594 833046 | High Street, GL16 8JS

www.tudorfarmhousehotel.co.uk

The charm-laden grey stone building looks the rustic part but, once inside, its stone walls, beams, wood panelling and inglenooks are overlaid with lashings of boutique bolt-hole style. Nor is the kitchen stuck in the past – its 20-mile menus are full of fresh, up-to-date ideas.

Chef Rob Cox **Seats** 36, Private dining 22 **Open** All year **Parking** 30 **Notes** Children welcome

See advertisement below

COLEFORD
The Miners Country Inn
MODERN BRITISH, TRADITIONAL **V**
01594 836632 | Chepstow Road, Sling, GL16 8LH
www.theminerssling.co.uk

The Miners is a family-run dining pub in a tiny village in the Forest of Dean. Beamed ceilings and stone floors come as standard, while the restaurant is simply but tastefully decorated. A daily changing menu selects from the best local produce available.

Chef Steven Jenkins **Seats** 50 **Open** All year **Parking** 40 **Notes** Children welcome

CORSE LAWN
Corse Lawn House Hotel
BRITISH, FRENCH **NOTABLE WINE LIST**
01452 780771 | GL19 4LZ
www.corselawn.com

The red-brick house dates from the Queen Anne period and stands on the village green in front of a large pond where coaches and their horses were once scrubbed clean. Today modern British cuisine is served in the smart principal dining room.

Chef Martin Kinahan **Seats** 50, Private dining 28 **Closed** 26–27 December **Prices from** S £5.50, M £17.50, D £7.50 **Parking** 60 **Notes** Children welcome

DAYLESFORD
Daylesford Farm Café
MODERN BRITISH
01608 731700 | GL56 0YG
www.daylesford.com

On the Gloucestershire farmland that spawned a mini-empire, the Daylesford Farmshop and Café occupies a smartly converted barn with a New England finish and an open-to-view kitchen. The food makes a virtue of simplicity, with quality ingredients allowed to shine.

Chef Gaven Fuller **Seats** 75, Private dining 60 **Closed** 25–26 December and 1 January **Prices from** S £7, M £12, D £6 **Parking** 100 **Notes** Vegetarian dishes, Children welcome

GLOUCESTERSHIRE

EBRINGTON
The Ebrington Arms
◎◎ MODERN BRITISH
01386 593223 | GL55 6NH
www.theebringtonarms.co.uk

Still very much a pub in the heart of the village by the green, the Ebrington has served its community for several hundred years, as is evident from its copious oak beams and flagged floors. The menu takes a contemporary line of original modern dishes.

Chef Ben Dulley **Seats** 50, Private dining 30 **Closed** 25 December **Parking** 13 **Notes** Vegetarian dishes, Children welcome

GLOUCESTER
Hatherley Manor Hotel & Spa
◎ TRADITIONAL BRITISH
01452 730217 | Down Hatherley Lane, GL2 9QA
www.hatherleymanor.com

A stylish brick and stone-built 17th-century house, Hatherley Manor has undergone sympathetic extension and refurbishment, and is popular as a wedding venue. The Dewinton Restaurant is a relaxed setting for contemporary dining, with rich gold drapes and upholstery and linen-clad tables.

Chef Terry Woolcock **Open** All year **Parking** 250

Hatton Court
◎ CLASSIC BRITISH, FRENCH **V**
01452 617412 | Upton Hill, Upton St Leonards, GL4 8DE
www.hatton-court.co.uk

A country-house hotel not far from the M5, Hatton Court is smothered with climbing foliage, its little windows barely peeping through the green. The formal dining room is kitted out with linen-clad tables, wood panelling and full-drop windows at one end.

Chef Jeff Lewis **Seats** 75, Private dining 50 **Open** All year **Parking** 100 **Notes** Children welcome

The Wharf House Restaurant with Rooms
◎ CONTEMPORARY BRITISH
01452 332900 | Over, GL2 8DB
www.thewharfhouse.co.uk

Perched alongside the River Severn on the outskirts of Gloucester, The Wharf House is owned/run by the Canal Trust, and is a soothing location for seasonal dining. The white-walled restaurant offers simple, well-balanced dishes with good contrasts of flavour and texture.

Chef David Penny, Maisy Smith, Tessa Berry **Seats** 40 **Closed** 24 December to 8 January **Prices from** S £6, M £14, D £6 **Parking** 32 **Notes** Vegetarian dishes

See advertisement on page 117

LECHLADE ON THAMES
The Bell Inn
◎ CLASSIC BRITISH
01367 860249 | Langford, GL7 3LF
www.thebelllangford.com

After a tasteful makeover, The Bell is a model for contemporary pub dining. Open fires, flagstone floors, rough-hewn beams and heritage colours draw in the punters to this welcoming local. There's real talent in the kitchen too, which shows its mettle in hearty Brit classics and wood-fired dishes – all hugely enjoyable.

Chef Tom Noest **Open** All year **Notes** Vegetarian dishes, Children welcome

LOWER SLAUGHTER
The Slaughters Country Inn
◎◎ MODERN BRITISH
01451 822143 | GL54 2HS
www.theslaughtersinn.co.uk

This artfully modernised, 17th-century Cotswold-stone inn makes good use of its riverside terrace in this peaceful village. In the 1920s the building was a crammer school for Eton College, thus it now has Eton's Restaurant. The modern British menu also covers the bar.

Chef Chris Fryer **Seats** 60, Private dining 30 **Open** All year **Parking** 40 **Notes** Vegetarian dishes, Children welcome

The Slaughters Manor House
◎◎◎ MODERN BRITISH **V**
01451 820456 | GL54 2HP
www.slaughtersmanor.co.uk

Built from golden Cotswold stone, this comfortable manor house may date from the 17th century, but it offers a stylish 21st-century interpretation of country living. Wonderful period features, like the ornate plaster ceiling in the drawing room, and the delightful formal gardens, rub shoulders with modern decorative touches and pale, soothing colours. The elegant dining room, partly set in the house's original chapel, is an airy, light-filled space, with chairs upholstered in silver-grey and nicely spaced, linen-clad tables. Head chef Nik Chappell originally studied fine art, and his dishes are often picture-perfect explorations of flavour and texture. At dinner you can choose between the set menu and an eight-course tasting menu, maybe starting with a complex dish of seared and raw scallop, green pepper juice, pickled rhubarb and crispy pork. A venison main course is accompanied to great effect by silky smooth celeriac purée, given a horseradish kick, along with baked celeriac and charred pineapple. At dessert, a delightfully light blackberry mousse works effectively with well-flavoured liquorice cake, pickled blackberries and coconut sorbet.

Chef Nik Chappell **Seats** 48, Private dining 24 **Open** All year **Parking** 30 **Notes** Children welcome

MORETON-IN-MARSH
Manor House Hotel
◉◉ MODERN BRITISH **V**
01608 650501 | High Street, GL56 0LJ
www.cotswold-inns-hotels.co.uk/manor

This Cotswold-stone hotel might date from the reign of Henry VIII, but careful renovation and updating have brought it squarely into the 21st century. The Mulberry Restaurant has generously spaced tables, comfortable chairs and on-the-ball staff, while the kitchen produces appealing dishes without over-complicating things.

Chef Nick Orr **Seats** 45, Private dining 120 **Open** All year **Parking** 32 **Notes** No children under 8 years

Redesdale Arms
◉ MODERN **V**
01608 650308 | High Street, GL56 0AW
www.redesdalearms.com

Dating from the 17th century, this inn has been sympathetically updated to give a contemporary edge. There are two dining rooms, one in a rear conservatory, the other overlooking the high street. A glance at the menu shows a kitchen seaming the modern British vein.

Chef Jack Jeffries-Marsh **Open** All year **Notes** Children welcome

White Hart Royal Hotel
◉ TRADITIONAL BRITISH
01608 650731 | High Street, GL56 0BA
www.whitehartroyal.co.uk

There's no shortage of period features to remind visitors of the long heritage of this building. The Courtyard restaurant – outside tables are a fair-weather treat – is a linen-free zone, the dark wood tables and bold colours creating a smart-casual space.

Chef Matthew Craven **Seats** 44, Private dining 12 **Open** All year **Prices from** S £6, M £13, D £6 **Notes** Vegetarian dishes, Children welcome

NAILSWORTH
Wilder
◉◉ MODERN BRITISH **V**
01453 835483 | Market Street, GL6 0BX
www.dinewilder.co.uk

The newly opened sister restaurant of Wild Garlic Restaurant with Rooms (located a one-minute walk away), this stylish place offers diners a relaxing evening with an eight-course tasting menu. All guests dine at 7.30pm and everyone enjoys the same courses (allergies need advance notification). Great attention to detail.

Chef Matthew Wilder **Open** All year

Wild Garlic Restaurant and Rooms
◉◉ MODERN BRITISH
01453 832615 | 3 Cossack Square, GL6 0DB
www.wild-garlic.co.uk

So prolific is wild garlic around these parts that the Beardshalls named their stylish restaurant with rooms after it. Cotswold tapas are one of the dining options, but it's on the main menus that the kitchen really shows its paces.

Chef Matthew Beardshall **Seats** 46 **Open** All year **Notes** Vegetarian dishes, Children welcome

NETHER WESTCOTE
The Feathered Nest Country Inn
◉◉◉ MODERN BRITISH
See pages 122–123

SELSLEY
The Bell Inn
◉◉ MODERN BRITISH
01453 753801 | Bell Lane, GL5 5JY
www.thebellinnselsley.com

New owners have transformed this 16th-century village Inn, which is now the hub of picturesque Selsley. Lunch or dinner can be taken in the comfortable bar or you can enjoy pleasant views from the conservatory-style dining area. Top quality local produce features in pub classics.

Chef Mark Payne **Seats** 55, Private dining 14 **Open** All year **Prices from** S £5, M £13, D £5 **Parking** 12 **Notes** Vegetarian dishes, No children

GLOUCESTERSHIRE

NETHER WESTCOTE
The Feathered Nest Country Inn
◉◉◉ MODERN BRITISH
01993 833030 | OX7 6SD
www.thefeatherednestinn.co.uk

An impressively busy kitchen in beautiful surroundings

The Timmers had what might be seen as a practice run at restaurateuring in southern Portugal, having for many years run a successful establishment on the Algarve. Now they have come to rest in the Edenlode Valley, a protected natural beauty spot in the Cotswolds, where they stumbled upon a village pub that had been converted from an old malthouse. A little more transformative magic, and the place is a rural inn with stylish guest rooms and grounds that take in all the soothing delectation the west of England has to offer. Kingham station isn't far away, for those tempted to hot-rail it out of Paddington for a breath of country air. A table on the garden terrace is a thing devoutly to be wished on a summer's day, but inside is rather enchanting too, with its stone walls, flagged floors and antique furniture.

Kuba Winkowski runs a very busy kitchen that bakes, ferments, churns, cures, dry-ages and smokes much of what the menus offer, as well as sending out battalions of cakes and sandwiches for an afternoon tea worthy of the name. His principal menu takes a

streamlined approach, offering a single list of dishes, from which you compile four or six that take your fancy.

Start perhaps in Italian fashion with partridge tortellini in game consommé, or with an on-trend Spanish pairing of octopus and chorizo garnished with purslane and saffron-yellow aïoli. Main dishes nod to tradition with classic presentations such as Dover sole and brown shrimps, albeit accompanied by today's indispensable cauliflower purée, or the fabulously rich beef fillet and foie gras in a truffle-laced Madeira sauce. At the more up-to-date end of the spectrum, a serving of beautifully tender sika venison with crosnes and salsify in a bilberry-strewn jus is a model of balanced combining. For dessert, it could be Valrhona chocolate ganache with peanut butter and goats' milk ice cream, or a sablé breton of apple in Calvados caramel. The simpler lunch menu offers a pair of options at each stage, perhaps rabbit and bacon terrine with celeriac and chanterelles, before cod and squid with noodles and nasturtiums, and then hazelnut nougatine in coffee sauce to conclude. Vegetarian and children's menus indicate a diligent willingness to please everybody, and the drinks department does the same, with hand-cranked cask-conditioned ales in the pub and a wine list that features some quality boutique bottlings from South Africa.

Chef Kuba Winkowski **Seats** 60, Private dining 14 **Closed** 2 weeks February and July, 1 week October, 25 December **Parking** 45 **Notes** Vegetarian dishes, Children welcome

GLOUCESTERSHIRE

STOW-ON-THE-WOLD
The Kings Head Inn
◉ BRITISH
01608 658365 | The Green, Bledington, OX7 6XQ
www.kingsheadinn.net

This mellow stone Cotswolds pub comes with a classic bar with wobbly floors, log fires, and head-skimming beams. It's a textbook example of a switched-on village pub that is still the local boozer while the cooking is a definite notch or two up.

Chef Michael Tozer **Seats** 60 **Closed** 25–26 December **Prices from** S £6, M £14, D £7 **Parking** 20 **Notes** Vegetarian dishes, Children welcome

Old Stocks Inn
◉ MODERN BRITISH
01451 830666 | The Square, GL54 1AP
www.oldstocksinn.com

An appealing package of bright and funky modern decor, a fun ambience, an array of regionally brewed craft beers and an inventive take on contemporary pub grub makes this revamped 17th-century Cotswolds inn worth checking out. Puddings deliver some deep comforts.

Chef Ian Percival **Seats** 37, Private dining 18 **Prices from** S £6.50, M £14, D £6.50 **Parking** 8 **Notes** Vegetarian dishes, Children welcome

The Porch House
◉ MODERN BRITISH
01451 870048 | Digbeth Street, GL54 1BN
www.porch-house.co.uk

Claiming to be the oldest inn in England, the original building has been dated to AD 947, although a 21st-century refurbishment has matched its undoubted period charm. The bar is stocked with real ales, while the restaurant turns out some impressive modern British dishes.

Chef Rob Chasteauneuf **Seats** 40, Private dining 12 **Open** All year **Parking** 4 **Notes** Vegetarian dishes, Children welcome

Wyck Hill House Hotel & Spa
◉◉ MODERN BRITISH
01451 831936 | Burford Road, GL54 1HY
www.wyckhillhousehotel.co.uk

With 100 acres of fabulous grounds, green-and-pleasant views over the Cotswold Hills and Windrush Valley, an oak-panelled bar and a glitzy spa, Wyck Hill House is a place to pamper yourself in. Main courses are put together with fine-tuned precision.

Chef Mark Jane **Seats** 50, Private dining 120 **Open** All year **Parking** 120 **Notes** Vegetarian dishes, Children welcome

STROUD
The Bear of Rodborough
◉ BRITISH, INTERNATIONAL
01453 878522 | Rodborough Common, GL5 5DE
www.cotswold-inns-hotels.co.uk

This Cotswold hotel with its own vineyard is a handsome beast, its identity emphasised by two stuffed bears in reception. The dining room enjoys ravishing countryside views and a menu of thoroughgoing British modernism.

Chef Felix Prem **Seats** 70, Private dining 50 **Open** All year **Parking** 100 **Notes** Vegetarian dishes, Children welcome

Burleigh Court Hotel
◉◉ BRITISH, MEDITERRANEAN
01453 883804 | Burleigh, Minchinhampton, GL5 2PF
www.burleighcourthotel.co.uk

Built of Cotswold stone early in the 19th century, this imposing, ivy-clad manor house overlooks Golden Valley and the River Frome. Its Georgian-style interior incorporates an oak-panelled lounge and a dining room where large windows reveal a beautiful garden.

Chef Adrian Jarrad **Seats** 34 **Closed** Christmas **Parking** 28 **Notes** Vegetarian dishes, Children welcome

TETBURY
Calcot
◉◉ MODERN BRITISH
01666 890391 | Calcot, GL8 8YJ
www.calcot.co

Calcot Manor is a boutique-style hotel of Cotswold stone with a health spa and a light-filled restaurant called The Conservatory. The kitchen works around a repertoire of imaginative modern dishes, and flavours have real punch. For dessert try the impeccable praline soufflé.

Chef Richard Davies **Seats** 72, Private dining 16 **Open** All year **Parking** 150 **Notes** Vegetarian dishes, Children welcome

The Close Hotel
◉◉ MODERN BRITISH
01666 502272 | 8 Long Street, GL8 8AQ
www.theclose-hotel.com

The Close Hotel is a handsome 16th-century pile, boasting period details and contemporary elegance. There are two dining options in the form of a brasserie and fine-dining restaurant. The modern British menu strikes the right balance in this setting, with creative combinations.

Chef Stuart Shaw **Seats** 54, Private dining 26 **Open** All year **Parking** 18 **Notes** Vegetarian dishes, Children welcome

Hare & Hounds Hotel

◉◉ MODERN BRITISH **V**
01666 881000 | Westonbirt, GL8 8QL
www.cotswold-inns-hotels.co.uk

The Beaufort Restaurant is the culinary heart of this Cotswold-stone hotel just outside Tetbury. There's an excellent selection of homemade breads (including a Guinness soda bread) to accompany the meal, and ice rhubarb parfait may be your choice of dessert,

Chef Dean Low **Seats** 60, Private dining 10 **Open** All year **Parking** 40 **Notes** Children welcome

THORNBURY
Ronnie's of Thornbury

◉◉ MODERN BRITISH
01454 411137 | 11 St Mary Street, BS35 2AB
www.ronnies-restaurant.co.uk

This 17th-century building wears its contemporary look well: stone walls, beams, wooden floors and neutral hues are pointed up with art by West Country artists. Kick start the day with coffee and eggs Benedict at Ronnie's, or end it with an excellent dinner.

Chef Ron Faulkner **Seats** 62, Private dining 30
Closed 25–26 December and 1–8 January
Prices from S £10, M £17, D £7 **Notes** Vegetarian dishes, Children welcome

Thornbury Castle

◉◉ MODERN BRITISH, EUROPEAN
01454 281182 | Castle Street, BS35 1HH
www.thornburycastle.co.uk

Step inside the oak doors and you'll find everything expected of a 500-year-old castle: log fires, panelling, stone staircases, suits of armour, tapestries. The menu in the hexagonal Tower restaurant is in the modern British pastoral style, with invention and heritage running side by side.

Chef Andrew Chan **Seats** 72, Private dining 22
Open All year **Parking** 50 **Notes** Vegetarian dishes, No children under 8 years

UPPER ODDINGTON
Horse & Groom

◉
01451 830 584 | GL56 OXH
www.horseandgroomoddington.com

An unreconstructed village inn with low beamed ceilings, flagstone floors and exposed stone walls, the Horse and Groom is a Cotswold Tudor charmer. An outdoor terrace with sunshades is just the job in good weather, and the menu mixes classics with seasonal specials, modern dishes as well as featuring pie nights.

Chef Jack Jeffries **Open** All year

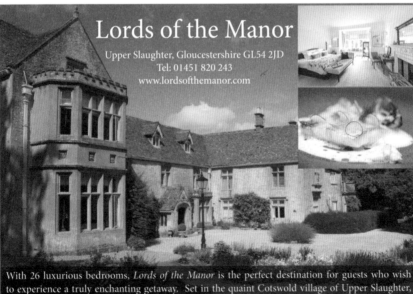

UPPER SLAUGHTER
Lords of the Manor
◉◉ MODERN BRITISH 🍷 NOTABLE WINE LIST

01451 820243 | GL54 2JD
www.lordsofthemanor.com

This traditional country-house hotel is a Cotswold gem. Overlooking the pretty gardens at the rear, the soft-focus neutral look of the dining room, with its double-clothed tables and a few pictures on plain white walls, makes for a relaxed setting for modern cooking rooted in the classics.

Chef Charles Smith **Seats** 50, Private dining 30 **Open** All year **Parking** 40 **Notes** Vegetarian dishes, No children under 7 years

See advertisement on page 125

WINCHCOMBE
The Lion Inn
◉ BRITISH

01242 603300 | 37 North Street, GL54 5PS
www.thelionwinchcombe.co.uk

A 15th-century coaching inn, The Lion has a Cotswold-stone facade and an abundance of original features. Alongside the period appeal is a contemporary attitude that sees the beams painted in fashionable grey and some well-chosen shabby-chic furniture.

Chef Thomas Law **Seats** 36, Private dining 20 **Open** All year **Prices from** S £3.50, M £14, D £6.50 **Notes** Vegetarian dishes, Children welcome

▶ GREATER MANCHESTER

BURY
Red Hall Hotel
◉ MODERN BRITISH

01706 822476 | Manchester Road, Walmersley, BL9 5NA
www.oscars.red-hall.co.uk

The hotel's conservatory-style restaurant goes by the name of Oscar's, and looks rather swish with its contemporary silver and grey tones and herringbone parquet floors. The modern British menu begins with an opener of cigar-like rolls of tuna sashimi filled with dressed white crab meat.

Chef Chris M Haddock **Seats** 45 **Open** All year **Parking** 60 **Notes** Vegetarian dishes, Children welcome

DELPH
The Old Bell Inn
◉ MODERN BRITISH

01457 870130 | 5 Huddersfield Road, OL3 5EG
www.theoldbellinn.co.uk

A traditional 18th-century coaching inn with a thoroughly contemporary attitude to dining, this pub holds a world record for its collection of 400 gins. In the modern restaurant, hearty, innovative food is created using an abundance of local raw materials.

Chef Ryan Dutson **Seats** 65 **Open** All year **Prices from** S £5.95, M £12.95, D £5.50 **Parking** 21 **Notes** Vegetarian dishes, Children welcome

The Saddleworth Hotel
◉ MODERN EUROPEAN

01457 871888 | Huddersfield Road, OL3 5LX
www.saddleworthhotel.co.uk

The Saddleworth feels like a real attempt to create a country inn for the modern era. Built of stone, with landscaped gardens, woodland, and sweeping views over the Lancashire moorland, it's not far from Oldham yet feels pleasingly remote from anywhere.

Chef Chris Chadwick **Seats** 30, Private dining 30 **Open** All year **Parking** 200 **Notes** Vegetarian dishes, Children welcome

DIDSBURY
HISPI
◉◉ CONTEMPORARY BRASSERIE

0161 445 3996 | 1C School Lane, M20 6RD
www.hispi.net

A third crowd-funded venture from the team behind Heswall's Burnt Truffle and Chester's Sticky Walnut, this one is named after the trendiest cabbage variety in British catering. It features stripped-back minimalist decor, an open kitchen, and a menu of inviting contemporary brasserie food.

Chef Richard Sharples **Notes** Vegetarian dishes

MANCHESTER
Adam Reid at The French
◉◉◉◉ MODERN BRITISH V 🍷 NOTABLE WINE LIST

0161 235 4780 | Peter Street, M60 2DS
www.the-french.co.uk

Adam Reid is the titular presence at The Midland Hotel and has been making his presence felt with a fully up-to-the-minute operation that embraces small-plate dining while sitting at the kitchen counter, as well as grand tasting processions served in the glitzy French restaurant, a handsome room done in moody blue and grey beneath giant crystal globes. Choose from four, six or nine courses, and expect energetic combinations such as truffled fried offals (duck heart and gizzards) with broccoli and a deeply flavoured mousse of Tunworth cheese, brill baked in beef butter with morel cream sauce and a meaty foam, and salt- and hay-aged duck on layers of beetroot in a sauce of pickled elderberries, even at the most modest end. Dessert could be positively flavoured rhubarb jelly topped with crumbled ginger biscuit and malt ice cream. On the nine-courser, there may also be veal sweetbreads with chopped carrot, hazelnuts and garlic, and an extra dessert based on 'easy peeler' citrus fruit with white chocolate and sea buckthorn. Don't miss the bread and butter, thick-sliced sourdough spread with beef dripping, served perhaps with a bowl of potato hash, and mushroom catsup made to a recipe by the Georgian cookery writer, Elizabeth Raffald.

Chef Adam Reid **Seats** 52 **Closed** Christmas, 2 weeks in August **Notes** No children under 8 years

Brasserie ABode

◉◉ EUROPEAN BRASSERIE **V**
0161 247 7744 | ABode Manchester, 107 Piccadilly, M1 2DB
www.abodemanchester.co.uk

Relaxed, all-day dining with a menu that features plats du jour with a comfortingly nostalgic nod and time-honoured classics. Generosity and value are at its heart whether it's Sunday lunch, classic dishes with plentiful sides or cocktails with a side serving of nibbles.

Chef Jamie Smith **Seats** 75, Private dining 24 **Open** All year **Notes** Children welcome

Chez Mal Brasserie

◉ MODERN BRITISH, INTERNATIONAL
0161 278 1000 | Piccadilly, M1 3AQ
www.malmaison.com

Plumb in the city centre, the interior of Chez Mal is boutiqued to the max, while cocktails and upscale brasserie food draw in the crowds. In the Smoak Bar Grill, the open-to-view kitchen produces surprising versions of modern comfort food.

Chef James Williams **Seats** 85, Private dining 18 **Open** All year **Notes** Vegetarian dishes, Children welcome

George's Dining Room & Bar

◉ MODERN BRITISH
0161 794 5444 | 17–21 Barton Road, Worsley, M28 2PD
www.georgesworsley.co.uk

The name of this gastropub pays homage to Victorian architect Sir George Gilbert Scott, but this place does not look backwards. The setting is stylish, with tan leather banquettes and neutral creamy hues, and the food is very much what you'd expect of a 21st-century kitchen.

Chef Joe McLeod **Seats** 140, Private dining 14 **Open** All year **Prices from** S £6.50, M £12.95, D £5.95 **Parking** 17 **Notes** Vegetarian dishes, Children welcome

Grafene

◉◉ MODERN BRITISH **V**
0161 696 9700 | 55 King Street, M2 4LQ
www.grafene.co.uk

Overlooking the busy city streets through full-length windows, Grafene features the produce of artisanal suppliers presented in a stylish space of industrial decor and exuberant colours. There's also a cocktail bar and an open pastry kitchen. The kitchen's broad-minded approach delivers lively modern ideas.

Chef Ben Mounsey

Greens

◉ MODERN VEGETARIAN **V**
0161 434 4259 | 43 Lapwing Lane, West Didsbury, M20 2NT
www.greensdidsbury.co.uk

TV chef Simon Rimmer's lively restaurant draws the crowds with exciting vegetarian cooking. Precisely flavoured cooking is the hallmark of the kitchen, with ideas picked up from around the globe in a menu that bursts with bright and appealing dishes.

Chef Simon Rimmer **Seats** 84 **Closed** 25–26 December and 1 January **Prices from** S £4.50, M £12.95, D £6 **Notes** Children welcome

Harvey Nichols Second Floor Bar and Brasserie

◉ MODERN INTERNATIONAL **NOTABLE WINE LIST**
0161 828 8898 | 21 New Cathedral Street, M1 1AD
www.harveynichols.com/manchester

Overlooking Exchange Square and the hustle and bustle of retail action in this central part of the city, the slick, contemporary second-floor brasserie provides a rather glamorous respite. An all-day menu means you can pop in for brunch and afternoon tea too.

Chef Matthew Horsfield **Seats** 140 **Closed** 25 December, 1 January and Easter Sunday **Prices from** S £6, M £12, D £6 **Notes** Vegetarian dishes, Children welcome

Hotel Gotham

◉◉ MODERN EUROPEAN
0161 413 0000 | 100 King Street, M2 4WU
www.hotelgotham.co.uk

The sleek art deco lines of a vintage bank building make a good setting for this hip restaurant in a glossy boutique hotel. Parquet floors, metal-topped tables and semi-circular windows all feed into the retro styling, while the menus are all about modern British combinations.

Chef Matthew Taylor **Open** All year **Notes** Vegetarian dishes, Children welcome

The Lowry Hotel
◉◉ CLASSIC, TRADITIONAL
0161 827 4000 | 50 Dearmans Place, Chapel Wharf,
Salford, M3 5LH
www.thelowryhotel.com

With floor-to-ceiling windows commanding
spectacular views over the canal and the Lowry
Bridge, The River Restaurant enjoys plenty of natural
light. The elegant surroundings are juxtaposed with
informal, chatty service.

Chef Andrew Green **Seats** 84, Private dining 24
Open All year **Prices from** S £7.50, M £16.50, D £7
Parking 88 **Notes** Vegetarian dishes, Children welcome

Mr Cooper's
◉◉ INTERNATIONAL
0161 235 4781 | The Midland Hotel, Peter Street,
M60 2DS
www.mrcoopers.co.uk

'Food for the flexitarian' is the stock-in-trade here,
another of the dining options in Manchester's
trendsetting Midland Hotel. The all-day cooking is
executed with great flair and attention to detail,
opening with a small plate section.

Chef Robert Taylor **Seats** 150 **Closed** 25–26
December and 1 January **Prices from** S £4.50,
M £9.50, D £6.50 **Notes** Vegetarian dishes,
Children welcome

See advertisement opposite

Sweet Mandarin
◉ CHINESE V
0161 832 8848 | 19 Copperas Street, M4 1HS
www.sweetmandarin.com

The Tse sisters, who run what has become one of the
most popular Chinese restaurants for miles around,
were awarded MBEs for their services to food in 2014.
It's relaxed and comfortable, where a mix of traditional
and less familiar Chinese dishes is offered.

Chef Lisa Tse **Seats** 85 **Closed** 25–26 December
Notes Children welcome

WOOD – Manchester
◉◉ MODERN BRITISH V
0161 236 5211 | Jack Rosenthal Street, First Street,
M15 4RA
www.woodmanchester.com

Dine out front by all means, although the main dining
space is inside, past the bar and the finishing kitchen.
Menu wording is economical: scallops, burnt
cauliflower and panch phoran (a sort of five-spice) is
an example. The chef here won the BBC's *Masterchef*
title in 2015.

Chef Simon Wood **Seats** 88, Private dining 22

Closed 25–26 December **Prices from** S £9.50, M £18,
D £7 **Notes** Children welcome

MANCHESTER AIRPORT
Best Western Plus Pinewood on Wilmslow
◉ MODERN, TRADITIONAL
01625 529211 | 180 Wilmslow Road, SK9 3LF
www.pinewood-hotel.co.uk

This good-looking red-brick hotel is home to the
thoroughly modern One Eighty restaurant, a sleek-
looking space with darkwood tables and fashionably
muted tones. The menu maintains the brasserie
attitude and reveals keen creativity in the kitchen.
There are sharing platters too.

Chef Colin Starkey **Seats** 80, Private dining **Open** All
year **Prices from** S £4, M £12.95, D £6.25 **Parking** 120
Notes Vegetarian dishes, Children welcome

OLDHAM
The Dining Room at The White Hart Inn
◉◉ MODERN BRITISH V
01457 872566 | 51 Stockport Road, Lydgate, OL4 4JJ
www.thewhitehart.co.uk

Following a full refurbishment, The Dining Room
restaurant is now the gastronomic centre of attention
inside this rambling village inn that overlooks
Manchester and the Cheshire plains. A seven-course
tasting option showcases the kitchen's expertise and
the seasonal menu.

Chef Mike Shaw **Seats** 50, Private dining 36
Closed 26 December and 1 January
Prices from S £8.50, M £18.50, D £7.50 **Parking** 75
Notes No children

ROCHDALE
Nutters
◉ MODERN BRITISH V 🍷 NOTABLE WINE LIST
01706 650167 | Edenfield Road, Norden, OL12 7TT
www.nuttersrestaurant.co.uk

Newly refurbished, this grand old house is run as a
family affair by the larger-than-life TV chef Andrew
Nutter and his parents. The menu takes a modern
British path, with plenty of flavours from Asia and
regional ingredients providing a sense of place.

Chef Andrew Nutter **Seats** 143, Private dining 100
Closed 1–2 days after both Christmas and New Year
Prices from S £5.40, M £20, D £5.40 **Parking** 100
Notes Children welcome

MR Cooper's

FOR INFORMATION OR TO BOOK
PLEASE CALL 0161 235 4781
OR VISIT WWW.MRCOOPERS.CO.UK

Mr Cooper's, The Midland Hotel,
Peter Street, Manchester, M60 2DS.
info@mrcoopers.co.uk 🐦 @MrCoopersMcr

WIGAN
Bennett's Restaurant
◉ MODERN INTERNATIONAL
01257 425803 | Moss Lane, Wrightington, WN6 9PB
www.bennettsrestaurant.com

This modern hotel is on the edge of Wigan within peaceful countryside. Bennett's Restaurant has a stylishly elegant look but a relaxed atmosphere and brisk young staff dispel any notion of formality. 'Lancashire Classics' are joined by a mix of the traditional and contemporary.

Chef Russel Norris **Seats** 75 **Closed** 25–26 December and 1 January **Parking** 220 **Notes** Vegetarian dishes, Children welcome

Riviera
◉ FRENCH, MEDITERRANEAN
01942 832895 | Haigh Hall Hotel, School Lane, Haigh, WN2 1PF
www.haighhallhotel.co.uk

A no-holds-barred refurb has overlaid the period magnificence of this Regency property with a touch of contemporary, boutique style. The restaurant fits the old-meets-new bill and has its heart in sunny Mediterranean dishes from France and Italy, taking top-class ingredients as the basis for uncomplicated, soundly executed dishes.

Chef Justin Williams **Open** All year **Notes** Vegetarian dishes

▶ HAMPSHIRE

ALRESFORD
Pulpo Negro
◉◉ MODERN SPANISH
01962 732262 | 28 Broad Street, SO24 9AQ
www.pulponegro.co.uk

Alresford – famous for its watercress, steam railway and clear-running chalk streams – has rather improbably added a sunny slice of the Med to its quintessentially English appeal with the arrival of Pulpo Negro. There's a smart-casual, modern feel-good vibe about the place.

Chef Andres Alemany **Seats** 40, Private dining 35 **Closed** 25–26 December, 1 January and Bank holidays **Notes** Vegetarian dishes, No children under 5 years

ALTON
The Anchor Inn
◉◉ MODERN, CLASSIC BRITISH
01420 23261 | Lower Froyle, GU34 4NA
www.anchorinnatlowerfroyle.co.uk

The 16th-century Anchor has all the elements of a traditional country inn down to its low beams, walls full of pictures and double-sided bar. It's a popular spot, attracting not just drinkers, but also takers for a wide-ranging menu displaying high levels of culinary skill.

Chef Josh Revis **Seats** 70, Private dining 24 **Open** All year **Prices from** S £6, M £12, D £6 **Parking** 30 **Notes** Vegetarian dishes, Children welcome

ANDOVER
Esseborne Manor
◉◉ MODERN BRITISH **V**
01264 736444 | Hurstbourne Tarrant, SP11 0ER
www.esseborne-manor.co.uk

In an Area of Outstanding Natural Beauty, Esseborne is a dignified Victorian country house where chef Dennis Janssen creates modern dishes that sparkle. It's not all whizz-bang, though, as there is evident classical thinking going on, and there's a tasting menu too.

Chef Dennis Janssen **Seats** 35, Private dining 80 **Open** All year **Prices from** S £6.50, M £14.50, D £6.50 **Parking** 40 **Notes** Children welcome

The George and Dragon
◉ BRITISH
01264 736277 | The Square, Hurstbourne Tarrant, SP11 0AA
www.georgeanddragon.com

Hurstbourne Tarrant now has its 16th-century coaching inn back, following its long and sympathetic renovation. Its light and airy, low-ceilinged spaces, bare tables and fires provide just the right setting for an essentially British menu of pub favourites and more innovative dishes.

Chef Paul Day **Seats** 65, Private dining 24 **Open** All year **Prices from** S £5.95, M £7.50, D £2.50 **Parking** 18 **Notes** Vegetarian dishes, Children welcome

BARTON-ON-SEA
Pebble Beach
◉ BRITISH, FRENCH, MEDITERRANEAN, SEAFOOD
01425 627777 | Marine Drive, BH25 7DZ
www.pebblebeach-uk.com

A clifftop perch gives this modern bar-brasserie a sweeping vista across Christchurch Bay to the Needles and the Isle of Wight. Inside is a buzzy split-level venue where high stools at the oyster bar allow views of the open-plan kitchen. An alfresco terrace is irresistible.

Chef Christian Rivron **Seats** 90, Private dining 8 **Open** All year **Prices from** S £7.20, M £14.95, D £7.95 **Parking** 20 **Notes** Vegetarian dishes, Children welcome

BASINGSTOKE
Audleys Wood Hotel
◉◉ MODERN BRITISH
01256 817555 | Alton Road, RG25 2JT
www.handpickedhotels.co.uk/thesimondsroom

This striking Victorian property stands in seven acres of grounds and woodland and has all the trappings of a luxury country-house hotel. The Conservatory Restaurant with its high vaulted ceiling and small minstrels' gallery has a seasonally changing menu.

Chef Gordon Neale Seats 55, Private dining 40 Open All year Parking 70 Notes Vegetarian dishes, Children welcome

Glasshouse Restaurant
◉◉ MODERN INTERNATIONAL V
01256 783350 | Oakley Hall, Rectory Road, Oakley, RG23 7EL
www.oakleyhall-park.com

Jane Austen enthusiasts will find references to Oakley Hall in her work. As a young woman, she was a frequent visitor. The new Glasshouse restaurant is the setting for classically based British menus that draw their raw materials from the kitchen garden.

Chef Salvatore Visaggio Seats 100, Private dining 300 Open All year Parking 100 Notes Children welcome

The Sun Inn
◉◉ MODERN CLASSIC
01256 397234 | Winchester Road A30, Dummer, RG25 2DJ
www.suninndummer.com

This popular, character gastro pub has a casual atmosphere and friendly service; modern British cuisine is given an inventive twist and dishes are presented with flair and exciting flavours. Posh pub classics are also available if you'd like to stay within your comfort zone.

Chef Gordon Stott Seats 44, Private dining 20 Closed 25 December Prices from S £5.50, M £11.95, D £6.25 Parking 20 Notes Vegetarian dishes, Children welcome

BAUGHURST
The Wellington Arms
◉◉ MODERN BRITISH
0118 982 0110 | Baughurst Road, RG26 5LP
www.thewellingtonarms.com

The Wellington Arms is a dining pub with a capital D. A good deal of what you eat will have found its way into the kitchen from the garden, and the rest won't have travelled very far. The old pub itself has scrubbed up nicely.

Chef Jason King Seats 40, Private dining 16 Open All year Parking 25 Notes Vegetarian dishes, Children welcome

BEAULIEU
The Master Builder's at Buckler's Hard
◉ MODERN BRITISH
01590 616253 | Buckler's Hard, SO42 7XB
www.themasterbuilders.co.uk

The master builder commemorated in the name of this rustic 18th-century hotel once built ships for Nelson's fleet on the grassy areas running down to the River Beaulieu. With those tranquil views as a backdrop, expect sound modern British cooking based on well-sourced local ingredients.

Chef Alicia Storey Seats Private dining 40 Open All year Parking 60 Notes Vegetarian dishes, Children welcome

The Montagu Arms Hotel
◉◉◉ MODERN EUROPEAN
01590 612324 | Palace Lane, SO42 7ZL
www.montaguarmshotel.co.uk

Named after the blue-blooded family who live across the river on the Beaulieu estate, the Montagu Arms sits in a prime New Forest spot. It's the quintessential wisteria-draped, 17th-century country hotel, and the sumptuous comforts within – including a spa and some seriously accomplished food courtesy of Matthew Tomkinson – do not disappoint. With its oak panels, linen-swathed tables and French windows opening onto a delicious garden, the Terrace Restaurant sets a suitably elegant tone for contemporary cooking shot through with uncommon culinary flair. Menus showcase fine ingredients from the New Forest, the south coast and the organic kitchen garden, opening with home-made black pudding with scallops, squid, crispy octopus and romesco sauce, then moving on to a main course of honey-roasted free-range duck breast, its richness balanced by the bitter note of caramelised endive tarte fine, celeriac purée, charred orange and lightly peppered sauce, or perhaps cod escalope with smoked chorizo, coco beans, salt-baked celeriac and lovage. To finish, there's a luscious combo of dark chocolate crémeux with stout ice cream, chocolate sable biscuit and blackcurrant sauce.

Chef Matthew Tomkinson Seats 60, Private dining 32 Open All year Prices from S £18, M £21, D £10 Parking 50 Notes Vegetarian dishes, No children under 12 years at dinner

HAMPSHIRE

Monty's Inn
⊛ TRADITIONAL BRITISH
01590 614986 | Palace Lane, SO42 7ZL
www.montaguarmshotel.co.uk
Specialising in hearty, unpretentious food that doesn't try to punch above its weight, Monty's Inn goes for a clubby look involving wood-panelled walls, wooden floors and unclothed tables – a posh country pub setting that opens with a home-made local pork Scotch egg.
Chef Robert McLean **Seats** 50 **Open** All year
Prices from S £6.95, M £13.95, D £6.50 **Parking** 40
Notes Vegetarian dishes, Children welcome

BRANSGORE
The Three Tuns
⊛ BRITISH, EUROPEAN
01425 672232 | Ringwood Road, BH23 8JH
www.threetunsinn.com
The picture-postcard 17th-century thatched inn deep in the New Forest is a delight in summer, festooned with flowers, and cosy in winter as blazing log fires warm the low beamed bar. The welcoming scene draws foodies and forest visitors for its charm and character.
Chef Colin Nash **Seats** 60, Private dining 50
Closed 25–26 and 31 December **Parking** 50
Notes Vegetarian dishes, Children welcome

BROCKENHURST
The Balmer Lawn Hotel
⊛⊛ MODERN BRITISH
01590 623116 | Lyndhurst Road, SO42 7ZB
www.balmerlawnhotel.com
This imposing pavilion-style Victorian hunting lodge in a charming New Forest setting does good business as a friendly, family-run operation with an excellent spa, sports and conference facilities. Expect modern cooking with prime-quality, often local, materials.
Chef Chris Wheeldon **Seats** 80, Private dining 100
Open All year **Prices from** S £7, M £18, D £7
Parking 100 **Notes** Vegetarian dishes, Children welcome

Cambium
⊛⊛⊛ MODERN BRITISH ⬩NOTABLE WINE LIST
01590 623551 | Careys Manor Hotel & SenSpa,
Lyndhurst Road, SO42 7RH
www.careysmanor.com/cambium
The Careys Manor Hotel is to be found in the New Forest, an environment its restaurant celebrates in every particular. Cambium is a technical botanical term for the inner tissue of plants or trees, and you only have to contemplate the decor, which incorporates leafy screens and a central bare-twigged tree with purple flowers stuck on it, to note the homage paid to the sylvan setting. Alastair Craig's cooking plays its

part too, with plates that look pretty and deliver convincing natural flavours. A starter serving of beef carpaccio dressed with capers and a soft quail egg is all about moistness and freshness, or there may be goats' cheese pannacotta garnished with cooked and raw garden beetroot. At main, roast venison haunch is sublimely pink and tender and comes with red cabbage and puréed swede, while plaice roasted on the bone is served in seaweed butter with crushed new potatoes and chard. Rhubarb parfait with gingery oat crunch and tonka bean ice cream is a dessert of pleasing textural contrasts, or there might be Baklava made with almonds and pistachios, with mascarpone ice cream.
Chef Alistair Craig **Seats** 94, Private dining 40
Open All year **Prices from** S £8, M £19, D £10
Parking 83 **Notes** Vegetarian dishes, No children under 8 years

THE PIG
⊛⊛ BRITISH V ⬩NOTABLE WINE LIST
01590 622354 | Beaulieu Road, SO42 7QL
www.thepighotel.com
This is a restaurant for our times, with cocktails served in jam jars and massages available in the old potting shed. Here in the wilds of the New Forest, the passion is for home-grown and foraged ingredients. It's a buzzy place with a retro interior.
Chef James Golding **Seats** 95, Private dining 14
Open All year **Parking** 40 **Notes** Children welcome

Rhinefield House Hotel
⊛⊛ CLASSIC, TRADITIONAL BRITISH V
01590 622922 | Rhinefield Road, SO42 7QB
www.handpickedhotels.co.uk/rhinefieldhouse
The present house sprang up in the late Victorian era. A Tudor-Gothic hybrid architecturally, the interiors are awash with finely crafted mouldings, copperwork, and beautiful examples of the lavatorialist's art, and a room modelled on the Alhambra.
Chef James Verity **Seats** 58, Private dining 20
Open All year **Prices from** S £8.50, M £22, D £8.50
Parking 150 **Notes** Children welcome

The Zen Garden Restaurant
⊛ THAI
01590 623219 | The SenSpa, Careys Manor Hotel,
Lyndhurst Road, SO42 7RH
www.careysmanor.com/zen-garden.html
Within the SenSpa at Careys Manor Hotel in the New Forest is a smart Thai eatery with its gold columns, bamboo ceiling and darkwood tables and chairs. Classic tom yam soup kick-starts the palate and proceedings end with a sharp, cleansing dessert of pineapple carpaccio.

Chef Thosporn Wongsasube **Seats** 50, Private dining 14 **Open** All year **Prices from** S £6.95, M £9.75, D £6.70 **Parking** 130 **Notes** Vegetarian dishes, No children

BROOK
The Bell Inn
MODERN BRITISH
023 8081 2214 | SO43 7HE
www.bellinn-newforest.co.uk
The Bell is in a picturesque New Forest village not far from Lyndhurst, and is more than a simple country inn: it has a pair of golf courses. The interior has blackboard menus, fires in winter, and plenty of gracefully presented local produce on offer.
Chef Mark Young **Seats** 60, Private dining 50 **Open** All year **Prices from** S £6.50, M £12.50, D £6 **Parking** 40 **Notes** Vegetarian dishes, Children welcome

BURLEY
Burley Manor
BRITISH, MEDITERRANEAN **V**
01425 403522 | Ringwood Road, BH24 4BS
www.burleymanor.com
Burley Manor was built in 1852 by a magistrate and custodian of the surrounding New Forest. A hotel since the 1930s and refurbished in 2015, this grand former home enjoys fabulous parkland views and a peaceful patio. In the restaurant, the menu has Mediterranean influences.
Chef Ben Johnson **Open** All year **Notes** Vegetarian dishes, No children under 13 years

Moorhill House Hotel
MODERN, TRADITIONAL BRITISH
01425 403285 | BH24 4AG
www.newforesthotels.co.uk
Deep in the ancient woodland of the New Forest, near the pretty village of Burley, this hotel sits in handsome gardens and is done out in light, attractive country-house style within, with log fires in winter. In the elegant dining room, straightforward, well-executed British dishes are served.
Chef Jonathan Davey **Seats** 60, Private dining 40 **Open** All year **Parking** 50 **Notes** Vegetarian dishes, Children welcome

CADNAM
Bartley Lodge Hotel
MODERN BRITISH
023 8081 2248 | Lyndhurst Road, SO40 2NR
www.newforesthotels.co.uk
In eight delightful Hampshire acres, the Grade II listed, 18th-century Bartley Lodge boasts many original

features. A 'flexible dining' approach means the menu is available throughout the hotel, including in the Crystal Restaurant, with its elegant centrepiece chandelier and delicate blue and gold colour scheme.
Chef Lee Wheeler **Seats** 60, Private dining 90 **Open** All year **Parking** 90 **Notes** Vegetarian dishes, Children welcome

DOGMERSFIELD
Four Seasons Hotel Hampshire
BRITISH **V**
01252 853000 | Dogmersfield Park, Chalky Lane, RG27 8TD
www.fourseasons.com/hampshire
Set within the expansive acreages of the Dogmersfield Estate, the Four Seasons' dining options include a bistro and café, but the main event is the Wild Carrot restaurant, a light-filled dining space with French windows and a view to the countryside beyond.
Chef Dirk Gieselmann, Adam Fargin **Seats** 100, Private dining 24 **Parking** 100 **Notes** No children under 8 years at dinner

DROXFORD
Bakers Arms
MODERN BRITISH
01489 877533 | High Street, SO32 3PA
www.thebakersarmsdroxford.com
The Bakers Arms is a whitewashed pub with a warmly welcoming atmosphere generated by hands-on young staff, an open fire and ceiling beams. The regularly changing menu (with favourites like sausage and mash remaining constant) concentrates on great British traditions with forays further afield.
Chef Adam Cordery, Kieron Rushworth **Seats** 45 **Open** All year **Prices from** S £6, M £11, D £6.50 **Parking** 30 **Notes** Vegetarian dishes, Children welcome

EMSWORTH
Fat Olives
MODERN BRITISH, MEDITERRANEAN
01243 377914 | 30 South Street, PO10 7EH
www.fatolives.co.uk
A 17th-century fishermen's cottage just a few steps from the quayside of pretty Emsworth harbour provides the setting for Lawrence and Julia Murphy's smart brasserie. The stripped-out interior of cream walls, wooden floors and unclothed tables is as unvarnished and honest as the food.
Chef Lawrence Murphy **Seats** 25 **Closed** 1 week Christmas and 2 weeks in June **Prices from** S £6.95, M £15.95, D £6.95 **Notes** Vegetarian dishes. No children under 8, no age restriction Saturday lunch

36 on the Quay
◉◉◉ MODERN BRITISH, EUROPEAN
01243 375592 | 47 South Street, PO10 7EG
www.36onthequay.co.uk
This well-known and long-running restaurant with rooms has a wonderful setting, in a 17th-century building right on the harbour in this lovely little fishing village. It's a great place to watch the sun go down – have a drink outside in the courtyard before heading in to the bright, airy dining room. The menu is quite traditional, with interesting contemporary interpretations of classic dishes and flavour combinations, and tasting menus are available at both lunch and dinner. A neatly presented starter of roast veal sweetbread comes with salt-baked celeriac, charred salsify, milk crumble and elderflower gel; or you might try the smoked eel with hazelnut and eel mousse with apple terrine, potato and eel croquette, and apple and eel sauce. A main course could be chalk stream trout with Cornish crab, Asian celery, roasted sprouts, seaweed crisp and dashi broth, or loin of South Downs vension with apple and beetroot relish, Magalitza black pudding and wild mushrooms. Muscovado and raspberry cannelloni with crème pâtissière, iced raspberry mousse and sour chocolate sticks is a great dessert – stylish and well conceived.
Chef Gary Pearce, Martyna Mysliwska-Pearce **Seats** 45, Private dining 12 **Closed** 1st 2/3 weeks January, 1 week end May, 1 week end October, 25–26 December **Notes** Vegetarian dishes, Children welcome

FAREHAM
Solent Hotel & Spa
◉ MODERN BRITISH, EUROPEAN, INTERNATIONAL
01489 880000 | Rookery Avenue, Whiteley, PO15 7AJ
www.thwaites.co.uk
This contemporary spa hotel in Whiteley near Fareham is fine-tooled for relaxation, whether your preferred element be pool, massage table or dining room. The cooking takes a brasserie approach, with international classics, pasta dishes, steaks from the chargrill, and seasonal daily specials.
Chef Peter Williams **Seats** 130, Private dining 40 **Open** All year **Prices from** S £6.50, M £14.50, D £3.95 **Parking** 200 **Notes** Vegetarian dishes, Children welcome

FARNBOROUGH
Aviator
◉◉ MODERN INTERNATIONAL **V**
01252 555890 | Farnborough Road, GU14 6EL
www.aviatorbytag.com
The TAG timepiece manufacturer's aviation-themed hotel has landed on the Hampshire-Surrey border, in the vicinity of the celebrated air show at Farnborough. The uncomplicated modern brasserie food is centred on a repertoire of classic cuts of steak, done on the charcoal grill.
Seats 120, Private dining 8 **Open** All year **Parking** 169 **Notes** Children welcome

HAMBLE-LE-RICE
The Bugle
◉ MODERN BRITISH
023 8045 3000 | High Street, SO31 4HA
www.buglehamble.co.uk
The Bugle's restored interiors with their solid brickwork, bare floorboards, low ceilings and beams are exactly what a country inn should look like, while the kitchen offers a clever mix of pub stalwarts and modern dishes. Fish and chips, roasts and sandwiches keep traditionalists happy.
Chef James Harrison **Seats** 28, Private dining 12 **Closed** 25 December **Notes** Vegetarian dishes, Children welcome

HAYLING ISLAND
Langstone Hotel
◉◉ MODERN BRITISH
023 9246 5011 | Northney Road, PO11 0NQ
www.langstonehotel.co.uk
A contemporary hotel on the north shore of Hayling Island enjoying sweeping views towards Chichester Harbour. There is brasserie cooking of real flair here. A speciality steak menu woos traditionalists, with fairground treats such as peanut parfait covered in popcorn and chocolate peanuts to finish.
Chef James Parsons **Seats** 120, Private dining 120 **Open** All year **Prices from** S £6, M £14, D £7 **Parking** 220 **Notes** Vegetarian dishes, Children welcome

HIGHCLERE
The Yew Tree
◉◉ MODERN BRITISH
01635 253360 | Hollington Cross, RG20 9SE
www.theyewtree.co.uk
A classic English country inn in a ravishing setting near Highclere Castle. Traditional English cooking is the order of the day, overlaid with modern flourishes. A list of 'The Usual Suspects' keeps the fish and chips and burger brigade content.
Chef Simon Davis **Seats** 68, Private dining 12 **Open** All year **Parking** 30 **Notes** Vegetarian dishes, Children welcome

HURSLEY
The King's Head
⊛ CLASSIC BRITISH
01962 775208 | Main Road, SO21 2JW
www.kingsheadhursley.co.uk

An ivy-clad Georgian inn at the heart of a village community near Winchester, The King's Head has a lightly worn touch of refinement, with candlesticks on wooden tables, equestrian prints, tartan banquette, and a menu of sound, regionally based cooking.

Chef Larry Pender **Open** All year **Notes** Vegetarian dishes, Children welcome

LYMINGTON
The Elderflower Restaurant
⊛⊛⊛ MODERN BRITISH, FRENCH
01590 676908 | 4A Quay Street, SO41 3AS
www.elderflowerrestaurant.co.uk

A Grade II listed building on a cobbled street close to the quayside is home to Andrew and Marjolaine Du Bourg's restaurant, where regional produce is centre stage. The antiquity of the building is evident through the old beams, but there is a contemporary neutrality to the interior, a confident charm that is matched by the output from Andrew's kitchen. Both the couple have experience in top-end addresses. Andrew is from Yorkshire (via South Africa) and Marjolaine hails from western France, and you may well notice evidence of this happy alliance on the menu, alongside a genuine creative streak. Via à la carte and two tasting menu options, expect winning flavour combinations such as wild nettle and dock leaf velouté, with braised Hereford snails and crispy bacon followed by crab lasagne with a delicious lobster bisque, or a celebration of Keyhaven lamb, with anchovy and celeriac purée and nori seaweed. Finish with lemon meringue soufflé with bouquet garni ice cream.

Chef Andrew Du Bourg **Seats** 40 **Open** All year **Prices from** S £8.50, M £23, D £8.50 **Notes** Vegetarian dishes, No children

The Mayflower
⊛ MODERN BRITISH
01590 672160 | King's Saltern Road, SO41 3QD
www.themayflowerlymington.co.uk

The first radio signal was transmitted to the Isle of Wight from the beacon ship after which this coastal pub is named. That nautical history is honoured in the design theming in the present-day restaurant, where seashells and ships' accoutrements abound.

Chef Edward Cracknell **Seats** Private dining 25 **Open** All year **Parking** 30 **Notes** Vegetarian dishes, Children welcome

Stanwell House Hotel
⊛⊛ MODERN BRITISH, EUROPEAN
01590 677123 | 14–15 High Street, SO41 9AA
www.stanwellhouse.com

'Tin' (and other metals) give the recently relaunched Etain restaurant its main theme, as it celebrates a decade of service. The contemporary style and cool pale colours set the scene for a seasonally changing menu with a good wine list.

Chef Matt Noonan **Seats** 70, Private dining 18 **Open** All year **Notes** Vegetarian dishes, Children welcome

LYNDHURST
The Crown Manor House Hotel
⊛⊛ MODERN BRITISH
023 8028 2922 | High Street, SO43 7NF
www.crownhotel-lyndhurst.co.uk

The fireplace just inside the entrance once provided instant defrosting for travellers who had braved the horse-drawn carriage transfer from the railway station. Such is the Crown's history, which extends from 15th-century beginnings to a late Victorian makeover, its panelled dining room a refreshing space today for contemporary brasserie cooking.

Chef Oli Richings **Seats** 60, Private dining 120 **Open** All year **Parking** 60 **Notes** Vegetarian dishes, Children welcome

Glasshouse Brasserie & Bar
⊛⊛ MODERN BRITISH
023 8028 6129 | BW Forest Lodge Hotel, Pikes Hill, Romsey Road, SO43 7AS
www.newforesthotels.co.uk/forest-lodge-hotel

On the outskirts of Lyndhurst, this hotel has had a thorough makeover, creating a hugely stylish environment. The menu covers a lot of ground, from burgers and light bites to a well-conceived starter of quail three ways (poached breast, confit leg and a Scotch egg).

Chef Alex Rodham **Seats** 60, Private dining 10 **Open** All year **Prices from** S £6, M £14, D £6 **Parking** 60 **Notes** Vegetarian dishes, Children welcome

Hartnett Holder & Co
⊛⊛⊛ ITALIAN V ⚑ NOTABLE WINE LIST
See page 136

HAMPSHIRE

LYNDHURST
Hartnett Holder & Co
◉◉◉ ITALIAN **V** ◣NOTABLE WINE LIST

023 8028 7177 | Lime Wood, Beaulieu Road, SO43 7FZ
www.limewood.co.uk

Refined Italian food and New Forest wellness

Lime Wood counts itself a 'wellness retreat', furnishing Thai-style spa facilities, fitness programmes and a technogym that looks out over the New Forest. The kitchen is in the hands of Luke Holder, and overseen by Italian food superstar Angela Hartnett. The seasonal menus work indeed to an Italian template, with antipasti and primi before the main course, and a wealth of respectfully treated natural ingredients running through them. A serving of Cornish crab with smoked eel, radish and apple is the perfect palate-primer for a pasta dish such as guinea fowl agnolotti with lardo di Colonnata, onion and sage. At main, there could be a copiously crammed fish stew incorporating monkfish, red mullet, langoustines and scallops. A fragrant dessert such as saffron pannacotta with rosewater and pistachios, or chocolate-orange tart with blood orange sorbet, make for memorable closing notes. The well-chosen wines include an inspired selection by the glass.

Chef Angela Hartnett, Luke Holder **Seats** 70, Private dining 16 **Open** All year
Prices from S £8.50, M £18, D £7 **Parking** 90 **Notes** Children welcome

MILFORD ON SEA
Verveine Fishmarket Restaurant
◉◉ MODERN SEAFOOD
01590 642176 | 98 High Street, SO41 0QE
www.verveine.co.uk

At the back of the fishmongers is the intimate, elegant dining room, reached by passing the kitchen, from which chef himself often emerges to bring your dish to table. Monkfish given the Madras treatment arrives with spiced carrot purée, plump raisins and sous-vide potato.

Chef David Wykes **Seats** 32 **Closed** 25 December to 18 January **Prices from** S £11.50, M £21, D £8.75 **Notes** Vegetarian dishes, No children under 8 years at dinner

NEW MILTON
The Dining Room
◉◉ MODERN BRITISH V ♦ NOTABLE WINE LIST
01425 282212 | Chewton Glen, Christchurch Road, BH25 6QS
www.chewtonglen.com

Whether you are drawn by the desire to play golf, or prefer being pampered in the spa, Chewton Glen is a luxurious bolt-hole. The menu aims to satisfy with an output that deals in classic British and European combinations, while incorporating some global flavours.

Chef Simon Addison **Seats** 164, Private dining 70 **Open** All year **Prices from** S £9, M £22, D £12 **Parking** 150 **Notes** Children welcome

See advertisement on page 138

The Kitchen
◉ ITALIAN, AMERICAN
01425 282212 | Chewton Glen, Christchurch Road, BH25 6QS
www.chewtonglen.com/thekitchen

Staff are friendly and service is polished at this modern venue, purpose-built as a restaurant and cookery school. Take a seat in one of the deep burgundy leather chairs or banquettes at copper-topped tables and peruse the menu of crowd-pleasing dishes.

Chef James Martin, Adam Hart **Seats** 50, Private dining 12 **Open** All year **Prices from** S £5, M £10, D £7 **Parking** 40 **Notes** Vegetarian dishes, Children welcome

NORTHINGTON
The Woolpack Inn
◉ CLASSIC BRITISH
01962 734184 | Totford, SO24 9TJ
www.thewoolpackinn.co.uk

In a tiny hamlet within the pretty Candover Valley, this Grade I listed flint-and-brick inn has retained its traditional country pub feel with open fires, flagstoned floors and real ales, although the emphasis is on food, a combination of pub grub and European influences.

Chef Alan Kaye **Seats** 50, Private dining 14 **Open** All year **Parking** 40 **Notes** Vegetarian dishes, Children welcome

OLD BURGHCLERE
The Dew Pond Restaurant
◉ BRITISH, EUROPEAN
01635 278408 | RG20 9LH
www.dewpond.co.uk

The Dew Pond was once a pair of 16th-century drovers' cottages, now welded into a very chic, pastel-hued country restaurant, not far from Highclere Castle (Downton Abbey). Cooking is founded on classical principles with the sort of personal overlay that has won many local devotees.

Chef Keith Marshall **Seats** 45, Private dining 30 **Closed** 2 weeks Christmas and New Year, 2 weeks August **Parking** 20 **Notes** Vegetarian dishes, Children welcome

OTTERBOURNE
The White Horse
◉ MODERN, TRADITIONAL BRITISH
01962 712830 | Main Road, SO21 2EQ
www.whitehorseotterbourne.co.uk

Descending from a hike along the spine of the South Downs, you couldn't ask for a more fortifying pitstop. This village hostelry looks every inch the modern dining pub with wooden and quarry-tiled floors, bare beams and mismatched tables. The mood is unbuttoned and family-friendly.

Chef Lucia Bozoganova **Seats** 90 **Open** All year **Prices from** S £6, M £11, D £5.75 **Parking** 25 **Notes** Vegetarian dishes, Children welcome

PETERSFIELD
JSW
◉◉◉ MODERN BRITISH V ♦ NOTABLE WINE LIST
01730 262030 | 20 Dragon Street, GU31 4JJ
www.jswrestaurant.com

Jake Saul Watkins has been cooking here in Petersfield for nearly 20 years, more than half of that time at this beautiful 17th-century former coaching inn. The pale, neutral colour palette in the dining room draws attention to the wealth of ancient beams above, and there's plenty of space for the smartly dressed tables. Everything's made in-house, from breads and ice cream to canapés, terrines and chocolates. JSW himself is a passionate advocate for allowing brilliant ingredients to speak for themselves, and dishes are carefully considered and precisely constructed. There's a choice of tasting menus, or you

CHEWTON GLEN
HAMPSHIRE

An English Original...

At Chewton Glen we are fortunate enough to have two fantastic dining options, The Dining Room and The Kitchen.

The Dining Room, is a truly cosmopolitan and quintessentially English restaurant. Offering a nexus of beautiful conservatories, intimate dining spaces and a stunning open wine room, The Dining Room is as formal or relaxed as the mood takes you. An open format grill menu has been carefully created for you to enjoy old Chewton Glen favourites as well as innovative creations from our present kitchen brigade.

The Kitchen, is a purpose-built cookery school and relaxed dining space for enjoying and learning about food. An informal dining experience with an open plan layout offers you the chance to watch the Chefs at work. The a la carte menu features wood-fired pizzas, gourmet burgers, superfood salads and much more.

Call 01425 282212 or email reservations@chewtonglen.com to book your table...

Chewton Glen | New Forest | Hampshire | BH25 6QS
chewtonglen.com

RELAIS &
CHATEAUX

PETERSFIELD continued

can stick with the carte – there's also a veggie menu. Maybe start with smoked mackerel, roots, brassicas and burnt hay oil, or scallops, spiced mussels, razor clams and ruby pearls – seafood is a particular strength. Main courses might include South Downs lamb three ways, accompanied by burnt hispi and winter veg, and the wonderful 72-hour beef cheeks with hops, marrow, dripping and chips. The blackberry, apple and cinnamon jammy dodger is a fun dessert, or try the honeycomb parfait with Valrhona ganache and raspberry.

Chef Jake Watkins **Seats** 58, Private dining 18 **Closed** 2 weeks in January, April and August **Parking** 19 **Notes** No children under 6 years

The Thomas Lord
◉ MODERN BRITISH
01730 829244 | High Street, West Meon, GU32 1LN
www.thethomaslord.co.uk

A proper pub with fine local ales, the Thomas Lord has a shabby-chic charm, kitted out with rustic pine tables, well-worn oak parquet floors, and church pews. Everything is made in-house, the garden supplies seasonal goodies, while others come from small-scale local producers.

Chef Joel Massey **Seats** 70 **Open** All year **Parking** 20 **Notes** Vegetarian dishes, Children welcome

PORTSMOUTH
Restaurant 27
◉◉ MODERN EUROPEAN V
023 9287 6272 | 27a South Parade, PO5 2JF
www.restaurant27.com

The whitewashed building may look like a storage-shed, but inside is a smartly appointed dining room where chef-proprietor Kevin Bingham runs a fixed-price carte or six-course tasting menus that showcase the kitchen's abilities. Flavours are captivating: 'umami duck' is juxtaposed with Ibérico chorizo and feta.

Chef Kevin Bingham, Annie Martin-Smith **Seats** 34 **Closed** Christmas and New Year **Notes** Children welcome

ROMSEY
The Three Tuns
◉ MODERN BRITISH
01794 512639 | 58 Middlebridge Street, SO51 8HL
www.the3tunsromsey.co.uk

Sympathetically remodelled, The Three Tuns retains its olden-times charm, with winter fires, exposed brickwork, and stuffed birds in glass cases. An extensive menu of pub classics aims to please all

comers. Meaty things are dependably satisfying but if it's fish you're after try devilled whitebait.

Chef Rob Price, Lee Burden **Seats** 35 **Closed** 25 December **Prices from** S £5.95, M £12.50, D £3.50 **Parking** 14 **Notes** Vegetarian dishes, Children welcome

The White Horse Hotel & Brasserie
◉◉ MODERN BRITISH
01794 512431 | 19 Market Place, SO51 8ZJ
www.thewhitehorseromsey.co.uk

This gleaming white Georgian hotel is where the future prime minister Lord Palmerston first cut his teeth in political debate. It now houses a very sleek contemporary Brasserie, with laminate floor and full-drop windows all around, where locally sourced modern British cooking is the main draw.

Chef Nick O'Halloran **Seats** 85, Private dining 100 **Open** All year **Prices from** S £7.50, M £14, D £7 **Notes** Vegetarian dishes, Children welcome

See advertisement on page 140

ROTHERWICK
The Oak Room Restaurant
◉◉ BRITISH, FRENCH V
01256 764881 | Tylney Hall Hotel, Ridge Lane, RG27 9AZ
www.tylneyhall.co.uk

Tylney Hall is the place for classical country-house dining, and the Oak Room Restaurant delivers the goods in a setting involving oak panels, a domed ceiling and a tinkling grand piano. What arrives on the plate is a gently updated take on the classics.

Chef Mike Lloyd **Seats** 80, Private dining 120 **Open** All year **Parking** 150 **Notes** Children welcome

ST MARY BOURNE
Bourne Valley Inn
◉ BRITISH
01264 738361 | SP11 6BT
www.bournevalleyinn.com

Known as BVI to its friends, this village pub has become a magnet for foodies, with its main dining area in a converted barn with beams and a rustic-chic look. The menu presses the comfort button with a mix of pub classics and down-to-earth cooking.

Chef Ryan Stacey **Seats** 100, Private dining 18 **Open** All year **Notes** Vegetarian dishes, Children welcome

"*Small things make perfection but perfection is no small thing*"

Sir Henry Royce

Set in the heart of Romsey, The White Horse has been a coaching inn for almost 600 years.

The 2 AA rosette awarded Brasserie & Grill is a wonderful place to enjoy every occasion from a romantic dinner for two to a robust family lunch, during the summer months the courtyard offers a perfect retreat for al fresco dining.

01794 512431
www.thewhitehorseromsey.com

SOUTHAMPTON
The Jetty
◉◉ MODERN
0238 110 3456 | 5 Maritime Walk, Ocean Village, SO14 3QT
www.southampton-harbour-hotel.co.uk

The Jetty is part of the rather spectacular Southampton Harbour Hotel and enjoys panoramic views across Ocean Village Marina. There's a terrace for outdoor dining, surrounded by sunshine and yachts. It's chic and elegant, with a bright airy feel and turquoise and yellow highlights.

Chef Alex Aitken **Open** All year

STOCKBRIDGE
The Greyhound on the Test
◉◉ MODERN BRITISH
01264 810833 | 31 High Street, SO20 6EY
www.thegreyhoundonthetest.co.uk

The Greyhound has no shortage of appeal, from upmarket, sumptuous bedrooms to a restaurant with that opened-up, country-chic vibe. The menu is a thoroughly up-to-date affair with regional produce at its heart. You're sure to go home happy after dark chocolate brownie with chocolate mousse.

Chef Chris Heather **Seats** 60, Private dining 16 **Closed** 25–26 December **Prices from** S £8.95, M £15.25, D £4 **Parking** 20 **Notes** Vegetarian dishes, Children welcome

The Peat Spade Inn
◉ MODERN BRITISH
01264 810612 | Village Street, Longstock, SO20 6DR
www.peatspadeinn.co.uk

A stolid-looking red-brick country inn where close-set tables add to the dining-room buzz. Rustic cooking with more than a soupçon of French influence proves abidingly popular, seen in the form of fried chicken livers on sourdough toast with charred sweetcorn in peppercorn sauce.

Chef Paul Dive **Seats** 53, Private dining 16 **Open** All year **Parking** 19 **Notes** Vegetarian dishes, Children welcome

The Three Cups Inn
◉ MODERN & TRADITIONAL BRITISH
01264 810527 | High Street, SO20 6HB
www.the3cups.co.uk

This 16th-century coaching inn is still very much a pub offering local ales, but it's also a dining destination with low-ceilinged dining room and an orangery extension opening up to the garden. The kitchen makes good use of local foodstuffs. There are bedrooms, too.

Chef Sebastian Edwards Smith **Seats** 50, Private dining 20 **Closed** 25–26 December **Parking** 15 **Notes** Vegetarian dishes, Children welcome

WINCHESTER
Avenue Restaurant at Lainston House Hotel
@@@ MODERN BRITISH **V** ♦ NOTABLE WINE LIST
01962 776088 | Woodman Lane, Sparsholt, SO21 2LT
www.lainstonhouse.com

The imposing red-brick manor house is of 17th-century vintage, with an avenue of mature lime trees leading to it. It's that arboreal feature that is referenced in the name of the dignified dining room, where varnished oak panels set with contemporary wall lights, a marble fireplace and simple modern table settings establish the mood. Open-air dining on the terrace will coax the sun-lovers out. A drink in the book-lined Cedar Bar sets the right tone for Andrew Birch's ingredient-focused cooking, served in straightforward, up-to-date dishes that fit the country-house ethos like a glove. An appetiser of densely rich crab mousse with crispy seaweed prepares the palate for a starter such as Orkney scallops with chicken wings, celeriac purée and watercress, strongly scented with truffle. Main could be a tasting plate of Mangalitsa pork cuts, the succulent belly topped with apple and pickled cabbage, with a muted aromatic note from juniper, or sea bass and Ibérico ham with pickled onion, sauced in red wine. A finale such as lemon parfait with meringue in warm griotte cherry sauce is a bold closing statement.

Chef Andrew Birch **Seats** 60, Private dining 120 **Closed** 25–26 December **Parking** 100 **Notes** Children welcome

The Black Rat
@@ MODERN BRITISH
01962 844465 | 88 Chesil Street, SO23 0HX
www.theblackrat.co.uk

In an inconspicuous white-fronted former pub on the edge of town, The Black Rat sets its sights firmly on culinary modernism. Lots of good technical skills and techniques – good flavours and consistency across all dishes and efficient service to boot.

Chef John Marsden-Jones **Seats** 40, Private dining 16 **Closed** Christmas and New Year **Prices from** S £9, M £19, D £7.50 **Notes** Vegetarian dishes, No children under 12 years at dinner

The Chesil Rectory
@@ FRENCH
01962 851555 | 1 Chesil Street, SO23 0HU
www.chesilrectory.co.uk

A beautiful half-timbered building dating from 1450, The Chesil Rectory is the oldest house in Winchester. Enter through a low door to be greeted by a brilliantly preserved interior with low beams, charming inglenook fireplaces and exposed brickwork. The kitchen puts a gently modernised spin on classic French dishes.

Chef Damian Brown **Seats** 75, Private dining 14 **Closed** 25 December and 1 January **Prices from** S £6.95, M £13.95, D £7.50 **Notes** Vegetarian dishes, No children under 10 years at dinner

Holiday Inn Winchester
@@ MODERN BRITISH
01962 670700 | Telegraph Way, Morn Hill, SO21 1HZ
www.hiwinchester.co.uk

On the edge of the South Downs National Park, the restaurant at this large purpose-built hotel goes to great lengths to source local produce. The high culinary standards elevate the cooking well above that you might normally see in hotel chains.

Chef Chris Keel **Seats** 128, Private dining 200 **Open** All year **Prices from** S £7, M £15, D £5 **Parking** 170 **Notes** Vegetarian dishes, Children welcome

Marwell Hotel
@@ MODERN EUROPEAN
01962 777681 | Thompsons Lane, Colden Common, Marwell, SO21 1JY
www.marwellhotel.co.uk

A pastoral retreat in the manner of an African safari lodge, Marwell is set in wooded grounds next door to a wildlife park, so the odd screech of a monkey is to be expected. The kitchen applies modern styling to mostly traditional dishes.

Chef Phil Yeomans **Seats** 60, Private dining 120 **Closed** 24–26 December **Parking** 100 **Notes** Vegetarian dishes, Children welcome

Running Horse Inn
@@ CLASSIC BRITISH
01962 880218 | 88 Main Road, Littleton, SO22 6QS
www.runninghorseinn.co.uk

The Running Horse is a revitalised village inn with a relaxed and informal dining environment: a wood-burning stove in a brick fireplace, some banquette seating and wooden tables. The kitchen delivers stimulating full-flavoured dishes.

Chef Simon James Lawrence **Seats** 60 **Open** All year **Prices from** S £6, M £13.50, D £5 **Parking** 40 **Notes** Vegetarian dishes, Children welcome

The Wykeham Arms

◉◉ MODERN BRITISH

01962 853834 | 75 Kingsgate Street, SO23 9PE

www.wykehamarmswinchester.co.uk

A coaching inn since the mid-1700s, The Wykeham Arms offers simple options, listed as 'Home Comforts' on the menu, but this is a kitchen that can turn out a starter as fashionable as boneless chicken wings with BBQ emulsion and blue cheese sauce.

Chef Allen Sorrell **Seats** 90, Private dining 25 **Open** All year **Notes** Vegetarian dishes, No children

WOODLANDS

Woodlands Lodge Hotel

◉ MODERN BRITISH

023 8029 2257 | Bartley Road, Woodlands, SO40 7GN

www.woodlands-lodge.co.uk

When we say this hotel is 'in the New Forest', we mean it. The ancient woodland can be accessed directly from the Lodge's gardens, making it the perfect spot for a walking break. Hunters restaurant serves capably rendered modern British dishes with plenty of verve.

Chef Andrew Smith **Seats** 30, Private dining 35 **Open** All year **Prices from** S £5.50, M £14, D £5.50 **Parking** 80 **Notes** Vegetarian dishes, Children welcome

▶ HEREFORDSHIRE

AYMESTREY

The Riverside at Aymestrey

◉◉ CLASSIC BRITISH

01568 708440 | The Riverside Inn, HR6 9ST

www.riversideaymestrey.co.uk

Close to Ludlow and Hereford on the edge of Mortimer Forest, this 16th-century black and white timber-framed inn features a kitchen that is serious about its food, with produce from their own garden. The menu changes daily and dishes are simple and honest.

Chef Andy Link **Seats** 60, Private dining 40 **Open** All year **Prices from** S £5.75, M £13.50, D £6.50 **Parking** 20 **Notes** Vegetarian dishes, Children welcome

EWYAS HAROLD

The Temple Bar Inn

◉◉ MODERN BRITISH

01981 240423 | HR2 0EU

www.thetemplebarinn.co.uk

Still a proper pub complete with a pool table, well-kept real ales, oak beams, flagstones and a blazing fire, this is an inviting spot with a friendly atmosphere and accomplished cooking. End with fig cake with a brandy snap and vanilla ice cream.

Chef Phillippa Jinman, Jo Pewsey, Aaron King **Seats** 30, Private dining 45 **Closed** 25 December, 1 week January to February and 1 week in November **Prices from** S £5, M £12, D £6 **Parking** 12 **Notes** Vegetarian dishes, Children welcome

LEDBURY

Feathers Hotel

◉ MODERN BRITISH

01531 635266 | High Street, HR8 1DS

www.feathers-ledbury.co.uk

The heavily timbered Feathers is a wonderful slice of Tudor England, its oak-panelled venerability thrown into relief by a modern brasserie named after the hop variety Fuggles, and an upmarket dining room, Quills. Sirloins and fillets of local beef are a big draw.

Chef Susan Isaacs **Seats** 55, Private dining 60 **Open** All year **Parking** 30 **Notes** Vegetarian dishes, Children welcome

LEINTWARDINE

The Lion

◉ MODERN BRITISH

01547 540203 | High Street, SY7 0JZ

www.thelionleintwardine.co.uk

Keen anglers will appreciate this village pub on the upper Teme, where trout and grayling are abundant. Others will just love the authentic air of a country inn, where the old beams and inviting leather sofas play their homely part.

Chef Paul Halmshaw **Seats** 50, Private dining 20 **Closed** 25 December **Prices from** S £5, M £11 **Parking** 20 **Notes** Vegetarian dishes, Children welcome

ROSS-ON-WYE

The Chase Hotel

◉ MODERN EUROPEAN

01989 763161 | Gloucester Road, HR9 5LH

www.chasehotel.co.uk

Every bit the contemporary dining room, Harry's Restaurant is named after the owner's grandson. Set in a large Georgian mansion with 11 acres of grounds, its modern decor blends with the original high ceilings and ornate plasterwork. The European comfort-oriented menu has something for everyone.

Chef Richard Birchall **Seats** 70, Private dining 300 **Closed** 24–27 December **Prices from** S £6, M £14, D £6 **Parking** 75 **Notes** Vegetarian dishes, Children welcome

Conservatory Restaurant

BRITISH

01989 763174 | King's Head Hotel, 8 High Street, HR9 5HL

www.kingshead.co.uk

Dating from the 14th century, the King's Head is woven into the historic high street's fabric and comes with all the fireplaces and oak beams you'd hope for in an inn of this vintage. The cooking takes a modern tack, letting prime local materials do the talking in flavour-led dishes.

Chef Ricky Barlow, Stewart Vale, Ashley Kibble **Seats** 32 **Open** All year **Prices from** S £5, M £12, D £6 **Notes** Vegetarian dishes, Children welcome

Glewstone Court Country House

TRADITIONAL BRITISH, EUROPEAN

01989 770367 | Glewstone, HR9 6AW

www.glewstonecourt.com

With pleasant views over the surrounding countryside, this family-owned Georgian retreat makes very good use of local and high quality produce. The Cedar Tree Restaurant offers seasonal fare with regularly changing tasting menus also available. The taster menu with wine flight is a very popular choice here.

Chef Vicky Lyons **Seats** 70, Private dining 32 **Closed** 26–29 December **Prices from** S £6, M £15, D £7 **Parking** 28 **Notes** Vegetarian dishes, Children welcome

Wilton Court Restaurant with Rooms

MODERN BRITISH

01989 562569 | Wilton Lane, HR9 6AQ

www.wiltoncourthotel.com

A riverside setting on the Wye makes for much natural diversion at Wilton Court. The house itself partly dates back to around 1500 and was once the local magistrate's court. Today the Mulberry Restaurant delivers an intelligent modern British repertoire.

Chef Rachael Williams **Seats** 40, Private dining 12 **Closed** 1st 2 weeks in January **Prices from** S £6.25, M £26.50, D £7.25 **Parking** 25 **Notes** Vegetarian dishes, Children welcome

SYMONDS YAT [EAST]
Saracens Head Inn

BRITISH

01600 890435 | HR9 6JL

www.saracensheadinn.co.uk

In a stunning location on the River Wye, The Saracens Head can be reached by its own ferry, operated by hand, just as it has for the past 200 years. There's a relaxed atmosphere throughout this 16th-century inn, from the dining room to two terraces.

Chef Michael Fowler **Seats** 60 **Closed** 25 December (all day); 24 December and 26 December to 4 January (evenings) **Prices from** S £6.25, M £13.95, D £7.50 **Parking** 30 **Notes** Vegetarian dishes, Children welcome

UPPER SAPEY
The Baiting House

MODERN BRITISH

01886 853201 | Stourport Road, WR6 6XT

www.baitinghouse.co.uk

Just 20 minutes from the M5, The Baiting House is set in the beautiful Teme Valley countryside and a popular stop for walkers. Refurbished by new owners, the property still has a traditional country pub feel but it is also thoroughly modern.

Chef Charles Bradley, Scott Harrison, Harry Tyler **Seats** 48 **Closed** 25 December, 7–20 January **Prices from** S £7, M £14, D £7 **Parking** 50 **Notes** Vegetarian dishes, Children welcome

HERTFORDSHIRE

BERKHAMSTED
The Gatsby

MODERN BRITISH

01442 870403 | 97 High Street, HP4 2DG

www.thegatsby.net

This stylish modern brasserie occupies a handsome art deco space with pictures of the golden age of British cinema. Chargrilled artichoke and Swiss chard risotto might have caught Fellini's interest while the smoked fish kedgeree might have been down Hitchcock's street.

Chef Matthew Salt **Seats** 65 **Closed** 25–26 December **Prices from** S £7.95, M £15.95, D £7.95 **Parking** 10 **Notes** Vegetarian dishes, Children welcome

Porters Restaurant

BRITISH, INTERNATIONAL

01442 876666 | 300 High Street, HP4 1ZZ

www.porters.uk.com

Porters had to up sticks and move when their Covent Garden home of more than 35 years was redeveloped in 2015. Their new, modern building is a mixture of glass and steel and there's also an outside terrace where guests can dine al fresco.

Chef James Rolt **Seats** 110 **Open** All year **Prices from** S £5.95, M £12.95, D £5.95 **Notes** Vegetarian dishes, Children welcome

HERTFORDSHIRE

BISHOP'S STORTFORD
Down Hall Hotel & Spa
CONTEMPORARY BRITISH
01279 731441 | Hatfield Heath, CM22 7AS
www.downhall.co.uk

The house originally dates from the 1300s, but its impressively grand Italianate exterior shows the mark of a Victorian makeover. With period details such as ornate cornices and white-painted columns, the dining room has a vibe reminiscent of an upmarket French brasserie.

Chef Chris Jones **Seats** 60, Private dining 200 **Closed** 24 and 31 December **Parking** 120 **Notes** Vegetarian dishes, Children welcome

CHANDLER'S CROSS
Colette's at The Grove
MODERN EUROPEAN V NOTABLE WINE LIST
01923 807807 | WD3 4TG
www.resdiary.com/restaurant/colettes

The Grove is a splendid Georgian country-house hotel and spa, set in 300 acres of parkland. Public areas are magnificent, with plenty of period features as well as smart contemporary touches. Colette's is the fine dining restaurant, located over two rooms in the original house, one with glowing yellow walls, the other blue, both with formal table settings and very well-trained, genuinely friendly and knowledgeable staff. Food is cutting-edge modern British in style with a firm basis in traditional French techniques. Head chef Russell Bateman has worked with some of the greats, and his food is picture-perfect – beautifully presented and precisely conceived. A choice of five- or seven-course tasting menus (including a vegetarian version) are offered in addition to the carte, and you might begin with poached and roasted Galician octopus, with chorizo, olives and rosemary cream sauce, before moving on to braised short rib and fillet of dry-aged Hereford beef, with onion marmalade, potato croquette, spinach and ceps. A perfect baked custard tart comes with poached Yorkshire rhubarb and rhubarb sorbet.

Chef Russell Bateman **Seats** 44 **Open** All year **Parking** 300 **Notes** No children

The Stables Restaurant at The Grove
MODERN BRITISH
01923 807807 | WD3 4TG
www.resdiary.com/restaurant/thestables

The stable block of the Georgian mansion has been given a makeover under its rafters and is now an informal eatery. The open-to-view kitchen is equipped with a wood-fired oven and chargrill, but the menu has more going for it than pizzas and steaks.

Chef Andrew Parkinson **Seats** 120, Private dining 16 **Closed** 25 December **Parking** 300 **Notes** Vegetarian dishes, Children welcome

DATCHWORTH
The Tilbury
MODERN BRITISH NOTABLE WINE LIST
01438 815550 | Watton Road, SG3 6TB
www.thetilbury.co.uk

A good local watering hole and a place to eat seriously good food, The Tilbury's kitchen is driven by quality, starting with carefully sourced produce. Pudding could be a cylinder of white chocolate parfait coated with pistachio crumbs.

Chef Thomas Bainbridge **Seats** 70, Private dining 36 **Closed** some Bank holidays **Prices from** S £6.50, M £12, D £6.50 **Parking** 40 **Notes** Vegetarian dishes, Children welcome

ELSTREE
Laura Ashley The Manor
MODERN BRITISH
020 8327 4700 | Barnet Lane, WD6 3RE
www.lauraashleyhotels.com

The Laura Ashley empire includes this 16th-century manor house restyled in plenty of contemporary beige. Setting off the mullioned windows in the Cavendish dining room, it makes for a cheering ambience in which to dine on some well-considered country-house cooking.

Chef Mick Butters **Seats** 40, Private dining 40 **Open** All year **Prices from** S £7, M £17.50, D £6.50 **Parking** 100 **Notes** Vegetarian dishes, Children welcome

See advertisement opposite

FLAUNDEN
Bricklayers Arms
BRITISH, FRENCH
01442 833322 | Black Robin Lane, Hogpits Bottom, HP3 0PH
www.bricklayersarms.com

The Bricklayers is a cheery Georgian pub with a cosy atmosphere, rustic oak beams, log fire and brick bar, with a garden and terrace. Food is a serious commitment, the kitchen sourcing locally and seasonally, supplementing the main menus with daily fish and vegetarian specials.

Chef Claude Paillet, Miro Schelling **Seats** 95, Private dining 50 **Closed** 25 December **Prices from** S £6.50, M £13.95, D £4.95 **Parking** 40 **Notes** Vegetarian dishes, Children welcome

A UNIQUE DINING EXPERIENCE

AT LAURA ASHLEY THE MANOR'S CAVENDISH RESTAURANT

Award-winning cuisine
Views across the London skyline
Elegant, designer interiors
Exceptional service

HE MANOR
208 3274700 | laurashleyhotels.com/themanor
arnet Lane, Elstree WD6 3RE

LAURA ASHLEY HOTEL

THE MANOR

ELSTREE

HERTFORDSHIRE

HATFIELD
Beales Hotel
MODERN BRITISH
01707 288500 | Comet Way, AL10 9NG
www.bealeshotels.co.uk

The contemporary brasserie-style dining room at Beales Hotel looks surprisingly small for a hotel, but such intimacy creates an aura of exclusivity. Served by well-informed staff, the food being served is a mix of modern British classics and Mediterranean magic.

Chef Phil Macrides **Seats** 60, Private dining 300 **Open** All year **Prices from** S £7, M £15, D £7 **Parking** 126 **Notes** Vegetarian dishes, Children welcome

HEMEL HEMPSTEAD
Aubrey Park Hotel
MODERN EUROPEAN
01582 792105 | Hemel Hempstead Road, Redbourn, AL3 7AF
www.aubreypark.co.uk

It stands in nine acres of rolling countryside, dates back to 1287 and has an Iron Age hillfort in the grounds. Old in parts indeed, but Aubrey Park's interiors are contemporary, particularly the light, bright Brasserie, where friendly staff serve bistro classics.

Chef Lee Robinson **Seats** 56 **Open** All year **Prices from** S £5.95, M £10.95, D £5.95 **Parking** 140 **Notes** Vegetarian dishes, Children welcome

ST ALBANS
Chez Mumtaj
FRENCH, ASIAN
01727 800033 | Centurian House, 136–142 London Road, AL1 1PQ
www.chezmumtaj.com

Partnerships of eastern and western culinary traditions have been one of the hallmarks of modern dining, and Chez Mumtaj effectively brings together pan-Asian cooking styles with influences from French gastronomic tradition. The wood-panelled dining room is gently lit and the huge menus afford plenty of choice.

Chef Chad Rahman **Seats** 100, Private dining 16 **Closed** 25 December **Prices from** S £6.50, M £14.95, D £5.50 **Notes** Vegetarian dishes, Children welcome

See advertisement opposite

The Restaurant at Sopwell House
MODERN BRITISH V
01727 864477 | Cottonmill Lane, Sopwell, AL1 2HQ
www.sopwellhouse.co.uk

A splendid stately hotel, equipped with spa and wedding facilities, with dining divided among conservatory, brasserie and restaurant, depending on your preferred style. The last is a glamorous, high-

ceilinged setting for modern cooking of great vigour. Desserts won't lack for takers.

Chef Gopi Chandran **Seats** 100, Private dining 320 **Open** All year **Parking** 300 **Notes** Children welcome

St Michael's Manor
MODERN BRITISH, EUROPEAN
01727 864444 | Fishpool Street, AL3 4RY
www.stmichaelsmanor.com

A handsome Georgian mansion standing in five acres of landscaped gardens, St Michael's Manor provides the setting for food with top-class provenance delivered by an ambitious team. Choose from an uncomplicated brasserie-style menu, or trade up to the carte for a main course.

Chef Jonathan Green **Seats** 130, Private dining 22 **Parking** 80 **Notes** Vegetarian dishes, Children welcome

THOMPSON St Albans
MODERN BRITISH V
See pages 148–149

See advertisement on page 150

TRING
Pendley Manor Hotel
TRADITIONAL BRITISH
01442 891891 | Cow Lane, HP23 5QY
www.pendley-manor.co.uk

The Victorian section at Pendley (there's also a modern annexe) offers period grandeur in spades, particularly in the Oak Restaurant where oak flooring, lofty ceilings, colourful patterned wallpaper, and swagged-back drapes at vast bay windows make an imposing setting. The cooking is totally 21st century.

Chef Martin White **Seats** 75, Private dining 200 **Open** All year **Prices from** S £7, M £15.50, D £6 **Parking** 150 **Notes** Vegetarian dishes, Children welcome

WELWYN
Auberge du Lac
MODERN BRITISH
01707 368888 | Brocket Hall Estate, Brocket Road, AL8 7XG
www.aubergedulac.co.uk

The 543-acre estate of Brocket Hall is the setting for this elegant restaurant in an old hunting lodge on the edge of a lake. After drinks in the reception area, dinner is served in the dining room with its beautiful views of the main house.

Chef Matt Edmonds **Seats** Private dining 18 **Closed** 27 December and some dates in January **Prices from** S £8.50, M £22.50, D £10 **Parking** 50 **Notes** Vegetarian dishes, Children welcome at lunch and Sundays only

HERTFORDSHIRE

ST ALBANS
THOMPSON St Albans
◉◉◉ MODERN BRITISH **V**
01727 730777 | 2 Hatfield Road, AL1 3RP
www.thompsonstalbans.co.uk

Classy contemporary cooking with interesting combinations

Set in a row of four weatherboarded cottages in the town centre, Phil Thompson's restaurant has put St Albans firmly on the gastronomic map. Now in his sixth year of running his own place (he was previously in the swish surrounds of the nearby Auberge du Lac) his cooking goes from strength to strength. Inside, it's a notch or two up from your average eatery, the dining room looking the business in restrained shades of grey, with linen-clad tables, and local artworks adding class to the walls.

Thompson's output is nothing if not inclusive, appealing to the local constituency with veggie versions of the taster and à la carte, plus a kids' menu, a 'Ladies that lunch' formula, a Sunday roast special menu, and if you want a budget way in, mid-week set-lunch and dinner deals are an absolute steal. Whichever tempts you in, it's all underpinned by sound classical technique and is all about sharply judged flavours, vivid combinations of on-trend ingredients and gorgeous presentation. Inspired starters might showcase yellowfin tuna loin, seared just so, with the lively flavours of pomelo, coriander,

marinated turnip and crème fraîche bringing it all to life, or a dish involving the full-on savoury smack of oxtail cannelloni intensified by parmesan custard and nicely balanced with pickled celeriac and chestnut. Sure-footed and technically astute cooking is also a hallmark of main courses, bringing on the likes of pan-roasted fillet of sea bream with razor clam, cured lardo and curried squash, while meat-based ideas often revolve around a two-way presentation of the prime ingredient – treacle-cured fillet of Dedham Vale beef, say, served with braised short rib, calçot onions, black garlic and shiitake mushroom. Vegetarians will be delighted to see that meat-free dishes are no mere afterthought: ricotta and fine herb tortellini with toasted almond and caper and lemon butter might lead on to butter-roasted baby cauliflower with charred calçots, shiitake mushroom and crisp shallot rings. Desserts show the same feel for astute flavour and texture combinations with a well-conceived composition involving dark 70% chocolate fondant with salt burnt almond ice cream and chocolate liqueur-soaked golden raisins providing an interesting finisher, or there may be fromage frais pannacotta, its lush creaminess offset by the tart bite of Sauternes-poached Yorkshire rhubarb and rhubarb sorbet, plus warm pistachio madeleines. An intelligently complied wine list delivers a global spread of bottles at sensible prices.

Chef Phil Thompson **Seats** 90, Private dining 50 **Prices from** S £10.50, M £25, D £9 **Notes** Children welcome

See advertisement on page 150

Mid-Week Dining

Luncheon

2 Course Set Lunch Menu £18.50

3 Course Set Lunch Menu £23.00

Main Course, Side & Beverage £14.50

Ladies That Lunch Package £35.00

Available Wednesday to Saturday

Evening Dining

2 Course Set Evening Menu £21.00

3 Course Set Evening Menu £25.00

Mid-Week Date Night Package £35.00

Available Tuesday to Thursday

Conservatory & Terrace Dining Availability

thompsondining
@thompsondining
thompsondining
www.thompsonstalbans.co.uk

WELWYN continued

The Waggoners
◉ FRENCH
01707 324241 | Brickwall Close, Ayot Green, AL6 9AA
www.thewaggoners.co.uk

With its venerable beams, inglenook fireplace and convivial ambience, the setting is that of a rather romantic, quintessentially English 17th-century inn, albeit with a nod to 21st-century tastes in the restaurant. There are seasonal influences drawn from the wider European cuisine.

Chef David Durand **Seats** 65, Private dining 35 **Open** All year **Prices from** S £5.50, M £13, D £7 **Parking** 70 **Notes** Vegetarian dishes, Children welcome

The Wellington
◉ MODERN BRITISH
01438 714036 | High Street, AL6 9LZ
www.wellingtonatwelwyn.co.uk

The Wellington, on Welwyn's pretty high street, is an old coaching inn with rustic-chic exposed brick walls, real fires and a bar stocked with proper beers. The focus is firmly on the gastro side of the pub spectrum, with a simple, unpretentious menu.

Chef Andris **Seats** 90 **Open** All year **Prices from** S £6.50, M £10.95, D £6.95 **Parking** 40 **Notes** Vegetarian dishes, Children welcome

The White Hart
◉ MODERN BRITISH
01438 715353 | 2 Prospect Place, AL6 9EN
www.whitehartwelyn.co.uk

Beside the river in the village of Welwyn, this 17th-century coaching inn had a full refurbishment in 2016. Owned and run by brothers James and Tom Bainbridge, it's an inn that oozes charm, from the cosy bar to the flagstoned restaurant.

Chef Gigi Putzu **Seats** 44, Private dining 40 **Open** All year **Prices from** S £6.50, M £10.50, D £5 **Parking** 20 **Notes** Vegetarian dishes, Children welcome

WELWYN GARDEN CITY
Tewin Bury Farm Hotel
◉◉ MODERN BRITISH V
01438 717793 | Hertford Road (B1000), AL6 0JB
www.tewinbury.co.uk

A complex of barns on a working farm has been skilfully converted into this characterful modern hotel. The restaurant is a handsome room with a beamed ceiling above rafters, mustard-yellow banquettes, and a boarded floor. Many of the kitchen's raw materials are produced on-site.

Chef Grant Tomkins **Seats** 60, Private dining 30 **Open** All year **Parking** 400 **Notes** Children welcome

WILLIAN
The Fox
◉◉ MODERN BRITISH
01462 480233 | SG6 2AE
www.foxatwillian.co.uk

If you lived in a village with just the one pub, you'd hope for it to be a stylish gastropub such as this, its bar bristling with real ales, an open-plan dining room and 25-seat conservatory, plus a kitchen whose ambition goes beyond pub grub.

Chef Aron Griffiths **Seats** 100, Private dining 25 **Open** All year **Prices from** S £5.95, M £11.95, D £6.95 **Parking** 40 **Notes** Vegetarian dishes, Children welcome

▶ ISLE OF WIGHT
NEWPORT
Thompsons
◉◉ MODERN BRITISH V
01983 526118 | 11 Town Lane, PO30 1JU
www.robertthompson.co.uk

Robert Thompson has long been an ambassador for the island and his eponymous restaurant has a genuine buzz to it. An open-plan kitchen ensures proper engagement with guests in the uncluttered dining room, and shows a serious commitment to island produce. Dishes are eloquently executed.

Chef Robert Thompson **Seats** 50 **Closed** Christmas and 10 days in both November and February to March (check website for exact dates)**Prices from** S £11, M £19, D £9 **Notes** Children welcome

SEAVIEW
Seaview Hotel
◉ MODERN BRITISH
01983 612711 | High Street, PO34 5EX
www.seaviewhotel.co.uk

In the picturesque fishing village of Seaview, on the island's northeast coast, this long-established hotel is just 50 metres from the sea that supplies much of the fish on the menu. The cooking is refined with classic techniques letting tip-top ingredients speak for themselves.

Chef Liam Howes **Seats** 50, Private dining 25 **Closed** Christmas **Parking** 10 **Notes** Vegetarian dishes, Children welcome

VENTNOR
The Royal Hotel
◉◉ MODERN BRITISH V
01983 852186 | Belgrave Road, PO38 1JJ
www.royalhoteliow.co.uk
The Royal is a handsome slice of Regency grandeur on the Isle of Wight's southeastern coast. Inside is a classic English tableau fully loaded with crystal chandeliers, parquet floors and decorative ironwork. The island's own Gallybagger cheese opens proceedings in a soaring soufflé.
Chef Jon Paul Charlo **Seats** 150, Private dining 40 **Open** All year **Parking** 50 **Notes** No children under 3 years

YARMOUTH
The George Hotel
◉◉ MODERN BRITISH, MEDITERRANEAN
01983 760331 | Quay Street, PO41 0PE
www.thegeorge.co.uk
This elegant 17th-century townhouse turned boutique hotel has two dining venues – Isla's Restaurant and Conservatory. Both have commanding views over manicured lawns to the sea. A meal in the elegant, stone-toned Isla's Restaurant ranges widely over the island's larder.
Chef Craig Davis **Seats** 70, Private dining 18 **Open** All year **Notes** Vegetarian dishes, Children welcome
See advertisement opposite

▶ KENT
BIDDENDEN
The West House Restaurant with Rooms
◉◉◉ MODERN EUROPEAN V ◀ NOTABLE WINE LIST
01580 291341 | 28 High Street, TN27 8AH
www.thewesthouserestaurant.co.uk
A charming 16th-century weaver's cottage in a picture-perfect village, this is a family business, with husband-and-wife team Graham and Jackie Garrett running the kitchen and front-of-house respectively. There's a relaxed, friendly atmosphere in the dining room, with fresh flowers on the unclothed tables and fantastically seasonal dishes on the menu. Graham is a passionate and enthusiastic advocate of using the best possible produce in the most interesting way, with an emphasis on simplicity and depth of flavour. A warm starter of thinly sliced and succulent oak-smoked haddock is accompanied by a soft-boiled quail's egg and creamy bacon dressing. To follow, a beautiful piece of turbot is set on smoothly rich and creamy potato purée with little cubes of crunchy pickled cucumber running through, along with light horseradish sauce that adds further complexity. Finish with an excellent mango cheesecake, accompanied by a divine mango sorbet and a refined and punchy mango salsa with a gentle kick of chilli.
Chef Graham Garrett, Tony Parkin **Seats** 32 **Closed** 24–26 December, 1 January **Parking** 7 **Notes** Children welcome

CANTERBURY
ABode Canterbury
◉◉◉ MODERN EUROPEAN V
01227 766266 | High Street, CT1 2RX
www.abodecanterbury.co.uk
An ornate arched portico announces the Canterbury branch of the go-ahead gastronomic hotel chain, which offers a champagne bar for that indispensable aperitif, and an expansive dining room with varnished floor, white walls and an appealing modern brasserie feel. There is also a chef's table, where up to a dozen inquisitive types can keep a beady eye on the kitchen flurry. The name of the game is well-balanced, technically accomplished cooking with much use of Kentish produce. Start with a lightly torched breast and confit leg of quail served with cheesy semolina gnocchi, puréed parsley and a truffled egg yolk, before moving on to a fish such as red mullet in south-east Asian garb with bok choi, sesame seeds and peanut butter in a chicken jus, or wonderful local beef fillet in a classical presentation with violet artichokes, roast garlic and ceps on a robust reduction of red wine. Simple combining of flavours confers class on a textbook raspberry soufflé with pistachio ice cream, or on strawberry bavarois with minted cucumber sorbet.
Chef Jauca Catalin **Seats** 76, Private dining 12 **Open** All year **Prices from** S £10.50, M £15.95, D £8.95 **Parking** 40 **Notes** Children welcome

Best Western Abbots Barton Hotel
◉ MODERN BRITISH
01227 760341 | New Dover Road, CT1 3DU
www.abbotsbartonhotel.com
Built in the mid-19th century as a large private house, this early Victorian Gothic pile has been a hotel since 1927. Although a second restaurant is mooted, diners currently eat in The Fountain Restaurant, whose modern British menu likes to declare Garden of England provenance.
Chef David Hoseason **Seats** 50, Private dining 20 **Open** All year **Parking** 40 **Notes** Vegetarian dishes, Children welcome

The George Hotel

Tel: 01983 760331
Email: info@thegeorge.co.uk
The George Hotel, Quay Street, Yarmouth,
Isle of Wight, PO41 0PE

The Goods Shed
BRITISH
01227 459153 | Station Road West, CT2 8AN
www.thegoodsshed.co.uk

This restaurant for the farmers' market next to Canterbury West station has chunky wood tables with views through majestic arched windows over the comings and goings below. It uses the market produce to the full, the selections changing with every service.

Chef Rafael Lopez **Seats** 80 **Closed** 25–26 December and 1–2 January **Prices from** S £6.50, M £14.50, D £6.50 **Parking** 40 **Notes** Vegetarian dishes, Children welcome

CRUNDALE
The Compasses Inn
MODERN BRITISH
01227 700300 | Sole Street, CT4 7ES
www.thecompassescrundale.co.uk

Run by Rob and Donna Taylor, this inn in a quiet hamlet has become a real destination dining spot, such is the growing reputation for Rob's accomplished cooking. Divided into two sections, the bar and restaurant, this has all the country pub attributes.

Chef Robert Taylor **Seats** 48 **Closed** Bank holidays **Prices from** S £7.50, M £17.95, D £7.50 **Parking** 30 **Notes** Vegetarian dishes, Children welcome

DARTFORD
Rowhill Grange Hotel & Utopia Spa
MODERN EUROPEAN **V**
01322 615136 | Wilmington, DA2 7QH
www.alexanderhotels.co.uk

A substantial 18th-century manor in acres of grounds that include a pond, Rowhill Grange is now an upmarket boutique hotel. RG's is the serious dining option, where roast hare (a welcome appearance) is served with textures of cauliflower and beer onions, for instance.

Chef Chris Man **Seats** 100, Private dining 16 **Open** All year **Parking** 300 **Notes** No children under 16 years at dinner

DEAL
Dunkerleys Hotel & Restaurant
MODERN BRITISH
01304 375016 | 19 Beach Street, CT14 7AH
www.dunkerleys.co.uk

Run with down-to-earth friendliness by Ian and Linda Dunkerley, this relaxed seafront hotel has a jauntily inviting air. Fuss-free dishes bring fresh local materials together in well-balanced combinations, and seafood is the main event.

Chef Ian and Ben Dunkerley **Seats** 38 **Open** All year **Notes** Vegetarian dishes, Children welcome

KENT

DOVER
The Marquis at Alkham
◉◉ MODERN BRITISH
01304 873410 | Alkham Valley Road, Alkham, CT15 7DF
www.themarquisatalkham.co.uk
Modern art, stylish furnishings and boutique bedrooms make a fine impression at this restaurant with rooms where the smart restaurant offers a carte and two tasting menus (one offering the best of Kentish produce). Desserts are a refined and comforting bunch.

Chef Stephen Piddock **Seats** 60, Private dining 20 **Open** All year **Parking** 26 **Notes** Vegetarian dishes, No children under 8 years

EGERTON
Frasers
◉◉ MODERN BRITISH
01233 756122 | Coldharbour Farm, TN27 9DD
www.frasers-events.co.uk
Guest house accommodation and a cookery school are part of the set up here, along with a barn-style dining room with high ceilings and exposed timbers. Proceedings could open with parsnip and apple soup, parsnip crisp and white truffle oil.

Chef Kevin Bennett **Seats** 30, Private dining 50 **Open** All year **Parking** 30 **Notes** Vegetarian dishes, No children

FAVERSHAM
Faversham Creek & Red Sails Restaurant
◉◉ MODERN BRITISH
01795 533535 | Conduit Street, ME13 7BH
www.favershamcreekhotel.co.uk
Once an 18th-century coaching inn, this hotel has had a modern makeover, with the Red Sails Restaurant sporting a suitably shipshape look involving brick walls and red stripy upholstery. The kitchen couldn't be in a better spot for hauling in Kent's rural and coastal bounty.

Chef Scott Pendry **Seats** 36 **Closed** 1st 2 weeks of January **Prices from** S £5.95, M £12.95, D £5.95 **Parking** 10 **Notes** Vegetarian dishes, Children welcome

Read's Restaurant
◉◉ MODERN BRITISH
01795 535344 | Macknade Manor, Canterbury Road, ME13 8XE
www.reads.com
Chef-patron David Pitchford's Georgian manor house has long been a Kentish destination for those in the know. Set in lush grounds, it feels like a country retreat, and is run with the friendly, grown-up affability we hope to find in such places.

Chef David Pitchford **Seats** 50, Private dining 30 **Closed** Bank holidays **Parking** 30 **Notes** Vegetarian dishes, Children welcome

FAWKHAM GREEN
Brandshatch Place Hotel & Spa
◉◉ MODERN BRITISH
01474 875000 | Brands Hatch Road, DA3 8NQ
www.handpickedhotels.co.uk/brandshatchplace
Modern brasserie cooking of informality and wit is the theme in this handsome Georgian manor house – how about a 'Battenberg' of salmon and cod with caviar and cucumber dressing? – and dishes reflect attention to detail with a visual dazzle.

Chef Carl Smith **Seats** 60, Private dining 110 **Open** All year **Prices from** S £8.50, M £19.50, D £6.95 **Parking** 100 **Notes** Vegetarian dishes, Children welcome

FOLKESTONE
Rocksalt Rooms
◉◉ MODERN BRITISH V
01303 212070 | 2 Back Street, CT19 6NN
www.rocksaltfolkestone.co.uk
Sitting on the harbour with a curving terrace cantilevered out over the water, a huge sliding glass wall to capitalise on the view and a classy, well-designed interior with oak floors, Rocksalt's menu has seafood at its heart. Save room for baked egg custart tart.

Chef Simon Oakley **Seats** 100, Private dining 24 **Open** All year **Notes** Children welcome

GRAFTY GREEN
Who'd A Thought It
◉◉ BRITISH V
01622 858951 | Headcorn Road, ME17 2AR
www.whodathoughtit.com
A champagne and oyster bar with rooms in a Kentish village not far from the M20 designed with racy opulence. As well as a menu of modern classics, shellfish platters and thermidor will please seafood purists, as will sticky toffee pudding with butterscotch sauce.

Chef David Kirby **Seats** 50 **Open** All year **Prices from** S £6, M £18, D £6 **Parking** 45 **Notes** Children welcome

HYTHE
Hythe Imperial
◉ MODERN, TRADITIONAL **V**
01303 267441 | Princes Parade, CT21 6AE
www.hytheimperial.co.uk
This elegant hotel stands looking out across the Channel from its prominent position on the seafront. Dishes are served on the finest tableware, in keeping with the grandeur of the setting, and menus include tried and tested favourites with a keen eye on seasonal produce.
Chef John Bingley **Seats** 60, Private dining 60 **Open** All year **Prices from** S £6, M £15, D £5 **Parking** 200 **Notes** Children welcome

LENHAM
Chilston Park Hotel
◉◉ MODERN BRITISH
01622 859803 | Sandway, ME17 2BE
www.handpickedhotels.co.uk/chilstonpark
Secluded in 22 acres of sublime landscaped gardens and parkland, Chilston Park brims with enough period authenticity, antiques and oil paintings that you might be inspired to dress as Mr Darcy or Elizabeth Bennet for dinner in the unique, sunken Venetian-style Culpeper's restaurant.
Chef Ross Pilcher **Seats** 45, Private dining 20 **Open** All year **Prices from** S £9.50, M £22, D £8.50 **Parking** 100 **Notes** Vegetarian dishes, Children welcome

LEYSDOWN-ON-SEA
The Ferry House Inn
◉ MODERN BRITISH
01795 510214 | Harty Ferry Road, ME12 4BQ
www.theferryhouseinn.co.uk
The Ferry House, a country inn alongside the Swale Estuary, has put the Isle of Sheppey on the culinary map. It's possible to eat in the bar, but the majority of diners book into the raftered Barn Restaurant. The kitchen's style is modern British.
Chef Vitalijs Kaneps **Seats** 40, Private dining 20 **Closed** 24–30 December **Parking** 70 **Notes** Vegetarian dishes

MAIDSTONE
Fish on the Green
◉◉ BRITISH, FRENCH
01622 738300 | Church Lane, Bearsted Green, ME14 4EJ
www.fishonthegreen.com
The pretty village green setting is quintessentially English and Fish on the Green has netted a strong local fan base with its fresh, unpretentious interior, clued-up staff, and the excellent fish and seafood on offer. Super-fresh materials are treated simply.
Chef Peter Baldwin **Seats** 50 **Closed** Christmas **Parking** 50 **Notes** Vegetarian dishes, Children welcome

MARGATE
The Ambrette
◉ MODERN INDIAN **V**
01843 231504 | 44 King Street, CT9 1QE
www.theambrette.co.uk
At both his Rye venue and here in Margate, Dev Biswal combines modern British and Indian flavours into an exciting fusion, amid decor that is more Anglo than Asian. Meanwhile, the presentation of dishes is more akin to European food.
Chef Dev Biswal **Seats** 52 **Open** All year **Prices from** S £6.95, M £14.95, D £6.95 **Parking** 10 **Notes** Children welcome

Sands Hotel
◉◉ MODERN EUROPEAN
01843 228228 | 16 Marine Drive, CT9 1DH
www.sandshotelmargate.co.uk
A breath of fresh air on the Margate seafront, Sands Hotel offers a contemporary experience with sweeping views of the sea. The team in the kitchen turn out impressive modern food that has classical foundations but there's no shortage of creativity.
Chef Eddy Seys **Seats** 64, Private dining 56 **Open** All year **Notes** Vegetarian dishes, Children welcome

ROCHESTER
Topes Restaurant
◉◉ MODERN BRITISH
01634 845270 | 60 High Street, ME1 1JY
www.topesrestaurant.com
On a corner of Rochester's high street, the castle and cathedral visible through side windows, Topes occupies a building that spans the 15th to 17th centuries replete with wonky, sagging timbers, carved beams, all relieved by an uncluttered modern decor.
Chef Chris Small **Seats** 45, Private dining 16 **Open** All year **Prices from** S £6, M £14, D £7 **Notes** Vegetarian dishes, Children welcome

KENT

SANDWICH

The Lodge at Prince's

◉◉ MODERN BRITISH

01304 611118 | Prince's Drive, Sandwich Bay,
CT13 9QB

www.princesgolfclub.co.uk

The Lodge occupies a substantial purpose-built
property of white walls and red roofs with a brasserie-
style restaurant, a coolly elegant space in shades of
pale blue/grey. Fashionable foams feature in some
starters. Puddings do the trick, especially the light
and delicate vanilla and coconut pannacotta.

Chef Ricky Smith **Seats** 55, Private dining 20 **Open** All
year **Parking** 100 **Notes** Vegetarian dishes, Children
welcome

STALISFIELD GREEN

The Plough Inn

◉◉ MODERN BRITISH

01795 890256 | ME13 0HY

www.theploughinnstalisfield.co.uk

High up on the North Downs, with far-reaching views,
stands this 15th-century, timber-framed, Wealden
hall house. Dining takes place in both a cosy pubby
area, where an impressive list of past landlords is
displayed, and a second space, more restaurant-like,
yet still informal.

Chef Richard Baker **Seats** 69 **Closed** 1st week
January **Prices from** S £5.75, M £12.50, D £6
Notes Vegetarian dishes, Children welcome

TENTERDEN

The Swan Wine Kitchen

◉◉ EUROPEAN

01580 761616 | Chapel Down Winery, Small Hythe
Road, TN30 7NG

www.swanchapeldown.co.uk

This striking, bare timber and galvanised steel building
lies in the grounds of Chapel Down Winery, one of
England's leading winemakers. Both bar and terrace
offer delightful countryside views, while from the
open-plan kitchen comes a short but appealing choice
of modern European dishes.

Chef Simon Ulph **Seats** 65, Private dining 18 **Open** All
year **Parking** 100 **Notes** Vegetarian dishes, Children
welcome

TUNBRIDGE WELLS (ROYAL)

Hotel du Vin Tunbridge Wells

◉ BRITISH, FRENCH 🍷 NOTABLE WINE LIST

01892 526455 | Crescent Road, TN1 2LY

www.hotelduvin.com

A Grade II listed Georgian mansion is home to HdV's
operation in Tunbridge Wells and the enormous wine
lists remain an integral part of the attraction of this
hotel chain. The cooking continues on a solid French
bistro basis, as well as more Anglo comfort-food.

Chef Jimmy Worrall **Seats** 80, Private dining 84
Open All year **Prices from** S £7.25, M £13.50, D £6.95
Parking 30 **Notes** Vegetarian dishes, Children welcome

The Kentish Hare

◉◉ MODERN BRITISH V

01892 525709 | 95 Bidborough Ridge, Bidborough,
TN3 0XB

www.thekentishhare.com

Brothers Chris and James Tanner have transformed a
closed-down pub into a dynamic, splendidly
refurbished contemporary restaurant. Dishes that are
squarely in the modern manner might include a starter
of seared scallops, wafer-thin cauliflower slices, pine
nuts and raisins in curry oil.

Chef C and J Tanner, Bobby Brown **Seats** 64
Closed 1st week in January **Parking** 24
Notes Children welcome

The Spa Hotel

◉◉ MODERN, TRADITIONAL BRITISH

01892 520331 | Mount Ephraim, TN4 8XJ

www.spahotel.co.uk

Tunbridge Wells has no shortage of buildings built in
the 18th century to capitalise on the spa business.
This hotel has a brasserie on site (Zagatos), while the
main Chandelier Restaurant provides something rather
more refined and worth the visit.

Chef Alan Irwin **Seats** 80, Private dining 200 **Open** All
year **Parking** 150 **Notes** Vegetarian dishes, Children
welcome

Thackeray's

◉◉◉ MODERN FRENCH V 🍷 NOTABLE WINE LIST

01892 511921 | 85 London Road, TN1 1EA

www.thackerays-restaurant.co.uk

Once home to the novelist William Makepeace
Thackeray, author of Vanity Fair, this lovely, white-
weatherboarded old building dates back more than
300 years and inside it's full of delightful period details.
The dining room is a great combination of ancient and
modern, with stylishly up-to-date touches and smart
table settings. The food, too, is elegantly contemporary
and intelligently constructed, with precise presentation

and refined, intricate re-workings of classic combinations. Service hits all the right notes of friendliness and professionalism. A pressing of ham hock and leek proves to be an elegant terrine, the meat tender and full of flavour, studded with leek and lightly curried potato. Main courses might include a highly satisfying corn-fed chicken breast with Beauvale blue macaroni cheese, salsify, roast shallots, mushroom and Madeira cream, providing a great balance of flavours and demonstrating a real lightness of touch. Bring down the curtain with rum soaked pineapple tart Tatin and a fabulous kafir lime ice cream.

Chef Pat Hill, Richard Phillips **Seats** 70, Private dining 16 **Open** All year **Notes** Children welcome

The Twenty Six
◉◉ MODERN BRITISH
01892 544607 | 15a Church Road, Southborough, TN4 0RX
www.thetwenty-six.co.uk
When it comes to the number of seats there are for diners in this cosy restaurant from Scott Goss, the clue is in the name. To keep things interesting for visitors and staff, the menu changes every day but dishes stick rigidly to the seasons.

Chef Scott Goss **Seats** 26, Private dining 22 **Open** All year **Notes** Vegetarian dishes, Children welcome

WEST MALLING
The Swan
◉◉ MODERN BRITISH
01732 521910 | 35 Swan Street, ME19 6JU
www.theswanwestmalling.co.uk
Refurbished in 2015, The Swan started life as a coaching inn back in the 15th century and it still draws the crowds. Inside, you'll find brasserie-style menus on offer, showcasing high-quality Kentish farm produce in carefully constructed dishes inspired by global flavours and techniques.

Chef Lee Edney **Seats** 90, Private dining 30 **Closed** 1 January **Prices from** S £6.50, M £15, D £7 **Notes** Vegetarian dishes, Children welcome

WHITSTABLE
The Sportsman
◉◉ MODERN BRITISH
01227 273370 | Faversham Road, Seasalter, CT5 4BP
www.thesportsmanseasalter.co.uk
The Sportsman has a distinctly rustic, unpretentious look, with scuffed floorboards and plain walls hung with pictures above half-panelling. Everything is made in-house, including the butter. You might choose to start with an appetiser of super-fresh oyster topped with warm chorizo.

Chef Stephen Harris, Dan Flavell **Seats** 50 **Closed** 25–26 December, 1 January **Prices from** S £8.95, M £21.95, D £8.95 **Parking** 20 **Notes** Vegetarian dishes, Children allowed at lunch only

WINGHAM
The Dog at Wingham
◉ MODERN BRITISH
01227 720339 | Canterbury Road, CT3 1BB
www.thedog.co.uk
Close to Canterbury, this lovely village pub is set in a former monastery that dates from the 13th century. The airy, wood-panelled restaurant is illuminated by leaded windows and the shabby-chic furniture adds a relaxed and rustic touch. Seasonal British-led ingredients drive the menu.

Chef Mark Kember, Tom Dawson **Seats** 50, Private dining 20 **Open** All year **Prices from** S £7.50, M £16, D £7 **Parking** 14 **Notes** Vegetarian dishes, Children welcome

WROTHAM
The Bull
◉◉ MODERN BRITISH 🍷 NOTABLE WINE LIST
01732 789800 | Bull Lane, TN15 7RF
www.thebullhotel.com
A 600-year-old country inn with a mix of wooden and leather-look chairs at unclothed wooden tables. From their newly conceived menus, perhaps kick off with an interesting starter of Colston Bassett Stilton pannacotta, cauliflower couscous and port jelly. Desserts should not be overlooked.

Chef James Hawkes **Seats** 60, Private dining 12 **Closed** 1 January **Prices from** S £7.50, M £16.95, D £7.50 **Parking** 30 **Notes** Vegetarian dishes, Children welcome

WYE
Wife of Bath
◉◉ MODERN SPANISH
01233 812232 | 4 Upper Bridge Street, TN25 5AF
www.thewifeofbath.com
Part of Mark Sargeant's growing collection of pubs and restaurants, The Wife of Bath was given a makeover in 2016 although there's been a restaurant here since the 1960s. The dining room's wood floors and grey wash walls give the place a cool Nordic look.

Chef Simon Oakley, Adam Ashley **Seats** 55, Private dining 12 **Open** All year **Parking** 8 **Notes** Vegetarian dishes, Children welcome

LANCASHIRE

▶ LANCASHIRE

BLACKBURN
The Millstone at Mellor
◉ MODERN BRITISH

01254 813333 | Church Lane, Mellor, BB2 7JR
www.millstonehotel.co.uk

Owned by Thwaites Brewery, whose ales are at the pumps, it's not all about beer at this old coaching inn. It also deals in feel-good menus that offer up pub classics, lunchtime sandwiches, locally sourced steaks cooked on the grill, and a few global flavours.

Chef Alan Holliday **Seats** 90, Private dining 20 **Open** All year **Parking** 45 **Notes** Vegetarian dishes, Children welcome

BURNLEY
Bertram's Restaurant
◉◉ BRITISH

01282 471913 | Crow Wood, Royle Lane, BB12 0RT
www.crowwood.com

Crow Wood, a modern hotel with extensive spa and leisure facilities, is set in 100 acres of woodland. Bertram's Restaurant, a stylish space with unclothed dark wood tables and smartly upholstered chairs, is popular with locals and guests alike. Get started with a prosecco cocktail.

Chef Spencer Burge, Gary Entwistle **Seats** 80, Private dining 42 **Closed** 1–3 January **Prices from** S £5.95, M £11.95, D £6.50 **Parking** 200 **Notes** Vegetarian dishes, No children

White Swan at Fence
◉◉ MODERN BRITISH

01282 611773 | 300 Wheatley Lane Road, Fence, BB12 9QA
www.whiteswanatfence.co.uk

Retaining all that makes the British pub such a national asset, while applying the highest standards in every department, the team at the White Swan create something special. It's a pub all right, but there's home-made damson vodka, and a chef delivering powerful flavours.

Chef Tom Parker **Seats** 40 **Closed** 26 December, 1 January **Prices from** S £6, M £16, D £6 **Parking** 20 **Notes** Vegetarian dishes, Children welcome

CHORLEY
Brookes Restaurant
◉ MODERN CLASSIC

01257 455000 | Park Hall Hotel, Park Hall Road, Charnock Richard, PR7 5LP
www.lavenderhotels.co.uk/park-hall

Brookes Restaurant is the principal dining room at Park Hall Hotel and is a smart venue done in salmon and blue tones, where friendly service is the norm. Modern brasserie cooking comes up trumps with dishes such as seared hake fillet in brown shrimp butter with curried cauliflower and chive mash.

Chef Jamie Kennard **Seats** 120, Private dining 50 **Open** All year **Prices from** S £6.95, M £17.95, D £4.95 **Parking** 400 **Notes** Vegetarian dishes, Children welcome

CLITHEROE
The Assheton Arms
◉ CONTEMPORARY SEAFOOD

01200 441227 | Downham, BB7 4BJ
www.seafoodpubcompany.com/the-assheton-arms

Although decidedly inland, this pub's ownership by Joycelyn Neve's Seafood Pub Company guarantees excellent Fleetwood-landed fish and seafood, although your dining choice extends way beyond what a trawler can net. For something light to finish, try passionfruit and blackberry mess with baby meringues.

Chef Antony Shirley **Seats** 90, Private dining 12 **Open** All year **Prices from** S £6.50, M £14.50, D £5.25 **Parking** 16 **Notes** Vegetarian dishes, Children welcome

The Parkers Arms
◉ MODERN BRITISH

01200 446236 | BB7 3DY
www.parkersarms.co.uk

Once the coach-house of next-door Newton Hall, the white-fronted Parkers Arms hides in a Ribble Valley village near the Trough of Bowland. Inside are stone floors and low ceilings, with a conservatory feel in the dining area. Nearly all produce is sourced within 30 miles.

Chef Stosie Madi **Seats** 100 **Closed** 25 December **Parking** 30 **Notes** Children welcome

COWAN BRIDGE
Hipping Hall
◉◉◉ MODERN BRITISH **V** NOTABLE WINE LIST

015242 71187 | LA6 2JJ

www.hippinghall.com

Pocket-sized Hipping Hall has been around since the 15th century, its name – since you ask – is an old term for the hipping, or stepping, stones across the little stream running through the mature gardens. The place has a classical elegance, and a real draw is its stylish restaurant, where boarded floors, walls done in local pigments, soaring oak beams and a rustic fireplace feel rooted into the area. Oli Martin is a sure-footed chef who takes a 21st-century line, teaming prime local produce with of-the-moment techniques in five- and eight-course tasters (with veggie alternatives). Celeriac barbecued over coals, served with black garlic and lovage shows the style. Seafood is handled with aplomb: a dish showcasing halibut is raised skywards by the addition of oyster foam, dill oil and kohlrabi. If it's meatier satisfaction you're after, beef comes with turnip and wild garlic, or venison loin might be supported by poached turnip and yeasted crab apple. Inspired desserts could involve Yorkshire rhubarb with buckwheat and sorrel ice, or off-the-wall ideas like malt loaf with pear and artichoke skin.

Chef Oli Martin **Seats** 34, Private dining 14 **Open** All year **Parking** 20 **Notes** No children under 12 years

GREAT ECCLESTON
The Cartford Inn
◉◉ MODERN BRITISH

01995 670166 | Cartford Lane, PR3 0YP

www.thecartfordinn.co.uk

On the banks of the River Fylde, this 17th-century coaching inn is enlivened by local artists' work and the owners' eye-catching memorabilia. The menu revels in Lancashire's fine produce with imaginative ideas that aim to comfort rather than challenge.

Chef Chris Bury **Seats** 90, Private dining 30 **Closed** 25 December **Prices from** S £4.95, M £13, D £6.95 **Parking** 50 **Notes** Vegetarian dishes, No children under 8 years after 8pm

See advertisement on page 160

LANCASTER
Lancaster House
◉ TRADITIONAL BRITISH

01524 844822 | Green Lane, Ellel, LA1 4GJ

www.englishlakes.co.uk

Practically on the doorstep of the Lake District, Lancaster House is an events and leisure hotel on the university campus. Foodworks is the promising name of its restaurant, and a relaxed, hang-loose brasserie feel predominates, offering a seasonal menu of readily understandable fare.

Chef Damien Ng **Seats** 90, Private dining 150 **Open** All year **Parking** 130 **Notes** Vegetarian dishes, Children welcome

LANGHO
Northcote
◉◉◉◉ MODERN BRITISH **V** NOTABLE WINE LIST

See pages 162–163

LOWER BARTLE
Bartle Hall Hotel
◉ MODERN BRITISH

01772 690506 | Lea Lane, PR4 0HA

www.bartlehall.co.uk

Between Blackpool and Preston, Bartle Hall is conveniently positioned for the M6 and the Lake District. Set within extensive gardens, this former private residence can be traced back to the 16th century although these days it's a comfortable modern hotel and wedding venue.

Chef Natasha Craven **Seats** 22 **Open** All year **Prices from** S £5.95, M £14.95, D £6.50 **Parking** 80 **Notes** Vegetarian dishes, Children welcome

LYTHAM ST ANNES
Bedford Hotel
◉ MODERN BRITISH

01253 724636 | 307–313 Clifton Drive South, FY8 1HN

www.bedford-hotel.com

The Bedford is a welcoming, family-run Victorian hotel with lots going on. Its Cartland Restaurant has plenty of period charm, with decorative plasterwork, warm pastel tones, black-and-white prints of film stars and neatly laid tables. The cooking steers sensibly clear of left-field flavours.

Chef Paul Curran **Seats** Private dining 120 **Open** All year **Parking** 20 **Notes** Vegetarian dishes, Children welcome

THE CARTFORD INN

Multi award-winning gastropub & boutique hotel at the heart of Lancashire's Fylde countryside.

'Estrella Damm top 50 best gastropubs'

" The focus is all about where we are and who we are - a reflection of traditional Lancashire with a swirling mix of French, plenty of creativity and eccentricity. "

   www.thecartfordinn.co.uk

call: (01995) 670166 email: info@thecartfordinn.co.uk
Cartford Lane, Little Eccleston, Lancashire, PR3 0YP

TOP 50 GASTROPUBS

THE GREAT BRITISH PUB AWARDS
WINNER

Rosette for
Culinary Excellence

AA
★★★★★
Inn

GOOD FOOD GUIDE
2018

EATING
IN PU
20

LYTHAM ST ANNES continued

Best Western Glendower Hotel

⚜ TRADITIONAL BRITISH

01253 723241 | North Promenade, FY8 2NQ

www.glendowerhotel.co.uk

A Victorian seafront hotel just along from the pier, the Glendower is home to Coast, a contemporary restaurant with a brasserie vibe. The kitchen turns out traditional British dishes with a twist – cottage pie, for example, arrives topped with truffle foam.

Chef Pascal Parisee **Seats** 70, Private dining 40 **Open** All year **Parking** 40 **Notes** Vegetarian dishes, Children welcome

Clifton Arms Hotel

⚜ BRITISH

01253 739898 | West Beach, Lytham, FY8 5QJ

www.cliftonarms-lytham.com

Chic table settings with good napery and floral adornments at this early Victorian red-brick building make the dining room look the part, and bay windows give wide sea views. The kitchen delivers contemporary cooking that moves with the seasons.

Chef Paul Howard **Seats** 60, Private dining 140 **Open** All year **Prices from** S £6, M £13.50, D £5.50 **Parking** 50 **Notes** Vegetarian dishes, Children welcome

Greens Bistro

⚜ MODERN BRITISH

01253 789990 | 3–9 St Andrews Road South, St Annes-on-Sea, FY8 1SX

www.greensbistro.co.uk

For a basement bistro venue Greens looks bright and airy, with ornate high-backed chairs in light wood at smartly clothed tables, and deep green carpeting. The cooking is straightforward bistro fare based on pedigree Lancashire produce, including the county's famous cheese.

Chef Paul Webster **Seats** 38 **Closed** 25 December, Bank holidays and 1 week in summer **Notes** Vegetarian dishes, Children welcome

MORECAMBE
Best Western Lothersdale Hotel

⚜ MODERN BRITISH

01524 416404 | 320–323 Marine Road, LA4 5AA

www.bfhotels.com

Run by the same family for more than 50 years, this refurbished seafront hotel on the promenade in Morecambe now has a separate bar and tapas area with an outside terrace area providing wonderful views across the bay to the Lakeland fells.

Chef Darren Tattersall **Seats Closed** 22–27 December

The Midland

⚜ MODERN BRITISH

01524 424000 | Marine Road West, LA4 4BU

www.englishlakes.co.uk/hotels/midland

An art deco gem, The Midland was built by the London, Midland and Scottish Railway in 1933 in the 'streamline modern' style. There's a sharp modernity to the restaurant that suits the space, with a contemporary finish and neat white tablecloths.

Chef Michael Wilson **Seats** 70, Private dining 20 **Closed** Christmas and New Year (non-residents) **Parking** 60 **Notes** Vegetarian dishes, Children welcome

ORMSKIRK
Moor Hall Restaurant with Rooms

⚜⚜⚜⚜⚜ MODERN BRITISH **V** ♦ NOTABLE WINE LIST

01695 572511 | Prescot Road, Aughton, L39 6RT

www.moorhall.com

The 'restaurant with rooms' concept here consists of seven rooms that form part of a major boutique transformation of the 16th-century manor into a foodie destination. It comprises a chic restaurant and state-of-the-art open kitchen in a modernist extension with soaring raftered roof and glass walls. The showstopping cooking of Mark Birchall, formerly of L'Enclume, means you can expect virtuoso creations built on unbeatable ingredients. The drill at dinner is five- and eight-course tasters, opening with home-grown carrots served in multifarious textures with ramsons and sea buckthorn cream bringing out their sweet notes. Next up, crab and turnip broth of remarkable clarity of flavour comes with anise leaves, hyssop and sunflower seed cream. Elsewhere, the technique is seriously impressive in the mesmerising combination of monkfish cooked on the bone pointed up with plump mussels in a light cream sauce, plus sea vegetables and silky artichoke purée, while Dorset Muntjac deer is showcased in another complex workout, the perfectly cooked loin and fillet alongside beetroot in various preparations, buttery kale, mushroom and a sauce of giddying depth of flavour. Desserts, too, are shot through with creativity, and there's a brace of them to end the show: a riff on gingerbread delivers a masterful ice cream with candied parsnips and brown sugar tuiles, and a filo basket of mead-flavoured cream matched with caramelised Bramley apple, sour apple purée and marigold leaves. Finally, Worcester Pearmain apple comes as terrine, ice cream and gel in the comforting company of woodruff cream, sweet whey caramel, almond and crisp pastry leaves. The wine list is a stunner with a knowledgeable sommelier team to guide the way.

Chef Mark Birchall **Seats** 50, Private dining 14 **Closed** From 31 July for 2 weeks, from 1 January for 2 weeks **Parking** 50 **Notes** No children under 12 years at dinner

LANCASHIRE

LANGHO
Northcote

◉◉◉◉ MODERN BRITISH **V** 🍾 NOTABLE WINE LIST

01254 240555 | Northcote Road, BB6 8BE

www.northcote.com

Fine dining with refined Lancashire sensibilities

Some years ago, Northcote dropped the designation 'Manor' from its name. Not that it has come down in the world – quite the reverse – but the Victorian red-brick house in the Ribble Valley, with the Forest of Bowland clustering in the view from the terrace, isn't as grandiloquent as many other manors. That said, it has been extended and decorated in discerning modern style, with an elegant bar overlooked by portrait photos of Brigitte Bardot and Frank Sinatra, and with contemporary paintings and sculpture abounding throughout. Before you arrive at the aperitif hour, take a gander at the kitchen gardens, from where much of the menu's wares emerge, ensuring that the kitchen moves to a seasonal pulse in its passage through the year.

The Lancashire accent established by Nigel Haworth at Northcote's inception remains firmly rooted, and has been consolidated by the appointment of Lisa Goodwin-Allen to head chef. Her deep understanding of the style produces dishes that have a cosmopolitan polish and broad range of reference, but that hasn't elbowed the likes of calf's liver and

onions in verjus, or Goosnargh duck cooked in beer with barley, off the menus. These have now been streamlined, so that there is now one six-course tasting slate in both omnivore and vegetarian (or 'plant-based') versions to supplement the carte at dinner, with the tasters only at lunch. Meanwhile, the splendid roast beef remains a constant of the Sunday lunch repertoire, A summer menu offers a bouquet of perfectly ripe tomatoes, in marinades, in tartare and fresh, dressed in nasturtium oil, accompanied by a garlic-buttered crumpet, garden cuisine if ever there was, before that liver turns up, timed to a nicety and matched with pickled shallots, sweet onion purée and all the thyme in the world. Fish cookery aims for bold complexity, as when John Dory with clams, cockles and dried scallop is treated to a welter of apple textures and crisped bacon too, and then there could be superlative smoked rare-breed pork dressed in pungent pesto with barbecued and puréed peach, pickled carrots and black garlic. The end-note comes with stunning strawberry shortcake, the buttery biscuit bedded on elderflower granita, the whole topped with a dome of pannacotta and strawberry sauce in a thin layer of cocoa butter, a clean, clear and perfectly balanced dish. The cheese trolley, compiled from Courtyard Dairies at Settle, is an aromatic temptation all its own. Accompanying it all is one of the region's outstanding wine lists, its glories revealed by a fine sommelier.

Chef Lisa Goodwin-Allen **Seats** 70, Private dining 60 **Closed** Food and Wine Festival **Prices from** S £13, M £28.50, D £14.50 **Parking** 60 **Notes** Children welcome

LANCASHIRE

RILEY GREEN
The Royal Oak
◉ TRADITIONAL BRITISH **V**
01254 201445 | Blackburn Old Road, PR5 0SL
www.royaloak-rileygreen.co.uk
Just a short distance from the Hoghton Tower in a beautiful part of Lancashire, this roadside inn has a proper pub atmosphere with traditional touches of open fires, stone walls and church pews. Modern British dishes are straightforward but cooked with confidence and flair.

Chef Chris Rawlinson **Seats** 75 **Closed** 25 December **Parking** 100 **Notes** Children welcome

THORNTON
Twelve Restaurant and Lounge Bar
◉◉ MODERN BRITISH
01253 821212 | Marsh Mill Village, Marsh Mill-in-Wyre, Fleetwood Road North, FY5 4JZ
www.twelve-restaurant.co.uk
Virtually under the sails of an 18th-century windmill, Twelve has a stylish, urban interior and a kitchen that works with regional producers and suppliers to deliver an appealing contemporary menu. The Market menu is terrific value, and cracking Sunday roasts include Bowland Forest beef.

Chef Graham Floyd **Seats** 106 **Closed** 1st 2 weeks January **Parking** 150 **Notes** Vegetarian dishes, Children welcome

See advertisement opposite

WHALLEY
Breda Murphy Restaurant
◉ MODERN BRITISH & IRISH **V**
01254 823446 | 41 Station Road, BB7 9RH
www.bredamurphy.co.uk
After a top-to-toe makeover in 2017, this vibrant enterprise comprises a contemporary restaurant, a gin bar and a casual daytime deli/café. Sitting cheek by jowl with the landmark Whalley Viaduct, it's ideally placed for friendly get-togethers accompanied by unfussy dishes with Irish and British accents.

Chef Gareth Bevan **Seats** 100, Private dining 34 **Closed** 25 December to 2 January **Prices from** S £5.25, M £12, D £5.75 **Parking** 12 **Notes** Children welcome

The Freemasons at Wiswell
◉◉◉ MODERN BRITISH **V** ⬥ NOTABLE WINE LIST
01254 822218 | 8 Vicarage Fold, Wiswell, BB7 9DF
www.freemasonswiswell.co.uk
Constructed from three little cottages in a village near Clitheroe, The Freemasons manages the clever balancing-act of being at once a country pub and a destination restaurant. Not that airs and graces are in conspicuous evidence, when napkins are rolled-up kitchen cloths and the furniture looks naturally weathered. Steven Smith's menus range from a six-course taster with extras to the core of the operation, a seasonally changing carte. A springtime offering might kick off with fresh young asparagus in a teacup of deep green soup strewn with puffs of Proctor's Kick Ass Lancashire Cheddar. Main courses may take their inspiration from French masters as for the salmon Troisgros brothers, served in a sauce of wild sorrel with whipped Jersey Royals, the fish water-bathed and dressed in orange zest and chives, or there could be majestic slow-cooked shoulder of spring lamb with peas à la française in a minted jus. The regional champion dessert has to be a square of deliciously rich egg custard, garnished with rhubarb sorbet, mousse and gel, as well as blobs of pistachio butter.

Chef Steven Smith, Matthew Smith **Seats** 70, Private dining 14 **Closed** 2nd January for 2 weeks **Prices from** S £10.95, M £22.95, D £9.95 **Notes** Children welcome

WREA GREEN
The Spa Hotel at Ribby Hall Village
◉◉ MODERN, TRADITIONAL
01772 674484 | Ribby Hall Village, Ribby Road, PR4 2PR
www.ribbyhall.co.uk/spa-hotel
As its name makes clear, there are some pretty swanky spa facilities at this classy adult-only retreat in 100 acres of Lancashire countryside. The Brasserie and its recently completed Orangery extension are another string to its bow, done out with orange and lime leather seats.

Chef Michael Noonan **Seats** 46, Private dining 30 **Open** All year **Parking** 100 **Notes** Vegetarian dishes, No children

The Villa Country House Hotel
◉ CLASSIC BRITISH
01772 804040 | Moss Side Lane, PR4 2PE
www.thevilla.co.uk
Built as a 19th-century gentleman's residence, this three-storey, gabled mansion stands in rolling parkland at the end of a sweeping drive. Its striking, carefully restored interior incorporates a part-oak-panelled restaurant, with high-backed, salmon-coloured chairs, and bare tables waited upon by white-shirted staff.

Chef Matthew Johnson **Seats** 80, Private dining 20 **Open** All year **Prices from** S £4.50, M £13.95, D £5.95 **Parking** 100 **Notes** Vegetarian dishes, Children welcome

TWELVE

RESTAURANT & LOUNGE BAR

for Culinary Excellence
2007-2018

Marsh Mill Village, Fleetwood Road North
Thornton Cleveleys, Lancashire, FY5 4JZ

T: **01253 82 12 12**
twelve-restaurant.co.uk
twelveeventmanagement.co.uk

OPENING HOURS:
Tuesday - Saturday for dinner | Sundays 12noon - 8.00pm

- Situated beneath a beautifully restored 18th century windmill
- 5 minute drive from Blackpool
- British cuisine with a modern twist

LEICESTERSHIRE

▶ LEICESTERSHIRE

LEICESTER
David Ferguson at The Belmont
◉◉ MODERN BRITISH **V**
0116 254 4773 | De Montfort Street, LE1 7GR
www.belmonthotel.co.uk

What started life as a B&B is now a stylish boutique hotel. Located on leafy New Walk, just a few minutes' stroll from Leicester's city centre, guests can enjoy a drink in contemporary Jamie's Bar before a meal in the sophisticated restaurant.

Chef David Ferguson **Seats** 60, Private dining 30 **Open** All year **Prices from** S £5.95, M £13.95, D £6.95 **Parking** 60 **Notes** Children welcome

LONG WHATTON
The Royal Oak
◉ MODERN BRITISH
01509 843694 | 26 The Green, LE12 5DB
www.theroyaloaklongwhatton.co.uk

The 21st-century incarnation of this thriving gastro pub is seen in a smart interior, some natty bedrooms and a focus on food. That said, real ale is part of the plan, and a few pub classics remain. The kitchen turns out some lively stuff.

Chef James and Charles Upton **Seats** 45 **Open** All year **Prices from** S £5.75, M £13, D £6.75 **Parking** 30 **Notes** Vegetarian dishes, Children welcome

MARKET HARBOROUGH
Three Swans Hotel
◉ MODERN, INTERNATIONAL
01858 466644 | 21 High Street, LE16 7NJ
www.threeswans.co.uk

Dating from the reign of Henry VIII, the Three Swans is a high-street hotel that has played host to various crowned heads over the generations. A makeover has produced a clean modern look that respects the original features, and smartly attired, tuned-in staff run the dining room with inspiring confidence.

Chef Marek Jani **Seats** 70, Private dining 50 **Closed** 1 January **Notes** Children welcome

MELTON MOWBRAY
Stapleford Park
◉◉ MODERN INTERNATIONAL, BRITISH 🍷 NOTABLE WINE LIST
01572 787000 | Stapleford, LE14 2EF
www.staplefordpark.com

Stapleford's lineage can be traced back to medieval times, the estate being owned by successive generations of the Earls of Harborough for nearly 500

years. Impeccable staff keep the elevated tone buoyant, and the cooking aims high too. Try the home-made breads.

Chef Tony Fitt **Seats** 70, Private dining 180 **Closed** Exclusive use days **Prices from** S £9.50, M £16.50, D £10 **Parking** 120 **Notes** Vegetarian dishes, Children welcome

MOUNTSORREL
John's House
◉◉ MODERN BRITISH **V**
01509 415569 | 139–141 Loughborough Road, LE12 7AR
www.johnshouse.co.uk

After working in a number of high profile establishments, John Duffin returned to his roots by opening his own restaurant on the family farm where he grew up. A chef committed to a 'farm to plate' philosophy, much of the produce comes from his family's land.

Chef John Duffin **Seats** 30 **Closed** Christmas and 2 weeks in August **Notes** Children welcome

NORTH KILWORTH
Kilworth House Hotel & Theatre
◉◉ MODERN BRITISH **V**
01858 880058 | Lutterworth Road, LE17 6JE
www.kilworthhouse.co.uk

A top-to-toe restoration overseen by the eagle eyes of English Heritage means period authenticity runs seamlessly through this Italianate 19th-century mansion. The Wordsworth Restaurant is the fine-dining option: a posh setting indeed, but the kitchen team certainly rises to the occasion.

Chef Carl Dovey **Seats** 70, Private dining 130 **Open** All year **Prices from** S £10, M £19, D £9.50 **Parking** 140 **Notes** Children welcome

SHAWELL
The White Swan
◉ MODERN EUROPEAN **V**
01788 860357 | LE17 6AG
www.whiteswanshawell.co.uk

Thoroughly refurbished, but retaining the welcoming ambience of a country pub, only with comfier sofas, the White Swan is run by a team that carries a weight of culinary experience on its young shoulders. A light-filled dining room with glass-fronted wine store is the restaurant setting.

Chef Rory McClean **Seats** 60, Private dining 25 **Closed** Early January **Prices from** S £9, M £22, D £7 **Parking** 30 **Notes** Children welcome

WYMESWOLD
Hammer & Pincers
◉◉ BRITISH, EUROPEAN **V**

01509 880735 | 5 East Road, LE12 6ST
www.hammerandpincers.co.uk

Having trained at The Savoy, this restaurant's owners know a thing or two about hospitality in the grand manner, but the mood here is decidedly more cutting edge. This is Stilton country, so Cropwell Bishop with quince paste might look appealing.

Chef Daniel Jimminson **Seats** 46 **Open** All year **Prices from** S £8.50, M £19, D £7.50 **Parking** 40 **Notes** Children welcome

▶ LINCOLNSHIRE
GRANTHAM
Harry's Place
◉◉◉ MODERN FRENCH

01476 561780 | 17 High Street, Great Gonerby, NG31 8JS

With the restaurant's 30th anniversary in September 2018, Harry and Caroline Hallam have surely proved you don't need a vast dining room or bespoke building to provide top notch cooking to discerning guests – when you visit Harry's Place you're visiting their home, a handsome old converted farmhouse, and eating in their dining room. There's space for just 10 guests at the three tables, so this is an intimate experience – and make sure you book – especially at weekends. Caroline expertly takes care of front-of-house duties, while Harry's in the kitchen, his classically inspired, hand-written menus offering a couple of choices at each course, always beginning with a soup, plus maybe fillet of roast Scottish salmon, served with vodka crème fraîche, and a wonderfully uplifting relish of mango, avocado, lime, ginger and basil. You might have local breed Lincoln Red beef fillet for a main course, perhaps, served with horseradish mayonnaise, spiced apricots, flame raisins and red onion, before concluding with chocolate mousse, mascarpone and blackberries, or prune and Armagnac ice cream with passionfruit.

Chef Harry Hallam **Seats** 10 **Closed** 2 weeks from 25 December, 2 weeks in August **Prices from** S £10.50, M £39.50, D £9 **Parking** 4 **Notes** Vegetarian dishes, No children under 5 years

GREAT LIMBER
The New Inn
◉◉ MODERN BRITISH, INTERNATIONAL

01469 569998 | 2 High Street, DN37 8JL
www.thenewinngreatlimber.co.uk

In the heart of the Brocklesby Estate, this Grade II listed inn has been welcoming guests for almost 240 years. It's undergone a stylish refurbishment, and offers modern lines and lots of period detail. The enthusiasm of the kitchen shows in the dishes.

Chef Chris Grist **Seats** 40, Private dining 18 **Closed** 25 December **Parking** 25 **Notes** Vegetarian dishes, Children welcome

HORNCASTLE
Magpies Restaurant with Rooms
◉◉ BRITISH EUROPEAN

01507 527004 | 73 East Street, LN9 6AA
www.magpiesrestaurant.co.uk

In a terrace of 200-year-old cottages, Magpies has decor of duck-egg blue, with mirrors, candlelight and drapes over the bay windows. If you've got room, finish with a trio of desserts: chocolate mousse, espresso crème brûlée and dark chocolate fondant.

Chef Andrew Gilbert **Seats** 34 **Closed** 26–30 December and 1–8 January **Notes** Vegetarian dishes, Children welcome

HOUGH-ON-THE-HILL
The Brownlow Arms
◉◉ BRITISH

01400 250234 | High Road, NG32 2AZ
www.thebrownlowarms.com

This Lincolnshire village inn has come up in the world, being as elegantly appointed as an interiors magazine country house, with tapestry-backed chairs and gilt-framed mirrors in a panelled dining room. Meanwhile, attentive, friendly service puts everyone at their ease.

Chef Ruarardh Bealby **Seats** 80, Private dining 26 **Closed** 25–26 December **Parking** 26 **Notes** Vegetarian dishes, No children under 8 years

LINCOLN
Branston Hall Hotel
◉ MODERN BRITISH **V**

01522 793305 | Branston Park, Branston, LN4 1PD
www.branstonhall.com

Branston Hall is a handsome old pile, with lofty decorative gables, pinnacle chimneys and interiors that evoke a more gentle pace of life. The Lakeside dining room follows the restful theme, with views over the park, and a culinary style which adds gently modernised twists.

Chef Miles Collins **Seats** 75, Private dining 28 **Open** All year **Prices from** S £6.25, M £20, D £6.25 **Parking** 75 **Notes** No children under 12 years

LINCOLNSHIRE

The Lincoln Hotel
◉ MODERN BRITISH **V**
01522 520348 | Eastgate, LN2 1PN
www.thelincolnhotel.com
Just a stone's throw away from Lincoln's 12th-century cathedral, The Green Room has a striking, design-led interior, with candles and fresh flowers adding a nice homely touch. The atmosphere is relaxed but the small restaurant retains an air of formality.
Chef Dale Gill **Seats** 30, Private dining 12 **Open** All year **Parking** 54 **Notes** Children welcome

The Old Bakery
◉◉ MODERN INTERNATIONAL
01522 576057 | 26–28 Burton Road, LN1 3LB
www.theold-bakery.co.uk
Ivano and Tracey de Serio's restaurant with rooms is a homely place, with the feel of a farmhouse kitchen. A five-course taster menu offers a comprehensive tour, and desserts include white chocolate and pistachio ganache with vanilla pannacotta and delicately flavoured star anise ice cream.
Chef Ivano de Serio **Seats** 65, Private dining 40 **Closed** 26 December, 1–16 January and 1st week August **Notes** Vegetarian dishes, Children welcome

Tower Hotel
◉ MODERN BRITISH
01522 529999 | 38 Westgate, LN1 3BD
www.lincolntowerhotel.com
In the Bailgate district of the cathedral quarter, the Tower benefits from all the charm of medieval Lincoln. The backbone of its operation is finely detailed, up-to-date cooking while gels, dusts and purées in profusion show understanding of fashionable textural variety.
Chef Mike Watts **Seats** 48 **Closed** 25–26 December, 1 January **Notes** Vegetarian dishes, Children welcome

Washingborough Hall Hotel
◉◉ TRADITIONAL BRITISH
01522 790340 | Church Hill, Washingborough, LN4 1BE
www.washingboroughhall.com
Set in three acres of a sleepy Lincolnshire village, with a garden to provide herbs for the kitchen, Washingborough delivers all you would hope for in a Georgian manor turned country-house hotel. The smart Dining Room exudes quietly understated class.
Chef Lucy Herring **Seats** 50, Private dining 110 **Open** All year **Parking** 40 **Notes** Vegetarian dishes, Children welcome

The White Hart
◉ BRITISH, FRENCH
01522 526222 | Bailgate, LN1 3AR
www.whitehart-lincoln.co.uk
The old hotel is a feature of the historic quarter of Lincoln, with splendid views of one of England's greatest cathedrals, and the castle not far off. Inside, a suave contemporary look brings wood flooring and large mirrors to the Grille restaurant and bar.
Chef Myles Mumby **Seats** 88, Private dining 100 **Open** All year **Prices from** S £4.25, M £12.50, D £5.80 **Parking** 40 **Notes** Vegetarian dishes, Children welcome

LOUTH
Brackenborough Hotel
◉ MODERN BRITISH
01507 609169 | Cordeaux Corner, Brackenborough, LN11 0SZ
www.oakridgehotels.co.uk
Just outside the historic town of Louth, this small hotel is set among beautifully maintained lawns and gardens and has lovely country views. The menu might be a crowd-pleaser, but the kitchen puts a great deal of effort and imagination into well-constructed, often unusual dishes.
Chef Anthony Hand **Seats** 78, Private dining 120 **Open** All year **Prices from** S £4.50, M £10, D £6 **Parking** 80 **Notes** Vegetarian dishes, Children welcome

MARKET RASEN
The Advocate Arms
◉◉ MODERN EUROPEAN, BRITISH
01673 842364 | 2 Queen Street, LN8 3EH
www.advocatearms.co.uk
The 18th-century restaurant with rooms in the centre of town has a contemporary finish and aims to impress with boutique styling and an open-plan interior. In the main restaurant, the output is broadly modern British, with some inventive combinations and plenty to satisfy traditionalists.
Chef Josh Kelly **Seats** 65, Private dining 20 **Open** All year **Prices from** S £4.95, M £11.95, D £5.25 **Parking** 6 **Notes** Vegetarian dishes, Children welcome

SCOTTER
The White Swan
◉ MODERN BRITISH
01724 763061 | 9 The Green, DN21 3UD
www.whiteswanscotter.com
The whitewashed facade looks the very image of the coaching inn that The White Swan once was, but

indoors the restaurant conforms to expectations with neutral shades, pale wood and glass panels. The approach is decidedly unaffected, with hospitable service matched by appealing, well-executed food.

Chef John Greenly **Seats** 120, Private dining 40 **Open** All year **Parking** 25 **Notes** Vegetarian dishes, Children welcome

SCUNTHORPE
Forest Pines Hotel & Golf Resort
@ MODERN BRITISH

01652 650770 | Ermine Street, Broughton, DN20 0AQ
www.qhotels.co.uk

The restaurant at this swish hotel is called Eighteen57, the year Grimsby's main fish dock opened. Its interior follows a piscine theme, with maritime pictures, reliefs and murals. The kitchen has an eye to sustainability; fish and seafood feature prominently on an enticing modern repertoire.

Chef Richard Yearnshire **Seats** 70 **Open** All year **Parking** 400 **Notes** Vegetarian dishes, Children welcome

San Pietro Restaurant Rooms
@@ MODERN MEDITERRANEAN

01724 277774 | 11 High Street East, DN15 6UH
www.sanpietro.uk.com

Pietro Catalano, who hails from Sicily, has created a restaurant with rooms in a former windmill that combines the best of Italian hospitality with a touch of boutique swagger. A first course dish of ballotine of rabbit and foie gras shows ambition.

Chef Pietro Catalano, Peter Garlick **Seats** 80, Private dining 14 **Closed** 25–26 December **Parking** 22 **Notes** Vegetarian dishes, Children welcome

SLEAFORD
The Bustard Inn & Restaurant
@ MODERN BRITISH

01529 488250 | 44 Main Street, South Rauceby, NG34 8QG
www.thebustardinn.co.uk

The bar, with an open fireplace, flagstones and real ales, is the hub of this Grade II listed inn. A typical main might be two ways with beef (fillet and rillette), accompanied by Madeira sauce, a fricassée of greens, pommes Anna and wild mushrooms.

Chef Phil Lowe **Seats** 66, Private dining 12 **Closed** 1 January **Prices from** S £5.50, M £9.95, D £5.75 **Parking** 18 **Notes** Vegetarian dishes, Children welcome

SOUTH FERRIBY
The Hope and Anchor Pub
@@ MODERN BRITISH **V**

01652 635334 | Sluice Road, DN18 6JQ
www.thehopeandanchorpub.co.uk

Tucked amidst creeks and moorings, the panoramic views from the patio and restaurant encompass the waterways and nearby Humber Bridge. An appealingly updated 19th-century inn, this is a popular stop for birdwatchers and dog-walkers.

Chef Slawek Mikolajczyk **Seats** 86 **Closed** 27–30 December and 1st week in January (check website) **Prices from** S £1.95, M £11.95, D £6.50 **Parking** 38 **Notes** Children welcome

STALLINGBOROUGH
Stallingborough Grange Hotel
@ ENGLISH, EUROPEAN **V**

01469 561302 | Riby Road, DN41 8BU
www.stallingboroughgrange.co.uk

Set in an 18th-century thatched building with modern extensions, this hotel restaurant takes an informal view of things with its oak panelling, bare brickwork, unclothed tables and garden views. When it comes to the food, local produce shows up well in capable dishes.

Chef Daniel Blow **Seats** 72, Private dining 26 **Closed** 26 December and 1 January **Prices from** S £6.95, M £9.95, D £6.95 **Parking** 80 **Notes** Children welcome

STAMFORD
The Bull & Swan at Burghley
@ TRADITIONAL BRITISH

01780 766412 | High Street, St Martins, PE9 2LJ
www.thebullandswan.co.uk

The old stone inn used to be a staging post for coaches on the Great North Road and is nowadays an informal dining pub. Within are beams, stone walls, rugs on dark wood floors and caramel-coloured leather dining chairs. Regional produce is the backbone.

Chef Phil Kent **Seats** 40 **Open** All year **Parking** 7 **Notes** Vegetarian dishes, Children welcome

The George of Stamford
@ TRADITIONAL BRITISH **V** ⚑ NOTABLE WINE LIST

01780 750750 | 71 St Martins, PE9 2LB
www.georgehotelofstamford.com

History seeps from the pores of every mellow stone of this venerable coaching inn which once fed and watered passengers on the Great North Road. The oak-panelled restaurant is a magnificent room with an old-world feel, and its menus are steadfastly traditional too.

Chef Paul Reseigh **Seats** 90, Private dining 40 **Open** All year **Prices from** S £8.75, M £18.95, D £8.95 **Parking** 110 **Notes** No children under 10 years

LINCOLNSHIRE

The William Cecil

⊛⊛ MODERN BRITISH

01780 750070 | High Street, St Martins, PE9 2LJ

www.thewilliamcecil.co.uk

The hotel is an interesting amalgam of three Georgian houses built at different times, named after the Elizabethan statesman otherwise known as Lord Burghley. It's a clever blend of old and new, the panelling done in lighter colours, with booth seating in the restaurant.

Chef Phil Kent **Seats** 72, Private dining 100 **Open** All year **Parking** 70 **Notes** Vegetarian dishes, Children welcome

WINTERINGHAM

Winteringham Fields

⊛⊛⊛⊛ MODERN BRITISH, EUROPEAN ⬩ NOTABLE WINE LIST

01724 733096 | 1 Silver Street, DN15 9ND

www.winteringhamfields.co.uk

A glimpse of the Humber Bridge means there's no need to geolocate – this is the Lincolnshire side of the Humber, the abundant flatlands that grow so much of what we eat in the UK, and it is home to Colin and Bex McGurran's inspiring restaurant with rooms. It sits within a village of just 1,000 or so souls and is the kind of place that once ensconced in one of the lavishly adorned bedrooms, you really won't want to leave. The restaurant is done out in an eye-catching contemporary style, with natural surfaces and designer touches, a space with a confident identity, watched over by a formally attired team who make you feel at home. A good deal of what appears on the menus comes from hereabouts, and much of it is actually grown on the owner's own farm – farm to fork in its purest form. Whether you choose from the carte or opt to follow the lead of the eight-course tasting menu, expect creative and modern food which maintains the integrity of the splendid produce. Dinner might begin with the heavenly combination of onions and mushrooms, with a tender boned chicken wing and rich black truffle sauce, before a mackerel dish of crisp skinned fillet and smoked tartare, matched with horseradish cream and ponzu gel. Pork belly is cooked long and slow (overnight as it happens), and arrives tender and full of flavour, matched with pineapple salsa and peanut satay in a winning combination, and, among sweet courses, Yorkshire rhubarb is the star of the show (poached, crème and sorbet). The wine list is as well-judged and thought-provoking as the food.

Chef Colin McGurran **Seats** 60, Private dining 12 **Closed** 2 weeks Christmas, last 2 weeks August **Prices from** S £12, M £22, D £12 **Parking** 20 **Notes** Vegetarian dishes, Children welcome

WOODHALL SPA

Petwood

⊛ MODERN BRITISH

01526 352411 | Stixwould Road, LN10 6QG

www.petwood.co.uk

Once a private residence, this secluded mansion opened as a hotel in 1933 and guests have included King George VI. It was also home of the legendary 617 Dambusters Squadron and proudly retains its links to aviation history. The formal dining room offers refined, ambitious dishes.

Chef Philip Long **Seats** Private dining 16 **Open** All year **Parking** 140 **Notes** Children welcome

WOOLSTHORPE

Chequers Inn

⊛ MODERN BRITISH

01476 870701 | Main Street, NG32 1LU

www.chequersinn.net

A beautifully preserved 17th-century inn, the Chequers stands cheek-by-jowl with Belvoir Castle in a pastoral spot where Lincs meets Leics and Notts. Interiors match old and new, with brasserie-style tables and banquettes in the dining room, while the pub retains its rustic ambience.

Chef Keith Martin **Seats** 70, Private dining 20 **Open** All year **Parking** 35 **Notes** Vegetarian dishes, Children welcome

▶ LONDON

LONDON E1

Blanchette East

◉ MODERN FRENCH, NORTH AFRICAN **V**

020 7729 7939 | 204 Brick Lane, E1 6SA

www.blanchettebricklane.co.uk

Opened in 2016 by brothers Maxime, Malik and Yannis, Blanchette East finds its home amongst trendy Brick Lane establishments and certainly has a quirky character of its own. The small venue has a striking mural, hanging plants, and eclectic music curated by Malik.

Chef Tam Storrar **Seats** 70, Private dining 14 **Closed** 25 December **Notes** Children welcome

Café Spice Namasté

◉ INDIAN, PAN ASIAN

020 7488 9242 | 16 Prescot Street, E1 8AZ

www.cafespice.co.uk

Set in an imposing red-brick Victorian Gothic building, the interior of this vibrant Indian has brightly painted walls and colourful fabrics that are matched by Cyrus Todiwala's refined, confidently spiced, inventive modern food, which draws on his Parsee roots and the best seasonal British ingredients.

Chef Cyrus Todiwala **Seats** 120 **Closed** Christmas and Bank holidays **Prices from** S £7.25, M £16.95, D £6.50 **Notes** Vegetarian dishes, Children welcome

Canto Corvino

◉◉ MODERN ITALIAN

020 7655 0390 | 21 Artillery Lane, E1 7HA

www.cantocorvino.co.uk

Canto Corvino ('song of the raven') brings modern Italian style to Spitalfields, with artwork on rough-hewn walls, comfortable chairs at well-spaced tables, soft lighting and a lively atmosphere. The menu is as fashionable as the surroundings, divided into eight sections of modestly portioned dishes.

Chef Tom Salt **Seats** 120, Private dining 24 **Closed** Christmas, New Year **Notes** Vegetarian dishes, Children welcome

The Culpeper

◉ MODERN EUROPEAN

020 7247 5371 | 40 Commercial Street, E1 6LP

www.theculpeper.com

This lively gastropub occupies a handsome Victorian boozer rejuvenated in hipster-friendly post-industrial style with bare-brick walls and a healthy dollop of period detail. The jam-packed ground-floor bar does an appealing line in switched-on modern food, while the first-floor Kitchen restaurant offers home-grown and European flavours on a thoroughly modern menu.

Chef Antonio Mota **Open** All year **Notes** Vegetarian dishes

The Frog Restaurant

◉◉◉ MODERN BRITISH TAPAS **V**

020 3813 9832 | 2 Ely's Yard, Old Truman Brewery, Hanbury Street, E1 6QR

www.thefrogrestaurant.com

In the former Truman Brewery yard in trendy Spitalfields, The Frog's back-to-basics dining room goes for an industrial, stripped-back look, with the de rigueur open kitchen at the back, edgy young artists' work, and an informal, boho mood that's pitched squarely at the hip local crew. Adam Handling deploys the techno arsenal in exciting cooking fizzing with ambition and creativity, delivered via a 'British tapas' menu and multi-course tasters that also come in veggie and vegan mode. To limber up the palate, finely honed miniature 'snacks' might see cannoli filled with smoked cod, crème fraîche and caviar, or punchy little crackers of BBQ beef, chilli and lovage. From the 'garden' section, dishes with sparkling flavours and lots of intricate detailing could involve burrata with smoked leeks, romesco and wild garlic; elsewhere, fish-based ideas run to the likes of roast cod with broccoli, miso and hazelnut, while meatier fare could be a partnership of pork belly with black lentils, hispi cabbage and apple. Desserts keep the vibrant flavours coming – perhaps dark chocolate tofu with blood orange.

Chef Adam Handling, Jamie Park **Seats** 70 **Closed** 25–26 December **Prices from** S £7, M £12, D £4 **Notes** Children welcome

Galvin HOP

◉◉ MODERN BRITISH, INTERNATIONAL

020 7299 0404 | 35 Spital Square, E1 6DY

www.galvinrestaurants.com

Galvin HOP is branded as a 'pub deluxe', with shiny copper tanks above the bar containing unpasteurised Czech lager. The menu could be described as modern pub or modern bistro, whatever floats your boat, with a repertoire that ranges from hot dogs to Dorset snails.

Chef Jeff Galvin **Seats** 70, Private dining 30 **Closed** 25–26 December and 1 January **Prices from** S £7.50, M £14.50, D £6 **Notes** Vegetarian dishes, Children welcome

Galvin La Chapelle

◉◉◉ FRENCH, EUROPEAN **V** 🍷 NOTABLE WINE LIST

See pages 172–173

LONDON E1
Galvin La Chapelle

◉◉◉ FRENCH, EUROPEAN 🅥 🍾 NOTABLE WINE LIST

020 7299 0400 | St Botolph's Hall, 35 Spital Square, E1 6DY

www.galvinrestaurants.com

A fantastic setting for classic-meets-modern French cooking

Set amid the shimmering modern glass buildings on Spital Square, La Chapelle is every bit a Spitalfields' top call, the converted red-brick Victorian former St Botolph's girls' school providing the brothers Galvin – the double-act with the Midas touch – a standout destination. Sweeping stone archways, marble pillars, arched windows and a roof open to the rafters some 30 metres up is a jaw-dropping smash-hit, while large iron chandeliers, art deco lamps, chocolate brown leather seating, huge velvety drapes and tables turned out in their best whites complete the dapper good looks and comforts to this awesome ecclesiastical backdrop. Throw in the razzmatazz of a smart zinc-topped bar by the entrance, a semi-open kitchen, striking private-dining mezzanine, an outdoor terrace, plus a platoon of attentive, well-drilled professional staff and you have friendly formality backed by slick service and a definite sense of occasion. No pressure then for the kitchen, but the cooking lives up to the billing, conforming purposefully to the Galvin genre: polished French cuisine underpinned by a classical base and given a light modern gloss.

Top-notch produce, uncluttered, sophisticated, fine-tuned cooking is the raison d'être, and pretty on the plate it is too. Take high-gloss signature starters like the lasagne of Dorset crab, perhaps turned out with a creamy beurre nantaise and pea shoots, or a ballotine of Landes foie gras twinned with burnt orange, granola and brioche. Classic desserts catch the eye too, like the ever-present and not-to-be-missed caramelised apple tarte Tatin with Normandy crème fraîche, or a perfectly timed hot Valrhona chocolate fondant served with a blood orange sorbet to cut through the richness. In between, perhaps sea-fresh fillet of Icelandic cod teamed with saffron potatoes, sea herbs and bouillabaisse flavours, while, for the City high-roller carnivores, another menu mainstay, roast chateaubriand of Cumbrian beef, perhaps teamed with silky truffle pomme purée and artichokes, or maybe roast loin and slow-cooked Hampshire venison served with butternut squash, chestnuts and jus grande veneur. Prices may lean toward the deep-wallets for carte and tasting options, but the prix fixe Menu de Chef (served at lunch and early evening) keeps budgets on track. (Commendably, vegetarians have their own menu and tasting version too.) The wine list is a corker, with French big guns leading the way on a knockout list. (Its popular adjoining Galvin HOP 'pub delux' can ramp-up the decibels in La Chapelle at busy times.)

Chef Jeff Galvin **Seats** 110, Private dining 16 **Closed** 24–26 December and 1 January
Prices from S £14.50, M £28.50, D £9.50 **Notes** Children welcome

E1 continued

Lyle's

◉◉ MODERN BRITISH **V**

020 3011 5911 | Tea Building, 56 Shoreditch High Street, E1 6JJ

www.lyleslondon.com

Lyle's coolly austere warehouse good looks – think whitewashed brick walls, subway tiles and industrial pendant lights – have made it a must-visit outfit since it first opened. The food certainly delivers on the hype and expectation, with some lesser-used gutsy cuts and innovative combinations

Chef James Lowe **Seats** 48 **Closed** Bank holidays, Christmas, New Year **Prices from** S £8, M £16, D £9 **Notes** Children welcome

Super Tuscan

◉ ITALIAN

020 7247 8717 | 8a Artillery Passage, E1 7LJ

www.supertuscan.co.uk

The cheery Italian enoteca in a Dickensian Spitalfields' alley is a hang-loose setting for inspired classic Italian home cooking. Antipasti sharing platters of salamis and/or cheeses are obvious ways to pique the appetite. Expect hearty mains such as chargrilled veal chop with rosemary-spiked potatoes.

Chef Nick Grossi **Seats** 30 **Closed** Christmas and New Year **Prices from** S £4, M £10.95, D £3.50 **Notes** Vegetarian dishes, Children welcome

LONDON E2
Brawn

◉◉ TRADITIONAL EUROPEAN ⚑ NOTABLE WINE LIST

020 7729 5692 | 49 Columbia Road, E2 7RG

www.brawn.co

Set among a strip of artisanal shops, the corner-sited restaurant is a hard-edged, pared-back neighbourhood outfit. The trendy interior goes for an unadorned look of whitewashed brickwork, high ceilings, and plain cafe tables and retro chairs, plus the de rigueur open kitchen at the back.

Chef Ed Wilson **Seats** 70 **Closed** Christmas, New Year and Bank holidays **Notes** Vegetarian dishes, Children welcome

Marksman

◉◉ MODERN BRITISH

020 7739 7393 | 254 Hackney Road, E2 7SJ

www.marksmanpublichouse.com

Once a run-down boozer, this was taken over by two chefs, both of whom previously worked at influential London restaurant St John. Restored to its former glory as a traditional pub downstairs, the first-floor restaurant is of a minimalist style.

Chef Tom Harris, Jon Rotheram **Seats** 45, Private dining 12 **Closed** 25–28 December **Prices from** S £7, M £18, D £6 **Notes** Vegetarian dishes, Children welcome

LONDON E8
Pidgin

◉◉◉ MODERN BRITISH **V**

020 7254 8311 | 52 Wilton Way, E8 1BG

www.pidginlondon.com

Set in a Hackney terrace, Pidgin could hardly be more of the moment. It's a small, rough-and-ready looking venue in which bare twigs adorn the walls beneath a bottle shelf, and bentwood chairs at café tables give notice that nobody expects you to come in your finery. On the other hand, the food, which issues from an open kitchen in tirelessly changing variations (it changes weekly) in the form of a fixed four-course menu, is something to be seen. A sample view for one week might be beetroot cashew, fermented tofu, shiso and rhubarb to start, followed by cod milt with Avruga caviar, apple, radish and yuzu kosho. Move on to pork with corn kernel, apricot, hibiscus and nettle and finish with a malted cajeta mousse, pine ice cream, preserved cherries and peanut. The weekly changing drinks list is also a nice approach, taking in anything from Tasmanian sparklers to Mexican reds.

Chef Adolfo De Cecco **Seats** 27 **Closed** Christmas **Notes** No children under 5 years

LONDON E9
The Empress

◉◉ MODERN BRITISH

020 8533 5123 | 130 Lauriston Road, Victoria Park, E9 7LH

www.empresse9.co.uk

This Victorian tavern fits right into its buzzy Victoria Park location. Red Chesterfields, fashionable retro lighting and bare-brick walls are suitably à la mode, and when it comes to food, the kitchen (headed up by an ex L'Ortolan man) delivers honest stuff made with quality ingredients.

Chef Harry Milbourne **Seats** 49 **Closed** 25–26 December **Notes** Vegetarian dishes, Children welcome

LONDON E14
Plateau
◉ MODERN FRENCH ⏷NOTABLE WINE LIST
020 7715 7100 | 4th Floor, Canada Place, Canada Square, Canary Wharf, E14 5ER
www.plateau-restaurant.co.uk

Bag a window table to enjoy the incredible view over Canary Wharf from this fourth-floor restaurant with minimalist decor and an open-plan kitchen. A skilful pastry cook is behind a crisp pastry case for salted caramel and chocolate tart with raspberry coulis.

Chef Jeremy Trehout **Seats** 120, Private dining 30 **Closed** 25 December, 1 January **Parking** **Notes** Children welcome

Quadrato
◉ ITALIAN
020 7510 1999 | 46 Westferry Circus, Canary Wharf, E14 8RS
www.canaryriversideplaza.com

Ensconced in a glossy white riverside hotel among the high-rise buildings of Canary Wharf, contemporary chic reigns in the Quadrato restaurant, while a terrace is a welcome bonus for fine weather dining. Simplicity is the watchword in an eclectic modern menu.

Chef Fabio Pellegrino **Seats** 90 **Open** All year **Notes** Vegetarian dishes, Children welcome

Roka Canary Wharf
◉◉ JAPANESE ⏷NOTABLE WINE LIST
020 7636 5228 | 1st Floor, 40 Canada Square, E14 5FW
www.rokarestaurant.com

A cool, ultra-modern interior of natural woods befits the setting in Canada Square. Contemporary Japanese robatayaki cuisine is the deal, based on the robata grill (diners sitting alongside can watch the chefs silently working), with first-class fresh produce.

Chef Libor Dobis **Seats** 129 **Closed** 25 December, 1 January **Prices from** S £4.30, M £14.90, D £7 **Notes** Vegetarian dishes, Children welcome

Tom's Kitchen Canary Wharf
◉ BRITISH
020 3011 1555 | 11 Westferry Circus, Canary Wharf, E14 4HD
www.tomskitchen.co.uk/canary-wharf

Tom Aiken's ground-floor restaurant in a modern building in Docklands is an all-day operation. It keeps things simple with British favourites and comfort food classics. Sharing boards, grills and vegetarian options are available too, while time-starved office workers grab their takeaways from the deli.

Chef Jon Snodgrass, Tom Aikens **Open** All year **Notes** Children welcome

LONDON EC1
Anglo
◉◉◉ MODERN BRITISH V
020 7430 1503 | 30 St Cross Street, EC1N 8UH
www.anglorestaurant.com

The blank grey frontage and spare office-canteen interior design are very much of the moment at Mark Jarvis's venue near the Hatton Garden jewellery quarter and Leather Lane market. Consecrated to the celebration of home produce, as is indicated by the name, the cooking matches contemporary ingenuity with a colourful, high-impact look on the plate, showing an essential lightness of touch but without any compromise on concentrated flavours. After a nibble of sourdough bread with yeast butter, the set tasting menus might open with optionally truffled potato dumplings in curds and whey, before pairing scallops with white asparagus, and then bathing Loch Duart salmon in buttermilk and wild garlic. Main course could be premium chicken accoutred with leeks and celeriac, a dish that rises out of the pub food ethos to produce something remarkable. A pre-dessert of Jerusalem artichoke in maple syrup leads on to a brace of sweeties – chocolate with cranberry and rhubarb, then coconut with lemon thyme and grapefruit. A vegetarian version is offered too, as are two grades of drinks pairing to accompany it all, with craft beers inveigling themselves among the wines.

Chef Mark Jarvis **Seats** 32, Private dining 5 **Closed** 24 December to 3 January and Bank holidays **Notes** Vegetarian dishes, No children

The Bleeding Heart
◉ MODERN FRENCH
020 7242 2056 | Bleeding Heart Yard, Off Greville Street, EC1N 8SJ
www.bleedingheart.co.uk

Named after the Dickensian courtyard where 17th-century 'It girl' Lady Elizabeth Hatton was killed by her jealous lover, this intimate cellar restaurant has atmosphere in spades, making it a hot spot for business lunches and romantic dinners. The kitchen deals in hearty Anglo-French fare.

Chef Julian Marshall **Seats** 110, Private dining 40 **Closed** Christmas and New Year (10 days) **Notes** Vegetarian dishes, No children under 7 years

Le Café du Marché

⊕ FRENCH

020 7608 1609 | Charterhouse Mews, Charterhouse Square, EC1M 6AH

www.cafedumarche.co.uk

The popularity of this classic cross-Channel country auberge-style venue remains undiminished. Bare-brick walls, French posters and candlelit tables set the tone in the rustic-chic converted Victorian warehouse. Food-wise, expect unreconstructed French provincial dishes on an ever-changing carte backed up by daily specials.

Chef Tony Pineda **Seats** 120, Private dining 65 **Closed** Christmas, New Year, Easter and Bank holidays **Prices from** S £5.95, M £21, D £5.95 **Notes** Vegetarian dishes, Children welcome

Chez Mal Brasserie

⊕ MODERN BRITISH

020 3750 9402 | 18–21 Charterhouse Square, Clerkenwell, EC1M 6AH

www.malmaison.com

Like other hotels in the group, this branch is done out in best boutique fashion, with dramatic crimson and purple interiors, a sultrily lit bar and a brasserie in deep brown tones. The order of the day is lively modern British cooking with interesting variations.

Chef John Woodward **Seats** 70, Private dining 14 **Open** All year **Prices from** S £5.50, M £14, D £4 **Parking** 4 **Notes** Vegetarian dishes, Children welcome

The Clove Club

⊕⊕⊕ MODERN BRITISH V

020 7729 6496 | Shoreditch Town Hall, 380 Old Street, EC1V 9LT

www.thecloveclub.com

The old Shoreditch Town Hall with its pilasters and pediments belonged by the 1960s to a past era of municipal bureaucratic grandeur, but has been reborn today as an arts venue staging theatrical productions and contemporary dance, as well as one of east London's vanguard culinary operations. The bare-boarded floor and unclothed tables in a white, high-ceilinged space have a certain dignity still, but it's the cutting-edge production of the kitchen that excites most notice. A multi-course taster is the principal business, though there is a shorter five-course deal for weekday evenings. If you're not up for one of the wine pairings, try a selection of ambient teas to go with the dishes.

Chef Isaac McHale, Chase Lovecky **Seats** 70 **Closed** 2 weeks at Christmas and New Year **Notes** Children welcome at lunch only

Club Gascon

⊕⊕⊕ FRENCH V ⌑ NOTABLE WINE LIST

020 7600 6144 | 57 West Smithfields, EC1A 9DS

www.clubgascon.com

When Pascal Aussignac opened Club Gascon two decades ago, his aim was to bring the cooking of his ancestral southwest France to a London that was familiar enough with foie gras and cassoulet, but in ways that creatively reimagined the possibilities of a region of gastronomic riches. He helped pioneer the small-plate approach that encourages experimentation, and constructed menus that successfully balance traditional combinations with thoroughgoing modernity. The formula remains a winner. Duck naturally features prominently, as in the immaculate duck confit with berries, and the opening taste of 'Ultimate Duck' with Aquitaine caviar, while fish options take in turbot with popcorn in Guinness and oyster sauce. Vegetarian offerings are as dynamic as the rest, as in smoked chestnut cappuccino or black-truffled potato spaghetti, and dessert might be pineapple soufflé with ginger and lemongrass sorbet.

Chef Pascal Aussignac **Seats** 42, Private dining 10 **Closed** Christmas, New Year, Bank holidays **Prices from** S £14.50, M £18.50, D £10 **Notes** Children welcome

Comptoir Gascon

⊕ TRADITIONAL EUROPEAN

020 7608 0851 | 61–63 Charterhouse Street, EC1M 6HJ

www.comptoirgascon.com

Comptoir deals in the gutsy food of southwest France, delivering simple comfort-driven cooking with full-on flavours. The decor fits the bill with its modern-rustic vibe; exposed brickwork and ducting, dinky elbow-to-elbow wooden tables, while the miniscule deli counter offers supplies to take away.

Chef Pascal Aussignac **Seats** 45 **Closed** 25–31 December, Bank holidays **Prices from** S £7, M £9.75, D £4.50 **Notes** Vegetarian dishes, Children welcome

The Green

⊕ TRADITIONAL BRITISH

020 7490 1258 | 29 Clerkenwell Green, EC1R 0DU

www.thegreenclerkenwell.com

The Green conforms to the trendy gastro pub template with its mismatched tables and chairs, art-laden walls and battery of real ales at the bar. Light streams in through windows upon a lively crew whose attention is focussed on the perky menu of fuss-free dishes.

Chef Sandy Jarvis **Seats** 35, Private dining 45 **Open** All year **Prices from** S £6.50, M £12, D £5.50 **Notes** Vegetarian dishes, Children welcome

Hix Oyster & Chop House
◉ MODERN BRITISH **V**

020 7017 1930 | 36–37 Greenhill Rents, Cowcross Street, EC1M 6BN

www.hixoysterandchophouse.co.uk

Mark Hix's first outfit in an ever-expanding portfolio perfectly embraces its cool Smithfield setting. Wooden floors, tiled walls and ceiling fans characterise the cool, pared-down space. The kitchen reflects the Hix credo of quality seasonal ingredients treated with simplicity, respect and flair.

Chef Jamie Guy **Seats** 65 **Closed** 25–26 December, Bank holidays **Notes** Children welcome

Luca
◉ ITALIAN

020 3859 3000 | 88 St John Street, EC1M 4EH

www.luca.restaurant

Another sizeable venue on the bustling entrepot of St John Street, Luca uses regional British produce in menus that look to Italy. Sharing plates for mixing and matching, and a boisterous, well-stocked bar are also in the now.

Chef Robert Chambers **Seats** 60, Private dining 10 **Closed** Christmas **Prices from** S £11, M £18, D £8 **Notes** Vegetarian dishes, Children welcome

The Modern Pantry Clerkenwell
◉◉ MODERN, FUSION

020 7553 9210 | 47–48 St John's Square, Clerkenwell, EC1V 4JJ

www.themodernpantry.co.uk

Set in two listed Georgian townhouses on St John's Square, this breezy all-day eatery is an intimate, relaxed backdrop for a lively trek through the world of fusion cooking. Expect influences from around the globe, delivered in inspired combinations.

Chef Anna Hansen, Robert McLeary **Seats** 110, Private dining 60 **Closed** Christmas, New Year and Summer Bank Holiday **Prices from** S £6.90, M £15, D £2.80 **Notes** Vegetarian dishes, Children welcome

The Montcalm London City at The Brewery
◉ TRADITIONAL BRITISH

020 7614 0100 | 52 Chiswell Street, EC1Y 4SB

www.themontcalmlondoncity.co.uk

Samuel Whitbread built up one of the UK's foremost beer brands on this spot, and part of his one-time Georgian brewery has been converted into this swanky hotel. There are a couple of dining options in situ, all entirely in keeping with the Georgian setting.

Chef Aarik Persaud **Seats** 70, Private dining 50 **Closed** Christmas, New Year and Bank holidays **Notes** Vegetarian dishes, Children welcome

Moro
◉ MEDITERRANEAN, NORTH AFRICAN

020 7833 8336 | 34–36 Exmouth Market, EC1R 4QE

www.moro.co.uk

Sam and Samantha Clark's Moorish food takes its cue from Spain via North Africa to the eastern Mediterranean, a popular formula with regulars who spill out onto pavement tables. Friendly staff keep it all together, while inventive menus deliver colourful dishes of big flavours.

Chef Samuel and Samantha Clark **Seats** 120 **Closed** Christmas to New Year, Bank holidays **Notes** Vegetarian dishes, Children welcome

St John
◉◉ BRITISH

020 7251 0848 | 26 St John Street, EC1M 4AY

www.stjohnrestaurant.com

St John is a pilgrimage spot for anyone claiming foodie credentials. Set up over 20 years ago in a former Georgian smokehouse by Smithfield Market, the 'nose-to-tail' eating philosophy championing unglamorous, lesser-used cuts has turned on a generation of chefs to the robust, gutsy style.

Chef Jonathan Woolway **Seats** 110, Private dining 18 **Closed** Christmas, New Year, Bank holidays **Notes** Vegetarian dishes, Children welcome

Smiths of Smithfield, Top Floor
◉◉ EUROPEAN

020 7251 7950 | 67–77 Charterhouse Street, EC1M 6HJ

www.smithsofsmithfield.co.uk

Opposite Smithfield Market, Top Floor offers rooftop views of the City skyscrapers from its long, light-filled room through full-drop sliding glass doors and fine-weather terrace. The kitchen produces light, modern dishes of flair and flavour. Funky chairs, semi-circular leather banquettes and unstuffy service are spot on.

Chef Liam Walsh **Seats** 80, Private dining 50 **Closed** 25–26 December and 1 January **Prices from** S £11, M £18, D £6.75 **Notes** Vegetarian dishes, Children welcome

Sosharu
◉◉◉ JAPANESE

020 3805 2304 | 64 Turnmill St, EC1M 5RR

www.sosharulondon.com

'Social' is the link that binds Jason Atherton's numerous culinary enterprises, pronounced here in the Japanese fashion as the banner for his unique take on the casual Japanese izakaya-style restaurant and bar theme. The traditional Japanese design influence is clear in the minimalist aesthetic of the whole operation, with latticed screens breaking up the space, and an urban-cool Tokyo-inspired cocktail bar in the basement. Alex Craciun is adept in Japanese culinary ways and leads the brigade of knife-wielding chefs who deliver exemplary sushi, sashimi and refined, highly detailed, Instagram-ready dishes. You might set out with broccoli tempura with pungent kimchi dressing and aged parmesan, or tuna tartare with caviar and brioche, then look to the hibachi grill for perfectly seared Wagyu rib-eye pointed up with ginger, garlic crisps, onion and sesame. Fish, too, is a strong draw – perhaps grilled cod marinated in sweet soy and boosted with pickled shimeji mushroom and seaweed salad. To finish, chocolate and sesame roll with warm whisky sauce might tempt. The impeccable wine list is rivalled by an impressive roster of 50-plus sakes.

Chef Alex Craciun, Jason Atherton **Seats** 74, Private dining 6 **Closed** Christmas, Bank holidays **Prices from** S £8, M £19, D £9 **Notes** Vegetarian dishes, Children welcome

LONDON EC2
Aviary Restaurant
® MODERN BRITISH
020 3873 4000 | Montcalm Royal London House, 22–25 Finsbury Square, EC2A 1DX
www.montcalmroyallondoncity.co.uk

Ten floors above Finsbury Square in the heart of the City, this ultra-modern restaurant with a centralised bar and excellent roof terrace features two stuffed peacocks and sundry birdcages, which explain the restaurant's name. The main draw, of course, is the British brasserie-style food.

Chef Dan Hodson **Seats** 65, Private dining **Open** All year **Notes** Vegetarian dishes, Children welcome

Boisdale of Bishopsgate
® TRADITIONAL BRITISH, FRENCH, SCOTTISH
020 7283 1763 | Swedeland Court, 202 Bishopsgate, EC2M 4NR
www.boisdale.co.uk

Down a Dickensian alley near Liverpool Street station, this Boisdale occupies an atmospheric vaulted basement. The soundtrack is live jazz, and the cooking is simple stuff founded on thoroughbred – often Scottish – meats and seafood, so starters include smoked salmon, or roast Blackface haggis.

Chef Philip Moore **Seats** 100, Private dining 44 **Closed** Christmas, 31 December, 1 January and Bank holidays **Notes** Vegetarian dishes, Children welcome

City Social
®®® MODERN EUROPEAN **V**
020 7877 7703 | Tower 42, EC2N 1HQ
www.citysociallondon.com

Up on the 24th floor of Tower 42, the setting is a glamorous contemporary art deco-inspired space with rosewood panelling, chrome, brass and smoked glass, and a couple of Warhols on the walls, all set against the lights of the Gherkin, the Cheesegrater and the Shard in the wraparound skyscape. The food is equally spectacular – inventive, detailed and bursting with entertaining combinations of taste and texture – courtesy of Paul Walsh, who brings authority and innovative impetus to the house style of classically founded modern European cooking, as seen in openers such as of Brixham crab teamed with pickled kohlrabi, nashi pear, coriander and pink grapefruit. Alternatively, you might kick off with pasta or risotto, perhaps wild garlic risotto with braised morels and aged parmesan, then move on to line-caught cod with octopus carpaccio, ratatouille and squid ink crisp, or rabbit saddle with Parma ham, chanterelles, spelt and black garlic. To finish, try banana soufflé with banana tartare and peanut ice cream, or two might sign up for apple tarte Tatin with vanilla ice cream and caramel sauce.

Chef Paul Walsh, Jason Atherton **Seats** 90, Private dining 24 **Closed** 25 December, 1 January and Bank holidays **Prices from** S £13, M £24, D £9.50 **Notes** Children welcome

Coq d'Argent
®® FRENCH **V**
020 7395 5000 | 1 Poultry, EC2R 8EJ
www.coqdargent.co.uk

A stylish, modern, sharp-suit confection that comes properly dressed for the accomplished, big-flavoured French cooking and City skyscraper views. Menus boast bags of luxury for City high rollers; from oysters, lobster or caviar to deep-wallet mains like slabs of prime beef.

Chef Damien Rigollet **Seats** 150 **Closed** Christmas and winter bank holidays **Prices from** S £3, M £24, D £8 **Notes** Children welcome

Duck & Waffle
®® BRITISH, EUROPEAN
020 3640 7310 | 110 Bishopsgate, EC2N 4AY
www.duckandwaffle.com

The view from the 40th floor of the City's Heron Tower is pretty amazing, and Duck & Waffle can sort you out for breakfast, lunch, dinner, cocktails, a late supper, in a casual space open 24/7. Food takes a broad sweep through contemporary European ideas.

Chef Daniel Doherty **Seats** 260, Private dining 18 **Open** All year **Notes** Vegetarian dishes, Children welcome

Eastway Brasserie
⊕ EUROPEAN
020 7618 7400 | ANdAZ Liverpool Street, 40 Liverpool Street, EC2M 7QN
www.eastwaybrasserie.com
There are numerous eating places to choose from here, including this take on a New York brasserie, with its own entrance, an open-to-view kitchen and massed ranks of tables. Open all day from breakfast to dinner, the carte offers up a wide selection of classic dishes.

Chef Sam Dunleavy **Seats** 96 **Open** All year **Prices from** S £9, M £16, D £7 **Notes** Vegetarian dishes, Children welcome

Manicomio City
⊕ MODERN ITALIAN
020 7726 5010 | Gutter Lane, EC2V 8AS
www.manicomio.co.uk
The city branch of Manicomio occupies a three-tiered, Sir Norman Foster-designed glass building with a buzzy ground-floor terrace and café-bar and a sleek first-floor restaurant dressed up with a decor as sober as the suited-and-booted city types at its black leather seats and white-linen-clad tables.

Chef Tom Salt **Seats** 95, Private dining 60 **Closed** 1 week at Christmas **Notes** Vegetarian dishes, Children welcome

Merchants Tavern
⊕⊕⊕ MODERN EUROPEAN
020 7060 5335 | 36 Charlotte Road, EC2A 3PG
www.merchantstavern.co.uk
Tucked down a slip of a back street in Shoreditch, the Tavern occupies the site of what was, in Victorian times, a warehouse and apothecary's premises. Music nights are a regular feature in a space that feels expansive enough for parties, with its parquet floor and convex mirrors, and in between funky jams and Balearic beats, the kitchen seems in permanent overdrive. With Angela Hartnett as one of the owners, there's a sure touch to the entire operation, no matter what time you rock up. Porridge-and-prune breakfasts, weekend brunches, and a solid repertoire of populist European food at lunch and dinner do their level best to cover all bases. In the evenings, it could be sea bream tartare with horseradish and Avruga to begin, prior to a cheeky pasta dish such as leek tortelli with oxtail ragout and parmesan. Main courses are comfortingly substantial, perhaps cod in mussel broth with monk's beard and turnips, or pork belly with apple, dates and parsley root purée. Desserts offer a cross-Channel list of Paris-Brest, gâteau basque with prunes and Armagnac, or rhubarb and custard.

Chef Philippa MacDonald **Seats** 120, Private dining 22 **Closed** 25–26 December, 1 January **Prices from** S £8.50, M £14, D £7.50 **Notes** Vegetarian dishes, Children welcome

Miyako
⊕ JAPANESE
020 7618 7100 | ANdAZ London, 40 Liverpool Street, EC2M 7QN
www.londonliverpoolstreet.andaz.hyatt.com/en/hotel/dining/Miyako.html
Miyako is within the ANdAZ London hotel, although it has its own entrance where queues form at lunchtime for takeaway boxes. The restaurant itself has a cool, uncluttered look, thanks to large windows, walls veneered in pale wood and bamboo, and black-lacquered tables and chairs.

Chef Kosei Sakamoto **Seats** 24 **Closed** Christmas, New Year **Prices from** S £4, M £12, D £7 **Notes** Children welcome

Popolo Shoreditch
⊕⊕ ITALIAN, MEDITERRANEAN
020 7729 4299 | 26 Rivington Street, EC2A 3DU
www.popoloshoreditch.com
A fashionable and young crowd are drawn to this small, modern restaurant that's spread over two levels. The service is informal but the staff are very knowledgeable, and you can sit at the bar to view the chefs producing excellent regional Italian tapas-style dishes.

Chef Jonathan Lawson **Seats** 33 **Closed** 24 December to 2nd January **Notes** Vegetarian dishes, Children welcome

SAGARDI London
⊕ BASQUE **V**
020 3802 0478 | Cordy House building, 95 Curtain Road, EC2A 3BS
www.sagardi.co.uk
Specialising in the cooking of the Basque country, Sagardi features a glass-walled meat-hanging room, wood-fired grilling and a copiously stocked wine wall. Steaks and pintxos (Basque tapas), plus fish from northern Spanish waters, comprise a menu replete with flavourful protein. The signature desserts include pastel vasco, a densely textured, crisp-shelled cake.

Chef Iñaki López de Viñaspre **Seats** Private dining 30 **Open** All year **Prices from** S £8, M £18, D £7 **Notes** Children welcome

LONDON EC2–EC3

SUSHISAMBA London
◉◉ JAPANESE, BRAZILIAN, PERUVIAN ◧ NOTABLE WINE LIST

020 3640 7330 | 110 Bishopsgate, EC2N 4AY
www.sushisamba.com

The glass lift whizzes up to the 38th floor of Heron Tower in a few queasy seconds, but Sushisamba offers nothing but pleasure to the digestion. Japan, Brazil and Peru provide inspiration for a fusion of straight-up sushi and all-day grazing plates of high-quality ingredients.

Chef Claudio Cardoso **Seats** 134, Private dining 40 **Open** All year **Notes** Vegetarian dishes, Children welcome

Temple and Sons
◉◉ MODERN BRITISH

020 7877 7710 | 22 Old Broad Street, EC2N 1HQ
www.templeandsons.co.uk

Jason Atherton's latest venture is a two-storey operation with a bar and deli at ground level, and the eaterie with open kitchen upstairs. Music pounds out and there's plenty of excited chatter in the air. Modernised British tradition is the name of the game.

Chef Keith Hooker **Seats** **Closed** Bank holidays **Notes** Vegetarian dishes, Children welcome

LONDON EC3
Caravaggio
◉ MODERN ITALIAN

020 7626 6206 | 107–112 Leadenhall Street, EC3A 4AF
www.caravaggiorestaurant.co.uk

Ornate ceilings, art deco light fittings and an imposing staircase leading to a mezzanine gallery lend a 1930s pizzazz to this Italian in a former banking hall. The pace is full-on at lunch, while evenings are more chilled. This is food of simplicity and flavour.

Chef Faliero Lenta **Seats** 150 **Closed** Christmas and Bank holidays **Notes** Vegetarian dishes, Children welcome

Chamberlain's Restaurant
◉ MODERN BRITISH, SEAFOOD

020 7648 8690 | 23–25 Leadenhall Market, EC3V 1LR
www.chamberlainsoflondon.co.uk

Spread over several floors amid the Victorian splendour of Leadenhall Market, Chamberlain's buzzes with the power-lunch crowd from the city skyscrapers. There's an all-weather terrace beneath the market's glass roof, while windows in the buzzy dining room and more intimate mezzanine make for good people-watching.

Chef Andrew Jones **Seats** 120, Private dining 55 **Closed** Christmas, New Year and Bank holidays **Prices from** S £11.50, M £16.50, D £7.50 **Notes** Vegetarian dishes, Children welcome

La Dame de Pic
◉◉◉ FRENCH V

020 3302 0310 | Four Seasons Trinity Square, 10 Trinity Square EC3N 4AJ
www.fourseasons.com/tentrinity

Anne-Sophie Pic may not be a household name on this side of la Manche, but she has earned her place in French culinary history at her renowned restaurant Maison Pic in the Rhône Valley in southeast France. Her base for conquering the UK's foodies is a sleek space done out with leather, wood and mirrors in the swanky Four Seasons Hotel by Tower Hill, and her fine-tuned culinary imagination produces some powerful and unexpected flavour combinations in the contemporary French style. The cooking is really on song in a starter of superb Scottish langoustine, sautéed in shellfish butter and served with cucumber, the citrus hit of kabosu, Granny Smith apple, and Chartreuse emulsion. Next up, a superbly crafted classic dish – Pithivier of venison and foie gras – delivers luxury in spades, alongside cocoa bean, salsify crisps and sake. The signature white millefeuille dessert made with Tahitian vanilla cream, jasmine jelly and voatsiperifery pepper foam is a triumphant finale.

Chef Anne-Sophie Pic, Luca Piscazzi **Closed** Sundays

James Cochran EC3
◉◉ MODERN BRITISH, CARIBBEAN V

020 3302 0310 | 19 Bevis Marks, Liverpool Street, EC3A 7JB
www.jcochran.restaurant

The Gherkin may be one of the instantly recognisable tower blocks, but James Cochran's restaurant isn't. But don't be put off by its lack of curb appeal; JC is a highly talented young chef with a stellar CV setting out on his first solo venture.

Chef James Cochran **Seats** 45, Private dining 30 **Closed** Bank holidays, Christmas, New Year **Prices from** S £6, M £14.50, D £7 **Notes** Children welcome

Mei Ume
◉◉ JAPANESE, CHINESE

020 3297 3799 | Four Seasons Trinity Square, 10 Trinity Square, EC3N 4AJ
www.meiume.com

Mei Ume is an impossibly chic Asian restaurant, showcasing dishes from China and Japan. Part of the incredibly impressive Ten Trinity Square hotel, the high-ceilinged dining room, with its pillars and curved banquettes, is a suitable venue for authentic dishes with a modern slant.

Chef Tony Truong **Seats** 50, Private dining 12 **Open** All year **Prices from** S £5, M £16, D £9 **Notes** Vegetarian dishes, Children welcome

LONDON EC4

Barbecoa

◉ MODERN

020 3005 8555 | 20 New Change Passage, EC4M 9AG
www.barbecoa.com

Expect a backing track of high-decibel chatter and banging music at this City temple to meat. It's a cool venue where show-stopping views of St Paul's mix with low-slung banquettes, polished floors and soaring wine walls. Cooking by fire, smoke and charcoal is the thing.

Chef Jamie Oliver, Adam Perry Lang, Sebastian La Rocca **Seats** 220, Private dining 30 **Open** All year **Notes** Vegetarian dishes, Children welcome

Bread Street Kitchen

◉◉ BRITISH, EUROPEAN

020 3030 4050 | 10 Bread Street, EC4M 9AJ
www.breadstreetkitchen.com

The name suggests a homely wholefood co-operative, but the reality is a cavernous, high-decibel, high-octane city-slicker operation. Expect a soaring, warehouse-like space that mixes retro and modern looks with art deco references and the feel of a film set from Fritz Lang's *Metropolis*.

Chef Erion Karaj, Paul Shearing **Seats** 250 **Open** All year **Notes** Vegetarian dishes, Children welcome

Chinese Cricket Club

◉ CHINESE **V**

0871 942 9190 | Crowne Plaza London – The City, 19 New Bridge Street, EC4V 6DB
www.chinesecricketclub.com

Occupying a neutral modern space enlivened with cricketing memorabilia, CCC combines modern techniques with traditional and authentic Szechuan flavours. From the dim sum list come three light and fluffy steamed dumplings packed with minced chicken, prawn and spinach with a fiery dipping sweet chilli sauce.

Chef Ken Wang **Seats** 80 **Closed** Christmas and Easter **Prices from** S £5.80, M £14, D £6.50 **Notes** Children welcome

Diciannove

◉◉ ITALIAN

0871 942 9190 | Crowne Plaza London – The City, 19 New Bridge Street, EC4V 6DB
www.diciannove19.com

The slick Italian operation at the Crowne Plaza City branch looks like the upscale café of a smart contemporary art gallery, all gleaming uncovered surfaces, striped upholstery, and a bar lit in throbbing

sunny yellow. Save room for warm amarena cherries, ricotta and sweet pistachios.

Chef Alessandro Bay **Seats** 100, Private dining 33 **Closed** Christmas, 24–30 January, Easter and Bank holidays **Prices from** S £7.50, M £17, D £5.50 **Notes** Vegetarian dishes, Children welcome

Lutyens Restaurant

◉◉ MODERN BRITISH ♣ NOTABLE WINE LIST

020 7583 8385 | 85 Fleet Street, EC4Y 1AE
www.lutyens-restaurant.com

The elegant Lutyens-designed building now bears the Conran stamp, with its cool pastel tones, pale wood, and elegant art deco lines. The modern European cooking is rooted in classic French technique but with a suitably light and refined touch to it.

Chef Daniel Mertl **Seats** 120, Private dining 26 **Closed** Christmas and Bank holidays **Prices from** S £9.50, M £19, D £7 **Notes** Vegetarian dishes, Children welcome

28–50 Wine Workshop & Kitchen

◉◉ MODERN EUROPEAN ♣ NOTABLE WINE LIST

020 7242 8877 | 140 Fetter Lane, EC4A 1BT
www.2850.co.uk

This wine-centric basement dining room has petrol-blue walls, exposed brickwork and bare wooden tables. Sitting at the bar gives a view into the efficiently run kitchen, while smartly dressed staff provide sleek, unobtrusive service to the buzzing room. The menu is accessible bistro-style fare.

Chef Julian Baris **Seats** 60, Private dining 12 **Closed** Christmas, New Year, Easter and Bank holidays **Prices from** S £8.50, M £16, D £7.50 **Notes** Vegetarian dishes, Children welcome

Vanilla Black

◉◉ MODERN VEGETARIAN **V**

020 7242 2622 | 17–18 Tooks Court, EC4A 1LB
www.vanillablack.co.uk

Tucked down an alley off Chancery Lane, Andrew Dargue and Donna Conroy's slick restaurant is a million miles from the initial bake school of vegetarianism. A minimalist contemporary look blends with dark floorboards, antique framed photos and rustic pine tables.

Chef Andrew Dargue **Seats** 45 **Closed** 2 weeks at Christmas and New Year, Bank Holiday Mondays **Notes** Children welcome

LONDON N1
Frederick's Restaurant
⦿ MODERN BRITISH

020 7359 2888 | 106–110 Islington High Street,
Camden Passage, Islington, N1 8EG
www.fredericks.co.uk

A spacious modern interior, with smart cocktail bar,
lofty conservatory dining space and garden out back,
proves a draw for the Islington set. Exposed or white-
painted brick walls are hung with bold contemporary
abstracts, and the light, modern Pan-European dishes
are a real crowd pleaser.

Chef Wilson Montoya **Seats** 150, Private dining 40
Closed Christmas, New Year and Bank holidays
Prices from S £8, M £13.50, D £7 **Notes** Vegetarian
dishes, Children welcome

Jamie Oliver's Fifteen
⦿ MODERN BRITISH

020 3375 1515 | 15 Westland Place, N1 7LP
www.fifteen.net

The original incarnation of Jamie Oliver's
philanthropic restaurant enterprise continues to draw
in the punters who come for the range of smaller and
larger plates for sharing. The place takes in young
unemployed people and prepare them for a career in
the kitchen.

Chef Robbin Holmgren **Seats** 130, Private dining 60
Closed 25 December, 1 January **Notes** Vegetarian
dishes, Children welcome

Radici
⦿⦿ ITALIAN

020 7354 4777 | 30 Almeida Street, Islington, N1 1AD
www.radici.uk

Francesco Mazzei's restaurant is located opposite the
Almeida Theatre, so it's a great spot to pop into before
or after the theatre. It's a big room with a large bar
and busy open kitchen that creates a great
atmosphere. Service is attentive without being stuffy.

Chef Francesco Mazzei **Seats** 100, Private dining 15
Closed 26 December, 1 January **Prices from** S £4.50,
M £8, D £6.50 **Notes** Vegetarian dishes, Children
welcome

Searcys St Pancras Grand
⦿ MODERN, NORTHERN EUROPEAN

020 7870 9900 | Grand Terrace, Upper Concourse, St
Pancras International, N1C 4QL
www.searcys.co.uk/stpancrasgrand

With Eurostar trains outside the window, it's fitting
that this sleek art deco-esque brasserie offers a menu
combining an entente cordiale of Pan-European

flavours. If you want to stay in Brit mode, there are
posh burgers, steaks, and fish and chips.

Chef Jack Norman, Andy Horsman **Seats** 160, Private
dining 14 **Closed** 25 December **Notes** Vegetarian
dishes, Children welcome

Smokehouse
⦿ MODERN AMERICAN

020 7354 1144 | 63–69 Canonbury Road, Islington,
N1 2DG
www.smokehouseislington.co.uk

The Smokehouse is an old Islington boozer reborn as a
temple to the elemental, Fred Flintstone principle of
subjecting hunks of meat to fire and wood-smoke. In
the yard are three giant smokers, and global culinary
influences add punch, fire and spice.

Chef Kevin Love **Seats** 70 **Closed** 24–26 December
Notes Vegetarian dishes, Children welcome

Trullo
⦿⦿ ITALIAN

020 7226 2733 | 300–302 St Paul's Road, N1 2LH
www.trullorestaurant.com

Just off Highbury Corner, Trullo is a cracking little
place, the setting for honest, ingredients-driven
modern Italian cooking and a menu that changes with
every sitting. Antipasti run to full-bore ideas such as
ox tongue with agretti and anchovy. Finish with
excellent almond tart.

Chef Conor Gadd, Tim Siadatan **Seats** 40, Private
dining 34 **Closed** 25 December to 3 January
Notes Vegetarian dishes, Children welcome

LONDON NW1
The Gilbert Scott
⦿⦿⦿ MODERN BRITISH ⏶ NOTABLE WINE LIST

020 7278 3888 | Renaissance St Pancras Hotel, Euston
Road, NW1 2AR
www.thegilbertscott.com

The Victorian era of the train was in full swing when the
grand Midland Hotel opened back in 1873, but our
illustrious forbears didn't have Eurostar trains that run
non-stop to the Continent. Now spectacularly restored
as the St Pancras Renaissance Hotel, it is once more a
London landmark at the heart of the rejuvenated Kings
Cross quarter. A masterpiece of Gothic Revival, from its
magnificent portico entrance to a sweeping double
staircase, the place displays the kind of opulence that
makes the perfect setting for a statement restaurant.
Enter Marcus Wareing, whose breathtakingly ornate and
glamorous cocktail bar and palatial dining room have put
St Pancras onto the map for 21st-century foodies. His
signature British-focused menus take prime UK produce
and a soupçon of French style to deliver a well-crafted,
gently contemporary repertoire that might open with

crispy Dorset snails with braised shallot, parsley and garlic, followed by venison haunch with roasted parsley root, black pudding and bitter leaves. To finish, cleverly conceived desserts include the likes of liquorice pannacotta with fig, and lemon thyme ice cream.

Chef Michael D'Adomo **Seats** 130, Private dining 18 **Open** All year **Prices from** S £9, M £18, D £6 **Notes** Vegetarian dishes, Children welcome

Meliã White House
◉◉ SPANISH, MEDITERRANEAN
020 7391 3000 | Albany Street, Regent's Park, NW1 3UP
www.melia-whitehouse.com

The Iberian-owned art deco hotel pays homage to its national cuisine in the elegant Spanish restaurant, L'Albufera. Serrano ham is carved from a trolley for traditionalists, otherwise try grilled octopus with black olive chimichurri dressing and salsify, or Spanish sausage cooked in cider with lavender.

Chef Ivan Jimenez Strzelecki **Seats** 62, Private dining 14 **Open** All year **Prices from** S £8, M £15, D £5.50 **Notes** Vegetarian dishes, Children welcome

Michael Nadra Primrose Hill
◉◉ MODERN EUROPEAN
020 7722 2800 | 42 Gloucester Avenue, NW1 8JD
www.restaurant-michaelnadra.co.uk

Nadra cooks on-the-money dishes of global cuisine, a reach that extends from tuna tartare and salmon céviche, through Ibérico presa (shoulder steak) and belly, wild mushrooms and mash in Madeira jus, to an apple and pear version of kataifi, the Greek shredded pasta dish.

Chef Michael Nadra **Seats** 100, Private dining 40 **Closed** 24–26 December, 1 January **Prices from** S £5, M £15, D £5 **Notes** Vegetarian dishes, Children welcome

Odette's
◉◉◉ MODERN BRITISH, EUROPEAN V
020 7586 8569 | 130 Regent's Park Road, NW1 8XL
www.odettesprimrosehill.com

Anybody looking to get a fix on the concept of the 'neighbourhood restaurant', look no further. Primrose Hill has always had its own distinct identity as a district, centred on a parade of smart shops and delis along Regent's Park Road, and Odette's has been part of the evolving scene since the late 1970s. Its open-air dining terrace conjures a sensation of the countryside out of the north London air, and the interior walls are crammed with diverting prints. Bryn Williams has moved with the times to the extent of offering a vegetarian tasting menu among the repertoire, but the core of his operation is elevated French bistro food of readily comprehensible appeal. Cured salmon with cabbage, apple and smoked roe, or a serving of crispy pig's head

with pickled mooli, pumpkin and black garlic, might lead on to halibut grenobloise in a sauce of potted shrimps. Welsh beef appears in two guises, the fillet and braised cheek, and sides include irresistible barbecued potatoes topped with cheese, onion and truffle. Finish with a pannacotta fragranced with bay leaf, garnished with blackberries, hazelnuts and olive oil.

Chef Bryn Williams, Tom Dixon **Seats** 70, Private dining 10 **Closed** 2 weeks from 24 December **Prices from** S £8, M £18, D £8 **Notes** Children welcome

Pullman London St Pancras
◉ MODERN EUROPEAN
020 7666 9000 | 100–110 Euston Road, NW1 2AJ
www.accorhotels.com/5309

This sleek hotel restaurant continues the cross-Channel link by refuelling Eurostar travellers at St Pancras International, five minutes away. This is a clean-cut 21st-century space constantly thrumming with activity. An open kitchen and Josper grill turn out an eclectic repertoire of uncomplicated modern European dishes.

Chef Mark Timms **Seats** 92 **Open** All year **Notes** Vegetarian dishes, Children welcome

The Winter Garden
◉◉ MODERN EUROPEAN
020 7631 8000 | The Landmark London, 222 Marylebone Road, NW1 6JQ
www.landmarklondon.co.uk/dining/winter-garden/

The Winter Garden is open all day, and the mood changes with the hour (and the weather), for it is in the heart of the eight-storey atrium that forms the nucleus of the Landmark Hotel. It's an impressive spot for classically minded modern food.

Chef Gary Klaner **Seats** 90 **Open** All year **Parking** 40 **Notes** Vegetarian dishes, Children welcome

LONDON NW3
Manna
◉ INTERNATIONAL VEGAN
020 7722 8028 | 4 Erskine Road, Primrose Hill, NW3 3AJ
www.mannav.com

Open for over 50 years, this pioneer in gourmet vegetarian and vegan dining sits in a residential street in well-heeled Primrose Hill. Relaxed decor has a touch of class. Carefully sourced produce is turned into vibrantly colourful dishes that take inspiration from far and wide.

Chef Robin Swallow, Marcin Janicki, Ioan Maftei **Seats** 50 **Closed** Christmas and New Year **Prices from** S £7, M £12, D £5 **Notes** Children welcome

LONDON SE1

The Anchor & Hope
🏅 BRITISH, EUROPEAN
020 7928 9898 | 36 The Cut, SE1 8LP
www.anchorandhopepub.co.uk

Rock up at this rollicking Waterloo gastro pub and try your luck for a table in the dining area. Every bit a proper no-frills boozer, food at the Anchor & Hope fits the no-nonsense mood, with big-hearted dishes on a menu that changes each session.

Chef Jonathon Jones, Alex Crofts **Seats** 58 **Closed** 25 December to 1 January and Bank holidays **Prices from** S £5, M £10.80, D £5.40 **Notes** Vegetarian dishes, Children welcome

Brasserie Joël
🏅🏅 MODERN FRENCH
020 7620 7200 | Park Plaza Westminster Bridge London, SE1 7UT
www.parkplaza.com

Park Plaza's dining options centre on a French venue called Brasserie Joël, a monochrome space with a large tree in the middle and funky music filling the air. A mix of traditional and lightly modernised French dishes brings plenty of lustre to the brasserie-style menu.

Chef Walter Ishizuka **Seats** 180, Private dining 80 **Open** All year **Notes** Vegetarian dishes, Children welcome

Chino Latino London
🏅🏅 MODERN PAN ASIAN, PERUVIAN V
020 7769 2500 | Park Plaza London Riverbank, 18 Albert Embankment, SE1 7TJ
www.chinolatino.eu/london

The London outpost of the east Asian/South American fusion venture is to be found in the Park Plaza Riverbank Hotel on the South Bank. A thoroughgoing glitziness sees an illuminated pink wall-sculpture preside over a soberly grey-toned dining room with the feel of a theatre set.

Chef Werner Seebach **Seats** 88 **Open** All year **Prices from** S £3.50, M £13, D £8.50 **Notes** Children welcome

See advertisement opposite

Hutong
🏅🏅 NORTHERN CHINESE V
020 3011 1257 | Level 33, The Shard, 31 St Thomas Street, SE1 9RY
www.hutong.co.uk

The view from the 33rd floor of The Shard is stunning, particularly at night with the shimmering lights below. The room is a bit of a looker, with red lanterns and an open-to-view wood-fired oven where ducks are cooking and drying.

Chef Fei Wang **Seats** 130, Private dining 26 **Closed** 25 December, 1 January **Notes** Children welcome

Oblix
🏅 MODERN INTERNATIONAL
020 7268 6700 | Level 32, The Shard, 31 St Thomas Street, SE1 9RY
www.oblixrestaurant.com

It goes without saying: the views from the 32nd floor of The Shard are terrific. Oblix holds its own too, with its slick, brasserie vibe, open kitchen, cool lounge bar and vibrant food that's driven by the grill and Josper oven.

Chef Marcus Eaves **Seats** 100 **Closed** 25 December **Notes** Vegetarian dishes, Children welcome

The Oxo Tower Restaurant
🏅🏅 MODERN BRITISH V 🍷 NOTABLE WINE LIST
020 7803 3888 | 8th Floor, Oxo Tower Wharf, Barge House Street, SE1 9PH
www.oxotowerrestaurant.com

On the eighth floor of the old Oxo building, this bar, brasserie and restaurant overlooks the river and St Paul's Cathedral, a world-class vista which never fails to impress. The cooking is modern British with a bit of globetrotting into Asian territory.

Chef Jeremy Bloor **Seats** 150 **Closed** 25 December **Prices from** S £11, M £21, D £8 **Notes** Children welcome

Park Plaza County Hall London
🏅 MODERN ITALIAN
020 7021 1919 | 1 Addington Street, SE1 7RY
www.parkplazacountyhall.com

Inside the snazzy modern hotel next to County Hall on the South Bank, L'Italiano restaurant is on a mezzanine level and has bags of style, including great views through the large glass wall. The heart of the culinary action is a wood-fired oven.

Chef Stephen Rey **Seats** 104, Private dining 50 **Open** All year **Notes** Vegetarian dishes, Children welcome

Pizarro
🏅🏅 TRADITIONAL SPANISH
020 7378 9455 | 194 Bermondsey Street, SE1 3TQ
www.josepizarro.com/restaurants/pizarro

Whole hams hanging at a Spanish tile-frieze bar, warm wood textures, and chefs at an open plancha are a nod to an Iberian mood, while a stripped back aesthetic appeals to local trendsters. At Pizarro, the tapas formula has evolved into gutsier regional fare.

Chef José Pizarro **Seats** 75, Private dining 10 **Closed** 4 days Christmas **Notes** Vegetarian dishes, Children welcome

Le Pont de la Tour

◉◉ MODERN FRENCH

020 7403 8403 | The Butlers Wharf Building,
36d Shad Thames, SE1 2YE
www.lepontdelatour.co.uk

Framed by the city skyscrapers, the view in front of
you might be of Tower Bridge but the well-executed
food at Le Pont de la Tour is rooted in the French
classics. Seafood is a strong suit and luxury
ingredients come thick and fast.

Chef Julien Imbert **Seats** 140, Private dining 20
Open All year **Prices from** S £3.50, M £19
Notes Vegetarian dishes, Children welcome

Restaurant Story

◉◉◉◉◉ MODERN BRITISH **V** ♦ NOTABLE WINE LIST

020 7183 2117 | 199 Tooley Street, SE1 2JX
www.restaurantstory.co.uk

Suppose a large wood shack with full-length windows
from somewhere in the wooded northerly reaches of
Scandinavia had been blown up in a tornado and set
down again not in the land of Oz, but on a traffic
island near the south end of Tower Bridge, with
London buses purring away in the logjams on either
side. Thus it is that Restaurant Story appears, its neat,
trim interior equipped with executive-style furniture,
the walls lined with books arranged according to the
colours of their spines (although the spring of 2018
was due to see a refurbishment of the look). It's the
creative lair of Tom Sellers, one of the capital's more
intensively experimental practitioners, whose stint at
René Redzepi's Noma in Copenhagen shines through
in much of the creative retooling of profoundly humble
ingredients that characterises the Nordic (and Tower
Bridge) style. The story concept of the menus isn't
applied too thickly – there is no need to fear any in-
character Jackanorying from the staff – even if the
successive stages are labelled 'chapters'. A harking
back to childhood, as long as yours was a childhood
that included bread and dripping and fairground
onions, sets the ball rolling, before a venture out into
the garden for some snails to cook in ravioli. At the sea
stage, cod comes partnered with brassicas and truffle,
before a waft of ash dresses a pairing of scallop and
cucumber. Yeast is one of the indispensable elements
of northern modernism, and reliably turns up here
with venison and cauliflower in the principal meat
dish, and then a trio of desserts files by in enticing
review, utilising strongly accented flavours from lemon
via chocolate and honey to almond and dill. A
condensed version of the above is offered at
lunchtime. It all adds up to what the menu calls 'a
kind of love story', one that can be taken home and
treasured on purchase of a signed copy of Sellers'
book of that title. The drinks list is not to be spurned

either, with fragrantly botanical cocktails, modern
wines and rare gin brands all contributing to a
singular experience.

Chef Tom Sellers **Seats** 37 **Closed** August bank
holiday weekend, 2 weeks Christmas
Notes No children under 6 years

Roast

◉ BRITISH **V**

020 300 6611 | The Floral Hall, Borough Market,
Stoney Street, SE1 1TL
www.roast-restaurant.com

Lording it above the global gourmet paradise of
Borough market, Roast occupies the ornate Victorian
Floral Hall, relocated from the old Covent Garden. With
pigeon's-eye views of the market, St Paul's Cathedral
and The Shard, it's a fantastic setting and, in true
market fashion, it's open for breakfast too.

Chef Stuart Cauldwell **Seats** 120 **Closed** 25–26
December, 1 January **Notes** Children welcome

Skylon

◉ MODERN BRITISH **V**

020 7654 7800 | Royal Festival Hall, Southbank Centre,
SE1 8XX
www.skylon-restaurant.co.uk

Knock-out Thames-side views and its setting inside the
Royal Festival Hall ensure that Skylon rocks. A real
looker, the Southbank set up incorporates a hotspot
centrepiece bar, swish grill and stellar restaurant, with
chandelier-style lighting, soaring pillars, dramatic
flower displays and low-slung contemporary seating.

Chef Kim Woodward **Seats** 100, Private dining 33
Closed 25 December **Notes** Children welcome

Ting

◉◉ BRITISH, EUROPEAN WITH ASIAN INFLUENCE **V** ♦ NOTABLE WINE LIST

020 7234 8008 | Shangri-La Hotel, at The Shard,
London, 31 St Thomas Street, SE1 9QU
www.ting-shangri-la.com

The Shangri-La occupies the 34th to 52nd floors of The
Shard, so the full-drop windows in Ting, the restaurant
on 35, pack quite a punch. The dining room is elegant,
with a Chinoiserie feel, and the modern European
menu has Asian influences.

Chef Gareth Bowen, **Seats** 95 **Open** All year
Parking 15 **Notes** Children welcome

Union Street Café

◉◉ ITALIAN, MEDITERRANEAN

020 7592 7977 | 47–51 Great Suffolk Street, SE1 0BS
www.gordonramsay.com/union-street-cafe

This café's casual, urban-chic warehouse sheen, with
funky lighting, buffed concrete, striking artwork and

an open kitchen, is a big hit, as is the cooking, driven by the best market produce. Skilled simplicity and a confident light modern touch keep the food high on flavour.

Chef Davide Degiovanni **Seats** 125, Private dining 22 **Open** All year **Prices from** S £7, M £19, D £7 **Notes** Vegetarian dishes, Children welcome

LONDON SE10
Craft London
◉◉ MODERN BRITISH

020 8465 5910 | Peninsula Square, SE10 0SQ
www.craft-london.co.uk

Café, bar, restaurant and shop, Craft London is a thriving enterprise in a modern construction of glass and steel next to the O2. The restaurant, on the first floor, has a striking contemporary finish with bold colours, cool lighting, floor-to-ceiling windows and an open-to-view kitchen.

Chef Stevie Parle **Seats** 90 **Closed** Christmas **Notes** Vegetarian dishes, Children welcome

The Peninsula Restaurant
◉◉◉ MODERN EUROPEAN **V**

020 8463 6868 | InterContinental London – The O2, 1 Waterview Drive, SE10 0TW
www.peninsula-restaurant.com

It's all happening on the Greenwich Peninsula, which has gradually been transformed into a smart London quarter with its own cultural milieu, and a swish InterContinental Hotel to boot. The Peninsula Restaurant on the second floor has views of the whole district, with Canary Wharf hovering behind it, and amid the sleek contemporary design, a menu of cutting-edge cooking completes the picture. A suitably luxurious lobster ravioli partnered with crosnes and Noilly Prat sauce, or seared foie gras with pickled dates, shiso and salted pancake might open proceedings. This is creative, confident cooking with a strong sense of freshness, flavour and balance. Next up, there may be beef in a sweet and sour composition involving fermented celeriac and calçot onions, or perhaps halibut with turnips and satay sauce. If you're keeping step with the vogue for meat-free ideas, leek quiche with smoked cheddar and lovage adds up to more than the spartan menu description. Desserts such as rhubarb with cream tea and vanilla, or sticky toffee pudding with caramel and popcorn maintain the creative momentum.

Chef Tomas Lidakevicius **Seats** 70, Private dining 24 **Closed** Bank holidays, Private hire **Prices from** S £12, M £18, D £9 **Parking** 220 **Notes** Children welcome

LONDON SE22
Franklins
◉ BRITISH

020 8299 9598 | 157 Lordship Lane, East Dulwich, SE22 8HX
www.franklinsrestaurant.com

British produce is celebrated zealously at Franklins, an exemplary neighbourhood eatery that combines the virtues of a pubby bar and a buzzy bistro at the rear that's all exposed brick, bare floorboards and big Victorian mirrors with an open view into the kitchen.

Chef Ralf Wittig **Seats** 42, Private dining 24 **Closed** 25–26 and 31 December, 1 January **Notes** Vegetarian dishes, Children welcome

The Palmerston
◉ MODERN BRITISH

020 8693 1629 | 91 Lordship Lane, East Dulwich, SE22 8EP
www.thepalmerston.co.uk

This classic Victorian corner pub in East Dulwich is an inviting prospect with its clubby wood panelling, racing-green leather banquettes and scrubbed-wood tables and chairs. A quick glance over the menu will show that this kitchen prizes seasonal British produce.

Chef Jamie Younger, Celia Dickerson **Seats** 70, Private dining 26 **Closed** 25–26 December, 1 January **Notes** Vegetarian dishes, Children welcome

LONDON SE23
Babur
◉◉ MODERN INDIAN

020 8291 2400 | 119 Brockley Rise, Forest Hill, SE23 1JP
www.babur.info

Extending the boundaries of Indian cooking since 1985, Babur's contemporary approach is bolstered by a classy modern look featuring striking artworks and funky lighting. The cooking delivers a bracing canter through some original ideas, backed by spice-friendly wine recommendations for each dish.

Chef Jiwan Lal **Seats** 72 **Closed** 26 December **Prices from** S £6.95, M £14.95, D £5.25 **Parking** 15 **Notes** Vegetarian dishes, Children welcome
See advertisement on page 188

LONDON SW1
Amaya
Rosettes suspended MODERN INDIAN ⧉ NOTABLE WINE LIST

020 7823 1166 | Halkin Arcade, Motcomb Street, SW1X 8JT
www.realindianfood.com

The Rosette award for this establishment has been suspended due to a change of chef and reassessment

continued on page 189

A smart,
comfortable,
space with
fantastic food

will take place in due course. In a plum spot just off Knightsbridge, Amaya is one of the new breed of Indian restaurants in London that has brought global glitz to the traditional cooking of the subcontinent. Inside, the mood is full of shimmer and glam, with vividly patterned decor and artworks in unapologetic colours. A classy wine list that extends into the firmament of premier cru burgundies and classed-growth Bordeaux is supplemented by a list of inventive cocktails.

Chef Sanchit Kapoor **Seats** 99, Private dining 14 **Open** All year **Prices from** S £9, M £24, D £8.50 **Notes** Vegetarian dishes, No children under 10 years at lunch Monday to Friday, no age restriction at dinner but must vacate table by 8pm
See advertisement on page 229

Ametsa with Arzak Instruction
MODERN BASQUE NOTABLE WINE LIST
020 7333 1234 | The Halkin by COMO, Halkin Street, Belgravia, SW1X 7DJ
www.comohotels.com/thehalkin/dining/ametsa

Part of the extremely fashionable and jaw-droppingly stylish Como The Halkin, deep in smartest Belgravia, the restaurant namechecks the famous Arzak family, whose San Sebastian restaurant is a global foodie destination. The minimalist dining room is a bright white space with pierced wooden screens and a real wow of a ceiling installation – 7,000 golden glass test tubes filled with spices. What you'll find on offer here is the 'New Basque cuisine' – stunningly beautiful dishes that reinterpret the earthy, robust tastes and textures of the region with a great deal of flair and imagination. As well as the thrilling tasting menu, there's an à la carte at lunch and dinner, and the set lunch gives a good idea of the style at a rather more affordable price. Terse but playful menu descriptions give little indication of the finely judged flavour combinations that can be expected in starters like the 'foie gras totem'. Main courses might include 'turbot beyond blackberries', or 'venison fractal with cherries'. The selection of Spanish cheese is tempting – but who could resist the 'passion of chocolate'?

Chef Sergio Sanz Blanco, Elena Arzak, Ruben Briones **Seats** 60, Private dining 24 **Closed** 24–26 December and 1 January **Prices from** S £18.50, M £27, D £13.50 **Notes** Vegetarian dishes, Children welcome

Aquavit
NORDIC
020 7024 9848 | St James's Market, 1 Carlton Street, SW1Y 4QQ
www.aquavitrestaurants.com

Sibling to New York's award-garlanded big-brother Aquavit, this London outpost brings sophisticated Nordic styling and cuisine to our capital. The handsome, double-height space comes bathed in light, and everything feels polished and image conscious – glossy, blond and golden with a posh, contemporary Scandi moniker.

Chef Henrik Ritzén **Seats** Private dining 79 **Closed** 24–29 December **Notes** Vegetarian dishes, Children welcome

Avenue
MODERN BRITISH, AMERICAN
020 7321 2111 | 7–9 St James's Street, SW1A 1EE
www.avenue-restaurant.co.uk

With its chic Manhattan-style attitude, Avenue's long bar sets a classy tone, while the glam restaurant spreads out around a 'wine-glass' chandelier and decanting bar, with semi-circular banquettes, low-back chairs and funky modern art. The kitchen sends out a lively take on modern American fare.

Chef Andras Katona **Seats** 150, Private dining 20 **Closed** 25–26 December, 1 January, Bank holidays **Notes** Vegetarian dishes, Children welcome

A. Wong
CHINESE
020 7828 8931 | 70 Wilton Road, Victoria, SW1V 1DE
www.awong.co.uk

In double-fronted premises beneath an anonymous office block in the purlieu of Victoria station, Andrew Wong has established one of the capital's more ambitious Chinese restaurants. The decor may be modest enough, with close-packed unclothed tables and bar seating, but when it comes to culinary ambition, the sky – or rather the almost equally vast range of China's regional cuisines – is the limit. A 10-course evening tasting menu indicates the modernity of the approach, its multifarious stages embarking with a cured scallop and stuffed crab claw with wasabi, passing through the undoubtedly challenging braised abalone with sea cucumber and shiitakes, and more familiar peanut-studded gong bao chicken, to arrive at a dessert plate of coconut sorbet with mochi, dried Xinjiang mulberries, blackberries and yogurt. Meanwhile, the regular menu is full of surprises: try goldfish (-shaped) dumplings with seared foie gras and chive flower oil. Lunchtime dim sum, including potsticker dumplings and Laughing Buddha buns, are an important resource for local office workers, while the Forbidden City bar offers stylish drinks and nibbles pairings to transition you into the nicer end of the day.

Chef Andrew Wong **Seats** 65, Private dining 12 **Closed** Christmas, New Year's Eve **Prices from** S £6, M £9, D £10 **Notes** Vegetarian dishes, Children welcome

Bar Boulud

FRENCH, AMERICAN | NOTABLE WINE LIST

020 7201 3899 | Mandarin Oriental Hyde Park, 66 Knightsbridge, SW1X 7LA
www.barboulud.com

Daniel Boulud's London restaurant bursts with contemporary glamour. The zinc-topped bar is a cool see-and-be-seen spot, staff whizz about, there's a contented hum in the dining rooms, complete with open kitchen, while the menu speaks French with English translations, and high-quality ingredients are prettily presented.

Chef Thomas Piat, Daniel Boulud **Seats** 168, Private dining 24 **Open** All year **Prices from** S £8, M £9, D £5 **Notes** Vegetarian dishes, Children welcome

Boisdale of Belgravia

MODERN BRITISH

020 7730 6922 | 15 Eccleston Street, SW1W 9LX
www.boisdale.co.uk

A combination of jazz venue, bar and restaurant, this warren of rooms in a Regency townhouse has a clubby decor and scarlet walls hung with jazz-related pictures. As at its Bishopsgate sibling, the cooking showcases fine Scottish produce, skilfully and accurately handled.

Chef Chris Zachwieja **Seats** 140, Private dining 22 **Closed** Christmas, New Year, Easter and Bank holidays **Prices from** S £12, M £22, D £8 **Notes** Vegetarian dishes, Children welcome

Café Murano

NORTHERN ITALIAN

020 3371 5559 | 33 St James's Street, SW1A 1HD
www.cafemurano.co.uk

Angela Hartnett's eatery is anything but a 'café', rather a sophisticated, albeit relaxed, take on a pop-in-every-day Italian. The room is a looker, from its marble-topped bar to wooden floors, banquettes and eye-catching lighting. The cooking is equally on cue.

Chef Sam Williams **Seats** 86, Private dining 22 **Closed** 25–26 December **Notes** Vegetarian dishes, Children welcome

Le Caprice

MODERN EUROPEAN V

020 7629 2239 | Arlington House, Arlington Street, SW1A 1RJ
www.le-caprice.co.uk

There's an ageless feeling to this iconic Mayfair favourite with smart linen-covered tables, crockery stamped with the restaurant's own logo. Main courses are often the highlight: and there are also Eastern influences.

Chef William Halsall **Seats** 86 **Closed** 25 December to 1 January **Notes** Children welcome

Caxton Grill

MODERN EUROPEAN

020 7222 7888 | St Ermin's Hotel, 2 Caxton Street, St James Park, SW1H 0QW
www.caxtongrill.co.uk

Situated in the audaciously grand St Ermin's Hotel, this is a surprisingly modern venue with a soothing colour scheme, striking contemporary artworks, and designer furniture. With Executive Head Chef Alexander Boyd at the helm, the Caxton Grill boasts an inspired à la carte menu.

Chef Alexander Boyd **Seats** 72, Private dining 10 **Open** All year **Prices from** S £8.50, M £16, D £8.50 **Notes** Vegetarian dishes, Children welcome

Le Chinois at Millennium Knightsbridge

CHINESE

020 7201 6330 | 17 Sloane Street, Knightsbridge, SW1X 9NU
www.millenniumhotels.com/knightsbridge

The Millennium is a modern Sloaneland hotel aimed at the style-conscious. Darkwood and plum-coloured pillars, as well as a row of birdcage light fittings, make a bright backdrop to the refined Cantonese-based cooking on offer, which veers between textbook traditionalism and newer ideas.

Chef Anthony Kong **Seats** 65 **Open** All year **Prices from** S £6, M £10, D £6 **Parking** 8 **Notes** Vegetarian dishes, Children welcome

Chutney Mary

MODERN INDIAN | NOTABLE WINE LIST

020 7629 6688 | 73 St James's Street, SW1A 1PH
www.chutneymary.com

Never one to stand still, Chutney Mary now opens on Sundays for brunch and dinner. Kick off with a drink in the cocktail bar, as luxurious as the dining room with its colourful fabrics and linen-free tables. The creative Indian cuisine runs to some inspiring combinations.

Chef Manav Tuli, Uday Salunkhe **Seats** 112, Private dining 32 **Open** All year **Prices from** S £10, M £17.75, D £7.50 **Notes** Vegetarian dishes, No children under 10 years at lunch Monday to Friday, 4–10 years at early dinner must leave by 8pm

See advertisement on page 229

The Cinnamon Club

MODERN INDIAN

020 7222 2555 | The Old Westminster Library, 30–32 Great Smith Street, SW1P 3BU
www.cinnamonclub.com

Former public buildings often make good venues, particularly those built with a bit of empire pomp, like the old Westminster Library with its handsome facade, book-lined galleries and high-end feel. Here, classy modern Indian cooking combines Asian and European techniques to deliver bang-on flavours.

Chef Vivek Singh, Rakesh Ravindran **Seats** 130, Private dining 60 **Closed** Bank holidays (some) **Notes** Vegetarian dishes, Children welcome

Colbert
◉ FRENCH V
020 7730 2804 | 50–52 Sloane Square, Chelsea, SW1W 8AX
www.colbertchelsea.com

Inspired by the grand boulevard cafés of Paris, the Colbert sits smack on Sloane Square and bustles with a wonderful feel-good vibe from breakfast to late evening, with a lengthy all-day menu that doesn't talk three-course formality. The essence of the cooking is clean simplicity.

Chef Stuart Conibear **Seats** 140 **Closed** Christmas **Notes** Children welcome

Céleste at The Lanesborough
◉◉◉ FRENCH, INTERNATIONAL
020 7259 5599 | Hyde Park Corner, SW1X 7TA
www.oetkercollection.com/destinations/the-lanesborough/restaurants-bars/restaurants/celeste/

A grand old mansion on Hyde Park Corner, The Lanesborough's world-class level of luxury and service tends to be the preserve of celebs and oligarchs. Assuming you're not up for its stratospherically priced rooms with a personal butler thrown in, you can buy into the hotel's glamour by dining at Céleste – not as inaccessible as you might think if you go for the set-price menu du jour – beneath a glass-domed ceiling, shimmering chandeliers, and Wedgwood-like blue and white friezes. Chef Florian Favario, a protégé of French super-chef Eric Frechon, cooks in the modern French style, blending classic techniques with a contemporary eye for light, fresh flavours in supremely elegant dishes that celebrate first-class British ingredients: poached native oysters come with confit leek in white wine, and lemon and brown butter sabayon, while exquisite halibut is matched with a riot of Jerusalem artichoke – crushed, puréed, crispy skin, and in a truffle-dusted bon bon – deftly aromatised with truffle shavings and chicken jus. Caramelised red apple, green apple sorbet, pine nut crumble and elderflower mousse provide a classy finish.

Chef Florian Favario, Eric Frechon **Seats** 100, Private dining 12 **Open** All year **Parking** 25 **Notes** Vegetarian dishes, Children welcome

Dinner by Heston Blumenthal
◉◉◉◉ BRITISH NOTABLE WINE LIST
020 7201 3833 | Mandarin Oriental Hyde Park, 66 Knightsbridge, SW1X 7LA
www.dinnerbyheston.co.uk

There's another branch in Melbourne, but the northern hemisphere iteration of Dinner is to be found within the ornate, balconied edifice of the Mandarin Oriental Hotel in Knightsbridge. A surprisingly unelaborate dining room is kitted out with unclothed tables, with views over Hyde Park as well as a centrally sited kitchen with open frontage allowing diners occasional glimpses behind the scenes. What Heston Blumenthal has created here is the culinary equivalent of a research institute, with dishes from British history – often quite distant history at that – offering quite as much novelty to today's globalised standard palate as the avant-garde goings-on at The Fat Duck. The starter known as Rice and Flesh dates from the troubled reign of Richard II and is in essence a painstakingly timed saffron risotto topped with mouthfuls of tender calf's tail richly glazed in red wine. Fast-forward to Churchill's day, before wartime austerity began to bite, and enjoy a goldenly caramelised piece of cod in opulent cider sauce, accompanied by flamed mussels and chard, or pause at the late Georgian era for 21-day-aged Hereford beef with mushroom ketchup and thrice-fried chips, perhaps followed by a gloriously elaborate raspberry tart lathered with Jersey cream, its sponge injected with olive oil, topped with corpulent raspberries filled with lovage cream and a pebble of gorgeously intense raspberry sorbet. A classic booze-sodden tipsy cake is garnished with a strip of sticky spit-roasted pineapple for a touch of exotic climes, while the cheeses come with gently spiced apple and plum chutney.

Chef Ashley Palmer-Watts **Seats** 149, Private dining 12 **Open** All year **Prices from** S £18.50, M £30, D £15 **Notes** Vegetarian dishes, No children under 4 years

The English Grill
◉◉ MODERN BRITISH
020 7834 6600 | The Rubens at the Palace, 39 Buckingham Palace Road, SW1W 0PS
www.redcarnationhotels.com

This elegant dining room is part of a hotel that has been run by the same family since 1912. Banquette seating along one wall provides views of large glass doors into the kitchen, where classic cooking techniques are employed for a menu that appeals to all.

Chef Ben Kelliher **Seats** 65, Private dining 60 **Open** All year **Notes** Vegetarian dishes, Children welcome

Enoteca Turi

◉◉ MODERN ITALIAN 🍷 NOTABLE WINE LIST

020 7730 3663 | 87 Pimlico Road, SW1W 8PH

www.enotecaturi.com

Run by the same family since 1990, Enoteca Turi has moved to Chelsea. The focus is on regional Italian flavours, with the menu highlighting the origins of each dish (Campania, Piedmont etc.). The whole place buzzes with life and the wine list champions Italian wines.

Chef Massimo Tagliaferri **Seats** 75, Private dining 28
Closed 25–26 December, 1 January
Prices from S £12.50, M £18.50, D £9
Notes Vegetarian dishes, Children welcome

Estiatorio Milos

◉◉ GREEK, MEDITERRANEAN, SEAFOOD

020 7839 2080 | 1 Regent Street, St James's, SW1Y 4NR

www.milos.ca/restaurants/london

The august surroundings of deep windows with voile coverings, frosted glass globe lighting and white linen here make a handsome backdrop for its modern Greek food. The cooking is full of both sea-fresh savour and hearty meaty robustness.

Chef Costas Spiliadis **Notes** Vegetarian dishes

The Game Bird at The Stafford London

◉◉ CLASSIC BRITISH 🍷 NOTABLE WINE LIST

020 7518 1234 | 16–18 St James's Place, SW1A 1NJ

www.thegamebird.com

Tucked away in a discreet street near Green Park, The Stafford is a luxurious St James's address that is worth tracking down. The kitchen takes top-notch British produce, subjects it to contemporary treatments and comes up with ambitious dishes glowing with Mediterranean colour.

Chef Jozef Rogulski **Seats** 60, Private dining 44
Open All year **Prices from** S £11.50, M £14, D £9
Notes Vegetarian dishes, Children welcome

The Goring

◉◉◉ TRADITIONAL BRITISH **V** 🍷 NOTABLE WINE LIST

020 7396 9000 | Beeston Place, SW1W 0JW

www.thegoring.com

Belgravia's Goring Hotel is a class act, and a family-owned one at that. Its century-long service to this elegant quarter of London has seen the titled and the improvident pass through its portals, and treated with flawless civility one and all. Brushing aside all thought of brutal modernism, the lustrous dining room is bathed in light from Swarovski chandeliers of an evening, and is still equipped with a fleet of trolleys, bearing their respective freights of cheeses, puddings and daily roasts, the last providing impeccable tableside theatre by means of, say, Thursday's roast rib of Ross County

beef and attendant Yorkshires. Executive chef Shay Cooper maintains a beady eye on British tradition, clearly, but not to the exclusion of more contemporary forays, so smoked eel risotto with preserved lemon and lovage oil might be the prelude to Romney salt marsh lamb and its sweetbreads with smoked aubergine, yogurt and spiced pinenuts. Trend-setters look to black fig trifle with gingerbread, caramel and buttermilk to finish, while doughty traditionalists will hardly pass up the chance of a bowl of rice pudding.

Chef Shay Cooper **Seats** 70, Private dining 50
Parking 7 **Notes** Children welcome

Hai Cenato

◉◉ NEW YORK ITALIAN

020 3816 9320 | Cardinal Place, 2 Sir Simon Milton Square, SW1E 5DJ

www.haicenato.co.uk

A 2017 arrival on the central London restaurant scene, Hai Cenato brings New York-Italian casual dining to Victoria's NOVA complex. The large theatre kitchen allows you to see two huge pizza ovens, where chefs serve up dishes on colourful artisan crockery.

Chef Jason Atherton, Paul Hood **Seats** 70
Closed Bank holidays **Notes** Vegetarian dishes, Children welcome

Il Convivio

◉◉ MODERN ITALIAN

020 7730 4099 | 143 Ebury Street, SW1W 9QN

www.ilconvivio.co.uk

A family-owned Italian in a Georgian townhouse, Il Convivio is a favourite of the Belgravia set. Its name is inspired by a Dante poem, which translates as 'a meeting over food and drink', and lines from his verse are inscribed on the walls.

Chef Cedric Neri **Seats** 65, Private dining 14
Closed Christmas, New Year and Bank holidays
Notes Vegetarian dishes, Children welcome

See advertisement opposite

Ken Lo's Memories of China

◉ CHINESE

020 7730 7734 | 65–69 Ebury Street, SW1W 0NZ

www.memories-of-china.co.uk

This sumptuous restaurant was created by the late Kenneth Lo, one of modern Chinese gastronomy's early movers and shakers. Oriental screen dividers, clothed tables and a bottle store create a fine-dining ambience for classy Chinese cooking. Accompaniments are spot on.

Chef Peter Shum Tsui **Seats** 120, Private dining 27
Closed 25–26 December **Notes** Vegetarian dishes, Children welcome

Kona

◎◎ MODERN EUROPEAN

020 7769 7766 | SW1E 6AF

www.taj51buckinghamgate.co.uk

At Kona, the stylishly smart decor shows there's obviously no expense spared. The culinary inspiration comes from southern Europe. A bowl of velvety lobster bisque with a quenelle of white crabmeat and crème fraîche seems a suitably opulent starting point.

Chef David Tilly **Seats** 44, Private dining 12 **Open** All year **Notes** Vegetarian dishes, Children welcome

Lorne Restaurant

◎◎ MODERN BRITISH AND EUROPEAN

020 3327 0210 | 76 Wilton Road, SW1V 1DE

www.lornerestaurant.co.uk

If you're looking to enjoy excellent cuisine in a relaxed atmosphere in central London, Lorne makes a fine choice. The restaurant has a bright and airy feel, with calming decor. Sommelier Katie Exton has created a wine list for enthusiasts of every taste and pocket.

Chef Peter Hall **Seats** 44 **Closed** Bank Holiday Mondays and 24 December to 1 January **Notes** Vegetarian dishes

Marcus

◎◎◎◎◎ MODERN EUROPEAN, BRITISH **V** NOTABLE WINE LIST

020 7235 1200 | Wilton Place,

Knightsbridge, SW1X 7RL

www.marcusrestaurant.com

It does make a nice change every once in a while to eat first-class modern British food in the kind of surroundings that would once have been the exclusive preserve of classical French gastronomy. Bare floorboards and rag-rolled walls are all very well, but sometimes it's deeply agreeable to the soul to step into a world of restrained elegance, where the tables are dressed in two layers of napery, muted light glows off burnished wood panelling, and little trolleys bear such goodies as bowls of petits fours or iced champagne. Not that there is anything overly stuffy about the ambience of Marcus Wareing's restaurant in Knightsbridge's Berkeley Hotel, but it is quality-signalling all the way. Wareing has been in the vanguard of modern cheffing for the past generation, and as well as being a familiar TV presence, is one of the great trainers of chefs. A highly commendable feature of the recent repertoire is a five-course lunch taster, in which each course is designed by a different chef. Head chefs Mark and Shauna Froydenlund contribute, respectively, an opener of sourdough crumpets with Essex cockle butter and a fish dish of turf-smoked trout with wild leek and sorrel. In between comes a version of chicken liver parfait with pain d'épices and rhubarb by a junior sous, while a more senior colleague has overseen the main course of short rib, slow-cooked for three days, and aromatised with wild garlic and onion. The Lancashire custard tart to finish is the recipe of Southport-born Marcus himself. In the evening, the lights are dimmed to a level that may take a little adjusting to, and the carte extends into the territory of Cumbrian rose veal neck with purple sprouting broccoli and winter savory, or benchmark Gigha halibut with a pickled egg, clams and monk's beard. They might follow a pitch-perfect offering of a brace of scallops with crisped shallots and verbena leaf in an emulsified beef dressing, while something of a signature dessert has been made from the pastry disc of piercing bergamot cream with soft meringues and a refreshingly unsweet ice made of Earl Grey tea. Seasonal tasting menus of five or eight courses represent terrific compilations of the main carte.

Chef Marcus Wareing, Mark and Shauna Froydenlund **Seats** 90, Private dining 16 **Open** All year **Notes** No children under 8 years

Osteria Dell'Angolo
🌟 ITALIAN
020 3268 1077 | 47 Marsham Street, SW1P 3DR
www.osteriadellangolo.co.uk
The warm tones of this Westminster Italian bring an air of Mediterranean sophistication to Marsham Street. Leather seating and white linen add class, and large windows fill the space with light, while a glass-panelled wall offers a glimpse of the chef in action.

Chef Demian Mazzocchi **Seats** 80, Private dining 22 **Closed** Christmas, New Year, last 2 weeks August and Bank holidays **Prices from** S £8, M £13, D £5.50 **Parking** 6 **Notes** Vegetarian dishes, Children welcome

Petrichor Restaurant
🌟🌟 MODERN EUROPEAN
020 7930 2111 | Cavendish London, 81 Jermyn Street, SW1Y 6JF
www.thecavendish-london.co.uk
The Cavendish is as chic as can be, with a plethora of striking paintings. The dining room may look over St James's, but conjures in its name the scent of freshly moistened earth after the first rains. The kitchen draws on thoroughbred suppliers for materials.

Chef Nitin Pawar **Seats** 80, Private dining 70 **Closed** 25–26 December and 1 January **Prices from** S £7.50, M £19.50, D £7.50 **Parking** 60 **Notes** Vegetarian dishes, Children welcome

Pétrus
Rosettes suspended MODERN FRENCH V ⬥ NOTABLE WINE LIST
020 7592 1609 | 1 Kinnerton Street, Knightsbridge, SW1X 8EA
www.gordonramsay.com/petrus
The Rosette award for this establishment has been suspended due to a change of chef and reassessment will take place in due course. Restaurant Gordon Ramsay in Royal Hospital Road may well be the flagship of Mr Ramsay's empire, but Pétrus runs it a very close second when it comes to delivering dynamic modern French food. The dining room is a sophisticated space with hues of copper, beige, silver, and splashes of claret red as a nod to the namesake wine, and well-spaced tables dressed up for the business of fine dining around a centrepiece walk-in glass wine room bristling with vintages.

Seats 55, Private dining 8 **Closed** 26–28 December **Prices from** S £25, M £40, D £20 **Notes** Children welcome

Quaglino's
🌟🌟 EUROPEAN
020 7930 6767 | 16 Bury Street, SW1Y 6AJ
www.quaglinos-restaurant.co.uk
Once the favoured watering-hole Evelyn Waugh and the future Edward VIII, Quaglino's is a masterpiece of art deco style on the cruise-ship scale, complete with golden-lit staircase to tempt out your inner Gloria Swanson. Flavours simply shine from the plate.

Chef Piero Leone **Seats** Private dining 36

Quilon
🌟🌟 INDIAN ⬥ NOTABLE WINE LIST
020 7821 1899 | 41 Buckingham Gate, SW1E 6AF
www.quilon.co.uk
Set in the swish St James' Court hotel, Quilon offers a designer-led, ultra-modern interior, and cooking that showcases the cuisine of India's southwest, mixing traditional and inventive ideas, with tip-top materials the backbone of the kitchen's output. Great care is given to rice and breads.

Chef Sriram Aylur **Seats** 90, Private dining 16 **Closed** 25 December **Prices from** S £11, M £12, D £10 **Notes** Vegetarian dishes, Children welcome

The Rib Room Bar and Restaurant

Rosettes suspended MODERN BRITISH

020 7858 7250 | Jumeirah Carlton Tower, Cadogan Place, SW1X 9PY

www.theribroom.co.uk

The Rosette award for this establishment has been suspended due to a change of chef and reassessment will take place in due course. On the ground floor of a luxury Knightsbridge hotel, The Rib Room has an air of affluence. The reputation of the place rests on the beef and steaks, as it has since it opened in 1961.

Chef Simon Young **Seats** 120, Private dining 20 **Open** All year **Prices from** S £10.50, M £18, D £8 **Parking** 78 **Notes** Vegetarian dishes, Children welcome

Roux at Parliament Square

MODERN EUROPEAN V NOTABLE WINE LIST

020 7334 3737 | Parliament Square, SW1P 3AD

www.rouxatparliamentsquare.co.uk

Near to the Houses of Parliament, the rather handsome Georgian building is also home to the Royal Institute of Chartered Surveyors, so you might be sharing the space with a bevy of politicians and architects at certain sittings. Its duo of dining rooms sport a fetching mix of modernity and clubby restraint, run by impeccably correct and professional staff, and if you're not one to miss out on a cocktail opportunity, start things at the Pembury Bar, with its elegant grand hotel opulence. Steve Groves fronts up the kitchen, interpreting the Roux house style to deliver light, modern, smartly engineered dishes that merge British, French and broader European ideas, where starters might see mackerel supported by smoked buttermilk, cucumber and quinoa. Mains courses could star dry-aged duck pointed up with beetroot, chicory and Yukon Gold potato, or offer a trip to the Hampshire terroir via Test Valley trout with watercress, leek and pine nut. It all looks pretty as a picture on the plate too, right through to desserts such as apple soufflé with muscovado, Calvados and oats.

Chef Steve Groves **Seats** 56, Private dining 10 **Closed** Christmas, New Year and Bank holidays **Notes** Children welcome

The Royal Horseguards

MODERN BRITISH

020 7451 9333 | 2 Whitehall Court, SW1A 2EJ

www.guoman.co.uk

Once home to the Secret Service in World War I, it now makes an upmarket base for London's attractions. Its posh restaurant comes kitted out with plush banquettes and deals in appealing modern brasserie-style food with its roots in French classics.

Chef Sandeep Chauhan **Seats** 100, Private dining 24 **Open** All year **Notes** Vegetarian dishes, Children welcome

Sake No Hana

MODERN JAPANESE V NOTABLE WINE LIST

020 7925 8988 | 23 Saint James's Street, SW1A 1HA

www.sakenohana.com

Part of the Hakkasan stable, this sleek Japanese restaurant is a striking L-shaped space with a wood lattice ceiling, bamboo columns and windows hung with screens. Perch at the sushi counter, or sit at low-slung leather banquettes for a menu offering contemporary and traditional dishes.

Chef Hideki Hiwatashi **Seats** 100, Private dining 32 **Closed** 25–26 December and New Year **Notes** Children welcome

Salloos Restaurant

PAKISTANI

020 7235 4444 | 62–64 Kinnerton Street, SW1X 8ER

www.salloos.co.uk

Salloos is a pukka, family-run outfit renowned for its tandooris. The atmosphere in the intimate first-floor dining room is traditional, and the service politely formal. Consistently sound Pakistani cooking is the kitchen's strength; the chef of 40 years assures confident spicing in well-tuned Mughlai cuisine.

Chef Abdul Aziz **Seats** 65 **Closed** Christmas **Prices from** S £10, M £22, D £7.50 **Notes** Vegetarian dishes, No children under 8 years

Santini Restaurant

TRADITIONAL ITALIAN

020 7730 4094 | 29 Ebury Street, SW1W 0NZ

www.santinirestaurant.com

The traditional values of a family-run Italian restaurant underpin this glossy Belgravia darling, and Latin style runs all the way from the recently refurbished interior to the waiters and the wine list. Impeccably sourced seasonal ingredients treated with a light touch are at the core.

Chef Cristian Gardin **Seats** 65, Private dining 30 **Closed** Christmas, 1 January **Notes** Vegetarian dishes, Children welcome

Seven Park Place by William Drabble

MODERN FRENCH NOTABLE WINE LIST

020 7316 1600 | St James's Hotel and Club, 7–8 Park Place, SW1A 1LP

www.stjameshotelandclub.com

Tucked away in St James's, the eponymously titled five-star hotel and club is home to one of London's most seductive dining opportunities, Seven Park Place, where the incomparable William Drabble has been producing dynamic and creative modern French cuisine since 2009. The dining room is a gem, small but perfectly formed, it positively shimmers with rich, warm colours and bold contemporary artworks. In such a sophisticated setting, top-end service is expected and duly delivered. The set lunch is a great introduction to William's work for anyone on a budget (two choices at each course), with an all-conquering Menu Gourmand at the other end of the spectrum (including a choice of three wine flights or a juice pairing). First-rate ingredients from trusted suppliers lead the way on the à la carte menu that might take you from an assiette of foie gras (seared, mousse and ballotine), via griddled fillet of John Dory or an assiette of pork with Madeira jus, to an apple crumble mousse. The technical virtuosity on display is impressive from start to finish, with attention to texture, flavour and temperature. The wine 'book' excels in France and does more than justice to the rest of the world.

Chef William Drabble **Seats** 34, Private dining 40 **Open** All year **Notes** Vegetarian dishes, No children

Sofitel London St James

◉◉ FRENCH

020 7968 2900 | 6 Waterloo Place, SW1Y 4AN
www.thebalconlondon.com

The Balcon restaurant at this imposing hotel is suitably capacious and stylish, done out in the grand Parisian manner with a duo of matching spiral staircases, plus a charcuterie and champagne bar. The menu ploughs a brasserie furrow with British and French influences.

Chef Matt Greenwood **Seats** 84, Private dining 20 **Open** All year **Prices from** S £11, M £16, D £4 **Notes** Vegetarian dishes, Children welcome

Zafferano

◉◉ MODERN ITALIAN

020 7235 5800 | 15 Lowndes Street, SW1X 9EY
www.zafferanorestaurant.com

Zafferano has always held its head high among the upper echelons of the UK's contemporary Italians since Giorgio Locatelli opened the place back in 1995. The kitchen gives classic dishes a sophisticated spin and well-sourced ingredients remain at the heart of it all.

Chef Daniele Camera **Seats** 140, Private dining 26 **Closed** 25 December **Prices from** S £14, M £24.50, D £6 **Notes** Vegetarian dishes, Children welcome

LONDON SW3
Admiral Codrington

◉ BRITISH

020 7581 0005 | 17 Mossop Street, SW3 2LY
www.theadmiralcodrington.co.uk

The Cod is a proper pub with real ales at the pumps, red leather stools and a wee terrace for supping outside. It's also a dining address with cosy booths, pretty banquettes and interesting wallpapers, plus private rooms upstairs. The menu offers globally inspired stuff.

Chef Chris Reeder **Seats** 40, Private dining 22 **Closed** 25–27 December **Notes** Vegetarian dishes, Children welcome

Bo Lang Restaurant

◉ CHINESE

020 7823 7887 | 100 Draycott Avenue, SW3 3AD
www.bolangrestaurant.co.uk

This is the Chelsea hangout for lovers of dim sum, a dimly lit space with lanterns dangling from the ceiling, and grey leather sofas and charcoal velvet chairs contrasting with lots of wood. Accompaniments are of the same high standards.

Chef Kai Wang **Seats** 60 **Open** All year **Notes** Vegetarian dishes, Children welcome

Claude Bosi at Bibendum

◉◉◉◉ CLASSIC FRENCH

020 7581 5817 | Michelin House, 81 Fulham Road SW3 6RD
www.bibendum.co.uk

At first glance, a returning visitor to Bibendum would hardly notice anything different about the place. Its ornate pillared entrance at the South Kensington end of the Fulham Road still leads into a ground-floor oyster bar, and the stairs still lead up to one of London's most serenely beautiful dining rooms, with its stained-glass window in cobalt blues depicting the Michelin Man on his bicycle. There's a nice contrast these days, though, between this soothing space and the peeks that the kitchen window affords of the culinary bustle, which is all to the good as the old stager received quite the new lease on life with the arrival in 2017 of Claude Bosi, ex-Hibiscus. This move could have embodied a certain tension. Bosi's trajectory from Ludlow via the West End was founded on the pursuit of vanguard French cooking in the experimental vein, food that abounded in curiosities and the unabashed counter-intuitive note, whereas Bibendum has for many years traded in unreconstructed cuisine bourgeoise. And yet the result has been a perfect fit. Undoubtedly, Bosi has trimmed his sails to the prevailing wind of culinary tradition here, but not at the expense of innovation and excitement, and not without the playful air we have come to associate with him. Start with dressed crab, a layer of the deliciously rich brown meat topped with the bracingly fresh white, under a diaphanous sheet of Cox's apple jelly threaded with lime zest, a dish that is all elegant understatement. The same nerveless simplicity is at work in another starter of gratinated veal sweetbreads with a crisp topping of Stilton and English mustard, served in autumn with new season's walnuts. Those cognisant with the Bosi style of old will find familiar notes picked out in a stunning main course of Breton rabbit – loin, leg and rib cuts – partnered with langoustine tails and braised artichoke barigoule, the dish doubly sauced with a glossy rabbit jus and langoustine bisque. In the same land-and-sea mode is the carved short rib of Galician beef that comes with oyster pannacotta generously topped with oscietra caviar. A constructivist approach to desserts produces lots of fun, as well as unexpected alliances: the vacherin is a spiked sphere of meringue that contains a parfait of banana and cep mushrooms with caramelised almonds.

Chef Claude Bosi **Open** All year

Le Colombier

◉ TRADITIONAL FRENCH

020 7351 1155 | 145 Dovehouse Street, SW3 6LB
www.le-colombier-restaurant.co.uk

The epitome of an old-school neighbourhood French restaurant, its blue-canopied terrace is a hot ticket, while the dining room is an equally sunny confection of cream and blues. Unfussy, unashamedly classic French brasserie-style dishes are so familiar they hardly need their translations.

Chef Philippe Tamet **Seats** 70, Private dining 28 **Open** All year **Prices from** S £6.90, M £19.50, D £8.20 **Notes** Vegetarian dishes, No children under 10 years

Eight Over Eight

◉ PAN ASIAN

020 7349 9934 | 392 King's Road, SW3 5UZ
www.rickerrestaurants.com

This King's Road branch of Will Ricker's oriental fusion trio is a sleek, high-ceilinged space flooded with light from huge windows by day and a soft-focus glow from oriental-style lights by night. Paper-clothed tables, slick banquettes and black lacquered chairs complete the on-trend, up-tempo vibe.

Chef Aaj Fernando, Jose Coetono **Seats** 95, Private dining 18 **Closed** 24–29 December, Easter **Notes** Vegetarian dishes, Children welcome

Elystan Street

◉◉◉ MODERN BRITISH V ◉ NOTABLE WINE LIST

020 7628 5005 | 43 Elystan Street, Chelsea, SW3 3NT
www.elystanstreet.com

With his long-running reputation as an A-list chef at The Square, Phil Howard hit the ground running in his next venture in this discreetly posh Chelsea neighbourhood gaff. Its bare tables, pale wood floors and curvy, pastel-hued seats have a Nordic simplicity that chimes well with the more relaxed culinary approach. Howard's right-hand man and head chef Toby Burrowes followed from The Square to lead the team on a day-to-day basis; his technical abilities are beyond question and the kitchen delivers brilliance at every turn. There's a tendency for vegetables to get star billing these days, perhaps in an opener of roasted and shaved cauliflower with cashew cream, pickled mushrooms, toasted almonds, truffle and Mimolette cheese. Next up, top-notch materials inspire a full-on dish of peppered rib-eye and glazed short rib of beef, the richness ramped up further by bacon and stout jam, potato galettes and chanterelles. Fish dishes might take in wild zander fillet with creamed lentils, smoked eel, leek hearts and grain mustard. To finish, maybe Brillat-Savarin cheesecake, its lush creaminess counterpointed by blood orange and cardamom.

Chef Philip Howard, Toby Burrowes **Seats** 64, Private dining 14 **Closed** Christmas **Prices from** S £19, M £25, D £10 **Notes** Children welcome

The Five Fields

◉◉◉◉ MODERN BRITISH V

See pages 198–199

Manicomio Chelsea

◉ MODERN ITALIAN

020 7730 3366 | 85 Duke of York Square, Chelsea, SW3 4LY
www.manicomio.co.uk

Manicomio presents a cool, calming image, with its darkwood floor, leather banquettes, dark blue walls and eye-catching artwork. Contemporary Italian cooking is the deal, with key ingredients imported from the Motherland and a menu evenly divided between fish and meat.

Chef Tom Salt **Seats** 70, Private dining 30 **Closed** Christmas and New Year **Notes** Vegetarian dishes, Children welcome

LONDON SW3

The Five Fields

◉◉◉◉ MODERN BRITISH V

020 7838 1082 | 8–9 Blacklands Terrace, SW3 2SP

www.fivefieldsrestaurant.com

Elegant setting for light-touch modern English cooking

In keeping with the Chelsea postcode, The Five Fields is the very template of discretion and elegance. The place might be billed as a 'neighbourhood restaurant', but images of a cosy, casual, budget eatery are wide of the mark – it exudes the kind of designer class that comes with a rather swish location indeed – just off Sloane Square to be exact. The bucolic name refers to the area as it was known back in the 18th century when cartographer John Rocque mapped the ever-expanding city of London, and while the pastoral scenes have gone, there is still a link to the countryside because chef-patron Taylor Bonnyman keeps a kitchen garden in Sussex for seasonal herbs and vegetables.

Bonnyman and his team – including head chef Marguerite Keogh who worked for Marcus Wareing – have all earned their stripes at some top addresses in New York, London and Paris, and continue to deliver intelligent, thrilling and sometimes playful contemporary food based on outstanding ingredients. The dining room is a soothingly

elegant space done out with neutral colours, plush designer leather chairs and coiling plant motifs. There's a swanky private dining room on the first floor too, with a grand fireplace and views into the impressive wine cellar.

Open for dinner only, this is not the sort of place that turns tables, so you can settle in and savour the seemingly never-ending parade of little extras from opening nibbles – for example crab tartlet with golden beetroot – to pre-desserts – cherry soda with lemon ice cream, say – and petits fours without watching the clock. You can expect artfulness and accuracy in equal measure in stunning looking plates, whether you go for the set-price menu or the eight-course tasting extravaganza.

A signature dish of foie gras parfait arrives covered in beetroot jelly alongside shimeji mushrooms, while there's more to a dish entitled 'cabbage' than its humble name suggests, since it comes with oxtail, oyster and dill. Elsewhere, there may be Herdwick mutton with butternut squash, pine nut and rapini, or superb Cornish turbot partnered by seaweed, cavolo nero and potato. This is cooking that shows an innate feel for what works with what, right through to desserts like rum baba, its sweetness offset by the sharp slap of grape and calamansi, or a riff on apple aromatised with green shiso leaves and jasmine. Slick service and a splendid, cleverly compiled wine list seal the deal.

Chef Taylor Bonnyman, Marguerite Keogh **Seats** 40, Private dining 10 **Closed** Christmas, 2 weeks January, 2 weeks August **Notes** No children under 6 years

Outlaw's at The Capital

◉◉◉ BRITISH, SEAFOOD 🍷 NOTABLE WINE LIST

020 7591 1202 | Basil Street, Knightsbridge, SW3 1AT
www.capitalhotel.co.uk

Nathan Outlaw's reach extends from the environs of his native Cornwall to the heart of Knightsbridge these days, but the specialist emphasis on premium fish and seafood survives the journey intact. In the beige-toned dining room of a smart backstreet hotel, there is something almost counter-intuitive about such an obviously maritime repertoire. The native oysters are as bracing as when they emerge from western waters, though, and make a fitting prelude to a menu that might skip nimbly from a composition of squid, mussels and salami with cauliflower and red onion salad, to hake with roast fennel in saffron-olive butter, or a cod and cuttlefish duo on a slew of beans. Meat-eaters and vegetarians are not neglected – there could be hogget cutlet to start, or ricotta dumplings for main – while desserts look the enticing part, in the form of honey custard tart with anise-scented quince and gingerbread ice cream. A five-course tasting menu explores the range, its successive stages encompassing pickled herring, octopus and bread sauce, brill in garlic hollandaise, and sea bass.

Chef Nathan Outlaw, Andrew Sawyer **Seats** 35, Private dining 24 **Open** All year **Parking** 8 **Notes** Vegetarian dishes, Children welcome

Restaurant Gordon Ramsay

◉◉◉◉ FRENCH **V** 🍷 NOTABLE WINE LIST

020 7352 4441 | 68 Royal Hospital Road, SW3 4HP
www.gordonramsayrestaurants.com

Over 20 years since it opened in Royal Hospital Road, the flagship of the Gordon Ramsay global empire remains a strong contender among the top dogs of London's high-end dining scene. The dining room is surprisingly intimate – just 45 or so seats – with clean-lined, art deco-influenced looks and plush, pastel-hued tones giving a sophisticated sheen to the space. As for the kitchen team, it has been many years since Gordon Ramsay led the action at the stoves; that task now falls to Matt Abé, who has spent over a decade absorbing and honing to perfection the classical French ways that are in this restaurant's DNA. What keeps this venue in the premier league is its rejection of pointless experimentation and tawdry effects: what you get is superb ingredients, harmoniously combined and executed with pin-sharp precision, as in a starter of lemon verbena-cured sea trout with Jersey Royals, dill, cucumber in various guises, and horseradish cream. Next up, roast Herdwick mutton sits atop potato purée enriched with ewe's milk and curd, alongside peas, broad beans, charred onions and punchy green herb pistou. Desserts maintain the impeccably haute tone via sublime custard tart with wild strawberries and basil sorbet. The fixed-price lunch menu provides an entry point for anyone looking to sample the RGR experience on a budget (relatively speaking...), while the Prestige and Seasonal Inspiration menus cater to the high rollers. Pitch-perfect service is supervised by Jean-Claude Breton, and sommelier Jan Konetzki and his team steer the way through a roll-call of the world's best producers.

Chef Matt Abé **Seats** 45 **Closed** 1 week at Christmas **Notes** Children welcome

Tom's Kitchen – Chelsea

◉◉ TRADITIONAL BRITISH

020 7349 0202 | 27 Cale Street, Chelsea, SW3 3QP
www.tomskitchen.co.uk/chelsea

Well placed for the still trendy Fulham and King's Roads, the decor here is modern, the ceilings high, the kitchen open-plan and the service good. Note that all starters and mains are for sharing, and as the menu recommends three to four dishes per person, prices might raise an eyebrow.

Chef Joel Chaudhuri **Seats** Private dining 40 **Open** All year **Notes** No children

LONDON SW4
Bistro Union

◉◉ BRITISH

020 7042 6400 | 40 Abbeville Road, Clapham, SW4 9NG
www.bistrounion.co.uk

This is exactly the sort of easy-going neighbourhood eatery we'd all like on our patch. You can perch on wooden bar stools, choosing from a menu of on-trend nibbles hand-written on a roll of brown paper. What leaves the kitchen is built with British-led ingredients.

Chef Adam Byatt **Seats** 40 **Closed** 24–27 December **Prices from** S £6, M £15, D £5 **Notes** Vegetarian dishes, Children welcome

The Dairy

◉◉ MODERN BRITISH **V**

020 7622 4165 | 15 The Pavement, Clapham, SW4 0HY
www.the-dairy.co.uk

This buzzy operation has a dinky bar and a bistro behind with a pared-back look and flag-stoned floors. The open kitchen produces well-crafted dishes with clean flavours and modern presentation. Kick off with sourdough bread with home-made smoked bone marrow butter.

Chef Robin Gill **Seats** 40 **Closed** Christmas **Notes** Children welcome

Trinity Restaurant

⊛⊛⊛ BRITISH, EUROPEAN 🍷 NOTABLE WINE LIST

020 7622 1199 | 4 The Polygon, Clapham, SW4 0JG
www.trinityrestaurant.co.uk

Adam Byatt's neighbourhood restaurant in the Old Town part of sprawling Clapham, just off the north-east corner of the Common, is well into its second decade now. The outdoor terrace and cool, clean monochrome tones inside, complete with open-to-view kitchen, are very much what modern London dining is about, with a light-touch, unstuffy service approach adding to the appeal. Limitlessly inventive modern European cooking is the order of the day, with careful judgment of balance notable throughout. The four-course dinner menu might start with an opener of bigeye tuna alongside crab salad, pickled cucumber and avocado, before progressing to a crispy pig's ear with sauce gribiche and crackling. Main-course meats are sensational, as in the tender, deeply flavoured Balmoral venison that comes with vivid pumpkin purée, salt-baked quince, toasted hazelnuts and an eloquently rich jus, while dessert could be a salt caramel outing, in the dual form of wobbly custard tart and intense ice cream, or perhaps rum-soaked baba with citrus salad. The vegetarian rendition might take in gorgonzola risotto with pear and walnuts, and then chanterelle pappardelle with aged parmesan.

Chef Adam Byatt Seats 50 Closed 24–27 December and 1–2 January Notes Vegetarian dishes, No children under 10 years

Tsunami

⊛ JAPANESE

020 7978 1610 | 5–7 Voltaire Road, SW4 6DQ
www.tsunamirestaurant.co.uk

This original branch of the two Tsunami outlets appeals to crowds of thirty-somethings eager for first-class sushi and sashimi and slick modern Japanese fusion. Okay, the open-planned space may be hard-edged and high-decibel, but it's sociable, with the kitchen delivering fresh, skilful, smart-looking classic-meets-contemporary dishes.

Chef Ken Sam Seats 75 Closed 24–26 December, 1 January Notes Vegetarian dishes, Children welcome

LONDON SW5
Cambio de Tercio

⊛⊛ MODERN SPANISH V

020 7244 8970 | 163 Old Brompton Road, SW5 0LJ
www.cambiodetercio.co.uk

Folding full-length glass windows open Tercio up to the street, while inside there's a dark, intimate feel – black slate floors, mustard yellow and fuchsia pink walls hung with striking modern artworks. The food is equally colourful and good looking, ranging from traditional tapas to more innovative dishes.

Chef Alberto Criado Seats 90, Private dining 18 Closed 2 weeks at Christmas, 15–31 August and New Year Prices from S £3.75, M £26, D £7.50 Parking 10 Notes Children welcome

Capote y Toros

⊛ SPANISH V

020 7373 0567 | 157 Old Brompton Road, SW5 0LJ
www.cambiodetercio.co.uk

A few doors away from sibling Cambio de Tercio, Capote y Toros describes itself as a tapas, ham and sherry bar. It has vivid decor with photographs of matadors and hams hanging from the ceiling above the bar. Live flamenco music adds to the fun.

Chef Luis Navacerrada Lanzadera Seats 25 Closed Christmas Notes Children welcome

LONDON SW6
The Harwood Arms

⊛⊛ BRITISH V

020 7386 1847 | 27 Walham Grove, Fulham, SW6 1QR
www.harwoodarms.com

On an unassuming backstreet in trendy Fulham, the stylish Harwood Arms is one of Britain's top gastro pubs. Inside you could almost forget you're in London, with photos of outdoor country pursuits hung on grey and cream walls, and rustic wooden tables. On the menu, first class, carefully sourced English produce is cooked with confidence.

Chef Sally Abé Seats 60 Closed 24–26 December Prices from S £12.50, M £28.50, D £10.50 Notes Children welcome

LONDON SW7
Bombay Brasserie

⊛⊛ INDIAN

020 7370 4040 | Courtfield Close, Courtfield Road, SW7 4QH
www.bombayb.co.uk

This classy South Ken institution cherry picks its culinary influences from all over India – Parsi, Bengali, Goan, Gujerati, Mughal, even Portuguese. There are two sumptuously styled dining rooms, one with banquettes under palatial chandeliers, the other an airy, conservatory-roofed space with widely spaced tables.

Chef Prahlad Hegde Seats 185, Private dining 16 Closed 25 December Prices from S £11, M £18, D £9 Notes Vegetarian dishes, Children welcome

Brunello

◉ MODERN ITALIAN

020 7368 5700 | Baglioni Hotel London, 60 Hyde Park Gate, Kensington, Kensington Road, Kensington, SW7 5BB

www.baglionihotels.com

The opulent restaurant is a haven of Italian chic, done in parquet and monochrome tiles, with chairs in lemon leather, and giant mirrored baubles suspended from the ceiling. Expect classic and modern dishes.

Chef Ivan Simeoli **Seats** 70, Private dining 60 **Open** All year **Parking** 2 **Notes** Vegetarian dishes, Children welcome

Olive Restaurant

◉ ITALIAN

020 7331 6308 | Millennium Bailey's Hotel London Kensington, 140 Gloucester Road, SW7 4QH

www.olivesrestaurant.co.uk

The main dining room of the elegantly restored Victorian townhouse hotel in upmarket South Kensington offers uncomplicated Italian cooking and a seasonally changing menu.

Chef Davide di Croce **Seats** 70 **Open** All year **Notes** Vegetarian dishes, Children welcome

190 Queen's Gate by Daniel Galmiche

◉◉ BRITISH, FRENCH V

020 7584 6601 | The Gore, 190 Queen's Gate, SW7 5EX

www.gorehotel.com

A revamped offering in the past year under the Daniel Galmiche's guidance – the modern European menus are continually evolving here and it has a real town house feel about it. A good range of wines too.

Chef Daniel Galmiche, Marco Bucciarelli **Seats** 45, Private dining 60 **Open** All year **Prices from** S £9, M £22, D £8 **Notes** Children welcome

Rivea London

◉◉◉ MODERN FRENCH, ITALIAN RIVIERA ⬥ NOTABLE WINE LIST

020 7151 1025 | Bulgari Hotel, London, 171 Knightsbridge, SW7 1DW

www.rivealondon.com

Discover the cuisine of Italy and Provence through the prism of Alain Ducasse, just about the most respected chef in the world, associated with full-works haute cuisine and some of the swankiest dining addresses in the world. The sweeping staircase makes for a grand entrance into a dining room with shades of art deco style and a pin-sharp service team on hand. Octopus, chickpeas and fennel combine in a first-course that is rich with flavours of the Mediterranean, land and sea, and the same can be said of stone bass carpaccio with pine nuts. Green asparagus and ricotta fill ravioli,

while langoustines and Amalfi lemons make for a delicious partnership in a risotto. Among main courses, seared John Dory arrives with seasonal vegetables, and tender braised veal cheeks with celeriac and black truffle. Two can share rib of beef or pan-seared Dover sole. To finish, tarte au chocolat or tiramisù hit the same sunny spot.

Chef Antonio Corsaro **Seats** 82, Private dining 24 **Open** All year **Prices from** S £8, M £25, D £6 **Notes** Vegetarian dishes, Children welcome

Zuma

◉◉ MODERN JAPANESE

020 7584 1010 | 5 Raphael Street, Knightsbridge, SW7 1DL

www.zumarestaurant.com

An effortlessly cool playground of the beau monde, Zuma appeals to lovers of contemporary Japanese food and slick design. The vibe is high octane, buoyed by the buzzing front bar-lounge offering 40 different sakes. A lengthy roster of in-vogue sharing plates feature; the sushi is exemplary.

Chef Bjoern Weissgerber, Ben Orpwood **Seats** 175, Private dining 14 **Closed** 25 December **Notes** Vegetarian dishes, Children welcome

LONDON SW8

FIUME

◉◉ ITALIAN

020 3904 9010 | Circus West, Battersea Power Station, SW8 5BN

www.fiume-restaurant.co.uk

This modern restaurant within the Battersea Power Station redevelopment offers a stripped back decor with industrial decor plus an open plan kitchen with a pizza oven that takes centre stage. The seasonally changing menus offer Italian dishes from Sardinia with a modern twist.

Chef Francesco Mazzei, Francesco Chiarelli **Open** All year

LONDON SW10

Maze Grill Park Walk

◉ MODERN AMERICAN, JAPANESE

020 7495 2211 | 11 Park Walk, SW10 0AJ

www.gordonramsayrestaurants.com/maze-grill-park-walk

On one side of the room at Maze Grill Park Walk is a neat line of marble tables at olive-green banquettes, on the other is a long bar. The place takes inspiration from Manhattan grill rooms, so beef is king here.

Chef Gabriele Zanini **Seats** 60 **Open** All year **Prices from** S £5, M £15, D £6 **Notes** Vegetarian dishes, Children welcome

Medlar Restaurant
◉◉◉ MODERN EUROPEAN 🍷 NOTABLE WINE LIST
020 7349 1900 | 438 King's Road, Chelsea, SW10 0LJ
www.medlarrestaurant.co.uk

Medlar is at the World's End end of Kings Road. Behind its small terrace area is an attractively simple interior, with spring-green banquettes and linened tables reflected in distressed mirror panels. Cheery staff create the right kind of ambience, while the kitchen specialises in modern bistro dishes of strong appeal. Most utilise a broad range of components, but in well-defined precision, beginning perhaps with crab raviolo, brown shrimps, leek fondue and samphire in bisque, or duck egg tart with a sautéed heart, lardons and turnip purée. Japanese and Italian notes inveigle themselves in, so fish might be turbot and baby squid in dashi with shimejis and sea kale, while the right royal treatment is reserved for meats such as roast quail glazed in soy sauce, maple syrup and lime, its legs confit, served with crêpe parmentier, foie gras, hazelnuts and a dollop of zhoug (Yemeni green chilli relish). Add a side of triple-cooked chips in a slather of béarnaise, and it's hard to see what else you could wish for, other than a chocolate tart and honeycomb ice cream to see you on your way.

Chef Joe Mercer Nairne Seats 85, Private dining 28 Closed Christmas and 1 January Notes Vegetarian dishes, Children welcome

The Painted Heron
◉ MODERN INDIAN
020 7351 5232 | 112 Cheyne Walk, SW10 0DJ
www.tphofchelsea.com

This upscale Chelsea Indian is a thoroughly modern affair with an understated, clean-lined interior. The cooking is smart and seasonal and plant-based dishes take the spotlight; no dairy products are used in the cooking process.

Chef Yogesh Datta Seats 70 Open All year Prices from S £8, M £11, D £5 Notes Vegetarian dishes, Children welcome

LONDON SW11
London House
◉◉ MODERN BRITISH
020 7592 8545 | 7–9 Battersea Square, Battersea Village, SW11 3RA
www.gordonramsayrestaurants.com/london-house

Smack on the corner of lovely Battersea Square, Gordon Ramsay's neighbourhood restaurant and bar is just the outfit everyone would love on their doorstep. The kitchen's creative modern British brasserie-style repertoire displays the same unmistakeable gloss; think simplicity, precision, flavour and flair.

Chef Will Stanyer Seats 63 Open All year Notes Vegetarian dishes, Children welcome

LONDON SW13
Sonny's Kitchen
◉◉ MODERN EUROPEAN
020 8748 0393 | 94 Church Road, Barnes, SW13 0DQ
www.sonnyskitchen.co.uk

Part restaurant, part food store, Sonny's has been a fixture for Barnes' foodies for almost 30 years, its neutral designer-chic decor involving textures of wood, leather, ceramic tiles, glass bricks and white walls hung with art. The inventive modern European food has a Mediterranean edge.

Chef Andrew Chelley Seats 85, Private dining 16 Closed Christmas, New Year Prices from S £6.50, M £16.95, D £6 Notes Vegetarian dishes, Children welcome

LONDON SW14
Rick Stein, Barnes
◉ SEAFOOD
020 8878 9462 | 125 Mortlake High Street, Barnes, SW14 8SN
www.rickstein.com/eat-with-us/barnes/

The Stein empire's first foray into London sees bottle-green banquettes and brass-edged tables add class to the conservatory-style space. The globetrotting menu parades fish and seafood dishes inspired by Rick Stein's TV travels: simple, light-touch treatments that let the top-class ingredients do the talking.

Chef Ian Salmon Open All year

LONDON SW17
Chez Bruce
◉◉◉ MODERN BRITISH 🍷 NOTABLE WINE LIST
020 8672 0114 | 2 Bellevue Road, Wandsworth Common, SW17 7EG
www.chezbruce.co.uk

Set in a parade of shops overlooking Wandsworth Common, the discreet aubergine-coloured frontage of Bruce Poole's high-flying neighbourhood restaurant has been a beacon of top-notch culinary achievement since 1995. The place doesn't need a celebrity chef, a social media storm or a glossy West End location to bring in the punters, preferring the unshouty approach of a white-walled dining room hung with tasteful art, furnished with linen-clad tables on herringbone parquet floors, and alive with the civilized hum of people reveling in splendid gastronomy. It's a setting that suits Poole's unfussy but highly classy cooking to perfection, the roots of the modern European menu deeply imbedded in France and the Mediterranean. Start, perhaps, with devilled lamb's kidneys with crisp potato, roast shallots and red wine, then move on to the indulgent sensuality of pot-roast pig's cheek with crisp boudin noir and pork fillet, the flavours all dialed up to 11 with celeriac, mustard and herbs. To finish, there's a peerless cheeseboard, or sweet delights along the lines of buttermilk pudding with poached Yorkshire rhubarb, lemon and pistachios.

Chef Bruce Poole, Matt Christmas **Seats** 75, Private dining 16 **Closed** 24–26 December and 1 January **Notes** Vegetarian dishes, Children welcome at lunch only

LONDON SW19
The Fox & Grapes
TRADITIONAL BRITISH
020 8619 1300 | 9 Camp Road, Wimbledon, SW19 4UN
www.foxandgrapeswimbledon.co.uk

On the edge of Wimbledon Common, the 18th-century Fox & Grapes has morphed into a contemporary food-oriented pub with an airy open-plan interior of oak floors, wood panelling, and chunky bare wooden tables and mismatched chairs wrapped around a central island bar.

Chef John Stanyer **Seats** 90 **Open** All year **Notes** Vegetarian dishes, Children welcome

Hotel du Vin Wimbledon
MODERN BRITISH, EUROPEAN
020 8879 1464 | Cannizaro House, West Side, Wimbledon Common, SW19 4UE
www.hotelduvin.co.uk

Located in Cannizaro House, an eye-poppingly posh late-Georgian mansion, this Bistro du Vin is split into two areas, the main part being the orangery. From the concise menu you might start with scallop ceviche marinated in lime juice, salt, sugar, pomegranate, chilli and coriander.

Chef Kauff Diop **Seats** 100, Private dining 120 **Open** All year **Parking** 55 **Notes** Vegetarian dishes, Children welcome

The Light House Restaurant
MODERN INTERNATIONAL, EUROPEAN
020 8944 6338 | 75–77 Ridgway, Wimbledon, SW19 4ST
www.lighthousewimbledon.com

The Light House is a beacon of fresh seasonal cooking just a short stroll from Wimbledon Common. Appealing menus of fresh, modern bistro-style dishes are the deal, with plenty of sunny, Mediterranean flavours being cooked up in the open kitchen.

Chef Chris Casey **Seats** 80, Private dining 12 **Closed** 25–26 December, 1 January **Prices from** S £6, M £12.95, D £6 **Notes** Vegetarian dishes, Children welcome

The White Onion
CONTEMPORARY FRENCH
020 8947 8278 | 67 High Street, Wimbledon, SW19 5EE
www.thewhiteonion.co.uk

This smart-casual bistro fits the bill for its well-heeled neighbourhood. With a sleek look of deep teal blue and white walls, bright modern artworks, buttoned leather banquettes and bare wood tables, it's a suitable setting for sparkily confident modern French cooking that gives star billing to excellent seasonal ingredients.

Chef Frédéric Duval **Seats** Private dining 22 **Closed** 30 July to 15 August and 24 December to 10 January **Prices from** S £9.10, M £14.50, D £8 **Notes** Vegetarian dishes, Children welcome

LONDON W1
Alain Ducasse at The Dorchester
CONTEMPORARY, MODERN FRENCH V NOTABLE WINE LIST
020 7629 8866 | The Dorchester, 53 Park Lane, W1K 1QA
www.alainducasse-dorchester.com

The notion of the maître cuisinier overseeing a flotilla of exclusive dining rooms across the known world may seem a little forbidding in these straitened times, but it remains a powerful exemplar of what aspirational restaurateuring is about. Alain Ducasse undoubtedly fits the model to a T, and The Dorchester makes a suitably grand setting for the London iteration of his culinary practice. It's an understated space, let it be said, elegant enough to be sure, but essentially pitched at the neutral end of the spectrum, the pierced curvilinear screen that shields the entrance. The kitchen here is the preserve of Jean-Philippe Blondet, who supervises a menu that remains a beacon of constancy in a changing culinary landscape. These are dishes burnished to a high degree of accomplishment through long acquaintance, from the crab tourteau with celeriac and caviar, through the halibut and oyster with seaweed, and dry-aged beef with artichoke and bone marrow, to the rum-laced babas to finish. That is not to suggest that the menu doesn't develop — look to rib and saddle of venison with parsnip and peanuts for a peek into the unfamiliar — but it reinforces the unfashionable idea that great kitchens become associated in the French tradition with a medley of signature dishes. The lunchtime menu offers appealingly simple options, perhaps salsify with smoked eel and Granny Smith, followed by Denbighshire pork and braised chicory, and a Menu Jardin vegetarian six-courser may be a pleasant surprise in the context. The quartet of French cheeses with individual dressings should not be missed.

Chef Jean-Philippe Blondet, Thibault Hauchard, Alberto Gobbo **Seats** 82, Private dining 30 **Closed** 1st week in January, Easter weekend, 3 weeks in August, 26–30 December **Parking** 20 **Notes** No children under 10 years

Alyn Williams at The Westbury
◉◉◉◉ MODERN EUROPEAN **V** 🍷NOTABLE WINE LIST
020 7183 6426 | 37 Conduit Street, W1S 2YF
www.alynwilliams.com

Since 2011, Alyn Williams' dedication and high-level artistry have been rewarded with his own name over the door of the top-end dining venue of The Westbury Hotel. A cocktail among the art deco-inspired Swarovski crystal fittings and Fendi-designed accoutrements of the Polo Bar is a good move to set the mood for the Alyn experience, which unfolds with impeccably correct, seamless and unobtrusive service in an unshouty yet unmistakably glossy space. Supported by a trusty and well-established kitchen team, Williams has had time to explore his own territory here, evolving a highly personal take on modern European cuisine, using unusual ingredients and pin-sharp techniques to produce creative and dynamic food. A seven-course tasting menu delivers the full works (a non-meat version means vegetarians are not sidelined) with optional wine or beer flights; otherwise, there's an à la carte option. High on flavour, thought, inspiration and – yes – fun, an opening course of roasted lobster with lobster taco, dirty guacamole, green gazpacho and chimichurri dressing is an explosion of well-balanced flavours coupled with high-quality ingredients. Prime ingredients and faultlessly composed flavours and textures also produce seductive results in a main course showcasing Salisbury Estate venison, alongside salt-baked celeriac, juniper, blueberries and the fruity pungency of mostarda. Desserts can make their point with the simple perfection of a chocolate and orange blossom tartlet or continue to explore thrilling juxtapositions of flavor and texture via an innovative play on the 'walnut whip' theme.

Chef Alyn Williams **Seats** 65, Private dining 20
Closed 1st 2 weeks of January, last 2 weeks of August
Prices from S £22.50, M £35, D £12.50 **Parking** 20
Notes Children welcome

Antidote
◉ MODERN EUROPEAN
020 7287 8488 | 12a Newburgh Street, W1F 7RR
www.antidotewinebar.com

Tucked away in a cobbled lane behind Carnaby Street, Antidote offers the perfect fix for organic/biodynamic wine lovers and foodies alike. Upstairs, the stylish dining room is a relaxed oasis, with a pared-back look – grey walls, floorboards; while the kitchen delivers imaginative modern dishes.

Chef Dan Whalan **Seats** 45 **Closed** Christmas and Bank holidays **Prices from** S £8, M £18, D £6
Notes Vegetarian dishes, Children welcome

Aqua Kyoto
◉◉ CONTEMPORARY JAPANESE
020 7478 0540 | 240 Regent Street, W1B 3BR
www.aquakyoto.co.uk

The rooftop views from the top floor of the former Dickins & Jones building are great, and Aqua Kyoto's dining room shimmers with contemporary style, complementing the knife-wielding theatre of a sunken centrepiece sushi bar and robata grill.

Chef Paul Greening **Seats** 110, Private dining 10
Closed 25–26 December and 1 January
Prices from S £4.50, M £6, D £7.50 **Notes** Vegetarian dishes, Children welcome

Aqua Nueva
◉◉ MODERN SPANISH
020 7478 0540 | 5th Floor, 240 Regent Street, W1B 3BR
www.aquanueva.co.uk

A lift whizzes you up from ground-floor street life to jet-set high life at this slick fifth-floor restaurant where people come to see and be seen while grazing on contemporary renditions of tapas based on top-class Spanish ingredients. Pick from a bilingual menu.

Chef Yahir Gonzalez **Seats** 100, Private dining 80
Closed 25–26 December and 1 January
Prices from S £5.50, M £8.50, D £8 **Notes** Vegetarian dishes, Children welcome

The Arch London
◉ MODERN BRITISH
020 7725 4825 | 50 Great Cumberland Place, W1H 7FD
www.thearchlondon.com

Just a short stroll from Marble Arch, The Arch is a charming hotel spread over seven Georgian townhouses. A stone oven comes into its own with some main courses, from game pie to whole sea bass with orange and rosemary butter.

Chef Gary Durrant **Seats** 66, Private dining 48
Open All year **Prices from** S £7, M £16, D £6.50
Notes Vegetarian dishes, Children welcome

Barrafina Dean Street
◉◉ SPANISH
020 7813 8016 | 26–27 Dean Street, W1D 3LL
www.barrafina.co.uk

Tapas is the name of the game here at this bustling plate-glass corner site. The no booking policy means queues are likely and, once in, you perch elbow-to-elbow at the marble counter and tuck into rapid-fire small plates bursting with flavour.

Chef Carlos Manuel Miranda Gomes **Seats** 28
Closed Bank holidays **Notes** Vegetarian dishes, Children welcome

The Beaumont
⚫ BRITISH, AMERICAN **V**
020 7499 9499 | 8 Balderton Street, Mayfair, W1K 6TF
www.colonygrillroom.com

On the south side of Oxford Street, not far from Selfridges, The Beaumont is a burnished slice of Mayfair elegance where bow-tied waiters bring brasserie food such as potted Morecambe Bay shrimps with brown bread and butter.

Chef Christian Turner **Seats** 100, Private dining 40 **Open** All year **Notes** Children welcome

Bellamy's
⚫ FRENCH
020 7491 2727 | 18–18a Bruton Place, W1J 6LY
www.bellamysrestaurant.co.uk

With its setting just off Berkeley Square, effortlessly classy good looks and slickly professional service, Bellamy's epitomises the chic, timeless French brasserie genre. Leather banquettes, pale yellow walls lined with tasteful French posters, and staff in bow ties and waistcoats add to the authentic look.

Chef Stephane Pacoud **Seats** 70 **Closed** Christmas, New Year, Bank holidays **Prices from** S £8.50, M £19.50, D £8.50 **Notes** Vegetarian dishes, Children welcome

Benares Restaurant
⚫⚫ MODERN INDIAN **V** 🍷 NOTABLE WINE LIST
020 7629 8886 | 12a Berkeley Square, W1J 6BS
www.benaresrestaurant.com

In the heart of Mayfair, Atul Kochhar's refurbished flagship has plenty of glamorous buzz, and takes a serious approach to dining. Combining high-end British ingredients with spices and aromatics, this crossover Anglo-Indian cooking always excites with its innovative ideas, precise technique and enticing presentation.

Chef Atul Kochhar **Seats** 120, Private dining 36 **Closed** 1 January **Prices from** S £14, M £26, D £10 **Notes** No children under 8 years after 7pm

Bentley's Oyster Bar & Grill
⚫ BRITISH, IRISH 🍷 NOTABLE WINE LIST
020 7734 4756 | 11–15 Swallow Street, W1B 4DG
www.bentleys.org

Over 100 years old, the illustrious oyster bar is a popular, feel-good rendezvous, while the grill restaurant upstairs takes a more formal, sophisticated approach. Portioning is light and prices lean toward West End grabby, but ingredients are excellent, service slick and wines a superb bunch.

Chef Richard Corrigan, Michael Lynch **Seats** 70, Private dining 60 **Closed** 25 December and 1 January **Notes** Vegetarian dishes, Children welcome

Berners Tavern
⚫⚫ MODERN BRITISH 🍷 NOTABLE WINE LIST
020 7908 7979 | The London EDITION, 10 Berners Street, W1T 3NP
www.bernerstavern.com

This palatial space with a magnificent plaster ceiling, chandelier, and walls crowded with pictures, is nothing like a tavern. Jason Atherton oversees the cooking, which is in his contemporary brasserie style. Restyled classics such as lobster and prawn cocktail get things going.

Chef Phil Carmichael, Jason Atherton **Seats** 130, Private dining 14 **Open** All year **Prices from** S £12.50, M £19, D £5 **Notes** Vegetarian dishes, Children welcome

Blanchette
⚫ MODERN, TRADITIONAL FRENCH TAPAS **V**
020 7439 8100 | 9 D'Arblay Street, Soho, W1F 8DR
www.blanchettesoho.co.uk

Opened by three brothers from across the Channel, Blanchette delivers imaginative bistro-style French cuisine served as sharing plates. The charcuterie and cheese selections show what this place is all about – salami-style Rosette de Lyon and truffled saucisson from the Rhône region for example.

Chef Tam Storrar, William Alexander **Seats** 54, Private dining 14 **Open** All year **Notes** Children welcome

Bocca di Lupo
⚫ ITALIAN 🍷 NOTABLE WINE LIST
020 7734 2223 | 12 Archer Street, W1D 7BB
www.boccadilupo.com

High-energy, high-octane and great fun, Bocca di Lupo rocks. Grab a stool at the long marble bar's 'chef's counter' to enjoy the culinary theatre, or head straight to the restaurant area proper, with its polished wood tables and feature lighting.

Chef Jacob Kenedy **Seats** 75, Private dining 32 **Closed** 25 December and 1 January **Notes** Vegetarian dishes, Children welcome

Bó Drake
⚫ KOREAN, JAPANESE, MODERN ASIAN
020 7439 9989 | 6 Greek Street, W1D 4DE
www.bodrake.co.uk

Tucked away at the top-end of Greek Street, the stripped-back space focuses on the long wood-slab dining counter, while the kitchen goes for a modern pan-Asian approach, delivering big umami-rich flavours in punchy slow-cooked and smoky barbeque dishes. Try pork belly bao – pillowy buns packed with melt-in-the-mouth Hampshire pork.

Chef Julio Cancedda **Seats** 55 **Closed** Christmas, New Year **Notes** Vegetarian dishes, Children welcome

Bonhams

◉◉ MODERN EUROPEAN

020 7468 5868 | 7 Haunch of Venison Yard, W1K 5ES
www.bonhams.herokuapp.com

Climb the wooden spiral staircase to the stark white dining room at the world-famous auction house in Mayfair to discover a menu of modernised classic dishes. The pristine monochrome of the restaurant is offset by jolting colour-field abstract paintings, and the odd art critic can be spotted among the clientele.

Chef Tom Kemble **Seats** 24 **Closed** Bank holidays and 10 days over Christmas **Notes** Vegetarian dishes, No children under 12 years

Brown's Hotel

CLASSIC ITALIAN ⚑ NOTABLE WINE LIST

020 7518 4004 | Albemarle Street, Mayfair, W1S 4BP
www.roccofortehotels.com

The Brown's Hotel dining room has undergone many manifestations, and as we were going to press it entered a new phase as Beck at Brown's with Heinz Beck bringing a casual dining menu of classic Italian dishes using the best British produce.

Chef Heinz Beck **Seats** 80, Private dining 70
Open All year **Notes** Children welcome

Casita Andina

◉ PERUVIAN

020 3327 9464 | 31 Great Windmill Street, Soho, W1D 7LP
www.andinalondon.com/casita

Canteen eating in the Peruvian style has to be another Soho first. Housed in a building that was a bolt-hole for actors and artists over the years, the Casita maintains links with its past – at least until the food starts emerging in dazzling array.

Chef Jakub Wilk, Vitelio Reyes **Open** All year
Prices from S £4, M £6, D £6 **Notes** Vegetarian dishes, Children welcome

Cecconi's

◉◉ TRADITIONAL ITALIAN

020 7434 1500 | 5a Burlington Gardens, W1S 1EP
www.cecconis.co.uk

Cecconi's is a classic, from the glamorous Mayfair crew slurping cocktails and cicchetti at the island bar to the black-and-white humbug-striped marble floors, green leather upholstery and slick Italian staff. Dedication to top-class seasonal produce is clear, and it's simply prepared to deliver full-on flavours.

Chef Simone Serafini **Seats** 80 **Closed** Christmas and New Year **Notes** Children welcome

The Chesterfield Mayfair

◉◉ TRADITIONAL BRITISH

020 7491 2622 | 35 Charles Street, Mayfair, W1J 5EB
www.chesterfieldmayfair.com

A fine Georgian property jam-packed with antiques and run with a touch of old-school charm. A suckling pig's cheek croquette looks pretty, with a sliver of black pudding and sweetcorn purée. There's a pre-theatre menu, and afternoon tea is served in the conservatory.

Chef Ben Kelliher **Seats** 65, Private dining 80
Open All year **Notes** Vegetarian dishes, Children welcome

China Tang at The Dorchester

◉◉ CLASSIC CANTONESE

020 7629 9988 | 53 Park Lane, W1K 1QA
www.thedorchester.com/china-tang

The basement of The Dorchester is home to this opulent homage to 1930s Shanghai. The kitchen's output is classic Cantonese, although the quality of the produce takes the menu of familiar dishes and all-day dim sum to a higher plane.

Chef Chong Choi Fong **Seats** 120, Private dining 80
Closed 24–25 December **Notes** Vegetarian dishes, Children welcome aged 5–10 years until 8pm

Clipstone

◉◉ MODERN

020 7637 0871 | 2 Clipstone Street, W1W 6BB
www.clipstonerestaurant.co.uk

Clipstone is the more casual sibling of the high-rolling Portland. The corner site has an informal vibe with an open kitchen and cheery, unstuffy service keeping things on course. The menu revolves around bistro-esque sharing plates of simplicity, precision and flavour, bound by a seasonal accent.

Chef Stuart Andrew **Seats** 35 **Closed** Christmas and New Year **Prices from** S £8, M £19, D £6
Notes Vegetarian dishes, Children welcome

C London

◉◉ ITALIAN

020 7399 0500 | 23–25 Davies Street, W1K 3DE
www.crestaurant.co.uk

C London is sibling to Venice's famous Harry's Bar and is a haunt of the international glitterati. The high-gloss dining room looks sleek with its art deco styling and mirror-sheen, panelled walls and white-jacketed, professional staff. The classic Italian cooking is founded on top-class produce.

Chef Giuseppe Marangi **Seats** 140, Private dining 32
Closed 25 December **Notes** Children welcome

Corrigan's Mayfair

◉◉◉ BRITISH, IRISH **V** ◢ NOTABLE WINE LIST

020 7499 9943 | 28 Upper Grosvenor Street, W1K 7EH
www.corrigansmayfair.co.uk

Richard Corrigan is a chef who likes to feed, to satisfy, and here, in his Mayfair flagship, he does just that in a dining room that is as buffed-up and glossy as you'd expect in the blue-chip postcode. There's a real feel of old-school grandeur as you take in the sleek art deco-style looks and sink into plush navy-blue leather seats and banquettes at linen-clothed tables; the front-of-house team are as slick as they come. Corrigan's Anglo-Irish food is grounded in honest-to-goodness gutsiness and robustness, allied to the pin-sharp techniques of haute cuisine and presented with modern swagger, whether you go for the six-course taster, the keenly priced seasonal set lunch, or the carte. To start, Carlingford oysters are a fixture, but if you prefer the chefs to do some proper work, consider seared Orkney scallops with cauliflower, vanilla and cocoa. At main-course stage there might be braised beef cheek, as meltingly tender as you'd like, with cauliflower and marrow croquette, while desserts such as blood orange soufflé with marmalade and sheep's yogurt are equally on the money.

Chef Richard Corrigan, Ross Bryans **Seats** 85, Private dining 30 **Closed** 25 December, Bank holidays **Prices from** S £14.50, M £18.50, D £9 **Notes** Children welcome

Coya

◉◉ MODERN PERUVIAN

020 7042 7118 | 118 Piccadilly, Mayfair, W1J 7NW
www.coyarestaurant.com

With its open kitchen, a céviche counter, a charcoal grill and a glamorous pisco bar, Coya is a hive of Peruvian-inspired activity. Expect classy food full of entertaining South American and Japanese fusion flavours and some spot-on ingredients.

Chef Sanjay Dwiveve **Open** All year

CUT at 45 Park Lane

◉◉◉ MODERN AMERICAN **V**

020 7493 4554 | 45 Park Lane, W1K 1BJ
www.dorchestercollection.com

The Park Lane glitz of a swanky hotel in the Dorchester stable makes a suitably top-end joint for one of US chef and restaurateur Wolfgang Puck's über-glam international steakhouses. With an extravagant decor of glitterball chandeliers, swathes of curtain, burnished wooden panels and a full set of Damien Hirst 'Psalm' artworks, no-one could fault the jet-set vibe of this temple to top-grade beef. Take your pick: Australian and Japanese Wagyu, South Devon Angus, USDA rib-eye steak with fries, all expertly aged, sold by weight, and precision timed on the grill, with eight sauces – Armagnac and green peppercorn, Argentinian chimichurri, or wasabi yuzu kosho butter, say – to go with it. The menu runs to seared foie gras with rhubarb purée and toasted brioche, then Dover sole meunière with preserved lemon and parsley, or sashimi-grade big-eye tuna steak. Puddings like sticky toffee medjool date cake with apricot gel and honeycomb ice cream are hard to resist.

Chef David McIntyre **Seats** 70, Private dining 14 **Open** All year **Prices from** S £12, M £28, D £12 **Notes** Children welcome

Dehesa

◉ SPANISH, ITALIAN

020 7494 4170 | 25 Ganton Street, W1F 9BP
www.dehesa.co.uk

Dehesa comes from the same stable as Salt Yard and Opera Tavern and, like them, is a charcuterie and tapas bar serving up a lively hybrid of Spanish and Italian dishes. It's a small, buzzy place where you sit elbow-to-elbow at high-level tables.

Chef William Breese **Seats** 40, Private dining 13 **Closed** 24–26 and 31 December and 1 January **Notes** Vegetarian dishes, Children welcome

Dinings

◉◉ JAPANESE, EUROPEAN

020 7723 0666 | 22 Harcourt Street, W1H 4HH
www.dinings.co.uk

There's scarcely room to swing a chopstick here, but exquisitely crafted Japanese tapas are the draw. The creative kitchen fuses Japanese and modern European dishes, so check out the blackboard specials, then tackle the lengthy menu by sharing a selection of small but perfectly formed dishes.

Chef Masaki Sugisaki, Keiji Fuku **Seats** 28 **Closed** 24–26 December, 31 December and 1 January **Prices from** S £3.05, M £7.45, D £6.20 **Notes** Vegetarian dishes, Children welcome

Ember Yard

◉◉ SPANISH, ITALIAN ◢ NOTABLE WINE LIST

020 7439 8057 | 60–61 Berwick Street, W1F 8SU
www.emberyard.co.uk

Ember Yard is the latest in the chain of uptempo tapas outfits that have been trending in the capital. The food comes inspired by Spain (the Basque country in particular) and Italy, and is smoked or cooked simply on a Basque-style wood and charcoal grill.

Chef Jacques Fourie **Seats** 120, Private dining 18 **Closed** 25–26 December **Notes** Vegetarian dishes, Children welcome

LONDON W1

L'Escargot
◎◎ FRENCH, MEDITERRANEAN
020 7439 7474 | 48 Greek Street, W1D 4EF
www.lescargotrestaurant.co.uk

This near-century-old Soho institution serves the rich comforts of classic French cuisine. Occupying a fine Georgian townhouse once home to the Duke of Portland, its sumptuous colours and serious art collection set an elegant old-school scene for cooking that reassures, comforts and thrills from the off.

Chef James Tyrrell **Seats** 80, Private dining 60 **Closed** 25–26 December, 1 January **Prices from** S £7, M £16, D £7 **Notes** Vegetarian dishes, No children under 10 years

Fera at Claridge's
◎◎◎ MODERN BRITISH **V**
020 7107 8888 | Brook Street, W1K 4HR
www.feraatclaridges.co.uk

The name is Latin for 'wild', a clue to the back-to-nature orientation that has been brought, however improbably, to a grand old West End hotel, Claridge's. A bare, white-limbed tree takes centre stage, with discreet sprays of foliage here and there, amid the art deco lamps and sober grey livery of the dining room. Matt Starling is able to draw on impeccable produce here to create technically dazzling dishes in shorter and longer tasting sequences, as well as a comprehensive carte. Crisply roasted veal sweetbreads come with caramelised violet artichokes and monk's beard in mussel cream for a bravura opener, and then poached turbot might appear in the delicate company of sprouting broccoli and sunflower seeds, or superlative fennel-seeded Cornish hogget saddle with hispi cabbage in a strong dill cream sauce. Vegetable-based desserts tease the unexpected sweetness out of such ingredients as Jerusalem artichoke, in an ice cream that accompanies toffee apple and salt caramel. The final witty note comes with a petit four styled on a certain brand of ambassadorial foil-wrapped chocolate, transformed into a hazelnut encased in sweet mushroom purée.

Chef Matthew Starling **Seats** 94, Private dining 12 **Open** All year **Prices from** S £19, M £30, D £14 **Notes** No children under 5 years

Four Seasons Hotel London at Park Lane
◎◎ ITALIAN **V**
020 7319 5206 | Hamilton Place, Park Lane, W1J 7DR
www.fourseasons.com/london/dining

Four Seasons stands in modern grandeur at Hyde Park Corner, a distinctly plutocratic node of London. In the restaurant, carefully crafted Italian dishes embrace the simplicity that everyone seeks in Italian food. Dessert

of retooled tiramisù is garnished with a salted tuile set with cocoa nibs.

Chef Romuald Feger, Eliano Crespi **Seats** 62, Private dining 10 **Open** All year **Parking** 10 **Notes** Children welcome

Galvin at The Athenaeum
◎◎ MODERN, CLASSIC BRITISH
020 7640 3333 | 116 Piccadilly, W1J 7BJ
www.athenaeumhotel.com

The Athenaeum Hotel's restaurant is another outpost in London chefs Chris and Jeff Galvin's empire. For the first time they've stepped away from their trademark French-inspired menus in favour of an array of menus including afternoon tea and private dining, and feature a modern take on classic British dishes.

Chef William Lloyd Baker **Seats** 90, Private dining 70 **Open** All year **Prices from** S £7, M £16, D £5 **Notes** Vegetarian dishes, No children

Galvin at Windows Restaurant & Bar
◎◎◎ MODERN FRENCH **NOTABLE WINE LIST**
020 7208 4021 | London Hilton on Park Lane, 22 Park Lane, W1K 1BE
www.galvinatwindows.com

Of the many different versions of glamour, one of the headiest is eating in the sky, especially when it begins with a greeting from TV celeb host, Fred Sirieix, star of Channel 4's *First Dates*. Whether you're dating or not, the views from the 28th floor of the Park Lane Hilton are bracing indeed, with London laid out like an architectural model during the day, and as a filigree of lights after dark. Joo Won steps up to the spectacle with a dazzling style of Asian-inflected modern European cuisine that scores many a hit. Kimchi risotto topped with a slow-cooked egg is sprinkled with spring onions, sesame seeds and parmesan shavings for a productive mixture of messages. Then comes a lamb treatment that mixes breast, rump and bolognese with goats' cheese in a jus gras, or perfectly timed seared halibut with plump, crisp king prawns and shimejis in dashi broth. Dessert might be rum and raisin baba with white chocolate cream and pickled pear.

Chef Joo Won, Chris Galvin **Seats** 130 **Closed** 26 December **Prices from** S £22, M £43, D £17 **Notes** Vegetarian dishes, Children welcome

Gauthier Soho
◎◎◎ MODERN FRENCH **V** **NOTABLE WINE LIST**
020 7494 3111 | 21 Romilly Street, W1D 5AF
www.gauthiersoho.co.uk

Ring or knock, whichever you deem more suitable, to gain entry, and the stolid black door, with its faint air of Downing Street, will be opened unto you. Alexis Gauthier's Soho address has a pleasingly refined ambience, expressed in a bright, cheery first-floor dining room with ostentatious floral displays on the mantelpiece, uplifting artworks and discreet street views over the windowboxes. A prix-fixe menu option of three, four or five courses changes seasonally, bringing affectionately regarded modern French cooking to the hearts of London. Smoked eel with a poached duck egg in watercress velouté is a vibrant spring opener, and could be followed by cod with broad beans, peas and creamed morels. Main meat dishes come with their own concentrated essences, as in the glossy jus that accompanies Highland venison with roast pumpkin, truffled celeriac and wine-poached pear. Vivid experimentation produces chickpea-crusted rhubarb vacherin with berry sorbet for dessert, but there is also a richly seductive and wildly popular creation called Golden Louis XV, layers of crunchy praline underneath a deliquescent coating of 70% dark chocolate.

Chef Gerard Virolle, Alexis Gauthier **Seats** 60, Private dining 32 **Closed** Christmas, Bank holidays **Notes** Children welcome

Le Gavroche Restaurant
@@@@ FRENCH V
020 7408 0881 | 43 Upper Brook Street, W1K 7QR
www.le-gavroche.co.uk

Now embarked on its sixth decade, Le Gavroche remains for many the gold standard of aspirational French dining, a place where everything is done with both correctness and courtesy, and the waiting list for tables speaks of the unwavering faith that an international clientele, as well as London regulars, maintain in such an approach. Two generations of the Roux family have built a culinary empire on classical French cuisine of the Escoffier era, with discreetly applied modernistic notes to taste, and Michel Roux Jnr, a genially familiar figure from food TV, is only too happy to make a tour of the dining room towards the end of service, dressed in his pristine whites for the selfies. Exquisite presentations elevate dishes as straightforward as lemon-marinated salmon with vodka jelly into the artworks they aspire to be, while the grilled scallops in clam minestrone are the last word in bracing sea-freshness. A main course of stone bass with red rice and fennel looks to north Africa for its pastilla presentation and seasoning with ras el hanout, its meat jus adding an extra resonant dimension, or there might be Cumbrian rose veal with creamed morels and mash, the ultimate in meaty comfort food. Meanwhile, the signature dishes for which the Gavroche has been noted over the decades – the soufflé suissesse in its bubbling cream bath, the lobster and Aquitaine caviar in champagne butter, the feather-light omelette Rothschild in its apricot and Cointreau sauce – remain touchstone manifestations

of an all but vanished culinary language, much as is the flawless service.

Chef Michel Roux Jnr **Seats** 60, Private dining 6 **Closed** Christmas, New Year and Bank holidays **Notes** Children welcome

Goodman
@ BRITISH, CLASSIC AMERICAN NOTABLE WINE LIST
020 7499 3776 | 26 Maddox Street, W1S 1QH
www.goodmanrestaurants.com

There's plenty of red meat action going on for die-hard carnivores in this upscale New York-inspired steakhouse serving prime slabs of US and UK beef. Choose your cut, from rib-eye, through bone-in sirloin to porterhouse, and it arrives precision timed and served with béarnaise, pepper or Stilton sauces.

Chef Lukasz Doktor **Seats** 95 **Closed** Christmas, New Year, Bank holidays **Prices from** S £8, M £16, D £5.50 **Notes** Vegetarian dishes, Children welcome

The Greenhouse
@@@@ MODERN FRENCH V NOTABLE WINE LIST
020 7499 3331 | 27a Hay's Mews, Mayfair, W1J 5NY
www.greenhouserestaurant.co.uk

The Mayfair mews location promises discreet, high-end pleasures, approached along a decked pathway lined with bamboo plants, box hedges, bay trees, sculptures and little fountains – a delightful, tranquil garden setting that makes you wish alfresco dining was on the cards. Inside, the soothing decor establishes a connection with nature via views of the garden from the serenely stylish dining room; restful shades of beige and ivory are offset by dark wood floors, avocado-coloured leather banquettes and chairs, tables dressed in their finest white linen, and a feature wall with a filigree display of tree branches to hammer home the garden theme. Extremely professional yet very friendly service plays its part in creating an oasis of calm and refinement. Arnaud Bignon cooks from the heart, starting with the best ingredients money can buy and combining techniques old and new in modern French dishes with a whiff of the Orient. Expect clean, precise flavours that look beautiful on the plate – witness luxurious native lobster that turns up with a delicately aromatic bisque incorporating carrot, parsley and lemongrass, or perhaps veal sweetbread with pineapple, black sesame and ginger. Exotic notes are again deployed to good effect in main courses, as when kaffir lime and dukkah spices enhance superlative monkfish served with onion shells packed with banana purée, or the gomasio, harissa and soya that come with organic Rhug Estate Welsh lamb. The aromatic note that distinguishes Bignon's cooking follows through to dessert stage too, when pineapple soufflé is scented with coriander and yellow chilli.

Chef Arnaud Bignon **Seats** 60, Private dining 12 **Closed** Christmas and Bank holidays **Notes** Children welcome

The Grill at The Dorchester

◉◉ MODERN BRITISH 🍷 NOTABLE WINE LIST

020 7317 6531 | Park Lane, W1K 1QA
www.dorchestercollection/london/the-dorchester

There's a been a Grill Room at the Dorchester since 1931 and today's new look version is a shimmering and elegant room. Save room for a contemporary lemon tart, or try one of the famous soufflés (Sicilian pistachio, for example, with salted caramel).

Chef Guillaume Katola **Seats** 65 **Open** All year **Prices from** S £12, M £17, D £10 **Parking** 20 **Notes** Vegetarian dishes, Children welcome

GYMKHANA

◉◉ CONTEMPORARY INDIAN V

020 3011 5900 | 42 Albermarle Street, W1S 4JH
www.gymkhanalondon.com

It may look like a colonial-era Indian gentlemen's club, but there's nothing retro about this restaurant's inventive new-wave Indian cooking. Wild boar vindaloo, or wild muntjac biryani with pomegranate and mint raita catch the eye, while game lovers might go for quail seekh kebab.

Chef Karam Sethi, Palash Mitra **Seats** 90, Private dining 15 **Closed** Christmas, 1 January

Hakkasan

◉◉ MODERN CHINESE 🍷 NOTABLE WINE LIST

020 7927 7000 | 8 Hanway Place, W1T 1HD
www.hakkasan.com

Escape the Oxford Street crowds in this chic basement and you're immediately captivated by its modern Chinoiserie design, super-cool cocktail bar, open kitchen and uptempo, nightclubby vibe. Innovative new-wave and classic Cantonese dishes cover all bases, and luxury ingredients abound.

Chef Tong Chee Hwee **Seats** 210, Private dining 20 **Closed** 25 December **Notes** Vegetarian dishes, Children welcome

Hakkasan Mayfair

◉◉◉ MODERN CANTONESE, CHINESE

020 7907 1888 | 17 Bruton Street, W1J 6QB
www.hakkasan.com

Hakkasan did such an effective job of rewriting the rulebook for Chinese cooking in the capital that it has become difficult to remember a time before it. In the Mayfair branch, just off Berkeley Square, a long corridor leads to a sharply lit room with long tables and seating at the well-stocked bar. Downstairs is a more intimate space, enclosed by intricately carved wood screens. Such is the sense of style that dress code strictures outlined on the website are worth attending to (the wearing of hats indoors is not encouraged), and the supercool approach extends to vivid reimaginings of traditional Cantonese dishes. Dim sum in their bamboo steamers are a riot of candy colours, encompassing gold-leafed lobster and lychee dumplings, caviar-dotted abalone and chicken shu mai, and truffled sole. House specialities among main dishes are silver cod glazed in Zhenjiang vinegar, wok-fried pork belly with plums and kumquat, and umami-dripping spiced okra with bonito flakes and shiitakes. Textured desserts are the last word in creativity: consider the Jivara chocolate bomb with praline and rice krispies.

Chef Tong Chee Hwee, Tan Tee Wei **Seats** 220, Private dining 16 **Closed** 24–25 December **Prices from** S £9, M £13, D £10 **Notes** Vegetarian dishes, Children welcome

Heddon Street Kitchen

◉ MODERN BRITISH

020 7592 1212 | 3–9 Heddon Street, Regent Street Food Quarter, W1B 4BD
www.heddonstreetkitchen.co.uk

In a pedestrianised oasis just off Regent street, Ramsay's contemporary take on the brasserie theme spreads over two floors, mingling industrial chic with macho leather and wood textures that suit the local vibe. The all-day menu aims to please all comers.

Chef Robert Mazur **Seats** 180, Private dining 12 **Closed** 25 December **Notes** Vegetarian dishes, Children welcome

HIX Soho

◉ BRITISH V

020 7292 3518 | 66–70 Brewer Street, W1F 9UP
www.hixsoho.co.uk

The mothership of Mark Hix's restaurant empire pays homage to Brit Art with an eclectic collection of artworks by celebrated artists like Damien Hirst and Sarah Lucas, while the patriotic brasserie fare celebrates seasonality and the UK's splendid regional produce.

Chef Simon Hicks **Seats** 80, Private dining 10 **Closed** 25–26 December and 1 January **Notes** Children welcome

Hélène Darroze at The Connaught

◉◉◉◉◉ FRENCH **V** ♦ NOTABLE WINE LIST

020 3147 7200 | Carlos Place, W1K 2AL
www.the-connaught.co.uk

Hélène Darroze has shuttled to and fro between her Parisian restaurant and The Connaught for over a decade, during which she has stamped her mark on both the interior of the venerable old dining room itself and the style of gastronomy that goes on within its burnished oak-panelled walls. There is all the grandeur you might imagine at such an iconic address, with places to sip champagne, tuck into a magnificent afternoon tea, or dine pretty much any time of the day. In the grand principal dining room, the more feminine, contemporary look uses swirly patterned fabrics that dovetail elegantly with the original panels and delicate plasterwork ceilings, but make no mistake, this is still very much an old-school high-class establishment, and it makes a suitable setting for Darroze's hyper-refined contemporary cooking. Once you've worked out how to order a multi-course menu by means of the solitaire board, its tiny balls each marked with one of the dishes, it's clear that the food is rooted in the rich gastronomic traditions of southwest France, but Asian influences are also woven into the mix – as seen in an opener of Cornish crab encased in avocado and transformed by a Vietnamese-inspired shiso-accented broth that is intense, light and complex all at once. The chef's origins in the Landes region mean foie gras will undoubtedly turn up, on this occasion in the company of black truffle and the balancing acidity of green apple. Darroze handles fish dishes boldly, using caviar to give halibut and oyster an extra layer of luxury, with potato and leek bringing welcome simplicity. Meat dishes, too, are approached with understated panache, so top-class venison is served pink, tender and highlighted with Sarawak pepper, but also has sweet Muscat grapes and Stichelton blue cheese to emphasise the superlative flavour of the meat. Desserts are also handled with uncommon artistry, as when the flavours and textures of pineapple, coconut and sesame are explored in a vibrant finale. Service strikes a really pleasing balance between slick professionalism and relaxed confidence, while wines meets expectations at this level, with a roll-call of big-hitters at big prices.

Chef Hélène Darroze **Seats** 60, Private dining 30 **Open** All year **Notes** No children under 7 years

Indian Accent

◉◉ MODERN INDIAN **V**

020 7629 9802 | 16 Albemarle Street, Mayfair, W1S 4HW
www.indianaccent.com

With outposts in New Delhi and New York, this swanky new Mayfair sibling brings merit to London's vibrant, high-end Indian dining scene. Opposite Brown's Hotel, its dining space, spread over two floors, is a magnet for the international jet-set. The decor mirrors the deep wallets.

Chef Manish Mehrotra **Seats** 70, Private dining **Open** All year **Prices from** S £9, M £16, D £5 **Notes** No children under 10 years

Jamavar

◉◉ INDIAN **V**

020 7499 1800 | 8 Mount Street, Mayfair, W1K 3NF
www.jamavarrestaurants.com

A smart Mayfair location suits this stylish restaurant. It's spread over two floors, with dark wood tables and Indian-inspired artwork and brass-framed mirrors. Staff are efficient and friendly, and menus showcase a wide array of flavours from across India.

Chef Rohit Ghai **Seats** 107, Private dining 8 **Prices from** S £8, M £18, D £8

JW Steakhouse

◉ AMERICAN

020 7399 8460 | Grosvenor House Hotel, Park Lane, W1K 7TN
www.jwsteakhouse.co.uk

The expansive JW brings American-style steakhouse dining to the Grosvenor House in an ambience of black-and-white ceramic floor tiles and parquet, dressers and a menu offering variations of cuts and sauces. The beef is either thoroughbred USDA-approved or grass-fed Aberdeen Angus.

Chef Simon Conboy **Seats** 120, Private dining 12 **Open** All year **Parking** 90 **Notes** Vegetarian dishes, Children welcome

Kai Mayfair

◉◉ MODERN CHINESE **V**

020 7493 8988 | 65 South Audley Street, W1K 2QU
www.kaimayfair.co.uk

This swanky Chinese restaurant is decorated in glossy Mayfair style, with arty photographs on the walls. Judicious use of spicing and seasoning, and subtle combinations of flavours and textures are hallmarks. The menu opens unusually with desserts, showing how seriously they are taken here.

Chef Alex Chow **Seats** 85, Private dining 12 **Closed** 25–26 December and 1 January **Notes** Children welcome

The Keeper's House
◉ MODERN BRITISH
020 7300 5881 | Royal Academy of Arts, Burlington House, Piccadilly, W1J 0BD
www.keepershouse.org.uk

The Keeper's House was installed in the 19th century as a grace-and-favour apartment for the steward of the Royal Academy collections. A strikingly attractive restaurant has been fashioned here, the recessed rooms imitating those of the galleries upstairs. Expect inspiring cocktails and English wines.

Chef Piotr Cizak **Seats** 65, Private dining 45 **Open** All year **Prices from** S £6.50, M £15.50, D £6.50 **Notes** Vegetarian dishes, Children welcome

Kitchen Table
◉◉◉ MODERN BRITISH V ♟ NOTABLE WINE LIST
020 7637 7770 | 70 Charlotte St, W1T 4QG
www.kitchentablelondon.co.uk

Plough through the hurly-burly of Bubbledogs, and through a curtain in the corner to what could be a meeting-place for a dissident cell. Sanctums don't come much more inner than this, as a venturesome 20 souls gather around a two-sided counter to watch a multi-course menu of modern concept food being prepared. The dishes, or at least a single-word summary of each, are chalked up on a board; the rest of it you can glean from conversing with the chefs and listening to James Knappett's announcements as each plate is served. This is avant-garderie at its sharpest: even the more recognisable dishes have mysterious flavour elements to them. A sautéed scallop is teriyaki-glazed, served with its dehydrated roe and kombu with a twizzle of pickled cucumber. A carrot is cooked in butter with coriander stems, and Indian-garnished with mango ketchup, peanuts, apple, yogurt and moilee. Other dishes rely on classic combinations, with the flavours turned up to 10 – spring lamb belly in its own jus with mint sauce and golden beetroot, or the delectable caramel ice cream sandwich.

Chef James Knappett **Seats** 20 **Notes** No children

Kitty Fisher's
◉◉ MODERN BRITISH
020 3302 1661 | 10 Shepherd Market, W1J 7QF
www.kittyfishers.com

Closely packed tables and stools at the bar offer diners two options in this low-lit, atmospheric, Bohemian-style restaurant with red velvet banquettes, retro light fittings and candles. The modern British food is driven by what's available at the market on the day.

Chef George Barson **Seats** 36 **Closed** 25 December, 1 January, Bank holidays **Notes** Vegetarian dishes, Children welcome

Levant
◉ LEBANESE, MIDDLE EASTERN V
020 7224 1111 | Jason Court, 76 Wigmore Street, W1U 2SJ
www.levant.co.uk

Levant delivers the authentic flavours of the Middle East, along with an exotic Aladdin's-cave decor of rich fabrics, carved wood, candlelight and lamps. Small plates for grazing and sharing are the way to start, while freshly cooked meat dishes are succulent and full of flavour.

Chef David Jones **Seats** 150, Private dining 12 **Closed** 25–26 December **Notes** Children welcome

Lima
◉◉ MODERN PERUVIAN
020 3002 2640 | 31 Rathbone Place, Fitzrovia, W1T 1JH
www.limalondon.com

Named after Peru's capital, this trendy, high-octane restaurant brings a refined take on that country's contemporary cuisine to the West End. Excellent British and Peruvian ingredients are the backbone, all handled confidently and skilfully to produce pretty little plates of knockout flavours.

Chef Robert Ortiz, Virgilio Martinez **Seats** 60, Private dining 25 **Closed** Christmas **Notes** Vegetarian dishes, Children welcome

Little Social
◉◉◉ FRENCH, MODERN EUROPEAN ♟ NOTABLE WINE LIST
020 7870 3730 | 5 Pollen St, W1S 1NE
www.littlesocial.co.uk

There are almost too many Jason Atherton venues to count now in London, so it helps when they cluster together a little, as here. The Little Social is just across the road from Pollen Street Social in its twisty back lane near Regent Street. What you get here is the bistro experience, in a dark-panelled setting with vintage Michelin posters and a vivacious pop soundtrack. Canonical dishes from the European repertoire are cooked with brio on a menu that furnishes plenty of choice. Ritz it up by starting off with copiously garnished black truffle risotto, or go the more austere route with a serving of grilled calçots in romesco dressing. Main courses are built to last, with whole Dovers roasted on the bone and slicked with meunière, cote de porc bulked with charcuterie and a pillow of mash, or aged Hereford rib-eyes arriving still asizzle from the Josper charcoal grill. Desserts are from the pudding end of the continuum – perhaps apple and blackberry crumble, sticky toffee, clementine Pavlova with passionfruit sorbet.

Chef Cary Docherty **Seats** 55, Private dining 8 **Closed** 25–26 December, 1–2 January, Bank holidays **Prices from** S £7.50, M £21.50, D £7.50 **Notes** Vegetarian dishes, Children welcome

Locanda Locatelli
◉◉◉ ITALIAN ♦ NOTABLE WINE LIST
020 7935 9088 | 8 Seymour Street, W1H 7JZ
www.locandalocatelli.com

TV star Giorgio Locatelli's culinary career began by the shore of Lake Comabbio in the Lombardy region of northern Italy, a provenance that attunes him so precisely to one of the prevalent currents of British gastronomy. Italian classical cooking, gently modernised but staying true to its principles of honesty and simplicity, will never lack for devotees. Curving booth seating in stone-coloured leather, etched glass screens and mirrors make for an ambience of refined civility, naturally, but the generously proportioned tables are designed with convivial family dining in mind. Traditionally structured menus open with compendious antipasti salads, before pasta makes its appearance via lobster linguine, or turnip-top orecchiette. Principal dishes command the attention with majestic fish – roast black bream in bagna cauda with wild chicory – or tender veal kidneys on a stew of lentils with a cloud of puréed potato. At the finish line, tradition (wine-poached pears with cinnamon ice cream) vies with a modern Britalian tendency, perhaps Earl Grey pannacotta with poached Yorkshire rhubarb and tarragon shortbread, for the toughest decision of all.
Chef Giorgio Locatelli **Seats** 85, Private dining 50
Closed 24–26 December, 1 January
Prices from S £13.50, M £21, D £8.50
Notes Vegetarian dishes, Children welcome

Magpie
◉◉ MODERN EUROPEAN V
020 3903 9096 | 10 Heddon Street, W1B 4BX
www.magpie-london.com

Tucked away just off Regent Street, Magpie brings a touch of Shoreditch hipster to deep-wallet Mayfair. A big warehouse-style room is the space with bar and open kitchen counter, dangling light-bulbs and funky seating embracing that pared-back look. A modern roster of snacks and grazing plates is very on-trend.
Chef Dan Graham, Sebastian Merry **Seats** 60
Closed Christmas, New Year **Prices from** S £5, M £13, D £7 **Notes** Children welcome

The Mandeville Hotel
◉ MODERN BRITISH
020 7935 5599 | Mandeville Place, W1U 2BE
www.mandeville.co.uk

Understated contemporary decor and a calming ambience are the hallmarks of this stylish boutique hotel, while unclothed tables and bottle-green banquettes set the tone in the restaurant. Familiar-sounding Black Forest cake and apple tart Tatin can be found among desserts.
Chef Gauri Shankar **Seats** 90, Private dining 12 **Open** All year **Notes** Vegetarian dishes, Children welcome

The Mayfair Chippy
◉ BRITISH
020 7741 2233 | North Audley Street, W1K 6WE
www.mayfairchippy.com

As a pairing, Mayfair and Chippy breaks new ground, and so it should. This wealthy quarter of W1 has as much right to a quintessentially British fish and chip restaurant as anywhere else. And it certainly looks the part too.
Chef Pete Taylor, Desiree Inezhaley **Seats** 45, Private dining 14 **Closed** 25 December and 1 January
Prices from S £5, M £10.50, D £5 **Notes** Vegetarian dishes, Children welcome

Maze
◉◉ EUROPEAN, ASIAN FUSION V
020 7107 0000 | London Marriott Hotel, 10–13 Grosvenor Square, W1K 6JP
www.gordonramsay.com/maze

Set on Mayfair's exclusive Grosvenor Square, Maze is enveloped within the London Marriott Hotel and is quite the vision of cool modernity. The restaurant is a light-filled, split-level affair punctuated by tall windows, bold colour, and cream leather seating. Service is professional and unstuffy.
Chef Owen Sullivan **Seats** 94, Private dining 90
Open All year **Notes** Children welcome

Mele e Pere
◉ ITALIAN
020 7096 2096 | 46 Brewer Street, Soho, W1F 9TF
www.meleepere.co.uk

Apples and Pears looks a riot of colour and conviviality on its Soho corner. At ground-floor level is a café area, but the main dining goes on downstairs in a dynamic, russet-walled basement room. Italian sharing plates are the principal draw to start.
Chef A Mantovani **Seats** 90 **Closed** 25–26 December and 1 January **Prices from** S £6.50, M £13, D £6.50
Notes Vegetarian dishes, Children welcome

Mere

⊕⊕⊕ MODERN EUROPEAN **V**

020 7268 6565 | 74 Charlotte Street, W1T 4QH

www.mere-restaurant.com

Monica Galetti (former Michel Roux Jr/Le Gavroche protégé, though better known to TV audiences as a feared *MasterChef: The Professionals* judge) has opened this her own restaurant with husband David (also a former Gavroche alumni [sommelier], like many of the key staff here). Okay, first up, the name; Mere is pronounced 'Mary', being both the French for mother and also Monica's mother's name. Next, the location – set at the less frenetic northern end of restaurant-jammed Charlotte Street and certainly adding to its profile. It's classily understated though; an impressive wooden door immediately shouts sophisticated, grown-up restaurant, and inside doesn't disappoint either. What really shines is the cooking; contemporary French (classically underpinned of course) yet sprinkled with touches from Monica's Western Samoan and Kiwi heritage. The expected consummate skill and attention to detail are obvious, though it comes with a light, refined, yet relatively straightforward approach, backed by flavour and panache. Take an opener of springy tender octopus, with a sweet-sharp tomato reduction and caper condiment, finished with parsley oil, or perhaps a star-turn squab pigeon mains (soft pink roasted breast and crispy skinned leg), with peach (adding a balanced sweetness), girolles and Earl Grey. Desserts might continue with signature 'banana and coconut' (cream pie with roasted bananas and rum caramel). Service is informed, professional but relaxed.

Chef Monica Galetti, Renee Miller **Seats** 60, Private dining 10 **Closed** Bank holidays **Prices from** S £12, M £23, D £11 **Notes** Children welcome

Le Meridien Piccadilly

⊕ MODERN BRITISH

020 7734 8000 | 21 Piccadilly, W1J 0BH

www.lemeridienpiccadilly.com

Within Le Meridien is a series of vast public rooms, including the impressive Terrace and Baran atrium-style space with a curved glass ceiling, columns and dark wood tables. The menu features grills from Red Poll rib-eye to lamb cutlets, but there's plenty more of interest.

Chef Stevel Ger **Seats** 80 **Open** All year **Prices from** S £8.50, M £20, D £9 **Notes** Vegetarian dishes, Children welcome

Mews of Mayfair

⊕ MODERN BRITISH

020 7518 9388 | 10–11 Lancashire Court, New Bond Street, Mayfair, W1S 1EY

www.mewsofmayfair.com

The Mayfair set converge on this stylish bar and restaurant, hidden from the Bond Street crowds on a narrow cobbled alleyway. With its terrace tables and roll-back doors, it feels more Mediterranean than West End. The cocktail bar and basement lounge make a glam statement.

Chef Michael Lecouteur **Seats** 70, Private dining 28 **Closed** 25 December **Notes** Vegetarian dishes, Children welcome

The Montagu

⊕⊕ MODERN BRITISH

020 7299 2037 | Hyatt Regency London, The Churchill, 30 Portman Square, W1H 7BH

www.themontagurestaurant.co.uk

With its liveried doormen out front and elegant proportions within, the swish five-star hotel is a classy act, and its Montagu restaurant meets international jet-set expectations with views over Portman Square, and an uncontroversial menu of smart ideas.

Chef Mark Sainsbury **Seats** 60 **Open** All year **Prices from** S £8, M £19, D £7.50 **Notes** Vegetarian dishes, Children welcome

Murano

⊕⊕⊕⊕ MODERN EUROPEAN, ITALIAN INFLUENCE ♦ NOTABLE WINE LIST

020 7495 1127 | 20–22 Queen Street, W1J 5PP

www.muranolondon.com

The single-width frontage on a side-street off Piccadilly, with its café chairs outside, looks a deceptively ordinary affair, but abandon any preconceptions, for Angela Hartnett's restaurant is one of the reference venues for sophisticated Italian food in the West End. Inside is a different kettle of fish altogether, with thick carpets, mirrored and marble surfaces and modern art providing a high-gloss backdrop to the culinary enticements. Well-pitched service is faultlessly efficient, with just the correct note of informality, ensuring everybody feels at home. The seasonally changing menus, including a top-value lunch carte, deal in sharply etched cooking of verve and energy, with simple but effective contrasts of flavour and texture throughout. Start with a serving of smoked eel, its meaty richess offset with semi-dried tomatoes, the pungency given lift with horseradish emulsion, or there may be grilled citrus-cured salmon with asparagus and blots of lemony crème fraîche. Main course might be a demonstration in how far to take an accompanying flavour without achieving overload: a welter of orange – compôte, torched segments, a purée of the burnt fruit, orange-braised baby fennel – add up to a harmonious supporting chorus for a sublime piece of succulent pork belly, the whole prettified with a flutter of nasturtium leaves. Fish might be hazelnut-crusted brill with a raviolo of prawns. At the end comes a sparingly topped apple tarte fine with salt caramel and thyme ice cream, or a luxurious pistachio soufflé anointed with hot chocolate sauce, worth the wait.

Chef Angela Hartnett, Oscar Holgado **Seats** 46, Private dining 12 **Closed** Christmas **Notes** Vegetarian dishes, Children welcome

Neo Bistro
◉◉ MODERN BRITISH
020 7499 9427 | 11 Woodstock Street, Mayfair, W1C 2AE
www.neobistro.co.uk
Ultra close to Oxford Street, this stripped-back new-wave bistro is a cut above. Here Mark Jarvis of Anglo fame has created a relaxed setting for some stellar, approachable cooking. An open kitchen and concise menu of deceptive simplicity delivers some slick modern cooking with informed, youthful service.

Chef Mark Jarvis, Alex Harper **Open** All year

The Ninth
◉◉◉ MODERN FRENCH, MEDITERRANEAN
020 3019 0880 | 22 Charlotte Street, W1T 2NB
www.theninthlondon.com
Okay, it may be called The Ninth, but it's definitely in our top 10-per-cent category. No mean feat for a first solo venture, but then New York-born chef-patron (and TV regular) Jun Tanaka has over two decades of working in starry kitchens. There's uncomplicated logic behind the outfit's name, as it's simply the ninth place he's worked in, but here he shuns past fine-dining pretension for relaxed, in-vogue good looks and an on-trend menu of stand-out sharing plates that shout precision, flavour and flair. Spread across two floors with a bar on each, the décor scores high in the stripped-back cool stakes, with exposed brick walls, decorated concrete and floorboards, while the space comes littered with eye-catching statement pieces like dangling glass lighting, metal wine cages and wine-glass racks, and arty wall displays of gleaming kitchen utensils. Leather banquettes and café-style chairs provide the chilled-out comforts alongside mahogany or white marble-topped tables. In-trend snacks head up the appealing carte roster, though these (witness knockout oxtail croquettes) are anything but bit-part scene filler, likewise statement vegetable dishes are so much more than 'sides' (think beetroot tarte tatin with feta and fresh walnuts). The light, inspired Mediterranean menu is understandably underpinned by Tanaka's classic French background, yet bursts with refined simplicity, confidence, flavour and seasonality

here. Take grilled pink-perfection lamb cutlets teamed with anchovy and charred hispi cabbage, or perhaps wild sea bass (with a basil crust) accompanied by salsify and tardivo (Italian radicchio). Desserts embrace the classics; take knockout pain perdu served with vanilla ice cream. Otherwise bag the fixed-price lunch menu (a steal for two or three plates at this level), and enjoy service that is fashionably relaxed yet as spot-on as everything else.

Chef Jun Tanaka **Seats** 84, Private dining 22 **Closed** Bank holidays **Prices from** S £8.50, M £23, D £8 **Notes** Vegetarian dishes, Children welcome

Nobu Berkeley ST
◉◉ JAPANESE, PERUVIAN ⬧NOTABLE WINE LIST
020 7290 9222 | 15 Berkeley Street, W1J 8DY
www.noburestaurants.com
Nobu draws in the Mayfair fashionistas who come for the see-and-be-seen buzz of the bar, or the cool minimalist restaurant. Traditionalists can head straight for the sushi bar, or for some fun DIY dining with chefs supervising your efforts around a sunken hibachi grill.

Chef Mark Edwards, Rhys Cattermoul **Seats** 180 **Closed** 25 December **Notes** Vegetarian dishes, Children welcome

Nobu Old Park Lane
◉◉ JAPANESE
020 7447 4747 | COMO Metropolitan London, Old Park Lane, W1K 1LB
www.noburestaurants.com
Londoners met Nobu Matsuhisa's brand of Japanese precision and South American spice back in 1977. It remains a fashionable and super-cool restaurant, and quality remains high. Seafood sparkles, from sea bass sashimi with dried red miso and yuzu sauce to salmon tartare with wasabi.

Chef Mark Edwards, Hideki Maeda **Seats** 160, Private dining 40 **Closed** 25 December, 1 January **Notes** Vegetarian dishes, Children welcome

NOPI
◉ MEDITERRANEAN
020 7494 9584 | 21–22 Warwick Street, W1B 5NE
www.nopi-restaurant.com
Inspired by the sun-drenched cuisines of the Middle East, North Africa and the Mediterranean, owner Yotam Ottolenghi's cooking is creative stuff, bursting with punchy flavours and delivered in dishes made for sharing in an all-white brasserie-style space, or in the basement.

Chef Yotam Ottolenghi, Ramael Scully **Seats** 100 **Closed** 25–26 December, 1 January **Notes** Vegetarian dishes, Children welcome

Novikov Asian Restaurant

◉ CHINESE, PAN ASIAN

020 7399 4330 | 50a Berkeley Street, W1J 8HA

www.novikovrestaurant.co.uk

The Asian venue of Russian restaurateur Arkady Novikov's see-and-be-seen Mayfair food palace offers a palate-tingling cornucopia of Pan-Asian dishes. A busy team of chefs behind a glass wall among mounds of super-fresh produce resembling an Asian street market takes centre-stage in the slick brasserie-style space.

Chef Luca Malacarne **Seats** 149 **Closed** 25 December **Prices from** S £7.25, M £11.50, D £8.50 **Notes** Vegetarian dishes, Children welcome

Novikov Italian Restaurant

◉ ITALIAN

020 7399 4330 | 50a Berkeley Street, W1J 8HA

www.novikovrestaurant.co.uk

The extravagant Novikov operation's Italian venue sprawls across a vast basement, where cornucopian buffet displays and a wood-fired oven dazzle on arrival. The Italian cooking is surprisingly rustic and simple.

Chef Marco Torri **Seats** 200, Private dining 40 **Closed** 25 December **Prices from** S £7, M £19.50, D £8.50 **Notes** Vegetarian dishes, Children welcome

Orrery

◉◉◉ MODERN FRENCH **V**

020 7616 8000 | 55–57 Marylebone High Street, W1U 5RB

www.orrery-restaurant.co.uk

Orrery may be pushing into its third decade, but it still cuts a contemporary dash with its classy good looks, polished service and skilful, modern take on classical French cuisine. Perched on top of the Conran store, it's a stylishly conceived space, lit by a full-length skylight and arched windows giving leafy views over Marylebone; a roof terrace adds further to its appeal. Igor Tymchyschyn's refined classic and modern French dishes exercise a powerful pull too, taking in cured sea bass, say, with cucumber, horseradish and kumquat as a refreshingly light way in, or perhaps fillet steak tartare with quail's egg, sourdough and truffle. Alluring main courses are similarly well conceived and beautifully presented, among them such classic ideas as tournedos Rossini with celeriac and sauce périgourdine, or turbot with asparagus, morels and wild garlic. A five-course taster with a veggie version gives a comprehensive tour of the repertoire.

Chef Igor Tymchyshyn **Seats** 110, Private dining 16 **Closed** 26–28 December, 1 January, Easter Monday, Summer bank holiday, quiet periods **Notes** Children welcome

The Palomar

◉◉ MODERN JERUSALEM

020 7439 8777 | 34 Rupert Street, W1D 6DN

www.thepalomar.co.uk

Quick-fire dishes that take inspiration from the Levant, North Africa and southern Spain are the deal in this high-octane operation in Theatreland. It's first come, first served for ringside seats at the open kitchen counter, where the Josper oven works overtime, delivering full-on, sun-drenched flavours.

Chef Tomer Amedi **Seats** 50 **Closed** 25–26 December **Notes** Vegetarian dishes, Children welcome

Park Chinois

◉◉ CHINESE

020 3327 8888 | 17 Berkeley Street, Mayfair, W1J 8EA

www.parkchinois.com

In the dining room, a piano, drums and microphone await the next jazz turn. White linen dresses the tables, red banquettes one side, floral-patterned tub seats the other. Lunch starts with a dim sum course. Entry level for wines is north of £40.

Chef Lee Che Liang **Seats** Private dining 12 **Closed** 25 December **Notes** Vegetarian dishes, No children under 8 years

Peyote

◉ MEXICAN

020 7409 1300 | 13 Cork Street, Mayfair, W1S 3NS

www.peyoterestaurant.com

Named after a hallucinogenic cactus native to the Chihuahuan desert, this cool, contemporary eatery spreads over two levels, with closely set wooden tables and grinning Day of the Dead skulls making a bold design statement. It's a lively, fun spot with well-informed staff on hand.

Chef Stamatios Loumousiotis **Seats** 110, Private dining 12 **Closed** Christmas, New Year **Notes** Vegetarian dishes, Children welcome

Picture

◉◉ MODERN EUROPEAN **V**

020 7637 7892 | 110 Great Portland Street, W1W 6PQ

www.picturerestaurant.co.uk

Set up by three talented deserters from the acclaimed Arbutus/Wild Honey stable, this switched-on outfit presses all the on-trend buttons. It has that sleek, neutral modern look – grey walls, abstract images, oak floors, and food that's more cheffy than the brown-paper menus might suggest.

Chef Alan Christie, Colin Kelly **Seats** 55 **Closed** Christmas, Bank holidays **Prices from** S £8, M £14, D £6 **Notes** Children welcome

LONDON W1

Pied à Terre
◉◉◉ MODERN FRENCH **V** 🍷 NOTABLE WINE LIST
020 7636 1178 | 34 Charlotte Street, W1T 2NH
www.pied-a-terre.co.uk

A top dining destination since the early 1990s,
David Moore's Pied à Terre is fittingly a Fitzrovia elder
statesman. Understated from the street, its bijou dining
room blends muted autumnal colours with copper tiles,
white linen and banquette seating in the chic-classic
rather than cool-pacesetter vogue. The cooking, by
contrast, is right on-trend; inventive, dressed-to-thrill
modern dishes of finesse, refinement and precision.
New head chef Asimakis Chaniotis has made the
kitchen his own, and can even be found delivering
dishes to tables in the progressive style. For tighter
budgets, the set lunch offers stonking value, with dishes
like sea-fresh Cornish cod with red wine sauce, oysters
Porthilly, orange baby carrots and monk's beard, while
the carte might strut its stuff via a saddle of venison
teamed with British pumpkin, pain d'epic and poivrade.
Desserts thrill too; take a millefeuille with Mouneyrac
apples, liquorice and celery. Tasting options up the ante,
while vegetarians and vegans commendably have their
own menus. The encyclopaedic wine list offers a galaxy
of stars as well as value, while service is unsurprisingly
professional, yet friendly and unstuffy.

Chef Asimakis Chaniotis **Seats** 40, Private dining 14
Closed 2 weeks at Christmas and New Year
Prices from D £15 **Notes** Children welcome

Plum Valley
◉ CHINESE
020 7494 4366 | 20 Gerrard Street, W1D 6JQ
www.plumvalleyrestaurant.co.uk

Plum Valley stands out on Gerrard Street with its sleek
black frontage and inside it has a dark, minimalist
contemporary gloss. Service is brisk but friendly. The
mainstay of the menu is classic Cantonese, with
familiar old favourites and some perky modern ideas.

Seats 150 **Closed** 25 December **Notes** Vegetarian
dishes, Children welcome

Podium
◉ MODERN EUROPEAN
020 7208 4022 | London Hilton on Park Lane,
22 Park Lane, W1K 1BE
www.podiumrestaurant.com

This swish all-day eatery in the Park Lane Hilton fits the
bill when you're tootling around Mayfair and fancy a
relaxed pit-stop with an eclectic, comfort-oriented menu.
Dishes show minimum posturing and can be as simple
as burgers, steaks or beer-battered cod and chips.

Chef Anthony Marshall **Seats** 80 **Open** All year
Parking 140 **Notes** Vegetarian dishes, Children
welcome

Pollen Street Social
◉◉◉◉◉ MODERN BRITISH **V**
020 7290 7600 | 8–10 Pollen Street, W1S 1NQ
www.pollenstreetsocial.com

The Atherton brand has gone global these days, with
outposts in Hong Kong, Shanghai, New York and
Dubai to name but four, but you don't need to fly
long-haul to sample the high-flying cuisine that
kickstarted this empire. Among the portfolio of London
venues, Pollen Street Social is still the flagship, and
you can rest assured that it remains one of the
capital's most in-demand foodie destinations. Tucked
away on a narrow Mayfair back-alley handy for Regent
Street's shopping, the decor is classy but far from
intimidating – it's a neutral, contemporary urban
space, with the familiar look of wooden floors, linen-
clothed tables and white walls punctuated by modern
British artworks, and a glass-fronted pass to the
kitchen for a touch of visual theatre. In contrast with
the high-tempo feeling of busy intensity, Atherton's
concept is 'relaxed fine dining', and Dale Bainbridge
interprets the house style with a high level of technical
competence, producing dishes that retain an inventive
edge, display enough complexity to be exciting, and
arrive looking dressed to thrill. There's an eight-course
tasting menu, the à la carte, dedicated vegetarian and
vegan options, and a set lunch offering that is well
worth the trip. Outstanding openers might include raw
Orkney scallop with a palate-priming array of pickled
kohlrabi, nashi pear, black olive and jalapeño granité,
while pressed Norfolk quail and duck liver gets a lift
from root vegetables, truffle, and braised quail taco.
The quality of the materials and the intense flavours
coaxed from them is endlessly astounding in main
courses like south coast turbot with its
accompaniments of potatoes baked in turbot stock,
morels, wild garlic, vin jaune and chicken skin;
elsewhere, pedigree meats such as Lake District lamb
and Goosnargh duck are given treatments that
showcase their inherent qualities, that lamb loin
coming with beetroot and blackcurrant, plus a hotpot
of braised shoulder, and mint sauce, while a whole
roasted duck for two arrives with braised swede,
quince, pesto, and a Moroccan-spiced salad of leg
meat. To finish, there might be bitter chocolate pavé
with olive biscuit and olive oil ice cream, or pistachio
soufflé with 70% chocolate and vanilla ice cream.

Chef Jason Atherton, Dale Bainbridge **Seats** 52,
Private dining 12 **Closed** Bank holidays
Prices from S £17.50, M £34, D £13 **Notes** Children
welcome

Portland

◉◉◉ MODERN BRITISH 🔖 NOTABLE WINE LIST

020 7436 3261 | 113 Great Portland Street, W1W 6QQ
www.portlandrestaurant.co.uk

Just up the road from the BBC, Portland scores high with unstuffy, spot-on service and an intimate, if rather spartan interior of wooden tables and chairs, plain white walls, retro lighting, and an upbeat ambience. Upfront, the must-have counter and high stools look out streetwise, while at the back, the open kitchen, headed up by Zach Elliott-Crenn, fires up the culinary action, sending out a faultlessly modern take on new-Brit cuisine. Brimming with innovation, a keen eye for seasonality, and executed with pin-sharp precision, things get going with Arctic char served with artfully arranged shavings of heritage carrot, and smoked cream finished with sprigs of dill; otherwise, raw scallops with cod's roe, kale and green apple might appeal. At main course, the well-judged balance of flavour, texture and colour interest continues with caramelised Sussex venison partnered with squash, purple kale, beetroot and elderberries, or fish fans might go for monkfish counterpointed with artichoke, parsnips and smoked mussel broth. For pudding, sweet pumpkin sorbet is contrasted with ethereal lime sabayon and muscovado crumble.

Chef Merlin Labron-Johnson, Zach Elliot-Crenn **Seats** 36, Private dining 16 **Closed** 23 December to 3 January **Notes** Vegetarian dishes, Children welcome

The Providores and Tapa Room

◉ INTERNATIONAL, FUSION 🔖 NOTABLE WINE LIST

020 7935 6175 | 109 Marylebone High Street, W1U 4RX
www.theprovidores.co.uk

There's plenty to keep the palate entertained on Kiwi Peter Gordon's inventive menus of Asian-accented fusion food. Head upstairs to the modern minimalism of the Providores dining room for a lively menu.

Chef Peter Gordon **Seats** 40, Private dining 40 **Closed** 25–26 December **Prices from** S £9, M £16, D £9.50 **Notes** Vegetarian dishes, Children welcome

Quo Vadis

◉◉ MODERN BRITISH

020 7437 9585 | 26–29 Dean Street, W1D 3LL
www.quovadissoho.co.uk

Tan banquettes, modern art and mirrors on the walls and stained-glass windows provide the backdrop for accomplished cooking at this Soho stalwart. Combinations are well considered so dishes maintain interest without over-elaboration.

Chef Jeremy Lee **Seats** 26, Private dining 32 **Closed** Bank holidays (excluding Good Friday), 25 December, 1 January **Notes** Vegetarian dishes, Children welcome

The Red Fort

◉ INDIAN

020 7437 2525 | 77 Dean Street, Soho, W1D 3SH
www.redfort.co.uk

This sleek, red-fronted Indian cuts a dash with its white linen, smart staff, leather seating and walls of inlaid sandstone and Mogul arch motif. It turns out classic Mogul cooking and more up-to-date dishes, combining fine British produce with authentic sub-continental flavours.

Chef Azadur Rahman **Seats** 84 **Open** All year **Notes** Vegetarian dishes, No children under 3 years

The Riding House Café

◉ MODERN EUROPEAN

020 7927 0840 | 43–51 Great Titchfield Street, W1W 7PQ
www.ridinghousecafe.co.uk

Handy for the Oxford Street shops, The Riding House Café is a big, high-decibel, all-day operation with an urban brasserie vibe. Head for a swivel seat at the white-tiled island bar overlooking the open kitchen, or park at a long refectory table.

Chef Etienne Bruwer **Seats** 115, Private dining 14 **Closed** 25–26 December and 1 January **Prices from** S £6, M £12, D £6 **Notes** Vegetarian dishes, Children welcome

The Ritz Restaurant

◉◉◉ BRITISH, FRENCH V

020 7300 2370 | 150 Piccadilly, W1J 9BR
www.theritzlondon.com

When César Ritz opened his latest hotel at the northern tip of Green Park in 1906, it bade fair to become one of the capital's most opulent lodgings, and so it would remain, from the Entente Cordiale to Cool Britannia. At its heart is the stunningly beautiful dining room, lined with French windows along the park side, topped with a ceiling fresco of sunlit clouds, overseen by a gilded statue of a reclining Poseidon. Many of the principles of the haute cuisine of yesteryear live on in John Williams' renditions of Dover sole véronique in champagne, tournedos and ox cheek in red wine, and the Mont Blanc dessert with its chestnut and rum ice cream. There are more contemporary doings afoot, though, too, so don't be surprised to start with a roast scallop with carrot purée and nasturtiums, prior to sika deer with elderberries and red cabbage, with tonka mousse and cocoa nibs to finish. Even if you don't opt for the crêpes suzette, hand-flamed by the maître d' at your table, you've got to hope somebody nearby does.

Chef John T Williams MBE **Seats** 90, Private dining 60 **Open** All year **Prices from** S £18, M £38, D £17 **Parking** 10 **Notes** Children welcome

LONDON W1

Roganic

◉◉◉ MODERN BRITISH

020 337 06260 | 5–7 Blandford Street, Marylebone, W1U 3DB

www.roganic.uk

Five years after the original pop-up Roganic closed back in 2013, Simon Rogan came back to Marylebone with a more permanent set-up. The new incarnation occupies a spartan space of bronze and white textured concrete walls, linen-clothed tables and design-classic chairs. As in Rogan's other ventures, the kitchen is tuned in to nature and its stunning ingredients – some sourced from his own Lake District farm. Tasting menu fans are in for a small-plate cavalcade of 11 or 17 courses, but if time is of the essence, the set lunch is a steal, and the inspired cooking driven by flavour, freshness and balance. Pulling out some highlights, a celebration of the humble celeriac yields delicious salt-baked discs with caramelised purée, dried enoki mushrooms, tarragon oil and whey foam, while duck comes three ways, the breast timed to perfection and pointed up with a honeyed sauce, a terrine matched with radish and onion, and seared duck hearts highlighted with cheese and potato foam. To finish, there's a sublime yogurt ice cream with blackcurrant syrup, tarragon oil and burnt milk shards.

Chef Simon Rogan, Oli Marlow **Notes** No children under 6 years at lunch or under 12 at dinner

Roka Charlotte Street

◉◉◉ JAPANESE

020 7580 6464 | 37 Charlotte Street, W1T 1RR

www.rokarestaurant.com

Stylish Japanese cooking doesn't show any sign of losing favour among London diners if this super-cool flagship of the Roka brand is anything to go by. Beloved of the fashion and media darlings of Fitzrovia since 2004, the light-flooded room's plate-glass frontage looks into a lively scene of chunky hardwood furniture around the beating heart of the robata counter, where ringside views of the kitchen action exert a strong pull. The menu's fusion temptations might run to black cod, crab and crayfish dumplings, octopus with seaweed and ponzu dressing, or soft-shell crab with cucumber, kimchi and chilli mayonnaise. As for the robata offerings, there may be cedar-roasted baby chicken with chilli and lemon, scallop skewers with wasabi and shiso, or sea bream fillet with ryotei miso and red onion. Try the fusion desserts – guava mousse with grilled papaya, mango biscuit and passionfruit sorbet. If choosing for yourself is a trial, there's a tasting menu, and an enthusiastic service team who are on hand to demystify any alien terminology.

Chef Hamish Brown **Seats** 350, Private dining 20 **Closed** Christmas **Notes** Vegetarian dishes, Children welcome

Roka Mayfair

◉◉◉ MODERN JAPANESE

020 7305 5644 | 30 North Audley Street, W1K 6ZF

www.rokarestaurant.com

Drop down a short hop from Oxford Street to find the Mayfair branch of London's Roka group, where busy shoppers refuel in the day and the cocktail set gathers at dusk. The same clean-lined functional contemporary design is found here as at other Rokas, the central focus being the open kitchen, where counter seats allow you to get close to the robatayaki action. These grilled dishes – lobster with yuzu and koshu wine mayonnaise and lotus crisps, spiced chicken wings seasoned with sea salt and lime, thoroughbred Wagyu beef with eryngii mushrooms and wasabi ponzu – are the stars of the show, but all the traditional Japanese things are done with exquisite attention to detail too. Chirashi maki offers a platter of spiced mixed sashimi with green beans and spring onion, and there's yellowfin tuna tataki dressed in apple mustard. Creative dessert ideas encompass citrus crème brûlée with Japanese granola and whisky ice cream. There are tasting menus for the financially intrepid, and an authoritative list of premium sake, still the best match for Japanese food old and new.

Chef Luca Spiga **Seats** 113 **Open** All year **Notes** Vegetarian dishes, Children welcome

Roti Chai

◉ MODERN INDIAN

020 7408 0101 | 3 Portman Mews South, W1H 6AY

www.rotichai.com

Here is a restaurant of two halves taking its inspiration from the street stalls and railway cafés of the Indian sub-continent. The ground-floor, canteen-style Street Kitchen serves homely 'street food', while the basement offers more refined nouveau Indian cooking.

Seats 75 **Open** All year **Notes** Vegetarian dishes, Children welcome

Roux at The Landau

◉◉ MODERN EUROPEAN, FRENCH Ⅴ ⬧NOTABLE WINE LIST

020 7636 1000 | The Langham, London, Portland Place, W1B 1JA

www.rouxatthelandau.com

The Roux dining room at the elegant Langham Hotel is a haven of traditional values. If things have gone dressed-down and laid-back elsewhere, here the elevated tone of the panelled oval room does justice to the highly polished cooking of the Roux ethos.

Chef Nicolas Pasquier **Seats** 100, Private dining 18 **Prices from** S £9, M £16, D £8 **Notes** Children welcome

AA Restaurant of the Year for London 2018–19

Sabor
◉◉ SPANISH
020 3319 8130 | 35–37 Heddon St, Mayfair, W1B 4BR
www.saborrestaurants.co.uk

This hot new Spanish ticket – from former Barrafina luminaries, Nieves Barragán Mohacho and José Etura – fairly rocks. Sabor (translating as 'flavour') delivers an authentic regional experience via its trio of dining options; from diminutive tapas bar to dining-counter restaurant facing a high-energy open kitchen. Head up the spiral staircase to the asador's communal tables for more regional delights; think Segovian roast suckling pig cooked in the wood-fired oven (asador) or pulpo a feira (octopus cooked in copper pots).

Chef Nieves Barragán Mohacho **Open** All year **Notes** Bookings for asador only

Salt Yard
◉◉ ITALIAN, SPANISH
020 7637 0657 | 54 Goodge Street, W1T 4NA
www.saltyard.co.uk

This buzzy restaurant deals in small-but-perfectly formed plates of vibrant food with a Spain-meets-Italy theme. The bar is the place for a glass of fizz with a plate of cured meats, or take a seat and graze, tapas-style, through a mix of the familiar and creative.

Chef Dan Sherlock, Joe Howley **Seats** 80 **Closed** 25 December, 1 January **Prices from** S £4, M £6, D £4.25 **Notes** Vegetarian dishes, Children welcome

Sartoria
◉ ITALIAN V
020 7534 7000 | 20 Savile Row, W1S 3PR
www.sartoria-restaurant.co.uk

Appropriately set in the fine suiting and booting world of Savile Row, Sartoria is an immaculately turned-out operation with a classy interior and switched-on, upbeat service from staff dressed to look the part.

Chef Francesco Mazzei **Seats** 100, Private dining 50 **Closed** 25–26 December, 1 January, Easter Monday, Bank holidays **Prices from** S £11.50, M £19.50, D £7 **Notes** Children welcome

Scott's
◉◉ SEAFOOD V ⚑ NOTABLE WINE LIST
020 7495 7309 | 20 Mount Street, W1K 2HE
www.scotts-restaurant.com

Glamour fills Scott's, from its charming service to the eye-catching mountain of seafood on ice in the swanky champagne bar. Apart from celebrities, there are mosaics, mirrors, oak-panelled walls, leather seats, and modern artworks to catch the eye, plus a menu brimming with top-notch seafood.

Chef Dave McCarthy **Seats** 150, Private dining 40 **Closed** 25–26 December **Prices from** S £9, M £20, D £9.50 **Notes** Children welcome

Sexy Fish
◉◉ ASIAN, SEAFOOD
020 3764 2000 | Berkeley Square House, Berkeley Square, W1J 6BR
www.sexyfish.com

This lavish new outfit reputedly cost a cool £15m, and the interiors are simply jaw dropping, from acres of onyx to aquatic-themed artworks by big names, and a water wall cascading behind the bar. The feel is glittering art deco with bags of bling.

Chef Bjoern Weissgerber **Seats** 138, Private dining 48 **Closed** 25–26 December **Notes** Vegetarian dishes, Children welcome

Sketch (The Gallery)
◉◉◉ MODERN EUROPEAN ⚑ NOTABLE WINE LIST
See pages 222–223

Sketch (Lecture Room & Library)
◉◉◉◉◉ MODERN EUROPEAN V ⚑ NOTABLE WINE LIST
See pages 224–225

Sketch (The Parlour)
◉◉ MODERN EUROPEAN
020 7659 4500 | 9 Conduit Street, W1S 2XG
www.sketch.london

Another of the options at style-conscious Sketch is The Parlour, open for breakfast and lunch before a DJ takes over for cocktail hour and on into the night. There is no booking, just turn up (although change out of your shorts first, if you don't mind).

Chef Pierre Gagnaire, Frederic Don **Seats** 50 **Closed** Christmas, 1 January **Notes** Vegetarian dishes, Children welcome

See advertisement on page 226

LONDON W1 continues on page 226

Sketch (The Gallery)
◉◉◉ MODERN EUROPEAN ⬩NOTABLE WINE LIST
020 7659 4500 | 9 Conduit Street, W1S 2XG
www.sketch.london

Virtuoso cooking in an artist-designed restaurant

It's all change again in the 'modern European gastro-brasserie' option at super-cool Sketch. They like to keep the design fresh here, so celebrated Brit artist David Shrigley's quirky, childlike drawings still fill the walls, but colourful images now take the place of his black-and-white cartoons; the crockery is designed by Shrigley too, so expect a few sardonic messages on the white ceramics to greet last mouthfuls. It all rubs along against a backdrop of designer glam from India Mahdavi in a striking open space that is an explosion of candy pink worthy of a teenage girl's boudoir, but accessorised with low-slung sponge finger-like barrel chairs and banquettes and clever lighting. As always, service remains a highlight, with charming, clued-up staff positively overflowing with sweetness and light.

Not intending to play second fiddle to the happening vibe, well-heeled, beautiful people and wry humour of the art, über-chef Pierre Gagnaire's food doesn't stint on creativity either, with vibrancy, sheer skill and a sense of fun evident throughout. The trademark Asian inspiration is still very much in evidence in an opener that teams pink burrata with

lychee, aloe vera, Thai grapefruit, and yellow mango velouté, all beautifully crafted, executed and presented; otherwise, stay in European mode with a highly inventive 'charcuterie'-themed riff that delivers an assemblage of duck foie gras, Parma ham, honey-roasted ham and sourdough, all leavened with a pungent mustard ice cream. Sophisticated technique, along with an intuitive grasp of flavours also distinguishes main-courses – Scottish fallow deer casserole might get a touch of Asian fusion sparkle via its accompaniment of pickled shiitake mushrooms, along with redcurrant, quince paste and a deftly wrought cube of red cabbage. The same meticulous craftmanship and complex layering of flavours also defines the likes of roasted Basque pork chop with prune paste, bacon and hay-roasted potatoes. The Sketch take on fish and chips could see pollock alongside crunchy French fries, coleslaw, green apple, mushy peas and 'sketchup'. Desserts are also highly technical workouts: expect fancy-pants creations such as Valrhona Abinao chocolate mousse with pistachio parfait, bitter chocolate leaves, roasted pear and cocoa, and aged rum water. The wine list brims with thoroughbred, wallet-denting treats, but cherry-pick the menu and you can eat here without the threat of insolvency. Afternoon tea is another treat on offer in The Gallery, with some spectacular cakes and more of Mr Shrigley's tableware providing a talking point.

Chef Pierre Gagnaire, Frederic Don **Seats** 126 **Closed** Christmas and 1 January
Prices from S £12, M £18, D £6 **Notes** Vegetarian dishes, Children welcome

LONDON W1

Sketch (Lecture Room & Library)

◉◉◉◉◉ MODERN EUROPEAN **V** ❦ NOTABLE WINE LIST

020 7659 4500 | 9 Conduit Street, W1S 2XG

www.sketch.london

Highly conceptualized food from a modern master

Something rather extraordinary lies in wait behind the sober facade of this Grade II listed townhouse in Mayfair. Built at the back end of the 18th century, the place has all the outward appearance of a bastion of traditional values, but within you'll find a venue as off-the-wall as any in the capital. With an approach to interior design that tears the rule book into a million tiny pieces and uses it as a decorative feature, designer Gabhan O'Keeffe's vision for Sketch is a one off. This is a dining room that sets the pulse racing, with its lavish red, pink, orange and gold colour scheme, padded cream leather walls and all-round air of theatricality. Like a Victorian salon as reimagined by Lewis Carroll, it's a suitably unforgettable spot for some ground-breaking cuisine.

The menus – à la carte and tasting – reveal dishes of complexity and imagination, and in an era of minimal elucidation, they actually come – hurrah! – with real descriptions that use lots of words to let you know what you're in for. The skill of this kitchen is beyond question: the French modern master Pierre Gagnaire still devises all menus here, with

head chef Johannes Nuding aiming to encompass a dizzyingly wide range of ingredients and techniques in a multitude of small plates. An opening course, Sea Garden, comprises transparent shellfish ravioli with almond, clams, leeks and potato cream, then hand-dived Scottish scallop glazed with a mandarin reduction, followed by pumpkin ice cream, seaweed jelly and shiitake mushroom, and a final salvo of razor clams with espardenya (sea cucumber), and squid in anchovy water with cava. Sure, it's a lot to take in, but the result is a beautiful progression of complementary flavours, appealing textures and visual impact. The ways the components work together produces an undeniable alchemy in mains too – a pork workout might bring grilled rack marinated with sage, cooked in hay and served with turnips and dry fruit marmalade, while line-caught sea bass could be poached in citrus butter then served with an assemblage of quince paste with saffron, fennel, candied beetroot and daikon. Desserts follow a similar complex route: choose a theme – Somerset Burrow Hill, say – and a riot of little dishes ensues: Bramley terrine with ice cider and Cox's apple juice, then cider-glazed cheesecake mousse, followed by perry jelly with pear and yogurt sorbet, and perhaps a finale of apple flambéd with Somerset cider brandy.

Chef Pierre Gagnaire, Johannes Nuding **Seats** 50, Private dining 40 **Closed** 2 weeks August, 2 weeks December, 1 January and Bank holidays **Prices from** S £45, M £50, D £17 **Notes** No children under 6 years

Social Eating House

◉◉◉ MODERN BRITISH **V** ◢ NOTABLE WINE LIST

020 7993 3251 | 58–59 Poland Street, W1F 7NS
www.socialeatinghouse.com

The Poland Street iteration of Jason Atherton's burgeoning empire looks very much the Soho part, the rather anonymous frontage leading into a racy cavern of bare brick walls and distressed leather stools at the copiously stocked bar. Draw up a bentwood chair at a café table if you prefer a menu that begins with sharing jars of smoked houmous and spiced aubergine, or confit duck rillettes with mango and coriander. The main menu deals in three-dimensional combinations that are more off the wall than at other Atherton venues, treacling côte de porc and salt-baking some white carrot for a main course that also incorporates cime di rapa and a spicy nut granola. Hake is smoked over applewood and served in seaweed butter with cured trout caviar and Charlottes, and anything can be further dolled up with a supplementary addition of truffle. Prior to those, look to octopus with charcoal mayonnaise and Padrón pepper in green sauce, and finish with a vibrant chocolate délice made with 70% cocoa gear,

sharpened with raspberry and star anise and served with milk and honey ice cream.

Chef Paul Hood **Seats** 75, Private dining 8
Closed 25–26 December and Bank Holidays
Prices from S £6.50, M £24.50, D £8.50
Notes Children welcome

Social Wine & Tapas

◉◉ MODERN TAPAS ◢ NOTABLE WINE LIST

020 7993 3257 | 39 James Street, W1U 1DL
www.socialwineandtapas.com

London purrs with Jason Atherton's inventive 'Socials', but his classy, convivial Marylebone tapas joint affords food and wine equal billing as its name implies. Factor in a wine shop, dynamic wine list and tasting room and you feel the love. Food doesn't play second fiddle.

Chef Marcus Rohlen, Jason Atherton **Seats** 60, Private dining 10 **Closed** 25 December, 1 January
Prices from S £3.50, M £7.50, D £6.75
Notes Vegetarian dishes, Children welcome

The Square

◉◉◉ MODERN FRENCH **V**

020 7495 7100 | 6–10 Bruton Street, Mayfair, W1J 6PU

www.squarerestaurant.com

The sense of having stepped into a contemporary art space makes a powerful initial impact at The Square, where monochrome abstracts and a strange headless sculptural group form the mise en scène for one of Mayfair's longest-running high fliers. Clément Leroy, formerly of Chantilly, cooking alongside his wife Aya Tamura, maintains the French-oriented style of the cuisine, which is as haute as it is moderne, with novel and challenging ideas coming thick and fast on the four-course menu format. First out of the traps might be a marinated Scottish langoustine with cauliflower in an aromatic welter of hibiscus and citrus, before the middle course offers foie gras seasoned with ginger in a fruity dashi broth. Main courses are essays in delicately considered balance, perhaps John Dory with sea-urchin and lychees, or the superlative matured meats that might be a three-way serving of 55-day aged pork, or 28-day Cumbrian beef fillet à la royale. If you're still feeling pretty royale at dessert stage, look to a creation of grand cru chocolate with pistachios and red shiso leaf, or salt-crusted pineapple with kombu caramel.

Chef Clément Leroy **Seats** 80, Private dining 18 **Closed** 24–26 December, 1 January **Notes** Children welcome

Street XO

◉◉ TAPAS

020 3096 7555 | 15 Old Burlington Street, W1S 2JR

www.streetxo.com/london

With its neon signage and pumping music, nobody could accuse this frenetic Mayfair restaurant and cocktail bar of lacking atmosphere. Descend the golden staircase to the black-and-red basement, where the cutting-edge fusion cooking is as vibrant as the decor, and small plates plunder the global larder.

Chef David Muñoz **Open** All year

Tamarind

◉◉ INDIAN

020 7629 3561 | 20 Queen Street, Mayfair, W1J 5PR

www.tamarindrestaurant.com

In the vanguard of design-led new-wave Indian restaurants when it opened in 1995, diners will find that Tamarind's expansive basement has expanded into the floor above when it reopens in Autumn 2018 following a multi-million pound refurbishment.

Seats 90 **Closed** 25–26 December and 1 January **Notes** Vegetarian dishes, No children under 5 years

10 Greek Street

◉◉ MODERN BRITISH, EUROPEAN

020 7734 4677 | W1D 4DH

www.10greekstreet.com

A Soho bistro reinvented for the present age, the lively cooking at number 10 has plenty to say for itself. Fish dishes in two sizes, such as gurnard with Jerusalem artichokes and black pudding, or mackerel chermoula with pomegranate and pistachio, indicate a flexible approach.

Chef Cameron Emirali **Seats** 30, Private dining 12 **Closed** Christmas **Prices from** S £7, M £18, D £7 **Notes** Vegetarian dishes, Children welcome

Texture Restaurant

◉◉◉◉ MODERN EUROPEAN **V**

020 7224 0028 | 4 Bryanston Street, W1H 7BY

www.texture-restaurant.co.uk

Texture is a compelling mix of Scandinavian style and traditional English charm. The former is down to the sheer blinding talent of Agnar (Aggi) Sverrisson, an Icelander who has brought his prodigious culinary talent to London and created one of the most divertingly appealing addresses in town. The latter is down to the splendid Georgian proportions of the space. It is this fusion of simple design and big-scale grandeur that makes dining chez Sverrisson such an appealing prospect. The cooking is a kind of fusion too, with Icelandic influences gliding through the modern European menu like skis through the snow. The splendid Champagne Bar at the front of the building is a good place to begin, where five champagnes are available by the glass and some 140 by the bottle. The space is adorned with impressive artworks, providing splashes of colour to the neutral walls, and the service is engaging and informed. Choose from the à la carte or tasting menus, which include fish and vegan versions. There is a lightness of touch in the cooking, a genuine depth of flavour achieved, and without the overuse of cream, butter (zero in the savoury courses) or sugar. Isle of Skye scallops shine in an opening course with textures of cauliflower, and there are Asian flavours running through a plate of new season Wye Valley asparagus. Among main courses, Icelandic cod is lightly salted, served with avocado, Romanesco and wild garlic, and Pyrenean milk-fed lamb arrives as saddle, shoulder and belly. The wine list shows the same level of attention to detail as the food, with great advice on hand if required.

Chef Agnar Sverrisson **Seats** 52, Private dining 16 **Closed** 2 weeks at Christmas, 2 weeks in August, 1 week at Easter **Prices from** S £18.75, M £43.50 **Notes** Children welcome

Trishna

◉◉ INDIAN **V** 🍷 NOTABLE WINE LIST

020 7935 5624 | 15–17 Blandford Street, W1U 3DG
www.trishnalondon.com

Trishna takes a minimalist decorative line in two dining rooms done out with oak floors and tables, painted brickwork, mirrored walls, and hues of cream and duck-egg blue. The kitchen celebrates the coastal cuisine of southwest India in fresh, flavour-packed contemporary dishes.

Chef Karam Sethi **Seats** 65, Private dining 12
Closed 24–27 December, 1–3 January **Notes** Children welcome before 7pm

Twist

◉◉ MEDITERRANEAN TAPAS

020 7723 3377 | 42 Crawford Street, W1H 1JW
www.twistkitchen.co.uk

Lively, intimate and fun, this Marylebone-hinterland 'kitchen and tapas' is smack on-cue. The in-vogue pared-back look keeps things relaxed while the Spanish-style tiled open kitchen draws top focus. Conversely, the downstairs room is quieter, quirkier and comes with a bar.

Chef Eduardo Tuccillo **Seats** 75, Private dining 35
Closed Christmas, 1 January, Easter, last 2 weeks in August, some Bank Holidays **Notes** Vegetarian dishes, Children welcome

Umu

◉◉◉ JAPANESE 🍷 NOTABLE WINE LIST

020 7499 8881 | 14–16 Bruton Place, W1J 6LX
www.umurestaurant.com

Press the buzzer to gain admittance to one of the West End's understated temples of Japanese elegance, a short glide from the hurly-burly of Berkeley Square. Inside, the prospect has what one might conventionally denote a Zen-like balance, with delicate wood screens and subdued lighting acting as a foil to the hyperactivity of the kitchen brigade. Almost alone among the world's classic cuisines, Japanese food has only very peripherally succumbed to the advancing tides of fashion, retaining a firm anchorage in the ancient ways. When that produces stunning fish and seafood dishes, ringing with resonant freshness and pinpoint seasoning, it's hard to argue: the zensai appetisers alone here are exquisite – try the sake-steamed abalone for one. Things might proceed to lightly grilled tuna cuts (back and belly) with a trio of dressings, or the famed Irish wild eel, charcoal-grilled and anointed with sweet soy. The Wagyu beef is inevitably superb, and inevitably comes at a terrific premium, but if funding is not an obstacle, go for the full Kyoto-style kaiseki menu, with

its monkfish hotpot, truffled sika deer, and sake-laced kumquat dessert.

Chef Yoshinori Ishii **Seats** 64, Private dining 10
Closed Christmas, New Year and Bank holidays
Notes Vegetarian dishes, Children welcome

Vasco & Piero's Pavilion Restaurant

◉ MODERN ITALIAN

020 7437 8774 | 15 Poland Street, W1F 8QE
www.vascosfood.com

This stalwart of the Soho dining scene has been plying its trade since 1971 but has a modern, clean-lined and arty look. The handwritten menu changes after each serving, so seasonality is a given. Rustic, home-style cooking delivers clear flavours; splendid pasta is made fresh.

Chef Vasco Matteucci **Seats** 50, Private dining 36
Closed Bank holidays **Prices from** S £6, M £14.50, D £6 **Notes** Vegetarian dishes, No children under 5 years

Veeraswamy Restaurant

◉◉ INDIAN **V**

020 7734 1401 | Mezzanine Floor, Victory House, 99 Regent Street, W1B 4RS
www.veeraswamy.com

Tucked away on a first floor at the bottom of Regent Street, Veeraswamy is London's oldest Indian restaurant, with a refined Mayfair feel; floral carpet, beamed ceiling and an ornate chandelier. Anglo-Indian dishes survive from the original 1926 menus, along with a more exploratory tendency.

Chef Uday Salunkhe **Seats** 114, Private dining 24
Open All year **Prices from** S £8.50, M £44, D £7.50
Notes No children under 10 years at lunch on weekdays, 4–10 years at early dinner must leave by 8pm

See advertisement opposite

Villandry Great Portland Street

◉ FRENCH, MEDITERRANEAN **V**

020 7631 3131 | 170 Great Portland Street, W1W 5QB
www.villandry.com

Embracing the all-day-dining concept with aplomb, the Great Portland Street Villandry offers something for everyone. Amble through to the casual café/bar, or take a seat in the more formal restaurant. It's bright and airy throughout and the food reflects this with a light Mediterranean vibe.

Chef Graham Thompson **Seats** 200, Private dining 14
Closed 25–26 December **Prices from** S £6.50, M £14.50, D £6.50 **Notes** Children welcome

London W1 continued

Wild Honey

◉◉◉ FRENCH INTERNATIONAL

020 7758 9160 | 12 Saint George Street, W1S 2FB
www.wildhoneyrestaurant.co.uk

Launched just over a decade ago, Anthony Demetre's Wild Honey feels as though it has been here for much longer. A long wood-panelled room with bar seating and small bistro tables evokes something of the feel of the Mayfair dining of old, the sort of place Anthony Powell's characters might repair to, although the menu is anything but stuck in a time-warp. A resourceful, creative approach sees a first-course serving of quail lacquered in sweet spice and grilled, then served with kumquat purée and roast carrots. Fashionable fragrances of the sea turn up in a main dish of cod with sea purslane and sprouting broccoli in seaweed vinaigrette, while the impeccably tender venison is sourced on Dartmoor, and earthily supported by sweet potato and puréed beetroot. The artisanal British and French cheeses are worth a gander as a transition to one of the sharply flavoured desserts, perhaps rosewater cheesecake with caramelised apple.

Chef Anthony Demetre, Greg Csaba **Seats** 65
Closed 25–26 December, 1 January and Bank holidays
Prices from S £8, M £17, D £9 **Notes** Vegetarian dishes, Children welcome

The Wolseley

◉ TRADITIONAL EUROPEAN **V**

020 7499 6996 | 160 Piccadilly, W1J 9EB
www.thewolseley.com

The Wolseley fizzes with energy. Staff rush about and happy customers chatter, from breakfast, brunch, lunch and afternoon tea, through to evening meals. Timeless brasserie classics fill the menu, and the all-day concept fits the bill.

Chef David Stephens **Seats** 150, Private dining 14
Open All year **Prices from** S £5.75, M £12.75, D £5
Notes Children welcome

Yauatcha

◉◉ MODERN CHINESE

020 7494 8888 | 15 Broadwick Street, W1F 0DL
www.yauatcha.com

A colourful array of pâtisserie opens the show in Yauatcha's ground-floor 'tea house', but in the basement dining room things are lively and loud. The menu impresses with its exciting blend of traditional Cantonese favourites and more intriguing contemporary compositions.

Chef Tong Chee Hwee **Seats** 120 **Closed** 24–25 December **Notes** Vegetarian dishes, Children welcome

Zoilo

◉◉ ARGENTINE

020 7486 9699 | 9 Duke Street, W1U 3EG
www.zoilo.co.uk

The mayhem of Oxford Street is close by but feels miles away in this racy outpost of South American cuisine. Bare brick walls, crimson banquettes and a midnight-blue palette around a central bar make a chic backdrop to dynamic food inspired by Argentina's regions.

Chef Diego Jacquet **Seats** 48, Private dining 12
Closed Christmas and bank holidays
Prices from S £6.90, M £14.90, D £7.50
Notes Vegetarian dishes, Children welcome

LONDON W2

Angelus Restaurant

◉ MODERN FRENCH

020 7402 0083 | 4 Bathurst Street, W2 2SD
www.angelusrestaurant.co.uk

A former pub which was transformed into a classy Parisian-style brasserie by renowned sommelier, Thierry Tomasin, Angelus Restaurant continues to impress with its luxe, art nouveau-inspired finish and ambitious, modern French cooking. The wine list offers some seriously good drinking.

Chef George Ng Fuk Chong **Seats** 40, Private dining 22
Closed 24–25 December **Notes** Vegetarian dishes, Children welcome

The Hyde

◉ MODERN BRITISH

020 7479 6600 | Roseate House London, 3 Westbourne Terrace, Lancaster Gate, Hyde Park, W2 3UL
www.roseatehouselondon.com

A boutique hotel occupying a row of townhouses a short walk from Paddington railway station, Roseate House is just a block away from Hyde Park and ideal for exploring central London's attractions. The hotel's contemporary food is worth a detour.

Chef Craig Van Der Meer **Open** All year
Prices from S £5.95, M £12.95, D £5.95 **Parking** 9
Notes No children

Island Grill & Bar

◉◉ MODERN BRITISH, EUROPEAN

020 7551 6070 | Royal Lancaster London, Lancaster Terrace, W2 2TY
www.islandrestaurant.co.uk

Island Grill & Bar is on the ground floor of the hotel with views over the busy road to Hyde Park opposite. Go for something from the grill – perhaps a steak with béarnaise or pork cutlets – or try salmon in a saffron-infused consommé.

Chef Adam Woolven **Seats** 68 **Open** All year **Prices from** S £7.50, M £15.50, D £7 **Notes** Vegetarian dishes, Children welcome

Kurobuta
◉ JAPANESE

020 7920 6440 | 17–20 Kendal Street, Marble Arch, W2 2AW

www.kurobuta-london.com

A modern, stripped-down look with dark and moody colours, exposed industrial ducting and wood-slab tables, plus a lively musical policy make Kurobuta a popular, buzzy place. Inspired by Japan's izakaya taverns, the kitchen takes a Japanese fusion approach and chucks a few lively global ideas in the mix for good measure.

Chef Francico **Seats** 100 **Open** All year **Notes** Vegetarian dishes, Children welcome

Nipa
◉◉ TRADITIONAL THAI

020 7551 6039 | Royal Lancaster London, Lancaster Terrace, W2 2TY

www.niparestaurant.co.uk

There's a cracking view over Hyde Park from this refined Thai restaurant with its wood panels and tables topped with Thai orchids. Set menus prevent the need to make difficult decisions, so for dessert, mango sticky rice with coconut cream is spot on.

Chef Sanguan Parr **Seats** 55 **Open** All year **Prices from** S £10, M £16, D £9 **Notes** Vegetarian dishes, Children welcome

LONDON W4
Hedone
◉◉◉ MODERN EUROPEAN

020 8747 0377 | 301–303 Chiswick High Road, W4 4HH
www.hedonerestaurant.com

It may not make the boldest of statements from the street – an understated grey awning above folding doors that open up to the Chiswick sunshine – but this is undoubtedly one of the nerve-centres of innovative cooking in west London. The open-plan kitchen is surrounded by a counter with high seating, ringside seats for the spectacular to come. Mikael Jonsson takes a spontaneous, intuitive approach to food, encouraging his brigade to work with the grain of the often recherché and constantly changing ingredients. A dish may not be cooked in the same way within the same session, while tasting menus vary a little from diner to diner. Some of the notable dishes have been the 45-day-aged beef with juniper-smoked potatoes

and cabbage, or the scallops that are topped with an emulsion dressing based on potato skins with beef jus. Vegetable dishes are quite as singular, perhaps Cévennes onions with pear shavings and Périgord truffle, while the extraordinary breads play havoc with traditional expectations of texture. Choose from the basic tasting menu, or the longer Carte Blanche format, and sign up for the imaginative wine pairings too.

Chef Mikael Jonsson **Seats** Private dining 16 **Open** All year **Notes** No children under 6 years

Restaurant Michael Nadra
◉◉ MODERN EUROPEAN

020 8742 0766 | 6–8 Elliott Road, Chiswick, W4 1PE
www.restaurant-michaelnadra.co.uk

A stalwart of the Chiswick dining scene, this classy restaurant's pan-European fixed-price repertoire offers bags of interest. Rabbit ballotine and cromesquis are combined with baby turnip, fresh peas and pea purée and fired up with a well-judged glow from spicy nduja sauce.

Chef Michael Nadra **Seats** 55 **Closed** 24–28 December and 1 January **Prices from** S £5, M £15, D £5 **Notes** Vegetarian dishes, Children welcome

La Trompette
◉◉ MODERN EUROPEAN ◀ NOTABLE WINE LIST

020 8747 1836 | 5–7 Devonshire Road, Chiswick, W4 2EU
www.latrompette.co.uk

La Trompette rocks...this neighbourhood restaurant par excellence has been playing to packed houses since 2001. The mood is relaxed, with a broad glass frontage opening onto a narrow street-side terrace, while inside white linen and a beige colour palette meet bright abstract artworks.

Chef Rob Weston **Seats** 88, Private dining 16 **Closed** 25–26 December and 1 January **Notes** Vegetarian dishes, Children allowed at lunch only

Le Vacherin
◉◉ FRENCH V

020 8742 2121 | 76–77 South Parade, W4 5LF
www.levacherin.com

Le Vacherin brings a hit of Gallic bonhomie to Chiswick, when you're in the mood for some classic French cooking. If you are after a real hit of rustic authenticity, how about sautéed veal sweetbreads with Burgundy snails, shallot purée and beurre noisette?

Chef Malcolm John **Seats** 72, Private dining 36 **Closed** Bank holidays **Prices from** S £7.50, M £14 **Notes** Children welcome

LONDON W6

L'Amorosa
◉ ITALIAN, BRITISH
020 8563 0300 | 278 King Street, Ravenscourt Park, W6 0SP
www.lamorosa.co.uk

This neighbourhood restaurant on Hammersmith's main drag has a man with pedigree at the stoves in the shape of ex-Zafferano head chef Andy Needham. The setting is smart-casual – darkwood floors, polished wood tables, buttoned brown leather banquettes and cream-painted walls hung with modern art.

Chef Andy Needham **Seats** 40 **Closed** 1 week Christmas, Bank holidays, 2 weeks August **Prices from** S £7, M £12, D £6 **Notes** Vegetarian dishes, Children welcome

Anglesea Arms
◉ MODERN BRITISH
020 8749 1291 | 35 Wingate Road, Ravenscourt Park, W6 0UR
www.angleseaarmspub.co.uk

The Anglesea Arms was one of the pioneering London gastro pubs, and it's as popular today as it ever has been. If you're in the mood for fish, there might be pan-roast whole lemon sole.

Chef Jasnobio Fardin **Seats** 37 **Closed** 24–26 December **Prices from** S £6, M £14, D £6 **Notes** Vegetarian dishes, Children accepted until 7.30pm

The River Café
◉ ◉ ◉ ITALIAN
020 7386 4200 | Thames Wharf Studios, Rainville Road, W6 9HA
www.rivercafe.co.uk

Things don't change much here – the River Café is perhaps the epitome of 'if it ain't broke…' – and it's been a wildly successful destination for 30 years. It's very busy, and still very popular indeed. It's not cheap, but you get what you pay for – timeless, pitch-perfect dishes conjured confidently from fabulous ingredients. Other places may be swayed by fashion but the River Café just keeps doing what it does best – hyper-seasonal, simple cooking. The atmosphere is informal and welcoming, the room light and relaxingly minimal – the building began life as the Duckhams oil storage facility. Kick things off with perfectly al dente mezzi paccheri, with the freshest langoustine, black pepper, butter and pecorino – utterly straightforward and delicious. Next up is branzino con vongole – wild sea bass roasted in vermentino with clams, swiss chard, chilli and parsley – a lovely piece of fish, accurately timed and

beautifully complemented by the sauce. Finish with 'the simplest tart ever' – a joyful example, almond and Mirabelle plums, served simply with a dollop of sour cream. Perfection.

Chef Ruth Rogers, Sian Wyn Owen, Joseph Trivelli **Seats** 120, Private dining 18 **Closed** 24 December to 1 January **Prices from** S £20, M £38, D £10 **Parking** 29 **Notes** Vegetarian dishes, Children welcome

Sagar
◉ INDIAN VEGETARIAN V
020 8741 8563 | 157 King Street, Hammersmith, W6 9JT
www.sagarveg.co.uk

Behind Sagar's glass frontage, this Indian restaurant has an almost Scandinavian feel with pale wood floors, chairs, tables and walls. Expect well-crafted dishes, smartly attired service and wallet-friendly prices. The roster focuses on South Indian staples such as crisp paper-thin dosas and uthappams.

Chef S Sharmielan **Seats** 60 **Closed** 25–26 December **Notes** Children welcome

LONDON W8

Belvedere
◉ ◉ BRITISH, FRENCH
020 7602 1238 | Holland House, Abbotsbury Road, Holland Park, W8 6LU
www.belvedererestaurant.co.uk

A dreamy location, surrounded by lawns and gardens, and a real looker of a dining room in the former summer ballroom of Holland House ensure Belvedere is a year-round hit. A top-value menu delivers the goods at lunch and early evening without gold card pricing.

Chef Gary O'Sullivan **Seats** 90 **Closed** 26 December and 1 January **Prices from** S £9, M £16, D £8 **Notes** Vegetarian dishes, Children welcome

Clarke's
◉ ◉ MODERN BRITISH, ITALIAN
020 7221 9225 | 124 Kensington Church Street, W8 4BH
www.sallyclarke.com

Sally Clarke's eponymous restaurant is a quietly elegant affair, with walls hung with abstract art. She takes the best, freshest produce available in the markets and her own garden each day and focuses on making it all taste resoundingly of itself, with Italian accents.

Chef Michele Lombardi **Seats** 90, Private dining 30 **Closed** 8 days Christmas and New Year, 2 weeks August **Notes** Vegetarian dishes, Children welcome

Kensington Place

◉ BRITISH

020 7727 3184 | 201–209 Kensington Church St, W8 7LX

www.kensingtonplace-restaurant.com

This glass-fronted brasserie championed a new brisk informality in high-end dining when it opened in 1987. In an atmosphere of infectious buzz, with a large communal table for the sociably inclined, the fish and seafood catches of the day receive due credit.

Chef Ian Waghorn **Seats** 110, Private dining 36 **Closed** 24–25 December, 1 January, Bank holidays **Notes** Vegetarian dishes, Children welcome

Kitchen W8

◉◉◉ MODERN BRITISH ▲ NOTABLE WINE LIST

020 7937 0120 | 11–13 Abingdon Road, Kensington, W8 6AH

www.kitchenw8.com

Even a locale as opulent as the one that surrounds Kensington High Street can lay claim to a neighbourhood restaurant, and the double-fronted venue that takes its postcode for a name fills the bill in fine style. Inside, the low-ceilinged room is furnished in determinedly monochrome array, with occasional splurts of colour from the modernist artworks, and tables are smartly got up in their best whites for a culinary production that fires on all cylinders. Mark Kempson's dishes look cleanly and neatly designed in the modern way, with a strong emphasis on the true flavours of their principal ingredients. Opening the show might be a double-act of grilled mackerel and smoked eel, accompanied by the sweetness of golden beetroot and mustard, before the main draw arrives in the form of lamb shoulder with winter pickles, calçots and Pink Firs, or roast cod with chestnut gremolata, pumpkin and hispi. Desserts make a commendable attempt to incorporate as much fruit as possible, rather than going wholesale for chocolate and caramel, the on-trend option being polenta and orange cake with passionfruit sorbet.

Chef Mark Kempson **Seats** 75 **Closed** 25–26 December, Bank holidays **Prices from** S £8.95, M £24.95, D £6.75 **Notes** Vegetarian dishes, Children welcome

Launceston Place

◉◉ MODERN EUROPEAN ▲ NOTABLE WINE LIST

020 7937 6912 | 1a Launceston Place, W8 5RL

www.launcestonplace-restaurant.co.uk

Consisting of four Victorian houses on the corner of an upmarket mews, Launceston Place offers first-class service in a series of sophisticated spaces in shades of grey. The kitchen's output is rooted in French classical cooking and incorporates contemporary techniques to good effect.

Chef Ben Murphy **Seats** 50, Private dining 12 **Closed** Christmas, Easter **Notes** Vegetarian dishes, Children welcome

The Milestone Hotel

◉◉ MODERN BRITISH ▲ NOTABLE WINE LIST

020 7917 1000 | 1 Kensington Court, W8 5DL

www.milestonehotel.com

A stolid red-brick corner edifice in affluent Kensington, formal service in the lead-windowed Cheneston dining room extends to a commis chef on hand to carve from the roast-of-the-day trolley. Incidentals offer a nod to modernism with foaming appetisers and pre-desserts.

Chef Alexandras Diamantis **Seats** 30, Private dining 8 **Open** All year **Notes** Vegetarian dishes, Children welcome

Min Jiang

◉◉◉ CHINESE

See pages 234–235

See advertisement on page 236

Park Terrace Restaurant

◉◉ MODERN EUROPEAN

020 7361 0602 | Royal Garden Hotel, 2–24 Kensington High Street, W8 4PT

www.parkterracerestaurant.co.uk

With leafy views over Kensington Gardens, the contemporary decor in the restaurant reflects the park-life theme, with a natural colour palate, wood veneer and large black-and-white images of trees. The modern cooking is light, clear-flavoured and uncomplicated, and shows commitment to local British suppliers and seasonality.

Chef Steve Munkley **Seats** 90, Private dining 40 **Open** All year **Parking** 200 **Notes** Vegetarian dishes, Children welcome

See advertisement on page 237

London W8 continues on page 237

LONDON W8
Min Jiang
◉◉◉ CHINESE
020 7361 1988 | Royal Garden Hotel, 2–24 Kensington High Street, W8 4PT
www.minjiang.co.uk

Authentic Chinese flavours and one of London's best views

This is a fabulous location for this smart Chinese restaurant, away up on the tenth floor of the Royal Garden Hotel, where you can enjoy views across the leafiest parts of Kensington, with all London's most iconic buildings spanning the horizon. It's particularly spectacular for autumn lunches, as the leaves change colour. The long dining room is decorated in red, black and cream, with displays of ceramics and well-spaced tables, all making the most of that wonderful view. There's also a private dining room, with mirrored walls and black-and-white photographs of China. Min Jiang is the name of a tributary of the Upper Yangzte River, which flows through the region of Sichuan.

There's a wide choice of both traditional and more contemporary Chinese dishes, including some from Sichuan – chicken with sesame, for example, dan dan noodles with minced pork, or hot and sour soup, as well as what is described as 'legendary' and 'truly authentic' wood-fired Beijing duck, for which the restaurant is justly famous (it's advised

to order this in advance). This is offered in two servings and carved at your table by one of the chefs. First the crispy skin, dipped in sugar, is served, accompanied by some of the meat, with pancakes and a choice of sweet sauce and shredded leek and cucumber or garlic paste with radish and Tientsin cabbage, followed by the rest of the meat, with rice or noodles, or maybe in soup, or minced with lettuce wrap.

Dim sum, including a vegetarian platter, is excellent, and there are other interesting vegetarian options, too, including tofu with morels in black bean sauce, and 'vegan abalone' with sakura cress. Sea bass might come steamed with preserved turnip and dried shrimp in soy sauce, roasted with soya bean paste, or stir-fried with sanpei sauce, or you might try the roasted Alaskan black cod in spicy sha cha sauce. A great dish of crispy fried salt-and-pepper squid makes a simple but harmonious beginning, while Sichuan double cooked pork belly with Chinese leek is served on a clay platter, with refined saucing and wonderful flavours, the leeks adding the perfect textural contrast. Desserts are more than mere afterthoughts – carefully considered and neatly constructed, the Min Jiang pancake with Cornish ice cream, for instance, is an outstanding finish, or perhaps try the poached black sesame dumplings, or the fresh mango cream with sago pearls and pomelo.

Chef Weng Han Wong **Seats** 80, Private dining 20 **Open** All year **Prices from** S £7, M £19.50, D £8 **Parking** 200 **Notes** Vegetarian dishes, Children welcome

See advertisement on page 236

LONDON W8 continued

Zaika of Kensington

⊛⊛ INDIAN **V**

020 7795 6533 | 1 Kensington High Street, W8 5NP

www.zaika-restaurant.co.uk

Comfortably in step with its postcode, this high-end Indian in a former bank has the feel of a Raj-era gentlemen's club, with its high ceilings, oak panels and colonial pictures. Taking classic, Moghul-inspired North Indian dishes as its starting point, the kitchen conjures scintillating flavours.

Chef Shoeb Haider **Seats** Private dining 18

LONDON W11

Core by Clare Smyth

⊛⊛⊛⊛⊛ BRITISH

020 3937 5086 | 92 Kensington Park Road W11 2PN

www.corebyclaresmyth.com

One of the UK's most lauded female chefs, there was always going to be a bit of a feeding frenzy around the opening, in 2017, of Clare Smyth MBE's first solo venture since cutting loose from her tenure of the top job at Restaurant Gordon Ramsay. Happily, it's a winner. The stripped-back setting is as precise and polished as the superlative service and food that is to come; fine glassware, cutlery and crockery are present

and correct, but some of the fine dining frippery you might expect – tablecloths and carpets, for example – have been kicked into touch, and the casual mood is miles from the hushed reverence of many an operation dealing in gastronomy at this rarefied level. Smyth and the kitchen team do their thing behind a glass partition, and what emerges is, of course, simply stunning – highly technical, eye-poppingly gorgeous in its presentation, but fun too, as in a signature opener starring a slab of the humble spud topped with crisps, herring and trout roe, and pointed up with dulse beurre blanc. Next up braised lamb and carrot come with a pesto of the vegetable's greens, sheep's milk yogurt and a mini brioche stuffed with shredded lamb. A dish of oxtail-stuffed Roscoff onion and braised short rib doesn't have the ring of an idea aimed at haute cuisine fireworks, but the results on the plate are memorable for their head-spinning depth of flavour and velvety saucing. This is cooking that is at once ingredients-led, unfussy and pursues a 'no-waste' environmental ethos. Desserts are also a masterclass in flavour and textural combinations: lemonade parfait with honeycomb and yogurt, then good old rhubarb and custard like you never dreamt possible, the rhubarb served on a pink peppercorn base with

continued on page 238

ridiculously good, rich golden custard. Incidentals, from a volley of snacks – pea and mint gougères; jellied eel, toasted seaweed and malt vinegar; crispy smoked duck wing, burnt orange and spices, and foie gras parfait and Madeira – through to sourdough with Isle of Wight butter are all sublime, as is the 450-bin wine list.

Chef Clare Smyth **Closed** Sunday and Monday

E&O

⦿ PAN ASIAN

020 7229 5454 | 14 Blenheim Crescent, Notting Hill, W11 1NN
www.rickerrestaurants.com

E&O is trend-central with the Notting Hill fashionistas. The decor is casually scuffed these days, but the high-octane vibe (ramped up by a lively bar) puts the experience-factor in overdrive. The young-at-heart pack the place plus there are great cocktails.

Chef AAJ Fernando **Seats** 86, Private dining 18 **Closed** 25–26 December, 1–2 January, Summer Bank Holiday **Prices from** S £4, M £10.50, D £5.50 **Notes** Vegetarian dishes, Children welcome

Edera

⦿ MODERN ITALIAN

020 7221 6090 | 148 Holland Park Avenue, W11 4UE
www.edera.co.uk

Decked out on tiered levels, with light walls hung with big mirrors and linen-dressed tables, this minimally styled Holland Park eatery pulls in a well-heeled crowd for its fashionable Sardinian-accented Italian cooking. The kitchen certainly knows its stuff, keeping things simple and straightforward.

Chef Carlo Usai **Seats** 70, Private dining 20 **Closed** 24 December to 1 January **Notes** Vegetarian dishes, Children welcome

The Ledbury

⦿⦿⦿⦿ MODERN BRITISH V 🍷NOTABLE WINE LIST
020 7792 9090 | 127 Ledbury Road, W11 2AQ
www.theledbury.com

Nobody could accuse Notting Hill of being behind the curve of London restaurant fashion over the past two or three decades. Many of the predominant trends found their footing here, and in The Ledbury the district has a flagship of exploratory modern cuisine to compete with any West End aristocrat. Brett Graham's modest beginnings in the harbour city of Newcastle (the one in New South Wales) launched one of the stellar careers. London is lucky to have him. A beautifully understated contemporary dining space has been conjured from a one-time pub, its sober purple frontage leading into an immaculately appointed room. The eight-course tasting menu offers a tour of dishes from the carte, itself a four-course

format replete with boundless creative energy. First up might be a tartare of Cumbrian veal, matched with grilled artichoke oil and aged beef fat on toast, an umami-laden prelude to a fish dish such as steamed cod with romanesco, anchovies and basil. Every element plays its allotted part in the symphony of flavours, none more resonantly than in a main course of fallow deer with rhubarb and smoked bone marrow, served against a ruffle of red leaves. A pair of diners might sign up for the majestic serving of Herdwick lamb, accompanied by tea-dusted aubergine and black olives. The signature dessert has long been the brown sugar tart with ginger ice cream, but consider too a simple but powerfully effective pairing of dark chocolate Chantilly and clementine leaf. The vegetarian menu is brimful of bright ideas.

Chef Brett Graham **Seats** 55 **Closed** 25–26 December, Summer bank holiday **Notes** No children under 12 years

LONDON W14

Cibo

⦿⦿ ITALIAN

020 7371 2085 | 3 Russell Gardens, W14 8EZ
www.ciborestaurant.net

The epitome of the authentic neighbourhood Italian, long-serving Cibo is a big hit with savvy Holland Park-ers. Breads and nibbles raise expectation from the off, and pasta is the real deal too. This is skilful Italian cooking showing respect of prime ingredients, flavour and precision.

Chef Piero Borrell **Seats** 50, Private dining 14 **Closed** Christmas, Easter Bank holidays **Prices from** S £10, M £17, D £6 **Notes** Vegetarian dishes, Children welcome

LONDON WC1

The Montague on the Gardens

⦿ BRITISH

020 7612 8416 | 15 Montague Street, Bloomsbury, WC1B 5BJ
www.montaguehotel.com

The bowler-hatted doorman at the entrance is a clue that this is a classy boutique hotel, on a quiet street near the British Museum. Its Blue Door Bistro is a welcoming and informal dining room, decorated with a frieze depicting London in around 1850.

Chef Martin Halls **Seats** 40, Private dining 100 **Open** All year **Notes** Vegetarian dishes, Children welcome

Otto's
◉◉ CLASSIC FRENCH
020 7713 0107 | 182 Gray's Inn Road, WC1X 8EW
www.ottos-restaurant.com

Small, intimate and owner-run, this old-school French restaurant feels like it has been around for decades. As befits a traditional French restaurant, the wine list is hefty in both range and price and the food displays confident cooking skills and high-quality ingredients.

Chef Abdul Cisse **Seats** 45, Private dining 30
Closed Christmas, Bank holidays, Easter
Prices from S £7, M £20, D £7 **Notes** Vegetarian dishes, No children under 8 years

Rosewood London
◉◉ MODERN EUROPEAN
020 3747 8620 | 252 High Holborn, WC1V 7EN
www.rosewoodhotels.com/london

This magnificent building on High Holborn is a fine setting, and the old East Banking Hall with its soaring marble pillars is now an elegant restaurant. The Mirror Room offers a relaxed and social dining experience.

Chef Martin Cahill **Seats** 70, Private dining 20 **Open** All year **Prices from** S £12, M £20, D £9 **Parking** 12 **Notes** Vegetarian dishes, Children welcome

LONDON WC2
L'Atelier de Joël Robuchon
◉◉◉ MODERN FRENCH **V**
020 7010 8600 | 13–15 West Street, WC2H 9NE
www.joelrobuchon.co.uk

Despite the location on an unprepossessing backstreet, L'Atelier is all about West End glitz. There are three floors of gastro-excitement going on, plus a rooftop bar, with the more formal restaurant on the first. Dramatic red and black tones, with splats of colour from the various food displays, as well as an open kitchen, make for a sense of theatre wholly appropriate in Covent Garden, and the food is modern French, an absorptive amalgam unabashed to draw on other traditions. Chicken and leek gyoza dumplings in sesame and hibiscus broth has plenty to say for itself, some of it in Japanese, while another starter of aubergine caviar in crispbread layers with goats' curd and tomato, strongly scented with smoked paprika and basil, is harder to place. Not so the signature main course of quail stuffed with foie gras and truffled pomme purée, which is inimitably French to its shinbones, while dessert may be a delightful combination of honey-roast peach with lemon verbena mousse and cottage cheese sorbet, or perhaps a tropical fruit soufflé with coconut ice cream.

Chef Jeremy Page **Seats** 55, Private dining 12
Closed 25 December **Prices from** S £19, M £29, D £17 **Notes** Children welcome

Balthazar
◉ FRENCH, EUROPEAN
020 3301 1155 | 4–6 Russell Street, WC2B 5HZ
www.balthazarlondon.com

The London offshoot of the legendary New York brasserie has played to packed houses since opening in 2013. It's a real looker, with mosaic floors, art deco lighting, leather banquettes and antique mirrors. The places buzzes from breakfast through to lunch, afternoon tea and dinner.

Chef Robert Reid **Seats** 175, Private dining 60
Closed 25 December **Notes** Vegetarian dishes, Children welcome

Barrafina Adelaide Street
◉◉ MODERN SPANISH
10 Adelaide Street, WC2N 4HZ
www.barrafina.co.uk

Tapas is the name of the game here and the place is cool and packed to the rafters. The no-booking policy means queues are likely and, once in, you sit at the marble counter and tuck into small plates full of flavour.

Chef Jose Antonio Ceballos Perez **Seats** 29, Private dining 32 **Closed** Christmas, New Year, Bank holidays **Notes** Vegetarian dishes, Children welcome

Barrafina Drury Lane
◉◉ SPANISH
43 Drury Lane, WC2B 5AJ
www.barrafina.co.uk

A lively repertoire of classic and modern tapas dishes and the perfect spot to grab and graze through a few little plates of big flavours in the pre- and post-theatre slots. There's a no-bookings policy and it takes groups of up to four people.

Chef Javier Duarte Campos **Seats** 31, Private dining 24 **Closed** 25–26 December, 1 January, Bank holidays **Notes** Vegetarian dishes, Children welcome

Café Murano Covent Garden
◉◉ ITALIAN
020 7240 3654 | 36 Tavistock Street, WC2E 7PB
www.cafemurano.co.uk

A long-raftered room with dark grey banquettes and an adjoining pastificio and coffee shop fits its Covent Garden location like a glove, with pre- and post-theatre menus on offer and a bustling lunchtime trade too. Northern Italian dishes under the aegis of Angela Hartnett are the stock-in-trade here.

Chef Angela Hartnett, Adam Jay **Seats** Private dining 50 **Open** All year **Notes** No children

Christopher's

⊛ CONTEMPORARY AMERICAN

020 7240 4222 | 18 Wellington Street, Covent Garden, WC2E 7DD

www.christophersgrill.com

This elegant eatery on the fringes of Covent Garden features a grand staircase, winding up from the uptempo street-level Martini Bar, while corniced high ceilings tower over the airy dining room, where chairs and banquettes in grey and lemon deliver bags of contemporary swagger.

Chef Francis Agyepong **Seats** 110, Private dining 40 **Closed** Christmas and 1 January **Notes** Vegetarian dishes, Children welcome

Cigalon

⊛ MEDITERRANEAN

020 7242 8373 | 115 Chancery Lane, WC2A 1PP

www.cigalon.co.uk

Cigalon's classy dining room certainly evokes memories of sun-drenched South of France dining rather than the dry legal world of Chancery Lane. But it's not all style over substance. The kitchen focuses on the grill to deliver its sunny, seasonal Provençal menu.

Chef Julien Carlon **Seats** 60, Private dining 8 **Closed** Christmas, New Year, Bank holidays **Notes** Vegetarian dishes, Children welcome

Clos Maggiore

⊛⊛⊛ FRENCH, MEDITERRANEAN ⬥ NOTABLE WINE LIST

See pages 242–243

The Delaunay

⊛ EUROPEAN **V**

020 7499 8558 | 55 Aldwych, WC2B 4BB

www.thedelaunay.com

The Delaunay, like its ever-popular Piccadilly sibling, The Wolseley, was conceived in the style of the grand café-restaurants of central Europe, making a vibrant, glamorous spot, great for people watching, with slick, service and an all-day dining repertoire. The Counter offers a fabulous takeaway service.

Chef Malachi O'Gallagher **Seats** 150, Private dining 24 **Closed** 25 December **Notes** Children welcome

Frenchie Covent Garden

⊛⊛ FRENCH, INTERNATIONAL **V**

020 7836 4422 | 16 Henrietta Street, WC2E 8QH

www.frenchiecoventgarden.com

Located in the heart of Covent Garden, this is a new venture for Chef Proprietor Gregory Marchand who splits his time chiefly between his Paris restaurant and here. The menus are simple, yet full of quality and the accuracy of the cooking is very good.

Chef Gregory Marchand **Seats** 72, Private dining 20 **Open** All year **Prices from** S £12, M £23, D £9 **Notes** Children welcome

Frog by Adam Handling

⊛⊛⊛ BRITISH, EUROPEAN

020 7199 8370 | 34–38 Southampton Street WC2E 7HF

www.frogbyadamhandling.com

Adam Handling's chic venue in Covent Garden is a dream of contemporary design, with bare wood floor, black granite tables, floor-to-ceiling street views and an open kitchen, exactly the disposition London expects to see when eating out today. The bar downstairs gets reliably buzzing of an evening. Artworks add eye-catching lustre to the place, including a depiction of Piccadilly Circus, and Handling's menus offer momentous, technically accomplished dishes that make big statements. Thinly sliced salt-baked celeriac comes with sweet dates, a slow-cooked egg yolk, shredded apple, powdered mushroom and lime for an impressive opening balancing-act, before lamb comes three ways – a Wellington of the loin with charred cabbage, spelt risotto with breaded neck, wild garlic and parmesan, and a slow ragout of the shoulder topped with creamy mash – for a virtuoso main-course performance. A thoroughgoing seafood exploration brings together hake with mussels and brown shrimps, and the closing turn could be caramelised apple in puff pastry with roasted peanuts and vanilla ice cream, or mango and coconut cheesecake. Pre- and post-theatre menus are a useful resource.

Chef Adam Handling, Jamie Park **Closed** Sundays

Great Queen Street

⊛ BRITISH, EUROPEAN

020 7242 0622 | 32 Great Queen Street, WC2B 5AA

www.greatqueenstreetrestaurant.co.uk

A long pub-like room with an open kitchen at the back, this is a busy, high-decibel place with an easy-going, friendly and completely unpretentious vibe. The twice-daily changing menu deals in quality produce where seasonality, sourcing and provenance are key. Expect unfussy fare with gutsy flavours.

Chef Sam Hutchins **Seats** 70 **Closed** Bank holidays **Notes** Vegetarian dishes, Children welcome

The Ivy
◉ BRITISH, INTERNATIONAL **V**
020 7836 4751 | 1–5 West Street, Covent Garden,
WC2H 9NQ
www.the-ivy.co.uk
The curtain opened on this theatreland dining
institution over a century ago and it's still a classy act.
Looking elegant after a redesign, the room's original
harlequin stained-glass windows, green leather
banquettes, mirrors and eye-catching modern artwork
set the scene for a wide-ranging menu of classic
British and international food.
Chef Gary Lee **Seats** 100, Private dining 60
Closed 25–26 December, 1 January **Notes** Children
welcome

J. Sheekey & J. Sheekey Atlantic Bar
◉ SEAFOOD **V**
020 7240 2565 | 32–34 St Martin's Court, WC2N 4AL
www.j-sheekey.co.uk
This enduring and much-loved seafood restaurant in
the heart of theatreland began life as a humble
seafood stall in the 1890s. Inside today is a seafood
and oyster bar, and a menu dealing in straightforward
fish and shellfish dishes whose impeccable credentials
speak for themselves.
Chef Andy McLay **Seats** 114 **Closed** 25–26 December,
1 January **Notes** Children welcome

Kaspar's Seafood Bar & Grill
◉ BRITISH, JAPANESE SEAFOOD **V**
020 7836 4343 | The Savoy, Strand, WC2R 0EU
www.fairmont.com/savoy-london/dining/kaspars
The centrepiece of Kaspar's striking, art deco-inspired
dining room is the seafood and oyster bar. You won't
meet Kaspar there, but if you are part of a table of 13,
the sculpted cat can make numbers up to 14,
maintaining an old Savoy tradition.
Chef Holger Jackisch **Seats** 114, Private dining 14
Open All year **Parking** 20 **Notes** Children welcome

Lima Floral
◉◉ MODERN PERUVIAN
020 7240 5778 | 14 Garrick Street, WC2E 9BJ
www.limafloral.com
Lima's Covent Garden outpost offers a more casual
setting than its Fitzrovia flagship, but the blast of
South American vivacity is still a big draw. Peru pretty
much invented the potato, and a fine tuber grown at
4,000 metres turns up in the mains.
Chef Patricia Roig **Seats** 60, Private dining 12
Closed Christmas and New Year **Notes** Vegetarian
dishes, Children welcome

AA Food Service Award 2018–19

Margot
◉◉ ITALIAN ❦ NOTABLE WINE LIST
020 3409 4777 | 45 Great Queen Street,
Covent Garden, WC2B 5AA
www.margotrestaurant.com
The dining room of this suave Italian looks as sharp as
an Armani suit with its black leather banquettes and
abstract artworks, and the slick service purrs along like
clockwork. The seasonal menu is full of promise, with
classic combinations and masterful home-made pasta.
Chef Massimiliano Vezzi **Seats** 105, Private dining 32
Closed 25 December **Prices from** S £9.50, M £18, D £6
Notes Vegetarian dishes, Children welcome
Read more about Margot on page 14

Massimo Restaurant & Bar
◉ MODERN, TRADITIONAL ITALIAN
020 7998 0555 | Corinthia Hotel London,
10 Northumberland Avenue, WC2N 5AE
www.massimo-restaurant.co.uk
Set in the glitzy Corinthia Hotel (though with its own
street entrance), Massimo's low-lit dining room is a
flamboyant show-stopper with its art deco lines,
candy-striped columns and vast glass globe lights. On
the menu, you'll find bold-flavoured, authentic regional
Italian cooking.
Chef Adriano Cavagnini **Seats** 140, Private dining 20
Open All year **Notes** Vegetarian dishes, Children
welcome

Mon Plaisir
◉ TRADITIONAL FRENCH
020 7836 7243 | 19–21 Monmouth Street,
WC2H 9DD
www.monplaisir.co.uk
Impervious to fads and fashion and about as French
as they come, the original front dining room has
changed little since the 1940s (unapologetically
Parisian bistro). Close-set tables, resolutely French
service and regional wines and cheeses add to the
authenticity and upbeat vibe.
Chef Xavier Dahan **Seats** 100, Private dining 25
Closed Christmas, New Year, Bank holidays
Notes Vegetarian dishes, Children welcome

LONDON WC2

Clos Maggiore

◉◉◉ FRENCH, MEDITERRANEAN 🍾 NOTABLE WINE LIST

020 7379 9696 | 33 King Street, Covent Garden, WC2E 8JD

www.closmaggiore.com

Franco-Italian cooking for true romantics

The official 'world's most romantic restaurant' isn't just a Valentine's Day pitch. Clos Maggiore is in the mood for love all year round, and to that end is got up a little like a stage production of *A Midsummer Night's Dream*, the vertical surfaces covered in foliage and hung with gilded baubles, opening to a glass-ceilinged courtyard area where a filigree mesh of twigs and blossoms is suspended overhead. Don't even think of noticing that none of it is real, it's safe to say it looks charming when darkness falls and the fairy-lights are twinkling.

The cooking is pitched in a metaphorical Alpine pass, halfway between France and Italy, with plenty of the classical underpinnings of the former allied to the bracing simplicity of the latter. Ingredients are well sourced and conscientiously treated, with highly professional presentations adding to the lustre. Duck liver from the Landes in southwest France is pan-roasted and served on an oat biscuit for textural contrast, with garnishes of smoked duck ham and roasted plum in flawless balance, or you may start instead with

octopus salad fragranced with lime zest and basil, accompanied by a pig trotter croquette and some salad leaves. At main course, fish is handled with all due respect, for Irish sea trout in a classic sauce maltaise with crushed new potatoes, braised leeks and a little brown crabmeat, while Scottish cod receives the bourguignon treatment, with potatoes and bacon in red wine sauce. The occasional modernist note creeps surreptitiously in, as in a serving of superlative slow-roast shoulder of milk-fed Pyrénées lamb for two, which comes with goats' cheese gnocchi and swede and prune gratin in a deeply meaty lamb jus, but there is more of old-school richness in serving a chicken leg stuffed with truffled duck liver in Madeira sauce spiked with green peppercorns. If you're a truffle nut, there are truffle-oiled saladings and truffled mash among the sides. Dessert traditionalists will likely be contented with beguilingly pretty Paris-Brest and hazelnut ice cream, but there are more avant-garde propositions at this stage than hitherto, such as Greek yogurt cheesecake with white chocolate and mandarin sorbet. The dessert for two is the caramelised Valrhona chocolate sensation, served with burnt honey ice cream and Armagnac jelly, which should seal the deal on any romantic business (though they do also have a fine digestif list).

Chef Marcellin Marc **Seats** 70, Private dining 23 **Closed** 24–25 December
Prices from S £9.90, M £21.20, D £8.90 **Notes** Vegetarian dishes, No children under 3 years at lunch

The National Dining Rooms
🍽 BRITISH
020 7747 2525 | Sainsbury Wing, The National Gallery, Trafalgar Square, WC2N 5DN
www.peytonandbyrne.co.uk

Overlooking Trafalgar Square from the National Gallery, this sleek all-day operation never struggles to fill its tables, but there's a lot more to the cooking than a simple pit-stop when you're checking out the art. Unfussy modern dishes draw on well-sourced seasonal materials.

Chef Gillan Kingstree **Seats** 84 **Closed** 24–26 December, 1 January **Notes** Vegetarian dishes, Children welcome

The Northall
🍽🍽 BRITISH
020 7321 3100 | Corinthia Hotel London, 10a Northumberland Avenue, WC2N 5AE
www.thenorthall.co.uk

The Northall is dedicated to all things British, with the produce of artisan growers and breeders showcased in the modern national culinary style. Savoury notes in desserts, often a minefield, are mobilised well for rosemary parfait with fig carpaccio, lemon verbena curd and honeycomb.

Chef Adriano Cavagnini **Seats** Private dining 30 **Open** All year **Notes** Vegetarian dishes, Children welcome

The Opera Tavern
🍽🍽 SPANISH, ITALIAN
020 7836 3680 | 23 Catherine Street, Covent Garden, WC2B 5JS
www.operatavern.co.uk

The Tavern is a classic London pub, repurposed as an upscale, two-storeyed tapas joint. You could go three-course but little dishes are the principal bill of fare. They pack a punch: truffle-buttered, panko-crumbed scallop with braised peas and prosciutto has a lot going for it.

Chef Michelle Fourie, Dan Sherlock **Seats** 45 **Closed** 25 December, 1 January **Notes** Vegetarian dishes, Children welcome

Roka Aldwych
🍽🍽 CONTEMPORARY JAPANESE
020 7294 7636 | 71 Aldwych, WC2B 4HN
www.rokarestaurant.com

Roka is characterised by top-drawer ingredients, with the freshest of seafood, to-the-second timings and artful presentation. The speciality is robatayaki: contemporary-style Japanese barbecued food.

Puddings include Japanese pancakes with banana, toffee and black sugar syrup, and cherry blossom ice cream accompanying almond crème brûlée.

Chef Hamish Brown **Closed** 25 December **Notes** Vegetarian dishes, Children welcome

Savoy Grill
🍽🍽 BRITISH **V**
020 7592 1600 | 1 Savoy Hill, Strand, WC2R 0EU
www.gordonramsayrestaurants.com

A handsome art deco room with lustrous panelling, antiqued mirrors, chandeliers and velvet banquettes, the Savoy's iconic Grill has always been the place to see and be seen. Built on classic Anglo-French foundations, the cooking aims for comfort. The wine list raises the bill skywards.

Chef Ben Waugh **Seats** 98, Private dining 40 **Open** All year **Prices from** S £9.50, M £24, D £8 **Notes** Children welcome

Spring
🍽🍽 EUROPEAN
020 3011 0115 | New Wing, Somerset House, Lancaster Place, WC2R 1LA
www.springrestaurant.co.uk

After winning much acclaim at the rustic glasshouse restaurant of Petersham Nurseries, Skye Gyngell has brought her trademark style to the grander stage of Somerset House. The regularly changing Mediterranean menu delivers good-looking plates of seasonal fare with flavours that shine.

Chef Skye Gyngell **Seats** 100, Private dining 36 **Closed** 24–29 December **Notes** Vegetarian dishes, Children welcome

Terroirs
🍽🍽 MEDITERRANEAN, FRENCH
020 7036 0660 | 5 William IV Street, Covent Garden, WC2N 4DW
www.terroirswinebar.com

Terroirs is a buzzy, split-level affair: you enter on the ground floor, the downstairs space is dominated by a big zinc-topped bar, and you can eat where you like. The style is provincial French cooking with a nod towards the Mediterranean.

Chef Michal Chacinski **Seats** 120, Private dining 50 **Closed** Christmas, New Year, Easter and Bank holidays **Notes** Vegetarian dishes, Children welcome

Tredwells

◉◉ MODERN BRITISH 🍷NOTABLE WINE LIST

020 3764 0840 | 4a Upper St Martin's Lane, Covent Garden, WC2H 9NY

www.tredwells.com

Tredwells spreads over three floors with a basement cocktail bar and two airy, retro-looking dining rooms lit by large windows. The menu describes itself as 'modern London cooking' which translates as good-quality British ingredients which have been livened up with globetrotting flavours.

Chef Chantelle Nicholson **Seats** 150, Private dining 60 **Closed** 25–26 December, 1 January **Prices from** S £6.50, M £18, D £6 **Notes** Vegetarian dishes, Children welcome

▶ GREATER LONDON

BARNET

Savoro Restaurant with Rooms

◉ MODERN EUROPEAN, BRITISH

020 8449 9888 | 206 High Street, EN5 5SZ

www.savoro.co.uk

Behind a rather quaint-looking shop front, the restaurant has a cool, contemporary interior. 'Simple execution of good technique' is the kitchen's mantra, with everything made in-house. Puddings are no afterthought when among them might be lemon crème brûlée with raspberries and ginger shortbread.

Chef Yiannis Avramidis **Seats** 100, Private dining 50 **Closed** 1 January, 1 week New Year **Parking** 6 **Notes** Vegetarian dishes, Children welcome

BROMLEY

Chapter One

◉◉◉ MODERN EUROPEAN Ⅴ 🍷NOTABLE WINE LIST

See page 246

HADLEY WOOD

West Lodge Park Hotel

◉ MODERN BRITISH

020 8216 3900 | Cockfosters Road, EN4 0PY

www.bealeshotels.co.uk

The restaurant at this imposing white mansion is named after the portraitist Mary Beale, whose works hang on the walls. It is a stylish room, with well-spaced tables and huge windows looking over the surrounding parkland, and the kitchen team cooks in confident, unfussy style.

Chef Wayne Turner **Seats** 92, Private dining 110 **Open** All year **Parking** 75 **Notes** Vegetarian dishes, Children welcome

HARROW ON THE HILL

Incanto Restaurant

◉ MODERN ITALIAN

020 8426 6767 | The Old Post Office, 41 High Street, HA1 3HT

www.incanto.co.uk

The former Victorian post office is delivering an altogether more sybaritic package to the local community these days, with a relaxed operation comprising a buzzy deli-café with a pizza oven, and a skylit, contemporary split-level restaurant where the main culinary action takes place.

Chef Stelian Scripcariu **Seats** 64, Private dining 30 **Closed** 24–26 December, 1 January, Easter Sunday **Notes** Vegetarian dishes, Children welcome

HEATHROW AIRPORT

La Belle Époque

◉◉◉ MODERN FRENCH 🍷NOTABLE WINE LIST

020 8757 5029 | Sofitel London Heathrow, Terminal 5, Wentworth Drive, London Heathrow Airport, TW6 2GD

www.la-belle-epoque.co

There's something a touch counter-intuitive about looking for seriously good cooking in the environs of Heathrow Airport, but put aside your preconceptions and head over the covered walkway from Terminal 5 into the swanky Sofitel hotel. With its lush hues of purple and royal blue, La Belle Époque offers a suave change of mood from the airport mayhem, with Mayur Nagarale leading the brigade in delivering bi-lingual menus of contemporary French cooking with intriguing Asian accents. Intelligent ideas and sympathetic flavours are there from the off, as typified by a pairing of pan-seared scallops and slow-cooked pork ribs served with pumpkin and ginger purée and marinated cabbage. Mains take in a wealth of choice from herb-crusted monkfish with Dorset crab, broccoli purée and crab bisque, to Irish beef, the fillet glazed with teriyaki and partnered with braised short rib, shiitake mushrooms, roasted potato mousseline and merlot jus. There's much to entertain here, and the kitchen keeps its eye firmly on the ball through to desserts like dark chocolate mousse with spiced blueberry, elderflower and fennel.

Chef Mayur Nagarale **Seats** 88, Private dining 20 **Closed** Christmas, Bank holidays **Prices from** S £9.50, M £19.50, D £9.50 **Parking** 400 **Notes** Vegetarian dishes, Children welcome

BROMLEY
Chapter One

◉◉◉ MODERN EUROPEAN V ⧫ NOTABLE WINE LIST

01689 854848 | Farnborough Common, Locksbottom, BR6 8NF

www.chaptersrestaurants.com

Enterprising chef-patron balancing quality and value

Situated snugly on the suburban cusp of Kent, Andrew McLeish's relaxing venue sees crisply linened tables and gastronomic prints set a refined tone. He has struck a nigh-perfect balance here between assured contemporary cooking with plenty of surprises and the pressing need to offer value. At the centre of operations, the tasting menu offers a tour of the territory in six enterprising stages, but choice on the main carte is extensive enough. Traditional potato gnocchi come with lobster, chestnuts and tarragon for a luxurious opener, among a welter of seafood options, while main courses run to the richly meaty roast red-leg partridge with choucroute, pancetta and liver parfait, as well as cod brandade in mussel butter with a poached egg. There is a deep understanding of combinations throughout and desserts see enlivening compositions such as pumpkin tart with honey-roast granola and cinnamon ice cream, or cardamom pannacotta vividly offset by blood-orange.

Chef Andrew McLeish **Seats** 120, Private dining 55 **Closed** 2–4 January **Parking** 90 **Notes** Children welcome

HEATHROW AIRPORT continued

Hilton London Heathrow Airport Terminal 5
◉ BRITISH, INTERNATIONAL

01753 686860 | Poyle Road, Colnbrook, Slough SL3 0FF

www.heathrowt5.hilton.com

Open all day and located on the mezzanine level of this hotel by Terminal 5, with views over the lobby, The Gallery's long, globally inspired menu features dishes that recall an altogether more pastoral existence, with dishes from the farm, the field and the sea.

Chef Jasbeer Dawar **Seats** 203 **Open** All year **Prices from** S £6, M £16.25, D £6.95 **Parking** 480 **Notes** Vegetarian dishes, Children welcome

Mr Todiwala's Kitchen
◉◉ PORTUGUESE, INDIAN, PAN ASIAN

01753 686860 | Hilton London Heathrow Airport Terminal 5, Poyle Road, Colnbrook, Slough SL3 0FF

www.hilton.com/heathrowt5

Cyrus Todiwala (of Café Spice Namaste) brings pan-Indian style to this airport hotel, in a clinically white atmosphere of lime-washed floors and café-style furnishings. Highly spiced, vividly seasoned food is the perfect antidote to corporate anonymity. Don't overlook the vegetarian dishes.

Chef Cyrus Todiwala, Arun Dev **Seats** 70 **Closed** Christmas **Prices from** S £6.95, M £7.25, D £6.50 **Parking** 480 **Notes** Vegetarian dishes, Children welcome

Vivre Restaurant
◉ INTERNATIONAL

020 8757 5027 | Sofitel London Heathrow, Terminal 5, Wentworth Drive, London Heathrow Airport, TW6 2GD

www.sofitelheathrow.com

The Sofitel at Heathrow Terminal 5 boasts more decent eating than many airport hotels. As an alternative to the fine French goings-on in La Belle Époque, Vivre offers informal dining in an open-plan room of colourful contemporary design, with the kitchen team on view.

Chef Anthony Roy **Seats** 235 **Open** All year **Notes** Vegetarian dishes, Children welcome

KESTON
Herbert's
◉◉ BRITISH, INTERNATIONAL

01689 855501 | 6 Commonside, BR2 6BP

www.thisisherberts.co.uk

Herbert's overlooks some of the 55 hectares of Keston Common and its oak floors, oval-backed chairs and wooden-topped tables create a warm, relaxing

atmosphere. The food is modern with a global spin. There's a wide range of bar snacks, too.

Chef Angela Herbert-Bell **Seats** 52, Private dining 32 **Open** All year **Notes** Vegetarian dishes, Children welcome

KEW
The Glasshouse
◉◉◉ MODERN INTERNATIONAL ⛊ NOTABLE WINE LIST

020 8940 6777 | 14 Station Parade, TW9 3PZ

www.glasshouserestaurant.co.uk

This perennially popular neighbourhood restaurant stands out in the parade of shops near Kew Gardens tube station. From the same stable as the equally high-achieving Chez Bruce in Wandsworth and La Trompette in Chiswick, its pedigree shines through from the off, with unshowy neutral tones, textured walls, white linen, polished-wood floors and colourful abstract artworks giving the space a smart modern sheen. But the main draw here is classy contemporary European cooking that hits the high notes without seeming to try too hard, with head chef Gregory Wellman leading the team in producing prettily presented dishes high on precision, flavour and intelligent simplicity. An eye-catching starter makes its mark, teaming glazed ox cheek with crisp polenta, mushroom purée, pickled red onion and bacon jam. Big, gutsy flavours are similarly on song in main-course lamb rump and belly highlighted with baby artichokes, potato gnocchi, anchovy, rosemary and garlic. Dessert is equally impressive: creamy malt custard with almond ice cream and cocoa nib. The wine list is a corker, and lunch a steal for cooking of this level.

Chef Gregory Wellman **Seats** 60 **Closed** 24–26 December, 1 January **Notes** Vegetarian dishes, Children permitted at lunch only

PINNER
Friends Restaurant
◉ BRITISH

020 8866 0286 | 11 High Street, HA5 5PJ

www.friendsrestaurant.co.uk

Occupying a 400-year-old timbered building in Betjeman's suburban Metro-Land, the decor is intimate and rather romantic, with a low-beamed ceiling and contemporary black leather seats at white linen tables. Local supply lines are strong, while top-grade meat and fish comes from Smithfield and Billingsgate markets.

Chef Stelian Scripcariu **Seats** 40, Private dining 10 **Closed** 25–26 December, 1 January, Bank holidays **Prices from** S £5.75, M £17.95, D £6.50 **Notes** Vegetarian dishes, Children welcome

RICHMOND UPON THAMES
Bacco Restaurant & Wine Bar
◉ ITALIAN
020 8332 0348 | 39–41 Kew Road, TW9 2NQ
www.bacco-restaurant.co.uk

This smart independent Italian next to the Orange Tree Theatre has built a loyal local fan base who come for its lively vibe and straight-talking contemporary cooking. There's a decked terrace on the pavement, and inside it's all bare floorboards, colourful artwork, and convivial tables.

Chef Valerio Cariotti **Seats** 50, Private dining 27 **Closed** Christmas, New Year and Bank holidays **Notes** Vegetarian dishes, Children welcome

Bingham
◉◉◉ MODERN BRITISH ⚲ NOTABLE WINE LIST
020 8940 0902 | 61–63 Petersham Road, TW10 6UT
www.thebingham.co.uk

Occupying a rather handsome pair of Georgian townhouses, with gorgeous Thames views making the covered balcony a hot ticket for alfresco dining during the balmy months, the Bingham sports a boutique look straight out of an interior design magazine. Easy-on-the-eye neutral hues and an ambience of calm set the tone in the mirrored and chandeliered dining room – it's all very glossy indeed, but not so much as to upstage the cooking of Andrew Cole, a skilful chef who coaxes sharply defined flavours and textures from top-drawer materials in his well-conceived modern British creations. A lively starter matches cured trout inventively with mildly pickled white asparagus and lovage pesto. Main-course pork belly comes in an elegant and harmonious composition involving white pudding, samphire, mashed potato and the balancing bitterness of chicory, or if you're up for fish, there might be a fresh and vibrant juxtaposition of salmon with squid, broccoli and ratte potatoes, all lifted by a pungent wasabi butter sauce. After that, a creative reworking of tiramisù partners mascarpone mousse with coffee ice cream and crunchy dehydrated sponge.

Chef Andrew Cole **Seats** 40, Private dining 110 **Open** All year **Parking** 20 **Notes** Vegetarian dishes, Children welcome

La Buvette
◉ FRENCH, MEDITERRANEAN V
020 8940 6264 | 6 Church Walk, TW9 1SN
www.labuvette.co.uk

If the sun is shining on Richmond, La Buvette's courtyard tables come into their own, but this place is a winner all year round when it comes to classic bistro dining. It's down a leafy walkway off the main high street, with closely packed tables.

Chef Buck Carter **Seats** 50 **Closed** 25–26 December, 1 January, Good Friday, Easter Sunday **Prices from** S £5.75, M £14.25, D £5.75 **Notes** Children welcome

The Dysart Petersham
◉◉ TRADITIONAL EUROPEAN V
020 8940 8005 | 135 Petersham Road, Petersham, TW10 7AA
www.thedysartpetersham.co.uk

The Dysart occupies a 1904 Arts and Crafts building with original leaded windows and wooden window frames facing south over Richmond Park. Sunshine streams in on bright days, and a low-key jazz soundtrack floats around the elegant room where dishes of top-class ingredients are served.

Chef Kenneth Culhane **Seats** 50, Private dining 40 **Closed** 25 December **Prices from** S £8.50, M £22.50, D £8.50 **Parking** 30 **Notes** Children accepted until 8pm

The Petersham Hotel
◉◉ MODERN V
020 8940 7471 | Nightingale Lane, TW10 6UZ
www.petershamhotel.co.uk

Built on the side of Richmond Hill in 1865, The Petersham's dining room has river views, comfortable banquette seating and smartly dressed tables. On the great value set menu the choice of desserts include rice pudding beignets with chocolate sauce.

Chef Jean-Didier Gouges **Seats** 90, Private dining 30 **Closed** 25 December **Prices from** S £8, M £26, D £9 **Parking** 45 **Notes** Children welcome

Petersham Nurseries Café
◉◉ MODERN BRITISH, ITALIAN ⚲ NOTABLE WINE LIST
020 8940 5230 | Church Lane, Petersham Road, TW10 7AB
www.petershamnurseries.com

This busy one-off restaurant is a romantically quirky, shabby-chic place, with its dirt floor and mismatched tables and chairs, but that's all part of the fun. The kitchen sends out a weekly changing menu of modern Italian-accented ideas with fresh produce plucked from the garden.

Chef Damian Clisby **Seats** 120, Private dining 20 **Closed** Easter Sunday, 25 December **Notes** Vegetarian dishes, Children welcome

RUISLIP
The Barn Hotel
◉◉ MODERN FRENCH V

01895 636057 | West End Road, HA4 6JB
www.thebarnhotel.co.uk

An expansive modern boutique hotel handy for inward-bound travellers at Heathrow, The Barn might sound rather agricultural, but stands in fact in three acres of attractive landscaped gardens. A Jacobean effect has been created in the dark-panelled dining room, Hawtrey's, to enjoy the bright, modern cooking.

Chef Vic Ramana **Seats** 44, Private dining 20
Open All year **Parking** 50 **Notes** Children welcome

SURBITON
The French Table
◉◉ MODERN EUROPEAN ▮ NOTABLE WINE LIST

020 8399 2365 | 85 Maple Road, KT6 4AW
www.thefrenchtable.co.uk

In a leafy quarter of Surbiton, The French Table is the sort of smart neighbourhood eatery we'd all like on our patch. Well-conceived modern French cooking is delivered via three-course, prix-fixe lunch and evening menus, supplemented by a five-course taster. Pastry skills are top-drawer here.

Chef Eric Guignard **Seats** 73, Private dining 32
Closed 25–26 December, 1–3 January
Notes Vegetarian dishes, Children welcome

TWICKENHAM
A Cena
◉ MODERN ITALIAN

020 8288 0108 | 418 Richmond Road, TW1 2EB
www.acena.co.uk

An informal neighbourhood bistro-style Italian dishing up comforting, authentic cooking. You might choose to open with a stimulating partnership of pan-fried Cornish mackerel fillet with grilled cucumber salad. Elsewhere on the menu, cheeses and wines all speak with an Italian accent.

Chef Nicola Parsons **Seats** 55 **Closed** Christmas and Bank holidays **Notes** Vegetarian dishes, Children welcome

▶ MERSEYSIDE

FRANKBY
Riviera at Hillbark
◉◉ FRENCH, MEDITERRANEAN

0151 625 2400 | Hillbark Hotel & Spa, Royden Park, CH48 1NP
www.rivierarestaurant.co.uk

This all-mod-cons spa hotel features a light-filled Riviera dining room, which embraces a sweeping Mediterranean arc all the way from Nice to Liguria, presented in the grazing format of little and large dishes, courtesy of a super-cool modern brasserie service.

Chef Craig Baker **Seats** 44, Private dining 16
Open All year **Parking** 160 **Notes** Vegetarian dishes, Children welcome

HESWALL
Burnt Truffle
◉ MODERN BRITISH

0151 342 1111 | 106 Telegraph Road, CH60 0AQ
www.burnttruffle.net

The sibling of the Sticky Walnut in Chester, Burnt Truffle follows a very similar and effective contemporary bistro vibe with its roster of intelligently updated classics, and good-looking decor featuring natural textures of wood, stone and slate. Expect inventive, well-executed dishes and bold flavours.

Chef William Cole **Seats** 53 **Closed** 25–26 December
Prices from S £5, M £14, D £6 **Parking** 10
Notes Vegetarian dishes, Children welcome

LIVERPOOL
The Art School Restaurant, Liverpool
◉◉ MODERN INTERNATIONAL V ▮ NOTABLE WINE LIST

0151 230 8600 | 1 Sugnall Street, L7 7EB
www.theartschoolrestaurant.co.uk

Located in the stunning Victorian setting of the lantern room (think immense skylights) of what was once the Home for Destitute Children. Dishes are carefully composed, full of imaginative juxtapositions, and confidently rendered.

Chef Paul Askew **Seats** 48, Private dining 28
Closed 25–26 December, 1–7 January, first week in August **Notes** Children welcome

MERSEYSIDE

Chez Mal Brasserie
◉ MODERN BRITISH
0151 229 5000 | 7 William Jessop Way,
Princes Dock, L3 1QZ
www.malmaison.com
On the landward side of Princes Dock, Malmaison's
first purpose-built hotel is a new landmark for the
maritime city. Echoing the city's industrial heritage,
are the exposed bricks, lighting gantries and air ducts
of the double-height brasserie.

Chef Duncan Anderson **Seats** 87, Private dining 10
Open All year **Notes** Vegetarian dishes, Children
welcome

The London Carriage Works
◉ MODERN BRITISH ▮NOTABLE WINE LIST
0151 705 2222 | Hope Street Hotel,
40 Hope Street, L1 9DA
www.thelondoncarriageworks.co.uk
The stripped-back interior of the old workshop at The
London Carriage Works is a very modern setting with
large windows to give a view of the street action. The
menu makes much of provenance and there's a
satisfying regional flavour to the food.

Chef Mike Kenyon **Seats** 100, Private dining 60
Open All year **Prices from** S £6, M £17.50, D £7
Notes Vegetarian dishes, Children welcome

Mowgli
◉ INDIAN V
0151 708 9356 | 69 Bold Street, L1 4EZ
www.mowglistreetfood.com
Restauranteur Nisha Katona brings Indian street and
domestic food to Liverpool, in a space with rough-
edged Stateside appeal. The menu features high-
concept recreations of popular subcontinental dishes.
There's a vegan menu too.

Chef Gavin Barker **Seats** 64 **Closed** 25–26 December,
1 January **Notes** Children welcome

Panoramic 34
◉ MODERN EUROPEAN
0151 236 5534 | 34th Floor, West Tower,
Brook Street, L3 9PJ
www.panoramic34.com
Panoramic 34 offers stunning views from the 34th floor
– the city, the Mersey flowing out to sea, and the
mountains of North Wales. The lift takes you to a
sleek, modern dining room with floor-to-ceiling
windows and contemporary takes on classic dishes.

Chef Dominic Grundy **Seats** 80 **Closed** 25–26
December, 1 January **Prices from** S £8.50, M £17,
D £8.50 **Notes** Vegetarian dishes, No children under
8 years at dinner

60 Hope Street Restaurant
◉ MODERN BRITISH
0151 707 6060 | 60 Hope Street, L1 9BZ
www.60hopestreet.com
A Liverpool dining fixture for two decades, this popular
Georgian townhouse restaurant still pulls in the
crowds. Occupying a convenient spot close to the
Philharmonic Hall, the unfussy modern decor is
reflected in the simple, seasonal modern food,
which puts an international spin on British ingredients.

Chef Neil Devereux **Seats** 90, Private dining 40
Closed 26 December **Prices from** S £7.95, M £15,
D £7.95 **Notes** Vegetarian dishes, Children welcome

The Vincent Café & Cocktail Bar
◉ INTERNATIONAL V
0151 236 1331 | Walker House, Exchange Flags, L2 3YL
www.vincentcafeandcocktailbar.com
An all-day café and cocktail bar in Exchange Flags, the
landmark 1930s building opposite Liverpool Town Hall,
The Vincent takes a global approach to food. Tapas,
sushi and a range of vegetarian dishes keep the
cocktail crowd happy, with the main menu offering
more ambitious choices.

Chef Don Hilario **Seats** 120, Private dining 12
Open All year **Prices from** S £4.50, M £13.50, D £7
Notes Children welcome

OXTON
Fraiche
◉◉◉◉ MODERN FRENCH, EUROPEAN V ▮NOTABLE WINE LIST
0151 652 2914 | 11 Rose Mount, CH43 5SG
www.restaurantfraiche.com
The discrete frontage of Fraiche, in the Wirral
conservation village of Oxton, gives no clue as to the
feast for the senses that awaits within. Dining chez
Marc Wilkinson is almost as much as a thrilling visual
experience as it is one of taste, with the LED lighting
changing throughout the meal, and projected images
of the seasons helping to set the mood. First and
foremost, the sense most stimulated will be taste, as
Marc and his team deliver a highly personal
experience that takes in contemporary cooking
techniques while never losing sight of the produce
itself – top-drawer ingredients from start to finish. An
opening salvo from the six-course signature menu
might be Nordic smoked salmon, bringing together
bergamot cream and pineapple granité in a compelling
combination, with fresh sea herbs, followed by
celeriac textures with ceps and pears. Fresh fish is
handled with skill, a fabulous piece of brill, say, with
crisp rice noodles and a spot-on dashi broth, plus
smoked yogurt and more sea herbs. Next up, Loire
Valley quail stars in another course with beetroot and
kohlrabi, and a wee bit of black pudding, and among

sweet courses, toasted coconut flakes and foam come with yuzu gel and shards of sesame tuiles. It's a joyful journey of texture and flavour, led by a hands-on chef who can be seen at the pass, ensuring the superb standard is maintained. The wine list has lots of interesting options at the lower end of the price spectrum alongside some outstanding vintages.

Chef Marc Wilkinson **Seats** 12, Private dining 12 **Closed** 25 December, 1 January, 2 weeks August **Notes** No children under 8 years

PORT SUNLIGHT
Riviera at Leverhulme
◉◉ FRENCH, MEDITERRANEAN
0151 644 6655 | Leverhulme Hotel, Central Road, CH62 5EZ
www.rivierarestaurant.co.uk

Lord Leverhulme opened the place in 1907 as a cottage hospital for soap works employees at his Port Sunlight garden village, and who wouldn't find their health restored amid such exquisite art deco surroundings? The French-Mediterranean menu is an experimental mix of small and large plates.

Chef Craig Baker **Seats** 60, Private dining 20 **Open** All year **Parking** 70 **Notes** Vegetarian dishes, Children welcome

SOUTHPORT
Bistrot Vérité
◉◉ FRENCH, INTERNATIONAL
01704 564199 | 7 Liverpool Road, Birkdale, PR8 4AR
www.bistrotverite.co.uk

Marc and Michaela Vérité's place is the essence of a neighbourhood bistro. Tables are closely packed, staff are clued-up, and the place generates a contented buzz. Start perhaps with a daily special such as baked crab thermidor jazzed up with some crispy samphire and croûtes.

Chef Marc Vérité **Seats** 45 **Closed** 1 week February and 1 week August **Notes** Vegetarian dishes, Children welcome

Gusto Trattoria
◉ MODERN ITALIAN
01704 544255 | 58–62 Lord Street, PR8 1QB
www.gustotrattoria.co.uk

Gusto is a trattoria with a nice line in cheerful bonhomie and some good and proper Italian cooking. The open kitchen adds to the buzz of the place. The food does not attempt to reinvent the wheel, just to do things properly.

Chef Giorgio Lamola **Seats** 38 **Open** All year **Notes** Vegetarian dishes, Children welcome

Vincent Hotel
◉◉ MODERN EUROPEAN
01704 883800 | 98 Lord Street, PR8 1JR
www.thevincenthotel.com

The V Café and Sushi Bar at this stylish contemporary hotel is the place to be in the evening, with lights dimmed and candles lit. Tables are closely packed and floor-to-ceiling windows look onto bustling Lord Street (alfresco dining is an option).

Chef Andrew Carter **Seats** 85, Private dining 30 **Open** All year **Prices from** S £5, M £13.50, D £6.50 **Parking** 50 **Notes** Vegetarian dishes, Children welcome

THORNTON HOUGH
The Lawns Restaurant at Thornton Hall
◉◉ MODERN EUROPEAN **V**
0151 336 3938 | Neston Road, CH63 1JF
www.lawnsrestaurant.com

This grand spa hotel on the Wirral peninsula has an unerring sense for an occasion. Head to The Lawns dining room for the full culinary package, where, amid a setting of teardrop chandeliers and ornate wood carvings, the modern British cooking makes very good use of local produce using modern techniques.

Chef Chad Hughes **Seats** 45, Private dining 24 **Open** All year **Prices from** S £10, M £22, D £11 **Parking** 250 **Notes** Children welcome

▶ NORFOLK

BAWBURGH
The Kings Head Bawburgh
◉◉ MODERN BRITISH
01603 744977 | Harts Lane, NR9 3LS
www.kingsheadbawburgh.co.uk

The pub itself dates from the early 17th century, but the king in question is Edward VII (born 1841), chosen for his reputation as a bon viveur. There are real ales and the likes of fish and chips up for grabs, plus low oak beams, real fires and plenty of character. Its reputation as a dining pub is confirmed by its well-judged output.

Chefs Jake Armes, Geoff Smith, Amber Burchinshaw, Tim Abbot **Seats** 62, Private dining 20 **Open** All year **Prices from** S £6, M £13, D £8 **Parking** 30 **Notes** Vegetarian dishes, Children welcome

BLAKENEY

The Blakeney Hotel

◉ MODERN BRITISH **V**

01263 740797 | The Quay, NR25 7NE

www.blakeneyhotel.co.uk

Those who like to be by the sea need look no further: this is in a perfect spot on the quay, with magnificent views over the estuary to Blakeney Point Area of Outstanding Natural Beauty. Well-sourced raw materials underpin the cooking.

Chef Martin Sewell **Seats** 100, Private dining 80 **Closed** 25–27 December **Parking** 60 **Notes** Children welcome

Morston Hall

◉◉◉◉ MODERN BRITISH **V** ⚑NOTABLE WINE LIST

01263 741041 | Morston, Holt, NR25 7AA

www.morstonhall.com

Galton and Tracy Blackiston's 17th-century country house opposite Morston Quay is truly an idyllic escape from the daily grind. The old manor is handsome enough without being overly grand, and the tone is set by the hosts who are passionate about the area and its magnificent produce. The conservatory dining room makes a soothing setting, all the better when the sun is up and the French doors are open. Dinner is served at a single setting, so it's aperitifs at 7pm before heading through to the dining room at 8pm where a single menu awaits. The seven-course tasting menu presents refined classical technique with contemporary verve and pretty presentation. An opening salvo might be smoked haddock in a light velouté, before a Scottish langoustine with Crown Prince squash. Those famous Brancaster mussels might partner poached wild brill, in a light flavoursome broth, while roe deer arrives in a rich sauce grand veneur with salt-baked celeriac and hen of the woods mushrooms. A couple of sweet courses are no less inventive; yogurt, yuzu and green tea, say, followed by Yorkshire rhubarb with white chocolate and honeycomb. Add cheese from the trolley if you can. There's no rush, it all happens at a civilised pace, until eventually it's time for coffee and the Morston Hall chocolate box. Sunday lunch is a cut above – four courses plus coffee and home-made chocolates, and afternoon is a treat if you've booked in advance. The wine list covers the globe and has lots of gems to find among its pages, and you're in safe hands if you opt for the wine flight.

Chef Galton Blackiston, Greg Anderson **Seats** 50 **Closed** 3 days at Christmas, January **Parking** 50 **Notes** Children welcome

BRANCASTER STAITHE

The White Horse

◉◉ MODERN BRITISH

01485 210262 | PE31 8BY

www.whitehorsebrancaster.co.uk

Here, the big skies of north Norfolk can be viewed over platefuls of fantastic regional produce, a sight made even better from a table in the refurbished conservatory area. In a location such as this, diners are bound to have fish and seafood in mind.

Chef Fran Hartshorne **Seats** 100 **Open** All year **Prices from** S £7.50, M £13.50, D £6 **Parking** 30 **Notes** Vegetarian dishes, Children welcome

COLTISHALL

Norfolk Mead Hotel

◉◉ MODERN BRITISH

01603 737531 | Church Lane, NR12 7DN

www.norfolkmead.co.uk

This handsome old house in the heart of the Norfolk Broads is looking dapper with its contemporary, country-chic finish. The smart restaurant follows the theme, seamlessly blending period features with an uncluttered style – white walls, abstract artworks, and simple flower arrangements.

Chef Anna Duttson, Damien Woollard **Seats** 40, Private dining 22 **Open** All year **Parking** 45 **Notes** Vegetarian dishes, Children welcome

CROMER

The Grove Cromer

◉◉ BRITISH, SEAFOOD

01263 512412 | 95 Overstrand Road, NR27 0DJ

www.thegrovecromer.co.uk

A private path leads through woodland to the beach from this north Norfolk hotel, a substantial white Georgian house partly covered in creepers. In the restaurant, it's all about clear, fresh flavours. You might try Norfolk cheeses with quince jelly as an alternative to dessert.

Chef Reis Khalil **Seats** 48, Private dining 30 **Closed** January (phone to check) **Parking** 15 **Notes** Vegetarian dishes, Children welcome

Sea Marge Hotel

◉◉ MODERN BRITISH

01263 579579 | 16 High Street, Overstrand, NR27 0AB

www.mackenziehotels.com

The Sea Marge is a family-run Edwardian hotel of great charm with terraced lawns sitting just above the coastal path, and glorious marine views from the panelled dining room. Chocolate and ginger terrine with salted caramel ice cream makes a satisfying dessert option.

Chef Rene Ilupar **Seats** 80, Private dining 40 **Open** All year **Prices from** S £7, M £13.50, D £6.25 **Parking** 50 **Notes** Vegetarian dishes, Children welcome

The White Horse Overstrand
◉◉ MODERN EUROPEAN, BRITISH
01263 579237 | 34 High Street, Overstrand, NR27 0AB
www.whitehorseoverstrand.co.uk

In a pretty village a short walk from the sea, this Victorian inn's restaurant occupies a converted barn, given a modern look within flint walls and oak ceiling trusses. The kitchen's a hive of industry, making everything on the premises, from breads to ice creams.

Chef Nathan Boon **Seats** 80, Private dining 40 **Open** All year **Parking** 6 **Notes** Vegetarian dishes, Children welcome

GREAT YARMOUTH
The Copper Kitchen
◉◉ MODERN BRITISH
01493 843490 | Andover House,
27–30 Camperdown, NR30 3JB
www.andoverhouse.co.uk

This boutique-styled Victorian terrace is a rather cool restaurant filled with blond wood with nary a tablecloth in sight. It's a bright and breezy environment for the contemporary cooking.

Chef Dave Nash **Seats** 22, Private dining 18 **Closed** 24–25 December **Prices from** S £5.25, M £12.25, D £4.75 **Notes** Vegetarian dishes, No children

Imperial Hotel
◉ MODERN BRITISH **V**
01493 842000 | North Drive, NR30 1EQ
www.imperialhotel.co.uk

Generations of the Mobbs family have run the Imperial since the 1930s, when one of its attractions was being seated at separate tables. Today frosted glass panels demonstrate that separate tables are still the elevated norm. Dishes from the brasserie repertoire feature.

Chef Peter Clarke **Seats** 60, Private dining 140 **Closed** 24–28 and 31 December **Prices from** S £5.95, M £11.50, D £4.95 **Parking** 45 **Notes** Vegetarian dishes, Children welcome

The Prom Hotel
◉ CONTEMPORARY BRITISH **V**
01493 842308 | 77 Marine Parade, NR30 2DH
www.promhotel.co.uk

Overlooking the seafront, Strollers is its newly extended, attractively furnished restaurant, with a bar,

perfectly positioned for pre-meal drinks. Yarmouth's trawler fleet has all but disappeared, but fish and seafood still have their place on the menu.

Chef Leigh Schofield **Seats** 40 **Open** All year **Prices from** S £6.50, M £10.75, D £6.40 **Parking** 30 **Notes** Children welcome

GRIMSTON
Congham Hall Country House Hotel
◉◉ MODERN BRITISH, EUROPEAN **V**
01485 600250 | Lynn Road, PE32 1AH
www.conghamhallhotel.co.uk

This Georgian house has gorgeous gardens, a swish spa and a restaurant full of period charm. A herb garden produces an astonishing 400 varieties. French windows look onto the garden, while the cooking that is gently modern in outlook.

Chef James O'Connor **Seats** 50, Private dining 18 **Open** All year **Parking** 50 **Notes** Children welcome

HEACHAM
Heacham Manor Hotel
◉ MEDITERRANEAN, EUROPEAN
01485 536030 | Hunstanton Road, PE31 7JX
www.heacham-manor.co.uk

The wide-open skies of Norfolk's fabulous coast make Heacham Manor an attractive prospect, and the place even comes with a coastal golf course. Built as an Elizabethan manor, the hotel has been brought smartly up-to-date and the Mulberry Restaurant extended and modernised.

Chef Richard Millar **Seats** 65, Private dining 16 **Open** All year **Prices from** S £5.25, M £13.95, D £5 **Parking** 30 **Notes** Vegetarian dishes, Children welcome

HETHERSETT
Park Farm Hotel
◉ MODERN BRITISH
01603 810264 | NR9 3DL
www.parkfarm-hotel.co.uk

Park Farm Hotel and its spa and conference facilities are surrounded by 200 acres of beautiful open countryside. The contemporary, open-plan Seasons Restaurant looks out over the gardens while uniformed staff deliver the kitchen's well-presented and well-timed modern British fare.

Chef David Bell **Seats** 60, Private dining 60 **Open** All year **Parking** 150 **Notes** Vegetarian dishes

HOLT

The Lawns

◉ MODERN EUROPEAN

01263 713390 | 26 Station Road, NR25 6BS
www.lawnshotelholt.co.uk

A small hotel dating from Georgian times, The Lawns offers a number of dining options: bar, conservatory, restaurant and south-facing garden. It's a warm and friendly place, reflected in a menu of largely comfortingly reassuring dishes pinned on East Anglian produce.

Chef Leon Brookes, Adam Kobialka **Seats** 60 **Open** All year **Prices from** S £6, M £12, D £6 **Parking** 18 **Notes** Vegetarian dishes, Children welcome

The Pheasant Hotel & Restaurant

◉ MODERN BRITISH

01263 588382 | Coast Road, Kelling, NR25 7EG
www.pheasanthotelnorfolk.co.uk

With the stretching beaches and marshland of the north Norfolk coast on hand, The Pheasant is plumb in one of the country's most fashionable resort areas. Cooking is modern British, with seafood a strong suit. Afternoon teas are an abiding part of The Pheasant's appeal.

Chef Matthew Gibson **Seats** 78, Private dining 30 **Open** All year **Prices from** S £7, M £14, D £6.50 **Parking** 50 **Notes** Vegetarian dishes, Children welcome

HUNSTANTON

Caley Hall Hotel

◉ MODERN BRITISH

01485 533486 | Old Hunstanton Road, PE36 6HH
www.caleyhallhotel.co.uk

Built around a manor dating from 1648, Caley Hall is a short walk to the wide beaches on The Wash, a twitcher's paradise. Its restaurant, in a former stable block, is a relaxing-looking room. It's a popular place offering precisely cooked East Anglian produce.

Chef Tom Heffer **Seats** 80 **Closed** 23–26 December, 7–18 January **Prices from** S £5.95, M £12.50, D £4.95 **Parking** 50 **Notes** Vegetarian dishes, Children welcome

The Neptune Restaurant with Rooms

◉◉◉ MODERN EUROPEAN **V**

01485 532122 | 85 Old Hunstanton Road, Old Hunstanton, PE36 6HZ
www.theneptune.co.uk

A former coaching inn just a short hop from the coast, The Neptune still has the look of an old inn, with its creeper-covered Georgian facade, but it's a top-notch restaurant with rooms these days.

Travellers are still met warmly by the hands-on Jacki, whose husband is the prodigiously talented Kevin Mangeolles. Much of the glorious regional bounty around these parts finds its way into Kevin's kitchen and onto a fixed-price carte and full-works tasting menu. The dining room is a smart, intimate space, with a neutral colour scheme and tables dressed in white linen. The cooking has its roots in sound classical thinking, with modern presentations, loads of good ideas and those local ingredients to the fore. Brancaster lobster, for example, in a mousse with star anise, or Norfolk quail with charred onion and pickled sultanas. Main course loin and shoulder of lamb is a fabulous summer offering, while a fishy number might be fillets of red mullet with broad beans and wild garlic. Peach is the centre of attention in a dessert with pistachio savarin and zesty lemon curd. The smart wine list has good options by the glass and half bottle.

Chef Kevin Mangeolles **Seats** 24 **Closed** January, 1 week May, 3 weeks November and 26 December **Parking** 6 **Notes** No children under 10 years

KING'S LYNN

Bank House

◉ MODERN BRITISH

01553 660492 | King's Staithe Square, PE30 1RD
www.thebankhouse.co.uk

This Georgian townhouse hotel on the quayside in the town's cultural district was once a bank. Inside, a trio of smart dining rooms have polished tables, candlelight and music, and trade in modernised traditional British fare. Try the lemon tart and raspberry sorbet for dessert.

Chef Stuart Deuchars **Seats** 100, Private dining 40 **Open** All year **Prices from** S £6, M £13, D £3.50 **Notes** Vegetarian dishes, Children welcome

The Duke's Head Hotel

◉ MODERN BRITISH

01553 774996 | 5–6 Tuesday Market Place, PE30 1JS
www.dukesheadhotel.com

The hotel occupies a prime spot on the main square, its frontage and period features making a fine first impression. There's a bistro-style restaurant called Gryffens and a fine-dining option, Turners Restaurant. The latter is an elegant space with a feeling of old meeting new.

Chef Trevor Clark **Seats** 52, Private dining 20 **Open** All year **Prices from** S £4.95, M £12.95, D £5.50 **Parking** 40 **Notes** Vegetarian dishes, Children welcome

LODDON
The Loddon Swan
◉◉ MODERN BRITISH
01508 528039 | 23 Church Plain, NR14 6LX
www.theloddonswan.co.uk

Close to the stunning River Chet, this 18th-century coaching inn reopened in 2012 after a refurbishment that retained its traditional charm while bringing it into the 21st century. While much is made of local sourcing of ingredients, the menu mixes modern British with Mediterranean classics.

Chef Jason Wright **Seats** 70, Private dining 30 **Closed** 26 December **Parking** 15 **Notes** Vegetarian dishes, Children welcome

NORTH WALSHAM
Beechwood Hotel
◉◉ MODERN BRITISH V
01692 403231 | 20 Cromer Road, NR28 0HD
www.beechwood-hotel.co.uk

Hospitality is top of the agenda at this charming country-house hotel, with hands-on owners and plenty of staff ensuring that guests are well looked after. The kitchen sources most ingredients from within 10 miles of the hotel and sends out contemporary British ideas.

Chef Steven Norgate **Seats** 60 **Open** All year **Prices from** S £7.25, M £15.50, D £5.95 **Parking** 20 **Notes** Children welcome

NORWICH
Benedicts
◉◉◉ MODERN BRITISH V
01603 926080 | 9 St Benedicts Street, NR2 4PE
www.restaurantbenedicts.com

Norwich is now firmly established on the UK's foodie firmament thanks to Benedicts, a switched-on operation where pared-back, Scandi-chic looks tick all the boxes of a big-city venue and make a suitably modernist setting for chef-patron Richard Bainbridge's innovative contemporary cooking. Devotees of *Great British Menu* may remember that Bainbridge was the 2015 winner, so diners can be assured of exciting 21st-century food that's brimful of revelations, courtesy of stimulating combinations of excellent materials. A starter of moist and super-fresh crisp-skinned mackerel is balanced with bracing bursts of cucumber, sour apple and dill ahead of a main course that sings of spring: hay-baked Blickling Hall Estate hogget matched with spring greens, chervil root and wild garlic. Otherwise, there may be dry-aged Gressingham duck with salted plums, shiitake mushrooms, red onions and thyme sauce. To finish, the nursery comforts of Nanny Bush's trifle with milk jam passed muster with the exacting standards of the

WI ladies on the telly and remains as a signature finisher, or you might go for an equally classic and perfectly rendered lemon tart, its heavenly pastry encasing a zingy lemon custard. It all comes via a seasonal à la carte, six- or eight-course tasting options, or a daily changing set lunch which offers remarkable value.

Chef Richard Bainbridge **Seats** 40, Private dining 14 **Closed** 31 July to 15 August, 24 December to 9 January **Notes** Children welcome

Best Western Annesley House Hotel
◉◉ MODERN BRITISH
01603 624553 | 6 Newmarket Road, NR2 2LA
www.bw-annesleyhouse.co.uk

Standing just outside the old city walls, Annesley's landscaped gardens impart a country-house feel, and an old vine supplies sweet red grapes to garnish the cheese plates. Perhaps try the roast guinea fowl with confit garlic and braised baby gem.

Chef Saul King **Seats** 30 **Closed** Christmas **Prices from** S £7.50, M £19.50, D £6.75 **Parking** 29 **Notes** Vegetarian dishes, Children welcome

Brasteds
◉◉ MODERN EUROPEAN
01508 491112 | Manor Farm Barns, Fox Road, Framingham Pigot, NR14 7PZ
www.brasteds.co.uk

In the village of Framingham Pigot, Brasteds occupies a converted barn, a charming room of raftered ceiling, oak floor and brick walls. Sure-footed experience brings the complex food together. Starter might be poached ray wing with grape gel, steamed clams and chorizo and truffle cream.

Chef Chris Busby **Seats** 40, Private dining 16 **Open** All year **Parking** 50 **Notes** Vegetarian dishes, Children welcome

Maids Head Hotel
◉◉ MODERN BRITISH
01603 209955 | Tombland, NR3 1LB
www.maidsheadhotel.co.uk

The brick-built hotel in the city centre lays claim to being the UK's oldest, having been feeding and watering East Anglian travellers for 800 years. Dining goes on in a glassed-in courtyard with a quarry-tiled floor and simple wooden tables.

Chef Magic Pomierny **Seats** 100, Private dining 130 **Open** All year **Prices from** S £8, M £17, D £8 **Parking** 60 **Notes** Vegetarian dishes, Children welcome

The Old Rectory

◉◉ MODERN BRITISH

01603 700772 | 103 Yarmouth Road,
Thorpe St Andrew, NR7 0HF
www.oldrectorynorwich.com

Creepers cover the large Georgian house at The Old Rectory, giving the impression the garden is attempting to reclaim the land – but this red-brick former rectory is here to stay. The daily changing menu has a good showing of regional produce.

Chef James Perry **Seats** 18 **Closed** Christmas, New Year **Parking** 16 **Notes** Vegetarian dishes, Children welcome

Roger Hickman's Restaurant

◉◉◉ MODERN BRITISH **V** 🍷 NOTABLE WINE LIST

01603 633522 | 79 Upper St Giles Street, NR2 1AB
www.rogerhickmansrestaurant.com

The location, in a quiet cul-de-sac near the cathedral, may be discreet, but Roger Hickman's calm and comfortable restaurant is a popular place, a refined and elegant setting for original artworks, smartly laid tables, and confident, attentive service. The modern British cooking is equally refined, stylishly presented and demonstrating a fine grasp of technique and seasonal opportunities. The wine list is well worth exploring, and fixed-price menus and tasting options are offered at both lunch and dinner. You might begin with a heritage carrot salad with lemon yogurt and dukkah crumb, or blowtorched mackerel with mackerel mousse, the flavours of gooseberry and horseradish a sharp contrast to the fish. Main course roast partridge comes with truffle mash, parsnips, sprouts and bacon, while butternut squash gnocchi with shiitake mushroom, cavolo nero and sage and chestnut crumb is an excellent wintery vegetarian option. A dessert of forced rhubarb with blood orange cake, custard and ginger ice cream shows spring is reassuringly just over the horizon.

Chef Roger Hickman **Seats** 40, Private dining 18 **Closed** 2 weeks January **Notes** Children welcome

St Giles House Hotel

◉◉ MODERN BRITISH

01603 275180 | 41–45 St Giles Street, NR2 1JR
www.stgileshousehotel.com

Beyond the hotel's magnificent pillared facade is a palatial interior of marble floors, oak panelling and elaborate plaster ceilings, all sharpened with stylish contemporary flair. The SGH Bistro is the setting for the kitchen's appealing repertoire of uncomplicated, up-to-date cooking.

Chef Michael Mann **Seats** 50, Private dining 50 **Open** All year **Parking** 24 **Notes** Vegetarian dishes, Children welcome

Stower Grange

◉ MODERN BRITISH

01603 860210 | 40 School Road, Drayton, NR8 6EF
www.stowergrange.co.uk

The ivy-covered country house in its own wooded grounds a few miles out of Norwich is a charming family-run hotel where contemporary cooking based on quality ingredients aims to satisfy rather than startle.

Chef Lee Parrette **Seats** 25, Private dining 100 **Closed** 26–30 December **Parking** 40 **Notes** Vegetarian dishes, Children welcome

Thailand Restaurant

◉ THAI **V**

01603 700444 | 9 Ring Road, Thorpe St Andrew, NR7 0XJ
www.thailandrestaurantnorwich.co.uk

Plants and hanging baskets add dash to the exterior of this well-established restaurant. Inside, the decor is as busy as the bamboo-framed upholstered seats are busy with customers: drapes over the windows, statues in niches, friezes on beams and lots of greenery.

Chef Anan Sirphas, Sampoin Jukjan **Seats** 55 **Closed** 25 December **Parking** 25 **Notes** No children under 5 years

Warwick Street Social

◉◉ MODERN BRITISH

01603 627687 | 2 Warwick Street, NR2 3LD
www.warwickstsocial.co.uk

The former Mad Moose pub, in Norwich's Golden Triangle, is reborn in contemporary style as the WSS. The Norfolk-inspired British cuisine is pretty modern too: sea-salt crackling belly pork with charred tenderloin. For a lip-smacking finale, choose dark chocolate fondant with salted caramel purée and amaretti ice cream.

Chefs Daniel Smith, Alex Clare **Seats** 95, Private dining 45 **Closed** 25 December **Prices from** S £7, M £12.50, D £6.50 **Notes** Vegetarian dishes, Children welcome

SHERINGHAM

Dales Country House Hotel

◉◉ BRITISH, EUROPEAN

01263 824555 | Lodge Hill, Upper Sheringham, NR26 8TJ
www.mackenziehotels.com

This step-gabled Victorian mansion has period charm in spades, although the cooking in Upchers restaurant takes a rather more contemporary European view of things. With the briny so near, a fillet of sea bass is a good bet, or try lamb kofta with spiced aubergine caviar.

Chef Rene Ilupar **Seats** 70, Private dining 40 **Open** All year **Prices from** S £6, M £12.95, D £6.25 **Parking** 50 **Notes** Vegetarian dishes, Children welcome

SNETTISHAM
The Rose & Crown
◉ MODERN BRITISH
01485 541382 | Old Church Road, PE31 7LX
www.roseandcrownsnettisham.co.uk

The interior of this country inn is all twisty passageways, low beams, flagged floors, and a busy bar. It isn't unknown for locals to dine here three or four times a week, returning for the likes of seared scallops with cauliflower and tonka bean purée.

Chef Jamie Clarke **Seats** 160, Private dining 30 **Open** All year **Prices from** S £5.50, M £12.50, D £4 **Parking** 70 **Notes** Vegetarian dishes, Children welcome

STOKE HOLY CROSS
The Wildebeest
◉◉ MODERN EUROPEAN
01508 492497 | 82–86 Norwich Road, NR14 8QJ
www.thewildebeest.co.uk

Set in a tranquil village, The Wildebeest continues to be a haven of refined eating. The interior is rich with beams, aged floorboards, wood-topped tables and leather-clad dining chairs. Much produce comes from a nearby farm.

Chef Daniel Smith, Charlie Wilson **Seats** 80 **Closed** 25–26 December **Prices from** S £7.95, M £16.95, D £7.25 **Parking** 30 **Notes** Vegetarian dishes, Children welcome

THORNHAM
The Chequers Inn
◉ MODERN BRITISH
01485 512229 | High Street, PE36 6LY
www.chequersinnthornham.com

This pretty village inn dates back to the 16th century and its location on the north Norfolk coast makes it a popular spot for people heading to the beautiful beaches of Brancaster and Holkham. Food is served throughout the pub, as well as a large heated terrace.

Chef Shayne Wood **Seats** 70, Private dining 14 **Open** All year **Notes** Children welcome

The Lifeboat Inn
◉ TRADITIONAL BRITISH V
01485 512236 | Ship Lane, PE36 6LT
www.lifeboatinnthornham.com

Down a quiet lane behind the church, this charming, white-painted inn has been providing hospitality for more than 500 years. The terrace is a tranquil spot to enjoy a pint in summer, while the coastal location means local seafood gets a strong showing.

Chef Mike Smith **Seats** 50, Private dining 18 **Open** All year **Parking** 60 **Notes** Children welcome

TITCHWELL
Titchwell Manor Hotel
◉◉◉ MODERN EUROPEAN
See pages 258–259

WIVETON
Wiveton Bell
◉◉ MODERN BRITISH
01263 740101 | The Green, Blakeney Road, NR25 7TL
www.wivetonbell.co.uk

An authentic Georgian country pub on the village green, the Bell is near Blakeney and the salt marshes of north Norfolk and is done up in light and airy modern fashion. The cooking has a pleasingly traditional air about it.

Chef Simon Haynes **Seats** 60 **Closed** 25 December **Parking** 5 **Notes** Vegetarian dishes, Children welcome

WYMONDHAM
Number Twenty Four Restaurant
◉ MODERN BRITISH
01953 607750 | 24 Middleton Street, NR18 0AD
www.number24.co.uk

Grade II listed, this comfortably furnished restaurant has been hewn out of a row of Georgian cottages and it retains a smart and homely feel to it. The atmosphere is welcoming, with efficient, friendly staff, and the regularly changing, thoughtfully constructed menus are stylish and appealing

Chef Jonathan Griffin **Seats** 50, Private dining 50 **Closed** 26 Decemnber, 1 January **Notes** Vegetarian dishes, Children welcome

▶ # NORTHAMPTONSHIRE
DAVENTRY
Fawsley Hall Hotel & Spa
◉◉ MODERN BRITISH
01327 892000 | Fawsley, NN11 3BA
www.handpickedhotels.co.uk/fawsleyhall

Plantagenets, Tudors and Georgians all played a part in the beguiling architectural mishmash seen today, and it screams 'grand' with its oak panels, stone arches and the Cedar Restaurant. However, a feeling of intimacy pervades the place, and the kitchen deals in imaginative 21st-century ideas.

Chef Richard Walker **Seats** 70, Private dining 20 **Open** All year **Prices from** S £11.50, M £16.50, D £10.50 **Parking** 140 **Notes** Vegetarian dishes, Children welcome

Northamptonshire continues on page 260

TITCHWELL
Titchwell Manor Hotel
◉◉◉ MODERN EUROPEAN
01485 210221 | PE31 8BB
www.titchwellmanor.com

Extensive repertoire in a delightful coastal hotel

Margaret and Ian Snaith celebrate 30 years at the helm of Titchwell Manor in 2018, a longevity that suggests they have come to think of the place as home. And why wouldn't they? Beautifully positioned on the north Norfolk coast, where stretching sands spiked with marram grass unroll to the sea and the great pale sky, it is a location worth travelling for. First-timers may be forgiven for thinking that the name of the place suggests a grandiose pile, and yet the hotel is built around a red-brick Victorian farmhouse, the interiors of which have been brought alive against the monochrome vistas with assertive patterns and colour combinations in fabrics and carpets.

When it comes to dining, it's worth heading to the Conservatory, an expansive tiled space built out into a glassed extension that looks over the walled garden, where much of the kitchen's produce is grown. The prospect is a treat in fair weather or not so fair, and staff run the place with confidence and flair. Head chef Chris Mann cooks to a number of menu formats, with Sunday brunch (help yourself from the laden starter and

dessert displays, with a main course served at the table) and afternoon tea solid fixtures of the repertoire.

The adventurous modern stuff is furnished forth on the Conversation Menu, where proceedings might open with a resonantly rich Epoisses quiche garnished with crisped shallots and apple chutney, or perhaps a restorative winter duck broth containing hispi cabbage, confit potato, chestnuts and frozen foie gras. Pedigree meats such as venison from Houghton Estate and grouse, the latter appearing as the breast and confit leg with a giblet black pudding, turnips, damsons and the scent of pine, are the mainstays of main courses, but fish is imaginatively handled too, as when turbot turns up à la Véronique, with salsify, rainbow kale, golden raisins and caper oil. For the grand finale, it could be golden Titchwell trifle, a groundbreaking version incorporating apple, honey and white chocolate, or there may be a Caribbean-inspired serving of pineapple – frozen ring, carpaccio and a fritter – with Jamaica ginger cake.

For those who prefer to keep their feet on culinary terra firma, a Classics menu offers the likes of Brancaster mussels in marinière guise, shepherd's pie made with lamb shoulder and duchesse potatoes, and lemon meringue pie. Less formal dining takes place in the Eating Rooms, but Titchwell is a delight throughout.

Chef Eric Snaith, Chris Mann **Seats** 80 **Open** All year **Prices from** S £7, M £14, D £7 **Parking** 50 **Notes** Vegetarian dishes, Children welcome

NORTHAMPTONSHIRE

KETTERING
Barton Hall Hotel
◎◎ TRADITIONAL BRITISH
01536 515505 | Barton Road, Barton Seagrave,
NN15 6SG
www.bartonhall.com

A charming hotel surrounded by splendid gardens and a Grade I listed orangery, Barton Hall dates from the 16th-century. The hotel's Vines Brasserie is a welcoming place with informal service matched by unclothed tables and modern background music to create a relaxed setting.

Chef Carl Long **Seats** 70, Private dining 50 **Open** All year **Parking** 150 **Notes** Vegetarian dishes, Children welcome

Kettering Park Hotel & Spa
◎ MODERN BRITISH
01536 416666 | Kettering Parkway, NN15 6XT
www.thwaites.co.uk

Kettering Park belies its business park location by having a degree of charming personality. The menu deals in the international stalwarts of today, but turned out with proficiency and style, and there is a buffet featuring local produce.

Chef Steven White **Seats** 90, Private dining 40 **Closed** Christmas, New Year (excluding residents and pre-booked) **Prices from** S £5.95, M £14.50, D £6.95 **Parking** 200 **Notes** Vegetarian dishes, Children welcome

Rushton Hall Hotel and Spa
◎◎◎ MODERN BRITISH
See opposite

NASSINGTON
The Queens Head Inn
◎ MODERN BRITISH
01780 784006 | 54 Station Road, PE8 6QB
www.queensheadnassington.co.uk

A delightful mellow stone inn with a relaxed vibe and a solid line in muscular modern cooking built on locally sourced ingredients. A charcoal-fired Josper grill takes pride of place in the kitchen.

Chef Mark Baker **Seats** 40, Private dining 70 **Open** All year **Prices from** S £5, M £11, D £5.50 **Parking** 45 **Notes** Vegetarian dishes, Children welcome

NORTHAMPTON
The Hopping Hare
◎◎ MODERN BRITISH V
01604 580090 | 18 Hopping Hill Gardens, Duston,
NN5 6PF
www.hoppinghare.com

The Hopping Hare is a 21st-century venue: the bar offers a stylish place to meet, while the restaurant is informal and atmospheric. The culinary output changes with the seasons, with chef's specials every day, and has been described as 'modern British with a playful twist'.

Chef Grant Wentzel **Seats** 80 **Open** All year **Prices from** S £6.95, M £14.95, D £4.95 **Parking** 40 **Notes** Children welcome

OUNDLE
The Talbot Hotel
◎ BRITISH
01832 273621 | New Street, PE8 4EA
www.thetalbot-oundle.com

If The Talbot looks ancient, that's maybe because its stone facades, mullioned windows and grand timber staircase were recycled from Fotheringhay Castle in the 17th century. Nowadays it does a brisk trade as a hotel, coffee house and eatery, aka the restaurant.

Chef Christian Koroma **Seats** 48, Private dining 64 **Open** All year **Parking** 30 **Notes** Vegetarian dishes, Children welcome

WEEDON BEC
Narrow Boat at Weedon
◎◎ MODERN BRITISH
01327 340333 | Stowe Hill, A5 Watling Street,
NN7 4RZ
www.narrowboatatweedon.co.uk

It's not actually on the water, but plenty of boats moor by this popular gastro pub. It offers watery rural views, and the kitchen offers everything from pub classics and stone-baked pizzas, to up-to-date ideas in the restaurant.

Chef Kirsty Collins **Seats** 100, Private dining 40 **Closed** 26 December **Parking** 40 **Notes** Vegetarian dishes, Children welcome

WHITTLEBURY
Whittlebury Hall
◎◎ MODERN BRITISH, EUROPEAN
01327 857857 | NN12 8QH
www.whittleburyhall.co.uk

This plush neo-Georgian hotel with a Rolls Royce of a spa and a sophisticated restaurant is just a Ferrari's roar away from Silverstone. While the slick front-of-house team help diners relax in the slow lane, the kitchen hits top gear with modern British cooking.

Chef Craig Rose **Seats** 32, Private dining 10 **Closed** selected dates at Christmas, 31 December **Parking** 460 **Notes** Vegetarian dishes

KETTERING
Rushton Hall Hotel and Spa
◉◉◉ MODERN BRITISH
01536 713001 | Rushton, NN14 1RR
www.rushtonhall.com

Stately surroundings for a contemporary repertoire

The Tresham Restaurant – named after the former owners – is the main formal dining room (the 1593 Brasserie is the more informal dining option), with acres of splendid oak panels and formally attired tables. It is a refined and elegant setting for food of an equally sophisticated demeanour. Head chef Adrian Coulthard's cooking is rooted in classic good sense while incorporating contemporary ideas in his precise, refined output. Regional ingredients play their part on the rigorously seasonal menus. Monkfish cheeks are seared and served up with cauliflower purée in an opener with a hint of curry flavour, while pheasant might appear as a pressing, with lovage mayonnaise, pickled onion shells and potato crisps. Among main courses, a trio of pork includes a classy sausage roll, and sea bass is delivered with mussels and wild sea herbs, and a potato dumpling. Finish with a rhubarb triptych (poached gel, jelly), or the fabulous array of English cheeses.

Chef Adrian Coulthard **Seats** 40, Private dining 60 **Open** All year **Parking** 140
Notes Vegetarian dishes, No children under 10 years at dinner

NORTHUMBERLAND

▶ NORTHUMBERLAND

BAMBURGH
Waren House Hotel
◉◉ MODERN, TRADITIONAL BRITISH
01668 214581 | Waren Mill, NE70 7EE
www.warenhousehotel.co.uk

Tradition is the watchword in the kitchen of this classic country-house hotel, starting with diligent sourcing of the region's finest ingredients, which are brought together in a broadly modern British style. Dishes are well conceived and fish cookery is handled with aplomb.

Chef Steven Owens **Seats** 30 **Open** All year
Prices from S £8.75, M £18.95, D £6.55 **Parking** 15
Notes Vegetarian dishes

BERWICK-UPON-TWEED
Magna
◉ INDIAN
01289 302736 | 39 Bridge Street, TD15 1ES
www.magnatandooriberwick.co.uk

Close to the bridge over the Tweed at the lower end of the walled town, Magna has earned a reputation for top-notch Indian cooking. Occupying a grand Victorian building, bright red chairs and marble-topped tables add a cheery glow to the place.

Chef Oliul Khan, Suman Ahmed **Seats** 85, Private dining 40 **Open** All year **Prices from** S £3.95, M £7.95, D £2.95 **Parking** 60 **Notes** Vegetarian dishes, Children welcome

Queens Head
◉ MODERN BRITISH, EUROPEAN
01289 307852 | Sandgate, TD15 1EP
www.queensheadberwick.co.uk

A traditional hotel overlooking Sandgate in the old part of Berwick, the Queens Head is a place with ambition. The principal dining room has a stripped wood floor, old beams and well-spaced tables, a relaxing place for upscale pub cooking founded on sound culinary logic.

Chef Gillet Libau, Alistair McGregor, Joanne Greenaway **Seats** 58, Private dining **Open** All year **Prices from** S £5.25, M £12.95, D £6.25 **Notes** Vegetarian dishes, Children welcome

BLANCHLAND
The Lord Crewe Arms Blanchland
◉ TRADITIONAL BRITISH
01434 675469 | The Square, DH8 9SP
www.lordcrewearmsblanchland.co.uk

Built for the residents of Blanchland Abbey in the 1100s, this wonderfully historic inn has served everyone from monks to lead miners. It seems unlikely that the latter would have been interested in the architecture, not least the vaulted stone crypt, now an atmospheric bar.

Chef Simon Hicks **Seats** 40, Private dining 14 **Open** All year **Parking** 30 **Notes** Vegetarian dishes, Children welcome

CHATHILL
Doxford Hall Hotel & Spa
◉◉ MODERN BRITISH **V**
01665 589700 | NE67 5DN
www.doxfordhall.com

Doxford Hall's restaurant has chandeliers in ornate ceilings, a stone fireplace, deep-red walls and menus reflecting 21st-century dining expectations. Seared scallops with two croquettes of slowly cooked pig's cheek and celeriac remoulade is just one possible starter of intense, distinct flavours.

Chef Michael Thorpe **Seats** 60, Private dining 200 **Open** All year **Parking** 100 **Notes** Children welcome

CORNHILL-ON-TWEED
Tillmouth Park Country House Hotel
◉ MODERN BRITISH
01890 882255 | TD12 4UU
www.tillmouthpark.co.uk

Close to the Scottish border, this splendid Victorian mansion is surrounded by 15 acres of landscaped grounds. Entry to the elevated Library Dining Room is via a beautiful wooden staircase around the edge of the tower. The kitchen turns out classically based modern British food.

Chef Mike Struthers **Seats** 40, Private dining 20 **Closed** 26–28 December and January to March **Prices from** S £4.95, M £14.95, D £5 **Parking** 50 **Notes** Vegetarian dishes, Children welcome

HEXHAM
The Barrasford Arms
◉ BRITISH
01434 681237 | Barrasford NE48 4AA
www.barrasfordarms.co.uk

Close to Hadrian's Wall in the tranquil village of Barrasford, this ivy-clad country inn has three dining rooms kitted out with rustic furniture. The kitchen works to a modern English template, the emphasis firmly placed on produce from local estates and punchy flavours.

Chef Michael Eames **Seats** 60, Private dining 10 **Open** All year **Prices from** S £6, M £12.50, D £6.50 **Parking** 30 **Notes** Vegetarian dishes, Children welcome

See advertisement opposite

Langley Castle Hotel
◉◉ CONTEMPORARY BRITISH, FRENCH
01434 688888 | Langley, NE47 5LU
www.langleycastle.com

Here you'll find a creative and modern output delivered via a table d'hôte menu; expect dishes based on top-quality, seasonal ingredients sourced from the Northumberland area. The kitchen's aim is to produce flavoursome food without unnecessary distractions.

Chef Mark Percival **Seats** 48, Private dining 28
Open All year **Parking** 57 **Notes** Vegetarian dishes, Children welcome

LONGHORSLEY
Macdonald Linden Hall, Golf & Country Club
◉ MODERN BRITISH
01670 500000 | NE65 8XF
www.macdonaldhotels.co.uk/lindenhall

This late-Georgian manor house sits in 450 acres amid views of the Cheviots and wild Northumberland landscapes. The upscale Dobson Restaurant, with its relaxed, professional service makes a refined setting for well-conceived dishes.

Chef Jerome Cogne **Seats** 78, Private dining 40
Open All year **Parking** 300 **Notes** Vegetarian dishes, Children welcome

MATFEN
Matfen Hall
◉◉ MODERN BRITISH **V**
01661 886500 | NE20 0RH
www.matfenhall.com

Matfen Hall, a creation of the Victorian era, within 300 acres of parkland, today offers all modern amenities. The panelled library, replete with shelves of old volumes, does duty as the dining room. The contemporary menus make a neat counterpoint to the surroundings.

Chef Paul Blakey **Seats** 52, Private dining 30
Open All year **Parking** 200 **Notes** Children welcome

MORPETH
Eshott Hall
◉◉ BRITISH, EUROPEAN
01670 787454 | Eshott, NE65 9EN
www.eshotthall.co.uk

Eshott Hall is a compact boutique hotel in a handsome Georgian property – a perfect base from which to explore the National Park and end the day with dinner in the elegant restaurant, with its soothing gold colour scheme and a fire in cooler weather.

Chef Mark Willis **Seats** 30, Private dining 30
Closed Private functions **Parking** 60 **Notes** Vegetarian dishes, Children welcome

NEWTON-ON-THE-MOOR
The Cook and Barker Inn
@ BRITISH
01665 575234 | NE65 9JY
www.cookandbarkerinn.co.uk
With great views of the Cheviot Hills and the coast from its elevated location, The Cook and Barker has turned from a traditional inn to a stylish place. Exposed brickwork, beams with fairy lights, upholstered chairs and wooden tables add up to a sophisticated look.

Chef William Farmer **Open** All year

STOCKSFIELD
The Duke of Wellington Inn
@ MODERN BRITISH
01661 844446 | Newton, NE43 7UL
www.thedukeofwellingtoninn.co.uk
An great extensive refurbishment has given 'The Wellie' an 18th-century country inn appeal. Views from the bar and restaurant are magnificent, especially so from the terrace on a sunny day. The menu is concise, but you'll still find a decent range of modern British dishes.

Chef Dave Mckie **Seats** 50 **Open** All year **Prices from** S £5.95, M £15.95, D £5.95 **Parking** 20 **Notes** Vegetarian dishes, Children welcome

▶ NOTTINGHAMSHIRE

BARNBY MOOR
Restaurant Bar 1650
@ MODERN EUROPEAN
01777 705121 | Ye Olde Bell Hotel, DN22 8QS
www.yeoldebell-hotel.co.uk
This hotel offers beauty therapies aplenty, and lots of room for functions. There's a bistro in the St Leger bar, but the main event is the oak-panelled Restaurant Bar 1650, with its art deco-style bar area and modern chandeliers to add a touch of glamour.

Chef Tim Stamp **Seats** 40, Private dining 200 **Open** All year **Prices from** S £6.50, M £12.50, D £7 **Parking** 200 **Notes** Vegetarian dishes, Children welcome

BLIDWORTH
The Black Bull
@@ MODERN BRITISH **V**
01623 490222 | Main Street, NG21 0QH
www.blackbullblidworth.co.uk
Not far from Sherwood Forest and Byron's Newstead Abbey is this classic Georgian timbered inn. Sand-blasted beams, a brick fireplace and checkered carpeting make for a modernised but still homely atmosphere for showcasing some creatively witty cooking. The inventive pace is sustained to the end.

Chef Lewis Kuciers, Craig Hadden **Seats** 35 **Open** All year **Prices from** S £7.50, M £15.50, D £6.95 **Parking** 12 **Notes** Children welcome

FARNDON
Farndon Boathouse
@@ MODERN BRITISH
01636 676578 | Off Wyke Road, NG24 3SX
www.farndonboathouse.co.uk
The leafy banks of the River Trent make an interesting contrast to the contemporary exposed ducting, industrial-style lighting, stone floors and glazed frontage of the stylish Boathouse. Modern cooking techniques, such as sous-vide, squeeze every molecule of flavour from the ingredients.

Chef Luke McGowan **Seats** 120 **Open** All year **Parking** 18 **Notes** Vegetarian dishes, Children welcome

GUNTHORPE
Tom Browns Brasserie
@@ MODERN BRITISH
0115 966 3642 | The Old School House, Trentside, NG14 7FB
www.tombrowns.co.uk
The homage to Thomas Hughes' plucky Victorian schoolboy denotes the fact that this large riverside building was a place of education in the 19th century. No risk of school dinners here now, though, this is a robustly complex, well-considered brasserie cooking in the modern style.

Chef Peter Kirk **Seats** 100, Private dining 20 **Open** All year **Prices from** S £5.95, M £12.50, D £6.50 **Parking** 28 **Notes** Vegetarian dishes, Children welcome

NOTTINGHAM

Hart's Restaurant

◉◉ MODERN BRITISH

0115 988 1900 | Standard Hill, Park Row, NG1 6GN
www.hartsnottingham.co.uk

With its contemporary good looks, booth seating and recently extended bar, Hart's is a welcoming restaurant with an approachable, daily changing menu. Dessert of poached Yorkshire rhubarb is matched with kaffir lime-flavoured pannacotta and pistachio brittle. There's an interesting wine list arranged by style.

Chef Daniel Burridge **Seats** 80, Private dining 100 **Closed** 1 January **Prices from** S £7, M £18, D £6.50 **Parking** 15 **Notes** Vegetarian dishes, Children welcome

MemSaab Restaurant

◉◉ INDIAN

0115 957 0009 | 12–14 Maid Marian Way, NG1 6HS
www.mem-saab.co.uk

A gigantic venue of 200 covers, there's a real vibrancy about this unique Nottingham establishment. A signature starter comes in the form of tandoori ostrich, roasted in garlic and red chilli. Meats benefit from the tenderising influence of slow cooking.

Chef Majid Ashraf **Seats** 200, Private dining 60 **Closed** 25 December **Prices from** S £5.25, M £9.95, D £4.95 **Notes** Vegetarian dishes, Children welcome

See advertisement on page 266

Merchants Restaurant

◉ MODERN EUROPEAN

0115 948 4414 | Lace Market Hotel, 29–31 High Pavement, NG1 1HE
www.lacemarkethotel.co.uk

The Lace Market Hotel occupies a handsome Georgian townhouse, carefully restored and retaining much of its period detail. The elegant Merchants restaurant is a light and airy room with large sash windows, vibrant modern art, and a confident, modern European menu.

Chef Luke Holland **Open** All year

Park Plaza Nottingham

◉◉ PAN ASIAN

0115 947 7444 | 41 Maid Marian Way, NG1 6GD
www.chinolatino.eu

Latin America meets the Far East in this Nottingham branch of the Park Plaza. Set across two levels, this buzzy restaurant and bar fuses pan-Asian cooking with international cuisine on the globe-trotting menu. Thai and Korean dishes appear in mains.

Chef Manol Dmitrov **Seats** 70 **Closed** 25–26 December **Prices from** S £4.50, M £14, D £6.95 **Parking** 30 **Notes** Vegetarian dishes, Children welcome

Restaurant Sat Bains with Rooms

◉◉◉◉ MODERN BRITISH V ◈ NOTABLE WINE LIST

0115 986 6566 | Lenton Lane, Trentside, NG7 2SA
www.restaurantsatbains.com

There is something about the approach to Restaurant Sat Bains that increases the anticipation. That's not because it is a glorious push through one of the UK's finest vistas, on the contrary, it is a trek through an out-of-town industrial state near a flyover…which is all the better, for it feels like you're heading to a secret hideaway. There is nothing 'secret' about Sat Bains. The man's reputation precedes him as one of a handful of super-chefs living and working in the country today. And if you want to know what makes him tick, get inside his head, get hold of a copy of *Too Many Chefs Only One Indian*, Sat's illuminating autobiographical cookbook. Once you pull up at the handsomely converted Victorian farmhouse and outbuildings, the journey can truly begin, and can be extended if you've booked one of the stylish bedrooms. An urban garden provides around 40% of the veg and herbs that make their way to the table, but RSB is not a rural experience, although a pre- or post-dinner drink in the small courtyard garden is perfectly charming. The dining option are multifarious: Chef's Table, Kitchen Bench, Conservatory, Nucleus (a table in the development kitchen), or the restaurant itself. The seven- and ten-course tasting menus are the mainstay of the restaurant, colour and size coded to inform about the taste elements of each dish (salt, sweet, sour, bitter and umami), and what arrives is an outstanding array of complex, thrilling and inspiring courses. Presentation is pretty thrilling too. A pressed poultry terrine may sound simple enough, but flavours and textures and imagination combine to elevate each course, the terrine with shiitake mushrooms, sweetbreads and a sauternes gelée, while Moroccan spices elevate an already outstanding Anjou pigeon, with dates and black olives. Monkfish 'bourguignonne' has the expected flavours, and so much more, with sweet courses delivering the same level of complexity and excitement; a chocolate marquise, for example with elements of coffee and salt, and 25-year-old balsamic. The wine list is a wise collection with lots to grab your attention, with the wine flights up for grabs to ensure food and drink matching is as perfect as everything else.

Chef Sat Bains **Seats** 46, Private dining 8 **Closed** 2 weeks in December to January, 1 week in April, 2 weeks in August **Parking** 16 **Notes** No children under 8 years

MEMSAAB
RESTAURANT

Winner
Best Front of House Team
Nottinghamshire Restaurant of the Year Runner up
Nottingham Restaurant & Bar Awards 2018

PRIVATE DINING • CANAPÉ & DRINKS RECEPTIONS
CELEBRATION DINNERS • OUTSIDE CATERING
£13.95 EARLY EVENING MENU AVAILABLE

0115 957 0009 12-14 MAID MARIAN WAY, NOTTINGHAM NG1 6HS WWW.MEM-SAAB.CO.UK CONTACT@MEM-SAAB.C

World Service

◉◉ MODERN BRITISH ⬛NOTABLE WINE LIST

0115 847 5587 | Newdigate House, Castle Gate, NG1 6AF

www.worldservicerestaurant.com

Renaissance-styled Newdigate House was built in 1675. Its idiosyncratic interior mines a colonial vein, the warm orange and copper hues of the main dining room offset with oriental artefacts: Buddha heads, Indian statuary and objets d'art in vitrines. The cooking has a gentle East-meets-West theme.

Chef James Nicholas **Seats** 80, Private dining 34 **Closed** 26 December and 1–7 January **Prices from** S £5, M £16.95, D £7.75 **Notes** Vegetarian dishes, No children under 12 years at dinner

OLLERTON

Thoresby Hall Hotel

◉ BRITISH, INTERNATIONAL

01623 821000 | Thoresby Park, NG22 9WH

www.warnerleisurehotels.co.uk

The principal restaurant at Thoresby has undergone a restyling. Now known as the Blue Grill, it has an informal feel, with a grill menu that embraces Wagyu, USDA and local beef. Inventive touches, extensive sides and sauces make for happy mixing and matching.

Chef Mark Maris, Gary Griffiths **Seats** 50, Private dining 50 **Open** All year **Parking** 140 **Notes** Vegetarian dishes,

RETFORD

Blacksmiths

◉ MODERN BRITISH

01777 818171 | Town Street, Clayworth, DN22 9AD

www.blacksmithsclayworth.com

A beautifully revamped inn in a village dating back to the 12th century, Blacksmiths is still a local pub, but with three attractively furnished bedrooms and a restaurant serving divertingly modern food, it's also a destination worth crossing county lines to visit.

Chef Peter Garlick **Seats** 70, Private dining 36 **Closed** 1st week January **Parking** 20 **Notes** Vegetarian dishes, Children welcome

▶ OXFORDSHIRE

BANBURY

Best Western Plus Wroxton House Hotel

◉◉ MODERN BRITISH

01295 730777 | Wroxton St Mary, OX15 6QB

www.wroxtonhousehotel.com

Wroxton House is a honey-stone beauty in a photogenic thatched village. Its restaurant occupies what was a row of cottages; all oak beams, columns and an inglenook fireplace. Table settings are smart and the kitchen turns out thoughtful modern brasserie dishes, founded on classic combinations.

Chef Jack Darbyshire **Seats** 60, Private dining 90 **Open** All year **Parking** 70 **Notes** Vegetarian dishes, Children welcome

The Three Pigeons Inn

◉ CONTEMPORARY BRITISH

01295 275220 | 3 Southam Road, OX16 2CD

www.thethreepigeons.com

This old red-brick inn has been servicing the needs of the community since the 17th century. Today's incumbents took over in 2011 and brought the place back to life. There's a light-filled dining room extension, panelled bar, cosy bedrooms and a smart courtyard garden.

Chef Patryk Taglewski **Seats** 40, Private dining 20 **Open** All year **Parking** 11 **Notes** Vegetarian dishes, Children welcome

The White Horse

◉◉ TRADITIONAL BRITISH, FRENCH INFLUENCE

01295 812440 | 2 The Square, Kings Sutton, OX17 3RF

www.whitehorseks.co.uk

This old pub has been given a makeover that ensures that you are reminded of its past. Clearly popular, it has received regional food accolades for its British and European cooking. A good choice of wines includes both the Old and New Worlds.

Chef Hendrik Dutson **Seats** 40, Private dining 7 **Open** All year **Parking** 14 **Notes** Vegetarian dishes, Children welcome

BURFORD

The Angel at Burford

◉ CLASSIC BRITISH

01993 822714 | 14 Witney Street, OX18 4SN

www.theangelatburford.co.uk

Just off the main street in pretty Burford, this welcoming Cotswold stone inn oozes character. Perfectly kept pints of Hook Norton lure drinkers to the cosy and bustling bar, with the all-day bar menu offering sandwiches, burgers and a charcuterie board alongside the main carte.

Chef Mike Burkert **Seats** 36, Private dining 14 **Open** All year **Prices from** S £6, M £14, D £6 **Notes** Vegetarian dishes, Children welcome

The Bay Tree Hotel
◉ MODERN BRITISH
01993 822791 | Sheep Street, OX18 4LW
www.cotswold-inns-hotels.co.uk/baytree
Built in Cotswold stone, this is a stylishly appointed place with a dining room that was fully refurbished in 2015, and a menu of modern-classic English food. Try scallops on cauliflower purée, with caramelisation bringing out the sweetness of the shellfish.

Chef Shawn Lovegrove **Seats** 70, Private dining 30 **Open** All year **Parking** 55 **Notes** Vegetarian dishes, Children welcome

The Bull at Burford
◉◉ MODERN TRADITIONAL
01993 822220 | 105 High Street, OX18 4RG
www.bullatburford.co.uk
The High Street of Burford is rich with historic buildings, including The Bull, which first opened its doors in 1610 as a coaching inn. The facade maintains the period character, of course, but inside there's a little more leeway to bring in an up-to-date touch.

Chef Pablo Romalde **Seats** 40 **Open** All year **Prices from** S £6.95, M £15.50, D £6.95 **Parking** 6 **Notes** Vegetarian dishes, Children welcome

The Lamb Inn
◉◉ MODERN BRITISH V
01993 823155 | Sheep Street, OX18 4LR
www.cotswold-inns-hotels.co.uk/lamb
Beautifully cosy and comfortable, with flagstone floors and open fires, The Lamb is your quintessential Cotswold inn, set in a quaint market town. The dining room, with its grey walls and skylight, makes a very classy setting for their chic food – complex, precise seasonal dishes.

Chef Pawel Stepien **Seats** 40, Private dining 20 **Open** All year **Notes** Children welcome

CHECKENDON
The Highwayman
◉ MODERN, TRADITIONAL BRITISH
01491 682020 | Exlade Street, RG8 0UA
www.thehighwaymaninn-checkendon.co.uk
Tucked away in a secluded hamlet, this rambling 16th-century inn is all brickwork, beams and wood-burner in a huge inglenook. Fine ales are on tap in the pubby bar, and all bases are covered in the food department by steaks from the grill, home-made pies.

Chef Paul Burrows, Evelyne Martin **Seats** 85, Private dining 40 **Closed** 25 December, 1 January **Parking** 30 **Notes** Vegetarian dishes, Children welcome

CHINNOR
The Sir Charles Napier
◉◉ MODERN BRITISH, EUROPEAN V ◢ NOTABLE WINE LIST
01494 483011 | Sprigg's Alley, OX39 4BX
www.sircharlesnapier.co.uk
Hidden down rural Oxfordshire lanes, this sublime flint-and-brick inn is named after the 19th-century British Army general who became commander-in-chief in India. Menus feature hedgerow and field-sourced herbs, mushrooms, berries and game. You can eat inside, on the vine-covered terrace or under the cherry trees.

Chef Ben Howarth **Seats** 75, Private dining 45 **Closed** 25–27 December **Prices from** S £11.50, M £22.50, D £9.50 **Parking** 60 **Notes** No children under 6 years at dinner

CHIPPING NORTON
The Chequers
◉ TRADITIONAL BRITISH
01608 659393 | Church Road, Churchill, OX7 6NJ
www.thechequerschurchill.com
A village pub with a focus on food, The Chequers has been done up with a bit of individuality and doesn't look the same as everywhere else. There's nothing fussy about the culinary output, but time has been taken to seek out good quality ingredients.

Chef James de Jong **Seats** 40, Private dining 12 **Closed** 25 December **Parking** 15 **Notes** Vegetarian dishes, Children welcome

FARINGDON
Magnolia Brasserie
◉◉ MODERN BRITISH
01367 241272 | Sudbury House,
56 London Street, SN7 7AA
www.sudburyhouse.co.uk
Close to the M4 between Swindon and Oxford, this smart hotel occupies an enviable spot on the edge of the Cotswolds. The contemporary Magnolia Brasserie is the more informal of the hotel's two restaurants and the room is dominated by the open kitchen with a wood-burning stove.

Chef Andrew Scott, Ben Bullen **Seats** 120, Private dining 40 **Open** All year **Prices from** S £6 D £6 **Parking** 100 **Notes** Vegetarian dishes, Children welcome

Restaurant 56

@@@ MODERN BRITISH V ♦NOTABLE WINE LIST

01367 245389 | Sudbury House, 56 London Street, SN7 7AA

www.restaurant56.co.uk

Perched at the edge of the Cotswolds between Oxford and Swindon, Sudbury House has been treated to an extensive refurbishment. The pick of its dining options is Restaurant 56, an elegantly appointed room with striped curtains, rococo gilt mirror-frames and tables got up in regal crimson. It makes an unexpectedly traditional framework for some thoroughly contemporary cooking, which Andrew Scott presents in the form of three menus. 'Choice' is a three-course carte, 'Prime' a seven-course taster, and 'Progressive' the full bells-and-whistles nine dishes. Innovation and excitement abound, as for 'Tongue in Cheek', a serving of veal tongue under a cannelloni roll of the cheek with crispy onions, nasturtium purée and honey vinegar gel. Norwegian cod might be poached with coconut, and served on peanut sauce with spring onions, or there may be a pair of porks, Royal Windsor and Ibérico, with creamed sweetcorn, girolles and a baby leek. Dessert could be a curd made of lulo (an orange-flavoured South American fruit) with smashed gingerbread, lime-leaf ice cream and cigarillos of meringue.

Chef Andrew Scott, Nick Bennett **Seats** 24, Private dining 12 **Open** All year **Parking** 70 **Notes** No children

The Trout Inn

@ MODERN BRITISH

01367 870382 | Buckland Marsh, SN7 8RF

www.troutinn.co.uk

This charming old inn has a smart country finish, with flagstone floors, beams, log burners, and country prints. The kitchen uses the region's best produce to deliver sharp, modern fare.

Notes Vegetarian dishes

FYFIELD
The White Hart

@@ MODERN BRITISH

01865 390585 | Main Road, OX13 5LW

www.whitehart-fyfield.com

Built as a chantry house, The White Hart offers traditionally based British food with contemporary flourishes. Sharing boards of fish, meze or antipasti might take your fancy. Dessert could be a study in cherry, with purée, tuile, sorbet and Kirsch-soaked fruit accompanying pistachio cake.

Chef Mark Chandler, James Wilkinson **Seats** 45, Private dining 32 **Open** All year **Prices from** S £7, M £15, D £8 **Parking** 60 **Notes** Vegetarian dishes, Children welcome

GORING
The Miller of Mansfield

@@ BRITISH V

01491 872829 | High Street, RG8 9AW

www.millerofmansfield.com

An 18th-century coaching inn with a makeover, The Miller offers sharp modern British output. Flickering candles on smart oak tables set the mood. Warm salmon bradan rost comes with hot and creamy horseradish mayonnaise and a sweet and sticky syrup of mirin and soy.

Chef Nick Galer **Seats** 60, Private dining 12 **Open** All year **Prices from** S £8, M £17.50, D £8.50 **Notes** Children welcome

GREAT MILTON
Belmond Le Manoir aux Quat'Saisons

@@@@@ MODERN FRENCH V ♦NOTABLE WINE LIST

01844 278881 | Church Road, OX44 7PD

www.belmond.com/lemanoir

It's hard to imagine now, but back in 1984 Raymond Blanc put everything on the line to open Le Manoir. Fast forward 35 years and the magnificence of the place and its renown as one of the UK's finest destinations seems set in stone. It stands as testament to his courage, passion and talent. It is part owned by the Belmond group these days, but Monsieur Blanc remains the life force of the place, with an amazing team of professionals by his side, including the long-standing executive head chef, Gary Jones. The pretty 15th-century manor stands at the heart of the grounds, with luxurious bedroom suites giving the opportunity to extend a stay (who would want to leave?), and a glorious garden to explore compete with sculptures, orchard, Japanese tea garden, and a kitchen garden that provides its bounty for us all to enjoy on the plate. The dining experience is never less than joyful, from the warm greeting, the charming attention, and the divertingly delicious French cuisine. The cooking is classic at its core, with technical precision and the pursuit of flavour preferred to chasing modern fashions. There is nothing old hat about the cooking by any means, though, and the attention to detail runs through from top to bottom. Five- and seven-course menus (including inspiring vegetarian versions) support the three-course à la carte – les spécialités du moment. Five perfectly formed agnolotti arrive filled with cheese and honey in a stellar combination, with tomato essence and seasonal peas and beans, or how about Cornish crab with hits of kaffir lime, coconut and passionfruit? Spiced monkfish and mussels with broccoli tempura and a sauce rich with Gewürztraminer is a main course full of flavour and verve, while assiette of Rhug Estate lamb has superb meat at its heart, and a rosemary jus that brings everything together in perfect harmony. The desserts offer the same degree of comfort and joy; a pistachio soufflé, say, with a bitter cocoa sorbet dropped in its centre. Even the bread basket is a thing of beauty. The wine list covers the globe but is at its very best when dealing with the French heavyweights. A cookery school and gardening school add to the mix and give everyone a chance to take knowledge home alongside wonderful memories.

Chef Raymond Blanc OBE, Gary Jones, Benoit Blin **Seats** 80, Private dining 50 **Parking** 60 **Notes** Children welcome

HENLEY-ON-THAMES
The Baskerville
 MODERN BRITISH **V**
0118 940 3332 | Station Road, Lower Shiplake, RG9 3NY
www.thebaskerville.com

This Baskerville is a handsome beast, a contemporary kind of inn that offers beer and bar snacks, comfortable rooms, and a restaurant that produces serious modern British grub. Pub classics like steak, ale and mushroom pie and Sunday roasts play to the gallery.

Chef Jamie Herridge **Seats** 58, Private dining 12 **Closed** 1 January **Prices from** S £7, M £14.50, D £6.50 **Parking** 15 **Notes** Children welcome

Hotel du Vin Henley-on-Thames
 EUROPEAN NOTABLE WINE LIST
01491 848400 | New Street, RG9 2BP
www.hotelduvin.com

Hotel du Vin always chooses impressive buildings, and the Henley branch is no exception: a Thames-side Georgian property that was the HQ of Brakspears brewery. Bistro classics plus a few less standard dishes are what to expect, all cooked just as they should be.

Chef Dominic Scott **Seats** 90, Private dining 72 **Open** All year **Prices from** S £5.95, M £10.50, D £6.50 **Notes** Vegetarian dishes, Children welcome

Orwells
 MODERN BRITISH **V**
0118 940 3673 | Shiplake Row, Binfield Heath, RG9 4DP
www.orwellsrestaurant.co.uk

A five-minute canter from the centre of Henley, in the rural enclave of Binfield Heath, Orwells is the labour of love of Ryan Simpson and Liam Trotman. It may look like a straightforward whitewashed country inn from the Georgian era, but all kinds of creative magic are going on here. A little along the road is the Orwells smallholding, where much of the fresh produce for the kitchens is grown, with honey from the resident apiary. Crisply linened tables and a modern wood floor make

a neat contrast to the unevenly beamed shell of the place, and the cooking is something else again. There is a distinct inclination to keep things straightforward rather than going for fiddly complexity, but the dishes are still possessed of inspirational modernist impetus. A starter of spider crab paired with smoked apple is a revealing combination of elements, while the Japanese katsu treatment of monkfish gains even sharper edge from rhubarb and spring onions. Main courses lean more towards classical treatments, as for lamb loin with turnips, broccoli and wild garlic, or muntjac venison with girolles and hazelnuts. The single fish offering could be a bracing preparation of Torbay brill in verjus with radish and cucumber. That honey then comes into its own as the anointment of a sponge pudding dessert served with salt caramel, or as the honeycomb that comes with tonka pannacotta, pistachios and rhubarb. Well-kept British cheeses are outlined on their own menu. Seasonal multi-course tasters run from an array of appetisers to a pair of desserts, with two exciting choices of wine flight.

Chef Ryan Simpson, Liam Trotman **Seats** 35, Private dining 16 **Closed** 2 weeks beginning January and 2 weeks beginning September **Prices from** S £10, M £23, D £9 **Parking** 30 **Notes** Children welcome

Shaun Dickens at The Boathouse
 MODERN BRITISH **V** NOTABLE WINE LIST
01491 577937 | Station Road, RG9 1AZ
www.shaundickens.co.uk

It would be a poor boathouse that didn't have watery views, and there's the River Thames, right on cue – all the better when the glass windows pull back. After experience gained at some top addresses, including Le Manoir aux Quat'Saisons and Per Se in New York, Shaun Dickens has his name above the door and his creative, contemporary food on the menu. The dining room is a smart and elegant space in the modern manner, watched over by an engaging service team. Classic and signature tasting menus support the carte and terrific value set lunch menus. Shaun is passionate about the ingredients he uses, building strong links with farmers and producers, which bears fruit in what arrives on the plate. A first-course chicken parfait arrives with smoked eel and the flavours of roast apple and mustard, while creamy burrata is matched with confit beetroot and venison cured in juniper. Among main courses, Blythborough pork comes with a moreish bacon croissant, plus braised chicory and prunes, and a fishy option might be stone bass with black olives and red peppers. The invention and impressive presentation continues into desserts.

Chef Shaun Dickens, James Walshaw **Seats** 45 **Open** All year **Prices from** S £12, M £21, D £9 **Notes** Children welcome

KINGHAM
The Kingham Plough
◉◉ MODERN BRITISH
01608 658327 | The Green, OX7 6YD
www.thekinghamplough.co.uk

The Plough presents a quintessentially English picture. Chef-proprietor Emily Watkins learned to revere fine ingredients during her stint in Heston's team at The Fat Duck, but there's no molecular wizardry going on in this kitchen, just a modernised take on country food.

Chef Emily Watkins, Darren Brown **Seats** 54, Private dining 20 **Closed** 25 December **Prices from** S £8, M £17, D £6 **Parking** 30 **Notes** Vegetarian dishes, Children welcome

The Wild Rabbit
◉◉◉ MODERN BRITISH V
01608 658389 | Church Street, OX7 6YA
www.thewildrabbit.co.uk

A stone-built, wisteria-draped Cotswold country inn on a village corner makes an appealing prospect when its outdoor tables under the sunshades fill up. Allied with the Daylesford Estate, an expansive organic farming business, it makes a virtue of the natural approach, with horsehair mattresses in the guest rooms and a menu informed by nose-to-tail butchery and locally grown produce. A crispy egg with truffled Jerusalem artichoke broth and watercress is a sound opening move, or you might plunge into a compendious salad of Crown Prince squash, whipped goats' curd, pickled walnuts and leaves. Notwithstanding the landlocked location, there are inspired fish dishes, as witness the skrei cod in shellfish sauce that comes with brown shrimps, roasted leeks and sea herbs, or there could be rabbit (of course), served with a ragout of its offals, hispi cabbage, carrots and black garlic. Charcoal-grilled steaks remain a favourite, and there are temptations galore at the finishing line, including passionfruit soufflé with dark chocolate ice cream, or an assemblage of walnut parfait and sponge with orange curd and crème fraîche. Or abdicate the need to choose with the six-course taster.

Chef Nathan Eades, Alyn Williams **Seats** 50, Private dining 20 **Open** All year **Prices from** S £13, M £22.50, D £8 **Parking** 15 **Notes** Vegetarian dishes, Children welcome

MILTON COMMON
The Oxfordshire
◉ MODERN BRITISH
01844 278300 | Rycote Lane, OX9 2PU
www.theoxfordshire.com

Whether you're at this new-build hotel in the Chilterns for golf or pampering, the Sakura restaurant has sweeping views of the course and countryside from its picture windows as a backdrop to a broad-ranging menu of modern dishes spiked with global influences.

Chef Craig Heasley **Seats** 50, Private dining 40 **Closed** Christmas, New Year **Prices from** S £6, M £18, D £6 **Notes** Vegetarian dishes, Children welcome

MURCOTT
The Nut Tree Inn
◉◉ MODERN EUROPEAN V ⟁ NOTABLE WINE LIST
01865 331253 | Main Street, OX5 2RE
www.nuttreeinn.co.uk

This place has retained its structure of stone walls and gnarled beams, a venerable backdrop for contemporary dishes that are designed to tease maximum flavour from exemplary ingredients. A salad of the Nut Tree's own garden roots in balsamic vinaigrette is an appealing simple opener.

Chef Michael North, Mary North **Seats** 70, Private dining 36 **Closed** 31 December **Prices from** S £9, M £20, D £8.50 **Parking** 30 **Notes** Children welcome

OXFORD
Bear & Ragged Staff
◉ MODERN, CLASSIC BRITISH
01865 862329 | Appleton Road, Cumnor, OX2 9QH
www.bearandraggedstaff.com

The Bear offers an appealing mixture of traditional atmosphere and contemporary design. Masses of artwork on cool green walls in the dining room offset the roughcast stone, and forward-thinking menus offer trend-conscious British food. Create a themed board with ingredients from sea, garden and butchery.

Chef James Durrant **Seats** 90 **Open** All year **Prices from** S £6, M £13.50, D £6.50 **Parking** 30 **Notes** Vegetarian dishes, Children welcome

Chez Mal Brasserie
◉ MODERN BRITISH, FRENCH
01865 268400 | Oxford Castle, 3 New Road, OX1 1AY
www.malmaison.com

Oxford's old slammer is now leading a reformed life as a classy hotel, with seductive bedrooms in the cells and a moodily lit brasserie in the former basement canteen. The cooking is a little bit French, a little bit British, and a little bit global.

Chef Jason Farbridge **Seats** 120, Private dining 35 **Open** All year **Prices from** S £5, M £14, D £6 **Parking** 30 **Notes** Vegetarian dishes, Children welcome

OXFORDSHIRE

Cotswold Lodge Hotel
⊛ BRITISH, EUROPEAN
01865 512121 | 66a Banbury Road, OX2 6JP
www.cotswoldlodgehotel.co.uk
This stately Victorian villa is replete with period style, all high ceilings, sweeping staircases and expansive bay windows, but given a modern facelift. The kitchen deals in contemporary food with clear European accents.

Chef Bruce Buchan **Seats** 50, Private dining 120
Open All year **Prices from** S £6, M £15, D £6.50
Parking 40 **Notes** Vegetarian dishes, Children welcome

Gee's Restaurant
⊛ MEDITERRANEAN
01865 553540 | 61 Banbury Road, OX2 6PE
www.gees-restaurant.co.uk
Gee's continues to delight townies and gownies on the northern edge of the city centre. The bright glasshouse setting sees potted olive trees and lightweight café-style furniture in a room flooded with natural light, and the style is very satisfying Med-influenced modern brasserie cooking.

Chef Russell Heeley **Seats** 74 **Open** All year
Prices from S £6.95, M £14.95, D £6.50
Notes Vegetarian dishes, Children welcome

Iffley Blue at Hawkwell House
⊛ BRITISH, EUROPEAN
01865 749988 | Church Way, Iffley Village, OX4 4DZ
www.hawkwellhouse.co.uk
Set within acres of gardens in the village of Iffley, Hawkwell House is a great base in Oxford. With its shaped glass ceiling, the hotel's open-plan Iffley Blue restaurant is light and spacious with a weeping fig tree taking pride of place in the centre.

Chef Andrew Carr **Seats** 72, Private dining 20
Open All year **Parking** 120 **Notes** Vegetarian dishes, Children welcome

No. 1 Ship Street
⊛ MODERN BRITISH BRASSERIE
01865 806637 | Ship Street, OX1 3DA
www.no1shipstreet.com
Tucked away in a side street, this smartly decorated restaurant creates a cosy atmosphere with its polished copper-topped tables, wooden chairs, creative lighting and soft ambient music. The Ground Floor dining space (there's a bar upstairs) offers modern British, brasserie-style food and a good selection of wines.

Chef Owen Little **Seats** 44 **Closed** 25–26 December and 1 January **Prices from** S £6.50, M £13, D £3
Notes Vegetarian dishes, Children welcome

The Oxford Kitchen
⊛⊛⊛ MODERN BRITISH V
01865 511149 | 215 Banbury Road, Summertown, OX2 7HQ
www.theoxfordkitchen.co.uk
A neighbourhood restaurant by a bus-stop on the Banbury Road, The Oxford Kitchen is a bustling, all-day venue with character to spare. Its chef, Paul Welburn worked under some of the luminaries of British cuisine, including Gary Rhodes and Richard Corrigan, and has done some TV time too. With comfortable brown banquettes inside and tables on the frontage for sunny days, he has created a relaxed setting for modern bistro eating that extends to a pair of tasting menus. Combinations are full of inventive elan, as for Cornish crab with Indian spices, compressed apple and radish, or gin-cured trout with puffed wheat, to start, ahead of breast and chestnut-stuffed leg of Cotswold White chicken with clementine jam, turnips and leeks. Presentations are exuberant and dramatic, and the balance of flavours always strong and true, through to baked rhubarb cheesecake with ginger and lemongrass, or maple syrup parfait garnished with pineapple, pecans and rosemary. The Express Lunch represents tremendous value, centred on a chef's seasonal special – pappardelle with pork ragù, pecorino and salsa verde in January – with an accompanying small glass of wine.

Chef Paul Welburn **Seats** 80, Private dining 50
Closed 1st 2 weeks January **Notes** Children welcome

SOUTH LEIGH
The Mason Arms
⊛⊛ BRITISH
01993 656238 | Station Road, OX29 6XN
www.themasonarms.co.uk
Tucked away in the countryside just outside of Oxford, the atmosphere is friendly and menus are a subtle, contemporary interpretation of British produce and flavours. A Scotch egg with the pub's own brown sauce goes down well with a pint.

Chef Tim Kewley **Seats** 60 **Open** All year
Notes Vegetarian dishes, No children under 10 years at dinner

STADHAMPTON
The English Restaurant
⊛⊛ MODERN BRITISH
01865 890714 | Bear Lane, OX44 7UR
www.crazybeargroup.co.uk
The Tudor inn is done out with pink-cushioned walls, a leopard-print carpet, big steel mirrors and a kind of herringbone overhead wine store set the scene for what's on offer here. The substantial list of

contemporary brasserie food majors in comfort-oriented classics.

Chef Craig Teasdale **Seats** 40, Private dining 140 **Open** All year **Parking** 100 **Notes** Vegetarian dishes, Children welcome

Thai Thai at The Crazy Bear

◉◉ MODERN THAI

01865 890714 | Bear Lane, OX44 7UR

www.crazybeargroup.co.uk

Crazy Bear's first outfit occupies a Tudor inn in an Oxfordshire village. As well as a British dining room, it boasts a Thai restaurant with crimson velvet beams, scatter cushions and tables that resemble brass platters balanced on boxes. There are forays beyond Thailand too.

Chef Chalao Mansell **Seats** 30, Private dining 140 **Open** All year **Parking** 100 **Notes** Vegetarian dishes, Children welcome

SWINBROOK
The Swan Inn

◉ MODERN BRITISH

01993 823339 | OX18 4DY

www.theswanswinbrook.co.uk

The wisteria-clad 16th-century Swan is the quintessential village pub, with an orchard to the rear and the Windrush River running by. The kitchen sources seasonal ingredients with care (traceability is a big deal here), and knows how to turn it into some skilfully rendered dishes.

Chef Matthew Laughton **Seats** 70 **Closed** 25–26 December **Parking** 12 **Notes** Vegetarian dishes, Children welcome

TOOT BALDON
The Mole Inn

◉ MODERN EUROPEAN

01865 340001 | OX44 9NG

www.themoleinn.com

In a quiet village on the outskirts of Oxford, The Mole Inn is everything a country inn should be, adorned with framed mirrors and run by a casual but professional team. A small conservatory to one side makes a pleasant summer retreat.

Chef Gary Witchalls **Seats** 70 **Closed** 25 December **Prices from** S £7.50, M £17.50, D £7.95 **Parking** 40 **Notes** Vegetarian dishes, Children welcome

WANTAGE
The Star Inn

◉◉ MODERN BRITISH

01235 751873 | Watery Lane, Sparsholt, OX12 9PL

www.thestarsparsholt.co.uk

Inside this solid 300-year-old inn in the quintessentially English village of Sparsholt, all is decluttered and open plan with chunky wooden furniture and plain white walls, and the food has a suitably modern accent.

Chef Matt Williams **Seats** 45, Private dining 40 **Open** All year **Parking** 20 **Notes** Vegetarian dishes, Children welcome

WATLINGTON
The Fat Fox Inn

◉ MODERN BRITISH

01491 613040 | 13 Shirburn Street, OX49 5BU

www.thefatfoxinn.co.uk

The Fat Fox lurks in a small market town on the edge of the Chilterns, and is a proper old country inn with an inglenook fireplace and wood-burning stove. The menu offers hearty portions of rustic, unfussy food with the right amount of modern tweaking.

Chef Stewart Lennox **Seats** 26 **Closed** 25 December **Prices from** S £6, M £12, D £6 **Parking** 20 **Notes** Vegetarian dishes, Children welcome

WITNEY
Hollybush Witney

◉ BRITISH

01993 708073 | 35 Corn Street, OX28 6BT

www.hollybushwitney.com

The Hollybush is a buzzy gastro pub run by a youthful team that successfully delivers the gastronomy part without neglecting that essential pub side of the equation. There are real ales at the hand pumps and a menu that comes up with pub classics.

Chef Liam Whittle **Seats** 71, Private dining 35 **Open** All year **Prices from** S £6, M £14, D £6 **Notes** Vegetarian dishes, Children welcome

Old Swan & Minster Mill

◉ MODERN BRITISH

01993 774441 | Old Minster, OX29 0RN

www.oldswanandminstermill.com

The quintessentially Cotswolds village of Minster Lovell makes the perfect history-steeped setting for the Old Swan, a smart country inn with rooms next door in the contemporary surrounds of Minster Mill. There's a local flavour to the menu (including produce grown in the kitchen garden).

Chef David Kelman **Seats** 110, Private dining 55 **Open** All year **Parking** 70 **Notes** Vegetarian dishes, Children welcome

The Restaurant at Witney Lakes Resort

◉ BRITISH, EUROPEAN

01993 893012 | Downs Road, OX29 0SY

www.witney-lakes.co.uk

The sprawling modern resort in west Oxfordshire caters for iron-pumpers, niblick-swingers and the nuptial trade, as well as offering contemporary brasserie cooking in a destination restaurant that has acquired a dedicated local following. Tables on a lakeside terrace embrace the sunnier months.

Chef Karl Franklin **Seats** 60 **Closed** 25 and 31 December, 1 January **Parking** 400 **Notes** Vegetarian dishes, Children welcome

WOODSTOCK

The Feathers Hotel

◉◉ MODERN BRITISH

01993 812291 | Market Street, OX20 1SX

www.feathers.co.uk

A brick-built inn in a handsome Cotswold market town, The Feathers has long been a local fixture. There can be no doubt about its having been coaxed into the boutique hotel era, including the dining room with its raspberry-red banquettes and bold artworks.

Chef Dominic Chapman, Wojciech Chodurski **Seats** 40, Private dining 24 **Open** All year **Notes** Vegetarian dishes, Children welcome

Macdonald Bear Hotel

◉◉ MODERN, TRADITIONAL BRITISH

01993 811124 | Park Street, OX20 1SZ

www.macdonaldhotels.co.uk/bear

This former coaching inn has its origins in the Middle Ages, although the kitchen clearly has its fingers on the pulse of today's tastes. Fish gets a decent airing, puddings can be a visual delight, and the kitchen's attention to detail extends to canapés.

Chef James Mearing **Seats** 65, Private dining 26 **Open** All year **Parking** 50 **Notes** Vegetarian dishes, Children welcome

WOOTTON

The Killingworth Castle

◉◉ MODERN BRITISH

01993 811401 | Glympton Road, OX20 1EJ

www.thekillingworthcastle.com

The inn has been an integral part of its community since the 1630s. When the Alexanders (who also run the Ebrington Arms near Chipping Campden) took over in 2012, it received the investment it needed. The kitchen produces imaginative cooking that isn't unduly fussy.

Chef Dan Watkins **Seats** 68, Private dining 20 **Closed** 25 December **Parking** 40 **Notes** Vegetarian dishes, Children welcome

▶ RUTLAND

CLIPSHAM

The Olive Branch

◉◉ BRITISH, EUROPEAN **V**

01780 410355 | Beech House, Main Street, LE15 7SH

www.theolivebranchpub.com

The Olive Branch serves a fine pint of local ale as well as home-made mulled wine, sloe gin and fruity cocktails flavoured with foraged berries and herbs. This is a kitchen with a passion for seasonal, local stuff with the easy-going atmosphere of a pub.

Chef Sean Hope **Seats** 45, Private dining 20 **Open** All year **Prices from** S £7.50, M £14.50, D £6.95 **Parking** 15 **Notes** Children welcome

LYDDINGTON

The Marquess of Exeter

◉ CLASSIC, MODERN EUROPEAN **V**

01572 822477 | 52 Main Street, LE15 9LT

www.marquessexeter.co.uk

The Marquess of Exeter has plenty of character and charm. Salt-and-chilli cuttlefish with Thai salad show globe-trotting tendencies, but equally you might go for black pudding fritters with home-made piccalilli. There are sharing dishes too. It's all good honest stuff with broad appeal.

Chef Brian Baker **Seats** 90, Private dining 14 **Closed** 25 December **Parking** 40

OAKHAM

Barnsdale Lodge Hotel

◉ MODERN BRITISH

01572 724678 | The Avenue, Rutland Water, North Shore, LE15 8AH

www.barnsdalelodge.co.uk

To one side of the Earl of Gainsborough's Exton estate, this is a handsome country seat on the shore of Rutland Water, with a main dining room, garden room and alfresco courtyard. It's host to simple modern British menus featuring produce from the vegetable garden.

Chef David Bucrowicki **Seats** 120, Private dining 200 **Open** All year **Parking** 250 **Notes** Vegetarian dishes, Children welcome

Fox & Hounds

◉◉ MODERN BRITISH, EUROPEAN **V**

01572 812403 | 19 The Green, Exton, LE15 8AP

www.afoxinexton.co.uk

Overlooking the green in the pretty village of Exton, this former coaching inn has been feeding people since the 17th century. Refurbished, and now a smart pub with rooms, it retains plenty of original character although the food is thoroughly contemporary. Puddings are worth exploring.

Chef David Graham, Glen Conul **Seats** 30, Private dining 16 **Open** All year **Parking** 20 **Notes** Children welcome

Hambleton Hall
◉◉◉◉ BRITISH **V**
See pages 276–277

UPPINGHAM
The Lake Isle
◉◉ BRITISH, FRENCH
01572 822951 | 16 High Street East, LE15 9PZ
www.lakeisle.co.uk

An 18th-century property is the setting for this restaurant with rooms in the market town of Uppingham. Oriental influences are apparent in a dish of grilled fillet of sea bass with Japanese mushrooms, toasted cucumber, prawn and sesame fishcakes and wasabi.

Chef Stuart Mead **Seats** 40, Private dining 16 **Closed** 1 January, Bank holidays **Prices from** S £5, M £15, D £8 **Parking** 6 **Notes** Vegetarian dishes, No children

WING
Kings Arms Inn & Restaurant
◉◉ TRADITIONAL BRITISH
01572 737634 | 13 Top Street, LE15 8SE
www.thekingsarms-wing.co.uk

Stone walls, beams and flagstones are reminders that this village inn dates from the 17th century. Real ales are dispensed in the bar, and there's an informal dining room. Everything is sourced from within 30 miles, and the place's own smokery contributes satisfying dishes.

Chef James Goss **Seats** 32 **Open** All year **Prices from** S £6, M £14, D £7 **Parking** 20 **Notes** Vegetarian dishes, Children welcome

▶ SHROPSHIRE
BISHOP'S CASTLE
The Coach House
◉◉ MODERN BRITISH
01588 650846 | Norbury, SY9 5DX
www.coachhousenorbury.com

Four miles from the market town of Bishop's Castle, this delightful 18th-century inn stands in the centre of a pretty conservation village in the beautiful Onny Valley. Monkfish, salmon and mussels poached in shellfish sauce with rouille and purple sprouting broccoli is one of the enticing mains.

Chef Harry Bullock

IRONBRIDGE
Number Ten
◉ MODERN BRITISH
01952 432901 | White Hart, The Wharfage, TF8 7AW
www.whitehartironbridge.com

Set just beyond Abraham Darby's famous bridge, The White Hart is located deep in the Severn Gorge and surrounded by reminders of the industrial revolution. Their Number Ten restaurant is a fine dining option with large windows that look out to the river.

Chef Kate Bradley **Seats** Private dining 40 **Open** All year **Prices from** S £7, M £15, D £7 **Notes** Vegetarian dishes, No children

Restaurant Severn
◉ BRITISH, FRENCH
01952 432233 | 33 High Street, TF8 7AG
www.restaurantsevern.co.uk

This small restaurant blends in with the terrace of souvenir and tea shops facing Abraham Darby's Iron Bridge World Heritage Site. Inside, however, the bare wooden floors, unclothed tables and high-backed toffee leather chairs make for an intimate brasserie look.

Chef Michelle Drayton, Connor Barns, Steve Cole **Seats** 30 **Open** All year **Notes** Vegetarian dishes, Children welcome

LUDLOW
The Charlton Arms
◉ MODERN BRITISH
01584 872813 | Ludford Bridge, SY8 1PJ
www.thecharltonarms.co.uk

On Ludford Bridge and a short walk from historic Ludlow Castle, this smart, modernised stone-built pub has a lovely tiered terrace overlooking the River Teme. Inside, the airy dining area is relaxed and informal with scrubbed wooden floorboards and mismatched chairs.

Chef Krisztian Balogh **Seats** 40 **Open** All year **Prices from** S £5.50, M £18.95, D £5.50 **Parking** 30 **Notes** Vegetarian dishes, Children welcome

The Cliffe at Dinham
◉◉ MODERN BRITISH
01584 872063 | Halton Lane, Dinham, SY8 2JE
www.thecliffeatdinham.co.uk

A handsome red-brick, Victorian mansion beside the River Teme with views across to Ludlow Castle, The Cliffe has morphed into a stylish restaurant-with-rooms with a breezily modern approach to its interior decor. The restaurant is a suitably contemporary spot for the kitchen's modern British bistro dishes.

Chef Ian Pugh **Seats** 60, Private dining 30 **Closed** 26 December, 1st 2 weeks January **Parking** 30 **Notes** Vegetarian dishes, Children welcome

RUTLAND

OAKHAM
Hambleton Hall

◉◉◉◉ BRITISH V 🍷 NOTABLE WINE LIST

01572 756991 | Hambleton, LE15 8TH

www.hambletonhall.com

Simple but powerfully effective country-house cooking

A gentleman of discernment, Walter Marshall, who had made his fortune in the shipping and brewing sectors, had Hambleton built for himself in 1881 as a bolt-hole for hunting expeditions. No boring old sweat of the shires, Marshall rather enjoyed the fast life, with its insalubrious gossip and the kinds of young ladies who didn't mind who saw their ankles. When ownership passed to his younger sister, the crowd got even racier, with Noël Coward and others of the sparkling set passing through its portals to be reliably amused by the goings-on. It remains a handsome property, its public rooms full of lively colour and opulent fabric, and the arrival of the Rutland Water reservoir in the 1970s added to the magnificence of its prospects.

As to that, Aaron Patterson has made a major contribution to Hambleton's charms since 1992, when he became head chef here following a tutelage under some of the conjurable names of 1980s gastronomy, Raymond Blanc and Anton Mosimann among them. Patterson has always favoured an understated, essentially uncluttered approach, with pure, true

flavours allowed to speak up in their own right, rather than being enveloped in layers of intricacy. This makes for a style of cuisine that everyone can understand, but that lacks nothing in technical flourish.

Opening courses are bold and bright – poached Scottish langoustines with asparagus in a chilled tomato essence of crystal clarity, or perfectly pink ballotine of foie gras with kumquats, Seville orange marmalade and sourdough toast, a flawless example of richness balanced by sharply delineated accompaniments. Thoroughbred meats and impeccably fresh fish are the mainstays of the principal business, perhaps poached halibut, cockles and clams in sauce bouillabaisse (a dish that also may be optioned as an intermediate course), or small slices of succulent veal fillet with its sweetbreads and violet artichokes on an invitingly fragrant truffled risotto. The house take on tiramisù remains a firm favourite of the dessert repertoire, a chocolate-topped, coffee-soaked sponge with mousse and honeycomb, but the soufflé technique is something to see too, in a flavour-drenched almond and amaretto version served with quince and honey ice cream. A separate vegetarian menu might centre on artichoke tartlet with a poached egg and hollandaise, and wild mushroom tagliatelle. Look to the sommelier for sound advice from the magisterial wine list, but service all round is irreproachable.

Chef Aaron Patterson **Seats** 60, Private dining 20 **Open** All year **Parking** 40 **Notes** No children under 5 years

LUDLOW continued

The Clive Bar & Restaurant with Rooms

@ MODERN BRITISH

01584 856565 | Bromfield, SY8 2JR

www.theclive.co.uk

Once the home of Clive of India, then a pub, this brick-built Georgian house has been imaginatively refurbished to form a restaurant with rooms. Seasonality dictates the modern British menu.

Chef Peter Mills **Seats** 90 **Closed** 26 December **Parking** 80 **Notes** Vegetarian dishes, Children welcome

The Feathers Hotel

@ BRITISH, EUROPEAN

01584 875261 | The Bull Ring, SY8 1AA

www.feathersatludlow.co.uk

Even in a town not short of timber-framed properties, this 17th-century inn stands out. Ornate panelling, plasterwork and venerable timbers attest to its history. The dining room has exposed stone walls, low beams and an inglenook, and the kitchen deals in uncontroversial modern British dishes.

Chef Gyorgy Szloboda **Seats** 50, Private dining 30 **Open** All year **Parking** 36 **Notes** Vegetarian dishes, Children welcome

See advertisement below

Fishmore Hall

Rosettes suspended MODERN BRITISH **V**

01584 875148 | Fishmore Road, SY8 3DP

www.fishmorehall.co.uk

The Rosette award for this establishment has been suspended due to a change of chef and reassessment will take place in due course. It's hard to believe that this handsome Georgian country pile just outside the foodie hub of Ludlow was falling apart until its current owners restored it in 2007 to the porticoed, pristine white boutique bolt-hole (with a spa tucked away in the garden). Housed in an orangery extension, Forelles restaurant enjoys views of the rolling Shropshire hills as a backdrop to the classic country-house cuisine.

Chef Joe Gould **Seats** 60, Private dining 20 **Open** All year **Parking** 30 **Notes** Children welcome

Old Downton Lodge

@@@ MODERN BRITISH **V**

01568 771826 | Downton on the Rock, SY8 2HU

www.olddowntonlodge.com

A short drive from foodie Ludlow, Old Downton Lodge is a rural idyll. The country-chic restaurant with rooms comprises a fascinating cluster of buildings – medieval, half-timbered, Georgian – around a courtyard filled with herbs and flowers overlooking the

Welsh Marches hills. Dating from Norman times, the restaurant has the feel of a medieval great hall with its stone walls, tapestry and chandelier. Dinner takes the form of a three-course market menu or daily changing six- and nine-course tasters, all built on superlative produce. What gives head chef Karl Martin's cooking its character is his use of sharp flavours to point up the main item – caviar and lardo boosting roasted celeriac, followed by wagyu beef highlighted with sweet beetroot and dill mayonnaise. There's an inherent simplicity and intuitive balance in main courses too: perfectly handled cod is counterpointed with hollandaise, kohlrabi, parsley and crisp puffed fish skin, or crisp-skinned duck breast with a bonbon of leg meat, squash purée, crisp kale and grapes. Everything is there for a good reason, all the way to a finale of hibiscus granita, white chocolate ice cream and fennel.

Chef Karl Martin **Seats** 25, Private dining 45
Closed Christmas **Parking** 20 **Notes** No children

MARKET DRAYTON
Goldstone Hall
◉◉ MODERN BRITISH ⬩ NOTABLE WINE LIST
01630 661202 | Goldstone Road, TF9 2NA
www.goldstonehall.com

The two stand-out elements to Goldstone Hall are its magnificent gardens and ambitious restaurant. The kitchen garden is a major part of the operation, providing seasonal produce, and dishes are bright and modern while avoiding jumping on the bandwagon of every contemporary fashion.

Chef David Jones **Seats** 60, Private dining 14
Open All year **Parking** 70 **Notes** Vegetarian dishes, Children welcome

MUCH WENLOCK
Raven Hotel
◉◉ MODERN BRITISH
01952 727251 | 30 Barrow Street, TF13 6EN
www.ravenhotel.com

Raven Hotel is a former coaching inn with plenty of period charm, with venerable beams, log fires and hand-pulled ales available in the bar. On the dining front, though, things are positively 21st century, for the kitchen turns out smart, modern dishes.

Chef Jani Celestino **Seats** 40, Private dining 14
Closed 25–26 December **Parking** 30 **Notes** Vegetarian dishes, Children welcome

MUNSLOW
Crown Country Inn
◉◉ MODERN BRITISH
01584 841205 | SY7 9ET
www.crowncountryinn.co.uk

In an Area of Outstanding Natural Beauty, the Crown dates from Tudor times and was first licensed in 1790. The kitchen has a 'Local to Ludlow' policy that might include a reworking of breakfast for black pudding croquettes with Boston beans, bacon and 'fried bread'.

Chef Richard Arnold **Seats** 65, Private dining 42
Closed some days during Christmas **Parking** 20
Notes Vegetarian dishes, Children welcome
See advertisement on page 280

NORTON
The Hundred House
◉ BRITISH, FRENCH
01952 580240 | Bridgnorth Road, TF11 9EE
www.hundredhouse.co.uk

Run by the Phillips family since the mid-1980s, The Hundred House is brimful of character and personality. The brasserie and restaurant produce classy dishes based on tip-top regional ingredients.

Chef Stuart Phillips **Seats** 80, Private dining 34
Open All year **Parking** 60 **Notes** Vegetarian dishes, Children welcome

OSWESTRY
Pen-y-Dyffryn Country Hotel
◉◉ MODERN BRITISH
01691 653700 | Rhydycroesau, SY10 7JD
www.peny.co.uk

A construction company built the rectory, church and village school here in 1840. Nowadays, the church is on the Welsh side of the border and the rectory is in England. With sweeping views over the valley, it is traditionally furnished in country-house style.

Chef Alex Lloyd **Seats** 25 **Closed** 20 December to 21 January **Parking** 18 **Notes** Vegetarian dishes, No children under 3 years

Sebastians
◉◉ FRENCH Ⅴ
01691 655444 | 45 Willow Street, SY11 1AQ
www.sebastians-hotel.com

In a 16th-century inn, full of cossetting beamed character, but not stuck in the past, monthly changing set-dinner menus take you through three courses of well-crafted, Gallic-influenced ideas, with an appetiser to set the ball rolling, and a sorbet before mains.

Chef Mark Fisher **Seats** 45 **Closed** 25–26 December, 1 January and all Bank holiday Mondays **Parking** 6
Notes Vegetarian dishes, No children

Crown Country Inn

The Crown is a Grade II listed building that has been transformed into a comfortable Bed and Breakfast and Restaurant. A gourmet's delight near Ludlow, Chef-patron Richard Arnold has earned many Awards and is a "Masterchef of Great Britain"

Munslow, Nr Craven Arms, Shropshire SY7 9ET • Tel: 01584 841205
Web: www.countryinn.co.uk • Email: info@crowncountryinn.co.uk

---

OSWESTRY continued

Waterside Restaurant
◎ MODERN
01691 684300 | Weston Rhyn, SY11 3EN
www.lionquays.com

Part of the luxurious Lion Quays Resort, the restaurant boasts fine views of the tranquil Shropshire countryside and there are good alfresco dining options.. Contemporary and welcoming, it draws a family-friendly weekend crowd for its Sunday roasts.
Chef Michael Batters **Seats** 134, Private dining 80 **Open** All year **Parking** 400 **Notes** Vegetarian dishes, Children welcome

Wynnstay Hotel
◎◎ BRITISH
01691 655261 | Church Street, SY11 2SZ
www.wynnstayhotel.com

The Wynnstay's Four Seasons restaurant has upped its game since a new head chef took the helm a few years back, producing modern British cooking based on reinvented versions of dishes taken from the Wynnstay's 1960s menus.
Chef Jamie Deery **Seats** 50, Private dining 200 **Open** All year **Parking** 80 **Notes** Vegetarian dishes, Children welcome

SHREWSBURY

Henry Tudor House Restaurant and Bar
◎ MODERN BRITISH
01743 361666 | Henry Tudor House, Barracks Passage, SY1 1XA
www.henrytudorhouse.com

Among the town's oldest half-timbered buildings, HTH's whimsical interior boasts a Parisian-style zinc bar bathed in ever-changing coloured light, while elegant chandeliers in the conservatory shine through delicate iron birdcages. The all-day menu offers a range of classics, while things are more elaborate in the evenings.
Chef Chris Conde, Dan Smyth **Seats** 34, Private dining 18 **Closed** 25–26 December, 1 January **Prices from** S £6.50, M £13.50, D £6.50 **Notes** Vegetarian dishes, Children welcome

House of the Rising Sun
◎ MODERN INTERNATIONAL **V**
01743 588040 | 18 Butcher Row, SY1 1UW
www.hotrs.co.uk

This restaurant is tucked away down a narrow lane where in medieval times, butchers plied their trade. The two dining areas vary greatly – upstairs is very clubby with dark walls and geisha-inspired artwork, while the ground floor is more open plan with long tables.

Chef Liam Watton **Seats** 52 **Closed** 25–26 December, 1 January **Notes** Children welcome

Lion & Pheasant Hotel
@@ BRITISH **V**
01743 770345 | 49–50 Wyle Cop, SY1 1XJ
www.lionandpheasant.co.uk

This coaching inn has stood since the 16th century before the street called Wyle Cop became a bridge over the River Severn. Its period facade gives way to a contemporary New England-style interior, with neutral tones and tongue-and-groove-panelling combining harmoniously with the brickwork and beams.

Chef Harri Alun Williams **Seats** 35, Private dining 45 **Closed** 25–26 December **Prices from** S £7, M £16, D £5.50 **Parking** 14 **Notes** Children welcome

The Mytton and Mermaid
@ MODERN BRITISH **V**
01743 761220 | Atcham, SY5 6QG
www.myttonandmermaid.co.uk

Alongside the River Severn, this handsome Grade II listed building has been tastefully updated. The pub's dining room is partially separated from the large open-plan bar but the atmosphere flows well across both areas. The modern British menu is split between pub favourites and specials which often lean towards the Far East.

Chef Chris Burt **Seats** Private dining 18 **Open** All year **Prices from** S £6, M £13, D £5 **Parking** 60 **Notes** Children welcome

The Peach Tree Restaurant
@ MODERN BRITISH, ASIAN FUSION **V**
01743 355055 | 18–21 Abbey Foregate, SY2 6AE
www.thepeachtree.co.uk

Modern flavours with influences from the East share the menu with more traditional dishes at this 15th-century building opposite Shrewsbury Abbey. Kick off with chicken liver paté, onion jam and artisan toast, with a rich and sweet cherry reduction, or start with a sharing board.

Chef Matthew Parry **Seats** 86, Private dining 80 **Closed** 1 January **Notes** Children welcome

The Royalist Restaurant
@ MODERN, CLASSIC
01743 499955 | Prince Rupert Hotel, Butcher Row, SY1 1UQ
www.princeruperthotel.co.uk

As befits a former home of the grandson of King James I, the Grade II listed Prince Rupert Hotel is a regal affair surrounded by cobbled streets and Tudor buildings. With tapestries and suits of armour, the oak-panelled Royalist Restaurant provides a medieval ambience.

Chef Justin Fenwick-Scott **Seats** 85, Private dining 16 **Open** All year **Notes** Vegetarian dishes, Children welcome

TELFORD
Chez Maw Restaurant
@@ MODERN BRITISH **V**
01952 432247 | Ironbridge, TF8 7DW
www.chezmawrestaurant.co.uk

On the bank of the Severn in Ironbridge, and barely a rivet's throw from the bridge, the Valley Hotel was owned by Arthur Maw and his family, suppliers of ceramic tiles, hence the name of its restaurant, which looks rather spiffy after a recent makeover.

Chef Barry Workman **Seats** 50, Private dining 30 **Closed** 26 December to 2 January **Prices from** S £5.50, M £13.50, D £6.95 **Parking** 100 **Notes** Children welcome

Hadley Park House
@ MODERN BRITISH
01952 677269 | Hadley Park, TF1 6QJ
www.hadleypark.co.uk

The origins of Hadley Park remain shrouded in mystery, but it seems likely to have been built in the mid-Georgian era, the 1770s perhaps. The conservatory extension dining room in the form of Dorrells is dedicated to the elegant pursuit of regionally sourced British cooking.

Chef Kevin Fellows **Seats** 80, Private dining 16 **Closed** 26 December **Notes** Vegetarian dishes, Children welcome

UPTON MAGNA
The Haughmond
@@ MODERN BRITISH **V**
01743 709918 | Pelham Road, SY4 4TZ
www.thehaughmond.co.uk

A refurbishment completed at the end of 2015 brought a contemporary feel to this traditional village inn. Family-run, it retains a pubby atmosphere, while drawing diners from afar. Classics can be enjoyed in the bar, while the new Basil's restaurant offers a fine-dining experience.

Chef Martin Board **Seats** 48, Private dining 20 **Open** All year **Parking** 30 **Notes** Children welcome

SOMERSET

AXBRIDGE
The Oak House
◎◎ CLASSIC BRITISH

01934 732444 | The Square, BS26 2AP

www.theoakhousesomerset.com

Parts of the Oak House date from the 11th century. Inside, a stylish mix of old and new places it at the boutique end of the design spectrum. Steaks are cooked on the grill – 10oz rib-eye, say – and arrive with triple-cooked chips.

Chef Jonathan Henderson **Seats** 40 **Open** All year **Notes** Vegetarian dishes, Children welcome

BATH
Bailbrook House Hotel
◎◎ MODERN BRITISH **V**

01225 855100 | Eveleigh Avenue, London Road West, BA1 7JD

www.bailbrookhouse.co.uk

Bailbrook is a handsome Georgian country mansion done out in classy contemporary boutique style. Its Cloisters Restaurant is the fine-dining option, an intimate split-level space. Flavours counterpoint well in fish dishes such as halibut fillet with pea and bacon fricassée, Jersey Royals and girolles.

Chef Jonathan Machin **Seats** 54, Private dining 14 **Open** All year **Prices from** S £7.50, M £17, D £9.50 **Parking** 100 **Notes** Children welcome

The Bath Priory Hotel, Restaurant & Spa
◎◎◎ MODERN EUROPEAN, FRENCH **V** ▲NOTABLE WINE LIST

01225 331922 | Weston Road, BA1 2XT

www.thebathpriory.co.uk

So named as it was built in 1835 on land owned by the priory of Bath Abbey, the present-day family-owned hotel and spa had a brief spell in the 1960s as a school dorm. Restored to its proper tranquillity on the western side of the Georgian city, it is dedicated today to the full range of creature comforts, from massages to modern cuisine, the latter courtesy of much-travelled executive chef Michael Nizzero. The dining room is all neutral hues and white linen, a relaxing setting for confident British cooking with a sense of style. An opening gambit is a soft-cooked duck egg with potato and pickled mushrooms, sauced in golden Jura wine, an opulent prelude to regally treated fish, perhaps sea bass with a medley of shellfish, puréed fennel and seaweed in champagne emulsion. Meats are typically offset with fruity notes, such as blackberries with the roast duck, or cranberries with venison loin, Amandine potatoes and wild mushrooms. The bravura finishing touch may be blackcurrant soufflé with matching sorbet, or figs roasted in red wine with caramelised walnuts.

Chef Michael Nizzero **Seats** 50, Private dining 72 **Open** All year **Parking** 40 **Notes** No children under 12 years

The Chequers
◎◎ MODERN BRITISH

01225 360017 | 50 Rivers Street, BA1 2QA

www.thechequersbath.com

The Chequers has been providing drink and victuals since 1776. Food is the core of the operation, and everything made from scratch. Why not step outside the box with something like seared scallops with smoked pork belly, cauliflower, candied lime and cumin velouté?

Chef Alex Betts **Seats** 74, Private dining 20 **Open** All year **Notes** Vegetarian dishes, Children welcome

The Circus Restaurant
◎ MODERN EUROPEAN **V**

01225 466020 | 34 Brock Street, BA1 2LN

www.thecircusrestaurant.co.uk

In a prime location between two of Bath's most iconic locations, The Circus and the Royal Crescent, this is an upmarket all-day eatery, with high-ceilinged dining rooms offering a bold, modern setting for the monthly changing, seasonally inspired menu, based on fine West Country produce.

Chef Alison Golden, Tom Bally, Tony Casey **Seats** 50, Private dining 32 **Closed** 3 weeks from 24 December **Prices from** S £5.90, M £11.50, D £4.70 **Notes** Vegetarian dishes, No children under 10 years

Dan Moon at the Gainsborough Restaurant
◎◎◎ MODERN BRITISH **V**

01225 358888 | Beau Street, BA1 1QY

www.thegainsboroughbathspa.co.uk

If it's a blowout stay in Bath you're after, its hotels don't come with a more blue-blooded pedigree than The Gainsborough Bath Spa Hotel. Named after the eponymous artist, an erstwhile Bath resident, the place spreads across a handsome Grade II listed building dating from the 18th century. Looking elegantly understated with its unclothed tables, blue-and-white walls and caramel leather seats, the dining room is a suitably contemporary setting for Dan Moon's impeccably up-to-date British food. Expect bright, fresh combinations and entertaining textures, all soundly rooted in an intuitive grasp of how things work together, as seen in openers such as smoked loin of rabbit with confit rabbit and foie gras terrine, balanced by pickled radish and sweetcorn, or chicken liver parfait with rhubarb sorbet, granola and red vein sorrel. Mains, too, are inspired by top-notch materials, perhaps roasted loin of Mendip venison with goats' curd, pommes Anna, salt-baked celeriac, chanterelles and black pudding. Desserts also aim for maximum impact, as when Valrhona chocolate ganache arrives alongside honeycomb, orange sorbet, ginger and sour citra cress.

Chef Daniel Moon **Seats** 70 **Open** All year **Prices from** S £10.50, M £25.50, D £9.50 **Notes** Children welcome

The Dower House Restaurant

◉◉◉ MODERN BRITISH **V** ♦NOTABLE WINE LIST
01225 823333 | The Royal Crescent Hotel & Spa, 16 Royal Crescent, BA1 2LS
www.royalcrescent.co.uk

Set in the heart of the grandiose sweep that is the Royal Crescent, the likewise-named hotel is a boutique establishment run with consummate professionalism. To the back of the building, The Dower House is home to the elegant main dining room, where a blossoming branch is printed along the wall and a blue and beige colour scheme prevails. This is the relaxing setting for some classically rooted modern British cooking that's sharp and precise, while featuring big flavours and the all-important inventive touch. Blowtorched mackerel with its own tartare comes with artichokes, pressed cucumber and lemon gel, the additional notes of genius being a cream of the smoked roe and a champagne-poached oyster. Then comes roasted brill with crispy ham hock and a hot Caesar salad incorporating fresh anchovies, blanched garlic and a fried quail egg, or perhaps loin and faggot of venison with a Stilton beignet and poached pear. A featherlight but intense anise parfait accompanies deeply caramelised pear Tatin to finish, while a tropical trio brings together mango mousse, passionfruit, and coconut sorbet.

Chef David Campbell **Seats** 60, Private dining 20 **Open** All year **Parking** 17 **Notes** Children welcome

The Hare & Hounds

◉ MODERN BRITISH
01225 482682 | Lansdown Road, BA1 5TJ
www.hareandhoundsbath.com

A mile and a half north of Bath, The Hare & Hounds is an enticing bolt-hole with glorious views from its hilltop location. Huge windows look over the terrace and allow light into the neat interior where wood proliferates: tables, chairs, panelling and floor.

Chef Pravin Nayar **Seats** 106, Private dining 14 **Open** All year **Prices from** S £5.50, M £13.50, D £6 **Parking** 30 **Notes** Vegetarian dishes, Children welcome

Macdonald Bath Spa

◉◉ MODERN BRITISH **V**
01225 444424 | Sydney Road, BA2 6JF
www.macdonald-hotels.co.uk/bathspa

A majestic Georgian facade sets a grand tone, running through to the Vellore Restaurant in the original ballroom, where pillars and a high-domed ceiling add to a stately air. Engaging staff and a helpful sommelier keep things on track.

Chef Andrew Britton **Seats** 80, Private dining 120 **Open** All year **Parking** 160 **Notes** Children welcome

The Marlborough Tavern

◉◉ MODERN BRITISH
01225 423731 | 35 Marlborough Buildings, BA1 2LY
www.marlborough-tavern.com

This straight-talking foodie pub has a pleasingly unstuffy vibe and local ales and ciders on tap. Fare could be as simple as home-made burgers or fish and chips, or at the more gastro end, a five-course tasting menu with matching wines.

Chef Daniel Edwards **Seats** 60 **Open** All year **Prices from** S £6.50, M £11.50, D £6.50 **Notes** Vegetarian dishes, Children welcome

Menu Gordon Jones

◉◉ MODERN BRITISH **V**
01225 480871 | 2 Wellsway, BA2 3AQ
www.menugordonjones.co.uk

Gordon Jones has form in Bath, having run the Royal Crescent Hotel kitchen. Now he's doing his own thing in an unassuming little spot with foodies beating down the door to enjoy what's put before them. The main concepts here are surprise and anticipation.

Chef Gordon Jones **Seats** 22 **Closed** 35 days a year (variable) **Notes** No children under 12 years

The Olive Tree at the Queensberry Hotel

◉◉◉ MODERN BRITISH **V** ♦NOTABLE WINE LIST
See pages 284–285

The Scallop Shell

◉ BRITISH
01225 420928 | 22 Monmouth Place, BA1 2AY
www.thescallopshell.co.uk

Behind a sky-blue frontage not far from Queen Square, this popular venue offers a versatile range of fish and seafood dishes in a relaxed café-style format where food is ordered at the counter. Freshness is everything at The Scallop Shell. There is no separate dessert menu, just one sweet thing per day.

Chef Garry Rosser, Peter Horn **Seats** 85 **Open** All year **Prices from** S £5.50, M £10, D £5.95 **Notes** Vegetarian dishes, Children welcome

SOMERSET

BATH

The Olive Tree at the Queensberry Hotel

◉◉◉ MODERN BRITISH V 🍷NOTABLE WINE LIST

01225 447928 | Russell Street, BA1 2QF

www.olivetreebath.co.uk

Accomplished cooking in chic boutique Georgian hotel

The West Country's most elegant city has more enviable locations for good hotels and restaurants than you can shake a Bath bun at, and this stylish bolt-hole in a magnificent Georgian townhouse terrace – built for the 8th Marquess of Queensbury in 1771 – is firmly in the top flight. Owners Laurence and Helen Beere have transformed the place into a top-ranking boutique hotel, driven by a passion for hospitality and a keen eye for interior aesthetics. All that, plus a sense of fun, apparent in the New Queensberry Rules asking that guests refrain from using 'stilts, pogo sticks, spacehoppers, flaming torches or whips at the bar'. The Olive Tree restaurant occupies a series of interconnecting basement rooms bathing in a light, minimalist look. Head chef Chris Cleghorn has honed his craft in some top-flight kitchens (stints chez James Sommerin, Michael Caines and Heston Blumenthal to name but three) and his dynamic cooking and sharp technical skills are showcased here via a choice of seasonal tasting menus, including an impressive one for vegetarians, and an admirably flexible approach allows you to cherry-pick a starter, main course and dessert if

you're not up for the full-on tasting experience. Whichever route you take, the modern British dishes are all built on the finest West Country produce. Flavour combinations are well considered and intelligently executed – scallops might be lifted with shiitake ketchup and leek, or beef tartare given a new spin with smoked egg yolk and caviar. Main ingredients are often given different stages of treatment, then deepened with layers of aromatic and assertively flavoured accompaniments in thoughtful combinations – mackerel, for example, might be cured and torched, then matched with cucumber, horseradish and apple to balance its assertive flavour. Other ideas could be robustly treated fish, perhaps brill served on the bone with celeriac, smoked eel and dashi broth, while venison might be partnered with barbecued cauliflower, raisin, sprout and bitter chocolate. If you're giving meat a swerve, intelligently composed dishes such as beetroot, frozen goats' curd, hazelnut and truffle, or chervil gnocchi with carrot, Roscoff onion and hen of the woods mushrooms are a lesson in texture and well-matched flavours. Scintillating desserts also bring superb displays of tastes, textures and temperatures – rhubarb, say, with sheep's yogurt, baked white chocolate and ginger, or Muscovado tart with coffee ice cream and walnuts. The wine list offers an eclectic international selection that bears the owners' hands-on stamp.

Chef Chris Cleghorn **Seats** 60, Private dining 30 **Closed** 1 week January, last week July, 1st week August and 1st week November **Prices from** S £13.50, M £26.50, D £9.50 **Notes** Children welcome

SOMERSET

BATH continued

Woods Restaurant
◉ MODERN BRITISH, FRENCH
01225 314812 | 9–13 Alfred Street, BA1 2QX
www.woodsrestaurant.com
Woods stands in a very 'Bath' setting, occupying the ground floor of five Georgian townhouses, and its comfortable bistro look is pretty much timeless. The cooking is broadly European, with French and Italy to the fore, and a British flavour here and there.
Chef Stuart Ash **Seats** 100, Private dining 40 **Closed** 25–26 December **Notes** Vegetarian dishes, Children welcome

BRIDGWATER
Walnut Tree Hotel
◉ MODERN BRITISH
01278 662255 | North Petherton, TA6 6QA
www.walnuttreehotel.com
The handsome former coaching inn is to be found in the town of North Petherton near Bridgwater, with the Quantock Hills not far. A traditional pub ambience prevails in the bar, and there is a cream-walled, airy dining room bright with fresh flowers and candles.
Chef Jakoby Phillips **Open** All Year

CASTLE CARY
The Pilgrims
◉◉ MODERN BRITISH
01963 240597 | Lovington, BA7 7PT
www.thepilgrimsatlovington.co.uk
The name honours those who passed this way on their quest to find King Arthur's tomb. The stone-built inn is now a restaurant with rooms, run with cheerful bonhomie by the Mitchisons – Sally presiding over front of house and Jools running the kitchen.
Chef Julian Mitchison **Seats** 25 **Open** All year **Parking** 40 **Notes** Vegetarian dishes, Children welcome

CHEDDAR
The Bath Arms
◉◉ MODERN BRITISH
01934 742425 | Bath Street, BS27 3AA
www.batharms.com
Smack in the centre of Cheddar village and within footslogging distance of the eponymous gorge and caves, The Bath Arms has kept faith with those essential pubby virtues – real ales, a genuine welcome and great food. The kitchen turns out some impressive culinary action.
Chef Sean Lee **Seats** 70 **Open** All year **Prices from** S £4.95, M £11.95, D £5.50 **Parking** 50 **Notes** Vegetarian dishes, Children welcome

CHEW MAGNA
The Pony and Trap
◉◉ MODERN BRITISH
01275 332627 | Knowle Hill, BS40 8TQ
www.theponyandtrap.co.uk
Chef/owner Josh Eggleton, known for his 2014 performance on the TV show *The Great British Menu*, is behind this revitalised 200-year-old country cottage pub in lush Chew Valley countryside. Ingredients arrive on the plate fresh from the herb and vegetable garden.
Chef Josh Eggleton **Seats** 64 **Open** All year **Parking** 40 **Notes** Vegetarian dishes, Children welcome

CORTON DENHAM
The Queens Arms
◉◉ MODERN BRITISH
01963 220317 | DT9 4LR
www.thequeensarms.com
This mellow stone 18th-century inn is set amid buxom hills on the Somerset-Dorset border, and a glance at the menu shows a clear love for local produce and a creative mind. The dining room is a cosy space; bare boards, dark walls and mis-matched, unclothed tables,
Chef Glen Banks **Seats** 78, Private dining 45 **Open** All year **Prices from** S £6.50, M £14, D £7.50 **Parking** 20 **Notes** Vegetarian dishes, Children welcome

DULVERTON
Woods Bar & Restaurant
◉◉ MODERN BRITISH, FRENCH **V**
01398 324007 | 4 Banks Square, TA22 9BU
www.woodsdulverton.co.uk
On the edge of Exmoor, Woods is a pub cunningly disguised on the outside to look like a café. The interior is cheered with a log fire, and wooden partitions divide the place between the drinking of local ales and the eating of locally sourced food.
Chef Ed Herd **Seats** 38 **Closed** 25 December **Notes** Children welcome

DUNSTER
The Luttrell Arms Hotel
◉◉ BRITISH
01643 821555 | Exmoor National Park, TA24 6SG
www.luttrellarms.co.uk
Located within the delightful setting of this 15th-century hotel, the restaurant offers relaxed and comfortable dining and a pleasing combination of traditional style with a more modern country-house feel. Hearty portions from an inspiring menu might include beef Wellington with truffle mash.
Chef Barrie Tucker **Seats** 45, Private dining 20 **Open** All year **Notes** Vegetarian dishes, Children welcome

FIVEHEAD
Langford Fivehead
◉◉ MODERN BRITISH **V**
01460 282020 | Lower Swell, TA3 6PH
www.langfordfivehead.co.uk
The Tudor manor house at Lower Swell stands in seven acres of mature grounds, full of cedars, box and yew. A contemporary dining room with modern artworks has a relaxed feel, and elegantly simple farm-to-plate eating is the order of the day.
Chef Olly Jackson **Seats** 22, Private dining 12 **Closed** 2 January for 2 weeks and 24 July for 2 weeks **Parking** 8 **Notes** No children under 8 years

FLAX BOURTON
Backwell House
◉◉
01275 794502 | Farleigh Road, BS48 3QA
www.backwellhouse.co.uk
Describing itself as 'thrillingly luxurious', Backwell House is a splendid Georgian mansion of golden Bath stone. There's a walled garden, the bedrooms are fab and the public rooms are quirky and stylish, so maybe you should treat yourself and go for the weekend.
Seats 40 **Open** All year **Notes** Vegetarian dishes, No children

HINTON CHARTERHOUSE
Homewood Park Hotel & Spa
◉◉ BRITISH **V**
01225 723731 | Abbey Lane, BA2 7TB
www.homewoodpark.co.uk
Homewood came to prominence during the first wave of the country-hotel movement in the 1980s. The chef takes the modern British bull by the horns with glazed pig's cheek with cheddar pommes purée and chard, a finely judged dish that is halfway to a main.
Chef Michael Ball **Seats** 70, Private dining 40 **Open** All year **Prices from** S £7.50, M £19.80, D £8.50 **Parking** 40 **Notes** Children welcome

HOLCOMBE
The Holcombe Inn
◉◉ BRITISH, INTERNATIONAL, FRENCH
01761 232478 | Stratton Road, BA3 5EB
www.holcombeinn.co.uk
A textbook country inn with fires, local ales and amicable staff. Regional ingredients, including the produce of its own garden, supply the menus of mostly traditional fare. Desserts might be a raspberry and nougat parfait choc ice with a Valrhona brownie.
Chef Shane Vant **Seats** 65 **Open** All year **Prices from** S £6.75, M £12.95, D £6.95 **Parking** 30 **Notes** Vegetarian dishes, Children welcome

HUNSTRETE
THE PIG near Bath
◉◉ MODERN BRITISH ▐ NOTABLE WINE LIST
01761 490490 | Hunstrete House, Pensford, BS39 4NS
www.thepighotel.com
At first sight, this is the archetypal English country-house hotel. Inside, however, the style is shabby-chic, the mood is chilled and hip and the whole operation has food at its heart, with much brought in from the gardens or foraged from fields and woods.
Chef Kamil Oseka **Seats** 90, Private dining 22 **Open** All year **Parking** 50 **Notes** Vegetarian dishes, Children welcome

LOWER GODNEY
The Sheppey
◉ MODERN BISTRO
01458 831594 | BA5 1RN
www.thesheppey.co.uk
Tucked away in the Somerset Levels, surrounded by peat moors, dairy farms and wildlife reserves, the delightfully quirky Sheppey attracts an eclectic mix of clientele. Many are drawn to the regular live music, others make a beeline here for the local ciders and ales.
Chef Kieron Ash, Matthew Creagh **Seats** 80 **Open** All year **Prices from** S £5.50, M £12.50, D £5.50 **Notes** Vegetarian dishes, Children welcome

MIDSOMER NORTON
Best Western Plus Centurion Hotel
◉◉ MODERN BRITISH **V**
01761 417711 | Charlton Lane, BA3 4BD
www.centurionhotel.co.uk
The restaurant in this modern family-run hotel is an inviting space, with a bright conservatory extension and menus full of appealing options. You'll want to conclude with one of the choose-me puddings such as an assiette of Yorkshire rhubarb, or caramelised pear rice pudding.
Chef Sean Horwood **Seats** 60, Private dining 120 **Closed** 25–26 December **Prices from** S £6, M £15, D £6 **Parking** 164 **Notes** Children welcome

MILVERTON
The Globe
◉ MODERN BRITISH
01823 400534 | Fore Street, TA4 1JX
www.theglobemilverton.co.uk
The Globe is still very much a pub, but it's a strong food destination too. The food is up-to-date country-pub fare and Sundays bring on traditionally garnished roasts – beef topside, lamb leg, pork – with roasties and Yorkshire puddings.
Chef Mark Tarry **Seats** 50 **Open** All year **Parking** 3 **Notes** Vegetarian dishes, Children welcome

SOMERSET

MONKSILVER
The Notley Arms Inn
◉ CLASSIC BRITISH
01984 656095 | Front Street, TA4 4JB
www.notleyarmsinn.co.uk
Chesterfields at an open fire, a mix of dining chairs and pew-style seating, and attentive staff add to the enjoyable experience of a visit to this whitewashed village inn. The kitchen turns out eloquently flavoured, well-executed dishes as well as some pub classics.
Chef Stephen Frost **Seats** 55 **Open** All year **Parking** 20 **Notes** Vegetarian dishes, Children welcome

NORTH WOOTTON
Crossways Inn
◉ MODERN BRITISH
01749 899000 | Stocks Lane, BA4 4EU
www.thecrossways.co.uk
A thoroughly contemporary kind of inn these days, the 18th-century Crossways looks much the same as it always has from the outside, but a 21st-century makeover has opened-up the place. It's the kind of place where you can eat what you want where you want.
Chef Barney Everett **Seats** 100, Private dining 86 **Open** All year **Parking** 120 **Notes** Vegetarian dishes, Children welcome

OAKHILL
The Oakhill Inn
◉ MODERN BRITISH
01749 840442 | Fosse Road, BA3 5HU
www.theoakhillinn.com
An ancient stone-built inn with hanging baskets is many people's idea of old England, and The Oakhill looks the part. The food itself edges more firmly into modern British territory than hitherto, although devotees of pub classics such as bubble-and-squeak have not been abandoned.
Chef Charlie Digney **Seats** 60, Private dining 50 **Closed** 25 December **Prices from** S £5.95, M £10.95, D £5.95 **Parking** 12 **Notes** Vegetarian dishes, Children welcome

RADSTOCK
The Redan Inn
◉◉ MODERN BRITISH
01761 258560 | Fry's Well, Chilcompton, BA3 4HA
www.theredaninn.co.uk
This whitewashed village inn has light wood tones and boarded walls in the dining area, a wood-burner in the bar, and comfortable seating outside. Pedigree Somerset produce underpins an innovative approach.

Luxurious desserts include rosemary pannacotta, apple granite, honeycomb and salted caramel.
Chef Tony Casey **Seats** 30, Private dining 12 **Open** All year **Parking** 16 **Notes** Vegetarian dishes, Children welcome

SHEPTON MALLET
Charlton House Hotel & Spa
◉ MODERN BRITISH
01749 342008 | Charlton Road, BA4 4PR
www.bannatyne.co.uk
A grand stone manor on the edge of Shepton Mallet, Charlton House combines period charm and contemporary style. A menu of modern British dishes includes flavours from beyond the European borders. For dessert try Asian flavours in rice pudding with chilli and lychee sorbet.
Chef Stephen Yates **Seats** 60, Private dining 80 **Open** All year **Prices from** S £7.50, M £12.50, D £6.50 **Parking** 70 **Notes** Vegetarian dishes, Children welcome

SOMERTON
The Devonshire Arms
◉ MODERN BRITISH
01458 241271 | Long Sutton, TA10 9LP
www.thedevonshirearms.com
This Georgian former hunting lodge turned restaurant with rooms is a convivial hub where people pop in for a jar of ale or cider in the bar, or for a full meal in the restaurant. Alfresco dining is pleasant in the courtyard and walled garden.
Chef Christopher Decourcey-Wheeler **Seats** 40, Private dining 16 **Closed** 25–26 December **Parking** 6 **Notes** Vegetarian dishes, Children welcome

STON EASTON
Ston Easton Park Hotel
◉◉ MODERN BRITISH **V**
01761 241631 | BA3 4DF
www.stoneaston.co.uk
A grand Palladian mansion in 36 acres of grounds landscaped by Humphry Repton – including a Victorian walled kitchen garden that provides seasonal organic fruit, veg, herbs and edible flowers. The team deliver light and confident modern country house-style cooking, bursting with luxurious ingredients, intense flavours and pin-sharp presentations.
Chef Ashley Lewis **Seats** 40, Private dining 80 **Open** All year **Parking** 60 **Notes** No children under 8 years at dinner

TAUNTON

Augustus

◎◎ BRITISH, FRENCH **V**

01823 324354 | 3 The Courtyard, St James Street, TA1 1JR

www.augustustaunton.co.uk

The repeated shrilling of the phone serves notice of the popularity of Richard Guest's stylish, friendly courtyard restaurant. There's a pared-down, contemporary look, with white-painted brick walls and unclothed, dark wood tables complementing the equally modern brasserie style food.

Chef Richard Guest **Seats** 40 **Closed** 25 December, 1 January **Prices from** S £6, M £12.95, D £6 **Notes** Children welcome

Castle Bow Restaurant

◎◎◎ MODERN BRITISH

01823 328328 | Castle Green, TA1 1NF

www.castlebow.com

In the ownership of the Chapman family, the Castle Hotel is the jewel in Taunton's crown. Firing on all cylinders in the culinary stakes, the principal dining room, Castle Bow, is the preserve of Liam Finnegan. He draws on the Castle's own orchard and herb garden, as well as meticulously selected local suppliers, to furnish a menu of vigorous modern British dishes that achieve real impact. Pasta work is good, as in an opener of Brixham crab tortellini scented with sea herbs, lemongrass and lime, while Quantock rabbit stars in a robust production with goose liver, celeriac and piccalilli. For main, there might be Exmoor venison with parsnip and red cabbage, opulently sauced in whisky, or a carefully considered fish dish such as Lyme Bay cod and grilled octopus in an assertive array of chicory, quince, bacon and tartare sauce. That orchard produce then turns up as apple mousse with pear and cinnamon ice cream, or there could be orange mascarpone cheesecake with macadamias and yogurt sorbet.

Chef Liam Finnegan **Seats** 30 **Closed** 7–24 January **Prices from** S £10, M £18 **Parking** 44 **Notes** Vegetarian dishes, No children under 5 years

The Mount Somerset Hotel & Spa

◎◎◎ BRITISH **V**

01823 442500 | Lower Henlade, TA3 5NB

www.mountsomersethotel.co.uk

Set in four acres of beautiful grounds and gardens, a cosseting air of luxury pervades the Mount Somerset, a fine Regency hotel with splendid views across the Quantock and Blackdown Hills. Inside you'll find all the original features you could wish for. In the kitchen, head chef Mark Potts has been making his presence felt, ensuring his menus bring a stylish and contemporary air to the high-ceilinged dining room.

Dishes are nicely judged, often featuring herbs, fruit and vegetables from the hotel's own garden. A starter of perfectly cooked veal sweetbreads, enhanced with thinly sliced cauliflower, hints of truffle and Mimolette cheese is a delicate dish, while a tasting of suckling pig makes a more robust main course, taking in pork belly, a lean, moist chop, and tender pork loin, all enhanced by choi sum and a sweet cider jus. 'Apples and Pears' is a soft, light apple and prune sponge, with poached pear and toast ice cream.

Chef Mark Potts **Seats** 60, Private dining 50 **Open** All year **Prices from** S £12.50, M £25, D £9.50 **Parking** 100 **Notes** Children welcome

TINTINHULL

Crown & Victoria

◎ BRITISH

01935 823341 | Farm Street, BA22 8PZ

www.thecrownandvictoria.co.uk

This is the kind of country pub that spurs urbanites to up sticks and move to a rural idyll. It's a proper pub, with a changing rota of ales and a serious approach to food. The kitchen keeps things local, seeking out organic, free-range ingredients.

Chef Rodney Scott, Daniel Hillyard, Oliver Harrison **Seats** 100, Private dining 45 **Open** All year **Prices from** S £6.25, M £10.95, D £6.50 **Parking** 50 **Notes** Vegetarian dishes, Children welcome

WELLS

Best Western Plus Swan Hotel

◎◎ MODERN BRITISH

01749 836300 | Sadler Street, BA5 2RX

www.swanhotelwells.co.uk

Once a coaching inn, The Swan is in the heart of Wells, close to the cathedral. The panelled restaurant is a smart and comfortable affair, with a short but ingenious menu. Check out the warm honey and stout tart for dessert.

Chef Adam Kennington **Seats** 50, Private dining 90 **Open** All year **Parking** 30 **Notes** Vegetarian dishes, Children welcome

Goodfellows

◎◎ MEDITERRANEAN, EUROPEAN

01749 673866 | 5 Sadler Street, BA5 2RR

www.goodfellowswells.co.uk

Look for the plum-coloured facade in the town centre. If it's first thing, breakfast is on hand in the café, or you might have a Danish and cappuccino at elevenses. Otherwise, sign up for some distinguished seafood-led cookery in the adjoining restaurant.

Chef Adam Fellows **Seats** 35, Private dining 20 **Closed** 25–27 December and 1 January **Notes** Vegetarian dishes, Children welcome

YEOVIL
Little Barwick House
◉◉◉ MODERN BRITISH
01935 423902 | Barwick, BA22 9TD
www.littlebarwickhouse.co.uk
This charming Georgian dower house is the perfect setting for a family-run restaurant with rooms. Public areas are relaxed and comfortable, and the Ford family (Tim and son Olly in the kitchen, wife Emma out front) have worked hard to create a delightfully civilized setting for their classically based, thoughtfully considered and precisely constructed dishes. The airy, gracious dining room overlooks the garden, and menus concentrate on wonderfully fresh produce, including fish from Cornwall. Menus are straightforward, and the main ingredient in each dish is given plenty of room to shine. A paupiette of Cornish lemon sole stuffed with Cornish lobster is a starter that signals the kitchen's intentions nicely, a delicate dish, full of flavour and elegant simplicity. A turbot main is another beautiful piece of fish, perfectly cooked and served with basil new potatoes, mini vegetables and champagne sauce. An Amaretto pannacotta is a fine example, thick and creamy and served with roasted pear and fig, and a slightly sharper pear sorbet for contrast. The wine list is exceptionally good.
Chef Timothy Ford Seats 40 Closed New Year, 2 weeks in January Parking 25 Notes Vegetarian dishes, No children under 5 years

▶ STAFFORDSHIRE
HOAR CROSS
The Ballroom Restaurant
◉ MODERN BRITISH
01283 575671 | Hoar Cross Hall, Maker Lane, DE13 8QS
www.hoarcross.co.uk
Guests at this 17th-century stately home in 50 deeply rural acres flock to the rather grand Ballroom, but not just for its food. Huge chandeliers hang from its lofty ceilings, the wallpaper is William Morris, the table settings are faultless, and the views are delightful.
Chef Tom Biddle Open All year Notes Vegetarian dishes, No children under 16 years

LEEK
Three Horseshoes Country Inn & Spa
◉◉ CLASSIC BRITISH
01538 300296 | Buxton Road, Blackshaw Moor, ST13 8TW
www.threeshoesinn.co.uk
The stone-built inn overlooked by lowering gritstone outcrops in the southern stretches of the Peak District covers many bases. Original oak beams, exposed brick walls and dark slate tiles are matched to create contemporary styling, with an open-to-view kitchen, augmenting the dynamic atmosphere.
Chefs Mark and Stephen Kirk, Gary Woolliscroft Seats 100, Private dining 150 Open All year Prices from S £5.45, M £10.95, D £3.50 Parking 100 Notes Vegetarian dishes, Children welcome

LICHFIELD
Swinfen Hall Hotel
◉◉◉ MODERN BRITISH **V**
01543 481494 | Swinfen, WS14 9RE
www.swinfenhallhotel.co.uk
Dating from 1757, this splendid mansion, complete with columns and pediment, is set in 100 acres of parkland, including a walled kitchen garden, deer park and formal gardens – hard to believe it's just half an hour from Birmingham's city centre. A careful restoration has created a stylish hotel, with elegant bedrooms and fine public areas with many period features. The oak-panelled dining room, with its ornate ceiling and heavily swagged drapes, enjoys views across the terrace and gardens to the deer park. Ryan Shilton's contemporary dishes are carefully considered, with thoughtful combinations of flavour and texture. Dinner might begin with sea-fresh barbecued mackerel with pickled apple and mustard 'snow', brightened with nasturtium flowers. A main course of Welsh lamb rump is served nicely pink, sweet and tender, with glazed belly offering a deeper flavour. Broad beans, mint and yogurt give a pop of green and good fresh flavour. Valrhona chocolate, bay leaf, popcorn is a smooth and silky ganache with a crisp tuile and creamy popcorn ice cream, popcorn crumb and chocolate popcorn.
Chef Ryan Shilton Seats 45, Private dining 22 Closed 26 December and 1 January Prices from S £10, M £25, D £8.50 Parking 80 Notes Children welcome

STAFFORD
The Moat House
◉◉ MODERN BRITISH
01785 712217 | Lower Penkridge Road, Acton Trussell, ST17 0RJ
www.moathouse.co.uk
The Moat House is indeed moated, a part-timbered manor dating from the 14th century. Main courses on the seasonally changing carte can be complex too but equally satisfying. For dessert try Turkish delight cheesecake with rose water gel and chocolate sorbet.
Chef Matthew Davies, James Cracknell Seats 120, Private dining 150 Closed 25 December Prices from S £6.25, M £15.50, D £6.50 Parking 200 Notes Vegetarian dishes, Children welcome

The Shropshire Inn
◉ TRADITIONAL BRITISH
01785 780904 | Newport Road, Haughton, ST18 9HB
www.theshropshireinnhaughton.co.uk
The family-run Shropshire hasn't decamped to Staffordshire, but has stood firm while county boundaries have flowed around it. Its physiognomy is a little different these days, with full-length windows looking on to the garden, and gathered curtains in the dining area creating an upscale ambience.
Chef Steve Kirkham **Seats** 100 **Open** All year **Parking** 60 **Notes** Vegetarian dishes, Children welcome

▶ SUFFOLK

ALDEBURGH
Brudenell Hotel
◉◉ MODERN BRITISH, EUROPEAN
01728 452071 | The Parade, IP15 5BU
www.brudenellhotel.co.uk
This privately owned hotel is virtually on Aldeburgh's beach so, naturally enough, seafood tops the bill, freshly delivered along with free-range meat each morning. Whole dressed crab with salad, new potatoes and lemon mayonnaise is just one of the tasty options.
Chef Ben Hegarty **Seats** 100, Private dining 20 **Open** All year **Parking** 15 **Notes** Vegetarian dishes, Children welcome

Regatta Restaurant
◉ MODERN BRITISH
01728 452011 | 171 High Street, IP15 5AN
www.regattaaldeburgh.com
A nautical-themed mural and piscine prints leave no doubt that fresh local seafood, often landed on the beach, is the main thrust of the Mabeys' restaurant on the High Street. It's a cheery, relaxed place, with a blackboard of daily specials supporting the carte.
Chef Robert Mabey **Seats** 90, Private dining 20 **Closed** 24–26 and 31 December and 1 January **Prices from** S £4.50, M £12, D £5.50 **Notes** Vegetarian dishes, Children welcome

The White Lion Hotel
◉ BRITISH, FRENCH
01728 452720 | Market Cross Place, IP15 5BJ
www.whitelion.co.uk
Sitting in beachfront splendour by the shingle banks of Aldeburgh's strand, The White Lion deals in unpretentious brasserie dining, built on fine Suffolk

ingredients – in fact, sourcing doesn't get more local than the fish landed a few steps away on the beach.
Chef James Barber **Seats** 80 **Open** All year **Prices from** S £5, M £12, D £6 **Parking** 10 **Notes** Vegetarian dishes, Children welcome

BILDESTON
The Bildeston Crown
◉◉ MODERN BRITISH
01449 740510 | 104–106 High Street, IP7 7EB
www.thebildestoncrown.co.uk
The Bildeston Crown has all the chocolate-box charm you'd hope for in a 15th-century former coaching inn, although there's a very 21st-century take on things, which means boutique bedrooms, an atmospheric beamed bar, a smart restaurant and classy food ranging from pub classics to more modern ideas from a kitchen that's on song.
Chef Chris Lee **Seats** 100, Private dining 30 **Prices from** S £8, M £14, D £8 **Parking** 20 **Open** All year **Notes** Vegetarian dishes, Children welcome

BROME
Best Western Brome Grange Hotel
◉◉ MODERN BRITISH
01379 870456 | Norwich Road, Nr Diss, IP23 8AP
www.bromegrangehotel.co.uk
It's easy to imagine horse-drawn carriages sweeping into the central courtyard of this 16th-century former coaching inn, with plenty of period details remaining inside and out. The Courtyard Restaurant, however, is a light and contemporary affair with vivid colours and well-spaced dark wood tables.
Chef Matthew Cooke **Seats** 60, Private dining 28 **Open** All year **Prices from** S £4.95, M £9.95, D £4.50 **Parking** 120 **Notes** Vegetarian dishes, Children welcome

BURY ST EDMUNDS
The Angel Hotel
◉◉ MODERN BRITISH
01284 714000 | Angel Hill, IP33 1LT
www.theangel.co.uk
Overlooking the cathedral and abbey walls, The Angel is a quintessential Georgian coaching inn with a creeper-curtained facade. Inside, the generous spaces have been overlaid with a contemporary boutique look. The Eaterie's kitchen shows equally 21st-century sensibilities in its repertoire of upbeat brasserie food.
Chef James Carn **Seats** 85, Private dining 16 **Open** All year **Notes** Vegetarian dishes, Children welcome

Best Western Priory Hotel
⚫ MODERN BRITISH, INTERNATIONAL
01284 766181 | Mildenhall Road, IP32 6EH
www.prioryhotel.co.uk

A peaceful atmosphere reigns throughout the Priory, including in the Garden Room restaurant, which offers soft lighting and a comforting feeling of being looked after by endlessly helpful staff. The kitchen produces dishes that pull in inspiration from across the globe.

Chef Matthew Cook **Seats** 72, Private dining 28 **Open** All year **Parking** 60 **Notes** Vegetarian dishes, Children welcome

The Leaping Hare Restaurant & Country Store
⚫⚫ CLASSIC, TRADITIONAL
01359 250287 | Wyken Vineyards, Stanton, IP31 2DW
www.wykenvineyards.co.uk

Set on a 1,200-acre farm complete with Shetland sheep and Red Poll cattle, plus a vineyard, The Leaping Hare occupies a splendid 400-year-old barn with a high raftered ceiling. What the farm doesn't provide is locally sourced, with fish landed at Lowestoft.

Chef Simon Woodrow **Seats** 47 **Closed** 2 weeks at Christmas reopening 6–8 January **Prices from** S £6.95, M £13.95, D £6.95 **Parking** 50 **Notes** Vegetarian dishes, Children welcome

Maison Bleue
⚫⚫ MODERN FRENCH
01284 760623 | 30–31 Churchgate Street, IP33 1RG
www.maisonbleue.co.uk

The Maison flies the tricolour for proudly French seafood cuisine in the bustling heart of Bury St Edmunds. The place is teemingly popular, indicating that the taste for unreconstructed Gallic cooking never went away. Meat dishes include beef featherblade which is a cut above.

Chef Pascal Canevet **Seats** 60, Private dining 33 **Closed** January, 2 weeks in summer **Notes** Vegetarian dishes, Children welcome

1921 Angel Hill
⚫⚫ BRITISH
01284 704870 | IP33 1UZ
www.nineteen-twentyone.co.uk

In a gloriously wonky period building, this decidedly up-to-date address turns out inspired modern British food with seasonal and local ingredients to the fore. It all takes place in a room with a slick contemporary finish and a knowledgeable service team setting the tone.

Chef Zack Deakins **Seats** 50, Private dining 14 **Closed** 23 December to 8 January **Prices from** S £7, M £17 **Notes** Vegetarian dishes, Children welcome

Pea Porridge
⚫⚫ MODERN BISTRO
01284 700200 | 28–29 Cannon Street, IP33 1JR
www.peaporridge.co.uk

Two cottages dating from 1820 have been converted into this unpretentious restaurant where 'Simplicity' is key, although plenty of expertise goes into the cooking. Snails with bone marrow, bacon, parsley, capers and garlic is a great way to kick things off.

Chef Justin Sharp **Seats** 46, Private dining 20 **Closed** 2 weeks September and 2 weeks Christmas **Notes** Vegetarian dishes, Children welcome

The White Horse
⚫ MODERN BRITISH
01284 735760 | Rede Road, Whepstead, IP29 4SS
www.whitehorsewhepstead.co.uk

This stylishly made over, mustard-yellow village inn sits comfortably at the gastro pub end of the spectrum, but without losing any of the features one hopes for – smart and cosy rooms with a copper-sheathed bar serving Suffolk ales, a huge inglenook and country-style tables.

Chef Craig Rice **Seats** 50, Private dining 25 **Open** All year **Prices from** S £4.50, M £11.95, D £5.50 **Parking** 30 **Notes** Vegetarian dishes, Children welcome

CAVENDISH
The George
⚫⚫ MODERN BRITISH
01787 280248 | The Green, CO10 8BA
www.thecavendishgeorge.co.uk

This handsome timbered 16th-century inn is rooted into the fabric of its ancient Suffolk village. The kitchen deals in no-nonsense modern comfort food with big, bold Mediterranean-inflected flavours that keep a keen eye on the seasons.

Chef Lewis Bennet **Seats** 50 **Closed** 25 December, 1 January **Notes** Vegetarian dishes, Children welcome

DUNWICH
The Ship at Dunwich
⚫ MODERN BRITISH
01728 648219 | St James Street, IP17 3DT
www.shipatdunwich.co.uk

Climbing foliage adorns this red-brick pub in a coastal village. Surrounded by heathland and nature reserves, with a beach on hand and Southwold nearby, it's got the lot, including a garden with an ancient fig tree and a courtyard for outdoor dining.

Chef Liam Davidson **Seats** 70, Private dining 35 **Open** All year **Parking** 20 **Notes** Vegetarian dishes, Children welcome

FRESSINGFIELD
Fox & Goose Inn
◉◉ MODERN BRITISH
01379 586247 | Church Road, IP21 5PB
www.foxandgoose.net

Fressingfield's timber-framed Tudor guild hall serves as the village inn, but if you want something more ambitious than well-crafted pub classics, head upstairs to the beamed restaurant for creative modern cooking driven by Suffolk's abundant larder. The kitchen aims higher than the average pub offering.

Chef P Yaxley, M Wyatt **Seats** 70, Private dining 35 **Closed** 25–30 December, 2nd week January for 2 weeks **Parking** 15 **Notes** Vegetarian dishes, No children under 9 years at dinner

HINTLESHAM
Hintlesham Hall Hotel
◉◉ MODERN BRITISH **V**
01473 652334 | George Street, IP8 3NS
www.hintleshamhall.com

Hintlesham Hall is a beautifully proportioned Grade I listed building of three wings, the facade a 1720 addition to the 16th-century core. The kitchen displays originality not commonly seen in such surroundings, producing thoughtfully constructed and elegant dishes eminently suited to the stylish dining room.

Chef Alan Ford **Seats** 80, Private dining 80 **Open** All year **Prices from** S £9, M £25, D £9 **Parking** 80 **Notes** No children under 12 years at dinner

HORRINGER
The Ickworth
◉◉ MODERN MEDITERRANEAN **V**
01284 735350 | IP29 5QE
www.ickworthhotel.co.uk

When Frederick Hervey, 4th Earl of Bristol, lived here in the early 18th century, he commissioned the impressive Rotunda to house his treasures. Frederick's, the restaurant named after him, is not without its delights either, not least its traditional style.

Chef Iain Inman **Seats** 78, Private dining 34 **Open** All year **Parking** 50 **Notes** Children welcome

INGHAM
The Cadogan Arms
◉ TRADITIONAL BRITISH
01284 728443 | The Street, IP31 1NG
www.thecadogan.co.uk

Flexibility is key in this smartly revamped former coaching inn, whether you just want a jar of real ale in the bar, a grazing board to snack on, or a full-blown meal. The decor is stylish with subdued lighting, upholstered sofas and chair.

Chef Karl Brunning **Seats** 72 **Closed** 25–26 December **Parking** 39 **Notes** Vegetarian dishes, Children welcome

IPSWICH
Mariners
◉◉ FRENCH, MEDITERRANEAN **V**
01473 289748 | Neptune Quay, IP4 1AX
www.marinersipswich.co.uk

Mariners has quite a history: built as a gunboat in Bruges in 1899, it was sunk in 1940, became a hospital ship in the 1950s and was an Italian restaurant in Ipswich before becoming a French brasserie. Mains might be pan-fried fillet of Scottish salmon with creamy wild mushroom Carnaroli risotto.

Chef Frederic Lebrun **Seats** 80, Private dining 30 **Closed** January **Notes** Children welcome

milsoms Kesgrave Hall
◉◉ MODERN INTERNATIONAL
01473 333741 | Hall Road, Kesgrave, IP5 2PU
www.milsomhotels.com

Hiding in woodland near Ipswich, this sparkling-white boutique hotel has verandah seating out front. Once inside the Brasserie dining room with its open kitchen and plain wooden tables, you write down your food order and take it to the bar for service.

Chef Stuart Oliver, Aarron Skerritt **Seats** 150, Private dining 24 **Open** All year **Prices from** S £4.50, M £14.50, D £6.75 **Parking** 150 **Notes** Vegetarian dishes, Children welcome

Salthouse Harbour Hotel
◉◉ MODERN BRITISH
01473 226789 | No 1 Neptune Quay, IP4 1AX
www.salthouseharbour.co.uk

A harbourside warehouse makeover with eye-popping interior collisions of lime-green and violet, the Salthouse deals in brasserie food with look-at-me flavours. A gin and tonic arrives later than is conventional, in a dessert of apple and Hendrick's jelly, with cucumber sorbet and lime granita.

Chef Chris McQuitty **Seats** 70 **Open** All year **Notes** Vegetarian dishes, Children welcome

SUFFOLK

IXWORTH
Theobald's Restaurant
◎◎ MODERN BRITISH
01359 231707 | 68 High Street, IP31 2HJ
www.theobaldsrestaurant.co.uk
Converted from a whitewashed Tudor inn in the early 1980s, Theobald's pulls in diners with its consistency and attention to detail. Ancient beams abound and tables are dressed in pristine white. There's a monthly changing carte, and locally reared meats and East Anglian fish are the mainstays.
Chef Simon Theobald **Seats** 32 **Closed** 10 days in spring/summer **Notes** Vegetarian dishes, No children under 8 years at dinner

LAVENHAM
The Swan at Lavenham Hotel and Spa
◎◎ MODERN, TRADITIONAL V ↓ NOTABLE WINE LIST
01787 247477 | High Street, CO10 9QA
www.theswanatlavenham.co.uk
Dating back to the 15th century, this characterful, asymmetrical timbered building is full of beams and period charm. The main restaurant is the Gallery, named for the medieval minstrels' balcony that can still be seen. The setting might be historic but the food is modern.
Chef Justin Kett **Seats** 90, Private dining 40 **Open** All year **Parking** 50 **Notes** No children under 5 years

LONG MELFORD
Long Melford Swan
◎◎ MODERN, CONTEMPORARY BRITISH V
01787 464545 | Hall Street, CO10 9JQ
www.longmelfordswan.co.uk
The Swan has now extended the restaurant to look out onto the garden and also opened the Duck Deli, full of East Anglian artisan produce. If you're eating in, the young team will kitchen conjure up innovative combinations from tip-top ingredients.
Chef Oliver Macmillan, Luke Parsons **Seats** 60, Private dining 8 **Open** All year **Prices from** S £8.50, M £16, D £5.50 **Notes** Children welcome

LOWESTOFT
The Crooked Barn Restaurant
◎◎ MODERN BRITISH
01502 501353 | Ivy House Country Hotel, Ivy Lane, Beccles Road, Oulton Broad, NR33 8HY
www.ivyhousecountryhotel.co.uk
A 16th-century barn, its ceiling exposed to the rafters, is the destination eatery of Ivy House Country Hotel, set in 20 acres of grounds on Oulton Broad. The kitchen makes excellent use of the region's produce in some eclectic dishes.
Chef Keith Parton **Seats** 45, Private dining 24 **Closed** 19 December to 6 January **Parking** 50 **Notes** Vegetarian dishes, Children welcome

MILDENHALL
The Bull Inn
◎ MODERN BRITISH
01638 711001 | The Street, Barton Mills, IP28 6AA
www.bullinn-bartonmills.com
The Bull provides some very enjoyable dishes using lots of local produce. There are also twists on traditional dishes as well as some British favourites. Look out for the chef's bread – a glossy crust with good crispness and light and fluffy inside.
Chef Cheryl Hickman, Shaun Jennings **Seats** 60, Private dining 30 **Closed** 25–26 December **Parking** 60 **Notes** Vegetarian dishes, Children welcome

NEWMARKET
Bedford Lodge Hotel & Spa
◎◎ BRITISH, MEDITERRANEAN
01638 663175 | Bury Road, CB8 7BX
www.bedfordlodgehotel.co.uk
This extended one-time Georgian hunting lodge has a prime position near the racecourse and enough top-end facilities to satisfy a modern epicure. Finish with a fun 'sweet shop' dessert comprising strawberry and bubble gum pannacotta, banana marshmallow, candyfloss, orange sherbet and macaroons.
Chef Sean Melville **Seats** 60, Private dining 150 **Open** All year **Prices from** S £6.50, M £19, D £7 **Parking** 150 **Notes** Vegetarian dishes, Children welcome

The Packhorse Inn
◎◎ MODERN BRITISH
01638 751818 | Bridge Street, Moulton, CB8 8SP
www.thepackhorseinn.com
Close to the racing at Newmarket, this modern country inn still pulls in local drinkers but it's the classy, inventive cooking that attracts foodies from far and wide. Suffolk produce is treated with respect in the kitchen and impressive pastry skills are evident in desserts.
Chef Greig Young **Seats** 65, Private dining 32 **Open** All year **Prices from** S £7, M £16, D £7 **Parking** 30 **Notes** Vegetarian dishes, Children welcome

Tuddenham Mill
◎◎◎ MODERN BRITISH V ↓ NOTABLE WINE LIST
See pages 296–297

ORFORD

The Crown & Castle

◉◉ ITALIAN, BRITISH **V** ♦ NOTABLE WINE LIST

01394 450205 | IP12 2LJ

www.crownandcastle.co.uk

There has been a hostelry on this site for 800 years, and today's incarnation is an easy-going, rustic-chic restaurant. There's genuine character to the spaces within, where unclothed wooden tables and comfortable cushioned chairs and benches help create a relaxed vibe.

Chef Rob Walpole, Ruth Watson (Food Director) **Seats** 50, Private dining 10 **Open** All year **Prices from** S £6.50, M £17.50, D £8 **Parking** 17 **Notes** No children under 8 years at dinner

SIBTON

Sibton White Horse Inn

◉◉ MODERN BRITISH

01728 660337 | Halesworth Road, IP17 2JJ

www.sibtonwhitehorseinn.co.uk

This fascinating pub's Tudor origins – low ceilings, mighty ships' timbers, quarry tiles – are impossible to miss. The bar has a raised gallery, an elegant dining room and a secluded courtyard. The kitchen produces globally influenced modern cooking that's won a heap of awards.

Chef Gill Mason, Gareth Knights, Matt Lee **Seats** 40, Private dining 18 **Closed** 25–26 December **Parking** 50 **Notes** Vegetarian dishes, No children under 6 years at dinner

SOUTHWOLD

Sutherland House

◉◉ MODERN BRITISH, SEAFOOD

01502 724544 | 56 High Street, IP18 6DN

www.sutherlandhouse.co.uk

A period property of genuine charm, Sutherland House has wooden beams, ornate ceilings, coving and real fireplaces, with fixtures and fittings creating a chic finish. Likewise, the cooking impresses with its modern ambitions, passion for seafood and loyalty to local ingredients.

Chef Carl Slaymaker **Seats** 50 **Closed** 25 December and 2 weeks January **Prices from** S £7.50, M £17, D £7.50 **Notes** Vegetarian dishes, No children

STOKE-BY-NAYLAND

The Angel Inn

◉ MODERN BRITISH

01206 263245 | Polstead Street, CO6 4SA

www.angelinnsuffolk.co.uk

A charming hostelry with quarry-tiled floors, exposed red-brick walls and a double-height ceiling in the dining area with oak beams and the original well. There are quality meats, like saddle and confit leg of rabbit, while veggies might opt for chickpea and bean curry.

Chef Daniel Russell **Seats** 60, Private dining 12 **Open** All year **Prices from** S £5.25, M £12.95, D £5.95 **Parking** 20 **Notes** Vegetarian dishes, Children welcome

The Crown

◉◉ MODERN BRITISH

01206 262001 | CO6 4SE

www.crowninn.net

Perfectly placed for exploring Constable country, the 16th-century Crown has morphed into a classy boutique inn with 11 swish bedrooms. The beamed bar and dining areas sport a smart contemporary look with cockle-warming log fires. Expect monthly changing modern British menus, supplemented by daily fish dishes.

Chef Nick Beavan **Seats** 125, Private dining 14 **Closed** 25–26 December **Prices from** S £5.75, M £11.50, D £6.75 **Parking** 49 **Notes** Vegetarian dishes, Children welcome

SUDBURY

The Black Lion

◉◉ MODERN BRITISH

01787 312356 | The Green, Long Melford, CO10 9DN

www.theblacklionhotel.com

Reopening after an impressive renovation in 2017, the Chestnut Group's imposing Black Lion has rapidly made a name for itself. There's no doubt that the discerning people of Suffolk have taken in a big way to the restaurant and its modern British cuisine.

Chef Nicholas Traher **Seats** 60, Private dining **Open** All year

The Case Restaurant with Rooms

◉ MEDITERRANEAN

01787 210483 | Further Street, Assington, CO10 5LD

www.thecaserestaurantwithrooms.co.uk

This charming country inn has a cosy little restaurant with a wood-burning stove, darkwood tables and ceiling beams; also there's a café and deli now. Host-led hospitality is the key to its success as well as the quality of the cooking. Puddings hit the mark.

Chef Barry and Antony Kappes **Seats** 40 **Open** All year **Prices from** S £5.95, M £11.95, D £5.95 **Parking** 30 **Notes** Vegetarian dishes, Children welcome

SUFFOLK

NEWMARKET

Tuddenham Mill

◉◉◉ MODERN BRITISH **V** ⌕ NOTABLE WINE LIST

01638 713552 | High Street, Tuddenham St Mary, IP28 6SQ

www.tuddenhammill.co.uk

Inventive regional cooking and a waterwheel taking centre stage

From the outside, the weatherboarded 18th-century mill looks solid enough to carry on its grinding career today, but a peek inside the doors reveals a seductive modern boutique hotel. Meticulous renovation means its heritage remains intact – the fast-flowing stream that turned its waterwheel is now a thriving wildlife habitat, while the impressive cast-iron wheel that was once its beating heart is atmospherically lit within glass walls to form a diverting centrepiece to the first-floor restaurant. With its framework of exposed beams, bare black tables, gauzy curtain partitions and bucolic views over the millpond, it's a classy setting for chef-patron Lee Bye's confident cooking, which has plenty of personality in its own right. As a local lad, he's in touch with his East Anglian roots and has an instinctive feel for combining ingredients from the surrounding region to striking effect, thus a typical opener strikes a balance between no-nonsense gutsiness and contemporary refinement via meltingly tender pig's cheek matched with hazelnuts, spring onions and a sweet-sour balsamic reduction. Another clever construction might see that old stalwart, chicken liver

parfait, transformed by accompaniments of roasted wings, marrow and beetroot ketchup. Cleverly constructed main courses owe their success to intricate detail and careful execution – malt-glazed guinea fowl, say, partnered with salt-baked beets, lovage, rainbow chard and sloe gin sauce, while fish dishes such as roasted halibut with chive beurre blanc, mussels, green fronds of agretti and escabeche sauce are equally well handled. Vegetarians might set about seaweed pommes Anna with king oyster mushrooms, roasted artichoke and wild honey. Desserts are executed with memorable dexterity, bringing entertaining plays of flavour and texture in ideas such as buttermilk pannacotta with poached Cox's apple, muscovado and crunchy flapjack, or a bitter chocolate pot counterpointed by Morello cherry sorbet and hazelnut oil; for a savoury finish, there are fine British artisanal cheeses with Garibaldi biscuits and chutney. The five-course tasting menu offers a leisurely paced tour through Bye's versatile repertoire, while some imaginative meat-free ideas should keep vegetarians entertained. If you're lucky enough to be staying over in order to loosen the belt and make the most of Tuddenham's excellent wine list, you can expect to get the next day off to a flying start with fortifying breakfasts built around Dingley Dell pork sausages, locally smoked kippers, and Goosnargh yogurt topped with almond granola. If you're passing by for a pitstop, set lunch menus offer cracking value.

Chef Lee Bye **Seats** 54, Private dining 36 **Open** All year **Prices from** S £7.50, M £19, D £7.50 **Parking** 40 **Notes** Children welcome

SUFFOLK

SUDBURY continued

The Mill Hotel
◉ BRITISH **V**
01787 375544 | Walnut Tree Lane, CO10 1BD
www.themillhotelsudbury.co.uk
The imposing white building on the edge of the Stour was once a working watermill, as witness the millpond opposite and the waterwheel that forms a focal point in the dining room. Views of nearby landscapes once inspired Thomas Gainsborough, and make a relaxing setting.

Chef Daniel Collins **Seats** 75, Private dining 60 **Open** All year **Prices from** S £6, M £16, D £6 **Parking** 35 **Notes** Children welcome

THORPENESS
Thorpeness Hotel
◉ MODERN BRITISH
01728 452176 | Lakeside Avenue, IP16 4NH
www.thorpeness.co.uk
The heathland golf course adjacent to the sea was opened in 1922 and there are views over the third tee from the traditional and roomy restaurant (there's also a wood-panelled bar and a terrace with a watery vista). The daily changing menu keeps things relatively simple.

Chef David Margas **Seats** 80, Private dining 30 **Open** All year **Prices from** S £7, M £13, D £5 **Parking** 80 **Notes** Vegetarian dishes, Children welcome

WESTLETON
The Westleton Crown
◉◉ MODERN BRITISH **V**
01728 648777 | The Street, IP17 3AD
www.westletoncrown.co.uk
This hotel, restaurant and pub, between Aldeburgh and Southwold, has its roots in the 12th century. 'Hearty yet sophisticated' cooking is the kitchen's aim and ambition doesn't falter among puddings: expect chocolate and pistachio cake with chocolate sorbet and cherries.

Chef James Finch **Seats** 85, Private dining 50 **Open** All year **Parking** 50 **Notes** Children welcome

WOODBRIDGE
The Crown at Woodbridge
◉◉ MODERN EUROPEAN
01394 384242 | 2 Thoroughfare, IP12 1AD
www.thecrownatwoodbridge.co.uk
An expensive facelift relaunched The Crown as a stylish 21st-century inn back in 2009. The look is decidedly boutique, combining 16th-century features with a fresh, contemporary design ethos. The kitchen raids the Suffolk larder for its unfussy, big-hearted modern cooking.

Chef Daniel Perjési **Seats** 60, Private dining 20 **Open** All year **Parking** 30 **Notes** Vegetarian dishes, Children welcome

Seckford Hall Hotel
◉◉ MODERN EUROPEAN, BRITISH
01394 385678 | IP13 6NU
www.seckford.co.uk
Approached by a sweeping drive through well-preened grounds, this blue-blooded Tudor pile impresses with its creeper-curtained brick facade, soaring chimneys and carved-oak front door. Culinary style is classical country house with a contemporary sensibility and the dessert menu offers old-school comforts.

Chef Luke Bailey **Seats** 85, Private dining 150 **Open** All year **Prices from** S £6, M £14.50, D £6 **Parking** 100 **Notes** Vegetarian dishes, Children welcome

The Unruly Pig
◉ BRITISH, ITALIAN **V**
01394 460310 | Orford Road, Bromeswell, IP12 2PU
www.theunrulypig.co.uk
Just five minutes from the market town of Woodbridge, this 16th-century pub is a lovely spot to enjoy a pint beneath original oak beams. Despite its age, The Unruly Pig has a contemporary look and feel with shabby-chic decor, a modern European menu, and relaxed, friendly service.

Chef Dave Wall **Seats** 90, Private dining 22 **Closed** 25 December **Prices from** S £6.95, M £10.95, D £7.50 **Parking** 40 **Notes** Children welcome

YAXLEY
The Auberge
◉◉ MODERN EUROPEAN
01379 783604 | Ipswich Road, IP23 8BZ
www.the-auberge.co.uk
Ancient beams, panelling and exposed brickwork dating back to medieval times are clear evidence that this was an inn for many centuries, but the name describes today's modern restaurant with rooms. The room is darkly intimate and French influences underpin skilfully rendered food.

Chef John Stenhouse, Mark Bond **Seats** 60, Private dining 20 **Open** All year **Parking** 25 **Notes** Vegetarian dishes, Children welcome

▶ SURREY

BAGSHOT
The Brasserie at Pennyhill Park
◉◉ MODERN BRITISH
01276 471774 | Pennyhill Park, London Road, GU19 5EU
www.exclusive.co.uk

The Brasserie is an informal and relaxed eating space that has been completely redesigned. A muted colour palette and stone walls set the scene and the mobile buffet stations offer a never-ending variety of food throughout the day from breakfast through to dinner.

Chef Daniel Lee **Seats** 150 **Open** All year **Parking** 500 **Notes** Vegetarian dishes, Children welcome

Matt Worswick at The Latymer
◉◉◉◉ MODERN EUROPEAN V ♦ NOTABLE WINE LIST
01276 471774 | Pennyhill Park, London Road, GU19 5EU
www.exclusive.co.uk

The original 19th-century mansion has been extended over the years, but it's still the heart and soul of the place, and it is where you'll find Matt Worswick at The Latymer, one of the UK's most compelling contemporary restaurants. The 120-acre estate offers all sorts of distractions, from a nine-hole golf course to a luxury spa, and it's even home to the England rugby union team when they gather to train for matches. Among a number of dining options at the hotel, The Latymer is a genteel and luxurious space with panelled walls and rich fabrics. In this formal and elegant setting comes food of diverting modernity, with contemporary cooking techniques showcased on five- or seven-course tasting menus. Flavour combinations are seldom less than thrilling, such as an opener of oyster emulsion, with cured sea trout and Yorkshire rhubarb, and playfulness with temperature brings excitement to salt-baked celeriac. The very best seasonal produce finds its way to the table and everything looks just beautiful as it is set gently before you. From the seven-course menu, veal sweetbread with heritage carrot and pickled shimeji mushrooms has a hint of liquorice running through it, while both menus get Gigha halibut with smoked almond pesto and seaweed beurre blanc. It may be technically clever cooking, but Matt Worswick never lets the fabulous produce get lost along the way, which is true right up to desserts such as a choux bun with vanilla mascarpone, rhubarb and hibiscus. The wine list is a global tour de force.

Chef Matt Worswick **Seats** 46, Private dining 8 **Closed** 1st 2 weeks January **Parking** 500 **Notes** No children under 12 years

CAMBERLEY
Macdonald Frimley Hall Hotel & Spa
◉◉ BRITISH, EUROPEAN
01276 413100 | Lime Avenue, GU15 2BG
www.macdonaldhotels.co.uk/frimleyhall

The handsome mansion not far off the M3 was home to William Valentine Wright, the man who gave Britain Coal Tar Soap. Its Linden restaurant has an intimate candlelit ambience in the evenings. Thoroughbred Scottish steaks are a popular feature, as are the intriguing desserts.

Chef James Lee **Seats** 62, Private dining 20 **Open** All year **Parking** 110 **Notes** Vegetarian dishes, Children welcome

CHOBHAM
Stovell's
◉◉◉◉ MODERN EUROPEAN ♦ NOTABLE WINE LIST
01276 858000 | 125 Windsor Road, GU24 8QS
www.stovells.com

The charming village setting, the wonky Tudor building, you may think you have the measure of Stovell's, but Fernando Stovell's place is pretty much unique…a union of Mexico and Britain in sleepy Surrey. Fernando hails from Mexico and has brought his culinary heritage to bear alongside his training in contemporary European cuisine. The result is creative, compelling and joyful. The dining room has plenty of beams to confirm the antiquity of the building, and a contemporary gloss to set the mood. Cookery lessons and a hand-crafted gin reveal a free-wheeling enterprising spirit. The flavours of Mexico are present, certainly on the Taste of Mexico menu, but there is nothing generic about the cooking here. The à la carte might get you started with aromatic foie gras, with burnt grelot onions, toasted hazelnuts, and a dressing made with hay-smoked tea and pennywort, before moving you onto pan-fried Cornish wild sea bass with pickled mushrooms, cardoons and yuzu. Presentation is always creative, usually pretty stunning, and the technical skills on show ensure everything works and flavours hit home. A céviche might be expected, and there it is, yellow fin tuna, say, with pickled radishes, while a vegetarian opener might be apple smoked aubergine with Isle of Wight tomatoes and winter leaves. Fermentation, a favoured contemporary technique with an ancient heritage, sees turnips treated thus, in a dish of 'nose to tail' rabbit, and again in a tepache dessert (fermented peel and rind of pineapples) with piloncillo sorbet (unrefined cane sugar) which is full of Mexican spirit. The wine list is a tour de force through Europe and South America in particular.

Chef Fernando Stovell **Seats** 60, Private dining 16 **Open** All year **Parking** 20 **Notes** Vegetarian dishes, Children welcome

SURREY

DORKING

Emlyn at The Mercure Burford Bridge
@@ MODERN BRITISH
01306 884561 | Burford Bridge, Box Hill, RH5 6BX
www.emlynrestaurant.co.uk
A new chef, joined by a brand-new kitchen team here at the Mercure Burford Bridge, plans to shake things up with a new concept for the restaurant, blending classic flavours with modern techniques. You can expect a fresh and stylish approach to the food.

Chef Nick Sinclair **Seats** 60, Private dining 200 **Closed** 1st week January **Prices from** S £7, M £16, D £6 **Parking** 140 **Notes** Vegetarian dishes, Children welcome

AA Restaurant of the Year for England 2018–19

Sorrel
@@@ MODERN BRITISH
01306 889414 | 77 South Street, RH4 2JU
www.sorrelrestaurant.co.uk
The setting for Steve Drake's latest enterprise certainly doesn't lack character with its wonky beams, wood floors, and linen-clad tables laid with fine glassware and herbs in little glass cloches adding to the all-round feel of a classy operation. Drake has form with creative contemporary ways when it comes to making an impact with his seasonal, ingredients-led cooking. Via a cracking value set lunch and five-and nine-course tasting menus, the kitchen delivers inspirational dishes starting with a celebration of the humble beetroot, served salt-baked, pickled and crisped alongside creamy Bosworth Ash goats' cheese mousse, toasted sesame seeds, crisp apple and mayonnaise, the latter aromatised with Douglas fir. Ingredients are combined in thoughtful and stimulating ways in dishes of robata-grilled monkfish topped with onion crumb and partnered by leeks, grelot onions and mushroom milk, or venison cooked in liquorice butter and served with carrots, black pudding purée and parsley purée and foam. Flavours are judged just so, through to a finale of pear poached in hibiscus syrup with crystallised gin, goats' milk cream and cardamom ice cream.

Chef Steve Drake, Richard Giles **Seats** 40, Private dining 10 **Closed** Sunday to Tuesday

EAST MOLESEY

Petriti's Restaurant
@@ MODERN EUROPEAN V
020 8979 5577 | 98 Walton Road, KT8 0DL
www.petritisrestaurant.co.uk
Tucked away in suburban East Molesey, not far from Henry VIII's Hampton Court palace, Petriti's is king in these parts. Smart in its relaxing hues of grey and cream, with matching modern seating and white linen, the dining room is enlivened by colourful artworks.

Chef Sokol Petriti **Seats** 70 **Closed** 1–15 January **Notes** No children under 6 years

EGHAM

The Estate Grill at Great Fosters
@@ MODERN BRITISH
01784 433822 | Stroude Road, TW20 9UR
www.greatfosters.co.uk
The Estate Grill chefs use Old Spot pigs reared in the grounds and honey from the apiary, as well as Cumbrian fell-bred lamb. Sharing platters are a possibility – charcuterie to start and a selection of estate-reared pork for main.

Chef Rob Chasteauneuf **Seats** 44, Private dining 20 **Open** All year **Prices from** S £9, M £20, D £9 **Parking** 200 **Notes** Vegetarian dishes, Children welcome

The Lock Bar and Kitchen at The Runnymede on Thames
@ MODERN
01784 220999 | Windsor Road, TW20 0AG
www.runnymedehotel.com
The scene could hardly be more *Wind in the Willows*, with the Thames burbling by, and outdoor tables and parasols set out by Bell Weir lock that lends its name to the kitchen and bar. The parquet-floored brasserie room has a light, breezy ambience.

Chef Adesh Bissonauth **Seats** 60 **Open** All year **Prices from** S £6.75, M £14.50, D £6.75 **Parking** 300 **Notes** Vegetarian dishes, Children welcome

The Tudor Room
@@@ MODERN EUROPEAN V ▮ NOTABLE WINE LIST
01784 433822 | Great Fosters, Stroude Road, TW20 9UR
www.greatfosters.co.uk
Great Fosters is a many-gabled red-brick Tudor mansion that once lay within the bounds of Windsor Great Park, and was originally the home of Sir John Dodderidge, James I's solicitor-general. Its 50 acres of gardens and parkland provide ample space for strolling, and make it a popular local resource for

stylish weddings, but the main dining room is an unexpectedly intimate space of just seven tables, with sconce lights on russet silk-lined walls and a large dramatic 17th-century Flemish tapestry, all reflected in an expansive mirror. Contemporary cooking of fascinating visual panache and careful balancing of elements is Douglas Balish's business, its three-course menu structure fleshed out with intermediate dishes such as an opening olive oil sorbet with pressed kohlrabi, peas and tarragon, and the wondrous langoustine tea, a bowl of crystal-clear shellfish consommé poured over a single plump shellfish garlanded with slivered radish. In among these extras, the principal dishes are all the more impressive: crisp-skinned sea bream with marine flora, cucumber and caviar, and a splendid presentation of pork loin, crackled belly and barbecue-sauced cheek, alongside finely shredded cabbage and bacon, caramelised shallots and piccalilli. Celebrate the opening of the strawberry season with gariguette berries in poached, jelly and ice cream guises, served with baked vanilla custard and goats' yogurt. Elsewhere, rhubarb is royally treated to accompaniments of bergamot, white chocolate and gingerbread, or you might opt for a quintet of British cheeses with truffle honey, fig chutney, quince and pecans. Well-chosen wines by the glass lead the charge on an authoritative list.

Chef Douglas Balish **Seats** 24 **Closed** 2 weeks in January, 1 week at Easter, 2 weeks in August **Parking** 200 **Notes** Children welcome

EPSOM
Dastaan
◉◉ INDIAN
020 8786 8999 | 447 Kingston Road, Ewell, KT19 0DB
www.dastaan.co.uk
A neighbourhood gem and anything but your regular curry house. There's an open kitchen and the atmosphere's much more Mumbai café than Surrey Indian. The intelligently compact menu delivers a succession of authentic flavours bursting with freshness, finesse and attitude.

Chef Sanjay Gour, Nand Kishor **Seats** 56 **Closed** New Year **Prices from** S £4.95, M £9.25, D £4.75 **Notes** No children

GUILDFORD
The Jetty
◉ CLASSIC BRITISH
01483 792300 | 3 Alexandra Terrace, High Street, GU1 3DA
www.guildford-harbour-hotel.co.uk
Located within the Harbour Hotel, The Jetty has a separate entrance leading into a jolly ambience of

sand- and sea-coloured seating. These signifiers announce a seafood bar and grill, the appealing menus built around main courses such as herby crab-crusted cod with creamy mash and peas.

Chef Steve Hubbert **Open** All year

The Mandolay Hotel
◉◉ MODERN EUROPEAN
01483 303030 | 36–40 London Road, GU1 2AE
www.guildford.com
The restaurant of this smart hotel certainly looks swish, and the kitchen delivers a menu suffused with creativity. You might start with a very tasty roast partridge with boudin and round off with a spot-on dessert of chocolate fondant with pistachio ice cream

Chef Mark Lawton **Seats** 60, Private dining 300 **Open** All year **Parking** 25 **Notes** Vegetarian dishes

MICKLEHAM
Running Horses
◉ TRADITIONAL BRITISH
01372 372279 | Old London Road, RH5 6DU
www.therunninghorses.co.uk
Dating from the 16th century, the Running Horses is a proper heart-warming village local, with a crackling fire in winter and a kitchen that knows what is required and delivers the goods without pretension. Accordingly, what arrives on the table is rustic, crowd-pleasing fare.

Chef Daniel Donohue **Seats** 72, Private dining 28 **Open** All year **Notes** Vegetarian dishes, Children welcome

OTTERSHAW
Foxhills Club & Resort
◉◉ MODERN, TRADITIONAL BRITISH ⓥ ⚑ NOTABLE WINE LIST
01932 704471 | Stonehill Road, KT16 0EL
www.foxhills.co.uk
A short hop from Heathrow, this 19th-century manor, built by George Basevi, architect of London's Belgrave Square, comes with a 400-acre estate, a spa, a championship golf course and other sporting pursuits to help work up an appetite for contemporary, ingredient-led cooking in the Manor Restaurant.

Chef Luke Davis **Seats** 100, Private dining 40 **Open** All year **Prices from** S £8.50, M £19, D £8 **Parking** 200 **Notes** Vegetarian dishes, Children welcome

See advertisement on page 302

Your table is waiting at Foxhills Club & Resort. Offering an à la carte selection and tasting menu, The Manor Restaurant - located in the historic Manor House - is the perfect setting for lunch and dinner. Discover what makes Foxhills a favourite.

Foxhills

Stonehill Road, Ottershaw, Surrey KT16 0EL

foxhills.co.uk

REDHILL
Nutfield Priory Hotel & Spa
⊕⊕ MODERN BRITISH **V**
01737 824400 | Nutfield, RH1 4EL
www.handpickedhotels.co.uk/nutfieldpriory

Standing in 12 acres on Nutfield Ridge, the Priory is classic Victorian neo-Gothic, dating from the 1870s. The Cloisters has mullioned windows offering expansive views over the grounds and lake, and makes an appropriate backdrop for a refined, modern take on country-house cooking.

Chef Alec Mackins **Seats** 60, Private dining 60
Open All year **Prices from** S £8, M £24, D £10
Parking 100 **Notes** Children welcome

RIPLEY
The Anchor
⊕⊕ MODERN BRITISH
01483 211866 | High Street, GU23 6AE
www.ripleyanchor.co.uk

The Anchor is a friendly gastro pub in the modern idiom with a dusting of pedigree, with dark-wood furniture, slate floors and armchairs by a log-burner. The kitchen delivers simple dining-pub fare with creativity and panache. Dishes cover all the bases with a contemporary touch.

Chef Michael Wall-Palmer **Seats** 46, Private dining 8
Closed 25 December and 1 January **Prices from** S £7, M £16, D £7 **Parking** 14 **Notes** Vegetarian dishes, Children welcome

The Clock House
⊕⊕⊕ MODERN BRITISH **V** ⬩NOTABLE WINE LIST
01483 224777 | High Street, GU23 6AQ
www.theclockhouserestaurant.co.uk

The great chronometer above the portico entrance on the high street is a graphic enough explanation of the name of a place that has seen a fair few years' service to Ripley. Inside, the dining room is done in defiantly plain but tasteful style, with the option of terrace seating in the Surrey sun, and with the emphasis on Fred

Clapperton's impressively confident contemporary cooking. A seasonally evolving carte is the core of the operation, with a seven-course taster drawn from it, and a vegetarian alternative too. There is a marked enjoyment of earthier flavours, parsley roots and leaves with a haddock and shrimp starter, alexanders with a pork belly and apple pairing, and kohlrabi and chanterelles to accompany a majestic main course of thoroughbred beef and sweetbreads. For the veggie option, the main matter might be a truffle-scented array of cauliflower with field mushrooms and sea beets, and the final stage mingles sweet and savoury notes productively for chocolate and orange with goats' milk and olive oil, or a daring combination of pineapple and white chocolate with the smoky fragrance of chamomile.

Chef Fred Clapperton **Seats** 40 **Closed** 1 week in January, 2 weeks in August, 1 week at Christmas and after Easter **Parking** 2 **Notes** Children welcome

STOKE D'ABERNON
Oak Room
◎◎ MODERN BRITISH

01372 843933 | Woodlands Lane, KT11 3QB
www.handpickedhotels.co.uk/woodlandspark

Money was clearly no object for William Bryant, son of one of the founders of the match company, when he built this magnificent pile in 1885. It's set in landscaped grounds and gardens, and the dining room is an elegant, formal background for the modern British food.

Chef Darren Edwards **Seats** 35, Private dining 150 **Open** All year **Parking** 150 **Notes** Vegetarian dishes, Children welcome

WARLINGHAM
India Dining
◎◎ MODERN INDIAN

01883 625905 | 6 The Green, CR6 9NA
www.indiadining.co.uk

India Dining features a stylish cocktail bar, black leatherette banquettes, polished-wood tables and highly contemporary artworks. The authentic Pan-Indian cooking takes an equally creative, modern and upmarket approach. Take monkfish tikka to open, cooked in the tandoor, its peppy spicing not overwhelming the sparkling-fresh fish.

Chef Asad Khan, Habibul Rahaman **Seats** 69 **Closed** 1 January **Notes** Vegetarian dishes, Children welcome

WEST END
The Inn West End
◎ MODERN BRITISH

01276 858652 | 42 Guildford Road, GU24 9PW
www.the-inn.co.uk

It has been said that Gerry and Ann Price's renowned village pub out-manoeuvres many a competitor; the kitchen brigade make great use of fish from the coast and game from Windsor Great Park, or shot by Gerry himself. The modern interior is open plan.

Chef Taylor Batey **Seats** 40 **Open** All year **Parking** 35 **Notes** Vegetarian dishes, No children under 5 years

WEYBRIDGE
Brooklands Hotel
◎◎ BRITISH, EUROPEAN

01932 335700 | Brooklands Drive, KT13 0SL
www.brooklandshotelsurrey.com

This thrillingly modern structure overlooks the first purpose-built car-racing circuit in the world, opening back in 1907. There's a creative modern brasserie feel to the food, with the kitchen team keenly producing dishes that arrive on the plate dressed to thrill.

Chef Adam Potten **Seats** 120, Private dining 150 **Open** All year **Prices from** S £6.95, M £16.50, D £6.95 **Parking** 120 **Notes** Vegetarian dishes, Children welcome

WONERSH
Oak Room Restaurant
◎◎ MODERN BRITISH

01483 893361 | Barnett Hill Country House Hotel, Blackheath Lane, GU5 0RF
www.alexanderhotels.co.uk/barnett-hill

A striking Queen Anne-style building set within 26 tranquil acres of woodlands and lovely gardens, the Barnett Hill Hotel is conveniently located just a 10-minute drive from Guildford. The wood-panelled Oak Room Restaurant overlooks a terrace and well-manicured lawns and it's an elegant setting.

Chef Lee Young **Seats** 32, Private dining **Open** All year **Prices from** S £8, M £18, D £8 **Parking** 50 **Notes** Vegetarian dishes, Children welcome

▶ EAST SUSSEX
ALFRISTON
Deans Place
◎◎ MODERN BRITISH **V**

01323 870248 | Seaford Road, BN26 5TW
www.deansplacehotel.co.uk

Once part of an extensive farming estate, Deans Place, with its elegant modern decor, makes a refreshing backdrop to the Victorian gardens and charming riverside location, while the stylish Dining Room offers the full-dress experience of fine table linen and glassware.

Chef Stuart Dunley **Seats** 74, Private dining 50 **Open** All year **Parking** 100 **Notes** Children welcome

BATTLE
The Powder Mills Hotel
◉◉ MODERN BRITISH **V**

01424 775511 | Powdermill Lane, TN33 0SP
www.powdermillshotel.com

Powder Mills was once the site of a major gunpowder-making operation that helped defeat Napoleon. It stands in 150 acres of lush parkland and woods with a seven-acre fishing lake. The owner's Springer Spaniels sometimes welcome arrivals and dining takes place in the Orangery Restaurant.

Chef Callum O'Doherty **Seats** 90, Private dining 20 **Open** All year **Parking** 100 **Notes** No children under 10 years at dinner

BODIAM
The Curlew Restaurant
◉◉ MODERN BRITISH **NOTABLE WINE LIST**

01580 861394 | Junction Road, TN32 5UY
www.thecurlewrestaurant.co.uk

The white-faced Curlew is perched on what was the old coaching-route from Hastings to London. A comfortably relaxed countrified atmosphere prevails, with a roaring log-burner and a fresh, open look to the decor and a smart, contemporary vibe to the thought-provoking modern British cooking.

Chef Gary Jarvis **Seats** 50 **Closed** 26 December, 1 January **Prices from** S £8, M £26, D £8.50 **Parking** 16 **Notes** Vegetarian dishes, Children welcome

BRIGHTON AND HOVE
The Chilli Pickle
◉ REGIONAL INDIAN

01273 900383 | 17 Jubilee Street, BN1 1GE
www.thechillipickle.com

The Chilli Pickle's open-plan interior works a casual, rustic look, with chunky wooden tables, blond-wood floors and vivid splashes of colour while full-length glass walls create the impression of dining alfresco. The vibe is breezy and buzzy, and the menu gives subcontinental clichés a swerve.

Chef Alun Sperring **Seats** 115 **Closed** 25–26 December **Notes** Vegetarian dishes, Children welcome

etch. by Steven Edwards
◉◉ MODERN BRITISH **V** **NOTABLE WINE LIST**

01273 227485 | 216 Church Road, Hove, BN3 2DJ
www.etchfood.co.uk

Local foodies hot-footed it to the door when etch opened in March 2017. And no wonder: the chef is a former BBC *MasterChef: The Professionals* winner, and the place is cool with its midnight-blue walls, brass-edged tables and air of all-round vitality. Set menus

(4, 6 or 8 courses) are the deal, and creative combos score hit after hit.

Chef Steven Edwards **Seats** 32, Private dining 8 **Open** All year **Notes** No children under 8 years

GB1 Restaurant
◉◉ MODERN BRITISH, SEAFOOD

01273 224300 | The Grand Brighton, 97–99 King's Road, BN1 2FW
www.grandbrighton.co.uk/dining-en.html

Turn your back on the stunning Italianate Victorian design at this seafront landmark and enter the cool, clean lines of the GB1 restaurant. Seafood is the thing, with a menu as bright and contemporary as the surroundings. Meat-eaters can choose from a selection of grills.

Chef Alan White **Seats** 90 **Open** All year **Notes** Vegetarian dishes, Children welcome

The Ginger Dog
◉ MODERN BRITISH

01273 620990 | 12–13 College Place, BN2 1HN
www.thegingerdog.com

A once run-down corner pub in Kemp Town village has been given a makeover, with clean white walls and bright pink banquettes in the main dining area. To finish, go for oat junket, with caramelised banana, toffee sponge and candied pecans.

Chef Dan Cropper **Seats** 45, Private dining 22 **Closed** 25 December **Prices from** S £6, M £19, D £7 **Notes** Vegetarian dishes, Children welcome

The Gingerman Restaurant
◉◉ MODERN BRITISH

01273 326688 | 21a Norfolk Square, BN1 2PD
www.gingermanrestaurants.com

The Gingerman is committed to dynamic modern British cooking with an inventive slant, notably incorporating touches of the Maghreb tradition. Maple-glazed pigeon breast with pine nuts and dates vies for first-course attention with salmon 'pastrami' served with caramelised parsnip and labneh, and an egg yolk.

Chef Ben McKellar, Mark Charker **Seats** 32 **Closed** 2 weeks from New Year's eve **Notes** Vegetarian dishes, Children welcome

Hotel du Vin Brighton
◉ TRADITIONAL BRITISH, FRENCH

01273 718588 | 2–6 Ship Street, BN1 1AD
www.hotelduvin.com

The Brighton branch of the chain has all the expected Francophile touches, its walls adorned with posters and risqué pictures, leather-look banquettes running back to back down the centre and small wooden tables. A glance at the menu reveals more than your average bistro fare.

Chef Rob Carr **Seats** 100, Private dining 90 **Open** All year **Notes** Vegetarian dishes, Children welcome

Isaac at
◎◎ MODERN BRITISH
07765 934740 | 2 Gloucester Street, BN1 4EW
www.isaac-at.com

'Local' and 'seasonal' is the mantra in this ambitious, pocket-sized outfit in the trendy North Laine quarter – even the wines are from Sussex vineyards. Serving just 20 or so diners from an open kitchen in a stripped-back space, the venue fits the youthful Brighton mood, and the food keeps step with modern trends.

Chef Isaac Bartlett-Copeland **Seats** 20, Private dining 22 **Notes** No children under 13 years

The Little Fish Market
◎◎◎ MODERN FISH
01273 722213 | 10 Upper Market Street, Hove, BN3 1AS
www.thelittlefishmarket.co.uk

Tucked away in a little side street off Hove's Western Road, chef-patron Duncan Ray's modest little operation certainly punches above its weight. After stints at The Fat Duck and Pennyhill Park, Ray knows a thing or two about top-end dining – here he works alone in the kitchen, and the results speak for themselves: stunning local and sustainable seafood cooked with exemplary attention to detail, accuracy and an intelligent creative edge. The setting is a light-filled space done out with a bare-bones contemporary look – neutral colours, bright, seafood-themed local art, wooden tables and quarry-tiled floors, and it is comfortable and atmospheric in the evening, with a charming solo server managing front of house for the lucky 20 diners. The tersely worded fixed-price menu offers five no-choice courses and delivers dishes of pure seafood flavour, a satiny mussel and bacon soup priming the palate for outstanding scallops pointed up with caper and cauliflower purées and crunchy beer-battered raisins. The bright, clean flavours continue in an outstanding piece of wild bass with dashi and Thai Morning Glory, then stunning turbot with crab cannelloni, sea herbs and shellfish sauce. To close the show, pineapple tarte Tatin is matched with a delicate coconut sorbet.

Chef Duncan Ray **Seats** 22 **Closed** 1 week in March, 2 weeks in September, Christmas **Notes** Vegetarian dishes, No children under 12 years

Pascere
◎◎ MODERN EUROPEAN, BRITISH Ⅴ
01273 917949 | 8 Duke St, BN1 1AH
www.pascere.co.uk

Spread over two floors on the edge of The Lanes, Pascere is a worthy newcomer to Brighton's flourishing restaurant scene. Stylish and cosy, the space sports a calming backdrop of teal blue panelling, and leather and suede banquettes, while an open kitchen creates intelligently dishes.

Chef Johnny Stanford **Seats** 53 **Closed** 25 December **Prices from** S £8, M £17.50, D £8.50 **Notes** Vegetarian dishes, No children under 5 years

Pike and Pine
◎◎
01273 686668 | 1d St James's Street, BN2 1RE
www.pikeandpine.co.uk

A coffee house by day, this chic Kemp Town eatery morphs into a hotbed of contemporary creativity for dinner. It's entirely in step with the Brighton vibe and its up-to-date culinary ways. A revamped menu format offers uncomplicated ideas, but rest assured that pin-sharp flavours are nailed from the off.

Chef Matt Gillan

The Salt Room
◎◎ MODERN BRITISH
01273 929488 | 106 Kings Road, BN1 2FU
www.saltroom-restaurant.co.uk

In a prime location on the seafront, this is a smart, contemporary space, with a terrace. The atmosphere is buzzing, the black-clad staff friendly, and the large dining room the perfect setting for modern British cooking. Simple presentation allows the main ingredient to shine.

Chef Dave Mothersil **Seats** 80, Private dining 14 **Closed** 25–26 December **Prices from** S £5, M £13, D £8.50 **Notes** Vegetarian dishes, Children welcome

SILO
◎ MODERN
01273 674 259 | 39 Upper Gardner Street, North Laine, BN1 4AN
www.silobrighton.com

Looking for solid eco-credentials? Restaurants don't come much more planet-saving than this outfit where the zero-waste ethos is embedded; from the recycled materials used to kit out the place through to the kitchen's emphasis on ethically sourced ingredients.

Chef Douglas McMaster **Open** All year **Notes** Vegetarian dishes

64 Degrees

◎◎ MODERN BRITISH

01273 770115 | 53 Meeting House Lane, BN1 1HB
www.64degrees.co.uk

In Brighton's famous Lanes, this bijou restaurant is big on small plates, the idea being tapas-style sharing. The menu's economically worded fish, veg and meat options – four of each – reveal nothing of how beautifully the open-kitchen team prepares them.

Chef Samuel Lambert **Seats** 20 **Closed** 25–26 December, 1 January **Prices from** S £8, M £16, D £8 **Notes** Vegetarian dishes, Children welcome

Terre à Terre

◎ MODERN VEGETARIAN **V**

01273 729051 | 71 East Street, BN1 1HQ
www.terreaterre.co.uk

This trendsetting restaurant serves creative, classy veggie-vegan food. It's just back from the seafront, and the pared-back dining area stretches back to a small terrace. The service team can help with the eccentric menu and the inspiration is worldwide.

Chef A Powley, P Taylor **Seats** 110 **Closed** 25–26 December **Prices from** S £8.95, M £15.98, D £8.95 **Notes** Children welcome

CAMBER
The Gallivant

◎◎ MODERN BRITISH **V** ♟NOTABLE WINE LIST

01797 225057 | New Lydd Road, TN31 7RB
www.thegallivant.co.uk

Overlooking the Camber shoreline near Rye, The Gallivant has its heart in New England, where that laid-back eastern seaboard style translates as oceans of space, light wood, and café furniture. Sourcing from within a 10-mile radius is an especially good idea when the radius takes in such impeccable stuff.

Chef Chris Baguley **Seats** 60, Private dining 100 **Open** All year **Prices from** S £7, M £17, D £7.50 **Parking** 24 **Notes** Children welcome

DITCHLING
The Bull

◎ MODERN BRITISH

01273 843147 | 2 High Street, BN6 8TA
www.thebullditchling.com

One of the oldest buildings in the village, The Bull has been central to this community for hundreds of years. Real fires, gnarled old beams: it's got the lot, and outdoors there's a garden that helps fuel the kitchen.

Chef Steve Sanger **Seats** 120, Private dining 16 **Open** All year **Prices from** S £5, M £12, D £5 **Parking** 40 **Notes** Vegetarian dishes, Children welcome

EASTBOURNE
Langham Hotel

◎ MODERN BRITISH

01323 731451 | 43–49 Royal Parade, BN22 7AH
www.langhamhotel.co.uk

The bracing seafront of Eastbourne fits this sparkling-white hotel like a glove, with marine views from the conservatory dining room. While old-fashioned courtesies abound, the kitchen doesn't just stick to heritage Englishry, although you can go from potato and herb soup to sirloin and chips.

Chef Michael Titherington **Seats** 24, Private dining 130 **Open** All year **Notes** Vegetarian dishes, Children welcome

The Mirabelle Restaurant

◎◎ MODERN, CLASSIC ♟NOTABLE WINE LIST

01323 412345 | The Grand Hotel, King Edwards Parade, BN21 4EQ
www.grandeastbourne.com

The Mirabelle ia appropriately ritzy, with cloches, trolleys and attentive service. And there's nothing passé about the kitchen's contemporary take on flavour combinations and textures, with dishes revealing modern European thinking..

Chef Keith Mitchell, Stephanie Malvoisin **Seats** 50 **Closed** 2–16 January **Parking** 70 **Notes** Vegetarian dishes

EAST CHILTINGTON
Jolly Sportsman

◎ MODERN BRITISH, EUROPEAN

01273 890400 | Chapel Lane, BN7 3BA
www.thejollysportsman.com

Located deep in the South Downs hinterland, a GPS comes in handy for hunting down chef-patron Bruce Wass's weatherboarded country inn. There's a cosy bar area with casks on trestles and a rustic-chic restaurant. The kitchen delivers full-flavoured, contemporary cooking.

Chef Bruce Wass, Vincent Fayat **Seats** 80, Private dining 20 **Closed** 25 December **Prices from** S £6.45, M £14.85, D £6.75 **Parking** 35 **Notes** Vegetarian dishes, Children welcome

FOREST ROW
The Anderida Restaurant
⊛⊛ MODERN BRITISH
01342 824988 | Ashdown Park Hotel, RH18 5JR
www.ashdownpark.com
Ashdown Park is a magnificent Victorian pile in acres of grounds, and the Anderida Restaurant, with its elegant drapes, sparkling glassware, double-clothed tables and grand piano, is a fine setting for sophisticated cooking.

Chef Byron Hayter **Seats** 120, Private dining 160 **Open** All year **Parking** 120 **Notes** Vegetarian dishes, Children welcome

RYE
Mermaid Inn
⊛⊛ BRITISH, TRADITIONAL FRENCH
01797 223065 | Mermaid Street, TN31 7EY
www.mermaidinn.com
This 600-year-old inn has bags of historic charm and atmosphere. The food in the restaurant, with its linen-fold panelling, takes an Anglo-French path, and there are appealingly contemporary dishes on the menu.

Chef Benjamin Fisher **Seats** 64, Private dining 14 **Open** All year **Parking** 26 **Notes** Vegetarian dishes, Children welcome

See advertisement below

Webbe's at The Fish Café
⊛ MODERN BRITISH
01797 222226 | 17 Tower Street, TN31 7AT
www.webbesrestaurants.co.uk
A brick-built warehouse constructed in 1907 houses this modern seafood restaurant. Exposed brickwork, high ceilings and fish-related artwork all feed in to the buzz of the ground-floor dining room where the chefs work their magic in the open-plan kitchen.

Chef Paul Webbe, Matthew Drinkwater **Seats** 52, Private dining 60 **Closed** 25–26 December, 2–17 January **Prices from** S £6.50, M £13, D £6.50 **Notes** Vegetarian dishes, Children welcome

TICEHURST
Dale Hill Hotel & Golf Club
⊛ MODERN EUROPEAN
01580 200112 | TN5 7DQ
www.dalehill.co.uk
With its pair of 18-hole courses, golf may be top of the agenda, but hill views and a pair of restaurants are reason enough for non-players to visit. The fine-dining Wealden View restaurant is the star attraction.

Chef Lloyd Walker **Seats** 60, Private dining 24 **Open** All year **Parking** 220 **Notes** Vegetarian dishes, Children welcome

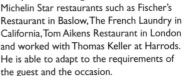

Welcome to the unique **Mermaid Inn**, rich in history, Cellars dating from 1156 and the building rebuilt in 1420. The Mermaid Inn offers a totally different experience, sloping ceilings, creaking floorboards and numerous staircases. A history and a rich tradition that is maintained by careful stewardship. Experience a drink in the Giant's Fireplace Bar and imagine how the Hawkhurst Gang, local smugglers in the 1730s and 1740s, caroused in the bar. Can you see the secret passageway entrance?

Dine in the Linen Fold Panelled Restaurant, where you can enjoy the ambience of the large restaurant, the cosiness of The Dr Syn Dining Room or the privacy of the Boardroom for your evening meal, lunch and breakfast.

Head chef Ben Fisher is very focused on using quality, seasonal, local ingredients and cooking them perfectly. He has a broad range of experience having worked in Michelin Star restaurants such as Fischer's Restaurant in Baslow, The French Laundry in California, Tom Aikens Restaurant in London and worked with Thomas Keller at Harrods. He is able to adapt to the requirements of the guest and the occasion.

The menu features local produce, such as Winchelsea Beef, Rye Bay Cod and Romney Marsh Lamb. There is an extensive wine list including wine from Chapel Down in nearby Small Hythe, Kent. All of these can be found on **www.mermaidinn.com**

Mermaid Inn, Mermaid Street, Rye, East Sussex, TN31 7EY
Tel: 01797 223065, Fax: 01797 225069

UCKFIELD
Buxted Park Hotel
@@ MODERN EUROPEAN V
01825 733333 | Buxted, TN22 4AY
www.handpickedhotels.co.uk/buxtedpark
A white mansion set in immaculate gardens, Buxted Park was built in early Georgian times and nowadays offers the full country-house package. The restaurant features a mixture of table and booth seating, with curved lilac-upholstered banquettes against a white background.
Chef Mark Carter **Seats** 40, Private dining 120
Open All year **Prices from** S £10.50, M £19, D £9.50
Parking 100 **Notes** Children welcome

East Sussex National Golf Resort & Spa
@@ MODERN BRITISH
01825 880088 | Little Horsted, TN22 5ES
www.eastsussexnational.co.uk
Overlooking the greens and the South Downs, the vast Pavilion Restaurant offers a concise menu with plenty of choice. Start, perhaps, with the earthy flavours of rabbit and leek terrine with pistachios, carrot and sourdough bread. Dishes bring out upfront flavours without being gimmicky.
Chef Hrvoje Loncarevic **Seats** 90 **Open** All year
Parking 500 **Notes** Vegetarian dishes, Children welcome

Horsted Place
@@ MODERN BRITISH
01825 750581 | Little Horsted, TN22 5TS
www.horstedplace.co.uk
In 1850, Gothic Revivalist architect Augustus Pugin was commissioned to work his wonders here, hard on the heels of his design for the interior of the new Palace of Westminster. Outside are 1,100 acres of verdant Sussex countryside. Inside is a rich green dining room.
Chef Allan Garth **Seats** 40, Private dining 80
Closed 1st week January **Prices from** S £9.90, M £23, D £9.50 **Parking** 50 **Notes** Vegetarian dishes, No children under 7 years

WESTFIELD
The Wild Mushroom Restaurant
@@ MODERN BRITISH
01424 751137 | Woodgate House, Westfield Lane, TN35 4SB
www.wildmushroom.co.uk
A converted 19th-century farmhouse surrounded by countryside just outside Hastings, Paul and Rebecca Webbe's restaurant is part of a local mini-empire. Original features like flagged floors and low beams

impart a smart country feel to the ground-floor restaurant, helped along by friendly service.
Chef Paul Webbe, Christopher Weddle **Seats** 40
Closed 25 December, 2 weeks beginning of January
Prices from S £8.50, M £17.50, D £8.95 **Parking** 20
Notes Vegetarian dishes, Children welcome

WILMINGTON
Crossways
@@ MODERN BRITISH
01323 482455 | Lewes Road, BN26 5SG
www.crosswayshotel.co.uk
Crossways' appeal lies in the standard of the cooking and in the interesting monthly changing four-course menu, with soup normally falling between the starter and main course. There's always a fish dish of the day, and puddings include Swiss roll with raspberries and cream.
Chef David Stott **Seats** 24 **Closed** 24 December to 24 January **Parking** 20 **Notes** Vegetarian dishes, No children under 12 years

▶ WEST SUSSEX

ALBOURNE
The Ginger Fox
@@ MODERN BRITISH, EUROPEAN
01273 857888 | Muddleswood Road, BN6 9EA
thegingerfox.com
The Brighton-based Ginger group of restaurants and refashioned pubs has given its country bolt-hole a stripped-down look with parquet and slate floors, chunky tables and brown leather banquettes, plus a beer garden and raised beds where the Fox's own vegetables are grown.
Chef Ben McKellar, Mark Bradley **Seats** 62, Private dining 22 **Closed** 25 December **Prices from** S £6.50, M £14, D £8.50 **Parking** 40 **Notes** Vegetarian dishes, Children welcome

AMBERLEY
Amberley Castle
@@@ MODERN EUROPEAN V ⭐ NOTABLE WINE LIST
01798 831992 | BN18 9LT
www.amberleycastle.co.uk
The Castle, for such it is, looks like the kind of place you'd happily pay the National Trust for the chance to look around, a nearly millennium-old fortification at the foot of the South Downs. It did time as a Royalist stronghold in the Civil War. Anywhere that is entered via a portcullis has more than a touch of class, an impression reinforced by the dining rooms with their armoury, tapestries, barrel-vault ceilings and lancet windows. Paul Peters produces assertive modern dishes with plenty to say for themselves, opening with confit

rabbit in a blackberry gel cylinder with pistachio granola, or gently charred barbecued eel dressed in wasabi with yuzu and cucumber, prior to halibut with apple, smoked raisins and capers in a spicy mussel sauce. Meat dishes look opulent, as with the carefully rendered mallard breast and leg that come with turnips, crosnes and chervil root in a light red wine jus. Finish with firmly set vanilla pannacotta, cinnamon ice cream and apple caramel, or the ultimate indulgence of mascarpone with flavours of chocolate, coffee and Tia Maria.

Chef Paul Peters **Seats** 56, Private dining 12 **Open** All year **Parking** 40 **Notes** No children under 8 years

ARUNDEL
The Parsons Table
◉◉ BRITISH, EUROPEAN
01903 883477 | 2 & 8 Castle Mews, Tarrant Street, BN18 9DG
www.theparsonstable.co.uk

Picture-perfect Arundel, laid out prettily beneath its majestic castle, is home to this bright, airy venue named after the chef-patron. White walls and unclothed light wood tables furnish a neutral backdrop to thoroughgoing modern British culinary wizardry.

Chef Lee Parsons **Seats** 34 **Closed** 24–28 December, February half term, Summer Bank Holiday to start of term **Notes** No children

The Town House
◉◉ MODERN **V**
01903 883847 | 65 High Street, BN18 9AJ
www.thetownhouse.co.uk

This smart restaurant with rooms is a place of enormous charm, its intimate dining room brought into the 21st century with high-backed black chairs, wooden floors and mirrors with funky striped frames. The kitchen takes the best of Sussex produce as the foundation.

Chef Lee Williams **Seats** 24 **Closed** 2 weeks Easter, 2 weeks October, Christmas **Notes** Children welcome

BOSHAM
The Millstream Hotel & Restaurant
◉◉ MODERN BRITISH
01243 573234 | Bosham Lane, PO18 8HL
www.millstreamhotel.com

Built of red brick and flint, this charming hotel was originally three 17th-century workmen's cottages. On a balmy evening, the gardens and millstream make an idyllic spot for drinks. The kitchen stays abreast of modern trends while keeping traditionalists happy.

Chef Neil Hiskey **Seats** 60, Private dining 40 **Open** All year **Parking** 40 **Notes** Vegetarian dishes, Children welcome

See advertisement on page 310

CHICHESTER
Chichester Harbour Hotel & Spa
◉ MODERN BRITISH SEAFOOD
01243 778000 | 57 North Street, PO19 1NH
www.chichester-harbour-hotel.co.uk

In the heart of Chichester, this hotel presents a sober, red-brick Georgian exterior, but inside the designers have unleashed a riot of boutique style. Murray's Restaurant is a split-level dining room that works a classy colonial look. Brasserie-style menus tick the right boxes.

Chef David Hunt **Seats** 80, Private dining 120 **Open** All year **Prices from** S £6.95, M £13.50, D £4.50 **Parking** 45 **Notes** Vegetarian dishes, Children welcome

Crouchers Restaurant & Hotel
◉◉ MODERN BRITISH **V**
01243 784995 | Birdham Road, PO20 7EH
www.crouchershotel.co.uk

Over the past two decades as a stalwart of the Chichester dining scene, Crouchers has traded upwards from a simple B&B to a smart modern hotel near Dell Quay and the marina. Desserts maintain the high standards, as shown by the well-balanced flavours and textures.

Chef Luke Gale **Seats** 80, Private dining 22 **Open** All year **Parking** 40 **Notes** Children welcome

Earl of March
◉ MODERN BRITISH
01243 533993 | Lavant Road, PO18 0BQ
www.theearlofmarch.com

Just a short drive out of Chichester, this 18th-century coaching inn looks out over the South Downs. There's a small patio garden, but most of the action takes place inside, in the large dining area or the snug bar area with a fire and sofas.

Chef Giles Thompson, Adam Howden **Seats** 60, Private dining 16 **Closed** 25 December **Parking** 30 **Notes** Vegetarian dishes, Children welcome

Halliday's
◉◉ MODERN BRITISH
01243 575331 | Watery Lane, Funtington, PO18 9LF
www.hallidays.info

At the foot of the South Downs in the peaceful village of Funtington, Halliday's occupies three flint-fronted thatched cottages dating from the 13th century. Chef and owner Andy Stephenson sources first-rate produce from the local area, shown off to advantage in his seasonally changing menus.

Chef Andrew Stephenson **Seats** 26, Private dining 12 **Closed** 1 week March, 2 weeks August **Prices from** S £7.50, M £18, D £6.75 **Parking** 12 **Notes** Vegetarian dishes, Children welcome

MILLSTREAM
HOTEL & RESTAURANT

CHICHESTER continued

Richmond Arms
◉◉ ECLECTIC
01243 572046 | Mill Road, West Ashling, PO18 8EA
www.therichmondarms.co.uk
The whitewashed Richmond is one of the glories of West Ashling, a peaceful village at the foot of the South Downs, only five minutes from Chichester. Daily specials are written up on the blackboard, and there's a wood-fired oven for traditional pizzas.
Chef William Jack, Theo Tzanis **Seats** 36, Private dining 60 **Prices from** S £4.95, M £15.95, D £4.95 **Parking** 9 **Notes** Vegetarian dishes, Children welcome

The Royal Oak
◉ CONTEMPORARY BRITISH
01243 527434 | Pook Lane, East Lavant, PO18 0AX
www.royaloakeastlavant.co.uk
A whitewashed village inn on a narrow lane in East Lavant, near Chichester, The Royal Oak is refreshingly allowed all its original character inside, with red-brick-and-flint walls and tiled and timbered floors. Modern pub cooking supplemented by daily specials. Sunday lunches are a local main attraction.
Chef James Bailey **Open** All year **Prices from** S £6.45, M £13, D £6.75 **Notes** No children

CHILGROVE
The White Horse
◉ BRITISH, EUROPEAN
01243 519444 | High Street, PO18 9HX
www.thewhitehorse.co.uk
This stylish pub boasts plenty of quirky touches, right down to sheepskin throws on the high-backed benches and deer skulls. A meal here showcases some modern British cooking of considerable poise and confidence.
Chef Robert Armstrong **Seats** 100, Private dining 25 **Open** All year **Parking** 50 **Notes** Vegetarian dishes, Children welcome

GATWICK AIRPORT
Arora Hotel Gatwick
◉ MODERN BRITISH
01293 530000 | Southgate Avenue, Southgate, RH10 6LW
www.arorahotels.com
Despite its name, this smart modern hotel is in Crawley town centre and its Grill restaurant is worth a visit in its own right. It's an airy open-plan room with clean-lined contemporary looks and diligently sourced British produce. Straight-up steaks keep the carnivores happy.
Chef Tony Staples **Seats** 70, Private dining 15 **Open** All year **Prices from** S £6, M £16, D £6 **Parking** 210 **Notes** Vegetarian dishes, Children welcome

Langshott Manor
◉◉◉ MODERN EUROPEAN $\mathbf{V}$
01293 786680 | Langshott Lane, RH6 9LN
www.langshottmanor.com
This Tudor mansion faced in exquisitely laid red brickwork with original beams and mullioned windows is a sight for travel-weary eyes if ever there was, not least for its garden tables under the trees, and Langshott's Elizabethan interiors – all low ceilings and blazing fireplaces – have been discreetly augmented with the accoutrements of the modern hotel. In the Mulberry Restaurant, views over the grounds are a welcome complement to Phil Dixon's assured country-house cooking. A gentle richness characterises many of his dishes, from a beginner of open lasagne heaped with rabbit, chestnuts, broccoli and tarragon, to mains such as Gigha halibut in truffled dashi stock with celeriac and cavolo nero. Meats are out of the top drawer – the Creedy Carver duck accompanied by gingered pear and hazelnuts, and the aged beef fillet with artichokes and roasted leeks in beer jus. Desserts aim to seduce with lashings of chocolate, caramel, peanuts and coffee in the enveloping forms of mousses, soufflés and parfaits, or there might be chilled cardamom-laced rice pudding with blood orange.
Chef Phil Dixon **Seats** 55, Private dining 60 **Open** All year **Parking** 30 **Notes** Children welcome

Sofitel London Gatwick
◉◉ BRITISH, INTERNATIONAL
01293 567070 | North Terminal, RH6 0PH
www.sofitel.com
An impressive central atrium makes a massive impact at this smart hotel close to Gatwick's North Terminal. The menu at La Brasserie, with its neatly laid tables and its contemporary artworks, takes a modern British path, with a French accent.
Chef David Woods **Seats** 120 **Open** All year **Parking** 565 **Notes** Vegetarian dishes, Children welcome

GOODWOOD
The Goodwood Hotel
◉◉ MODERN BRITISH
01243 775537 | PO18 0QB
www.goodwood.com
Part of the 12,000-acre Goodwood Estate, the newly named Farmer, Butcher, Chef restaurant at this luxurious hotel uses pork, lamb and beef from the estate's organic home farm. Although there are plenty of fish and vegetarian options on the menu, home-reared meat dominates.
Chef Mark Forman, Matt Vidal **Seats** 84, Private dining 50 **Open** All year **Prices from** S £7, M £16, D £7 **Parking** 200 **Notes** Vegetarian dishes, Children welcome

SUSSEX, WEST

HASSOCKS
The Glass House Restaurant & Terrace
◉ BRITISH
01273 857567 | Wickwoods Country Club Hotel & Spa,
Shaveswood Lane, Albourne, BN6 9DY
www.wickwoods.co.uk

The contemporary Glass House restaurant occupies an
orangery overlooking the landscaped grounds within
the South Downs National Park. The crowd-pleasing
modern European menu includes local steaks cooked
on the chargrill, burgers and ribs, although there's
plenty of other options.
Chef Dale Lapperts **Seats** 50, Private dining 24
Open All year **Prices from** S £6.50, M £9.95, D £5.95
Parking 160 **Notes** Vegetarian dishes, No children

HAYWARDS HEATH
Jeremy's at Borde Hill
◉◉ MODERN EUROPEAN, PAN ASIAN
01444 441102 | Balcombe Road, RH16 1XP
www.jeremysrestaurant.com

It is hard to imagine a more idyllic setting than this
contemporary restaurant in Borde Hill Gardens.
Occupying a stylishly converted stable block overlooking
the Victorian walled garden and south-facing terrace,
it's a wide open, bright space. The kitchen delivers bold
flavours and vibrant, Mediterranean-inflected food.
Chef Jimmy Gray, Eliott Buchet **Seats** 55, Private
dining 120 **Closed** after New Year for 14 days
Prices from S £9, M £16, D £8 **Parking** 30
Notes Vegetarian dishes, Children welcome

HORSHAM
Restaurant Tristan
◉◉◉ MODERN BRITISH, FRENCH V ♦ NOTABLE WINE LIST
01403 255688 | 3 Stan's Way, East Street, RH12 1HU
www.restauranttristan.co.uk

The 16th-century building in the heart of old Horsham
looks pretty historic, but chef-patron Tristan Mason's
food is bang up-to-date stuff. The first-floor dining room
blends ancient and modern with panache, its striking
beamed vaulted ceiling, wall timbers and oak
floorboards sitting alongside sleek contemporary decor.
As is often the way with this kind of innovative,
creative, technically skilful cooking, menus make a
virtue of conciseness, listing the components of each
composition, but whether you go for three, four, six or
eight courses, you can be sure that the full gamut of
taste categories, textural contrasts and temperatures
will be deployed. Clever stuff, then, but this isn't just
about techno flim-flam; having trained with Marco
Pierre White, Mason's ideas are solidly grounded in
classic French technique. Foie gras with mango,
hazelnut and honeycomb is an impressive, highly
detailed starter that wows with its contrasting textures

and richness offset with fruity tartness. Fish and meat
combinations are favoured, as in the crisp chicken
wings and turbot that arrive beautifully cooked
alongside trompette mushroom foam and jelly, and
parsley root purée and crisps. Elsewhere, an idea might
explore the textures and flavours of lamb, kid and goat.
Things end with a thought-provoking dessert of white
chocolate mousse with dill sorbet and black olive.
Chef Tristan Mason **Seats** 34 **Closed** 25–26 December,
1 January **Notes** No children under 10 years

Wabi
◉ MODERN JAPANESE
01403 788140 | 38 East Street, RH12 1HL
www.wabi.co.uk

Wabi is stylish to the hilt. The ground floor is a trendy
cocktail bar with a waterfall curtain, while the first-
floor restaurant goes for a minimal, calming Zen
garden vibe, with tatami-screened booths above
spotlit beds of white pebbles.
Chef Kha Wai Pang **Seats** 62, Private dining 14
Closed 25–26 December, Bank holidays
Notes Vegetarian dishes, Children welcome

KIRDFORD
The Half Moon Inn
◉◉ MODERN BRITISH V
01403 820223 | Glasshouse Lane, RH14 0LT
www.halfmoonkirdford.co.uk

Owned by TV presenter and international model Jodie
Kidd, it ticks all the 'quintessential village pub' boxes
– oak beams, red-brick floors, an inglenook fireplace
and friendly staff. A tasty, indeed attractively
presented, opener is salmon and langoustine ravioli
with rich shellfish cream, peas and broad beans.
Chef Johnny Stanford **Seats** Private dining 20
Open All year **Prices from** S £7.25, M £14.50, D £7
Parking 20 **Notes** Children welcome

LICKFOLD
The Lickfold Inn
◉◉◉ BRITISH V
01789 532535 | GU28 9EY
www.thelickfoldinn.co.uk

By the time the nearby National Trust property of
Petworth House was built, The Lickfold Inn had already
been up and running for a century. Its origins in the
Tudor period are apparent in the ground-floor bar, but
it's upstairs, in the low-beamed dining room, where a
modern design sensibility has installed parquet
tabletops and high-backed chairs, that its present-day
identity comes into sharpest focus. Here, executive
chef Tom Sellers oversees a menu of contemporary but
refreshingly direct cooking that brings its ingredients

into stimulating conjunctions. Cornish crab with burnt gem lettuce and the scent of tarragon might open the bidding, prior to earthily treated fish such as halibut with cauliflower, pickled sloes and yeast, or a more traditional seasonal game option like pheasant with smoked bacon, hazelnuts and capers. The technical panache at dessert stage produces a soufflé of roasted quince with walnut sorbet, or a razor-sharp medley of Yorkshire rhubarb, blood orange and yogurt. A five-course taster drawn from the main menu is bookended by ingenious nibbles and a 'petits fours box', and optionally accompanied by imaginatively chosen wines by the glass.

Chef Tom Sellers, Graham Squire **Seats** 40 **Closed** 25 December **Prices from** S £9, M £19, D £7 **Parking** 20 **Notes** Children welcome

LODSWORTH
The Halfway Bridge Inn
@ MODERN BRITISH

01798 861281 | Halfway Bridge, GU28 9BP
www.halfwaybridge.co.uk

This classy 18th-century roadside inn makes an inviting pitstop after a hike on the South Downs Way or a leisurely perusal of Petworth's antique emporia. The ambience is friendly and unbuttoned, while the kitchen deals in pub classics given a contemporary tweak.

Chef Clyde Hollett **Seats** 55, Private dining 16 **Open** All year **Prices from** S £6.50, M £14, D £7 **Parking** 30 **Notes** Vegetarian dishes, Children welcome

LOWER BEEDING
The Camellia Restaurant at South Lodge
@@ BRITISH V ▲ NOTABLE WINE LIST

01403 891711 | South Lodge Hotel, Brighton Road, RH13 6PS
www.exclusive.co.uk

South Lodge is a handsome Victorian mansion hotel in the Sussex countryside featuring The Pass (see below) and The Camellia. Fresh vegetables come straight from the hotel's walled garden and help shape the central components in the contemporary, seasonal cooking.

Chef Richard Mann **Seats** 100, Private dining 140 **Open** All year **Prices from** S £9, M £19.50, D £9 **Parking** 200 **Notes** Children welcome

The Pass Restaurant
@@@ MODERN BRITISH V ▲ NOTABLE WINE LIST

01403 891711 | South Lodge Hotel, Brighton Road, RH13 6PS
www.exclusive.co.uk

Many establishments offer a chef's table for those who like to glean plating and garnishing tips from the professionals, but at the South Lodge Hotel's Pass Restaurant, chef's tables are all there are. And quite the show it is, with seating for over two dozen, watching the action in the flesh or on plasma-screen monitors, depending which way you're facing. Ian Swainson has given the menus an extra streak of inventiveness, with dishes exquisitely composed of textural and colour contrasts and given conceptual titles. 'The Colour Merge' is an abstract-expressionist assemblage of tuna sashimi, burrata and tomato from the hotel garden, while the more gently watercolourish 'By The Sea' offers an almost classical mix of clams, sea vegetables and caviar, but with the rakish angle of a white chocolate sauce to boot. The format is six or eight courses, with main dishes like suckling pig, nettle purée, balsamic and garlic full of striking resonance. A dessert called 'Food Porn' is in the event a blameless activity involving strawberries and cream in red wine with elderflower sorbet.

Chef Ian Swainson **Seats** 28 **Closed** 1st 2 weeks January **Parking** 200 **Notes** No children

ROWHOOK
The Chequers Inn
@ BRITISH

01403 790480 | RH12 3PY
www.thechequersrowhook.com

A proper village local with flagstones, oak beams, chunky wooden tables, open fires and well-kept real ales on hand pump. The Chequers has been around since the 15th century, but it is in tune with modern tastes, with no pretensions, just bang-on-the-money modern ideas.

Chef Yves Noel (Head chef), Tim Neal (Chef Proprietor) **Seats** 40 **Closed** 25 December **Parking** 40 **Notes** Vegetarian dishes, Children welcome

RUSPER
Ghyll Manor
@ MODERN BRITISH

0330 123 0371 | High Street, RH12 4PX
www.ghyllmanor.co.uk

A timbered manor house in picture-perfect Sussex countryside, Ghyll Manor is an ideal retreat from the city. Inside, an appealing mixture of period features and modern styling creates a harmonious impression. The kitchen team maintains a steady hand at the tiller for assured country-house cooking.

Chef Barry Scarborough **Seats** 48, Private dining 40 **Open** All year **Parking** 50 **Notes** Vegetarian dishes, Children welcome

SUSSEX, WEST

SIDLESHAM
The Crab & Lobster
◉◉ MODERN BRITISH
01243 641233 | Mill Lane, PO20 7NB
www.crab-lobster.co.uk
The whitewashed 17th-century pub has become an upscale restaurant with rooms, and is looking spruce from top to bottom. On the edge of the Pagham Harbour nature reserve, it offers a stylish restaurant that aims to impress with ambitious, upscale modern British food.

Chef Dan Storey, Clyde Hollett **Seats** 54 **Open** All year **Prices from** S £6.95, M £16.85, D £7.50 **Parking** 12 **Notes** Vegetarian dishes, Children welcome

TANGMERE
Cassons Restaurant
◉◉ MODERN BRITISH
01243 773294 | Arundel Road, PO18 0DU
www.cassonsrestaurant.co.uk
Chef-patronne Viv Casson ran a successful restaurant in France, so you can expect Gallic culinary influences to her work. Inside, the place gains character from the huge inglenook fireplace and low-beamed ceilings, while the modern menu takes in classically influenced ideas.

Chef Viv Casson **Seats** 36, Private dining 14 **Closed** Christmas to New Year **Prices from** S £8, M £23, D £8 **Parking** 30 **Notes** Vegetarian dishes, Children welcome

TILLINGTON
The Horse Guards Inn
◉◉ TRADITIONAL BRITISH
01798 342332 | Upperton Road, GU28 9AF
www.thehorseguardsinn.co.uk
The Horse Guards is a relaxed and friendly pub dating back 350 years, with open fires, wooden tables, beams and a boarded floor. It's a foodie destination with a daily changing menu showcasing what's been bought or foraged locally or dug up from the garden.

Chef Mark Robinson **Seats** 55, Private dining 18 **Closed** 25–26 December **Notes** Vegetarian dishes, Children welcome

TURNERS HILL
AG's Restaurant at Alexander House Hotel
◉◉◉ BRITISH, FRENCH V
01342 714914 | East Street, RH10 4QD
www.alexanderhouse.co.uk
With 120 acres of Sussex countryside all to itself, Alexander House is in a Goldilocks spot, close enough to Gatwick Airport for those jetting in and out, but

tranquil enough as a getaway in its own right. The handsome red-brick hotel has glam bedrooms, a spa to pamper you into submission, and two smart dining options. Royal-blue upholstery and white linen reinforce the fine dining mood in AG's, the principal dining room (there's also a sleek brasserie called Reflections). The cooking is contemporary, with striking combinations of ingredients and heaps of visual artistry. First off, pan-fried scallops are matched harmoniously with a cauliflower beignet, baby globe artichokes and Serrano ham crisp. The precision can be remarkable, as when well-rested venison loin is teamed with crispy pommes Anna and given a luxuriant gloss with macerated cherries and bitter chocolate. An impressive show is topped off by banana soufflé with toffee ice cream, banana jam and 100% chocolate. The kitchen has all the millennial dietary bases covered with vegetarian, vegan and dairy-free versions of both its set-price and tasting menus.

Chef Darrel Wilde **Seats** 30, Private dining 12 **Open** All year **Parking** 100 **Notes** No children

Reflections at Alexander House
◉◉ MODERN BRITISH V
01342 714914 | Alexander House Hotel, East Street, RH10 4QD
www.alexanderhouse.co.uk
The handsome 17th-century mansion has moved into boutique territory after a thoroughly modern makeover, with pampering facilities to delight spa enthusiasts and a buzzy brasserie – Reflections – to lift the spirits still further (the fine-dining option is AG's Restaurant).

Chef Darrel Wilde **Seats** 70, Private dining 12 **Open** All year **Parking** 100 **Notes** Children welcome

WEST CHILTINGTON
The Roundabout
◉ BRITISH
01798 817336 | Monkmead Lane, RH20 2PF
www.southcoastinns.co.uk
One of several buildings in the tranquil village of West Chiltington designed in the 1920s and 1930s by sculptor Reginald Wells, the Tudor-style Roundabout Hotel has a traditional, beamed restaurant with drapes and red carpet is an elegant setting for the modern British cooking.

Chef Andrew Lee **Open** All year **Notes** No children

WEST HOATHLY
Graveye Manor Hotel
◉◉◉ MODERN BRITISH V 🍷 NOTABLE WINE LIST
See pages 316–317

WORTHING
Indigo Seafood & Grill
◉ MODERN BRITISH, EUROPEAN
01903 230451 | Steyne Gardens, BN11 3DZ
www.indigorestaurant.info
Just outside the town centre, and a few minutes' walk from the seafront, Indigo is a contemporary seafood and grill restaurant. Red leather banquettes and lavish chandeliers add a luxurious touch to the proceedings, although the vibrant, globally influenced food is simple and well-defined.

Chef Luca Mason, John Wheatland **Closed** 25 December to 4 January

▶ TYNE & WEAR

NEWCASTLE UPON TYNE
Blackfriars Restaurant
◉ MODERN, TRADITIONAL BRITISH
0191 261 5945 | Friars Street, NE1 4XN
www.blackfriarsrestaurant.co.uk
Once the refectory for monks at the Dominican friary, the restaurant dates back to the 13th century. Recently completely refurbished, a cookery school and tasting room have been added, and the kitchen deals in gutsy modern and classic brasserie dishes made from local ingredients.

Chef Christopher Wardale **Seats** 80, Private dining 50 **Closed** Good Friday, Bank holidays **Prices from** S £6, M £15, D £5 **Notes** Vegetarian dishes, Children welcome

Cal's Own
◉ ITALIAN, MEDITERRANEAN
0191 281 5522 | 1–2 Holly Avenue West, Jesmond, NE2 2AR
www.calsown.co.uk
When you're up for a slice of pizza nirvana, this family-run joint delivers the authentic goods, courtesy of a hand-built wood-fired pizza oven imported from Naples sitting centre stage amid a no-nonsense setting of unclothed tables and bare brick walls.

Chef Calvin Kitchin **Seats** 65, Private dining 20 **Closed** 25–26 December **Prices from** S £5.95, M £7.85, D £5.95 **Parking** 2 **Notes** Vegetarian dishes, Children welcome

Chez Mal Brasserie
◉ FRENCH
0191 245 5000 | 104 Quayside, NE1 3DX
www.malmaison.com
The urban-cool boutique chain has taken a quayside warehouse as the starting point for its glamorous Newcastle outpost. The classy Chez Mal Brasserie

serves up a splendid view over the Gateshead Millennium Bridge as well as a cracking feel-good menu of globetrotting contemporary fare.

Chef Sandeep Singh **Seats** 100, Private dining 20 **Open** All year **Prices from** S £5.50, M £14, D £4 **Parking** 60 **Notes** Vegetarian dishes, Children welcome

Horton Grange Country House Hotel
◉◉ MODERN BRITISH
01661 860686 | Berwick Hill, Ponteland, NE13 6BU
www.hortongrange.co.uk
Set within a privately owned Grade II country-house hotel in the heart of Northumberland, Horton Grange's open-plan restaurant boasts some elegant touches with high quality crockery on the well-spaced tables. A meal here showcases some ambitious modern British cooking.

Chef Lee Williams **Seats** 60, Private dining 40 **Open** All year **Prices from** S £5.95, M £19.95, D £5.95 **Parking** 50 **Notes** Vegetarian dishes, Children welcome

Hotel du Vin Newcastle
◉ BRITISH, FRENCH 🍷 NOTABLE WINE LIST
0191 229 2200 | Allan House, City Road, NE1 2BE
www.hotelduvin.com
The converted red-brick Edwardian warehouse of the Tyne Tees Steam Shipping Company enjoys commanding views of the city's many bridges, while, as might be expected from this well-established chain, the restaurant has the look of a French bistro, with dark wood floors and wooden-topped tables.

Chef Kevin Bland **Seats** 86, Private dining 22 **Open** All year **Parking** 15 **Notes** Vegetarian dishes, Children welcome

House of Tides
◉◉◉◉ MODERN BRITISH V 🍷 NOTABLE WINE LIST
See pages 318–319

Jesmond Dene House
◉◉ MODERN BRITISH, EUROPEAN
0191 212 3000 | Jesmond Dene Road, NE2 2EY
www.jesmonddenehouse.co.uk
Part of the allure of Jesmond Dene House is that it has the feel of a grand country house sitting in a tranquil wooded valley, yet is actually within the city limits of Newcastle. There is refinement, creativity and skill in the execution of dishes.

Chef Michael Penaluna **Seats** 80, Private dining 24 **Open** All year **Prices from** S £6.50, M £15.50, D £7.50 **Parking** 64 **Notes** Vegetarian dishes, Children welcome

Newcastle upon Tyne continues on page 320

315

WEST HOATHLY
Gravetye Manor Hotel
◉◉◉ MODERN BRITISH V 🍷NOTABLE WINE LIST

01342 810567 | Vowels Lane, RH19 4LJ

www.gravetyemanor.co.uk

Dynamic modern cooking in a brand new dining room

Gravetye has seen it all. Originally built as an Elizabethan love nest by one Richard Infield for his new bride, Katharine, the manor has not always been an oasis of Sussex serenity. A smugglers' bolt-hole and a foundry supplying 12-pound cannon to the Woolwich arsenal in its time, it nonetheless faces the present day as a perfect blend of Tudor architectural style, exquisite Victorian gardens laid out by one of its former owners, the celebrated landscapist William Robinson, and the full rash of expected modern elegances. Inside, there are perfectly preserved age-dark oak panels and graceful plaster mouldings to emphasise the Manor's venerability, but change has also been in the air of late.

Its closure in the first few months of 2018, its sixtieth anniversary as a hotel, was in aid of building the stylish new dining room for George Blogg to showcase his dynamic modern British cooking, which is plentifully supplied by Gravetye's own walled kitchen garden, itself undergoing painstaking restoration. In addition to this, there are a thousand acres of grounds from which to forage, as well as an on-site smokehouse,

glasshouses and orchards, while contented chickens do their bit by reliably supplying the breakfast eggs.

Blogg's menus are naturally seasonal, changing monthly with the rhythms of the horticultural year, and his sharply etched culinary style is absolutely not about resting on any laurels, but strives for innovation and novelty all the way. A crisped quail egg and caramelised onion might adorn a successful starter of roasted quail in verjus, or there may be cured chalkstream trout with beetroot and winter marigolds in a dashi stock teeming with garden vegetables. After these, rose veal and tongue turn up with cauliflower, charred leeks and truffled sweetbread purée in a main course full of earthy notes, but flavours are just as clearly defined and true in fish dishes such as the beautifully balanced halibut and lobster pairing that comes with coral ravioli and pak choi in a basil-scented sauce.

Desserts aim for distinctiveness in the form of roasted acorn soufflé and matching ice cream, or perhaps an effusively fragrant combination centred on a set custard of rose geranium with shortbread, wild sorrel and hibiscus, all lit up with sloe gin sorbet. A seven-course tasting menu that steers a strategic path through the highlights of the carte can easily become eight with the option of a raid on the cheese trolley.

Chef George Blogg **Seats** 60, Private dining 30 **Open** All year **Parking** 40 **Notes** No children under 7 years

TYNE & WEAR

NEWCASTLE UPON TYNE
House of Tides
◉◉◉◉ MODERN BRITISH V ♦ NOTABLE WINE LIST

0191 230 3720 | 28–30 The Close, NE1 3RF

www.houseoftides.co.uk

Prime modern British cooking right beside the Tyne Bridge

A four-storey brick townhouse built for a well-to-do merchant in the 16th century, lurking just next to one of the towering arches of the Tyne Bridge, the House of Tides is pretty much peak Newcastle. It wasn't that long ago that it was sadly derelict, but since the beginning of 2014, it has been the latest centre of operations of local man Kenny Atkinson, one of Britain's foremost exponents of imaginative contemporary food. It's worth taking your time to move through the spaces here, from a drink in the stone-flagged ground-floor bar before heading upstairs to the dining room, which extends along the full breadth of the building. The gnarled wooden columns and fireplace speak eloquently of the venerability of the place, but the pale yellow banquettes, white walls and gentle landscape pictures keep things feeling light and easy on the eye. Probably the most exciting aspect of Atkinson's cooking is that it is very much still developing, taking on new challenges, exploring new ideas, and yet maintaining the firm commitments to depth of flavour and overall culinary balance.

Tasting menus are the standard offering, and it's as well to allow virtually as much time at lunch as you would in the evening, as there is only one course fewer during the day. Appetisers give the earliest notice of the quality to come: airily light gougères, a carrot meringue with fennel, smoked cod's roe on a squid ink cracker with lemon. The first course may be a Lindisfarne oyster adorned with caviar, cucumber and ginger, before the bread arrives, a fermented rye dough with cultured butter to spread on it. Then come a succession of novel and surprising dishes, often mobilising quite straightforward combinations – sea bass with a chicken wing and white asparagus, veal sweetbreads in beef fat crumbs with onion, Cumbrian lamb with hen of the woods and hazelnuts – but achieving unearthly resonance on the palate from first-rate materials and pin-sharp attention to detail of each nuance of seasoning.

At dessert, rhubarb finds a new best friend in dulce de leche with brown butter and rosewater to lubricate it, while the pastry offering combines perfect puff with Bramleys, raisins and cinnamon.

Needless to say, the wine pairing is well worth the extra for rounding out the whole experience, but if you're determined to light out on your own, wines by the glass are particularly well chosen, and there are some great cocktails to open the bidding.

Chef Kenny Atkinson **Seats** 60, Private dining 12 **Closed** 2 weeks Christmas and New Year **Parking** 70 **Notes** No children under 9 years

NEWCASTLE UPON TYNE continued

Peace and Loaf
◉◉ MODERN BRITISH
0191 281 5222 | 217 Jesmond Road, Jesmond, NE2 1LA
www.peaceandloaf.co.uk

In the fashionable Jesmond district of Newcastle, this is a thoroughly 21st-century place, with bare-wood floor and brick walls offset by kooky decorative touches. Bag a table on the mezzanine floor for views of the kitchen pass and the folks below.

Chef David Coulson **Seats** 53 **Closed** 25 December, 1 January **Prices from** S £11, M £18, D £8 **Notes** Vegetarian dishes, Children welcome

21
◉ MODERN BRITISH **V**
0191 222 0755 | Trinity Gardens, Quayside, NE1 2HH
www.21newcastle.co.uk

The spacious, glass-fronted brasserie, with its polished wooden floor, leather banquettes and neatly clothed tables, remains as buzzy as ever, with slick and smooth service ensuring that all is as it should be, and the appealing brasserie-style dishes play a big part in the attraction.

Chef Chris Dobson **Seats** 130, Private dining 44 **Closed** 25–26 December, 1 January **Prices from** S £6.60, M £16, D £6.50 **Notes** Children welcome

Ury Restaurant
◉ INDIAN
0191 232 7799 | 27 Queen Street, NE1 3UG
www.uryrestaurants.com

An ury is a clay pot used for storing preserved food, a traditional feature of Keralan homes in south India, which is where the regional specialities hail from in this large, exuberantly decorated restaurant just off the quayside. Mains run from turmeric-spiked lamb cooked with coconut and curry leaves to chemmeen masala.

Chef Yusuf Mukkat, Naseer Chennad **Open** All year **Notes** No children

Vujon
◉ INDIAN
0191 221 0601 | 29 Queen Street, Quayside, NE1 3UG
www.vujon.com

Set in the fashionable quayside area, Vujon has long been the smart place to go for new-wave Indian cuisine. A stylish contemporary-looking dining room is the backdrop to a creative mix of classic and up-to-date Indian dishes. Spicing is expert and can be delicate.

Chef Ataur Rahman, Anhar Mohammed **Seats** 80 **Closed** 25 December **Notes** Vegetarian dishes

NORTH SHIELDS
The Staith House
◉ MODERN BRITISH
0191 270 8441 | NE30 1JA
www.thestaithhouse.co.uk

Since it was taken over by former *MasterChef: The Professionals* finalist John Calton, this venerable pub on the regenerated North Shields fish quay has established itself as a foodie hotspot. Rubbing shoulders with the fish merchants, the quality of the piscine produce is beyond question.

Chef John Calton, James Laffan **Seats** 45 **Closed** 25–26 December **Prices from** S £5, M £10.50, D £5 **Parking** 10 **Notes** Vegetarian dishes, Children accepted until 7.30pm

TYNEMOUTH
Buddha Lounge
◉ PAN ASIAN
0191 270 8990 | 76 Front Street, NE30 4BP
www.buddhatynemouth.co.uk

The setting is memorable: a converted church where a huge Buddha statue surveys a galleried upper floor beneath the soaring timber roof. Local ingredients and seafood from day boats shine through, appearing in vibrant ideas that take their cue from Indian, Japanese, Thai and Chinese cuisines.

Chef Simon Li **Seats** 92 **Closed** 25 December **Notes** Vegetarian dishes, Children welcome

▶ WARWICKSHIRE

ALDERMINSTER
The Bell at Alderminster
◉ BRITISH
01789 450414 | Shipston Rd, CV37 8NY
www.thebellald.co.uk

Part of the Alscot Estate, The Bell is a free house with classy bedrooms and a bar stocked with the estate's own ales, and a restaurant, now extended to cover two floors, that successfully brings contemporary elements into the traditional space. Service is upbeat.

Chef Karol Szmigiel **Seats** 85, Private dining 20 **Open** All year **Prices from** S £4.75, M £15.95, D £4.75 **Parking** 50 **Notes** Vegetarian dishes, Children welcome

Ettington Park Hotel
◉◉ MODERN, TRADITIONAL BRITISH **V**
01789 450123 | CV37 8BU
www.handpickedhotels.co.uk/ettingtonpark

A magnificent example of mid-Victorian Gothic architecture, Ettington Park stands in 40 acres of grounds in the Stour Valley. The interior bursts with antiques and walls hung with paintings, plus several friezes. Staff are friendly as they serve up some modern contemporary cooking.

Chef David Guest **Seats** 50, Private dining 80 **Open** All year **Parking** 80 **Notes** Children welcome

ANSTY
Macdonald Ansty Hall
🏵 BRITISH
024 7661 2888 | Main Road, CV7 9HZ
www.macdonald-hotels.co.uk/anstyhall
Ansty Hall is a handsome, red-brick 17th-century mansion house set in eight acres of grounds. The emphasis is on British food wrought from good-quality seasonal produce, cooked without pretension and served without undue fanfare and fuss.

Chef Paul Kitchener **Seats** 60, Private dining 40 **Open** All year **Parking** 100 **Notes** Vegetarian dishes, Children welcome

ARMSCOTE
The Fuzzy Duck
🏵🏵 SEASONAL MODERN BRITISH
01608 682635 | Ilmington Road, CV37 8DD
www.fuzzyduckarmscote.com
This upmarket gastro pub is looking pretty swanky these days after a makeover that made the most of the original character of the place (it's been doing the business as a coaching inn since the 18th century) and injected a bit of contemporary style.

Chef Ben Tynan **Seats** 60, Private dining 20 **Open** All year **Parking** 15 **Notes** Vegetarian dishes, Children welcome

EDGEHILL
Castle at Edgehill
🏵 MODERN BRITISH
01295 670255 | Main Street, OX15 6DJ
www.castleatedgehill.co.uk
Built in 1742 to mark the centenary of the battle of Edgehill (the first major battle of the English Civil War), the Castle was converted to a pub in 1822. Expect creative modern cooking.

Chef Matthew Ayers **Seats** 60, Private dining 24 **Open** All year **Parking** 22 **Notes** Vegetarian dishes, Children welcome

HENLEY-IN-ARDEN
The Bluebell
🏵🏵 MODERN, CLASSIC
01564 793049 | 93 High Street, B95 5AT
www.thebluebell-henley.co.uk
The Bluebell occupies a half-timbered coaching inn on Henley's uncommercialised High Street. Within are

uneven flagged floors, beamed ceilings, draught beers in the bar and an enterprising restaurant menu. Expect starters along the lines of braised pig's cheek with lobster bisque.

Chef Joe Adams **Seats** 46, Private dining 15 **Open** All year **Prices from** S £6, M £16, D £6 **Parking** 16 **Notes** Vegetarian dishes, Children welcome

ILMINGTON
The Howard Arms
🏵 BRITISH
01608 682226 | Lower Green, CV36 4LT
www.howardarms.com
History seeps from every stone of the Howard, a 400-year-old inn on a Warwickshire village green to the south of Stratford. A big old stone fireplace, weathered armchairs and unclothed tables make for a relaxing ambience, and the cooking is in the modern country-pub mould.

Chef Gareth Rufus **Seats** 45 **Open** All year **Parking** 20 **Notes** Vegetarian dishes

KENILWORTH
The Cross at Kenilworth
🏵🏵 MODERN BRITISH V 🍷 NOTABLE WINE LIST
01926 853840 | 16 New Steet, CV8 2EZ
www.thecrosskenilworth.co.uk
This former inn dating from the 19th century has had a new lease of life under the auspices of regional big-hitter Andreas Antona. Refurbishment has made the best of the original features while introducing a smart decor. The menu includes classic Pan-European cooking.

Chef Adam Bennett **Seats** 74, Private dining 12 **Closed** 25–26 December, 1 January **Prices from** S £10, M £28, D £11 **Parking** 25 **Notes** Children welcome

LEA MARSTON
Lea Marston Hotel & Spa
🏵 MODERN BRITISH
01675 470468 | Haunch Lane, B76 0BY
www.leamarstonhotel.co.uk
The modern Lea Marston Hotel sits in tranquil Warwickshire countryside buffered by 54 acres of grounds. Decked out in shades of aubergine and grey, it's a swish, low-lit and romantic space with an unbuttoned vibe. The kitchen deals in unpretentious contemporary ideas.

Chef Richard Marshall **Seats** 100, Private dining 120 **Open** All year **Parking** 220 **Notes** Vegetarian dishes, Children welcome

WARWICKSHIRE

LEAMINGTON SPA (ROYAL)
The Brasserie at Mallory Court Hotel
🏵🏵 MODERN BRITISH **V**
01926 453939 | Harbury Lane, Bishop's Tachbrook, CV33 9QB
www.mallory.co.uk
As well as the main dining room, Mallory Court boasts a more contemporary-looking brasserie a short stroll from the main house. No mere adjunct to the main action, this is a fine venue in its own right, with art deco-style lines and glass-topped wicker tables.
Chef Jim Russell **Seats** 80, Private dining 24 **Open** All year **Parking** 100 **Notes** Children welcome

The Dining Room at Mallory Court Hotel
🏵🏵🏵 MODERN BRITISH **V** 🍷NOTABLE WINE LIST
01926 330214 | Harbury Lane, Bishop's Tachbrook, CV33 9QB
www.mallory.co.uk
A charming manor house not far from Leamington Spa, set in 10 acres of grounds including a kitchen garden where they grow some of the produce for the restaurant, Mallory Court has a comfortable country-house feel with plump sofas and wooden floors adorned with Chinese rugs. There are lovely garden and countryside views from the smart, panelled restaurant where floral drapes and elegantly dressed tables all add up to a classy setting, ideal for the smart, grown-up cooking style. The highly trained staff are attentive without being intrusive, and in addition to the seasonal carte and daily changing set price menus there is a choice of 5- or 7-course tasting menus – and vegetarians also get their own menu. You might kick things off with a cleanly presented duck liver pressing, pickled blackberries, hazelnut, and Sauternes jelly – a classic pairing of flavours. Move on to pan-braised halibut, with pickled, puréed and roasted cauliflower, a nicely conceived combination of textures, before finishing with a delightfully refined apple and vanilla cheesecake with Pedro Ximenez and apple sorbet.
Chef Paul Evans **Seats** 56, Private dining 14 **Open** All year **Parking** 100 **Notes** Children welcome

Queans Restaurant
🏵 MODERN EUROPEAN
01926 315522 | 15 Dormer Place, CV32 5AA
www.queans-restaurant.co.uk
This is a delightful establishment with a good deal of genteel charm, where a smartly neutral decor meets an appealing menu of unpretentious dishes based on high-quality regional produce. Save room for a dessert of strawberry and pink champagne cheesecake.
Chef Laura Hamilton **Notes** Vegetarian dishes

The Tame Hare
🏵 MODERN BRITISH
01926 316191 | 97 Warwick Street, CV32 4RJ
www.thetamehare.co.uk
Understated on the outside, this is a contemporary restaurant with wooden floors, soft downlighting and a mirrored wall that creates the illusion of a large space. The modern British menu follows the seasons and the short descriptions of the dishes can keep you guessing.
Chef Jonathan Mills **Seats** 40 **Closed** 2 weeks in January and 2 weeks in the autumn **Prices from** S £6, M £16, D £6 **Notes** Vegetarian dishes, Children welcome

SHIPSTON ON STOUR
The Red Lion
🏵 TRADITIONAL BRITISH
01608 684221 | Main Street, Long Compton, CV36 5JS
www.redlion-longcompton.co.uk
Built as a coaching stop in 1748, The Red Lion is a textbook country inn, right down to its inglenook fireplace, settles and eclectic furniture and local artwork. The cooking takes traditional pub food to a higher level, both in terms of preparation and presentation.
Chef Sarah Keightley **Seats** 70 **Closed** 25 December **Prices from** S £5.50, M £15, D £6 **Parking** 70 **Notes** Vegetarian dishes, Children welcome

STRATFORD-UPON-AVON
The Arden Hotel
🏵🏵 MODERN BRITISH **V**
01789 298682 | Waterside, CV37 6BA
www.theardenhotelstratford.com
Just across the river from the theatres of the Royal Shakespeare Company, this contemporary brasserie offers a champagne bar and enterprising modern cooking. Dark chocolate pavé with a deconstructed garnish of griottine cherries, cherry sorbet and Chantilly cream is a fashionable twist on a classic.
Chef Abhijeet Dasalkar **Seats** Private dining 28 **Open** All year **Notes** Children welcome

Hallmark Hotel The Welcombe
🏵 MODERN BRITISH, FRENCH
Warwick Road, CV37 0NR
www.hallmarkhotels.co.uk
The formal garden outside this splendid Victorian house brings a stately presence to the Jacobean-style property. The restaurant matches the setting with its grandeur. Start with a pre-dinner drink in the lounge and eat alfresco if the weather is fine.
Chef Brian Henry **Seats** 70, Private dining 150 **Parking** 150 **Notes** Vegetarian dishes, Children welcome

Macdonald Alveston Manor
@ MODERN BRITISH
01789 205478 | Clopton Bridge, CV37 7HP
www.macdonald-hotels.co.uk/alvestonmanor
A Tudor manor house only a few minutes' walk from the centre of the Shakespeare action in Stratford, Alveston brims with old-school charm. Traditional service from table-side trays is the vehicle for the kitchen's contemporary output.
Chef George Thomas **Seats** 110, Private dining 40 **Open** All year **Parking** 120 **Notes** Vegetarian dishes, Children welcome

Salt
@@@ MODERN BRITISH V
01789 263566 | 8 Church St, CV37 6HB
www.salt-restaurant.co.uk
Three cheers for crowdfunding, without which the lucky residents of Stratford-upon-Avon would not be able to revel in this high-flying new addition to the local gastronomic scene. The bijou dining room is shoehorned into a snug space, all low beams, bare brick and wood and a tiny open kitchen. Chef-patron Paul Foster brings a sound pedigree from world-class kitchens, conveying a clear passion for the very best ingredients and a sound grasp of contemporary cooking techniques in his captivating à la carte and tasting menus. His clear vision of how flavours and textures work together is amply demonstrated in a vibrant dish of cured halibut with pickled cucumber, grapes, almonds and sea purslane, all deftly offset with suave dill emulsion. Meat is also handled with impressive dexterity, as in a pairing of deeply flavoured Herdwick hogget shoulder and tender lamb rump served with minted goats' curd, charred hispi cabbage and pink slivers of pickled onion. At the end, a deliciously refreshing rendering of Wye Valley rhubarb appears poached and puréed with granita-like buttermilk ice, ginger crisp and sorrel.
Chef Paul Foster **Seats** 35 **Closed** Christmas **Notes** Children welcome

WARWICK
The Brasserie
@ MODERN BRITISH
01926 843111 | Ardencote, The Cumsey, Lye Green Road, Claverdon, CV35 8LT
www.ardencote.com
The all-day dining venue at Ardencote, The Brasserie, is another string to the bow of this establishment. Situated in an extension to the original grand Victorian house, The Brasserie is open for light lunches and sandwiches, and ups the ante in the evening.
Chef Ian Buckle **Seats** 65 **Open** All year **Prices from** S £5.95, M £13.95, D £6.95 **Parking** 350 **Notes** Vegetarian dishes, Children welcome

Tailors Restaurant
@@ MODERN BRITISH V
01926 410590 | 22 Market Place, CV34 4SL
www.tailorsrestaurant.co.uk
In a pint-sized room centred on an old brick fireplace, the cooking is complex, with much technical skill. The seafood cocktail consists of prawns and brown shrimps, Marie Rose dressing deep-fried in breadcrumbs, red pepper purée and a gel of preserved lemon; a conceptual triumph.
Chef Dan Cavell **Seats** 28 **Closed** Christmas **Notes** No children under 8 years at lunch

WISHAW
The Belfry
@ MODERN BRITISH, EUROPEAN
01675 238600 | B76 9PR
www.thebelfry.com
The Belfry has more than 300 bedrooms, a nightclub and four eating places, including the lively Ryder Grill. Enjoy views across the famous Brabazon golf course, and in summer relax on its outdoor terrace. Steaks and spit-roasts, fish and lobster are the stock in trade.
Chef Robert Bates **Seats** 220, Private dining 16 **Open** All year **Prices from** S £6.95, M £19.95, D £6.95 **Parking** 1,000 **Notes** Vegetarian dishes, Children welcome

▶ **WEST MIDLANDS**

BALSALL COMMON
Nailcote Hall
@ TRADITIONAL EUROPEAN
024 7646 6174 | Nailcote Lane, Berkswell, CV7 7DE
www.nailcotehall.co.uk
Built on the eve of the Civil War, Nailcote is a stately home on a modest scale, with 15 acres of grounds containing, reputedly, some of England's oldest yew trees. Old-school service extends to tableside steak-flambéing, but otherwise the mood is modern.
Chef Daniel Topa **Seats** 50, Private dining 300 **Closed** 31 December **Parking** 200 **Notes** Vegetarian dishes, Children welcome

BIRMINGHAM
Adam's
@@@ MODERN BRITISH V ▨ NOTABLE WINE LIST
0121 643 3745 | New Oxford House, 16 Waterloo Street, B2 5UG
www.adamsrestaurant.co.uk
Originating as a peripatetic pop-up, Adam and Natasha Stokes' restaurant moved into its permanent residence in early 2016 and set about making itself at home. The principal dining room on the ground floor is

a distinctly elegant space with large annular light fittings, unclothed tables and comfortable seating. Service moves with discreet efficiency over the thick-pile carpet, delivering thrillingly presented dishes of confident and refined modern British food. An opening course of accurately timed monkfish comes with thinly tempura-battered eel, Roscoff onion petals and slivered grapes, as well as a foam-light onion purée with capers and dill, as a possible prelude to breast and smoked heart of duck with hispi cabbage, shiitakes and parsley root, or rare-breed Hampshire pork with black pudding, quince and crisp-topped potato terrine. A reimagined tarte Tatin has expert caramelisation with a hit of Calvados, along with a tart granita of Pink Lady apple, or go for the CasaLuker 70% chocolate fix, served with salted pecans and 'Horlicks'. The tasting menu aims to win you over with eight ingeniously constructed dishes, and there are some imaginative wine pairings to accompany.

Chef Adam Stokes, Tom Shepherd **Seats** 34, Private dining 16 **Closed** 2 weeks in summer, 3 weeks at Christmas

Carters of Moseley
◉◉◉ MODERN BRITISH **V**
0121 449 8885 | 2c Wake Green Road, Moseley, B13 9EZ
www.cartersofmoseley.co.uk

The unassuming location amid a parade of shops belies this high-flying neighbourhood restaurant's ambition. Chef Brad Carter's operation sticks to the contemporary template of calculated neutral decor, the buzz of an open kitchen, and relaxed, on-the-ball staff whose enthusiasm for the food is palpable. The moreish 'pigs butter' (whipped Tamworth pork dripping flavoured with caramelised onions) and splendid home-made sourdough are stalwarts to prime the palate, together with a barrage of on-trend 'snacks' – chicken liver cereal, Dorset clam with fermented ramsons, house charcuterie, raw kohlrabi with pine and salad burnet – before an array of bang-on-the-money dishes of inventive and clever pairings. Clarity and freshness define it all, from an opener of deeply flavoursome oat, spelt and barley porridge laden with pine mushrooms (foraged from Lapland) boosted by a broth laced with Moliterno al tartufo (truffled cheese), to top-drawer Skrei cod with leek and buttermilk. Elsewhere, meatier influences come into play. Dry-aged Cornish lamb is pointed up with vivid green wheat grass sauce and bone marrow, or there might be red deer with kabocha squash and quince. The imaginative approach at Carters continues through to desserts. For example, an unusual eggless ice cream infused with kombu seaweed and black rice, say, or chocolate ganache

finished with dried cardamom, orange zest and minty shiso oil.

Chef Brad Carter **Seats** 32 **Closed** 1–17 January, 24 April to 3 May and 3–23 August **Parking** 4 **Notes** No children under 8 years

Chez Mal Brasserie
◉ MODERN, TRADITIONAL
0121 246 5000 | 1 Wharfside Street, The Mailbox, B1 1RD
www.malmaison.com

The Malmaison team bring their boutique venue to the Mailbox, a swanky shopping destination. The brasserie, with its floor-to-ceiling windows and contemporary finish, is a relaxed and lively spot offering a menu of globally inspired contemporary dishes.

Chef Pete Brown **Seats** 120, Private dining 20 **Open** All year **Notes** Vegetarian dishes, Children welcome

Circle Restaurant Birmingham Hippodrome
◉ MODERN BRITISH
0844 338 9000 | B5 4TB
www.birminghamhippodrome.com/eatanddrink

Pre-theatre dining doesn't get much closer to curtain-up than at this large, open-plan restaurant on the second floor of the Hippodrome. You can even save your dessert for the interval; a uniquely quirky touch. Service is friendly and the modern British cooking is confident.

Chef Melissa Menns **Seats** 95, Private dining 25 **Closed** Non-performance days, 25 December, 1 January **Notes** Vegetarian dishes, Children welcome

Hotel du Vin & Bistro Birmingham
◉ BRITISH, FRENCH
0121 200 0600 | 25 Church Street, B3 2NR
www.hotelduvin.com

Sip an aperitif in the Bubble Lounge Bar or head downstairs to the vaulted Pub du Vin before dining in the stylish restaurant, with its Gallic-inspired decor of bare floorboards and round-backed wooden chairs.

Chef Greg Pryce **Seats** 85, Private dining 108 **Open** All year **Notes** Vegetarian dishes, Children welcome

Lasan Restaurant
◉◉ INDIAN
0121 212 3664 | 3–4 Dakota Buildings, James Street, St Paul's Square, B3 1SD
www.lasangroup.co.uk

Set in the Jewellery Quarter, Lasan is a stylish contemporary Indian restaurant. A vibrant atmosphere pervades the light and spacious split-level dining room, where the menu takes a broad sweep across the subcontinent to deliver regional authenticity alongside modern fusion touches.

Chef Aktar Islam, Gulsher Khan Seats 66 Closed 25 December, 1 January Notes Vegetarian dishes, Children welcome

Opus Restaurant

◎◎ MODERN BRITISH V

0121 200 2323 | 54 Cornwall Street, B3 2DE

www.opusrestaurant.co.uk

With girder-framed, full-length windows, this stylish, big-city venue has leather banquettes and linen-clothed tables, drawing in execs from the financial and legal chambers nearby, as well as lunching shoppers. Add a menu with broad appeal built on top-quality British ingredients and its appeal becomes clear. Chef Ben Ternent Seats 85, Private dining 32 Closed between Christmas and New Year, Bank holidays Notes Vegetarian dishes, Children welcome

See advertisement below

Purnell's

◎◎◎ MODERN BRITISH ♟ NOTABLE WINE LIST

0121 212 9799 | 55 Cornwall Street, B3 2DH

www.purnellsrestaurant.com

Glynn Purnell's personality shines through on his menus, where playful puns and little details give insight into his development as a chef; his journey if you like. The building in the financial district has been on a journey as well, and it's looking fine and dandy right now; the old red-brick warehouse has surely never looked so dapper within – a fashionably muted colour palette with the occasional splash of something more daring, and stylish artworks. In this smart and confident setting, Glynn's menus include a fixed-price carte and tasting menus: '10 Years in the Making', 'Brummie Tapas', and 'A Purnell's journey...', the latter featuring the BBC *Great British Menu* winning monkfish masala (which is also a regular on the carte). The creative output might get going with Herefordshire beef carpaccio with bresaola, with red wine-braised octopus, chive crème fraîche and sweet-and-sour onions, while main courses extend to Wiltshire pork belly, paired with burnt apple purée and confit turnip. Desserts follow a similar modern British/pan-European theme, with millefeuille of lemon and chocolate alongside burnt English surprise (a rhubarb and custard number also seen on *Great British Menu*). The impressive wine list features staff favourites.

Chef Glynn Purnell Seats 45, Private dining 12 Closed 1 week Easter, 2 weeks late July to early August, Christmas and New Year Notes Vegetarian dishes, No children under 10 years

BIRMINGHAM continued

Simpsons

◉◉◉ MODERN BRITISH **V** 🍷 NOTABLE WINE LIST
0121 454 3434 | 20 Highfield Road, Edgbaston, B15 3DU
www.simpsonsrestaurant.co.uk

The gradual evolution of Simpsons has been one of the more fascinating trajectories of the Birmingham dining scene over the years. Housed in a Georgian mansion in well-heeled Edgbaston, it has been made over into a thoroughly modern dining space, all wood and stone textures in an expansive airy room that looks out on to the landscaped garden. There's also a chef's table in the middle of the kitchen action, and the Eureka development hub, where members of the brigade are encouraged to unleash their creative skills. The result is cooking of bright, sculpted flavours and inspired combinations, as in the opener of pork cheek in smoked eel cream garnished with crisped onions and chicory, and mains such as Skrei cod with burnt leek, monk's beard and truffled potato purée, or cheek and bavette of Aberdeenshire beef in a charcoal emulsion with salsify, nasturtiums and shallots. Taster menus distil the carte into seven stages of loveliness, ending perhaps with passionfruit curd and yogurt sorbet, followed by Guanaja chocolate with blood orange and burnt marmalade ice cream.

Chef Luke Tipping **Seats** 70, Private dining 14 **Closed** Bank holidays **Parking** 12 **Notes** Children welcome

The Wilderness

◉◉ BRITISH
0121 233 9425 | 7 Warstone Lane, Jewellery Quarter, B18 6JQ
www.wearethewilderness.co.uk

Tucked down an alleyway in the Jewellery Quarter of the city, The Wilderness is a monochrome venue with skylight panels and an open kitchen, decked with foliage to bring a sense of sylvan repose to city eating. Foraged ingredients and allotment produce provide the building-blocks for playful, inspired modern cooking.

Chef Stuart Deeley, Alex Claridge **Open** All year

DORRIDGE

Hogarths Hotel

◉◉ MODERN BRITISH
01564 779988 | Four Ashes Road, B93 8QE
www.hogarths.co.uk

A little Midlands village is the setting for Hogarths, a picturesque location that also manages to be handy for the NEC and the airport. Fresh Mediterranean-influenced brasserie food is the bill of fare here, with quality produce in simple preparations.

Chef Alex Alexandrov **Seats** 80, Private dining 100 **Open** All year **Parking** 120 **Notes** Vegetarian dishes, Children welcome

HOCKLEY HEATH

Nuthurst Grange Hotel

◉◉ MODERN BRITISH **V**
01564 783972 | Nuthurst Grange Lane, B94 5NL
www.nuthurst-grange.com

Nuthurst's long tree-lined avenue approach leads to a brick-built Victorian mansion in private woodland, so allow time for exploring. A judicious balance of culinary modernism and traditional ideas is evident on the menus. Dishes have a lot in them but manage not to look crowded.

Chef Andrew Glover **Seats** Private dining 70 **Open** All year **Notes** Children welcome

SOLIHULL

Hampton Manor

◉◉◉◉ MODERN BRITISH **V** 🍷 NOTABLE WINE LIST
01675 446080 | Swadowbrook Lane, Hampton-in-Arden, B92 0EN
www.hamptonmanor.com

Towers and turrets mark the spot within the 45 acres of land surrounding this impressive stately manor, built by a son of Sir Robert Peel. These days it's a divertingly stylish restaurant with rooms, a moniker that signifies the importance of dining to the operation, with a kitchen garden providing its bounty and the dynamic contemporary cooking of Rob Palmer in the offing. The design of the place is timelessly tasteful; the part-panelled dining room is a mix of traditional comfort and contemporary sophistication, while the staff are just as engaging as the setting. The format sees three tasting menus vying for your attention – two four-course options, the more expensive of which features Wagyu beef – and a full-throttle seven-course menu that includes all the bells and all the whistles. Flavour combinations are not designed to shock – beetroot and goats' cheese for example – but what arrives on the plate is creative, pretty as a picture, and never less than delicious. A fish course sees monkfish with barbecue sauce and salsify, or smoked eel with samphire and kohlrabi, while game could crop up as hare with black garlic, seeds and grains. Chocolate, sherry and vanilla come together in an outstanding finale, and if you've room, the artisan cheese course, with apricot and walnut bread, should not be missed. A drinks flight is chosen with genuine care and attention. The afternoon tea, taken in the stylish parlour and beginning with a bit of live chef action, is a proper treat.

Chef Rob Palmer **Seats** 28, Private dining 14 **Open** All year **Parking** 30 **Notes** No children under 12 years

The Regency Hotel
◉ MODERN, CLASSIC
0121 745 6119 | Stratford Road, Shirley, B90 4EB
www.corushotels.com/solihull
Less than 20 minutes from Birmingham Airport and the NEC, The Regency is a well-positioned base for visitors, but the hotel's stylish restaurant appeals equally to Solihull locals. A contemporary space with its own courtyard, the restaurant offers inventive British dishes inspired by international flavour combinations.
Chef Nigel Cooke **Seats** 64, Private dining 20 **Open** All year **Prices from** S £5.50, M £10, D £4.50 **Parking** 320 **Notes** Vegetarian dishes, Children welcome

SUTTON COLDFIELD (ROYAL)
The Bridge at New Hall
◉◉ MODERN BRITISH
0121 378 2442 | Walmley Road, B76 1QX
www.handpickedhotels.co.uk/newhall
Before Birmingham's sprawl engulfed the village of Sutton Coldfield, this 800-year-old moat house stood in empty countryside. Nowadays, it's surrounded by 26 acres of grounds. The Bridge Restaurant is the top-end dining option, where mullioned stained-glass windows blend with modern decor.
Chef Matthew Brooker **Seats** 52, Private dining 12 **Open** All year **Parking** 60 **Notes** Vegetarian dishes, Children welcome

The Oak Room Restaurant
◉◉ MODERN BRITISH
0121 308 3751 | Moor Hall Hotel & Spa, Moor Hall Drive, Four Oaks, B75 6LN
www.moorhallhotel.co.uk
A family-run country-house hotel set in parkland, Moor Hall's panelled Oak Room restaurant has a real sense of grandeur and lovely views over the grounds, including the golf course. Contemporary British cooking from a young kitchen team emphasises quality ingredients.
Chef Nigel Parnaby **Seats** 70, Private dining 30 **Open** All year **Parking** 170 **Notes** Vegetarian dishes, Children welcome

WALSALL
Restaurant 178
◉◉ MODERN BRITISH V
01922 455122 | Fairlawns Hotel & Spa, 178 Little Aston Road, Aldridge, WS9 0NU
www.fairlawns.co.uk
Well placed to reach virtually anywhere in the West Midlands, the spa hotel near Walsall is family-owned

and a refreshing antidote to corporate anonymity. The dining room is the place to sample an extensive Market Menu of modern and seasonal British ideas.
Chef Chris Morris **Seats** 80, Private dining 100 **Closed** 25–26 December, 1 January, Good Friday, Easter Monday, May Day, Bank holiday Monday **Prices from** S £8.50, M £15.50, D £6 **Parking** 120 **Notes** Children welcome

WOLVERHAMPTON
Bilash
◉ INDIAN, BANGLADESHI
01902 427762 | 2 Cheapside, WV1 1TU
www.thebilash.co.uk
Bilash has been pushing beyond the confines of mere curry since 1982. The stylishly clean-cut interior works a neutral colour palette with cream chairs, seating booths, tables with crisp white linen and walls hung with sparkling mirrors, a smart contemporary setting.
Chef Sitab Khan **Seats** 48, Private dining 30 **Closed** 25–26 December, 1 January **Prices from** S £5.90, M £9.90, D £5.90 **Parking** 15 **Notes** Vegetarian dishes, Children welcome

Drawing Room, Bar and Grill
◉◉ MODERN EUROPEAN
01902 752055 | The Mount Hotel Country Manor, Mount Road, Tettenhall Wood, WV6 8HL
www.themount.co.uk
In a stately Victorian mansion overlooking the canal, the dining room wears a more understated modern look. Expect a brasserie buzz and food that satisfies most modern tastes. Chocolate and raspberry delice sprinkled with amaretti crumbs is a classy finisher.
Chef Craig Thomas **Seats** 38, Private dining 100 **Open** All year **Parking** 120 **Notes** Vegetarian dishes, Children welcome

▶ WILTSHIRE
BEANACRE
Beechfield House Restaurant
◉◉ MODERN BRITISH
01225 703700 | SN12 7PU
www.beechfieldhouse.co.uk
Built in 1878 in the Venetian style, Beechfield House has been gently updated for 21st-century requirements. Soft classical music is just right for the handsome restaurant, with its chandelier, rug on the wooden floor, large gilded mirror above the mantelpiece and Roman blinds.
Chef Mike Bain **Seats** 70, Private dining 20 **Closed** 1 January **Prices from** S £6.95, M £19.50, D £7.50 **Parking** 70 **Notes** Vegetarian dishes, Children welcome

WILTSHIRE

BOX

The Northey Arms
◉ BRITISH, EUROPEAN
01225 742333 | Bath Road, SN13 8AE
www.ohhpubs.co.uk

Looking rather swish after top-to-toe renovation, this old stone-built inn has been brought up to full 21st-century spec with seagrass chairs and boldly patterned wallpaper in the split-level dining area. Locally reared 32-day-aged steaks get star billing.

Chef Chris Alderson **Seats** 70 **Closed** 25–26 December **Parking** 40 **Notes** Vegetarian dishes, Children welcome

BRADFORD-ON-AVON

The George
◉ MODERN BRITISH
01225 865650 | 67 Woolley Street, BA15 1AQ
www.thegeorgebradfordonavon.co.uk

This is a smart and comfortable inn with an emphasis on food. Seasonal produce from the South West drives the menu, combining classics with more inventive dishes. Try the impressive homemade bread.

Chef Alex Venables **Seats** 90, Private dining 16 **Closed** 25 December **Prices from** S £6.50, M £13.50, D £6.50 **Parking** 11 **Notes** Vegetarian dishes, Children welcome

The Kitchen
◉ MODERN BRITISH
01225 864750 | Widbrook Grange,
Trowbridge Road, BA15 1UH
www.widbrookgrange.co.uk

Built of Bath stone in the early 18th century and recently refurbished, Widbrook Grange lies on the outskirts of picturesque Bradford-on-Avon. In the dining room a menu of modern European cooking is given added fragrance from an on-site herb garden.

Chef Sandor Szucs **Open** All year **Notes** Vegetarian dishes, Children welcome

CALNE

Strand Room
◉◉ MODERN BRITISH
01249 812488 | The Lansdowne, The Strand, SN11 0EH
www.lansdownestrand.co.uk

Dating from the 16th century, The Lansdowne pub has been rejuvenated by Arkell's Brewery and the Strand Room restaurant is at the very heart of the place. The modern cooking keeps things simple on the plate, allowing local produce to shine.

Chef Joel Lear **Seats** 50, Private dining 12 **Closed** 25 December **Prices from** S £6, M £13.50, D £6 **Notes** Vegetarian dishes, Children welcome

CASTLE COMBE

The Bybrook at The Manor House, an Exclusive Hotel & Golf Club
◉◉◉ MODERN BRITISH V ⬥NOTABLE WINE LIST
01249 782206 | SN14 7HR
www.exclusive.co.uk

Set in 365 acres of parkland with its own golf course and high-flying contemporary country-house cooking to draw in 21st-century sybarites, the 14th-century manor house ticks all the right boxes for Cotswolds exclusivity. Named after the river that flows through the grounds, The Bybrook restaurant does a nice line in heritage and class with its mullioned windows, sober colours and pristine white linen, but there's nothing old-fashioned about the food here – Rob Potter's cooking is defined by well-thought-out and enterprising ideas, clear flavours and razor-sharp accuracy. As you'd hope, it's all based on top-drawer ingredients, often sourced from the vicinity, and what doesn't carry the 'local' tag is tracked with due diligence – the Newlyn mackerel, for example, that stars in a starter with Cornish crab, Exmoor caviar, pickled mooli radish and avocado purée. Next up, first-class line-caught sea bass is teamed with an entertaining medley of Jerusalem artichokes, ceps, crosnes and kale, all bathed in a sultry chicken jus. The sure-footed display ends with banana torte with caramel, banana mousse, nougatine and cocoa sorbet.

Chef Robert Potter **Seats** 60, Private dining 100 **Open** All year **Parking** 100 **Notes** No children under 11 years

COLERNE

The Brasserie
◉◉ MODERN BRITISH
01225 742777 | Lucknam Park Hotel & Spa, SN14 8AZ
www.lucknampark.co.uk

The Brasserie is the less formal dining option at Lucknam Park. Located within the walled garden, with a wall of glass of its own, it has a classy finish and serves up classy food from its open kitchen and a wood-burning oven.

Chef Hywel Jones **Seats** 40 **Open** All year **Parking** 80 **Notes** Vegetarian dishes, Children welcome

Restaurant Hywel Jones by Lucknam Park
◉◉◉ MODERN BRITISH V ⬥NOTABLE WINE LIST
01225 742777 | Lucknam Park Hotel & Spa, SN14 8AZ
www.lucknampark.co.uk

Lucknam Park is a beautiful, symmetrical Palladian mansion set in 500 acres of unspoilt parkland. For the last 30 years it has been a splendidly luxurious hotel and spa, offering an indulgent escape from the daily grind into a world of elegant country-house living. From the mile-long drive lined with beech trees to the delightful public spaces, it's all effortlessly sumptuous. The dining room, with its curved walls, cloud-painted ceiling and pristine double-clothed tables, is the perfect setting for Hywel Jones' sophisticated, focused cooking. This is not fanciful stuff at the whim of fashion, but mature and well directed, where great produce is treated with respect. To begin, roast duck liver comes with caramelised chicory tart and an intense mandarin purée, with textural interest contributed by cob nuts and pomegranate. A main course of line-caught sea bass with crab bon bon and Trealy Farm chorizo makes for a fine, complex dish of contrasting flavours. Madagascan vanilla crème brûlée with glazed blackberries and ginger doughnuts is a delightful finale, light and fragrant.

Chef Hywel Jones **Seats** 70, Private dining 28 **Open** All year **Parking** 80 **Notes** No children under 5 years

CORSHAM
Guyers House Hotel
◉◉ MODERN EUROPEAN, BRITISH
01249 713399 | Pickwick, SN13 0PS
www.guyershouse.com

An elegant country house in handsome grounds with a relaxing dining room patrolled by friendly staff, and menus with a real sense of creative elan. Save room for an up-to-the-minute Earl grey and lavender crème brûlée with pistachio brittle and mullet wine sorbet.

Chef Phillip Low **Seats** 66, Private dining 56 **Closed** 30 December to 3 January **Parking** 60 **Notes** Vegetarian dishes, Children welcome

The Methuen Arms
◉◉ BRITISH, ITALIAN **V**
01249 717060 | 2 High Street, SN13 0HB
www.themethuenarms.com

In 1805 the former Red Lion took the Methuen family's name when it was rebuilt in Bath stone with three storeys and a fine portico. The food boasts British roots with strong Italian influences.

Chef Leigh Evans **Seats** 60, Private dining 50 **Open** All year **Parking** 40 **Notes** Children welcome

CRICKLADE
The Red Lion Inn
◉ MODERN BRITISH
01793 750776 | 74 High Street, SN6 6DD
www.theredlioncricklade.co.uk

A 17th-century inn with cosy beams, log fires and real ales from its own Hop Kettle microbrewery. Food is taken as seriously as beer – the pub rears pigs, and veggies come from locals' allotments. Choose the bar or the contemporary country-chic dining room.

Chef James Maulgue **Seats** 70, Private dining 16 **Closed** 25–26 December **Notes** Vegetarian dishes, Children welcome

DEVIZES
The Peppermill
◉◉ BRITISH **V**
01380 710407 | 40 Saint John's Street, SN10 1BL
www.peppermilldevizes.co.uk

This family-run restaurant with rooms impresses with its contemporary, feel-good menu. In the evening you might start with BBQ-infused slow-roasted pork belly with carrot 'slaw', or potted shrimps with home-made brioche. It is a popular place so it's worth booking ahead.

Chef Costinel Velicu **Seats** 60 **Open** All year **Prices from** S £6, M £14, D £5 **Parking** 5 **Notes** Children welcome

EDINGTON
The Three Daggers
◉◉ MODERN BRITISH
01380 830940 | Westbury Road, BA13 4PG
www.threedaggers.co.uk

A pub with its own microbrewery, farm and farm shop, there's plenty to offer both locals and destination diners. Bare tables, exposed brick and heritage colours add to the informal country pub feel, as does the seasonal modern cooking.

Chef Matt Gillard **Open** All year **Notes** Vegetarian dishes, Children welcome

FOXHAM
The Foxham Inn
◉ MODERN BRITISH
01249 740665 | SN15 4NQ
www.thefoxhaminn.co.uk

Dinner is served in both the small bar and the purpose-built restaurant at this red-brick country inn. There's variety aplenty on the enticing menu, with starters including snails with noodles in a light soya broth. Dishes have clear, distinct flavours.

Chef Neil Cooper **Seats** 60 **Closed** 1st 2 weeks January **Prices from** S £7, M £13.95, D £7 **Parking** 16 **Notes** Vegetarian dishes, Children welcome

HORNINGSHAM
The Bath Arms at Longleat
◉ MODERN BRITISH
01985 844308 | Longleat Estate, BA12 7LY
www.batharms.co.uk

A creeper-covered stone building, The Bath Arms is in a delightfully picturesque village within the Longleat Estate. The kitchen takes pride in sourcing produce from within 50 miles of the estate and all the bread is made in-house.

Chef Brian Hall **Seats** 45, Private dining 60 **Open** All year **Prices from** S £4.95, M £11.95, D £5.50 **Parking** 8 **Notes** Vegetarian dishes, Children welcome

WILTSHIRE

LACOCK

Sign of the Angel
◉◉ BRITISH
01249 730230 | 6 Church Street, SN15 2LB
www.signoftheangel.co.uk

This 500-year-old, timbered inn is the very personification of classy Cotswold charm. Low-beamed ceilings, walk-in fireplaces and cosy nooks and crannies are all present and correct, and candlelit tables add to the cossetting mood. On the food side, the kitchen takes local sourcing seriously.

Chef Jon Furby **Seats** 50, Private dining 16 **Open** All year **Prices from** S £6, M £16, D £6.50 **Notes** Vegetarian dishes, Children welcome

LITTLE BEDWYN

The Harrow at Little Bedwyn
◉◉◉ MODERN BRITISH **V** ⬤ NOTABLE WINE LIST
See pages 332–333

MALMESBURY

The Dining Room
◉◉◉ MODERN BRITISH **V** ⬤ NOTABLE WINE LIST
01666 822888 | Whatley Manor Hotel and Spa, Easton Grey, SN16 0RB
www.whatleymanor.com

A feeling of anticipation builds as the gated entrance opens into Whatley's cobbled courtyards of honeystone Cotswold buildings – and that's as it should be because the Victorian manor house has long sat in the top flight of the UK's country-house hotels. The principal dining room is an understated modern place, with cream walls, bare floors and a good measure of space around each table. Niall Keating now leads the kitchen team here and his blend of refined contemporary cooking with Asian influences has created a new dining experience. Delivered via a 12-course tasting menu, including a vegetarian version, phenomenal precision and flavours are there from the off in a spiced cracker pointed with lime and Parmesan, then the purity of raw oyster with seaweed mignonette dressing. Produce is, naturally, as good as you can get, and flavours and textures come razor sharp – tempura eel with kimchi aigre-doux, or pigeon with kohlrabi, spiced date purée and wood ear mushrooms, while fish puts in an appearance as halibut supported by charred alliums, pear and shrimp. A trio of desserts offers ideas such as apple with caramel, passionfruit and honeycomb, and wine flights of revelatory pairings line up to enhance the whole experience further.

Chef Niall Keating **Seats** 46, Private dining 30 **Open** All year **Parking** 120 **Notes** No children

The Refectory
◉ MODERN BRITISH
01666 822 344 | The Old Bell Hotel, Abbey Row, SN16 0BW
www.oldbellhotel.co.uk

Originally a 13th-century hostelry for dignitaries visiting Malmesbury Abbey, The Old Bell is possibly England's oldest hotel. Behind its largely wisteria-covered Edwardian exterior is a rich architectural mix, uncompromised by contemporary interior decor and furnishings. Some dishes belong in gastro-pub territory while others have classic heritage.

Chef Frédéric Fetiveau **Open** All year **Notes** Children welcome

MARLBOROUGH

Three Tuns Freehouse
◉ BRITISH
01672 870280 | 1 High Street, Great Bedwyn, SN8 3NU
www.tunsfreehouse.com

A welcoming and dog-friendly pub on the edge of the Savernake Forest, the Three Tuns combines the traditional charms of a local village inn with an excellent selection of carefully prepared tempting dishes. Everything from bread to ice cream is made on the premises.

Chef James Wilsey **Seats** 48, Private dining 34 **Closed** 25 December **Prices from** S £5, M £13, D £2.50 **Parking** 11 **Notes** Vegetarian dishes, Children welcome

PEWSEY

Red Lion Freehouse
◉◉◉ MODERN BRITISH
01980 671124 | East Chisenbury, SN9 6AQ
www.redlionfreehouse.com

Along a narrow lane in a slip of a Wiltshire village, Guy and Brittany Manning's thatched pub is what most of us hope to find in a country inn. Inside, a big brick fireplace and bare-boarded floors, with menus chalked up on blackboards, set the tone, and the place is run with appreciable charm and cheer. A new private dining room and tied guest house add to the range of hospitality, but it's the regionally based menus of sharply defined country cooking that exercise the most obvious appeal. Beetroot-cured salmon in dill and citrus dressing with pickled cucumber might raise the curtain for Creedy Carver duck breast with potato millefeuille, braised fennel and griottines in red wine, or an Asian-inspired dish of wreckfish and mussels with a crisp spring roll, bok choi and shiitakes. At the end, there might be incomparable Passe Crassane pear, poached and accompanied by candied walnuts and sage ice cream. Sunday lunches are a locally revered amenity, and the breakfasts are a thing of beauty too, with eggs Benedict or cinnamon waffles and mascarpone among the temptations.

Chef Guy and Brittany Manning **Seats** 45, Private dining 23 **Open** All year **Prices from** S £8, M £19, D £8 **Parking** 14 **Notes** Vegetarian dishes, Children welcome

RAMSBURY
The Bell at Ramsbury
◉◉ MODERN BRITISH, EUROPEAN
01672 520230 | The Square, SN8 2PE
www.thebellramsbury.com

A whitewashed coaching inn dating back 300 years, The Bell is a popular pitstop for walkers and visitors to nearby Marlborough. It has its own brewery, distillery and smokehouse, with much of the produce used in the kitchen coming from the estate and walled garden.

Chef Jonas Lodge **Seats** 42, Private dining 22 **Closed** 25 December **Parking** 25 **Notes** Vegetarian dishes, Children welcome

ROWDE
The George & Dragon
◉◉ SEAFOOD **V**
01380 723053 | High Street, SN10 2PN
www.thegeorgeanddragonrowde.co.uk

This Tudor coaching inn in the unassuming village of Rowde has a reputation as a destination dining venue. The rustic country finish is part of its charm, while the menu makes a speciality of seafood hauled in from the boats at St Mawes in Cornwall.

Chef Christopher Day, Tom Bryant **Seats** 35, Private dining 18 **Closed** 25 December **Prices from** S £6, M £14, D £6 **Parking** 14 **Notes** Children welcome

SOUTH WRAXALL
The Longs Arms
◉◉ SEASONAL MODERN BRITISH
01225 864450 | BA15 2SB
www.thelongsarms.com

Across the road from the church in the picturesque village of South Wraxall, The Longs Arms is a welcoming stone-built pub with traditional flagstone floors and a wood-burning stove in the fireplace. Everything here is made on the premises including the delicious bread.

Chef Robert Allcock **Seats** 46, Private dining 38 **Closed** 3 weeks January and 2 weeks September **Prices from** S £6, M £12, D £2.25 **Parking** 15 **Notes** Vegetarian dishes, Children welcome

SWINDON
The Angel
◉ MODERN BRITISH
01793 851161 | 47 High Street, Royal Wootton Bassett, SN4 7AQ
www.theangelhotelwoottonbassett.co.uk

Ancient oak panelling and flagstone floors confirm the pedigree of this veteran coaching inn, which continues life as a high-street hub of local goings-on into the 21st century. The kitchen keeps with the times, sending out starters such as seared pigeon breast with Merlot-poached pear.

Chef Stephen Newton **Open** All year

Chiseldon House Hotel
◉ MODERN EUROPEAN, BRITISH
01793 741010 | New Road, Chiseldon, SN4 0NE
www.chiseldonhouse.com

The grand Regency manor house is a popular wedding venue, with the Marlborough Downs and attractive gardens providing a stunning backdrop, and the M4 nearby. The restaurant is a bright space with crisp white linen on the tables and a cheerful service team.

Chef Paul Suter **Seats** 100, Private dining 32 **Open** All year **Parking** 40 **Notes** Vegetarian dishes, Children welcome

TOLLARD ROYAL
King John Inn
◉◉ BRITISH
01725 516207 | SP5 5PS
www.kingjohninn.co.uk

You might expect a Victorian country inn on the Wiltshire-Dorset border to be a good bet for hearty English food, and the King John obliges. The chef is there all the way from field to plate, shooting most of the game himself.

Chef Lloyd Bartlett **Seats** 50 **Open** All year **Parking** 20 **Notes** Vegetarian dishes, Children welcome

TROWBRIDGE
The Milking Parlour
◉◉ SEASONAL BRITISH
01225 777393 | The Moonraker Hotel, Trowle Common, BA14 9BL
www.moonrakerhotel.com

The restaurant here was once the 500-year-old Moonraker Hotel's milking barn. A large kitchen garden, orchard and on-site smokery are key to the menus' offerings. The five-course tasting menu is highly tempting.

Chef Dean Toon **Open** All year

WILTSHIRE continues on page 334

WILTSHIRE

AA Wine Award for England 2018–19

LITTLE BEDWYN

The Harrow at Little Bedwyn

◉◉◉ MODERN BRITISH V 🍾 NOTABLE WINE LIST

01672 870871 | SN8 3JP

www.theharrowatlittlebedwyn.com

Highly polished cooking with the accent on fun

Little Bedwyn itself, as its name suggests, tends to the diminutive, a peaceable village on the River Dun not far from Marlborough. Its neighbour, Great Bedwyn, actually retains a railway station, but the junior sibling is a mere slip of a thing distributed among narrow country lanes. On the corner of two of these is to be found Roger and Sue Jones's erstwhile village pub, built of two-tone brick with a little sparse creeper cladding, reborn practically 20 years ago as an ambitious country restaurant.

The tone is deeply relaxing in the best country manner, the dining room a white-linened space with high-backed black chairs, framed prints and a giant mirror. Roger Jones has made a name for the place with lustrously polished cooking of exemplary energy, presented with all the novelty and fun of cutting-edge city dining, and maintaining formidable consistency from one season to the next.

Multi-course menus are the order of the day, with tasters in six or eight stages, including vegetarian and vegan versions, and a five-course lunch offering. Dishes arrive on wavy glass platters and gutters, in eggcups and Kilner jars, and sometimes even on big white plates, and nothing looks less than thrilling. The quality of prime materials is unimpeachable, as witness a single perfectly succulent scallop that comes with ozoney samphire and pungent wild garlic, while carefully judged Indian spicing points up all the exhilarating richness of deep-fried Pembroke lobster. January king cabbage cooked in ham stock makes an umami-laden accompaniment to Cornish turbot, before the main business of the taster arrives in the form of Périgord-truffled Highland beef with parsnip purée. The signature pre-dessert that still evokes gasps of delight is what looks like a breakfast boiled egg, a meringue-topped intense mango delight with a thick tuile to represent the finger of toast. Dessert itself could be a majestically airborne cherry soufflé, or perhaps an ingenious reimagining of bread-and-butter pudding. If you're on the vegan trail, expect a parade of equally imaginative dishes. Wine has always been taken very seriously here, and the pairings with the menus – with the option of upgrading to Coravin servings of the likes of decades-old Mosel Riesling, mature-vine burgundies and aged Napa Cabernet – are reliably spot-on.

Chef Roger Jones, John Brown **Seats** 34 **Closed** Christmas and New Year
Notes Children welcome

WILTSHIRE continued

WARMINSTER
The Bishopstrow Hotel & Spa
◉◉ MODERN BRITISH **V**
01985 212312 | Borenam Road, BA12 9HH
www.bishopstrow.co.uk

Surrounded by 27 acres of grounds alongside the River Wylye, this creeper-clad Regency mansion is now a glossy country-house hotel with a cool contemporary spa. The kitchen team creates vibrant contemporary menus, supported by top-class ingredients from the estate and local area.

Chef Jon Los **Seats** 65, Private dining 30 **Open** All year **Parking** 70 **Notes** Children welcome

▶ WORCESTERSHIRE

ABBERLEY
The Elms Country House Hotel & Spa
◉ MODERN BRITISH
01299 896666 | Stockton Road, WR6 6AT
www.theelmshotel.co.uk

Dating from 1710, this grand Queen Anne manor house has been a country-house hotel since 1946, with 10 acres of grounds including tennis courts and croquet lawns. Produce from the hotel's kitchen garden forms the basis of seasonal menus in the elegant fine-dining Brookes restaurant.

Chef John Brandon **Seats** 50, Private dining 60 **Open** All year **Prices from** S £9, M £20, D £7.50 **Parking** 150 **Notes** Vegetarian dishes, No children under 10 years at dinner

The Manor Arms
◉ MODERN BRITISH **V**
01299 890300 | The Village, WR6 6BN
www.themanorarms.co.uk

Originally dating from the 17th century, today's pub is a valuable part of the community, appreciated by locals and visitors alike (note the six classy bedrooms). The traditional decor inside is entirely in keeping and the finish is smart but informal.

Chef Stuart Foreman **Seats** 90, Private dining 36 **Open** All year **Parking** 30 **Notes** Children welcome

BEWDLEY
The Mug House Inn
◉ MODERN BRITISH
01299 402543 | 12 Severnside North, DY12 2EE
www.mughousebewdley.co.uk

This Georgian inn is an entirely pleasing place, with hanging baskets adorning the white facade, and views of river traffic on the Severn. Lively ideas see a dessert of 'Pimm's Mess', a mash-up of meringue, cream, Pimm's syrup, strawberries, mint and cucumber sorbet.

Chef Drew Clifford, Jamie Stampe **Seats** 26, Private dining 12 **Open** All year **Prices from** S £5.50, M £10, D £5.50 **Notes** Vegetarian dishes, No children under 10 years

Royal Forester Country Inn
◉ MODERN EUROPEAN
01299 266286 | Callow Hill, DY14 9XW
www.royalforesterinn.co.uk

This historic inn has ancient beams and plenty of nooks and crannies, but with boutique bedrooms and an on-trend bar, it chimes with our times. The restaurant is the setting for classically inspired dishes featuring Cornish seafood and some items foraged by the chef himself.

Chef Mark Hammond **Seats** 60, Private dining 18 **Open** All year **Prices from** S £5, M £14, D £6 **Parking** 25 **Notes** Vegetarian dishes, Children welcome

BROADWAY
The Broadway Hotel
◉◉ TRADITIONAL BRITISH
01386 852401 | The Green, High Street, WR12 7AA
www.cotswold-inns-hotels.co.uk/broadway

The Broadway Hotel, overlooking the green, has its roots in the 16th century, so Tattersall's Brasserie, in a contemporary light-filled atrium, is in sharp contrast to its traditional surroundings. The kitchen focuses on quality seasonal produce and has an assured sense of what will work.

Chef Eric Worger **Seats** 60 **Open** All year **Prices from** S £6.50, M £17, D £6.50 **Parking** 15 **Notes** Vegetarian dishes, Children welcome

Dormy House Hotel
◉◉◉ MODERN **V** ⚐ NOTABLE WINE LIST
01386 852711 | Willersey Hill, WR12 7LF
www.dormyhouse.co.uk

Owned by the same family for over 40 years, Dormy House perches on a hill above Broadway, its origins as a 17th-century former farmhouse evident in its golden stones, beams and panelling; these days the place is a swish bolt-hole with looks worthy of an interiors magazine, plus the de rigueur spa for 21st-century hedonists. Done out in sleek, modern style, the airy Garden Room looks through floor-to-ceiling windows onto a verdant backdrop; this is where the chefs get to show what they are made of, and under the leadership of head chef Sam Bowser, the culinary bar has been raised considerably. Delivered via five- or seven-course menus of cleverly constructed, contemporary British dishes, dinner might begin with caramelised veal sweetbreads with asparagus, truffled almond pesto

and wild garlic, then progress through a fish course
– butter-poached halibut, say, with shellfish broth,
razor clam and sea lettuce – to poached chicken
highlighted by manzanilla sherry, glazed morels and
asparagus. A tricksy rice pudding moelleux soufflé
might come with textures of apple and puff pastry to
end on an indulgent note.

Chef Sam Bowser **Seats** 50, Private dining 14
Open All year **Parking** 70 **Notes** Children welcome

The Fish
◉◉ BRITISH
01386 858000 | Farncombe Estate, WR12 7LJ
www.thefishhotel.co.uk
The sea is miles away, no river flows past, for The Fish
is named after the hill on which it stands, because
monks once cured fish in caves on the hillside. Part of
a 400-acre estate, today's boutique hotel has an
informal Scandi-chic style restaurant.

Chef Carl Holmes **Notes** Vegetarian dishes

Russell's
◉◉ MODERN BRITISH
01386 853555 | 20 High Street, WR12 7DT
www.russellsofbroadway.co.uk
In a prime spot on the High Street of this pretty,
touristy village, Russell's is smartly decked out in
contemporary style. Puddings get heads turning: a
light plum soufflé, say, with subtle Earl Grey
pannacotta, poached plums and frothy almond foam.

Chef Jorge Santos **Seats** 60, Private dining 14
Closed Bank holiday Monday and 1 January
Prices from S £7, M £15, D £7 **Parking** 7
Notes Vegetarian dishes, Children welcome

CHADDESLEY CORBETT
Brockencote Hall Country House Hotel
◉◉◉ MODERN BRITISH V
01562 777876 | DY10 4PY
www.brockencotehall.com
Victorian Brockencote stands in 70 acres of landscaped
gardens and parkland overlooking the waters of its
ornamental lake. The place has been made over with a
light touch that blends original features with a sprinkle
of contemporary pizzazz. Sweeping pastoral views are
best appreciated from either a seat in the Colonial
lounge-bar or a table in the linen-swathed elegance of
the Chaddesley dining room, or if you are going about
things in the right spirit, one after the other. Tim
Jenkins is in charge of the gastronomic show, setting
high standards with precisely executed modern dishes
composed with intuitive culinary logic – an opener of
pan-fried scallops and confit belly pork lifted with
passionfruit being a case in point. Main courses might

see roasted venison loin haunch next to Jerusalem
artichoke, chestnut mushroom and hazelnut jus, or
another idea might match pan-fried cod fillet with
roasted cauliflower, caper and raisin and sea veg.
Technical dexterity is once again in abundance at
dessert, when white chocolate pannacotta is delivered
with apple textures and white chocolate crumb.

Chef Tim Jenkins **Seats** 40, Private dining 16
Open All year **Parking** 50 **Notes** Children welcome

EVESHAM
Wood Norton Hotel
◉◉ MODERN FRENCH V
01386 765611 | Wood Norton, WR11 4YB
www.thewoodnorton.com
The hall was built in the late 19th century as an
upmarket hunting lodge to attract European royalty.
Interiors are fabulously rich, with chandeliers and
wood panelling everywhere, and the dining room is
no exception. Dishes combine sharply focused flavour
and thoughtful combination.

Chef Kieran Hunt **Seats** 20, Private dining 140
Closed December to February **Parking** 100
Notes Children welcome

KIDDERMINSTER
The Granary Hotel & Restaurant
◉ MODERN BRITISH
01562 777535 | Heath Lane, Shenstone, DY10 4BS
www.granary-hotel.co.uk
Set in the countryside, the boutique-style Granary
Hotel boasts a market garden to supply the kitchen
with low-mileage produce. The key players in the
kitchen brigade have worked together for a decade,
developing a contemporary style to bring great
seasonal ingredients together in well-considered
compositions.

Chef Anthony Phillips **Seats** 60, Private dining 16
Open All year **Parking** 95 **Notes** Vegetarian
dishes, Children welcome

Stone Manor Hotel
◉ TRADITIONAL
01562 777555 | Stone, DY10 4PJ
www.hogarths.co.uk/stone-manor
In its newly refurbished Fields restaurant, Stone
Manor makes space for appealing modern brasserie
food. Flambé dishes cooked before your delighted eyes
have been productively revived, so that beef fillet or
chicken breast can be set alight with vodka or brandy.

Chef Paul Harris **Seats** 96, Private dining 26
Open All year **Parking** 300 **Notes** Vegetarian
dishes, Children welcome

MALVERN

L'Amuse Bouche Restaurant

◉◉ CLASSIC FRENCH **V**

01684 572427 | The Cotford Hotel, 51 Graham Road, WR14 2HU

www.cotfordhotel.co.uk

Built in the mid-19th century as a summer bolt-hole for the Bishop of Worcester, The Cotford Hotel is still in the rest-and-recreation business, its chapel now L'Amuse Bouche restaurant. Loch Fyne scallops are flamed in anisette and served on a bed of wild mushrooms.

Chef Christopher Morgan **Seats** 40 **Open** All year **Parking** 12 **Notes** Children welcome

Colwall Park Hotel

◉◉ MODERN BRITISH

01684 540000 | Walwyn Road, Colwall, WR13 6QG

www.colwall.co.uk

Colwell Park is a half-timbered inn on the borders of Herefordshire and Worcestershire. In a chapel-like dining room, the menu of locally reared meats, Evesham fresh produce and own-grown herbs is full of modern style where mains could be tenderloin and belly of superlative pork, teamed with a black pudding Scotch egg and apple purée.

Chef Richard Dixon **Open** All year

The Cottage in the Wood

◉◉ MODERN BRITISH

01684 588860 | Holywell Road, Malvern Wells, WR14 4LG

www.cottageinthewood.co.uk

This delightful Georgian property has a panoramic view across the Severn Valley from its position high up on a wooded hillside. The aptly named Outlook Restaurant makes the best of its situation while the kitchen's rather refined classically inspired output is a distraction in itself.

Chef Mark Redwood **Seats** 80, Private dining 50 **Open** All year **Prices from** S £8, M £16, D £8 **Parking** 45 **Notes** Vegetarian dishes, Children welcome

Holdfast Cottage Hotel

◉ TRADITIONAL, MODERN BRITISH

01684 310288 | Marlbank Road, Welland, WR13 6NA

www.holdfast-cottage.co.uk

Built in the 17th century and extended by the Victorians, Holdfast Cottage Hotel is surrounded by magnificent gardens with spectacular views of the Malvern Hills. The hotel is an ideal base to explore Worcester, Gloucester and Hereford and there is a no-frills approach to cooking.

Chef Andrew Evans **Seats** 30 **Parking** 15 **Notes** Vegetarian dishes, Children welcome

The Malvern

◉ MODERN BRITISH

01684 898290 | Grovewood Road, WR14 1GD

www.themalvernspa.com

The Malvern, the first spa resort in the town, opened in 1910. Its brasserie is a fresh-looking space of neutral tones, wooden tables and a tiled floor. You might start with Indian flavours of pan-fried scallops on squash purée with an onion bhaji.

Chef James Wilson **Seats** 52 **Open** All year **Prices from** S £5.25, M £12, D £6.25 **Parking** 82 **Notes** Vegetarian dishes, No children

OMBERSLEY

The Venture In Restaurant

◉◉ BRITISH, FRENCH

01905 620552 | Main Road, WR9 0EW

www.theventurein.co.uk

Behind the half-timbered facade of this 15th-century property is a bar with a open fire, comfortable sofas and low tables and a restaurant with bags of ancient character from its ceiling beams and standing timbers. Chef-patron Toby Fletcher stamps his style on the Anglo-French repertoire.

Chef Toby Fletcher **Seats** 32, Private dining 32 **Closed** 25 December to 1 January, 2 weeks summer, 2 weeks winter **Parking** 15 **Notes** Vegetarian dishes, No children

▶ EAST RIDING OF YORKSHIRE

BEVERLEY

The Pipe and Glass Inn

◉◉ MODERN BRITISH **V** ⬥ NOTABLE WINE LIST

01430 810246 | West End, South Dalton, HU17 7PN

www.pipeandglass.co.uk

The rustic bar has a smart finish with Chesterfield chairs and sofas, and a wood-burning stove, while the restaurant is dominated by horse-themed prints and chunky wooden tables. The industrious and creative team in the kitchen deliver some arresting options.

Chef James Mackenzie **Seats** 100, Private dining 28 **Closed** 25 December, 2 weeks January **Parking** 60 **Notes** Children welcome

The Westwood Restaurant
◉◉ MODERN BRITISH **V**
01482 881999 | New Walk, HU17 7AE
www.thewestwood.co.uk

Owned by twins Matt and Michelle Barker, the Westwood began life as a courthouse and the building is full of character. Decorated in dark colours with copper and gold highlights, it has a contemporary feel, with an open kitchen and a terrace for outdoor dining.

Chef Matt Barker **Seats** 70, Private dining 20 **Closed** 27 December to 15 January **Prices from** S £6.50, M £14.95, D £5.50 **Parking** 32 **Notes** Children welcome

▶ NORTH YORKSHIRE

ALDWARK
Aldwark Manor Golf & Spa Hotel
◉ CLASSIC BRITISH
01347 838146 | YO61 1UF
www.qhotels.co.uk/our-locations/aldwark-manor-golf-spa-hotel-york

When you're all done with golf and pampering, the contemporary, split-level brasserie of this grand Victorian manor in 120 acres of parkland will see you right on the gastronomic front. The kitchen delivers tasty combinations and there's a bustling vibe with attentive and engaging staff..

Chef Lucy Hyder **Seats** 85, Private dining 18 **Open** All year **Parking** 200 **Notes** Vegetarian dishes, Children welcome

ARKENGARTHDALE
Charles Bathurst Inn
◉ BRITISH
01748 884567 | DL11 6EN
www.cbinn.co.uk

The CB – to its friends – is named after a Georgian parliamentarian, and the beamed dining room is done out with pale wood and generously spaced tables. Local farmers and fishermen supply its seasonally changing menus of modern Yorkshire cooking.

Chef Gareth Bottomley **Seats** 70, Private dining 60 **Closed** 25 December **Parking** 25 **Notes** Vegetarian dishes, Children welcome

ASENBY
Crab & Lobster Restaurant
◉◉ MODERN BRITISH **V**
01845 577286 | Dishforth Road, YO7 3QL
www.crabandlobster.co.uk

The Crab & Lobster restaurant offers various settings in which to dine, from a garden terrace to a room hung with a profusion of fishing nets and pots.

Traditional seafood specialities cooked with flair include fresh plump blue-shelled mussels in a hearty marinière.

Chef Steve Dean, Stephen Thomas **Seats** 85, Private dining 16 **Open** All year **Parking** 80 **Notes** Children welcome

AUSTWICK
The Traddock
◉◉ MODERN BRITISH
01524 251224 | Settle, LA2 8BY
www.thetraddock.co.uk

The Yorkshire Dales extend gloriously all around the character stone house, where a vigorous rendition of British modernism is the stock-in-trade, with overlays of various Mediterranean traditions. A white-truffled pumpkin and chestnut risotto is one way to start off proceedings.

Chef Thomas Pickard **Seats** 36, Private dining 16 **Open** All year **Parking** 20 **Notes** Vegetarian dishes, Children welcome

AYSGARTH
The Aysgarth Falls
◉ MODERN **V**
01969 663775 | DL8 3SR
www.aysgarthfallshotel.com

When you're exploring the Yorkshire Dales, schedule a pitstop at this traditional pub with rooms in the pretty village of Aysgarth, whether it's for a pint of locally brewed Black Sheep ale or a meal in the contemporary restaurant overlooking the lovely garden.

Chef Gavin Swift **Seats** 45, Private dining 14 **Parking** 25 **Notes** Children welcome

BAINBRIDGE
Yorebridge House
◉◉◉ MODERN BRITISH **V** 🍷 NOTABLE WINE LIST
See pages 338–339

BIRSTWITH
The Station Hotel
◉ MODERN BRITISH
01423 770254 | Station Road, HG3 3AG
www.station-hotel.net

The Station is a venerable building in a village on the edge of Nidderdale, near Harrogate. The pick of the eating areas is the smart room that looks over the garden, but the main menu is served throughout. Classical cooking is given a high shine.

Chef Benjamin Doyle **Seats** 60 **Open** All year **Prices from** S £5.95, M £14.95, D £5.95 **Parking** 30 **Notes** Vegetarian dishes, Children welcome

BAINBRIDGE
Yorebridge House
◉ ◉◉ MODERN BRITISH V 🍾 NOTABLE WINE LIST
01969 652060 | DL8 3EE
www.yorebridgehouse.co.uk

High-impact modern dining in the former headmaster's residence

Founded by a local philanthropist at the dawn of the 17th century, the old Yorebridge grammar school is deeply rooted into this gorgeous location, although the present schoolhouse and headmaster's residence date from around 1850. Today, the trim greystone buildings make a living as a fine country hotel, and you can imagine that the bucolic delights of such a soul-soothing spot must have provided some relief from the grim, disciplinarian regime of those days. Legend has it that one long-gone headmaster was rather more interested in fishing the local waters than improving the educational standards of his pupils. And who can blame him, with the luxuriant Yorkshire Dales unfolding all around, and Yorebridge's five acres bracketed by the rivers Bain and Ure flowing peacefully by. The main building and guest rooms have indeed been boutiqued to perfection, some kitted out with their own terrace and hot tub, while an understated palette of charcoal-grey against louvred doors makes for a stylishly neutral contemporary look in the dining room. Dan Shotton and his brigade favour a straightforward,

unpretentious approach to the modern British repertoire, founded on ingredients of unimpeachable quality in regionally based dishes executed with skill and creativity, but without undue complication. The kitchen's flair for comforting, intuitive flavour combinations is clear from the off, as when rabbit is lifted by the earthy notes of watercress and carrot, or when a scallop starter is teamed with meaty pork and the contrasting sharpness of Granny Smith apple. Sound northern meats such as Gressingham duck and Dexter beef fillet from local suppliers (duly name-checked on the menu) appear in intuitive, immensely appealing combinations, the former, perhaps, with red cabbage and parsnip purée, the latter with turnips and king oyster mushrooms. Likewise, fish is sourced from trusted local suppliers, and might appear in the shape of superb halibut with brown shrimp and sea kale. The finale could be an impressive array of British cheeses, including some fine local specimens from Swaledale or the Wensleydale creamery, with quince, chutney and lavoche crispbread, or there may be a coffee-based idea accessorised with amaretti and mascarpone. If you're an aficionado of rhubarb, you're in the right county, and could well find it starring in contemporary fusion mode with yuzu and blackberry. The wine list sources some imaginative choices from the New World as well as doing justice to the classic regions of Europe, with helpful notes to guide the way.

Chef Daniel Shotton **Seats** 35, Private dining 18 **Open** All year **Prices from** S £15, M £30, D £15 **Parking** 30 **Notes** Children welcome

BOLTON ABBEY

The Burlington Restaurant

⊛⊛⊛⊛ MODERN BRITISH V ◣ NOTABLE WINE LIST

01756 718100 | The Devonshire Arms Hotel, BD23 6AJ
www.thedevonshirearms.co.uk

The Devonshire Arms may sound like a cosy village pub but is actually a country-house hotel set in 30,000 acres of the Duke of Devonshire's estate with a swish spa and a restaurant that has put it well and truly on the gastronomic map. The Burlington Restaurant is the star of the show, where chef Paul Leonard delivers food of craft and creativity, making good use of the estate's excellent produce (dining during the game season is a good idea) and the kitchen garden for herbs, vegetables and fruits. Presented in six- and nine-course tasting menus (there's a veggie version of the latter), his dishes are colourful, full of presentational artistry and precisely composed flavours, opening with a burst of freshness from raw Isle of Skye scallops with apple, turnip, caviar and apple dashi. Meat and fish are both handled with top-level skills, whether it's aged Yorkshire beef with various preparations of leek, onion, garlic and morels, all lifted by smoked bone marrow and a sauce of great depth, or superlative turbot seared crisp and golden and presented with fat mussels, sea kale and velvety potato purée. The final flourish delivers high-flying technical panache via blood orange mousse encased in a chocolate sphere, dusted with grapefruit powder and matched with pistachio and toasted rice for texture, and the sour kick of crème fraîche ice cream. Superlative nibbles and amuses punctuate the whole experience in imaginative style. Simpler dining is available in the brasserie, with its roughcast white walls and vibrantly coloured furnishings.

Chef Paul Leonard **Seats** 70, Private dining 90
Closed Christmas and New Year **Parking** 100
Notes Children welcome

The Devonshire Brasserie & Bar

⊛ TRADITIONAL BRITISH

01756 710710 | The Devonshire Arms Hotel, BD23 6AJ
www.thedevonshirearms.co.uk

The Devonshire Arms has a lot going for it, from its fabulous position on the 30,000-acre estate, the luxe bedrooms and the high-end restaurant (see above), but don't forget about the Brasserie & Bar. The menu deals in upscale modern brasserie food, with a Yorkshire flavour.

Chef Sean Pleasants **Seats** 60 **Open** All year
Prices from S £5.50, M £14.95, D £6 **Parking** 40
Notes Vegetarian dishes, Children welcome

BOROUGHBRIDGE

The Crown Inn

⊛⊛ MODERN BRITISH V

01423 322300 | Roecliffe, YO51 9LY
www.crowninnroecliffe.co.uk

In this 16th-century coaching inn you'll find stone-flagged floors, roaring fires, fashionably mismatched furniture and a kitchen that churns out generous dishes with unmistakably French accents. If you hanker for fish, try hake steamed with king prawns over a stock of tomato, chorizo and mussels.

Chef Steve Ardern **Seats** 60, Private dining 20
Open All year **Parking** 30 **Notes** Children welcome

BURNSALL

The Devonshire Fell

⊛ MODERN BRITISH V

01756 729000 | BD23 6BT
www.devonshirefell.co.uk

This place presents a sober face to the world, but inside, a contemporary boutique makeover displays vibrant shades of lilac and blue, sensuous fabrics and attractive artwork in the funky bar and conservatory bistro. Informal, friendly service feeds into the easy-going vibe.

Chef Rob Harrison **Seats** 40, Private dining 70
Open All year **Parking** 40 **Notes** Children welcome

GILLING EAST

The Fairfax Arms

⊛⊛ CLASSIC BRITISH

01439 788212 | Main Street, YO62 4JH
www.thefairfaxarms.co.uk

Popular with the local farming community, The Fairfax guards the village crossroads, one of which leads to Gilling Castle, prep school for the well-known Ampleforth College. The pub's black-beamed open-plan bar and dining area leads out to a beer garden bordered by a stream.

Chef Ben Turner **Seats** 90, Private dining 50
Open All year **Prices from** S £5.25, M £13.50, D £5.50
Parking 12 **Notes** Vegetarian dishes, Children welcome

GOATHLAND

Mallyan Spout Hotel

⊛ MODERN BRITISH

01947 896486 | YO22 5AN
www.mallyanspout.co.uk

Named after the tumbling 70-ft waterfall behind the hotel, the Mallyan Spout clings comfortably to a traditional style of furnishing and decor – textured wallpaper, mirrors, high-backed upholstered chairs, that sort of thing. Old and New World wines are well balanced on the 50-bin list.

Chef Richard Taylor **Seats** 50, Private dining 12 **Closed** 25–26 December **Prices from** S £6.50, M £12.95, D £6.50 **Parking** 30 **Notes** Vegetarian dishes, Children welcome

GOLDSBOROUGH
Goldsborough Hall
◉◉ BRITISH

01423 867321 | Church Street, HG5 8NR
www.goldsboroughhall.com

Princess Mary, one of the Queen's aunts, lived in this 1620s stately home until 1929. The Dining Room is small, with formally laid tables, a baby grand, and a splendid marble fireplace. White-gloved staff serve from the informal Garden menu, a seven-course taster, or the carte.

Chef Adam Thur **Seats** 60, Private dining 110 **Closed** 24–26 December **Parking** 50 **Notes** Vegetarian dishes, Children welcome

GRASSINGTON
Grassington House
◉◉ MODERN BRITISH

01756 752406 | 5 The Square, BD23 5AQ
www.grassingtonhouse.co.uk

This stone-built Georgian house boasts a new state-of-the-art, eco-friendly kitchen producing modern food with the accent on sharply etched flavours. Imaginative side orders take in roast courgettes in honey, garlic and chilli, and desserts include classic apple Tatin with vanilla cream.

Chef John Rudden **Seats** 40 **Closed** 25 December **Prices from** S £5.50, M £14.50, D £6.25 **Parking** 20 **Notes** Vegetarian dishes, Children welcome

GUISBOROUGH
Gisborough Hall
◉ MODERN BRITISH V

01287 611500 | Whitby Lane, TS14 6PT
www.gisborough-hall.com

The hall is an imposing creeper-covered country-house hotel situated in well-kept grounds, and Chaloner's restaurant occupies a large space with pillars and a fireplace in what was once the billiard room. The kitchen team turns out some rather interesting dishes.

Chef Karl Rochford **Seats** 75, Private dining 36 **Open** All year **Prices from** S £6.75, M £18.50, D £6.75 **Parking** 180 **Notes** Children welcome

HAROME
The Star Inn
◉◉ MODERN BRITISH V ⚑ NOTABLE WINE LIST

01439 770397 | YO62 5JE
www.thestaratharome.co.uk

This thatched pub in a moorland village boasts a rustic bar, a dining room with chunky tables, a real fire and knick-knacks galore, and a more modern restaurant. Andrew Pern's country cooking places a high premium on big, rugged flavours. A great wine list, too.

Chef Andrew Pern, Steve Smith **Seats** 70, Private dining 10 **Open** All year **Prices from** S £8, M £18.50, D £6 **Parking** 30 **Notes** Children welcome

HARROGATE
Clocktower
◉◉ MODERN BRITISH

01423 871350 | Rudding Park, Follifoot, HG3 1JH
www.ruddingpark.co.uk/dine/clocktower

Rudding Park boasts food that's worth a detour in the Clocktower Restaurant. It's all vibrant, colourful spaces, from the long limestone bar to the grand conservatory with its Catalonian olive tree, and a dining room complete with eye-catching pink glass chandelier.

Chef Eddie Gray **Seats** 110, Private dining 14 **Open** All year **Prices from** S £9.50, M £21, D £9.50 **Parking** 350 **Notes** Vegetarian dishes, Children welcome

Horto Restaurant
◉◉◉ MODERN BRITISH V

01423 871350 | Rudding Park Hotel, Spa & Golf, Rudding Park, Follifoot, HG3 1JH
www.ruddingpark.co.uk/dine/horto-restaurant

The handsome stone-built Rudding Park is master of the 300 acres of landscaped gardens and woodland that it surveys, and has been refashioned for the present day as a spa hotel with all the luxury accoutrements one could wish. As is the way nowadays, it incorporates a productive kitchen garden, the Latinised name of which is conferred on the fine-dining restaurant, where its steward Adrian Reeve works in close conjunction with head chef Murray Wilson to furnish a menu built on unimpeachable seasonal freshness. The format is six or eight courses for food that pulls out all the modernising stops and then some. In autumn, the opening gambit could be stone bass with pickled leek in sake, before pork cheek with celeriac and apple makes an appearance. The various sweetnesses of cherries and carrots add depth to a principal dish of succulent mallard breast, and then the longer menu offers a cavalcade of three desserts arriving in single file: bergamot-fragrant yuzu tart, pear with ginger and maple syrup, and a chocolate treat offset with blackberries and sheep's milk.

Chef Murray Wilson **Seats** 45 **Open** All year **Parking** 350 **Notes** Children welcome

Hotel du Vin & Bistro Harrogate
◉ BRITISH, FRENCH, EUROPEAN
01423 856800 | Prospect Place, HG1 1LB
www.hotelduvin.com/locations/harrogate

The Harrogate outpost of the HdV chain occupies a luxuriously converted terrace of eight Georgian townhouses opposite the 200-acre Stray Common. With hops around the windows and mustard-coloured walls, the place bears the group's corporate stamp, and the kitchen makes a virtue of simplicity.

Chef Walter Marskamp **Seats** 86, Private dining 60 **Open** All year **Parking** 33 **Notes** Vegetarian dishes, Children welcome

Nidd Hall Hotel
◉◉ MODERN BRITISH **V**
01423 771598 | Nidd, HG3 3BN
www.warnerleisurehotels.co.uk

Built in the 1820s, Nidd Hall is a glorious hodge-podge of architectural and stylistic references that take in everything from stained window panels to Tuscan columns. The fine-dining option of the Terrace restaurant manages a light decorative tone in keeping with graceful modern British cooking.

Chef Andrew Mangan **Seats** 42 **Open** All year **Parking** 300 **Notes** No children

Studley Hotel
◉◉ PACIFIC RIM
01423 560425 | 28 Swan Road, HG1 2SE
www.orchidrestaurant.co.uk

In the Studley Hotel's Orchid restaurant, a multinational brigade of chefs delivers authentic regional flavours in an eclectic Pan-Asian melting pot of cuisines. Mango and darkwood interiors divided by Japanese lattice-style screens make for a classy contemporary setting.

Chef Kenneth Poon **Seats** 72, Private dining 20 **Closed** 25–26 December **Parking** 15 **Notes** Vegetarian dishes, Children welcome

West Park Hotel
◉ TRADITIONAL BRITISH
01423 524471 | West Park, HG1 1BJ
www.thewestparkhotel.com

This contemporary boutique hotel occupies a lovely spot overlooking the Harrogate Stray, an open area of 200 acres of grassland in the centre of the historic spa town. In the comfortable modern dining room or

in the alfresco courtyard, everything looks good on the plate.

Chef Pawel Cekala **Seats** 70, Private dining 55 **Open** All year **Prices from** S £5.95, M £11.95, D £5.95 **Notes** Vegetarian dishes, Children welcome

White Hart Hotel
◉ CLASSIC BRITISH
01423 505681 | 2 Cold Bath Road, HG2 0NF
www.whitehartharrogate.com

The White Hart is a Harrogate landmark, having provided bed and sustenance to travellers since the Georgian era. The recently refurbished Fat Badger Grill is its main eating space, serving up classic British food with a bit of a contemporary twist.

Chef Richard Ferebee **Seats** 100, Private dining 90 **Open** All year **Parking** 80 **Notes** Vegetarian dishes, Children welcome

HAWES
Drawing Room Restaurant
◉ MODERN BRITISH
01969 667255 | Simonstone Hall Hotel, Simonstone, DL8 3LY
www.simonstonehall.com

An old stone manor house, built to last, Simonstone Hall is a country-house hotel with a few contemporary surprises in store. The rural aspect may be timeless, and the decor soothingly traditional, but the restaurant's food is very much of our times.

Chef Christopher Hemsworth **Seats** 40, Private dining 22 **Open** All year **Prices from** S £7, M £16, D £7 **Parking** 20 **Notes** Vegetarian dishes, Children welcome

HELMSLEY
Black Swan Hotel
◉◉◉ CLASSIC BRITISH, FRENCH **V**
01439 770466 | Market Place, YO62 5BJ
www.blackswan-helmsley.co.uk

Set in a trio of ancient houses spanning the centuries from Elizabethan to Georgian to Victorian, the Black Swan is still a focal point of this lovely little market town in the 21st century, albeit with a rather smart country-chic look these days to offset the old-world charm of its open fires and antiques. The Gallery restaurant (so named because it doubles up as a daytime gallery showcasing original artworks for sale) is where head chef Matt Tyler gets to show off his skills and creative flair. Respecting the integrity of top-drawer Yorkshire ingredients is one of the secrets, as seen in a starter that pairs local ham hock with duck egg and the refreshing acidity of Cox's apple purée, celeriac remoulade, pickled shallots and watercress salad. Next up, slow-cooked pork belly partnered with boudin noir, pommes Anna, crisp sage leaves and apple purée has impressive depth and clarity of flavour, every component with something to say. For pudding, a heavenly millefeuille of flaky, golden pastry is complemented by salted caramel, almonds and banana ice cream.

Chef Matt Tyler **Seats** 65, Private dining 50 **Open** All year **Prices from** S £8.50, M £28, D £9.50 **Parking** 40 **Notes** Children welcome

Feversham Arms Hotel & Verbena Spa

◉◉ MODERN BRITISH V
01439 770766 | 1–8 High Street, YO62 5AG
www.fevershamarmshotel.com

Sophisticated cooking built on fine regional ingredients is the order of the day here in The Weathervane Restaurant. The seared scallop with warm apple jelly, black pudding and smoked roe emulsion seems appropriate for a hotel in an affluent market town.

Chef Christopher Hobley **Seats** 65, Private dining 32 **Open** All year **Parking** 50 **Notes** Children welcome

The Pheasant Hotel

◉◉ MODERN BRITISH V
01439 771241 | Mill Street, Harome, YO62 5JG
www.thepheasanthotel.com

The Pheasant has been carved out of a blacksmith's, village shop and barns, all around a courtyard. The conservatory is mainly used for dining, and the cooking style is an updated British version of the classical French repertory, with an expert's skill behind judicious combinations.

Chef Peter Neville **Seats** 60, Private dining 30 **Open** All year **Parking** 15 **Notes** Children welcome

HETTON
The Angel Inn

◉◉ BRITISH, INTERNATIONAL
01756 730263 | BD23 6LT
www.angelhetton.co.uk

A 500-year-old inn with food at the heart of everything, The Angel was among the first pubs to break away from the chips-with-everything mentality back in the 1980s. The smart restaurant has linen-clad tables and pretty, country-style decor, while the kitchen offers a gently contemporary repertoire.

Chef Naem Rafiq **Seats** 65, Private dining 24 **Closed** 25 December, 1 week January **Prices from** S £7.50, M £21, D £6.95 **Parking** 40 **Notes** Vegetarian dishes, Children welcome

HOVINGHAM
The Worsley Arms Hotel

◉◉ BRITISH
01653 628234 | High Street, YO62 4LA
www.worsleyarms.co.uk

This Victorian hotel is well positioned in a pretty Yorkshire village set against a backdrop of the spectacular Howardian Hills. With its red walls, white linen and floral drapes, the restaurant is an elegant and traditional setting for fine-tuned dishes.

Chef Andrew Jones **Seats** 40, Private dining 30 **Open** All year **Parking** 40 **Notes** Vegetarian dishes, Children welcome

KETTLEWELL
King's Head Restaurant

◉ MODERN BRITISH V
01756 761600 | The Green, BD23 5RD
www.thekingsheadkettlewell.co.uk

Owner-run inn, located in the peaceful but popular village of Kettlewell. Nestled within the Yorkshire countryside, it's perfect for leisure guests and keen walkers alike. Meals can be enjoyed in the cosy bar.

Chef Michael Pighills **Seats** 34 **Closed** 1 week in November, 2 weeks in January **Prices from** S £6, M £14, D £7 **Notes** Children welcome

KIRKBY FLEETHAM
Black Horse Inn

◉ MODERN BRITISH
01609 749010 | 7 Lumley Lane, DL7 0SH
www.blackhorseinnkirkbyfleetham.com

A short spin from the whirling traffic at Scotch Corner, this stone-built traditional inn pushes all the right buttons. The main dining room overlooks the back garden and delivers classic and modern British dishes.

Chef David Davies **Seats** 60, Private dining 12 **Open** All year **Prices from** S £5.50, M £10.50, D £6.50 **Parking** 100 **Notes** Vegetarian dishes, Children welcome

KNARESBOROUGH
General Tarleton Inn

◉◉ MODERN BRITISH
01423 340284 | Boroughbridge Road, Ferrensby, HG5 0PZ
www.generaltarleton.co.uk

Not far from the castle, and with Harrogate barely five miles away, the GT is a country inn with character. When the chef entitles his menus 'Food with Yorkshire Roots' here, he means it. Twice-baked Wensleydale soufflé with tomato relish is a regionally unimpeachable starter.

Chef John Topham, Marc Williams **Seats** 64, Private dining 40 **Open** All year **Prices from** S £6.95, M £13.95, D £5.95 **Parking** 40 **Notes** Vegetarian dishes, Children welcome

YORKSHIRE, NORTH

LEYBURN
Thirteen
◉ MODERN BRITISH
01969 622951 | 13 Railway Street, DL8 5BB
www.thirteenatleyburn.co.uk
Located just off the main square in the quiet town of Leyburn, this small enterprise is very unassuming from the outside. Having gained experience at some of the top restaurants in North Yorkshire, Michael and Sarah McBride haven't looked back since opening three years ago.
Chef Michael McBride **Seats** 24 **Closed** 2 January for 3 weeks **Prices from** S £5.95, M £14.95, D £6.50 **Notes** Vegetarian dishes, Children welcome

MASHAM
Samuel's at Swinton Park
Rosettes suspended MODERN BRITISH
See opposite

The Terrace
◉ MODERN, INTERNATIONAL
01765 680900 | Swinton Park, HG4 4JH
www.swintonestate.com
The Swinton Park estate is well known for the impressive Samuel's in the main hotel (see opposite), but if you're looking for casual dining with a relaxed atmosphere then The Terrace restaurant is probably your best bet. It serves a globally inspired menu throughout the day.
Chef Chris McPhee **Seats** 50, Private dining **Open** All year **Prices from** S £3.50, M £10, D £4.50 **Parking** 50 **Notes** Vegetarian dishes, Children welcome

Vennell's
◉◉ MODERN BRITISH
01765 689000 | 7 Silver Street, HG4 4DX
www.vennellsrestaurant.co.uk
Jon Vennell's self-named neighbourhood eatery has become a destination for out-of-towners. Four dinners and one lunch a week keep things on a tight rein. Some of the local ale goes into a majestic suet pudding of beef and mushrooms, and desserts maintain the pace.
Chef Jon Vennell **Seats** 30, Private dining 16 **Closed** 26–29 December, 1–14 January, 1 week August **Notes** Vegetarian dishes, No children under 4 years

MIDDLESBROUGH
Chadwicks Inn Maltby
◉◉ MODERN BRITISH V
01642 590300 | High Lane, Maltby, TS8 0BG
www.chadwicksinnmaltby.co.uk
Food is the focus at this traditional 19th-century inn on the edge of the moors. Dine in the bar, with its wood-burner and sofas, or in the comfortable restaurant. The dinner menu is a slate of ambitiously enterprising dishes.
Chef Steve Lawford **Seats** 47 **Closed** 26 December and 1 January **Prices from** S £6, M £20, D £6 **Parking** 50 **Notes** Children welcome

MIDDLETON TYAS
The Coach House
◉◉◉ SEASONAL MODERN BRITISH V
01325 377977 | Middleton Lodge, DL10 6NJ
www.middletonlodge.co.uk
The Georgian house at the heart of the 200-acre estate is a handsome pile, and even its coach house is on a grand scale. In fact, The Coach House restaurant is the heart and soul of this operation, and with its smart, rustic finish, soothing natural colours and a ceiling opened to the rafters, it is a stylish spot to tuck into fine Yorkshire produce treated with respect. The hard-working kitchen kicks off with breakfast (eggs Benedict with Yorkshire ham), before lunches such as classy sandwiches or fish and chips, or sea bream with heritage salad carrot. The kitchen garden provides a good deal of the salads, veg and herbs. In the evening, the chargrill comes into its own for top-notch steaks (côtes de boeuf for two to share, say), served with a choice of sauces and sides. This kitchen has a sure touch, with starters like torched mackerel with sweet-and-sour apple, and main courses such as that bream or soy-glazed duck with sweet potatoes and toasted seeds. Finish with baked pistachio Alaska. A new dining addition is on the way: The Forge will be adding to Middleton Lodge's culinary output.
Chef Gareth Rayner **Seats** 80, Private dining 24 **Open** All year **Prices from** S £5, M £11, D £5 **Parking** 100 **Notes** Children welcome

MONK FRYSTON
Monk Fryston Hall
◉ MODERN BRITISH V
01977 682369 | LS25 5DU
www.monkfrystonhallhotel.co.uk
Set within 30 acres of lawns and woodlands in the Vale of York, Monk Fryston Hall dates back to the 13th century and retains much of its original character. Despite being only a few minutes from the A1, it's a tranquil spot.
Chef Steven Bowerbank **Seats** 50, Private dining 80 **Open** All year **Notes** Children welcome

MASHAM
Samuel's at Swinton Park
Rosettes suspended MODERN BRITISH
01765 680900 | Swinton, HG4 4JH
www.swintonpark.com

Modern cooking in a glorious country estate

The Rosette award for this establishment has been suspended due to a change of chef and reassessment will take place in due course.

With its baronial tower and castellated walls hung with creeper, Swinton Park makes quite an impression. Within, there's no let up in its opulent public areas festooned with antiques and family portraits, and millions have been lavished recently on grafting on a glitzy spa. Samuel's restaurant is the jewel in its culinary crown, a suitably grand space, with its high gilded ceilings, carved fireplace and views onto the 20,000-acre estate. The kitchen celebrates the produce from Swinton's four acres of walled kitchen garden and the local area.

For casual dining, try The Terrace (see opposite), where seasonally changing menus are focused around small gazing plates and items cooked through the Josper Grill.

Chef Jake Jones **Seats** 60, Private dining 20 **Closed** 2 days January **Parking** 80 **Notes** Vegetarian dishes, No children under 8 years at dinner

OLDSTEAD
The Black Swan at Oldstead
◉◉◉◉ MODERN BRITISH V ⚑ NOTABLE WINE LIST
01347 868387 | YO61 4BL
www.blackswanoldstead.co.uk
Down on the farm on the edge of the North York Moors, is where the Banks family calls home. With foraging forays to supplement the growing of fresh produce, it's a very modern enterprise, which is to say it has taken on many of the attributes of the rural life of 200 years ago. There's nothing like a family affair to bring a sense of collaborative cohesion to a place, and while James Banks runs a tight ship out front, his brother Tommy works wonders in the kitchen. It's certainly worth a wander around the kitchen gardens to get a handle on how your dinner will eventually come together, with rare varieties and prime specimens on hand to lend distinction. The tasting menu, which is the standard bill of fare, opens with the customary nibbles, and posts notice of the intent straight away: a sliver of raw Dexter beef, langoustine with salted strawberry, a luscious chicken dumpling. Some sour butter is offered for spreading on the sourdough bread, and then it's into a serving of dry-aged duck leg with onion in Madeira. A scallop cured in rhubarb juice marries sweetness and sourness productively and is followed by the signature beetroot (or 'meatroot', if you prefer), cooked for five hours in beef fat. Cod receives its modern-traditional pairing with cauliflower, prior to more of that dry-aged duck, the breast now adorned with smoked sloe. The concluding stages then arrive in three waves, perhaps centring on blackened apple with rye, with a final savoury of root vegetable panettone.

Chef Tommy Banks, Will Lockwood **Seats** 50 **Open** All year **Parking** 20 **Notes** No children

OSMOTHERLEY
The Cleveland Tontine
◉◉ MODERN BRITISH
01609 882671 | Staddlebridge, DL6 3JB
www.theclevelandtontine.com
Once an overnight stop for travellers using the London to Sunderland mail coach, this has been an iconic restaurant for the past four decades. Now modernised for contemporary diners, the candlelit dining room oozes atmosphere with its stone fireplace and rustic carvings.

Chef Luke Taylor **Seats** 88, Private dining 50 **Open** All year **Prices from** S £6.95, M £14.95, D £5.95 **Parking** 60 **Notes** Vegetarian dishes, Children welcome

PICKERING
Fox & Hounds Country Inn
◉ MODERN BRITISH
01751 431577 | Main Street, Sinnington, YO62 6SQ
www.thefoxandhoundsinn.co.uk
This stone-built country inn at the hub of its own little Yorkshire community is all cosiness and cheer within, from the snug bar with its wood-burner to the dining room that looks onto the back garden. Well-wrought pub food based on fine prime materials.

Chef Mark Caffrey **Seats** 36, Private dining 10 **Closed** 25–27 December **Prices from** S £5.50, M £13.50, D £5.95 **Parking** 35 **Notes** Vegetarian dishes, Children welcome

The White Swan Inn
◉◉ MODERN, TRADITIONAL
01751 472288 | Market Place, YO18 7AA
www.white-swan.co.uk
A venerable stone-built Tudor coaching inn where the kitchen philosophy is all about good Yorkshire produce. Rare-breed meats from the celebrated Ginger Pig butcher in nearby Levisham, local cheeses, fish from Whitby and veg from the allotment all feature proudly.

Chef Darren Clemmit **Seats** 50, Private dining 30 **Open** All year **Prices from** S £6, M £27, D £7 **Parking** 45 **Notes** Vegetarian dishes, Children welcome

SALTBURN-BY-THE-SEA
Brockley Hall Boutique Hotel & Fine Dining Restaurant
◉◉ MODERN BRITISH V
01287 622179 | Glenside, TS12 1JS
www.brockleyhallhotel.com
Located close to the seafront in the heart of Saltburn, this hotel has been lovingly restored, and the restaurant has a dark and opulent theme that works really well. For dessert how about a wickedly sweet apple tart Tatin, apple textures and ginger?

Chef Scott Miller **Seats** 60, Private dining 20 **Closed** 25–26 December **Parking** 14 **Notes** Children welcome

See advertisement opposite

BROCKLEY HALL

BOUTIQUE HOTEL · SALTBURN

Modern British Food providing an exciting gastronomic journey through each course

Brockley Hall Boutique Hotel and Restaurant is situated in the beautiful town of Saltburn By The Sea, which has just been recognised as one of the top 10 places to live in Britain.

Saltburn is famous for its Pier, water powered funicular Cliff Lift and Victorian pleasure gardens as well as its vibrant arts scene and huge variety of eating places celebrated in the annual food festival.

Brockley Hall is a beautiful Victorian building which has been restored in an individual and quirky style with a range of double, twin and family rooms and individually designed suites with freestanding feature baths, perfect for romantic breaks.

The Hotel has a spectacular restaurant in which to enjoy our award winning fine dining menu, we also serve well known favourites from our a la carte menu. Our delightful hand painted conservatory and sumptuous lounge are ideal for sampling our lunch menu and handcrafted afternoon teas.

Our restaurant was awarded 2 rosettes in the first year of opening for its fine dining menu.

Our head chef, Scott Miller, and his team of talented and inventive chefs will take you on a journey of taste with our unique menus which make the most of fabulous, locally sourced, ingredients. We are working with some of the UK's finest wine suppliers to provide exciting wines to complement your dining experience.

www.brockleyhallhotel.com

Reservations: 01287 622179

YORKSHIRE, NORTH

SCARBOROUGH

Lanterna Ristorante

🏵 ITALIAN SEAFOOD

01723 363616 | 33 Queen Street, YO11 1HQ

www.lanterna-ristorante.co.uk

It has been honoured by Italian newspaper La Stampa as 'the English temple of Italian cuisine', which seems an extraordinary accolade for an unassuming, albeit heartily convivial restaurant. Chef-patron, tireless Giorgio Alessio, oversees a venue done out in reds and oranges, sunny yellow and sky-blue.

Chef Giorgio Alessio **Seats** 35 **Closed** 2 weeks in October, 25–26 December, 1 January **Prices from** S £7.95, M £15.95, D £7.50 **Notes** Vegetarian dishes, Children welcome

Palm Court Hotel

🏵 MODERN BRITISH

01723 368161 | St Nicholas Cliff, YO11 2ES

www.palmcourtscarborough.co.uk

This grand old Victorian hotel has a modern decor that sits comfortably beside its elegant period features. Dinner is served in the elegant, neutral-toned restaurant, where tables swathed in floor-length linen sit beneath chandeliers. The kitchen relies on top-class local produce.

Chef Will Howes, Mike Stead **Seats** 85, Private dining 60 **Closed** 25 December **Notes** Vegetarian dishes, Children welcome

SCAWTON

The Hare Inn

🏵🏵🏵 MODERN BRITISH V

01845 597769 | YO7 2HG

www.thehare-inn.com

The Hare is the jewel in the crown of wee Scawton, a moorland village near Thirsk. It's been around since the 13th century, but wears its age well, with a fresh whitewashed exterior, and a pleasantly understated split-level dining room of rough-hewn stone walls and unclothed tables. Liz Jackson runs the show with effortless warmth, while Paul cooks up a Yorkshire storm out back. Abandon any expectations of standard pub fare: there are tasting menus all the way, sourced from the pick of local suppliers, and presented with dramatic flair. The shorter six-course option might run from a serving of sea bass with mussels and shimejis, through buttermilked and horseradished beetroot, a two-way fish course, often mackerel, and then a sumptuous main course of duck with truffled cauliflower and Tunworth. The signature frozen milk balls with honeycomb make a perfect entrée to the final dessert, perhaps rhubarb with marigolds and sheep's milk ice cream. On the longer menu, a razor clam and crayfish pairing with kohlrabi and pistachios

might intervene, with an extra dessert in the form of chocolate, salt caramel and hazelnuts.

Chef Paul Jackson **Seats** 16 **Closed** Annual holidays vary (see The Hare Inn website for details) **Parking** 12 **Notes** No children

TIMBLE

The Timble Inn

🏵🏵 MODERN BRITISH V

01943 880530 | LS21 2NN

www.thetimbleinn.co.uk

Retaining all that makes a village pub an asset, this Grade II listed 18th-century coaching inn is squirrelled away in the beautiful Washburn Valley inside the Nidderdale Area of Outstanding Natural Beauty. Five miles from the Yorkshire Dales National Park, it's a popular pit stop.

Chef Jamie Cann **Seats** 45 **Open** All year **Prices from** S £8, M £16, D £7 **Parking** 10 **Notes** No children under 10 years

See advertisement opposite

WEST WITTON

The Wensleydale Heifer

🏵 MODERN BRITISH, SEAFOOD V

01969 622322 | Main Street, DL8 4LS

www.wensleydaleheifer.co.uk

Dining on super-fresh fish and seafood isn't the first thing that comes to mind when you're in the heart of the beautiful Yorkshire Dales National Park, but this chic 17th-century inn with boutique rooms draws foodies from far and wide for its piscine pleasures.

Chef David Moss **Seats** 70 **Open** All year **Prices from** S £9.50, M £16.75, D £8 **Parking** 30 **Notes** Children welcome

WHITBY

Estbek House

🏵🏵 MODERN BRITISH

01947 893424 | East Row, Sandsend, YO21 3SU

www.estbekhouse.co.uk

Overlooking the North Sea just north of Whitby, Estbek House is perfectly positioned to source its materials from the chilly waters out front and the rolling moors behind. It all takes place in a handsome Regency house that operates as a restaurant with charming rooms.

Chef Tim Lawrence **Seats** 40, Private dining 20 **Closed** 1 January–10 February **Parking** 6 **Notes** Children welcome

The Timble Inn

"Hidden away in the quiet, beautiful village of Timble, nestling in the stunning Washburn Valley, The Timble Inn is a romantic Grade II listed 18th Century Coaching Inn with foundations dating back to 1200AD.

Now family owned and having been awarded a 5 Star Silver Award rating and 2 culinary Rosettes by the AA, we aim to provide a home-from-home for our guests. With our friendly service and superb food, you're sure to have the relaxing break you deserve with us here."

Timble nr Harrogate
North Yorkshire
LS21 2NN

Tel: 01943 880530

ail: info@thetimbleinn.co.uk

Web: thetimbleinn.co.uk

YARM

The Conservatory

◉◉ MODERN BRITISH

01642 789000 | Judges Country House Hotel, Kirklevington Hall, TS15 9LW
www.judgeshotel.co.uk

Dating from 1881, the Judges Country House Hotel occupies a magnificent edifice within 22 acres of well-maintained grounds that include a walled kitchen garden. First-class ingredients underpin the kitchen's output, and the short Market Menu is particularly good value in the opulent circumstances.

Chef Scott Papprill Seats 30, Private dining 50
Open All year Prices from S £15.50, M £34.50, D £14
Parking 110 Notes Vegetarian dishes, Children welcome

Crathorne Hall Hotel

◉ MODERN BRITISH

01642 700398 | Crathorne, TS15 0AR
www.handpickedhotels.co.uk/crathorne-hall

While the decor and furnishings of the Leven Restaurant are all early 20th century – oak half-panelled walls, heavy drapes at tall windows, oil paintings, and a gilt-edged coffered ceiling – the cuisine tends towards modern British sensibilities, with sound, classical technique on display.

Chef Alan Robinson Seats 45, Private dining 26
Open All year Parking 80 Notes Vegetarian dishes, Children welcome

YORK

The Churchill Hotel

◉◉ MODERN BRITISH

01904 644456 | 65 Bootham, YO30 7DQ
www.churchillhotel.com

The set-up is rather civilised in this Georgian mansion, which blends its airy period elegance with the look of a contemporary boutique city hotel. The dining room looks through vast arching windows into the garden, where the trees are spangled in fairy lights.

Chef Andrew Carr Seats 30, Private dining 30
Open All year Parking 35 Notes Vegetarian dishes, Children welcome

Dean Court Hotel

◉ MODERN BRITISH

01904 625082 | Duncombe Place, YO1 7EF
www.deancourt-york.co.uk

Sitting on the corner of Petergate, Dean Court is an amalgam of Victorian buildings. The dining room is a clean-lined, light-coloured contemporary space. The modern styling gives a clue to the orientation of the cooking.

Chef Benji Thornton Seats 60, Private dining 40
Open All year Notes Vegetarian dishes, Children welcome

The Grand Hotel & Spa, York

◉◉◉ MODERN BRITISH V NOTABLE WINE LIST

01904 380038 | Station Rise, YO1 6HT
www.thegrandyork.co.uk

The grand old Edwardian pile by the city's medieval walls started life as the HQ of the North Eastern Railway and its handsome features and lavish scale were ripe for reinvention as today's luxurious hotel. The place boasts the sort of swish facilities we expect in the 21st century – classy bedrooms, a glossy spa, and an elegant cocktail bar for a sharpener before dining in Hudson's, a brasserie-style venue with a sophisticated sheen and professional service to match. Head chef Craig Atchinson and his team turn out contemporary, well-crafted dishes with a local flavour, delivered via an ever-evolving set menu or five- and nine-course tasters. A five-course workout might open with smoked cod roe with seaweed and sea buckthorn, then progress via Jerusalem artichoke partnered by wild mushrooms, Wensleydale cheese and brassicas to a lively fish idea like stone bass and langoustine with fennel and buckwheat. Meat, too, is handled deftly – glazed beef cheek, say, alongside hen of the woods mushrooms, alliums and truffle. Finish on local ground with Yorkshire blackberries, apple, buttermilk and brown butter.

Chef Craig Atchinson Seats 24 Closed 25 December (check web for additional closure dates) Notes No children

The Grange Hotel

◉◉ MODERN

01904 644744 | 1 Clifton, YO30 6AA
www.grangehotel.co.uk

A classic 1829 townhouse with a designer-led interior of some panache, with inviting sofas and open fires. The cooking makes an impact, with the kitchen clearly taking a broad-based attitude, moving with the times and picking up ideas from near and far.

Chef Will Nicol Seats 60, Private dining 70 Open All year Prices from S £6.50, M £16.50, D £6.25
Parking 19 Notes Vegetarian dishes, Children welcome

Guy Fawkes Inn

◉ BRITISH

01904 466674 | 25 High Petergate, YO1 7HP
www.guyfawkesinnyork.com

The gunpowder plotter was born here in 1570, in the shadow of York Minster. It is a darkly atmospheric den with an interior akin to stepping into an 'old master' painting, with log fires, wooden floors, gas lighting, cosy nooks and crannies.

Chef Adrian Knowles **Seats** 34 **Open** All year **Prices from** S £3.95, M £9.95, D £5.95 **Notes** Vegetarian dishes, Children welcome

Hotel du Vin & Bistro York
⊛ EUROPEAN, FRENCH
01904 557350 | 89 The Mount, YO24 1AX
www.hotelduvin.com
The York billet of the HdV group is a late Georgian townhouse in the vicinity of the Minster's Gothic splendour and the city racecourse. Bare tables and floor fit in with the unbuttoned ethos, and the menu offers sturdy French domestic fare..

Chef James Skinner **Seats** 80, Private dining 24 **Open** All year **Parking** 18 **Notes** Vegetarian dishes, Children welcome

The Judge's Lodging
⊛ MODERN BRITISH
01904 638733 | 9 Lendal, YO1 8AQ
www.judgeslodgingyork.co.uk
The Georgian townhouse hard by the Minster has been reinvented as a modern hotel with a plethora of eating and drinking options. Dining can be elegantly panelled or domestic-cosy, and the all-day menus offer a wide range of international favourites.

Chef James Peyton **Seats** 100 **Open** All year **Notes** Vegetarian dishes, Children welcome

Lamb & Lion Inn
⊛ MODERN BRITISH
01904 654112 | 2–4 High Petergate, YO1 7EH
www.lambandlioninnyork.com
Seamlessly grafted into the ancient city walls of medieval York, the Lamb & Lion pleases all, young and old, locals and visitors. The undisputed classic of the kitchen is the chef's pie of the day with green beans and bacon, chips and real ale gravy.

Chef Leslie Leak **Seats** 40 **Open** All year **Notes** Vegetarian dishes, Children welcome

Middlethorpe Hall & Spa
⊛⊛ MODERN BRITISH ⬛ NOTABLE WINE LIST
01904 641241 | Bishopthorpe Road, Middlethorpe, YO23 2GB
www.middlethorpe.com
This majestic old building stands in 20 acres of gardens and parkland. The kitchen offers a fashionable surf and turf combination of diver-caught roasted scallop with sticky pork belly, kohlrabi and apple

purée. The cracking wine list offers good advice on food and wine matching.

Chef Ashley Binder **Seats** 60, Private dining 56 **Open** All year **Prices from** S £11, M £23, D £8 **Parking** 70 **Notes** Vegetarian dishes, No children under 6 years

Oxo's on The Mount
⊛⊛ MODERN EUROPEAN V
01904 619444 | The Mount Royale Hotel, 119 The Mount, YO24 1GU
www.oxosrestaurantyork.com
Cobbled together from a pair of Regency-era houses, The Mount Royale Hotel brings a country-house atmosphere to the city. The kitchen combines simple flavours to good effect. Save room for lemon pannacotta with milk ice cream, honey, almonds and oat crumb.

Chef Russell Johnson **Seats** 70, Private dining 18 **Open** All year **Prices from** S £5.95, M £14.50, D £7.50 **Parking** 15 **Notes** Children welcome

The Park Restaurant
⊛⊛⊛ MODERN, TRADITIONAL BRITISH V
01904 540903 | Marmadukes Town House Hotel, 4–5 St Peters Grove, Bootham, YO30 6AQ
www.marmadukestownhousehotelyork.com
Marmadukes is a boutique townhouse hotel of the latest vintage, conjured from a Victorian gentleman's residence a little way from the medieval city walls. Antique furniture fills the public spaces, and The Park Restaurant is a bright conservatory space with a skylight and glass frontage, grey wood tables and matching walls hung with modern artworks. The drill here is Adam Jackson's six-course dinner menu, an extended showcase of quality Yorkshire produce and the kind of ingredient-centred approach that brings the concentrated best out of all elements in a dish. Principal components of each course are listed on the menu, which might open with burrata, beetroot and balsamic, served with focaccia. Successful compositions include crisp-skinned mackerel partnered with pickled radish, peas and nasturtiums, a main dish of tenderly pink pork fillet, braised cheek and crackled ear with romanesco, tart apple and puréed cauliflower, and a simple but memorable dessert of chocolate parfait with cherry variations – puréed, macerated and dried sour fruits. For a supplement, there's the option of a cheese course, perhaps deliciously oozy Vacherin Mont d'Or with truffle honey.

Chef Adam Jackson **Seats** 28, Private dining 25 **Closed** 25–29 October and 1–16 January **Parking** 12 **Notes** No children

Skosh

◉◉ MODERN INTERNATIONAL

01904 634849 | 98 Micklegate, YO1 6JX

www.skoshyork.co.uk

Skosh has made a big splash on the local and national food radar. Occupying a former shop in central York, a slate grey and vivid yellow colour scheme adds a bright and cheery vibe, as does the jeans and T-shirt attire of the relaxed staff.

Chef Neil Bentinck **Seats** 45 **Closed** 25–26 December, 1 week January, May and September
Prices from S £5, M £10, D £3.50 **Notes** Vegetarian dishes, Children welcome

The Star Inn The City

◉ MODERN BRITISH

01904 619208 | Lendal Engine House, Museum Street, YO1 7DR

www.starinnthecity.co.uk

This former pump engine house in a stunning riverside setting in the centre of York has been redeveloped into a modern bustling restaurant. There are various dining spaces, including a terrace and a cellar.

Chef Matt Hunter **Seats** 140, Private dining 36
Open All year **Prices from** S £6, M £14, D £6
Notes Vegetarian dishes, Children welcome

▶ SOUTH YORKSHIRE

SHEFFIELD

Best Western Plus Aston Hall Hotel

◉ MODERN BRITISH V

0114 287 2309 | Worksop Road, Aston, S26 2EE

www.astonhallhotel.co.uk

Just a minute from the M1 and at the gateway to the Peak District, Aston Hall dates from 1772 but has been tastefully restored over the years. Surrounded by 55 acres of gardens, it's a magnificent and luxurious setting on the edge of Sheffield.

Chef Craig Simpson **Seats** 40, Private dining 40
Open All year **Parking** 100 **Notes** Children welcome

1855 Restaurant

◉ CONTEMPORARY BRITISH

0114 252 5480 | Copthorne Hotel Sheffield, Sheffield United Football Club, Bramall Lane, S2 4SU

www.millenniumhotels.co.uk/copthornesheffield

Bramall Lane, home of Sheffield United football club, is also home to the Copthorne Hotel. The stylishly contemporary 1855 Restaurant is close to the stadium and five minutes from The Crucible. The menu offers broad appeal and the modern British dishes have a pronounced Yorkshire accent.

Chef Mark Jones **Open** All year

Jöro Restaurant

◉◉◉ BRITISH, SCANDINAVIAN V

0114 299 1539 | Krynkl, 294 Shalesmoor, S3 8UL

www.jororestaurant.co.uk

A converted shipping container off a roundabout on the outskirts of Steel City doesn't sound too inviting a prospect, but Jöro's urban edginess is bang in tune with the contemporary trend for neo-Nordic-influenced eating. Inside, the space has a minimalist feel with barewood floors and tables decorated with flowers and baby vegetables, and the buzz of an open kitchen adding to the convivial vibe. Despite the urban surrounds, the kitchen team maintains a close bond to nature, working with local farms and foragers to provide a steady flow of seasonal materials – a 'surprise' box from one vegetable supplier means the kitchen builds the menus around what turns up that week and the small plate concept encourages diners to try a salvo of different dishes. Expect pin-sharp techniques and combinations that pack a punch, starting with a perfect piece of mackerel in miso-boosted broth alongside kohlrabi pickled in buttermilk whey, intensely sweet and smoky wood-fired onions, and roasted yeast purée. Salt-baked celeriac Lincolnshire poacher cheese, black truffle and elder capers is another winning partnership, followed by mallard with red cabbage ketchup and blackcurrant jam. The good ideas flow through to a sweet dish uniting brown butter and muscovado parfait with parkin, apple and Pedro Ximenez jam.

Chef Luke French **Seats** 40 **Closed** 15–21 April, 22–28 July, 16–22 September, 1–15 January (2019)
Prices from S £5.50, M £15, D £5.50 **Notes** Children welcome

Nonnas

◉ MODERN ITALIAN V

0114 268 6166 | 535–541 Ecclesall Road, S11 8PR

www.nonnas.co.uk

Nonnas is a bustling, good-natured Italian restaurant with friendly staff, café-style marble-topped tables and green walls. This is an imaginative kitchen turning out properly cooked, highly original dishes. Inspired puddings have included chocolate and beetroot cake with sweet beetroot and balsamic ripple ice cream.

Chef Ross Sayles **Seats** 80, Private dining 30
Closed 25 December and 1 January
Prices from S £5.75, M £14, D £7 **Notes** Children welcome

Rafters Restaurant
◉◉ MODERN BRITISH
0114 230 4819 | 220 Oakbrook Road,
Nethergreen, S11 7ED
www.raftersrestaurant.co.uk

After more than two decades, Rafters continues to
deliver the goods as a Sheffield dining hotspot.
Located on the first floor of a shop in a leafy
neighbourhood, the contemporary, grey-hued room is
smart and formal, while the set menu is packed with
interesting combinations.

Chef Thomas Lawson **Seats** 34 **Closed** 25–27
December, 1–9 January, 27 August to 4 September
Notes Vegetarian dishes, No children under 10 years

Whitley Hall Hotel
◉◉ MODERN BRITISH
0114 245 4444 | Elliott Lane, Grenoside, S35 8NR
www.whitleyhall.com

Surrounded by rolling countryside, Whitley Hall is a
solid stone mansion dating from the 16th century, set
in 20 acres of immaculate grounds. The restaurant
may have a whiff of formality, but the kitchen keeps
ahead of the game with a thoroughly modern menu.

Chef Ian Spivey **Seats** 80, Private dining 16 **Open** All
year **Prices from** S £8.95, M £19.95, D £7.50
Parking 80 **Notes** Vegetarian dishes, Children welcome

WORTLEY
Ruddy Duck Restaurant
◉◉ BRITISH
0114 2882100 | Wortley Hall, S35 7DB
www.wortleyhall.org.uk

Wortley Hall is a grand Regency building in golden
stone, with pillars and portico, set in 26 acres of lovely
gardens and splendid parkland. The walled garden
provides some of the fruit and veg used in the
restaurant, where modern British cooking is
underpinned by classic techniques.

Chef Matt Robinson **Seats** Private dining
Closed 25–26 December and 1 January **Parking** 40
Notes Vegetarian dishes

The Wortley Arms
◉ MODERN BRITISH V
0114 288 8749 | Halifax Road, S35 7DB
www.wortley-arms.co.uk

The Wortley Arms is an appealing spot for a pint of local
ale and some modern gastro-pub cooking. Timeless
staples (beer-battered fish and chips with home-made
tartare sauce, or gammon steak with griddled
pineapple) rub shoulders with more up-to-date ideas.

Chef Andy Gabbitas **Seats** 80, Private dining 12
Open All year **Parking** 30 **Notes** Children welcome

▶ WEST YORKSHIRE
BRADFORD
Prashad
◉◉ INDIAN VEGETARIAN V
0113 285 2037 | 137 Whitehall Road, Drighlington,
BD11 1AT
www.prashad.co.uk

There is strong competition in Bradford when it comes
to authentic Indian cooking, but Prashad's meat-free
repertoire ensures a loyal local following. The food
has its roots in the vegetarian cuisine of the Gujarat.

Chef Minal Patel **Seats** 75, Private dining 10 **Closed** 25
December **Parking** 26 **Notes** Children welcome

HALIFAX
Holdsworth House Hotel
◉◉ TRADITIONAL BRITISH
01422 240024 | Holdsworth Road, Holmfield, HX2 9TG
www.holdsworthhouse.co.uk

Built during the reign of Charles I, Holdsworth House
looks fit for a king with its handsome creeper-covered
facade and charming period interior. Sunday lunches
are classic, afternoon tea is the real deal, and the grill
cooks steaks, lamb rump, pork chop and the like.

Chef Simon Dyson **Seats** 45, Private dining 120
Open All year **Prices from** S £6.50, M £14.95, D £7.95
Parking 60 **Notes** Vegetarian dishes, Children welcome

Shibden Mill Inn
◉◉ MODERN BRITISH V
01422 365840 | Shibden Mill Fold, Shibden, HX3 7UL
www.shibdenmillinn.com

A corn and spinning mill in the 17th century, this inn is
the sort of place we'd all like as our local: a warren of
rooms with beams, exposed stone, and mismatched
tables and chairs. Service is friendly and the kitchen
turns out an inviting menu.

Chef Adam Harvey **Seats** 50, Private dining 12
Closed Christmas **Parking** 60 **Notes** Children welcome
See advertisement on page 354

HUDDERSFIELD
315 Bar and Restaurant
◉◉ MODERN V
01484 602613 | 315 Wakefield Road, Lepton, HD8 0LX
www.315barandrestaurant.co.uk

This place brings a touch of metropolitan chic to
Huddersfield. The menu bursts with bright, modern
ideas. The main courses are no less original and
puddings are attractively presented.

Chef Jason Neilson **Seats** 90, Private dining 115
Open All year **Prices from** S £5, M £12.50, D £6.95
Parking 97 **Notes** Children welcome

www.shibdenmillinn.com

Nestling in the fold of West Yorkshire's picturesque Shibden Vall

For over 350 years *The Shibden Mill Inn* has been at the heart of life i
West Yorkshire's Shibden Valley. It's a magical place where generation
after generation of locals have enjoyed time well spent with friends an
family, sharing in life's special moments and shaping memories
to last a life time.

The inn's reputation for warm hospitality, premier 2 Rosette gastro dini
and 5 Star Inn accommodation draws people to the Shibden Valley fro
far and wide, and the Mill has naturally become a popular choice for
those wishing to savour a sumptuous weekend break or mid-week sta

Stunning countryside walks are in easy reach, as too are the bright ligh
and city centre shopping on offer in Leeds. From its unique location,
Shibden Mill Inn offers easy access to the very best to be found in this
delightful part of West Yorkshire.

Opening times for breakfast, morning coffee & cake, afternoon teas,
lunch and dinner can be found on the food page of the website:
www. shibdenmillinn.com

Tel. 01422 365840
enquiries@shibdenmillinn.co.uk
www.shibdenmillinn.co.uk

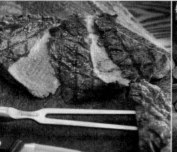

ILKLEY

Box Tree
◉◉◉ MODERN, TRADITIONAL FRENCH NOTABLE WINE LIST
01943 608484 | 35–37 Church Street, LS29 9DR
www.theboxtree.co.uk

A name to conjure with since first opening as a restaurant in the 1960s, this traditional stone building, one of the oldest in Ilkley, is recognisable by its jolly hanging baskets and flower-filled front garden (it won 'Ilkley in Bloom' in 2017). Inside it's equally traditional – no pale contemporary tones here – it's all antiques, curly light fittings and ornately framed paintings, giving a richly luxurious feel. Simon Gueller's classically inspired food, though, is bang on and firmly up to date, with refined dishes showing an elegant grasp of modern French style. Dinner might begin with a delicious amuse bouche of spiced parsnip velouté with salted apple, followed by a starter of east coast mackerel, Whitby crab, and heritage beetroot, or butter-roasted cauliflower, hazelnut, winter truffle, cauliflower and coconut purée. Main course fillet of turbot comes with leek fondue, silky parmesan pommes mousseline, crosnes and jus noisette. Dishes are beautifully presented and flavours clear and uncluttered. At dessert, look out for the seasonal soufflés – prune and Armagnac is a warming winter version, accompanied with crème anglaise.

Chef Simon Gueller, Kieran Smith **Seats** 50, Private dining 20 **Closed** 27–31 December, 1–7 January **Prices from** M £70 **Notes** Vegetarian dishes, No children under 5 years at lunch, 10 years at dinner

LEEDS

Calverley Grill
◉ MODERN BRITISH V
0113 282 1000 | Rothwell Lane, Oulton, LS26 8HN
www.qhotels.co.uk/oultonhall

Surrounded by beautiful Yorkshire countryside, this handsome 18th-century mansion is well positioned for junction 30 of the M62. Named after the championship golf course outside, the elegant Calverley Grill is at the heart of the hotel and offers a seaonsal and soundly conceived British menu.

Chef Stephen Collinson **Seats** 150 **Open** All year **Prices from** S £6, M £14, D £7 **Parking** 300 **Notes** Children welcome

Chez Mal Brasserie
◉ MODERN BRITISH
0113 398 1000 | 1 Swinegate, LS1 4AG
www.malmaison.com

The Malmaison group's Leeds branch is decorated and furnished to a high standard after refurbishment and the brasserie is no exception, with plush leather booths and fireplaces under its elegant ceiling. The cooking is built on quality ingredients, and talented professionals are clearly at work.

Chef Simon Silver **Seats** 85, Private dining 12 **Open** All year **Notes** Vegetarian dishes, Children welcome

Fourth Floor Café
◉ BRITISH, MODERN MEDITERRANEAN
0113 204 8888 | 107–111 Briggate, LS1 6AZ
www.harveynichols.com/restaurant/leeds-dining

As the name suggests, the restaurant is located on the fourth floor and it has a similarly chic, minimalist style as other in-store restaurants in the Harvey Nichols collection. The gold-clad dining area is flanked by the bar and an open kitchen.

Chef Lee Heptinstall **Seats** 70 **Closed** 25 December, 1 January, Easter Sunday **Notes** Vegetarian dishes, Children welcome

The Man Behind The Curtain
◉◉◉◉ MODERN EUROPEAN V
0113 243 2376 | 68–78 Vicar Lane, Lower Ground Floor Flannels, LS1 7JH
www.themanbehindthecurtain.co.uk

The determinedly monochrome basement room of Michael O'Hare's contemporary restaurant is in stark contrast to the culinary approach. While black marble tables and floor tiles offset the grey-veined walls, which are lightened with vertical displays of skateboards, marble surfboards and scrawls of incoherent graffiti, the black-shaded lamps illuminate plates – and many another receptacle – of cutting-edge experimental food that manages to avoid a lot of what have become the modern clichés. The standard offering is a taster of 10 to 14 'sequences', with a digested version at lunchtime, built around a repertoire of dazzlingly imaginative dishes. A single octopus tentacle in butter emulsion has a strong hit of paprika, while a pâté of perfect crab is balanced on a crisp cracker and topped with a quail egg. Coarsely sliced, eloquently fatted Wagyu beef in olive juice with a sheet of potato paper is extraordinary in its impact, and the delicacy of judgment extends to a hake dumpling covered in hair-fine filaments of chilli for discreet heat. A dish that proved controversial on the BBC's *Great British Menu*, O'Hare's fish and chips, is a model of concentrated refinement, expressively flavoured cod in miso broth with salt-and-vinegar straw potatoes, while a new spin on Rossini made with ox cheek is full of savoury, sticky richness. Creativity is unflagging to the end, which might feature milk chocolate mousse with honey and violet ice cream, cardamom and lemongrass soup with chilli sorbet, or potato puffs sprinkled with beetroot powder. It's all served forth to a soundtrack of throbbing rock.

Chef Michael O'Hare **Seats** 42 **Closed** 21 December to 13 January **Notes** No children

Salvo's Restaurant & Salumeria
◉ ITALIAN
0113 275 5017 | 115 Otley Road, Headingley, LS6 3PX
www.salvos.co.uk
Salvo's is a lively, family-friendly and family-run restaurant that will sort you out for some rustic and hearty Italian cooking. If you come for a pizza or a plate of pasta, you are spoiled for choice and won't leave disappointed. But there's much more besides.

Chef Geppino Dammone, Oliver Edwards **Seats** 88, Private dining 24 **Closed** 25–26 December and 1 January **Prices from** S £5, M £8.50, D £5.50 **Notes** Vegetarian dishes, Children welcome

Thorpe Park Hotel & Spa
◉ BRITISH, FRENCH
0113 264 1000 | Century Way, Thorpe Park, LS15 8ZB
www.thwaites.co.uk/hotels-and-inns/hotels/thorpe-park-hotel-leeds
With quick access into Leeds or the countryside, the modern Thorpe Park Hotel is a handy base for exploring the area. The split-level dining room has a contemporary finish with artwork on the walls and black leather-type chairs. The populist menu offers feel-good stuff.

Chef Paul Woodward **Seats** 120, Private dining 50 **Open** All year **Parking** 200 **Notes** Children welcome

LIVERSEDGE
Healds Hall Hotel & Restaurant
◉ MODERN BRITISH
01924 409112 | Leeds Road, WF15 6JA
www.healdshall.co.uk
This stone-built, family-owned hotel is definitely worth leaving the M62 for, in order to dine in either the open-plan Bistro or its conservatory extension, furnished with wicker-style chairs and tables with tea lights. There's a more formal restaurant, which fills up on busy evenings.

Chef Andrew Ward **Seats** 46, Private dining 30 **Closed** 27–29 December, 1 January, Bank holidays **Parking** 50 **Notes** Vegetarian dishes, Children welcome

PONTEFRACT
Wentbridge House Hotel
◉◉ MODERN BRITISH V ♦ NOTABLE WINE LIST
01977 620444 | The Great North Road, Wentbridge, WF8 3JJ
www.wentbridgehouse.co.uk
Set in 20 acres of landscaped grounds in a West Yorkshire conservation village, Wentbridge is a stone-built grand manor house. There's a degree of glossy formality, where candy-coloured upholstery creates a light, bright effect, and the cooking reaches out in all directions for its references.

Chef Ian Booth **Seats** 60, Private dining 36 **Open** All year **Prices from** S £6.95, M £15.95, D £5.95 **Parking** 100 **Notes** Children welcome

WAKEFIELD
Waterton Park Hotel
◉ MODERN, TRADITIONAL BRITISH V
01924 257911 | Walton Hall, The Balk, Walton, WF2 6PW
www.watertonparkhotel.co.uk
This Georgian hotel stands on an island in a 26-acre lake, with a modern extension on the shore accessed via a bridge, which explains how the attractive Bridgewalk restaurant was named. Dishes are admirably understated and flavours are to the fore.

Chef Armstrong Wgabi **Seats** 50, Private dining 40 **Open** All year **Parking** 200 **Notes** Children welcome

WETHERBY
Wood Hall Hotel & Spa
◉◉ MODERN BRITISH V
01937 587271 | Trip Lane, Linton, LS22 4JA
www.handpickedhotels.co.uk/woodhall
High on a hill with fine views, the Georgian Wood Hall retains much of its original detailing. Its dining room is an elegant, relaxing space where a rigorous dedication to Yorkshire produce is observed, and the cooking is marked by clear, distinct flavours.

Chef Rohan Nevins **Seats** 40, Private dining 100 **Open** All year **Parking** 100 **Notes** Children welcome

CHANNEL ISLANDS

▶ GUERNSEY

ST MARTIN
The Auberge
◉◉ MODERN BRITISH
01481 238485 | Jerbourg Road, GY4 6BH
www.theauberge.gg
A clifftop position overlooking the neighbouring islands draws people to this sleek contemporary restaurant near St Peter Port. The menu is big on fish and seafood, as in the Guernsey crab and cold-water prawn tian, bois boudran dressing and pickled cucumber and avocado purée.

Chef Pavel Florin **Seats** 70, Private dining 20 **Closed** 25–26 December, 1 January **Prices from** S £5, M £12.80, D £6.80 **Parking** 30 **Notes** Vegetarian dishes, Children welcome

La Barbarie Hotel
◉ TRADITIONAL BRITISH
01481 235217 | Saints Road, Saints Bay, GY4 6ES
www.labarbariehotel.com
This former priory is now a comfortable hotel with a soothing vibe and a restaurant that uses the fresh produce of Guernsey's coasts and meadows. The kitchen looks to the French mainland for inspiration in their repertoire of simply cooked and presented dishes.

Chef Colin Pearson **Seats** 70 **Closed** mid November to mid March **Prices from** S £6.95, M £13.25, D £5.95 **Parking** 50 **Notes** Vegetarian dishes, Children welcome

Bella Luce Hotel, Restaurant & Spa
◉◉ FRENCH, MEDITERRANEAN **V**
01481 238764 | La Fosse, GY4 6EB
www.bellalucehotel.com
With its 12th-century granite walls, period charm and luxe boutique finish, Bella Luce is a class act. The culinary action takes place in the romantic restaurant, where there's some sharp, contemporary European cooking built on a good showing of local produce.

Chef Seb Orzechowski, Seb Laskowy, Richard Waller, Chris Harworth, Simon MacKenzie **Seats** 70, Private dining 20 **Closed** 2–22 January **Parking** 38 **Notes** Children welcome

ST PETER PORT
The Duke of Richmond Hotel
◉ MODERN, BRITISH, FRENCH
01481 726221 | Cambridge Park, GY1 1UY
www.dukeofrichmond.com
The Leopard Bar and Restaurant, with its distinctive style and excellent quality ingredients, has developed a unique identity. Guests might choose to dine al fresco on the large terrace, but those who dine inside will have a view through to the open kitchen.

Chef Rafal Baranski **Seats** 90, Private dining 25 **Closed** 1st 6 weeks after New Year **Prices from** S £8, M £14 **Parking** 5 **Notes** Vegetarian dishes, Children welcome

GUERNSEY–HERM–JERSEY

The Old Government House Hotel & Spa
MODERN EUROPEAN
01481 724921 | St Ann's Place, GY1 2NU
www.theoghhotel.com
The beautiful white Georgian building was once the island governor's harbourside residence, converted into a hotel in 1858. Among several dining options at the hotel, The Brasserie is the place to be, offering fresh Guernsey fish as part of the menu.
Chef Robert Newall **Seats** 60, Private dining 12 **Open** All year **Prices from** S £9, M £18, D £9 **Notes** Vegetarian dishes, Children welcome

St Pierre Park Hotel, Spa and Golf Resort
BRITISH
01481 736676 | Rohais, GY1 1FD
www.handpickedhotels.co.uk
One mile from St Peter Port, this peaceful hotel is surrounded by 35 acres of grounds and a nine-hole golf course. Overlooking the garden and with its own terrace and water feature, the bright, contemporary Pavilion Restaurant offers something for everybody.
Chef Aaron Sarre **Seats** 70 **Open** All year **Parking** **Notes** Vegetarian dishes, Children welcome

▶ HERM

HERM
White House Hotel
EUROPEAN, TRADITIONAL BRITISH V
01481 750000 | GY1 3HR
www.herm.com
The island's only hotel is a real time-warp experience, dispensing with TVs, phones and clocks. Every table has a sea view in the Conservatory Restaurant, where pin-sharp technique and peerless raw materials combine to impressive effect in the contemporary European menu.
Chef David Hook **Seats** 100, Private dining 12 **Closed** November to April **Notes** Children welcome

▶ JERSEY

GOREY
The Moorings Hotel & Restaurant
TRADITIONAL
01534 853633 | Gorey Pier, JE3 6EW
www.themooringshotel.com
Smack on Gorey's picturesque harbour front, The Moorings has a continental feel with its pavement terrace overlooking the sea and the ruins of Mont Orgueil Castle. With the smell of the sea in the air, it's no surprise to see plenty of local seafood.
Chef Simon Walker **Seats** 65, Private dining 35 **Open** All year **Notes** Vegetarian dishes, Children welcome

Sumas
MODERN BRITISH V
01534 853291 | Gorey Hill, JE3 6ET
www.sumasrestaurant.com
Overlooking the harbour, and with fab views of Mont Orgueil, terrace tables at Sumas are in high demand when the sun shines. Needless to say, there's plenty of seafood on the menu, from local hand-dived scallops to brill or crab ravioli. There's a vegan menu too.
Chef Dany Lancaster **Seats** 40 **Closed** late December to mid January (approximately) **Prices from** S £8, M £16.50, D £2 **Notes** Children welcome

ROZEL
Château la Chaire
CLASSIC TRADITIONAL V
01534 863354 | Rozel Bay, JE3 6AJ
www.chateau-la-chaire.co.uk
Snuggled into a wooded valley, and yet only moments from the seashore, La Chaire is an early Victorian edifice with grounds laid out by the Kew Gardens luminary Samuel Curtis, and interiors full of oak panelling and intricate plaster scrollwork. A newly added conservatory dining room extension capitalises fully on the majestic green views. Marcin Ciechomski's menus make a strong feature of the island's bounteous seafood, as well as plenty of locally grown fresh produce in dishes that have potent impact. A perfectly constructed first course of ham hock and foie gras croquette on crushed peas comes with Serrano ham, apple purée and a piece of crackling to keep the palate engaged, before main course might deliver roasted monkfish with cannellini beans, chorizo and basil gnocchi, or fine Barbary duck breast with super dripping-cooked potatoes and red wine shallots in whisky jus. A thick-shelled custard tart is garnished with blackberries and pear sorbet for a bravura finish, or there may be dark chocolate ganache with confit lemon, yogurt sorbet and clementine purée, if the fully loaded cheese trolley doesn't distract you.
Chef Marcin Ciechomski **Seats** 60, Private dining 28 **Open** All year **Prices from** S £8.95, M £22.95, D £8.95 **Parking** 30 **Notes** Children welcome

ST AUBIN
The Boat House
◉ BRITISH
01534 744226 | 1 North Quay, JE3 8BS
www.theboathousegroup.com
With its full-drop glass walls overlooking the harbour and town, The Boat House has staked its claim to the best spot in St Aubin. Light and airy with an open kitchen, the first-floor restaurant celebrates fresh, Jersey produce, mixing fine ingredients and confident technique.

Chef Filipe Vieira Ribeiro

ST BRELADE
L'Horizon Beach Hotel and Spa
◉◉ MODERN BRITISH
01534 743101 | St Brelade's Bay, JE3 8EF
www.handpickedhotels.co.uk/lhorizon
The view over the bay is a big draw here but the Grill restaurant really puts the place on the map. It's a smart room with neutral colours, and a menu making excellent use of the island's bounty, in bright, modern dishes.

Chef Andrew Soddy **Seats** 44, Private dining 300 **Open** All year **Prices from** S £9.50, M £22.50, D £8.50 **Parking** 70 **Notes** Vegetarian dishes, Children welcome

Ocean Restaurant at The Atlantic Hotel
◉◉◉ MODERN BRITISH V ⓘ NOTABLE WINE LIST
01534 744101 | Le Mont de la Pulente, JE3 8HE
www.theatlantichotel.com
There is a timelessness to a sea view of which it is impossible to tire, and the prospect over the hotel gardens to the blue briny beyond from the louvred windows of the Ocean Restaurant is the jewel in the crown of The Atlantic Hotel. Staff run the place with well-polished pride, doing things properly without pomp or undue circumstance, and new chef Will Holland capably maintains the stellar culinary reputation the place enjoys. A taste of the sea is a virtual must, seen to great distinction in an opener of accurately seared scallops with salt cod brandade, carrot remoulade and sweet-and-sour carrot purée, a sensational marriage of sweet and salty savour. That could be followed by tenderly juniper-roasted venison loin with a breaded bonbon of the meat, smoked bacon choucroute, salsify and pickled blueberries, in a glossy, deeply resonant bitter chocolate jus. The showstopping finale is an apple study combining fresh diced fruit, flavoured marshmallow, sorbet and a tuile with praline crémeux and layered almond dacquoise. Chocoholics will gravitate to cacao streusel coated with Guanaja, with 70% chocolate gelée and coffee ice cream.

Chef Will Holland **Seats** 60, Private dining 60 **Closed** January **Parking** 60 **Notes** Children welcome

Oyster Box
◉◉ MODERN BRITISH
01534 850888 | St Brelade's Bay, JE3 8EF
www.oysterbox.co.uk
The views of St Brelade's Bay are unbeatable from the Oyster Box, whether you're dining on the terrace or in the cool, contemporary dining room. If you can resist grilled lobster with garlic butter and chancre crab with mayonnaise, there may be brill 'chop'.

Chef Tony Dorris **Seats** 100 **Closed** 25–26 December **Notes** Vegetarian dishes, Children welcome

ST CLEMENT
Green Island Restaurant
◉ MEDITERRANEAN SEAFOOD
01534 857787 | Green Island, JE2 6LS
www.greenisland.je
This laid-back beach café and restaurant claims to be the most southerly eatery in the British Isles, so kick back and bask in sun-kissed views over the sandy bay. The emphasis is on fish and shellfish, and the kitchen treats them with a light touch.

Chef Paul Insley **Seats** 40 **Closed** Christmas, New Year, January **Parking** 20 **Notes** Vegetarian dishes, Children welcome

ST HELIER
Best Western Royal Hotel
◉ MODERN EUROPEAN
01534 726521 | David Place, JE2 4TD
www.morvanhotels.com
In the hotel's Seasons restaurant, a predominantly white colour scheme, with lightwood flooring, flowers on the tables and comfortable leather chairs, creates a coolly elegant atmosphere, appropriate surroundings for some polished cooking. A decent choice of bread, all made on the premises, is offered.

Chef Robert Scott **Seats** 90, Private dining 12 **Open** All year **Parking** 14 **Notes** Vegetarian dishes, Children welcome

JERSEY

Bohemia Restaurant

🏵🏵🏵🏵🏵 MODERN FRENCH, BRITISH **V** 🍷NOTABLE WINE LIST

01534 880588 | The Club Hotel & Spa, Green Street, JE2 4UH

www.bohemiajersey.com

Not far from the Maritime Museum, The Club Hotel and Spa is poised to dispense refreshment of all kinds, from gentle abrasions of the skin to wholesale seductions of the palate. Cocktail masterclasses for budding shakers and stirrers are a must, and the bountiful views from the rooftop bar terrace offer the best kind of orientation. When it comes to dining, a booth-style table on the edge of the kitchen action will be a strong draw, and there are more private dining spaces than you can shake a cocktail stick at. The core of the operation, though, is the Bohemia Restaurant, where against a gently lit background of sleek wood and scribbly patterned banquettes, Steve Smith continues to produce the most outstanding food in the Channel Islands. At its root, this is classic cooking, but excitingly reworked to create novel and innovative dishes. Everything on the menus is ingredient-led, utilising thoroughbred produce. Execution is sharp and precise, with bold flavours that can be complex, but are always carefully considered. The first consideration is to decide what you want to eat: the multi-course tasters are classified according to vegetable, fish and omni regimens, with a Prestige Menu of nine courses (plus the option of Bordier's artisan cheeses). Whichever route you opt for, there are discoveries to be made. The vegetarian menu might centre on successive courses of Roscoff onion with chanterelles and kale, and then a composition of heritage carrots, sea veg and citrussy sea buckthorn, while fish builds through the wonderful crab custard tart with mango and coriander, followed by sea bass and smoked eel with rock samphire (the choicest kind), leading to turbot and mussels, with more of that abundant sea buckthorn. At the Prestige tables by then, they could be on to a serving of Goosnargh duck glazed in blood orange with chicory and medjool dates, having earlier been treated to a showstopping steak tartare made with Belted Galloway beef, its fatty richness counterpointed by raisins and capers. Calling a Kir Royale a pre-dessert sounds like the best kind of euphemism, while the dessert dishes themselves play variations on spiced apple and blackberry, or cranberries, lychees and lime spiked with rose-attar Lanique liqueur.

Chef Steve Smith **Seats** 60, Private dining 24 **Closed** 24–30 December **Prices from** S £17.50, M £35, D £12.50 **Notes** Children welcome

Doran's Courtyard Bistro

🏵 BRITISH, FRENCH, STEAKS, SEAFOOD

01534 734866 | The Hotel Revere, Kensington Place, JE2 3PA

www.reverehoteljersey.com

It's easy to see why Doran's is popular with the locals as well as with guests staying at The Hotel Revere. Service is relaxed in the cosy restaurant with stone-flagged floors and exposed oak beams, and the menu is simple but well done.

Chef Krzysztof Kuczynski **Seats** 50 **Closed** Christmas, New Year, Bank holidays **Prices from** S £6.50, M £13.95, D £4.95 **Notes** Vegetarian dishes, Children welcome

Hampshire Hotel

🏵 MEDITERRANEAN

01534 724115 | 53 Val Plaisant, JE2 4TB

www.hampshirehotel.je

The Hampshire Hotel has a contemporary restaurant sporting a colonial look with rattan chairs, ceiling fans and pot plants. There are simple steaks as well as more refined options and a terrific value daily menu, with desserts running to the likes of sticky toffee pudding.

Chef Edwin Ombunah **Seats** 100 **Open** All year **Parking** 28 **Notes** Vegetarian dishes, Children welcome

Restaurant Sirocco@The Royal Yacht

🏵🏵🏵 MODERN BRITISH

See pages 362–363

See advertisement on page 364

Samphire

🏵🏵🏵 MODERN EUROPEAN **V** 🍷NOTABLE WINE LIST

01534 725100 | 7–11 Don Street, JE2 4TQ

www.samphire.je

Gorgeously done out with clean art deco-style lines worthy of a 1920s ocean liner, Samphire looks stunning with its wooden floors, plush blue velvet banquettes and mustard yellow leather seating, and darkwood tables simply decorated with small lamps. There's a lively ground-floor bar, a see-and-be-seen terrace on the street out front and, up on the roof, a garden terrace for those balmy Jersey days. And so to the food: head chef Lee Smith's menus showcase the island's finest materials in modern European dishes that are memorable for their depth of natural flavour and beautiful presentation – Jersey lobster ravioli deftly aromatised with ginger and coriander and boosted with rich crab and tomato bisque and puffed black rice making a thrilling starter. Next up, a posh surf and turf pairing brings spanking fresh brill and the powerful meaty punch of glazed pig's cheek matched with celeriac and parsley. Attention to detail is spot-on, all the way through to a masterfully executed tangerine baked Alaska with chocolate and cardamom ice cream and the clean citrussy hit of kumquat and orange curd.

Chef Lee Smith **Seats** 50, Private dining 14 **Closed** 25 December **Prices from** S £9, M £16, D £9 **Notes** Children welcome

Tassili

⊚⊚⊚⊚ BRITISH, FRENCH **V**

01534 722301 | Grand Jersey, The Esplanade, JE2 3QA
www.handpickedhotels.co.uk/grandjersey

The Grand Jersey is a rather splendid late-Victorian hotel with all the glamour and confidence of the Belle Epoque. There are wonderful views from the terrace, just a stone's throw from the waters of St Aubin's Bay, and a deeply indulgent spa. But that's all a bonus – you're here for the food. The restaurant, Tassili, is a darkly luxurious space that comes into its own in the evenings. Service is excellent, with a great eye for detail, and you can expect high-level French technique from Nicolas Valmagna and his team, taking inspiration from the island's produce and ideas from further afield. A starter of Scottish langoustine (a hugely plump, fresh example) with asparagus and morels is a fine spring dish, and perfectly timed turbot is an equally well-conceived main course, accompanied by saffron risotto, mussels, wonderful sea vegetables and a squid ink crisp. Moving on, a pre-dessert of almond ice and blood orange is a great introduction to dessert proper – Valrhona chocolate pistachio cake with yuzu cremeaux and chocolate sorbet proving a truly brilliant combination of flavours and textures.

Chef Nicolas Valmagna **Seats** 24 **Closed** 25 December, 1–30 January **Parking** 32 **Notes** No children under 12 years

ST PETER
Greenhills Country Hotel

⊚ MODERN MEDITERRANEAN, BRITISH, FRENCH

01534 481042 | Mont de L'Ecole, JE3 7EL
www.greenhillshotel.com

There is much to admire about this relaxed country hotel with its riotously colourful gardens, heated outdoor pool and bags of traditional charm. The kitchen team turns out a wide-ranging menu taking in everything from a classic straight-up fillet steak to more ambitious ideas.

Chef Lukasz Pietrasz **Seats** 90, Private dining 40 **Closed** 17 December to 9 February **Prices from** S £6, M £15.50, D £4.95 **Parking** 45 **Notes** Vegetarian dishes, Children welcome

Mark Jordan at the Beach

⊚⊚ ANGLO FRENCH

01534 780180 | La Plage, La Route de la Haule, JE3 7YD
www.markjordanatthebeach.com

A pleasant white-walled space with wicker chairs and fish pictures gives you a clue as to what the forte is. But you won't be neglected if you're set on meat, with the likes of honey-roasted duck breast with griottine cherries. The style is contemporary Anglo-French.

Chef Mark Jordan **Seats** 50 **Closed** 23 December to 15 January **Prices from** S £7.50, M £15.50, D £7.50 **Parking** 16 **Notes** Vegetarian dishes, Children welcome

ST SAVIOUR
Longueville Manor Hotel

⊚⊚⊚ MODERN ANGLO-FRENCH **V** ♨ NOTABLE WINE LIST

01534 725501 | JE2 7WF
www.longuevillemanor.com

Set on a lovely 18-acre estate, with woodland walks, restored Victorian kitchen garden, and a lake, Longueville Manor has been the grande dame of the Jersey hotel scene since the 1940s. Andrew Baird's kitchen focuses on local produce – plenty of which comes from that beautiful kitchen garden – and the cooking is a refined, innovative Anglo-French take on classic techniques. The Oak Room is a wonderfully atmospheric panelled dining room, a delightful setting for compelling dishes inspired by wonderful produce. Grilled hand-dived scallops with garden shoots, potato rösti, crisp pancetta, cauliflower and truffle is a well-balanced starter with great textural contrast, while a main course of grilled fillet of Angus beef with slow-cooked sticky rib showcases very good quality meat, accompanied by an oxtail bon bon which is 'packed with goodness', along with tartiflette potato and béarnaise sauce. For dessert, keep things local with Longueville honey with Jersey milk pannacotta, honeycomb and Jersey milk sorbet. The new state-of-the-art wine cellar, home to some 4,000 bottles, needs to be seen to be believed.

Chef Andrew Baird **Seats** 65, Private dining 40 **Open** All year **Parking** 45 **Notes** Children welcome

JERSEY

ST HELIER
Restaurant Sirocco@The Royal Yacht
◉◉◉ MODERN BRITISH
01534 720511 | The Weighbridge, JE2 3NF
www.theroyalyacht.com

Bright Jersey cooking with harbour view

If you're thinking 'floating restaurant', you're on the wrong course with this royal yacht, although the waters of the marina are glittering below, and its curvaceous, wave-shaped balconies do lend a maritime air to the glossy harbourfront bolt-hole. It's a slick, upmarket affair, with expanses of plate glass facing the harbour, and high-end facilities including a glitzy spa centre to pamper away the cares of the world, plus ample dining and drinking opportunities to keep you refueled and refreshed, running from a grill restaurant to the casual all-day Zephyr eatery, the pick of the bunch being the snazzy Sirocco with its huge terrace opening up sweeping views over the harbour through full-drop windows. A cosmopolitan ambience and designer chic looks conjure a fittingly slick setting for pin-sharp modern British cooking.

Steve Walker's menus are big on flavour and technical panache and put together with an acute eye on the seasons. A starter of succulent seared scallops comes in a feisty surf and turf pairing with oxtail, alongside silky cauliflower purée and cheddar cheese beignet.

As you would hope in the island setting, fish gets star billing among main courses – witness a luxurious partnership of well-timed turbot, scattered with pistachio crumb, and a sweet medallion of lobster supported by puréed and caramelised Jerusalem artichoke, or perhaps a classic treatment of Dover sole, simply grilled and served up with caper butter sauce and Jersey Royals. The kitchen also delivers well-rehearsed meat dishes in which prime ingredients and sympathetic combinations produce seductive results – perhaps tender cannon of lamb with potato terrine, peas, lamb's lettuce and onions, or if you're a sucker for timeless tableside theatre, go for a classic steak Diane, flambéed at the table and partnered with Lyonnaise potatoes and green beans. Desserts are also handled with impressive dexterity, as seen in a zesty tropical alliance of super-light coconut mousse with passionfruit ice cream, fresh mango and meringue. If you don't want to envy your partner's pudding, two might go for a sharing assiette and have a taste of everything or conclude on a savoury note with a plate of expertly ripened local, British and continental cheeses. The evident balance and thoughtful composition in the food is reflected in a pedigree wine list that takes off in France then spreads its wings around carefully chosen bottles from all over the world, with a couple of dozen by the glass.

Chef Steve Walker **Seats** 65, Private dining 20 **Open** All year **Prices from** S £9.50, M £17.50, D £9 **Notes** Vegetarian dishes, Children welcome

See advertisement on page 364

AWARD-WINNING
BRITISH CUISINE

With views out to the marina, Sirocco is the perfect setting for a relaxed meal with friends and family or an informal business dinner. Watch as head chef, Steve Walker and his team prepare contemporary dishes that burst with island flavour.

Choose à la carte or the three course table d'hôte menu; there's an exciting wine list to match. Sirocco is also open for delicious breakfasts, with dining available inside or out on the heated terrace. What's not to enjoy!

FIRST FLOOR
THE ROYAL YACHT

DINNER
7PM - 9.30PM
EVERY DAY

RESTAURANT
Sirocco

▶ SARK

SARK
La Sablonnerie
◉ MODERN, TRADITIONAL INTERNATIONAL
01481 832061 | Little Sark, GY10 1SD
www.sablonneriesark.com

Reaching this small hotel is an adventure: a horse-drawn carriage collects guests arriving on the ferry. The building itself is ancient, with beams and stone walls as evidence. Seafood draws the attention, from lobster to grilled fillets of sea bass.

Chef Colin Day **Seats** 39 **Closed** mid October to Easter
Prices from S £9.80, M £14.50, D £9.80
Notes Vegetarian dishes, Children welcome
See advertisement below

Stocks Hotel
◉◉ MODERN BRITISH
01481 832001 | GY10 1SD
www.stockshotel.com

One of only two hotels on the island, the family-owned Stocks is a tranquil bolt-hole with a comfortable country-house style. With its opulent drapes and white tablecloths, the panelled dining room provides a traditional and formal setting for the technically solid cooking that plays to the gallery. The kitchen has close links with local fishermen and farms so the menu is ingredient driven.

Chef Ben Smith, Dan Wood **Seats** 60, Private dining 12 **Closed** 2 January to 1 March
Prices from S £10.50, M £25, D £10.50 **Parking** 36
Notes Vegetarian dishes, Children welcome

SCOTLAND

▶ ABERDEEN

ABERDEEN

Chez Mal Brasserie

◉ MODERN FRENCH

01224 327370 | 49–53 Queens Road, AB15 4YP
www.malmaisonaberdeen.com

Built from the solid granite that gives the city its moniker, the Aberdeen Mal is suitably dashing, with boutique allure and a cool industrial-chic finish. The brasserie is at the heart of the operation, with an open-to-view kitchen revealing the Josper grill.

Chef John Burns **Seats** 120, Private dining 30
Open All year **Parking** 30 **Notes** Vegetarian dishes, Children welcome

Fusion

◉ INTERNATIONAL, EUROPEAN

01224 652959 | 10 North Silver Street, AB10 1RL
www.fusionbarbistro.com

Blurring the line between bar and restaurant, Fusion's upstairs Gallery restaurant is a chic spot to see and be seen in, with its seats upholstered in blackberry or grey, and stylish wall panels. The creative menu suits the upbeat vibe and staff deliver pin-sharp service.

Chef Murray Dawson **Seats** 50, Private dining 8
Closed Christmas (4 days), New Year (4 days)
Prices from S £7, M £14, D £7 **Notes** Vegetarian dishes, Children welcome

IX Restaurant

◉◉ MODERN SCOTTISH

01244 327777 | The Chester Hotel, 59–63 Queens Road, AB15 4YP
www.chester-hotel.com

The kitchen team behind this glossy contemporary grill are on a mission to be one of Aberdeen's top restaurants, and their switched-on menu is heading straight for that target. Happily, the food here is about great flavours rather than ego.

Chef Kevin Dalgleish **Seats** 85, Private dining 22
Open All year **Notes** Vegetarian dishes, Children welcome

Mercure Aberdeen Ardoe House Hotel & Spa

◉ MODERN SCOTTISH, FRENCH

01224 860600 | South Deeside Road, Blairs, AB12 5YP
www.mercure.com

The Scots certainly knew how to build grand houses in the 1870s. This once-staid old pile in 30 acres of grounds is now a smart hotel and spa with a jazzy contemporary look that extends to the sleekly designed Blair's Restaurant.

Chef Richard Yearnshire, Alan Clarke **Seats** 100, Private dining 25 **Open** All year **Parking** 90
Notes Vegetarian dishes, Children welcome

Moonfish Café
◉ MODERN BRITISH
01224 644166 | 9 Correction Wynd, AB10 1HP
www.moonfishcafe.co.uk

Chef-patron Brian McLeish was a finalist on *MasterChef: The Professionals* a few years back, although his Moonfish Café has been on the local foodie radar since 2004. It's a relaxed set-up, its pared-back looks enlivened by changing artworks and fish motifs on the large windows.

Chef Brian McLeish **Seats** 36 **Closed** 25–26 December, 1 January, 1st 2 weeks January **Notes** Vegetarian dishes, Children welcome

Norwood Hall Hotel
◉◉ MODERN BRITISH
01224 868951 | Garthdee Road, Cults, AB15 9FX
www.norwood-hall.co.uk

Built in 1881, Norwood is a magnificent Victorian mansion with all of its period grandeur – stained glass, grand fireplaces, oak panels – still present and correct. The restaurant is a suitably baronial oak-panelled room hung with tapestries, while cuisine is contemporary with a strong Scottish element.

Chef Roland Tokaji, Matthew Moore **Seats** 48, Private dining 180 **Open** All year **Prices from** S £7.50, M £18, D £9 **Parking** 120 **Notes** Vegetarian dishes, Children welcome

The Silver Darling
◉◉ FRENCH, SEAFOOD
01224 576229 | Pocra Quay, North Pier, AB11 5DQ
www.thesilverdarling.co.uk

As befits its location at the mouth of Aberdeen harbour, The Silver Darling focuses on seafood, and you can watch the trawlers come and go from the conservatory-style restaurant atop a stocky granite building. The kitchen produces menus of French-accented contemporary ideas.

Chef Didier Dejean **Seats** 50, Private dining 14 **Closed** Christmas to New Year **Notes** Vegetarian dishes, Children welcome

▶ ABERDEENSHIRE

BALLATER
Loch Kinord Hotel
◉ TRADITIONAL SCOTTISH
01339 885229 | Ballater Road, Dinnet, AB34 5JY
www.lochkinord.com

Built in granite in Victorian times, Loch Kinord has homely lounges with real fires, a small bar and a dining room done out with tartan wallpaper and plush red and gold carpets. There's a classical leaning to the kitchen's output.

Chef Maciej Jaworski **Seats** 40 **Open** All year **Parking** 20 **Notes** Vegetarian dishes, Children welcome

BALMEDIE
Cock & Bull
◉ MODERN SCOTTISH, BRITISH
01358 743249 | Ellon Road, Blairton, AB23 8XY
www.thecockandbull.co.uk

The Cock & Bull is a low-slung establishment full of 19th-century character with wooden beams and real fires, but there's nothing stuck in the past about this gastro-pub: modern food and local artworks ensure that. Eat in the conservatory dining room or the main restaurant.

Chef Graham Mitchell **Seats** 80, Private dining 30 **Closed** 26 December, 2 January **Prices from** S £5, M £10.95, D £5.95 **Parking** 50 **Notes** Vegetarian dishes, Children welcome

BANCHORY
The Falls of Feugh Restaurant
◉ MODERN BRITISH
01330 822123 | Bridge of Feugh, AB31 6NL
www.thefallsoffeugh.com

In a bucolic spot by the river, surrounded by trees, the sound of running water is particularly evocative if you're sitting on the small terrace. There's a charming café, but the main draw is the modern French- and Scottish-inflected food on offer.

Chef John Chomba **Seats** 96, Private dining 40 **Closed** 1 January **Prices from** S £5, M £14, D £6 **Parking** 20 **Notes** Vegetarian dishes, Children welcome

The Tornacoille Restaurant
◉◉ MODERN BRITISH
01330 822242 | Inchmarlo Road, AB31 4AB
www.tornacoille.com

Peeping out from the trees in acres of wooded grounds, the Victorian granite mansion has become a smart country-house hotel, with a classy but relaxed restaurant providing appetising views of the surrounding countryside. It's a glorious setting for seasonally astute menus of modern food with sound classical roots.

Chef Colin Lyall **Seats** 50 **Open** All year **Notes** Vegetarian dishes, Children welcome

ABERDEENSHIRE

ELLON
Eat on the Green
◉◉ BRITISH, SCOTTISH, EUROPEAN
01651 842337 | Udny Green, AB41 7RS
www.eatonthegreen.co.uk

It's all change at Eat on the Green, with a new chef and a refurbishment of the restaurant. They've even moved the bar, and there's a new garden/champagne lounge, all demonstrating how seriously they take things here. The kitchen turns out stylish modern dishes from top Scottish ingredients.

Chef Craig Wilson **Seats** 48, Private dining 16 **Closed** 1 week January **Parking** 7 **Notes** Vegetarian dishes, Children welcome

INVERURIE
Macdonald Pittodrie House
◉◉ MODERN, TRADITIONAL SCOTTISH
01467 622437 | Chapel of Garioch, Pitcaple, AB51 5HS
www.macdonaldhotels.co.uk/our-hotels/macdonald-pittodrie-house

A few miles off the main road, Pittodrie House has a wonderfully peaceful position, plus 2,000 acres to call its own. Inside all is rich, warm decor and period detail, including the restaurant with its classical proportions and large oil canvases on the walls.

Chef Zack Brotherton **Seats** 28, Private dining 22 **Open** All year **Prices from** S £6.50, M £19.50, D £6.50 **Parking** 150 **Notes** Vegetarian dishes, Children welcome

KILDRUMMY
Kildrummy Inn
◉◉ MODERN SCOTTISH
01975 571227 | AB33 8QS
www.kildrummyinn.co.uk

Kildrummy Inn has an authenticity that appeals to tourists and locals, while the output from its dynamic kitchen has put it on the foodie map. Menus reveal classical sensibilities and a contemporary touch and flavours hit the mark when it comes to desserts, too.

Chef Alexandria Hay, Sarah Morris **Seats** 32, Private dining 12 **Closed** January **Notes** Vegetarian dishes, Children welcome

OLDMELDRUM
Meldrum House Country Hotel & Golf Course
◉◉ MODERN SCOTTISH
01651 872294 | AB51 0AE
www.meldrumhouse.com

Even if you're not nifty with a niblick, Meldrum House is a good place to marinate in the luxury of a turreted baronial pile. The traditional country-house hotel has 350 acres of wooded parkland and is a lovely setting for the Scottish country-house cooking.

Chef Paul Grant **Seats** 70, Private dining 30 **Open** All year **Prices from** S £8, M £30, D £12 **Parking** 70 **Notes** Vegetarian dishes, Children welcome

PETERHEAD
Buchan Braes Hotel
◉ MODERN SCOTTISH, EUROPEAN
01779 871471 | Boddam, AB42 3AR
www.buchanbraes.co.uk

The low-slung Buchan Braes won't win any architectural prizes, but it's a splendid contemporary hotel with a rural aspect and up-to-date wedding and conference facilities to boot. There's also the Grill Room restaurant, with its open kitchen and warmly colourful decor.

Chef Gary Christie **Seats** 70, Private dining 80 **Open** All year **Parking** 100 **Notes** Vegetarian dishes, Children welcome

STONEHAVEN
The Tolbooth Seafood Restaurant
◉ MODERN BRITISH, SEAFOOD
01569 762287 | Old Pier, Stonehaven Harbour, AB39 2JU
www.tolbooth-restaurant.co.uk

There can't be many better spots than this for tucking into seafood: it's right on the harbour wall, with a museum on the ground floor and the upstairs restaurant giving sea views. What you eat depends on what's been landed that day.

Chef Craig Somers **Seats** 46 **Closed** 1st 3 weeks in January **Notes** Vegetarian dishes, Children welcome

TARLAND
Douneside House
◉◉◉ MODERN SCOTTISH
013398 81230 | Tarland, AB34 4UL
www.dounesidehouse.co.uk

Initially bought as a holiday home by the MacRobert family in the 1880s, Douneside was creatively enhanced with a crenellated tower and extra rooms, and presents a pleasingly asymmetrical facade to the world. The family trust still oversees the running of the place, from its excellent gardens to the fully equipped spa hotel. Completing the picture is a dynamic kitchen supplied by an industrious kitchen garden, fish from the Peterhead boats, and meat from a local butcher with a royal warrant. David Butters combines forward-looking culinary dash with plenty of old-school opulence in dishes that might embrace a truffled egg with wild mushrooms in artichoke velouté to begin, and then a pairing of halibut and braised oxtail with anise-spiked carrots in citrus beurre blanc, or Gressingham duck with bok choi and orange. An appealing light touch at dessert produces lemon posset with marshmallow, poppyseed meringue and blackberry sorbet, or there are artisan cheeses with oatcakes and quince. The five-course tasting menu, framed by canapés and petits fours, perhaps centring on Highland venison with kohlrabi, chervil roots and dauphinoise, should be reserved 24 hours ahead.

Chef David Butters **Open** All year **Notes** Vegetarian dishes, Children welcome

▶ ANGUS

CARNOUSTIE
Carnoustie Golf Hotel & Spa
◉ BISTRO, SCOTTISH, EUROPEAN
01241 411999 | The Links, DD7 7JE
www.bespokehotels.com/carnoustiegolfhotel

Calder's Bistro enjoys a stunning location overlooking the 1st tee and 18th green of the world-famous Carnoustie Links golf course. With floor-to-ceiling windows providing impressive views of the golf course, this makes a pleasant place to sample an eclectic range of dishes.

Chef Andrew McQueen **Seats** 80 **Open** All year **Parking** 120 **Notes** Vegetarian dishes, Children welcome

FORFAR
Drovers
◉ MODERN SCOTTISH
01307 860322 | Memus By Forfar, DD8 3TY
www.the-drovers.com

Surrounded by beautiful glens, Drovers is the kind of wild place you want to be stranded when the weather closes in. Although a modern pub in many ways, the walls of antlers remind you this rustic bolt-hole has been around for many years.

Chef Richard Young **Seats** 60, Private dining 16 **Open** All year **Parking** 35 **Notes** Vegetarian dishes, Children welcome

INVERKEILOR
Gordon's
◉◉◉ MODERN SCOTTISH
01241 830364 | Main Street, DD11 5RN
www.gordonsrestaurant.co.uk

Blink, and you'd miss the tiny coastal hamlet of Inverkeilor, were it not for the discreet restaurant with rooms along the high street that has established the village on the map of gastronomic destinations. Thanks to the Watsons family's efforts over 30-odd years, the place ticks all the boxes for a food-and-sea-themed getaway, with boutique rooms and a beamed and stone-walled dining room making an inviting prospect with its contemporary good looks. These days, Gordon's son Garry Watson heads up the kitchen side of things, keeping all-comers on side with his precise modern Scottish cooking. The drill is a fixed-price menu of four courses at dinner, opening with Isle of Skye scallops, say, with pea purée, duck ham and an aromatic dressing of curry spices to bring it all together. An intermediate soup course offers the likes of smoked red pepper and tomato velouté, then mains might showcase Angus beef fillet partnered by artichoke and truffle ravioli, bacon jam, hay-baked celeriac and Rioja jus. Finish with pistachio crème brûlée lifted with rhubarb compôte and mascarpone sorbet.

Chef Garry Watson **Seats** 24, Private dining 8 **Closed** January **Parking** 6 **Notes** Vegetarian dishes, No children under 12 years

▶ ARGYLL & BUTE

COVE
Knockderry House
◉◉ MODERN SCOTTISH
01436 842283 | Shore Road, G84 0NX
www.knockderryhouse.co.uk

Standing on the shore of Loch Long, this much-altered Victorian house is a period treat inside, with a billiard room, intricate wood panelling and magnificent stained windows in the dining room. Gloved staff serve Scottish food that embraces modern techniques.

Chef Jonathan Evans **Seats** 30, Private dining 50 **Closed** 12–28 December **Parking** 15 **Notes** Vegetarian dishes, Children welcome

HELENSBURGH
Sugar Boat
◉◉ MODERN SCOTTISH
01436 647522 | 30 Colquhoun Square, G84 8AQ
www.sugarboat.co.uk

On a square in the heart of town, with tables out front and back, Sugar Boat is done out in natural colours of earth and sea, with a marble-topped bar and viewable kitchen. The hearty modern bistro cooking features big flavours and an essentially simple approach.

Chef Scott Smith **Seats** 65 **Closed** 25–26 December and 1–2 January **Prices from** S £6.50, M £10.50, D £6.50 **Notes** Vegetarian dishes, Children welcome

ARGYLL & BUTE

INVERARAY

Clansman Restaurant

◉ CLASSIC TRADITIONAL **V**

01499 302980 | Loch Fyne Hotel & Spa, Shore Street, PA32 8XT

www.crerarhotels.com/loch-fyne-hotel-spa

On the bonny banks of Loch Fyne, the restaurant goes for the time-honoured stone-walls-and-tartan-carpet school of cosiness, with slate mats on burnished mahogany tables to boost the sense of well-being. In such a location you'd hope for seafood, and the menu duly obliges.

Chef James Sharp, Craig Thomson **Seats** 150, Private dining 20 **Open** All year **Prices from** S £5.95, M £11.95, D £7 **Parking** 60 **Notes** Children welcome

KILCHRENAN

Taychreggan Hotel

◉◉ CLASSIC FRENCH, SEAFOOD **V**

01866 833211 | PA35 1HQ

www.taychregganhotel.co.uk

The whitewashed 17th-century hotel lies a short drive from Oban on a peninsula jutting into Loch Awe, framed by timeless Highland landscapes. The kitchen delivers five-course set dinner menus beginning with a soup such as courgette, with perch and tarragon oil.

Chef Ondrej Kasan **Seats** 45, Private dining 18 **Closed** 3–21 January **Parking** 40 **Notes** Children welcome

LOCHGOILHEAD

The Lodge on Loch Goil

◉◉ MODERN SCOTTISH

01301 703193 | Loch Goil, PA24 8AE

www.thelodge-scotland.com

At the head of a sea loch, the beautifully restored Lodge offers three dining spaces: the Orangery, the Treehouse and the lochside Arts & Crafts restaurant. Scottish produce leads the menu; indeed, many ingredients are grown in the Lodge's gardens or at least locally foraged. Expect seafood too.

Chef Daniel Holleren **Seats** Private dining **Open** All year **Notes** No children

LUSS

The Lodge on Loch Lomond

◉◉ MODERN INTERNATIONAL

01436 860201 | G83 8PA

www.loch-lomond.co.uk

Situated on the edge of Loch Lomond, The Lodge occupies a peaceful woodland setting. The unbeatable loch views and sense of tranquillity in the balcony restaurant give the impression that you are floating on water. The modern food is underpinned by classic technique.

Chef Stephano Cifaldi **Seats** 100, Private dining 100 **Open** All year **Prices from** S £4.95, M £11.95, D £5.30 **Parking** 70 **Notes** Vegetarian dishes,

OBAN

Coast

◉ MODERN BRITISH

01631 569900 | 104 George Street, PA34 5NT

www.coastoban.co.uk

Next door to the art gallery, Coast is the very image of a modern brasserie, with a seasonally changing menu of vivacious dishes. You might finish with apple and honeycomb parfait with toffee ice cream or a ginger sponge pudding with spiced pears.

Chef Richard Fowler **Seats** 46 **Closed** 25 December, 2 weeks January **Prices from** S £4.50, M £13.50, D £5.95 **Notes** Vegetarian dishes, Due to licensing restrictions, children aged under 10 years are required to leave the restaurant by 8pm

Manor House Hotel

◉◉ SCOTTISH, EUROPEAN

01631 562087 | Gallanach Road, PA34 4LS

www.manorhouseoban.com

Built for the Duke of Argyll in 1780, the Manor House Hotel sits in a commanding position overlooking the harbour at Oban. Fine regional Scottish produce is celebrated in menus that aim for a soft-focus country-hotel approach.

Chef Gerard McCluskie **Seats** 34 **Closed** 25–26 December **Parking** 20 **Notes** Vegetarian dishes, No children under 12 years

PORT APPIN

Airds Hotel and Restaurant

◉◉◉ MODERN SCOTTISH **V** ♦ NOTABLE WINE LIST

01631 730236 | PA38 4DF

www.airds-hotel.com

The short drive from Fort William to Port Appin is a tonic in itself, but the location of the Airds Hotel, on the shore of Loch Linnhe, looking over to the Isle of Lismore, is guaranteed to unwind the troubled mind. In a long, low-ceilinged dining room, an atmosphere of considerate civility reigns, and the cooking is characterised by classical techniques delivered with polish and the kind of simplicity that allows quality to shine through. A single crisply toasted Tarbet scallop is joined by its best friend, an intensely flavoured Mull langoustine, in a starter further enriched by crumbled egg yolk and vivid watercress purée. That makes a fine prelude to a main dish of lamb – roast loin and breast and braised neck – simply served with buttery fondant potato, baby vegetables and another vibrant green purée, this time of peas. Fish could be Wester Ross salmon with tomato tortellini and lightly spiced houmous, while desserts such as sticky toffee soufflé with salt caramel sauce, given a jolt by assertive pickled apple and gentled by clotted cream ice cream, aim to send you away happy.

Chef Chris Stanley **Seats** 30 **Open** All year **Prices from** S £5, M £8.95, D £4.50 **Notes** No children under 8 years

The Pierhouse Hotel
@ SEAFOOD
01631 730302 | PA38 4DE
www.pierhousehotel.co.uk

Tucked away on a quiet arm of Loch Linnhe, this waterside restaurant is a simple, magnolia-painted space – there's no point fretting over interior design when all eyes are turned towards the peaks marching across the skyline above the loch.

Chef Laura Milne **Seats** 45, Private dining 25 **Closed** 25–26 December **Parking** 25 **Notes** Vegetarian dishes, Children welcome

PORTAVADIE
Portavadie Marina Restaurant
@@ SCOTTISH
01700 811075 | PA21 2DA
www.portavadie.com

A spa resort hotel in a fantastic location overlooking Loch Fyne makes a great setting for this restaurant, the floor-to-ceiling windows giving every table a view. Staff are friendly, knowledgeable and passionate about the region's produce, which features prominently.

Chef Liam Murphy **Open** All year

RHU
Rosslea Hall Hotel
@ MODERN SCOTTISH
01436 439955 | Ferry Road, G84 8NF
www.rossleahallhotel.co.uk

Views over the Firth of Clyde offer a stunning backdrop to this comfortable, stylish hotel. In the smart restaurant, friendly but informed staff cut through any hint of formality. The kitchen works with modern ideas.

Chef James Quinn **Seats** 48, Private dining 40 **Open** All year **Parking** 60 **Notes** Vegetarian dishes

STRACHUR
Inver Restaurant
@@@ MODERN BRITISH
01369 860537 | Strathlachlan, PA27 8BU
www.inverrestaurant.co.uk

The isolated spot on the shore of Loch Fyne is the first plank of Inver's campaign of seduction. It isn't in the slightest bit grand as a venue, but the idyllic and wild setting are a good preparation for some trend-conscious cooking that showcases wild and regional produce in contemporary style. At simple little wood tables, with bench seating around the walls, the Scandinavian inspiration (Pam Brunton did a stint at Copenhagen's Noma) is plain to see, and the food is full of sharp-edged, enlivening flavours. Appetise yourself with shellfish from nearby lochs – perhaps Otterferry oysters and horseradish – before an opener such as fried fennel and smoked cod's roe sprinkled with dill salt leads into one of the larger dishes like confit duck leg with fermented cabbage and lemon thyme, or Gigha halibut in smoky mussel butter with monk's beard. Desserts are straight out of the Nordic canon, with rye doughnuts, bone marrow caramel and wild pepper ice cream among the enticements. The fixed-price taster looks a cinch, but must be booked in advance.

Chef Pamela Brunton **Seats** 40 **Closed** Christmas and January to February **Prices from** S £6.50, M £13.50, D £7.50 **Parking** 20 **Notes** Vegetarian dishes, Children welcome

TARBERT
Stonefield Castle Hotel
@ SCOTTISH
01880 820836 | PA29 6YJ
www.bespokehotels.com/stonefieldcastle

This 19th-century Scottish baronial architecture sits proudly on the Kintyre peninsula overlooking Lock Fyne. Richly decorated public spaces speak of a long history, while open fires and stunning views set the scene for simple cooking with a country-house feel.

Chef Stephen Gibb **Open** All year **Notes** Children welcome

▶ SOUTH AYRSHIRE
AYR
Enterkine Country House
@@ MODERN BRITISH V
01292 520580 | Annbank, KA6 5AL
www.enterkine.com

Dating from the 1930s, Enterkine is approached via a tree-lined avenue running through its 300 acres. Three sides of Browne's restaurant have huge windows with views of the estate. It's a handsome room, with high-backed upholstered chairs, a polished floor and swagged curtains.

Chef Paul Moffat **Seats** 40, Private dining 14 **Open** All year **Prices from** S £7, M £21, D £7 **Parking** 20 **Notes** Children welcome

Fairfield House Hotel
◉ MODERN BRITISH
01292 267461 | 12 Fairfield Road, KA7 2AS
www.fairfieldhotel.co.uk

A Glasgow tea merchant built Fairfield House as a seaside retreat affording views over the firth towards the Isle of Arran. Confident modern Scottish cooking is the kitchen's forte, with pedigree Scots produce used as the bedrock of an appealing menu of big flavours.

Chef Ryan Petterson **Seats** 80, Private dining 12 **Open** All year **Prices from** S £6, M £14, D £6 **Parking** 50 **Notes** Vegetarian dishes, Children welcome

BALLANTRAE
Glenapp Castle
◉◉◉ MODERN BRITISH V
01465 831212 | KA26 0NZ
www.glenappcastle.com

Glenapp is a Victorian creation in the Scottish baronial style, of the same vintage as Balmoral and almost as turrety. There's something counter-intuitive, but delightfully so, about gazing out to sea from an oak-panelled room, with Holy Island visible on crystal-clear days. The principal business of the kitchen is a six-course dinner menu, including a pre-dessert, with a choice at main and another for either cheese or dessert. A smooth velouté soup, perhaps celeriac with parsley oil, is the start of it, with seared scallops and fennel in dramatic sauce nero to follow. Goosnargh duck breast is served pink with unrendered fat, but gains from sweet-sour red cabbage, butternut purée and a restrained ginger and coriander jus, while fish may be sea bass with goats' cheese agnolotti in blood-orange and star-anise. Dessert may be a sinuously wobbly lemongrass pannacotta with poached pineapple, lime gel and crushed gingernuts. If you've gone for the Scottish cheeses instead, leave room for wholemeal crackers, oatcakes and walnut bread too.

Chef Tyron Ellul, David Alexander **Seats** 34, Private dining 20 **Open** All year **Parking** 20 **Notes** No children under 5 years

TROON
Lochgreen House Hotel
◉◉◉ MODERN FRENCH
01292 313343 | Monktonhill Road, Southwood, KA10 7EN
www.lochgreenhouse.com

Dating back to 1905, this splendid white-painted house enjoys a stunning setting, overlooking the Ayrshire coast and the fairways of Royal Troon. With beautiful gardens and 30 acres of woodland, it's a gloriously quiet and comfortable place to escape the rat race. Service is very efficient and friendly in the formal Kintyre Restaurant, a high-ceilinged, airy room, with elegant table settings and crystal chandeliers. The modern cooking has a firm basis in classic French technique, and presentation is very stylish. You might begin with Ayrshire pork with Troon langoustines, pear, vanilla and celeriac, or a perfectly constructed lobster bisque, accompanied by native crab croûton, saffron aïoli and parmesan. At main, pancetta-wrapped monkfish comes with salsify, poached grapes and red wine fish sauce, another very precise and stylish dish; or you might plump for rack of Scottish lamb with roasted artichoke, Provençal vegetables, basil and red pepper sauce. Finish with a classic custard tart, with clean, simple lines and a rich and tasty custard, accompanied by delicious liquorice and fig compôte and clotted cream.

Chef Andrew Costley, Iain Conway **Seats** 80, Private dining 40 **Open** All year **Prices from** S £9.50, M £17, D £7.50 **Parking** 90 **Notes** Vegetarian dishes, Children welcome

MacCallums of Troon
◉ INTERNATIONAL, SEAFOOD
01292 319339 | The Harbour, KA10 6DH
www.maccallumsoftroon.co.uk

There should really only be one thing on your mind when dining at the Oyster Bar. It's all about the bass, the turbot, the sole... for this is a seafood restaurant in a glorious harbourside setting within a converted pump house.

Chef Ross Auld **Seats** 43 **Closed** Christmas, New Year **Notes** Vegetarian dishes, Children welcome

TURNBERRY
Trump Turnberry
◉◉ TRADITIONAL FRENCH
01655 331000 | Maidens Road, KA26 9LT
www.turnberry.co.uk

The 1906 restaurant at this luxurious golf-centric hotel, with sweeping views across greens and fairways to the hump of Ailsa Craig, is named after the year it opened. The setting resembles a giant wedding cake, and the kitchen puts a luxury modern spin on Escoffier's classics.

Chef Callum Dow **Seats** 120, Private dining 16 **Open** All year **Prices from** S £10, M £24, D £6 **Parking** 200 **Notes** Vegetarian dishes, Children welcome

▶ DUMFRIES & GALLOWAY

AUCHENCAIRN
Balcary Bay Hotel
◉◉ MODERN EUROPEAN
01556 640217 | Shore Road, DG7 1QZ
www.balcary-bay-hotel.co.uk
The solid-looking white hotel stands on the shore of the Solway Firth with views across the water to Heston Isle and the Lake District beyond. The hotel might be in a secluded spot, but the kitchen team proves to be a forward-looking lot.
Chef Craig McWilliam **Seats** 55 **Closed** December to January **Parking** 50 **Notes** Vegetarian dishes, Children welcome

GATEHOUSE OF FLEET
Cally Palace Hotel
◉ TRADITIONAL BRITISH **V**
01557 814341 | Cally Drive, DG7 2DL
www.callypalace.co.uk
Old-school opulence is the order of the day in this Georgian country manor in 150 acres of parkland on the Solway coast, where a pianist tinkles away in formal restaurant. The kitchen delivers gently modernised country-house cooking built on soundly sourced Scottish produce.
Chef Callum Harvey **Seats** 110, Private dining 25 **Closed** 3 January to early February **Parking** 70 **Notes** Children welcome

GRETNA
Smiths at Gretna Green
◉◉ MODERN BRITISH, INTERNATIONAL
01461 337007 | Gretna Green, DG16 5EA
www.smithsgretnagreen.com
Smiths certainly extends the options for those fleeing here with marriage on their minds, and makes a stylish stay to celebrate a landmark anniversary. The imaginative menus are especially good at game. Don't miss the excellent bread, which comes in a plant-pot.
Chef Phillip Woodcock **Seats** 60, Private dining 18 **Closed** 25 December **Parking** 115 **Notes** Vegetarian dishes, Children welcome

MOFFAT
Brodies
◉ MODERN BRITISH
01683 222870 | Holm Street, DG10 9EB
www.brodiesofmoffat.co.uk
Just off the high street, there's a contemporary sheen to Brodies that really pays off in the evening when it becomes quite a smart dining spot. The bistro-style menu offers some interesting stuff made with high-quality ingredients. Sunday lunch is a classic affair.
Chef Russell Pearce, Ross Birrel **Seats** 40 **Closed** 25–27 December **Notes** Vegetarian dishes, Children welcome

PORTPATRICK
Knockinaam Lodge
◉◉◉ MODERN SCOTTISH ♨ NOTABLE WINE LIST
01776 810471 | DG9 9AD
www.knockinaamlodge.com
For a small country hotel, Knockinaam is something of a knockout. About three miles out of Portpatrick, it stands in 30 of its own acres, with access to a private shingle beach. A handsome greystone building, it's decorated in elegant but homely style, with panoramic views of the brooding briny from the dining room windows. Tony Pierce's career began with waitering gigs in Manchester while he trained, and after compiling a star-studded CV, he has brought distinction to the kitchens here. The evening agenda is a four-course table d'hote, beginning on a winter's night with grilled turbot in a pink grapefruit emulsion sauce with pak choi, before a cappuccino soup of turnip and thyme intervenes. Main course is roast loin of red deer with puréed celeriac, winter greens and a potato gaufrette in a reduction of sloe gin, before the final course requires a choice between British and French cheeses with walnut bread, or a vibrantly flavoured hot prune and Armagnac soufflé with vanilla ice cream. Sunday lunches bring on the likes of Galloway pork loin with black pudding bonbon in red wine.
Chef Anthony Pierce **Seats** 32, Private dining 18 **Open** All year **Parking** 20 **Notes** No children

SANQUHAR
Blackaddie House Hotel
◉◉ MODERN BRITISH
01659 50270 | Blackaddie Road, DG4 6JJ
www.blackaddiehotel.co.uk
This stone-built house on the east bank of the River Nith is in the perfect location for sourcing top-drawer produce. Firm classical underpinnings produce a Scotch beef study that combines sautéed fillet, a sticky ragoût and beef terrine with accompanying greens.
Chef Ian McAndrew **Seats** 20, Private dining 20 **Open** All year **Parking** 20 **Notes** Vegetarian dishes, Children welcome

THORNHILL
The Buccleuch and Queensberry Arms Hotel
◉ MODERN SCOTTISH **V**
01848 323101 | 112 Drumlanrig Street, DG3 5LU
www.bqahotel.com
The BQA to its friends, this family-run hotel has
undergone an extensive refurbishment and emerged
looking good, with a satisfying Scottish-ness to the
place which extends to the culinary output. The
region's produce figures large on menus that show
Pan-European leanings and no lack of ambition.
Chef Will Pottinger **Seats** 52, Private dining 22
Open All year **Prices from** S £5, M £9, D £3.50
Parking 100 **Notes** Children welcome

▶ WEST DUNBARTONSHIRE
CLYDEBANK
Golden Jubilee Conference Hotel
◉ MODERN BRITISH
0141 951 6000 | Beardmore Street, G81 4SA
www.goldenjubileehotel.com
A hotel and conference centre next to the Jubilee
hospital, the Golden Jubilee Conference Hotel is a
multi-purpose hub for business meetings, fitness
workouts and aspirational dining with a new spin on
some classics. Ecclefechan tart with toffee ice cream
is a fine regional speciality.
Chef Iain Ramsay **Seats** 50, Private dining 200
Open All year **Parking** 300 **Notes** Vegetarian
dishes, Children welcome

▶ DUNDEE
DUNDEE
Castlehill Restaurant
◉◉ MODERN SCOTTISH
01382 220008 | 22–26 Exchange Street, DD1 3DL
www.castlehillrestaurant.co.uk
Close to the city's booming waterfront, Castlehill is a
sophisticated spot with a decorative style evoking the
colours and textures of Scotland. There's a real sense
of place to the menu, too, with Scottish ingredients
to the fore, while the cooking is thoroughly modern
and creative.
Chef Graham Campbell **Seats** 40 **Closed** 25–26
December, 1 January **Notes** Vegetarian
dishes, Children welcome

Chez Mal Brasserie
◉ BRITISH, FRENCH
01382 339715 | 44 Whitehall Crescent, DD1 4AY
www.malmaison.com
The Dundee branch of the chain is a majestic old hotel
with a domed ceiling above a central wrought-iron
staircase, with the Malmaison trademark sexy looks,
which run through to the candlelit brasserie's darkly
atmospheric colour scheme. The menu plays the
modern brasserie game.
Chef Steven Urquhart **Seats** 110, Private dining 12
Open All year **Prices from** S £5, M £16.50, D £6.50
Notes Vegetarian dishes, Children welcome

The Tayberry
◉◉ SCOTTISH **V**
01382 698280 | 594 Brook Street, Broughty Ferry,
DD5 2EA
www.tayberryrestaurant.com
This relaxed, contemporary operation has made quite
a splash on the local culinary scene. Spread over two
floors, its purple-toned decor is a nod to the namesake
berry, and views across the River Tay from the first
floor are a real bonus.
Chef Adam Newth **Seats** 36, Private dining 16
Closed 25–27 December **Notes** No children accepted
after 8pm

▶ EDINBURGH
EDINBURGH
Bia Bistrot
◉ BRITISH, FRENCH
0131 452 8453 | 19 Colinton Road, EH10 5DP
www.biabistrot.co.uk
The 'Bia' element of the name is the Gaelic for food,
the 'Bistrot' part more self-evident, and it's the
winning setting for the cooking of husband-and-wife
team Roisin and Matthias Llorente. Their Irish/Scottish
and French/Spanish backgrounds are apparent in well-
crafted and satisfying food.
Chef Roisin & Matthias Llorente **Seats** 60, Private
dining 24 **Closed** 1 January, 2nd week in July, 1 week
at Easter, 1 week in October **Prices from** S £3.75,
M £13.50, D £2 **Notes** Vegetarian dishes, Children
welcome

EDINBURGH

Bistro Deluxe
@@ MODERN SCOTTISH
0131 550 4500 | Macdonald Holyrood Hotel, Holyrood Road, EH8 8AU
www.macdonaldhotels.co.uk/our-hotels/macdonald-holyrood-hotel/eat-drink/
In Edinburgh's historic old town, just a couple of minutes from Royal Mile, this modern hotel is well positioned and the elegant, brasserie-style Bistro Deluxe restaurant is a destination in itself. The kitchen makes good use of prime Scottish ingredients.
Chef Paul Tamburrini **Open** All year

The Brasserie – Norton House Hotel & Spa
@ MODERN BRITISH
0131 333 1275 | Ingliston, EH28 8LX
www.handpickedhotels.co.uk/nortonhouse
Buffered by 50-odd acres of well-tended grounds, you'd hardly know that this Victorian country house is handy for motorways and the airport. After you've worked up an appetite in the spa, the brasserie offers an unbuttoned, contemporary setting and modern Scottish food to match.
Chef Graeme Shaw **Seats** 110, Private dining 40 **Open** All year **Prices from** S £6, M £12.50, D £6 **Parking** 100 **Notes** Vegetarian dishes, Children welcome

Britannia Spice
@ INDIAN, THAI, BANGLADESHI V
0131 555 2255 | 150 Commercial Street, EH6 6LB
www.britanniaspice.co.uk
Named after the famous ship that is docked a short distance away, the award-winning Britannia Spice occupies a former whisky warehouse, with some nautical themed adornments adding to the seafaring vibe. That said, it's a simple and stylish place, with wooden tables and banquette seating.
Chef Abu Zaman **Seats** 130 **Open** All year **Prices from** S £3.95, M £8.95, D £2.25 **Parking** 16 **Notes** Children welcome

The Café Royal
@ MODERN SCOTTISH
0131 556 1884 | 19 West Register Street, EH2 2AA
www.caferoyaledinburgh.co.uk
The Café Royal's Victorian-baroque interiors simply cry out to be the scene of grand dining with their gilt pillars, panelled ceilings and stained windows. These days, traditional Scots fare mingles with modern thinking on menus.
Chef Anil Colasco **Seats** 40 **Open** All year **Notes** Vegetarian dishes, No children under 5 years

Castle Terrace Restaurant
@@@ SCOTTISH, FRENCH V NOTABLE WINE LIST
0131 229 1222 | 33–35 Castle Terrace, EH1 2EL
www.castleterracerestaurant.com
A venue in the environs of the castle has got to have a head start in Edinburgh, and the sibling restaurant to the much-lauded Kitchin at Leith steps up to the challenge. In a dark blue room with a spacious modern feel and an outline image of the castle picked out on the wall, Dominic Jack plies a contemporary Scottish nature-to-plate style, with enough brio to offer a Land and Sea surprise menu with optional wine pairings, opening with a glass of champagne. The carte itself furnishes a heartening spread of choice, perhaps beginning with flawlessly timed Orkney scallops given the Indian treatment with a light curry sauce and garnishes of miniaturised naan and poppadum, mango chutney, pineapple and sultanas. Main course might be fillet, belly and cheek of Ayrshire pork with black pudding, fondant potato and creamed cabbage, or the house take on paella, served on spelt risotto. A signature dessert of apple mascarpone cheesecake with caramelised sesame seeds and apple sorbet competes with dark chocolate and orange délice for attention.
Chef Dominic Jack **Seats** 75, Private dining 16 **Closed** 3–7 April, 24–28 July, 9–13 October, 25 December to 14 Janaury **Notes** No children under 5 years

Chaophraya
@ THAI
0131 226 7614 | 4th Floor, 33 Castle Street, EH2 3DN
www.chaophraya.co.uk/edinburgh/
Located on the 4th floor, this panoramic restaurant offers magnificent rooftop views of Edinburgh all the way to the Forth. Helpful, courteous staff offer a traditional welcome and explain the lengthy menu, which combines traditional Thai dishes with more modern interpretations. Great cocktails, too.
Chef Chef Min **Open** All year **Notes** Vegetarian dishes

Chez Mal Brasserie
@ BRITISH, FRENCH
0131 468 5000 | One Tower Place, Leith, EH6 7BZ
www.malmaison.com
This was the first opening for the Malmaison chain, housed in a renovated seamen's mission on the waterfront in the old part of Leith, and is nowadays the grande dame of the boutique chain. The restaurant overlooks the docks with a terrace for alfresco dining.
Chef Andrew Mcconnell **Seats** 60, Private dining 60 **Open** All year **Parking** 45 **Notes** Vegetarian dishes, Children welcome

The Dining Room

◉◉ MODERN FRENCH, SCOTTISH **V**

0131 220 2044 | 28 Queen Street, EH2 1JX

www.thediningroomedinburgh.co.uk

Climb the spiral staircase to the restaurant of the Scotch Malt Whisky Society, where a light, smart room is furnished with linened tables, primrose hued walls and colourful food and drink-themed pictures. The cooking has more than a hint of French classicism to it.

Chef James Freeman **Seats** 66, Private dining 20 **Open** All year **Notes** No children under 14 years

Divino Enoteca

◉ MODERN ITALIAN, INTERNATIONAL

0131 225 1770 | 5 Merchant Street, EH1 2QD

www.divinoedinburgh.com

A hip venue with contemporary artworks on the walls, exposed brickwork and displays of wine bottles wherever you look: it's dark, moody, and a lot of fun. The kitchen's Italian output includes an excellent range of antipasti plus some more modern interpretations of the classics.

Chef Francesco Ascrizzi **Seats** 50, Private dining 14 **Open** All year **Prices from** S £7, M £12.50, D £7 **Notes** Vegetarian dishes, Children welcome

The Dungeon Restaurant at Dalhousie Castle

◉◉ TRADITIONAL EUROPEAN

01875 820153 | Bonnyrigg, EH19 3JB

www.dalhousiecastle.co.uk

Dalhousie Castle is a 13th-century fortress in wooded parkland on the banks of the River Esk, so you know you're in for something special at The Dungeon Restaurant. The cooking here has its roots in French classicism based on top-class Scottish ingredients.

Chef Francois Giraud **Seats** 45, Private dining 100 **Open** All year **Parking** 150 **Notes** Vegetarian dishes, No children under 10 years

l'escargot blanc

◉ FRENCH

0131 226 1890 | 17 Queensferry Street, EH2 4QW

www.lescargotblanc.co.uk

A West End fixture for more than 20 years, the first floor l'escargot blanc is accessed via the restaurant's own standalone wine bar. The intimate restaurant is classic bistro through and through, from the stripped wooden floors and distressed furniture to the Gallic objets d'art.

Chef Frederic Berkmiller **Seats** 56, Private dining 18 **Closed** 1st week January, 2nd week July **Notes** Vegetarian dishes, Children welcome

l'escargot bleu

◉ FRENCH, SCOTTISH

0131 557 1600 | 56 Broughton Street, EH1 3SA

www.lescargotbleu.co.uk

L'Escargot Bleu is indeed blue – on the outside at least, and snails are present and correct among les entrées. The bilingual menu deals in classic bistro dishes such as those snails, which come from Barra in the Outer Hebrides, and there's a Scottish flavour.

Chef Fred Berkmiller **Seats** 55, Private dining 18 **Closed** 1 week January, 1 week July **Notes** Vegetarian dishes, No children after 9pm

La Favorita

◉ MODERN ITALIAN, MEDITERRANEAN

0131 554 2430 | 325–331 Leith Walk, EH6 8SA

www.la-favorita.com

The Vittoria group's Leith pizzeria provides upscale Italian food for a vibrant crowd seated at booth tables. The deal is a compendious list of pizzas and platters of cured meats, while multi-ingredient pasta dishes and risottos broaden the choice.

Chef Jarek Splawski **Seats** 120, Private dining 30 **Closed** 25 December **Notes** Vegetarian dishes, Children welcome

Galvin Brasserie de Luxe

◉ FRENCH

0131 222 8988 | The Caledonian, A Waldorf Astoria Hotel, Princes Street, EH1 2AB

www.galvinrestaurants.com

The luxurious Caledonian Waldorf Astoria is the home of the Galvin brothers in Edinburgh, and this iteration of their cross-Channel classicism pleases diners with its Parisian brasserie-styled looks including waiting staff in time-honoured black-and-white uniforms. As for the food, it's all you'd expect and more.

Chef Jamie Knox **Seats** 150, Private dining 24 **Open** All year **Prices from** S £8, M £21, D £8 **Parking** 42 **Notes** Vegetarian dishes, Children welcome

The Gardener's Cottage

◉ BRITISH

0131 558 1221 | 1 Royal Terrace Gardens, London Road, EH7 5DX

www.thegardenerscottage.co

With its blackboard menu in the gravel outside, this restaurant with full-on royal connections is an oasis of pastoral calm in the bustling city. Cosy up in wicker chairs at big communal tables for Scottish cooking that takes pride in its prime materials.

Chef Edward Murray, Dale Mailley **Seats** 30, Private dining 10 **Closed** Christmas and New Year **Notes** Vegetarian dishes, Children welcome

La Garrigue
⊛⊛ FRENCH, MEDITERRANEAN ▮ NOTABLE WINE LIST
0131 557 3032 | 31 Jeffrey Street, EH1 1DH
www.lagarrigue.co.uk
La Garrigue is the name given to the wild, herb-scented scrubland in Provence and Languedoc in the south of France. Chef-patron Jean-Michel Gauffre (who hails from down that way) has brought the region's honest rustic cooking to his smart neighbourhood restaurant in Edinburgh's old town.

Chef Jean-Michel Gauffre **Seats** 48, Private dining 11 **Closed** 26–27 December, 1–2 January **Prices from** S £4.95, M £15.95, D £6.50 **Notes** Vegetarian dishes, Children welcome

Hadrian's Brasserie
⊛ MODERN SCOTTISH
0131 557 5000 | The Balmoral Hotel, 1 Princes Street, EH2 2EQ
www.roccofortehotels.com
This large, bustling brasserie-style restaurant is within The Balmoral Hotel and creates a cool, modern vibe. Scottish classics range from haggis, neeps and tatties to whisky pannacotta. Sourdough bread is so good as to be moreish.

Chef Jeff Bland **Seats** 100, Private dining 26 **Open** All year **Notes** Vegetarian dishes, Children welcome

Harajuku Kitchen
⊛ JAPANESE
0131 281 0526 | 10 Gillespie Place, EH10 4HS
www.harajukukitchen.co.uk
Named after an area of Tokyo, this bistro offers authentic Japanese dishes with a touch of panache in an informal café-like atmosphere of chunky wood chairs and bare tables. The menu is a mix of small plates and signature main dishes.

Chef Kaori Simpson, Rui Macedo **Seats** 30 **Closed** 25 December, 1 January **Prices from** S £3.50, M £7.50, D £4 **Notes** Vegetarian dishes, Children welcome

Harvey Nichols Forth Floor Restaurant
⊛ MODERN EUROPEAN V ▮ NOTABLE WINE LIST
0131 524 8350 | 30–34 St Andrew Square, EH2 2AD
www.harveynichols.com/restaurants
With views of the castle and the Forth Bridge, the top floor of Harvey Nic's Edinburgh restaurant serves up the city on a plate. The restaurant is a slick contemporary space with linen on the tables, leather seats and a smart line in seasonal dishes.

Chef Robert Meldrum **Seats** 47, Private dining 14 **Closed** 25 December, 1 January **Notes** Vegetarian dishes, Children welcome

The Honours
⊛⊛ MODERN FRENCH
0131 220 2513 | 58a North Castle Street, EH2 3LU
www.thehonours.co.uk
Martin Wishart is a shining star of the Scottish restaurant firmament, his self-named restaurant in Leith his flagship. Here, he's brought his dedication to high quality and his attention to detail to French brasserie classicism. There's a contemporary sheen to the place.

Chef Rikki Preston **Seats** 65 **Closed** Christmas and 1–3 January **Prices from** S £8.50, M £22, D £8 **Notes** Vegetarian dishes, Children welcome

Hotel du Vin Edinburgh
⊛ CLASSIC FRENCH
0131 247 4900 | 11 Bristo Place, EH1 1EZ
www.hotelduvin.com
The former city asylum is the setting for HdV's Edinburgh outpost. The setting is considerably more cheerful thanks to the group's trademark gentleman's-club look of well-worn leather seats and woody textures. There's a splendid tartan-clad whisky snug, plus a buzzy mezzanine bar overlooking the bistro.

Chef Ross Edgar **Seats** 88, Private dining 33 **Open** All year **Prices from** S £6.50, M £14.50, D £4.50 **Notes** Vegetarian dishes, Children welcome

Kanpai Sushi
⊛ JAPANESE
0131 228 1602 | 8–10 Grindlay Street, EH3 9AS
www.kanpaisushiedinburgh.co.uk
Just around the corner from the Usher Hall and the Traverse Theatre, Kanpai is a diminutive but elegant sushi place with an open kitchen counter where you can watch its well-drilled artistry take place. Attention to fine detail, and exemplary freshness are hallmarks.

Chef Max Wang **Seats** 45, Private dining 8 **Open** All year **Prices from** S £2.50, M £9.90, D £4.90 **Notes** Vegetarian dishes, No children under 6 years

The Kitchin
⊛⊛⊛⊛⊛ SCOTTISH, FRENCH V ▮ NOTABLE WINE LIST
0131 555 1755 | 78 Commercial Quay, Leith, EH6 6LX
www.thekitchin.com
There could be no more fitting venue for a restaurant devoted to celebrating the very best in Scottish gastronomy than a repurposed bonded whisky warehouse. Built of stone in the Leith docklands, it has been Tom Kitchin's address since 2006, and has been for virtually all that time one of the top destinations in the country. The interior still looks a little starker than first-timers may be expecting, low-lit, faintly cavernous, with exposed stone walls and grey-painted

brick pillars. It's comfortable enough, but unrepentantly monochrome. That of course is all part of the plan, since the focus is firmly on the distinctiveness of Scottish ingredients, on which topic front-of-house staff are superbly well versed. The ethos is encapsulated in the motto, 'From Nature to Plate', articulated through cooking that lacks nothing in refinement and technical skills, but never forgets that these fine prime materials are what it's about. The short set lunch menu is one way in, delivering a starter such as Orkney scallops baked in the shell and topped with a pastry seal, which is breached at the table to release their aromas, served with pasta-like ribbons of carrot and courgette in a light but precise fish velouté. Next comes roasted loin of Borders roe deer, seasoned with cracked pink peppercorns, the braised haunch incorporated in a cottage pie, alongside extraordinarily concentrated root vegetable mash, with braised apple and an outstanding, classically French red wine sauce. The production closes with a thin-shelled chocolate ganache tart, with bitter orange worked in throughout, in the chocolate, as a purée, diced whole fruit, and a splendid buttermilk ice cream. The principal carte is supplemented by daily seasonal specials, which might run in autumn to Isle of Lewis woodcock in salmis sauce with roasted and puréed pumpkin, while the main menu offers poached Scrabster monkfish with squid ink pasta in a sauce of capers and saffron, or the benchmark hare royale, served with gnocchi and baby turnips. Desserts utilise today's trending flavours to resonant effect, as in the sea buckthorn consommé that comes with orange meringue, set yogurt and Granny Smith sorbet, but the apple and pear crumble soufflé with rich vanilla ice cream remains hard to forgo.

Chef Tom Kitchin **Seats** 75, Private dining 20 **Closed** 10–14 April, 31 July to 4 August, 16–20 October, 25 December to 12 January **Parking** 30 **Notes** No children under 5 years

Locanda De Gusti

◉◉ ITALIAN, MEDITERRANEAN, SEAFOOD
0131 346 8800 | 102 Dalry Road, EH11 2DW
www.locandadegusti.com

Translating loosely as 'inn of taste', this Haymarket award-winner has more than a hint of an Italian domestic kitchen about it. The mixed Scottish seafood feast is a starter full of the freshest squid, king prawns, langoustines, scallops and more.

Chef Rosario Sartore **Seats** 30 **Closed** 1 week in January, 1 week at Easter, 2 weeks in July, 1 week in October **Prices from** S £5.95, M £9.95, D £4.95 **Notes** Vegetarian dishes, Children welcome

Mother India's Cafe

◉ INDIAN TAPAS
0131 524 9801 | 3–5 Infirmary Street, EH1 1LT
www.motherindia.co.uk

Open since 2008 and boisterous Edinburgh sibling to the Glasgow mothership, this bustling Indian café is tucked away behind the university buildings but it's well worth going off the beaten track for. With its mismatched furniture, unclothed tables and disposable napkins, it's chaotic and unpretentious.

Chef Ajay Kumar Sharma **Seats** 110 **Closed** 25–26 December and 1 January **Prices from** S £3.50, M £5, D £3.50 **Notes** Vegetarian dishes, Children welcome

The Mumbai Mansion

◉◉ MODERN INDIAN **V**
0131 229 7173 | 250 Morrison Street, EH3 8DT
www.themumbaimansion.com

Mumbai Mansion is an Indian restaurant, under new ownership since 2015, where both the interior design and menu take a glamorous and contemporary approach. A statement chandelier, plum-coloured columns and chairs, and chunky wooden designer tables make for an appealing space.

Chef Pramod Kumar Nawani **Seats** 85 **Open** All year **Prices from** S £4.50, M £9.95, D £4.95 **Notes** Children welcome

NAVADHANYA

◉ MODERN INDIAN **V**
0131 281 7187 | 88 Haymarket Terrace, EH12 5LQ
www.navadhanya-scotland.co.uk

Compact and informal with simple Indian objets d'art, unclothed tables and good quality crockery, Navadhanya has become a popular spot for locals in Edinburgh's Haymarket area since it opened in 2014. The modern Indian food steers clear of the usual high street curry dishes.

Chef I Tharveskhan **Seats** 42 **Closed** Christmas and New Year **Prices from** S £6.25, M £14.95, D £4 **Notes** Children welcome

New Chapter

◉◉ SCOTTISH, EUROPEAN
0131 556 0006 | 18 Eyre Place, EH3 5EP
www.newchapterrestaurant.co.uk

A godsend for the neighbourhood, this cheery venue combines a laid-back demeanour with clean-cut, contemporary looks, breezy service, and a kitchen that produces unfussy, full-flavoured dishes with European leanings. If you're after top value, the lunch menu is a steal.

Chef Maciej Szymik **Seats** 96, Private dining 20 **Open** All year **Notes** Vegetarian dishes, Children welcome

Number One, The Balmoral
◉◉◉◉ MODERN SCOTTISH **V** ♦ NOTABLE WINE LIST
0131 557 6727 | 1 Princes Street, EH2 2EQ
www.roccofortehotels.com

Red-jacketed porters no longer meet The Balmoral's guests off the trains in Waverley Station, but modern guests can't really find fault with the luxury on offer at this magnificent Edinburgh landmark. Lavish public areas have as much marble and fancy plasterwork as anyone could reasonably ask of a masterpiece of imperial Edwardian pomp, and the Number One dining room looks classy with its oak flooring offset by dove-grey banquettes, and striking artworks on loan from the Royal College of Art adding interest to its red lacquered walls. Executive chef Jeff Bland and head chef Brian Grigor send out reliably sophisticated food full of creative modern panache, delivered via a carte or seven- and ten-course tasting workouts. Seasonal Scottish ingredients are given star billing, as in the hand-dived Dingwall scallops that open the show, dusted with gentle curry spicing, and matched with puréed and roasted cauliflower and kaffir lime oil. Next up, grouse is handled with aplomb, the breast roasted and topped with crunchy pistachio, the leg meat placed atop a square of roasted celeriac, all supported by a classy combination of earthy girolles, crisp game chips, truffled potato purée and bramble jus. A Black Forest-themed dessert is a paragon of dashing artistry and well-managed textures and flavours involving an expertly crafted chocolate financier made with Amadei's blue-chip products, as well as cherry mousse and a splendid almond ice cream. Otherwise, the cheese trolley hums with perfectly ripened items. It's all backed by a heavyweight wine list and a knowledgeable, pitch-perfect service team.

Chef Jeff Bland, Brian Grigor **Seats** 60 **Closed** 2 weeks in January **Notes** Children welcome

Ondine Restaurant
◉◉ SEAFOOD ♦ NOTABLE WINE LIST
0131 226 1888 | 2 George IV Bridge, EH1 1AD
www.ondinerestaurant.co.uk

Ondine has earned a loyal following in a few years, and it's not hard to see why: just off the Royal Mile, it's a contemporary space with great views out over the old town. Sustainable seafood amid an atmosphere of cheerful bustle is the draw.

Chef Roy Brett **Seats** 82, Private dining 10 **Open** All year **Notes** Vegetarian dishes, Children welcome

One Square
◉ MODERN SCOTTISH
0131 221 6422 | Sheraton Grand Hotel & Spa, 1 Festival Square, EH3 9SR
www.onesquareedinburgh.co.uk

The views of Edinburgh Castle give a sense of place to this slick, modern dining option. The floor-to-ceiling windows add a cool, classy finish. The lunch and dinner menus have a sharp focus on Scotland's fine produce in their crowd-pleasing medley of modern ideas.

Chef Craig Hart **Seats** 90, Private dining 40 **Open** All year **Parking** 125 **Notes** Vegetarian dishes, Children welcome

The Pompadour by Galvin
◉◉◉ MODERN FRENCH **V** ♦ NOTABLE WINE LIST
0131 222 8975 | Waldorf Astoria Edinburgh, The Caledonian, Princes Street, EH1 2AB
www.galvinrestaurants.com

The name gives a little clue as to the other-worldly grandeur of the setting, a lavishly appointed dining room at the Waldorf Astoria with hand-blocked floral wall designs, a gigantic oval mirror, and views through half-moon windows towards the Castle. Here, the Galvin brothers have made themselves a very comfortable home north of the border, and the menus, which embrace multi-course specials with vegetarian counterparts, as well as a shorter seasonal offering and the standard carte, deal in modern Anglo-French dishes of impact and finesse. A first course brings together perfectly timed monkfish cheeks with hand-rolled macaroni and smoked marrow in a crisp red wine vinaigrette, while main courses subtly step things up with roast veal sweetbreads, pearl barley and pea risotto and morels, strongly accented with wild garlic, or turbot poached in dashi and partnered with an oyster and slivered radish. Incomparable technique distinguishes a salt caramel soufflé with a scoop of bourbon vanilla ice cream dropped into it, or there could be a bang-up-to-date mousse of Manjari chocolate and praline with toasted hay ice cream and almond gel.

Chef Daniel Ashmore **Seats** 60, Private dining 20 **Closed** 2 weeks in January **Parking** 42 **Notes** Children welcome

Restaurant Mark Greenaway
◉◉◉ MODERN BRITISH ♦ NOTABLE WINE LIST
See pages 380–381

EDINBURGH
Restaurant Mark Greenaway
❀❀❀ MODERN BRITISH 🍷 NOTABLE WINE LIST
0131 226 1155 | 69 North Castle Street, EH2 3LJ
www.markgreenaway.com

Astonishing modern cooking at a handsome Georgian address

Mark Greenaway's has been one of the more industrious careers in Scottish gastronomy of the last several years. He is a TV regular to begin with, as well as prolific charity ambassador, a cookbook author and teacher, and still finds time to run the present venue in former bank premises in the stone-built Georgian purlieus of the capital. It remains a rather sober place within, the walls in light blue, punctuated by a backlit steel beam used as shelving. Downstairs, in what was the safe deposit room, is the space for private dining. Greenaway cooks in an exuberant, creative style, mobilising playful, even theatrical flourishes to keep diners fascinated, with the result that dishes never look less than extraordinary, while remaining founded on unimpeachable Scottish produce.

An opening course features a smoke-shrouded double-decker arrangement with a herb-buttered cannelloni roll of white Loch Fyne crabmeat on shredded lettuce on the plate above; from beneath it emerges a bowl of smoked cauliflower custard with some of the brown crabmeat and pearls of lemony caviar gel. It's a breathtaking, labour-intensive

beginning that is worth all the conceptual effort that has gone into it. A curry-scented celeriac velouté with matching crisps is another triumph of textural contrasts and resonant flavours. At main course, imaginatively treated duck is always a strong bet, the indispensable Gartmorn Farm bird preferred for a serving of the crisp-skinned breast and a complex poppyseed tart, its undulations of pastry filled with diced leg meat, together with aubergine purée, cherry gel and salsify, as well as the crumbled bacony duck skin. The vegetarian proposal may be roast polenta of silky smoothness, offset with goats' cheese, parsnip and spinach.

Viewers with long memories may well recognise the Knot chocolate tart from a 2013 episode of the BBC's *Great British Menu*: it comprises custard jelly, frozen cookies, a stick of crème fraîche parfait, salted caramel and streaks of kumquat purée, arranged around the tightly wound knot of dark chocolate itself, an undoubtedly rich but mightily effective plate. If you're not of the sweet-toothed persuasion, the cheese trio may be ordered with confidence. It comes with lavosh crackers, oatcakes and frozen grapes. Little wonder that the eight-course taster, perhaps centring on a main dish of 11-hour slow-cooked pork belly with pork cheek pie and sweetcorn in toffee apple jus, is a popular recourse. A sterling wine list has been carefully compiled to do justice to the ambitious nature of the food.

Chef Mark Greenaway **Seats** 60, Private dining 14 **Closed** 25–26 December, 1–2 January **Notes** Vegetarian dishes, No children under 5 years

Restaurant Martin Wishart

🏵🏵🏵🏵 MODERN FRENCH V ⬛NOTABLE WINE LIST
0131 553 3557 | 54 The Shore, Leith, EH6 6RA
www.restaurantmartinwishart.co.uk

The port area of Leith is rich with bars and restaurants, but that wasn't always the case, and Martin Wishart was one of the trailblazers who breathed life back into the neglected area. It was a brave move, much rewarded, and the restaurant is now one of the top dining addresses in the UK. The chef hasn't let the grass grow under his feet either after opening a number of other dining destinations. An empire built on a passion for French cuisine, where experience working with the Roux brothers and Marco Pierre White was a grounding that has taken him to the very top. The dining room is elegant and stylish, but understated, and the attention to detail in everything that arrives on the plate is breathtaking at times. Scottish produce leads the line on menus that combine French classical ways with contemporary creativity; choose from a fixed-price four-course carte or six- or eight-course tasting menus, including outstanding vegetarian versions. A guinea fowl mousse might get things going, in a refined yet earthy dish, with morels and cabbage, or how about an emmental soufflé, rising to the occasion with creamed Swiss chard? A second course on the à la carte might be ravioli of snails in a stunning partnership with Shetland mussels and white onion velouté. Among main courses, halibut is cooked to perfection in a water bath, served with a deliciously sharp hollandaise, while roast breast and pastilla of Goosnargh duck shows balance and superb technical skills. That goes for desserts, too, such as brown butter pannacotta with blackcurrant crémeux and Granny Smith granité. The wine list is out of the top drawer, covering the globe and truly excelling itself in the French regions.

Chef Martin Wishart, Joe Taggart **Seats** 50, Private dining 10 **Closed** 25–26 December, 1 January, 2 weeks in January **Notes** No children under 7 years

Rhubarb at Prestonfield House

🏵🏵 TRADITIONAL BRITISH ⬛NOTABLE WINE LIST
0131 225 1333 | Priestfield Road, EH16 5UT
www.rhubarb-restaurant.com

One of the city's most visually impressive dining rooms, Rhubarb at Prestonfield House is a real stunner. Classical preparations mix with contemporary ideas in a menu with broad appeal. Have a classic Scottish steak followed by tarte Tatin for two.

Chef John McMahon **Seats** 90, Private dining 500 **Open** All year **Parking** 200 **Notes** Vegetarian dishes, No children under 12 years

The Scran & Scallie

🏵 TRADITIONAL SCOTTISH V ⬛NOTABLE WINE LIST
0131 332 6281 | 1 Comely Bank Road, EH4 1DT
www.scranandscallie.com

Tom Kitchin and Dominic Jack's pub is done out in fashionable shabby-chic, just the right sort of setting for a menu of modern classics combined with traditional preparations. The feel-good factor extends right through to desserts.

Chef James Chapman, Tom Kitchin, Dominic Jack **Seats** 75, Private dining 14 **Closed** 25 December **Prices from** S £8, M £11.50, D £7.50 **Notes** Children welcome

The Stockbridge Restaurant

🏵🏵 SCOTTISH, EUROPEAN
0131 226 6766 | 54 Saint Stephen Street, EH3 5AL
www.thestockbridgerestaurant.com

The Stockbridge is a charming restaurant where the walls are hung with vivid modern artwork and mirrors, and spotlights in the low ceiling create pools of light on crisply clothed tables. The cooking goes from strength to strength, producing well-conceived dishes from fine Scottish produce.

Chef Jason Gallagher **Seats** 40 **Closed** 24–25 December, 1st 2 weeks January **Notes** Vegetarian dishes, No children after 8pm

Taisteal

🏵 MODERN SCOTTISH
0131 332 9977 | 1–3 Raeburn Place, Stockbridge, EH4 1HU
www.taisteal.co.uk

Gaelic for a journey, Taisteal is the younger but larger sibling to Field across town in Southside and it shares a similar farm-to-fork philosophy when it comes to local provenance. It has a relaxed style with stripped wood and animal-themed artwork.

Chef Gordon Craig **Seats** 44 **Closed** Christmas **Prices from** S £6, M £14, D £6.50 **Notes** Vegetarian dishes, No children under 5 years

Ten Hill Place Hotel

🏵 MODERN, TRADITIONAL BRITISH
0131 662 2080 | 10 Hill Place, EH8 9DS
www.tenhillplace.com

Can there be another hotel that uses its profits to help train the world's would-be surgeons? That's what this part-Georgian hotel owned by The Royal College of Surgeons of Edinburgh does. Try a starter of haggis pastilla.

Chef Alan Dickson **Seats** 54 **Open** All year **Prices from** S £7, M £16, D £6 **Notes** Vegetarian dishes, Children welcome

AA Wine Award for Scotland 2018–19

Timberyard

◉◉◉ MODERN BRITISH V ♦ NOTABLE WINE LIST

See pages 384–385

21212

◉◉◉◉ MODERN FRENCH ♦ NOTABLE WINE LIST

0131 523 1030 | 3 Royal Terrace, EH7 5AB

www.21212restaurant.co.uk

In case the name isn't enough of a clue, Paul Kitching and Katie O'Brien's sumptous restaurant with rooms is not one to follow the herd. The sandstone Georgian townhouse on Royal Terrace seems par for the course for a high-end joint, but the idiosyncratic side of things is revealed on the inside, with contemporary design and classic elegance combining in a true one-off operation. The four bedrooms have a glossy finish, and the swish restaurant works a dramatic look, mingling ornate plasterwork, curvaceous banquettes and quirky design touches like giant moths on the carpet; a glass partition lets you eyeball the open-to-view kitchen where Paul gives full rein to his off-the-wall culinary artistry. The place's quirky name derives from the five-course menu format: a choice of two starters, two mains and two desserts, punctuated by one soup course and a cheese course – that's if you're doing lunch – the line-up jumps to 31313 at dinner. Cryptic menu descriptions will need some elucidation from Katie, who orchestrates front-of-house with charm and efficiency, but you can expect creative and dynamic modern cooking in dishes that inspire and amaze. A complex starter layers gazpacho with various vegetables and wild rice with horseradish foam, then comes celeriac soup topped with red pepper foam, vegetables, tomato crisp and curried meringue. Scallops and truffles with 'fake moss' appear as a main course dish, or perhaps chicken and artichoke with garlic and smoked figs. Next up is cheese, before the finale, a creative confection involving ginger, coconut, apple, rice and sultanas.

Chef Paul Kitching **Seats** 36, Private dining 10 **Closed** 2 weeks in January, 2 weeks in summer **Notes** Vegetarian dishes, No children under 5 years

The Witchery by the Castle

◉ TRADITIONAL SCOTTISH ♦ NOTABLE WINE LIST

0131 225 5613 | Castlehill, The Royal Mile, EH1 2NF

www.thewitchery.com

This 16th-century merchant's house by the gates of the castle makes a strikingly atmospheric, even Gothic-looking restaurant. The cooking follows a contemporary route built on Scottish traditions, with the kitchen using quality native produce. Seafood gets a strong showing, and puddings are worth a punt.

Chef Douglas Roberts **Seats** 110, Private dining 60 **Closed** 25–26 December **Notes** Vegetarian dishes, Children welcome until 7pm

RATHO
The Bridge Inn at Ratho

◉ MODERN BRITISH

0131 333 1320 | 27 Baird Road, EH28 8RA

www.bridgeinn.com

Right by the Union Canal, with views over the water from both garden and restaurant, The Bridge Inn is the perfect spot for watching the passing boats. If the canal-side action doesn't float your boat, there are cask ales, regional whiskies, and an appealing menu.

Chef Ben Watson **Seats** 72, Private dining 12 **Closed** 25 December **Parking** 50 **Notes** Vegetarian dishes, Children welcome

▶ FALKIRK

BANKNOCK
Glenskirlie House & Castle

◉◉ MODERN BRITISH V

01324 840201 | Kilsyth Road, FK4 1UF

www.glenskirliehouse.com

A castle for the 21st century, Glenskirlie is a bright white pile, kitted out with a conical-roofed turret here, a little step-gabling there. The restaurant has a good ambience and a friendly and brisk service from staff.

Chef Richard M Leafe **Seats** 54, Private dining 150 **Closed** 26–27 December, 1–4 January **Parking** 100 **Notes** Children welcome

POLMONT
Macdonald Inchyra Hotel and Spa

◉ MODERN, TRADITIONAL

01324 711911 | Grange Road, FK2 0YB

www.macdonald-hotels.co.uk

The solid-stone Inchyra is a smart hotel with a plush spa and all mod cons. It's home to The Scottish Steak Club, a brasserie-style dining option done out in swathes of rich leather, animal prints and dark wood. The menu is a foray into brasserie-land.

Chef Kevin Semple **Seats** 90 **Open** All year **Notes** Vegetarian dishes, Children welcome

AA Wine Award for Scotland 2018–19

EDINBURGH
Timberyard
◉◉◉ MODERN BRITISH **V** 🍾 NOTABLE WINE LIST
0131 221 1222 | 10 Lady Lawson St, EH3 9DS
www.timberyard.co

On-trend regional cooking in an old warehouse

The Radford family have taken a brick-built, 19th-century warehouse (the place was once a lumber merchant's premises, hence the name), and left it fashionably stripped back and spartan, all hard surfaces and a rough-and-ready approach to interior aesthetics. You enter through postbox-red garage doors into a high-ceilinged dining space of whitewashed brick walls. Wine – quirky and interesting natural bottles, of course, sourced from artisan producers – is stacked in racks alongside the bar, the upper levels reached by ladder. The set-up also incorporates an in-house smokery and butcher, as well as finding little nooks for growing herbs and edible flowers. There are a couple of tables outside under the birch saplings and an area sheltered by a lean-to (Scottish weather, obvs) in the yard. Dishes arrive on chunky unglazed pottery, the bread on a slab of varnished wood, and ingredients

provided by Lothian growers, breeders and foragers lead the way. If you're dropping by for a light lunch or pre-theatre grazing, a menu of 'bites', small and main-course-sized plates offers up the likes of octopus with burnt apple, kohlrabi and nasturtium, or cured pork belly alongside ramsons, onion, potato and horseradish. Otherwise, the full-works options take the shape of four-, six- or eight-course tasters, with omnivore, pescatarian, veggie and vegan versions covering all the bases.

Led by Ben Radford, the kitchen sends out inventive dishes assembled from intriguing components: sea-fresh raw scallop, for example, is matched with apple, elderflower and dill, followed by rabbit with a sensory slalom of salsify, hazelnut, brown butter and sage. Next up, perhaps venison starring with a cast of ramsons, beetroot, juniper and onion in various textural guises, or if you're in the mood for fish, trout and plump mussels supported by the earthy notes of turnip, wild leek, crow garlic and the refreshing sharpness of yogurt might fit the bill. The finisher might be a simple ingredients-led compilation of dynamic flavours, poached rhubarb, say, with sheep's milk yogurt, cream cheese and a crunchy biscuit for textural variety. Enthusiastic and knowledgeable staff make sure everything ticks along smoothly.

Chef Ben Radford **Seats** 65, Private dining 10 **Closed** 1 week in April, October, 24–26 December, 1st week in January **Prices from** S £7.50, M £12.50, D £5 **Notes** No children under 12 years at dinner

FIFE

FIFE

ANSTRUTHER
The Cellar
@@@ MODERN BRITISH
01333 310378 | 24 East Green, KY10 3AA
www.thecellaranstruther.co.uk

The 17th-century house just off the harbourfront was once a cooperage and a smokehouse so it is fitting that it now houses a destination restaurant run by chef-patron Billy Boyter who's keen on drying, fermenting, salting and smoking his ingredients. The ambience is rustic-chic, with beamed ceilings, rough stone walls and wood-burning stoves, and friendly staff playing their part in its appeal, while Boyter's intelligent modernist cooking draws the faithful for seven-course tasting menus at dinner (five if you're in for lunch). A winter workout might include slow-cooked beef cheek with Fearn Abbey cheese and pickled onion, then introduce a hint of the Orient in a plate of local crab with toasted rice, squid and seaweed jelly. Main meat might be red deer matched with pear, chocolate, turnip, peanut and tonka bean, and the finale arrives in the form of an imaginative assemblage of apple and sorrel, bramble, brown butter curd and lemon thyme. The Cellar does wine equally well, and the clever pairings to go with each course are well worth signing up for.

Chef Billy Boyter **Seats** 28 **Closed** 25–26 December, 1 January, 3 weeks January, 1 week May, 10 days September **Notes** Vegetarian dishes, No children under 5 years at lunch, 12 years at dinner

CAIRNEYHILL
The Restaurant and Acanthus
@@ MODERN BRITISH
01383 880505 | Forrester Park Leisure, Pitdinnie Road, KY12 8RF
www.forresterparkresort.com

Forrester Park is a chic, contemporary take on a traditional Scottish mansion. There are two dining rooms, The Restaurant is smaller and more modern in style, while the much larger Acanthus is all starched white linen and chandeliers. The same set-price dinner menu is served in both.

Chef Alistair Clark **Seats** 240 **Open** All year **Notes** Vegetarian dishes, Children welcome

CUPAR
Ostlers Close Restaurant
@@ MODERN SCOTTISH V
01334 655574 | Bonnygate, KY15 4BU
www.ostlersclose.co.uk

This one-time scullery of a 17th-century Temperance hotel has been a popular destination since 1981.

With red-painted walls and linen-clad tables, it's an intimate space run with charm and enthusiasm. Concise handwritten menus showcase produce from the garden and wild mushrooms from local woods.

Chef James Graham **Seats** 26 **Closed** 25–26 December, 1–2 January, 2 weeks January, 2 weeks April **Prices from** S £8, M £24, D £8 **Notes** No children under 6 years at dinner

NEWPORT-ON-TAY

AA Restaurant of the Year for Scotland 2018–19

The Newport Restaurant
@@ MODERN SCOTTISH V
01382 541449 | 1 High Street, DD6 8AB
www.thenewportrestaurant.co.uk

There's not much better publicity than winning *MasterChef: The Professionals*, so 2014 winner Jamie Scott got off to a flyer when he opened his own restaurant. Cheerful and enthusiastic service and a breezy contemporary decor make for a relaxed dining experience, while pin-sharp contemporary cooking from Scott and his team make it a hot ticket. Choose between the small plates or go for a pre-ordained tasting menu, and expect the likes of a glorious veggie number with violet artichoke, goats' curd and pickled carrots. The ingredients impress throughout – local hogget, say, with aubergine prepared three ways, or sea trout with a divine mussel emulsion.

Chef Jamie Scott **Seats** 52, Private dining 30 **Closed** 24–26 December, 1–8 January **Parking** 10 **Notes** Children welcome

ST ANDREWS
The Adamson
@@ MODERN BRITISH
01334 479191 | 127 South Street, KY16 9UH
www.theadamson.com

Once home to photographer and physician Dr John Adamson, the handsome building is a cool restaurant with exposed bricks, darkwood tables and a bar serving up nifty cocktails. The menu brings vim and vigour to the brasserie format..

Chef Stewart MacAulay **Seats** 70 **Closed** 25–26 December, 1 January **Notes** Vegetarian dishes, Children welcome

Ardgowan Hotel

⊛ STEAKHOUSE, SCOTTISH

01334 472970 | 2 Playfair Terrace, North Street, KY16 9HX

www.ardgowanhotel.co.uk

The Argowan's Restaurant and Steakhouse is located under the reception, and the configuration means that diners can often find themselves eating close to drinkers using the bar. It all makes for a relaxed atmosphere, while linen-clothed tables in the restaurant add a touch of formality.

Chef Duncan McLachlan **Seats** 45 **Closed** Christmas, New Year **Prices from** S £4.50, M £11.95, D £4.95 **Notes** Vegetarian dishes, Children welcome

Hotel du Vin St Andrews

⊛ FRENCH, BRITISH

01334 845313 | 40 The Scores, KY16 9AS

www.hotelduvin.com

The kitchen delivers the trademark menu of French impressionism, where Gallic and British classics sit side by side. Expect a compelling mix of stylish boutique rooms, lively and informal bistro and good wine list.

Chef Hugh Drysdale **Seats** 45, Private dining 27 **Open** All year **Prices from** S £6.50, M £10.50, D £5.50 **Parking** 5 **Notes** Vegetarian dishes, Children welcome

Road Hole Restaurant

⊛⊛⊛ MODERN STEAK, SEAFOOD

See pages 388–389

Rocca Restaurant

⊛⊛⊛ MODERN BRITISH

See page 390

The Peat Inn

⊛⊛⊛ MODERN BRITISH

01334 840206 | KY15 5LH

www.thepeatinn.co.uk

This inn has been enough of a local landmark since the mid-18th century that the village in which it stands was named after it, rather than the other way round. It's a handsomely white-fronted stone-built former coach-stop, the dining room now redecorated in sleek contemporary fashion with light woods, thick cloths and smart tableware. Geoffrey Smeddle has maintained the place in the upper ranks of Scottish gastronomy over an impressive stretch, and the modernist flourishes and precise presentations confer real character on the cooking. A meaty starter full of gentle richness sees wood-pigeon breast and roast veal sweetbreads teamed with a smooth liver parfait, along with discreet support from quince purée and smoked almonds. For main, there may be seared stone bass in champagne butter with the varied

accompaniments of cauliflower cheese, pink grapefruit and poached lettuce, or perhaps glazed breast and confit leg of wild mallard on a slew of Puy lentils with walnuts, figs and pancetta. A perfectly rendered prune and Armagnac soufflé comes with warm madeleines aromatic with five spice, or consider the Scottish farmhouse cheeses.

Chef Geoffrey Smeddle **Seats** 50, Private dining 12 **Closed** 25–26 December, 1–14 January **Prices from** S £9, M £17, D £8.50 **Parking** 24 **Notes** Vegetarian dishes, Children welcome

St Andrews Bar & Grill

⊛ SCOTTISH

01334 837000 | Fairmont St Andrews, Scotland, KY16 8PN

www.fairmont.com/standrews

A free shuttle bus takes you from the Fairmont Hotel to this dining option in the clubhouse, but it is a lovely walk. Spectacularly situated on a promontory overlooking St Andrews Bay, the evening sees the seafood bar and grill come into their own.

Chef Trevor Kliaman **Seats** 80 **Open** All year **Parking** 40 **Notes** Vegetarian dishes, Children welcome

Sands Grill

⊛ MODERN SCOTTISH

01334 474371 | The Old Course Hotel, Golf Resort & Spa, KY16 9SP

www.oldcoursehotel.co.uk

Overlooking the world-famous golf course and the coast beyond, The Old Course Hotel occupies a desirable position and offers a wide range of dining options. The Sands Grill is the more informal option, a contemporary brasserie run by slick, unstuffy staff.

Chef Martin Hollis **Seats** 75, Private dining 40 **Open** All year **Parking** 100 **Notes** Vegetarian dishes, Children welcome

Seasons at Rufflets St Andrews

⊛⊛ MODERN BRITISH, EUROPEAN ⬛ NOTABLE WINE LIST

01334 472594 | Strathkinness Low Road, KY16 9TX

www.rufflets.co.uk/wine-dine/seasons-restaurant/

The creeper-covered turreted mansion has been in the same family ownership since 1952, sitting in 10 acres of exquisite gardens. Its name refers to the 'rough flat lands' that once comprised the local landscape. The cooking is as modern as can be.

Chef David Kinnes **Seats** 60, Private dining 130 **Open** All year **Prices from** S £8, M £18, D £7 **Parking** 50 **Notes** Vegetarian dishes, Children welcome

FIFE restaurants continue on page 391

FIFE

ST ANDREWS
Road Hole Restaurant
◉◉◉ MODERN STEAK, SEAFOOD
01334 474371 | The Old Course Hotel, Golf Resort & Spa, KY16 9SP
www.oldcoursehotel.co.uk

Steaks, seafood and modern dishes with views of the golf

If you're a golf-made gourmet, a pilgrimage to the illustrious granddaddy of them all, the St Andrews Old Course, and a stopover at the eponymous hotel should be on your bucket list, allowing you to indulge both passions in one fell swoop. The Old Course Hotel will certainly keep you fed and watered in grand style while basking in a spectacular location with views of West Sands beach and the majestic coastline. The grand property also towers above the famous golf links, specifically the 17th hole, the 'Road Hole', so it seems only right that the main dining room here has been named after it.

It's a civilized, upmarket spot with an open kitchen providing an alternative theatre for those who have no interest in the stick-swinging action outside. Not short on luxurious items, Martin Hollis's menus are built on the finest produce from Scotland's seasonal larder, including some classic local seafood and steak options, so you might choose to open with some thoroughbred shellfish, perhaps oysters with the customary shallot vinegar and lemon, langoustines with garlic mayonnaise, or why not have the lot in

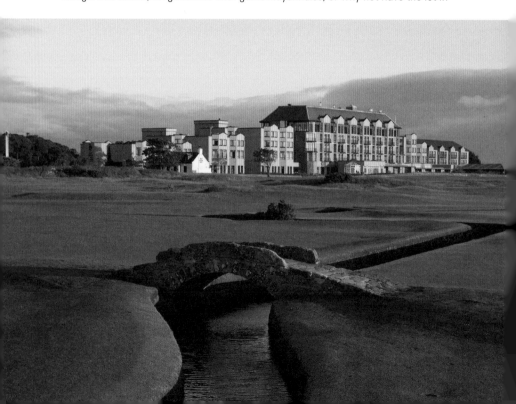

seafood platters laden with lobster, cockles, scallops, dressed crab and all the trimmings. If you would rather the chefs did something more onerous than opening shells, a more modernist route might set out with ballotine of foie gras with chilli, peppered pineapple and brioche, or you could stick to the luxuriant classicism of lobster bisque ramped up with aïoli and crostini.

As for main courses, red meat aficionados can expect prime cuts of pedigree Black Isle rib-eye or fillet, or a surf and turf pairing of rib-eye chops and lobster. Elsewhere, straightforward main dishes take in the likes of herb-crusted loin and braised shoulder of lamb with aubergine purée and courgettes, or perhaps spanking-fresh halibut with cockle risotto, samphire, parsley oil and coriander. Waiting at the end are superb artisanal cheeses that come with truffle honey and black grapes, or those with a sweet tooth should look to a dessert list that takes in the alluring flavours of liquorice pannacotta with strawberry sorbet, coconut foam and lime, as well as a zesty combo of lemon meringue soufflé with yogurt sorbet and lemon jelly.

Highly professional, genuinely engaged staff deliver perfectly pitched service, and as for wine, it's a rich man's world with a deeply classical wine list offering a mind-boggling trip through fine Burgundies, clarets and big-hitters from the New World.

Chef Martin Hollis **Seats** 70, Private dining 16 **Open** All year **Prices from** S £7, M £15.50, D £8.50 **Parking** 100 **Notes** Vegetarian dishes, Children welcome

ST ANDREWS
Rocca Restaurant
◉◉◉ MODERN BRITISH

01334 472549 | Macdonald Rusacks Hotel, Pilmour Links, KY16 9JQ

www.macdonaldhotels.co.uk

Fine Scottish dining next to the 18th hole

For many people, St Andrews is all about golf. If you happen to be a golf-mad foodie, both passions are catered for here where front-row balcony seats for the golfing action at the 18th hole of the Old Course are available for the price of a meal in the Rocca restaurant amid a chic contemporary decor of richly coloured fabrics and darkwood tables. The kitchen's food is modern, ingredients-led from the best local supply lines, and provides deep satisfaction, the six-course taster opening, perhaps, with cured salmon supported by pressed cucumber, lemon, hazelnuts and fennel, followed by trompette mushroom risotto with parmesan crisp and cep foam. Classy fish dishes may include halibut served with clams, seafood chowder and chorizo, while meatier ideas take in braised beef cheek with Savoy cabbage, potato mash, Puy lentils and confit shallot. Desserts aim for the same level of straight-talking impact with the likes of lemon curd sponge with raspberry ice cream.

Chef Tony Borthwick **Seats** 70, Private dining 35 **Open** All year **Parking** 23
Notes Vegetarian dishes, Children welcome

FIFE continued

ST MONANS
Craig Millar@16 West End
⊚⊚ MODERN SCOTTISH ▮NOTABLE WINE LIST

01333 730327 | 16 West End, KY10 2BX
www.16westend.com

Sweeping views of the Firth of Forth and St Monans harbour can get dramatic when winter waves surge over the sea wall, but the proximity of the sea is a reminder of the business here: serving seafood with an exciting modern spin.

Chef Craig Millar **Seats** 40, Private dining 24 **Closed** 25–26 December, 1–2 January, 2 weeks January **Parking** 6 **Notes** Vegetarian dishes, No children under 12 years at dinner

▶ GLASGOW

GLASGOW
Blythswood Square
⊚⊚ MODERN BRITISH

0141 248 8888 | 11 Blythswood Square, G2 4AD
www.blythswoodsquare.com

Built in 1821 as the grand headquarters for the Royal Scottish Automobile Club, this building has been injected with a good dollop of boutique style. The restaurant in the former ballroom features contemporary decor with food that follows suit.

Chef Zoltan Szabo **Seats** 120, Private dining 80 **Open** All year **Prices from** S £6.50, M £16.50, D £7 **Notes** Vegetarian dishes, Children welcome

La Bonne Auberge
⊚ FRENCH, MEDITERRANEAN

0141 352 8310 | Holiday Inn Glasgow,
161 West Nile Street, G1 2RL
www.labonneauberge.co.uk

This ever-popular venue is kitted out in contemporary style with exposed brickwork, tiled and wooden flooring and lamps on wooden tables, and has attentive and friendly staff. Meats including BBQ pork loin and rib-eye steak are cooked on the grill.

Chef Gerry Sharkey **Seats** 90, Private dining 100 **Open** All year **Prices from** S £7.50, M £14.50, D £6 **Notes** Vegetarian dishes, Children welcome

Cail Bruich
⊚⊚⊚ MODERN SCOTTISH **V**

0141 334 6265 | 752 Great Western Road, G12 8QX
www.cailbruich.co.uk

It isn't always necessary to head out into the Highlands in search of country cuisine. Here in Glasgow's swinging West End, the Charalambous brothers bring it to the city doorstep, in a modern bistro setting where hanging baskets flank the door, and rows of tables at crimson banquettes form a long, informal space. The vegetarian dishes alone are inspired, offering salt-baked celeriac with onion and truffle, or spelt with Jerusalem artichoke, lettuce and Brinkburn goats' cheese, for mains. Elsewhere, stimulating combinations distinguish the seasonally changing menus, perhaps Loch Fyne scallop with smoked eel, sour cabbage and apple, and then lamb with sprouting broccoli, anchovies and black olives, or stone bass with langoustine, clementine and pumpkin. For the seven-course taster, there are fish or meat alternatives at two stages, and caramelised whey with sea buckthorn, apple and fennel pollen makes for a thoroughly modern finale. A single cheese option might be Baron Bigod with potato bread and truffle honey. Speciality beers and a tempting list of imaginative cocktails supplement the commendable wine list.

Chef Chris Charalambous **Seats** 48 **Closed** 25–26 December, 1 January, 1 week January **Notes** No children under 5 years

Chez Mal Brasserie
⊚ MODERN FRENCH

0141 572 1001 | 278 West George Street, G2 4LL
www.malmaison.com

The Glasgow Mal has made its home in a deconsecrated Greek Orthodox church. A mix of traditional and modern French brasserie cooking is the draw, with select breeds and cuts of thoroughbred beef the backbone. Soufflé du jour is worth a look at dessert.

Chef John Burns **Seats** 106, Private dining 56 **Open** All year **Notes** Vegetarian dishes, Children welcome

The Fish People Café
⊚ MODERN SEAFOOD

0141 4298787 | 350a Scotland Street, G5 8QF
www.thefishpeoplecafe.co.uk

A lively little fish restaurant run by the fishmonger next door sounds like an irresistible proposition, and the skilled team in the kitchen know how to handle the peerless piscine produce, turning out uncomplicated dishes with pin-sharp technique and timings.

Chef John Gillespie **Seats** 32 **Closed** 25–26 December, 1st week January (including 1 January) **Prices from** S £5.50, M £16.50, D £6.50 **Notes** Vegetarian dishes, Children welcome

Gamba

◉◉ SCOTTISH, SEAFOOD

0141 572 0899 | 225a West George Street, G2 2ND

www.gamba.co.uk

This perennial favourite enjoys a well-deserved reputation as the go-to place for top-notch fish and seafood. The kitchen is passionate about sourcing the best seasonal produce, with fish from sustainable stocks cooked with simplicity and style. Desserts include some impressive stuff.

Chef Derek Marshall **Seats** 66 **Closed** 25–26 December, 1st week January **Prices from** S £8, M £10.50, D £7 **Notes** Vegetarian dishes, Children welcome

The Gannet

◉◉◉ MODERN SCOTTISH

0141 204 2081 | 1155 Argyle Street, G3 8TB

www.thegannetgla.com

Conceived on a research trip to the Hebridean west of Scotland, the Reid brothers' venue in the Finnieston district of the city is a continuous tribute to the produce of the growers, breeders and gatherers of the islands and coasts. Transposed into the more obviously urban setting of a modern bistro with walls of bare brick and stone, it takes on a new identity in the form of lively European dishes that mobilise up-to-date technique but without undue complication. Cured sea trout with charred and pickled cucumber in herb dressing sits alongside black pudding made in-house and served with lamb sweetbreads and caramelised onion among starters. Main courses might reach to the northerly extremities for Scrabster cod with mussels and salsify in pancetta sauce, or partner superb red deer with cavolo nero, wild mushrooms and burnt carrot purée in a gamey reduction. At the finish, there are farmhouse cheeses in tip-top condition, or tempters such as blood orange, almond and basil tart with cardamom ice cream.

Chef Peter McKenna, Ivan Stein **Seats** 45, Private dining 14 **Closed** 25–26 December, 1–2 January **Prices from** S £6.50, M £16, D £7 **Notes** Vegetarian dishes, Children welcome

The Hanoi Bike Shop

◉ VIETNAMESE V

0141 334 7165 | 8 Ruthven Lane, G12 9BG

www.hanoibikeshop.co.uk

Sister restaurant to the Ubiquitous Chip and Stravaigin, this colourful West End venture is set across two buzzing floors. The canteen-style vibe suits the authentic street food menu of dazzling flavours.

Chef Jesse Stevens **Seats** 75, Private dining 35 **Closed** 25 December, 1 January **Notes** Children welcome

See advertisement opposite

Hotel du Vin at One Devonshire Gardens

Rosettes suspended MODERN FRENCH **V**

0141 339 2001 | 1 Devonshire Gardens, G12 0UX

www.hotelduvin.com

The Rosette award for this establishment has been suspended due to a change of chef and reassessment will take place in due course. The HdV group has always done a nice line in suave boutique luxury, and this supremely elegant Victorian terrace in the West End – with a long-standing foodie reputation to maintain – is the jewel in the crown. The Bistro – as the restaurant is named, in keeping with the rest of the group – is a rather grander affair than its name denotes, with glitzy chandeliers illuminating polished wood floors, chocolate-brown banquettes and a classy, neutral decor.

Chef Gary Townsend **Seats** 78, Private dining 80 **Open** All year **Prices from** S £9.75, M £23.95, D £9 **Notes** Children welcome

Mother India

◉ INDIAN

0141 221 1663 | 28 Westminster Terrace, Sauchiehall Street, G3 7RU

www.motherindia.co.uk

This landmark restaurant, launched in 1990, continues to draw the crowds with its inventive, flavour-packed Indian food. Spread over three floors, Mother India avoids cliché in its decor. The menu takes a step away from curry-house standards to deliver broadly appealing dishes.

Chef Amar Kumar Maurya **Seats** 145, Private dining 8 **Closed** Christmas, New Year **Notes** Vegetarian dishes, Children welcome

Number Sixteen

◉◉ MODERN INTERNATIONAL

0141 339 2544 | 16 Byres Road, G11 5JY

www.number16.co.uk

This dinky neighbourhood restaurant has a strong local following. It's an elbow-to-elbow sort of place with a pocket-sized downstairs area, and a mini-mezzanine above, decorated with colourful artwork, and kept ticking over by casually dressed staff. The chefs experiment with a vibrant barrage of flavours.

Chef Sean Currie **Seats** 36, Private dining 17 **Closed** 25–26 December, 1–2 January **Prices from** S £5.95, M £13.50, D £7.50 **Notes** Vegetarian dishes, Children welcome

VIETNAMESE CANTEEN

RUTHVEN LANE GLASGOW G12 9BG HANOIBIKESHOP.CO.UK 0141 334 7165

111 by Nico
◉ MODERN EUROPEAN V
0141 334 0111 | 111 Cleveden Road, Kelvinside,
G12 0JU
www.111bynico.co.uk

Nico Simeone's altruism in employing youngsters who didn't get the best start in life is thoroughly commendable. Together, they produce contemporary cooking for a city-smart audience, the kind that appreciates ingenious duck leg croustillants with textures of parsnip including an Indian-spiced purée.

Chef Nico Simeone, Modou Diagme **Notes** No children

Opium
◉ CHINESE, ORIENTAL FUSION
0141 332 6668 | 191 Hope Street, G2 2UL
www.opiumrestaurant.co.uk

A pin-sharp, contemporary-styled Asian-fusion restaurant in the heart of Glasgow. Big picture windows allow light to flood into a slick space where communal tables share the space with conventional seating. Kwan Yu Lee has honed an on-trend mix of classical and modern Asian fusion dishes.

Chef Kwan Yu Lee **Seats** 54 **Open** All year
Notes Vegetarian dishes, Children welcome

Ox and Finch
◉◉ MODERN BRITISH V
0141 339 8627 | 920 Sauchiehall Street, G3 7TF
www.oxandfinch.com

Tapas-size portions are the deal at this buzzing venue. Bare brick walls, roughly painted wooden floors, banquette and booth seating and unbuttoned service create a casual, laid-back atmosphere. The menu is divided into such headings as 'snacks' and 'raw, cured and cold'.

Chef Daniel Spurr, Aurelien Mourez **Seats** 70, Private dining 14 **Closed** 25–26 December, 1–2 January
Notes Children welcome

Shish Mahal
◉ BRITISH, INDIAN
0141 339 8256 | 60–68 Park Road, G4 9JF
www.shishmahal.co.uk

Opened in the 1960s by the charismatic 'Mr Ali', Shish Mahal is a Glaswegian institution which has moved with the times. There's a smart modern feel to the restaurant, while the menu takes in old favourites as well as plenty of intriguing new ideas.

Chef I Humayun **Seats** 84, Private dining 14 **Closed** 25 December **Prices from** S £3.25, M £11.15, D £3.95
Notes Vegetarian dishes, Children welcome

Stravaigin
◉◉ MODERN INTERNATIONAL, SCOTTISH V
0141 334 2665 | 28–30 Gibson Street, Kelvinbridge, G12 8NX
www.stravaigin.co.uk

In a busy street near the university, this popular all-day bar/restaurant draws the crowds to eat and drink among the contemporary decor, modern art and quirky antiques. Expect innovative and exciting fusion food cooked from top-quality, seasonal Scottish ingredients.

Chef Nathan Kidney **Seats** 62 **Closed** 25 December, 1 January **Notes** Children welcome

See advertisement opposite

Ubiquitous Chip Restaurant
◉◉ SCOTTISH V ♦ NOTABLE WINE LIST
0141 334 5007 | 12 Ashton Lane, G12 8SJ
www.ubiquitouschip.co.uk

The Chip will celebrate its 50th birthday in a couple of years, its longevity due in part to an instinct for keeping abreast of the times without chasing culinary fashion. The cooking is imaginative, soundly conceived, and has always been based on superb Scottish ingredients.

Chef Andrew Mitchell **Seats** 120, Private dining 45 **Closed** 25 December and 1 January **Notes** Children welcome

See advertisement on page 397

Wee Lochan
◉ MODERN SCOTTISH
0141 338 6606 | 340 Crow Road, Broomhill, G11 7HT
www.an-lochan.com

The black frontage gives a distinguished look to a neighbourhood restaurant in the quiet, leafy reaches of the West End, its wide terrace allowing pleasant outdoor dining in summer. The contemporary Scottish cooking scores a hit with precise, defined flavours.

Chef Chris Bryers **Seats** 50 **Closed** 25–26 December, 1–2 January **Prices from** S £4.50, M £12.50, D £5.25
Notes Vegetarian dishes, Children welcome

THINK GLOBAL

Stravaigin

WANDERING
SINCE 1994

EAT LOCAL

28 GIBSON ST KELVINBRIDGE GLASGOW G12 8NX
STRAVAIGIN.CO.UK 🅕 🅓 🅘 0141 334 2665

HIGHLAND

▶ HIGHLAND

ACHARACLE
Mingarry Park
◉◉ MODERN BRITISH
01967 431202 | Mingarry, PH36 4JX
www.mingarryparkhouse.co.uk

The relaxing dining room at Mingarry Park enjoys spectacular views, setting the scene for a bold menu. Creativity is shown in dishes such as sous-vide Moidart venison loin accompanied by carrot purée, maple-glazed Chantenay carrots, a summer greens sponge and an intense red wine jus.

Chef David Punter **Seats Closed** November to April **Parking** 20 **Notes** Vegetarian dishes

CROMARTY
The Factor's House
◉ MODERN BRITISH
01381 600394 | Denny Road, IV11 8YT
www.thefactorshouse.com

This attractive red sandstone house on a coastal inlet features a wood-floored dining room with walls in burgundy and grey. A daily changing four-course dinner menu, including Scottish cheeses, is the offering, and there is a real personality to the dishes.

Chef Fiona Deakin **Seats** 10, Private dining 10 **Closed** 15 December to 5 January **Parking** 4 **Notes** Vegetarian dishes, No children under 5 years

DORNOCH
Links House at Royal Dornoch
◉◉ CLASSIC SCOTTISH
01862 810279 | Links House, Golf Road, IV25 3LW
www.linkshousedornoch.com

Links House is single-mindedly devoted to the pursuit of golf and pictures of fairways and bunkers adorn the dining room, where a peat-burning fireplace is a feature. A new head chef brings his classical French training to the newly expanded Orangery restaurant.

Chef Javier Santos **Seats** 33 **Closed** Christmas, 3 January to 25 March **Parking** 6 **Notes** Children welcome

FORT AUGUSTUS
The Inch
◉◉ TRADITIONAL SCOTTISH
01456 450900 | Inchnacardoch Bay, PH32 4BL
www.inchhotel.com

The Inch occupies an old hunting lodge above Inchnacardoch Bay and the hotel's restaurant boasts one of the best views over the iconic Loch Ness. The food has a strong sense of place, with Scottish produce dominating the impressive menu.

Chef Philip Carnegie **Seats** 36 **Open** All year **Parking** 18 **Notes** Vegetarian dishes, Children welcome

FORT WILLIAM
Inverlochy Castle Hotel
◉◉◉ MODERN FRENCH V ♦ NOTABLE WINE LIST
01397 702177 | Torlundy, PH33 6SN
www.inverlochycastlehotel.com

This very grand baronial castle is set in a wonderfully verdant valley at the foot of Ben Nevis. Views are spectacular, and there's a real sense of history and opulence in the richly decorated public spaces, with all the high ceilings, antiques and crystal chandeliers you could wish for. The restaurant is more intimate and extremely formal in approach – white gloves are worn by smartly attired staff and gentlemen guests will need their jackets. Don't be intimidated, though – the team are wonderfully hospitable. The style is modern British with French influences as one might expect from the consultant chefs, father and son Albert and Michel Roux Jr. Dishes are complex, with many elements, which means you'll experience wonderful textural contrasts and clean, clear flavours. Tartare of Highland beef with chestnut mushrooms is a robust beginning, served with super crisp croûtons, sliced chestnut and pickled shiitake and a wonderful truffle mayonnaise. Sea bass comes with courgette tagliatelle and shrimp consommé, poured at the table. A precisely plated ginger cake with white chocolate and orange sorbet brings things to a refined conclusion.

Chef Dan Barker **Seats** 40, Private dining 20 **Open** All year **Parking** 20 **Notes** No children under 8 years

GLENFINNAN
The Prince's House
◉◉ MODERN BRITISH
01397 722246 | PH37 4LT
www.glenfinnan.co.uk

Kieron and Ina Kelly's white-fronted house has charm in bucket loads. The dining room is hung with a fine art collection and the small conservatory has ravishing views over the glen. Kieron Kelly's cooking steps up to the regional plate in four-course set menus.

Chef Kieron Kelly **Seats** 30 **Closed** Christmas, October to March **Parking** 18 **Notes** Vegetarian dishes, Children welcome

INVERGARRY

Glengarry Castle Hotel

◉ SCOTTISH, INTERNATIONAL

01809 501254 | PH35 4HW

www.glengarry.net

The Glengarry, overlooking Loch Oich, is a slice of Victorian Scottish baronial, built in the 1860s. Spotless white linen and quality glassware glow beneath the chandelier in the opulent dining room, where lightly modernised traditional fare is the order of the day.

Chef Romuald Denesle **Seats** 40 **Closed** mid November to mid March **Parking** 30 **Notes** Vegetarian dishes, Children welcome

INVERGORDON

Kincraig Castle Hotel

◉ MODERN SCOTTISH

01349 852587 | IV18 0LF

www.kincraig-castle-hotel.co.uk

Pretty gables and wee turrets give this former ancestral seat of Clan MacKenzie a bit of gravitas, while its lush lawn sweeps down towards the Cromarty Firth. The house is decorated to suit the grand baronial setting, and the traditional Alexander Restaurant matches the mood.

Chef Stuart Thomson **Seats** 30, Private dining 50 **Open** All year **Parking** 40 **Notes** Vegetarian dishes, Children welcome

INVERNESS

Bunchrew House Hotel

◉◉ MODERN BRITISH

01463 234917 | Bunchrew, IV3 8TA

www.bunchrewhousehotel.com

Bunchrew House is a magnificent 17th-century mansion, complete with turrets and a pink facade, on the water's edge of the Beauly Firth. Modern British with a basis of classical influence is the kitchen's view of its culinary world. There is a daily changing menu.

Chef J P Saint **Seats** 32, Private dining 14 **Closed** 23–26 December **Parking** 40 **Notes** Vegetarian dishes, Children welcome

Contrast Brasserie

◉ SCOTTISH **V**

01463 223777 | Glenmoriston Town House Hotel, 20 Ness Bank, IV2 4SF

www.glenmoristontownhouse.com

In the evening, with a pianist playing soft, funky music, the low lighting and modern decor, the atmosphere is rather romantic. Scottish produce is used here in, for example, Shetland mussels and seared carpaccio of Ardgay venison, but overall we're talking modern British cooking.

Chef David Toward **Seats** 56, Private dining 90 **Open** All year **Prices from** S £4.95, M £14, D £5.95 **Parking** 45 **Notes** Children welcome

Loch Ness Country House Hotel

◉◉ MODERN BRITISH

01463 230512 | Loch Ness Road, IV3 8JN

www.lochnesscountryhousehotel.co.uk

This creeper-covered Georgian house in lovely grounds is not actually on Loch Ness, and is three miles outside Inverness. The classy interiors are all stripes and tartan, with three dining rooms, each with only a few tables, decorated in restrained greys and browns.

Chef Adam Dwyer **Seats** 42, Private dining 24 **Open** All year **Parking** 70 **Notes** Vegetarian dishes, Children welcome

The New Drumossie Hotel

◉◉ MODERN SCOTTISH

01463 236451 | Old Perth Road, IV2 5BE

www.drumossiehotel.co.uk

A few miles out of Inverness, the hotel is a sparkling-white art deco beauty in acres of well-tended grounds framed by the Scottish Highlands. Its charm is due in no small part to the staff who treat guests with engaging politeness.

Chef Stewart Macpherson **Seats** 40, Private dining 40 **Open** All year **Parking** 200 **Notes** Vegetarian dishes, Children welcome

Rocpool

◉◉ MODERN EUROPEAN

01463 717274 | 1 Ness Walk, IV3 5NE

www.rocpoolrestaurant.com

This buzzy brasserie on the banks of the River Ness has floodlit views of the river and castle at night. The interior is an exercise in contemporary design flair featuring lots of wood and natural tones. The food is an appealing cast of modern European dishes built on top-class Scottish produce.

Chef Steven Devlin **Seats** 55 **Closed** 25–26 December, 1–3 January **Prices from** S £4.95, M £13.95, D £7.45 **Notes** Vegetarian dishes, Children welcome

Rocpool Reserve and Chez Roux

◉◉ FRENCH, SCOTTISH **V**

01463 240089 | 14 Culduthel Road, IV2 4AG

www.rocpool.com

With the hallowed Roux name above the door (Monsieur Albert in this case), the auld alliance is alive and well at this contemporary, riverside restaurant. A vein of French classicism runs through the cooking, while the impeccable Scottish credentials of the produce is trumpeted too.

Chef Javi Dominguez Santos **Seats** 60, Private dining 14 **Open** All year **Prices from** S £10.50, M £18.50, D £8 **Parking** 14 **Notes** Children welcome

Table Manors Restaurant
◉◉ TRADITIONAL SCOTTISH
01463 831878 | Kirkhill, IV5 7PD
www.perfect-manors.com

Table Manors is part of the Achnagairn Estate, whose luxury lodges are nicknamed the 'perfect manors'. Designed in contemporary style, the restaurant demonstrates the importance of space and light. Wordplay on the compact menu includes 'Crabbing the Nettle' – sweetcorn pannacotta, white crab, hazelnut, avocado and nettle.

Chef Euan Walker **Closed** Monday to Tuesday (winter and spring) **Prices from** S £7, M £16, D £7 **Parking** 24 **Notes** Vegetarian dishes

KINGUSSIE
The Cross
◉◉◉ MODERN SCOTTISH **V** 🍷 NOTABLE WINE LIST
01540 661166 | Tweed Mill Brae, Ardbroilach Road, PH21 1LB
www.thecross.co.uk

Formed from an old tweed mill that stood on the crossroads of the Highland village of Kingussie, The Cross is now a restaurant with rooms on the human scale, with eight brightly designed bedrooms and a beamed restaurant with undressed tables and landscape prints. The mood is one of informal tranquillity, and the kitchen matches the pastoral surroundings with locally reared meats a speciality. Lamb is served two ways, as the roast loin and cannelloni of the shoulder, with violet artichoke and glazed shallots in jus gras, while venison makes up a double-act with braised oxtail, alongside a delicately fashioned beetroot tart and creamed cabbage in red wine sauce. Prior to those, there may be confit salmon sharply dressed with horseradish cream and orange, anointed with splashes of fine olive oil, while the covetable dessert is a complex construction of chocolate and Grand Marnier millefeuille with marmalade ice cream, clementines and toasted almonds. A tasting menu picks out some of the main menu's highlights, complete with appetiser and pre-dessert, while the three-course lunch menu, with three choices at each stage, represents exemplary value.

Chef David Skiggs **Seats** 26 **Closed** Christmas and January (excluding New Year) **Parking** 12 **Notes** Children welcome

LOCHALINE
The Whitehouse Restaurant
◉◉ MODERN SCOTTISH **V**
01967 421777 | PA80 5XT
www.thewhitehouserestaurant.co.uk

This must be one of the remotest restaurants in Scotland, reached via a single track road. The kitchen cooks whatever its suppliers have provided on the day. This local bounty is turned into dishes that maintain integrity through simplicity.

Chef Michael Burgoyne, Lee Myers **Seats** 26 **Closed** November to March **Parking** 10 **Notes** Children welcome

LOCHINVER
Inver Lodge and Chez Roux
◉◉ FRENCH **V**
01571 844496 | Iolaire Road, IV27 4LU
www.inverlodge.com

In a prime position above the fishing village of Lochinver, Chez Roux has breathtaking views of the loch and local area, making window seats highly prized. The menu changes regularly but three of Monsieur Roux's signature dishes remain on the menu.

Chef Albert Roux, Patryk Stanalowski **Seats** 45 **Closed** November to March **Parking** 25 **Notes** Children welcome

NAIRN
Golf View Hotel & Spa
◉ TRADITIONAL, INTERNATIONAL **V**
01667 452301 | Seabank Road, IV12 4HD
www.golfviewhotel.co.uk

In case you get the impression there's only golf to look at, this hotel's seaside location looks out over the Moray Firth. The Fairways Restaurant is a half-panelled room with chandeliers, serving a six-course fixed-price menu as well as the carte.

Chef Martin Ewart **Seats** 70 **Open** All year **Prices from** S £6, M £14, D £6 **Parking** 30 **Notes** Children welcome

SPEAN BRIDGE
Russell's at Smiddy House
◉◉ MODERN SCOTTISH
01397 712335 | Roy Bridge Road, PH34 4EU
www.smiddyhouse.com

Occupying a corner spot on the main road through Spean Bridge, four smart bedrooms mean you can stop over and spoil yourself with top seasonal cooking. Russell's is in the 'Smiddyhouse', once the village blacksmith's, an intimate spot for well-presented food.

Chef Glen Russell **Seats** 38 **Parking** 15 **Notes** Vegetarian dishes, No children under 12 years

HIGHLAND

STRONTIAN
Kilcamb Lodge Hotel
◉◉◉ MODERN SEAFOOD V ♦ NOTABLE WINE LIST
01967 402257 | PH36 4HY
www.kilcamblodge.co.uk

Standing on the shore of Loch Sunart in 22 acres of sumptuous grounds, Kilcamb offers unruffled tranquillity and seclusion, the journey alone providing a delightful taste of the wild Ardnamurchan Peninsula. With just 12 rooms, the Georgian house is an intimate hideaway that delivers old-school country-house comforts all the way to the elegant dining room, where linen is crisp, cutlery and glassware sparkle, and the loch views paint an unforgettable backdrop to modern cooking with its distinct Scottish accent. Gary Phillips provisions the larder from local crofts, estates and fishing boats, the latter's catch showcased on a daily changing speciality seafood menu. Hand-dived scallops open the show in a vibrant medley with black pudding, apple bonbon, salt-baked beetroot, pickled cauliflower and caramelised apple purée, then roast loin of superb local lamb comes crusted with garlic and pistachio, alongside shepherd's pie of slow-cooked leg meat, creamed cabbage and bacon, carrot and apricot purée, and caper and mint butter. The finale is a riff on lemon comprising lemon and ginger cheesecake, white chocolate and lemon parfait, mini lemon meringues and lemon jelly.

Chef Gary Phillips **Seats** 40, Private dining 14 **Closed** 1 January to 1 February **Parking** 28 **Notes** Children welcome

THURSO
Forss House Hotel
◉◉ MODERN SCOTTISH
01847 861201 | Forss, KW14 7XY
www.forsshousehotel.co.uk

You can't get much further away from urban bustle in the mainland British Isles than the northern Highlands, where this Georgian country-house hotel luxuriates in tranquillity below a waterfall on the River Forss, amid acres of woodland. Plenty of pedigree Highland produce is on parade.

Chef Andrew Manson **Seats** 26, Private dining 14 **Closed** 23 December to 4 January **Prices from** S £6.50, M £12.50, D £6.50 **Parking** 14 **Notes** Vegetarian dishes, Children welcome

TORRIDON
The Torridon
◉◉◉ MODERN SCOTTISH V ♦ NOTABLE WINE LIST
01445 791242 | By Achnasheen, Wester Ross, IV22 2EY
www.thetorridon.com

You do have to be pretty determined to track down The Torridon, but who wouldn't be? The reward for the hunt is a turreted Victorian lochside lodge that still offers plenty of sporting activity, a copiously stocked whisky bar, and a panelled and leathered ambience for sinking into while you forget the rigorous journey. Ross Stovold has the produce of a two-acre kitchen garden at his disposal in the 1887 Restaurant, where he offers contemporary Scottish cuisine in dishes that are presented with artful simplicity. Textures and flavours come into exquisite harmony in a starter of seared sea bass with smoked butternut squash, garnished with herring roe, chicken skin and samphire. At main, pedigree meats such as Beinn Eighe venison with textures of parsnip, sprouts and fermented rosehip make strong statements, while fish might be Mallaig halibut with Skye mussels, pink firs and seaweed. To finish, the several richnesses of double cream custard with heather honey and meringue are offset with nippy little pickled raspberries, or go for brown butter cake with oats and nutmegged plum.

Chef Ross Stovold **Seats** 38, Private dining 16 **Closed** 2 January for 5 weeks **Parking** 20 **Notes** No children under 10 years

WICK
Mackay's Hotel
◉ MODERN SCOTTISH V
01955 602323 | Union Street, KW1 5ED
www.mackayshotel.co.uk

Mackay's is home to the No. 1 Bistro, a contemporary restaurant with a relaxed vibe. The kitchen makes good use of quality local ingredients, and there's a modernity to the output. There's a buzzy bar for real ales, cocktails and a terrific range of whiskies.

Chef Jason Woods **Seats** 40, Private dining 30 **Closed** 24–25 December and 1–2 January **Notes** Children welcome

NORTH LANARKSHIRE

CUMBERNAULD
The Westerwood Hotel & Golf Resort
◉ MODERN SCOTTISH
01236 457171 | 1 St Andrews Drive, Westerwood,
G68 0EW
www.qhotels.co.uk
A sharply modern construction of brick and glass,
Westerwood House's restaurant – Flemings – matches
the contemporary mood of the hotel and its colour
scheme recalls the natural Scottish landscape. There's
a modern-minded menu, and tasting menu, too, with
wine flight option.
Chef Russell Johnstone **Seats** 150, Private dining 60
Closed December to January **Parking** 250
Notes Vegetarian dishes, Children welcome

SOUTH LANARKSHIRE

BLANTYRE
Crossbasket Castle
◉◉◉ CLASSICAL FRENCH
01698 829461 | Crossbasket Estate,
Stoneymeadow Road, G72 9UE
www.crossbasketcastle.com
Not far from Glasgow, Crossbasket was conjured out
of a much older castle in the 17th century, complete
with crenellated facade and spiral turret staircases. An
elegant dining room of pale yellow wallpaper, a winter
fire and linened tables under an ornate gold-leafed
plasterwork ceiling, offering superb views over the
gardens, is a refined backdrop for a Roux operation,
père et fils, in which the classical French dishes are
finished with some innovative touches. Highland game
pâté comes shoehorned into a croûte casing with a
layer of savoury jelly, accompanied by spiced pear and
raisin chutney, or you might begin with a great fat
Orkney scallop that has truffled leek and potato
velouté poured over it at the table. Confident meat
cookery produces Gartmorn duck breast with sherried
prunes in a glossy jus, or fine pink venison in red wine
with richly creamy pomme purée, Savoy cabbage and
beetroot. Crisp-glazed lemon tart with bramble sorbet
is from the vintage Albert Roux playbook, while
Valrhona chocolate pavé with salt caramel and
popcorn ice cream is distinctly more de nos jours.
Chef Albert and Michel Roux Jnr, Aaron Sobey
Seats 30, Private dining 250 **Open** All year
Prices from S £10, M £18, D £8 **Parking** 120
Notes Children welcome

EAST KILBRIDE
Macdonald Crutherland House
◉◉ BRITISH
01355 577000 | Strathaven Road, G75 0QZ
www.macdonald-hotels.co.uk
Dating from the early 1700s, Crutherland House
stands in nearly 40 acres of peaceful grounds. The
restaurant keeps things traditional, with its panelled
walls, paintings and burnished darkwood tables. The
menu takes a classical approach to things, with plenty
of Scottish ingredients on show.
Chef Richard Dickson **Seats** 80, Private dining 300
Open All year **Parking** 200 **Notes** Vegetarian
dishes, Children welcome

EAST LOTHIAN

ABERLADY
Ducks Inn
◉◉ MODERN BRITISH
01875 870682 | Main Street, EH32 0RE
www.ducks.co.uk
Located in the heart of a small village, Ducks Inn
covers all the bases with its bar-bistro, restaurant and
smart accommodation. The good-looking dining area,
recently refurbished, is matched by the attractiveness
of what arrives on the plate. The kitchen turns out
appealing combinations.
Chef Michal Mozdzen **Seats** 26, Private dining 22
Closed 25 December **Parking** 15 **Notes** Vegetarian
dishes, Children welcome

GULLANE
Greywalls and Chez Roux
◉◉ MODERN FRENCH COUNTRY **V**
01620 842144 | Muirfield, EH31 2EG
www.greywalls.co.uk
Located on the East Lothian coast, Chez Roux has its
home in a country house with magnificent gardens.
The dining room displays an eclectic mix of cartoons,
photos and artwork that enhance the formal decor.
The menu features classic dishes from the Albert
Roux repertoire.
Chef Ryan McCutcheon **Seats** 80, Private dining 20
Open All year **Prices from** S £11, M £23.50, D £8
Parking 40 **Notes** Children welcome

La Potinière

◉◉ MODERN BRITISH

01620 843214 | Main Street, EH31 2AA
www.lapotiniere.co.uk

A double-act operation with Mary Runciman and Keith Marley at the stoves. Menus change regularly and the deal is just a couple of choices per course. A high level of skill is evident: perhaps braised salmon partnered by crushed new potatoes with spring onion.

Chef Mary Runciman, Keith Marley **Seats** 24 **Closed** Christmas, January, Bank holidays **Parking** 10 **Notes** Vegetarian dishes, Children welcome

NORTH BERWICK
Macdonald Marine Hotel & Spa

◉◉ EUROPEAN

01620 897300 | Cromwell Road, EH39 4LZ
www.macdonaldhotels.co.uk/marine

The Marine Hotel is an upscale Grade II listed Victorian manor overlooking the East Lothian golf course. The Craigleith Restaurant surveys the action through the sweeping bay windows. The kitchen follows contemporary culinary style, while showing respect for classical thinking.

Chef David Quinn **Seats** 80, Private dining 20 **Open** All year **Parking** 50 **Notes** Vegetarian dishes, Children welcome

▶ WEST LOTHIAN

LINLITHGOW
Champany Inn

◉◉ TRADITIONAL BRITISH

01506 834532 | Champany Corner, EH49 7LU
www.champany.com

Close to Linlithgow Palace, this cluster of buildings dates from the 16th century and the candlelit restaurant occupies a former flour mill complete with bare stone walls and vaulted roof. It is the destination of choice for fans of properly hung, expertly butchered slabs of top-quality meat.

Chef D Gibson, G Stoddart **Seats** 50, Private dining 30 **Closed** 25–26 December, 1–2 January **Parking** 50 **Notes** Vegetarian dishes, Children welcome

UPHALL
Macdonald Houstoun House

◉◉ TRADITIONAL BRITISH, MODERN SCOTTISH

01506 853831 | EH52 6JS
www.macdonaldhotels.co.uk/our-hotels/
macdonald-houstoun-house

The white-painted house, surrounded by 22 acres of woodlands, dates from the 16th century. The restaurant sports deep burgundy walls, chandeliers

and elegant unclothed tables. The kitchen presents its Scottish ingredients in a modern, unfussy style.

Chef Jeremy Wares **Seats** 65, Private dining 30 **Open** All year **Parking** 200 **Notes** Vegetarian dishes, Children welcome

▶ MIDLOTHIAN

DALKEITH
The Sun Inn

◉ MODERN, TRADITIONAL

0131 663 2456 | Lothian Bridge, EH22 4TR
www.thesuninnedinburgh.co.uk

'Eat, drink, relax' is the motto of this gastro pub, and it's made easy by a dose of rustic-chic style with the original oak beams, exposed stone and panelling. Expect welcoming log fires, a bright patio, and Scotland's larder forming the backbone of the output.

Chef Ian Minto, Lee Coulter, Christy McNiven **Seats** 90, Private dining 100 **Closed** 26 December, 1 January **Prices from** S £6, M £10, D £7 **Parking** 115 **Notes** Vegetarian dishes, Children welcome

▶ MORAY

FORRES
Cluny Bank

◉ TRADITIONAL EUROPEAN

01309 674304 | 69 St Leonards Road, IV36 1DW
www.clunybankhotel.co.uk

A substantial Victorian mansion in lush gardens, Cluny Bank has traditionally styled decor and a small, smart restaurant called Franklin's. There is a lot of period charm to the restaurant and an air of sophistication. The menu name-checks the local Moray suppliers.

Chef Lloyd Kenny **Seats** 24 **Open** All year **Prices from** S £5.25, M £19.25, D £6.50 **Parking** 10 **Notes** Vegetarian dishes, No children under 8 years

▶ PERTH & KINROSS

ABERFELDY
Thyme Restaurant

◉◉ SCOTTISH, INTERNATIONAL

01887 820850 | Errichel House, Crieff Road, PH15 2EL
www.errichel.co.uk

Thyme is located within the Roundhouse at Errichel, a very impressive contemporary building. The weekly changing menu features lamb, beef and pork from the surrounding working farm itself, along with many other ingredients – real 'farm to fork' in action.

Chef Paul Newman **Seats** 40 **Closed** Last week of November, 25–26 December, 1st week of January **Parking** 10 **Notes** Vegetarian dishes, No children under 12 years

AUCHTERARDER
Andrew Fairlie at Gleneagles
@@@@ MODERN FRENCH, SCOTTISH **V** 🍷 NOTABLE WINE LIST
01764 694267 | The Gleneagles Hotel, PH3 1NF
www.andrewfairlie.co.uk

The five-star hotel and its three championship golf courses need little introduction, and, after so many years at the top of the Scottish dining table, neither does Andrew Fairlie's restaurant. An independent business in the heart of the hotel, the lavish windowless dining room is a deeply cossetting space, a shimmering haven with atmospheric lighting and original artworks, watched over by a passionate team who make you feel at ease. Fairlie won the first ever Roux scholarship and got to work with French culinary icon, Michel Guérard, and the legacy of bold French classical cooking can be seen in today's finally crafted, dazzlingly creative contemporary French cuisine...with a Scottish soul, naturally. Choose between the à la carte or eight-course dégustation menus. Roasted veal sweetbread might get the ball rolling, with truffled polenta and Madeira sauce, or go for whipped Scottish crowdie cheese in another opening salvo with beetroot, spiced nuts and aged balsamic. If you're going the way of the à la carte, you might opt for an intermediate course before the main – oven-baked scallop, say, with seaweed butter and lemongrass. Among main courses, roast lamb loin and slow-cooked shoulder comes with a potato and confit lamb pressé, butter-poached fillet of halibut with clams and langoustine bisque, and Goosnargh duck breast with confit leg bonbon and a rich port sauce. To finish, passionfruit soufflé with Pina Colada and exotic fruits is a ray of sunshine. The wine list is a mighty tome with expert advice on hand if required.

Chef Andrew Fairlie, Stephen McLaughlin **Seats** 54 **Closed** 25–26 December, 3 weeks in January **Prices from** S £38, M £54, D £18 **Parking** 300 **Notes** No children

The Strathearn
@@ BRITISH, FRENCH
01764 694270 | The Gleneagles Hotel, PH3 1NF
www.gleneagles.com

The Strathearn is a splendid art deco room with columns and moulded ceilings. The number of trolleys wheeled to the tables may create the impression that the restaurant is in some time warp, but the kitchen embraces the contemporary as well as the classics.

Chef Jonathon Wright **Seats** 250 **Open** All year **Parking** 300 **Notes** Vegetarian dishes, Children welcome

COMRIE
Royal Hotel
@ TRADITIONAL SCOTTISH
01764 679200 | Melville Square, PH6 2DN
www.royalhotel.co.uk

The 18th-century stone building on the main street of this riverside village is now a plush small-scale luxury hotel, with a restaurant split into two areas linked by double doors. Trustworthy sourcing for the seasonally changing menu is clear in pink slices of excellent quality venison.

Chef David Milsom **Seats** 60, Private dining 40 **Closed** 24–26 December **Prices from** S £5.25, M £11.50, D £5.95 **Parking** 18 **Notes** Vegetarian dishes, Children welcome

FORTINGALL
Fortingall Hotel
@ MODERN SCOTTISH
01887 830367 | PH15 2NQ
www.fortingall.com

Fortinghall is very much a tourist destination, and many end up at this Victorian country-house hotel. Dining takes place in two rooms, the main one done out in Arts and Crafts style, with a red carpet, open fire, paintings on the walls and tartan-effect curtains.

Chef David Dunn **Seats** 30, Private dining 30 **Closed** January **Prices from** S £6.50, M £13.50, D £5.95 **Parking** 20 **Notes** Vegetarian dishes, Children welcome

KILLIECRANKIE
Killiecrankie Hotel
@@ MODERN BRITISH **V** 🍷 NOTABLE WINE LIST
01796 473220 | PH16 5LG
www.killiecrankiehotel.co.uk

Built for some blessed church minister back in 1840, the views across the Pass of Killiecrankie and the River Garry will soothe the troubled soul of any visitor. The kitchen delivers a fixed-price à la carte that comes with suggestions for accompanying wines.

Chef Mark Easton **Seats** 36, Private dining 12 **Closed** January to February **Parking** 20 **Notes** Children welcome

PERTH & KINROSS

KINCLAVEN
Ballathie House Hotel
◎◎ MODERN BRITISH V
01250 883268 | PH1 4QN
www.ballathiehousehotel.com
This turreted mansion overlooking the River Tay hosts a restaurant that impresses with its dedication to local ingredients. The dining room has a classical elegance. Traditional flavours combine with a moderated degree of invention to create dishes that seem entirely in keeping with the setting.
Chef Scott Scorer **Seats** 60, Private dining 35 **Open** All year **Parking** 100

PERTH
Deans Restaurant
◎◎ MODERN SCOTTISH
01738 643377 | 77–79 Kinnoull Street, PH1 5EZ
www.letseatperth.co.uk
Right in the centre of town, the family-run, recently refurbished Deans is ever-popular. Here you'll find modern Scottish flavours in a vibrant but easy-going atmosphere. Willie Deans is a highly accomplished chef and his kitchen turns out skilfully executed, elegant dishes.
Chef Willie and Jamie Deans **Seats** 70 **Closed** 1st 2 weeks in January, 1 week in November
Notes Vegetarian dishes, Children welcome

Murrayshall House Hotel & Golf Course
◎ MODERN BRITISH
01738 551171 | New Scone, PH2 7PH
www.murrayshall.co.uk
With two golf courses, Murrayshall doesn't do anything by halves. The main dining option is the Old Masters restaurant, a series of elegant spaces with views over the Perthshire landscape. The menu is rich with Scottish ingredients.
Chef Craig Jackson **Seats** 55, Private dining 40 **Open** All year **Parking** 120 **Notes** Vegetarian dishes, Children welcome

The North Port Restaurant
◎ SCOTTISH V
01738 580867 | 8 North Port, PH1 5LU
www.thenorthport.co.uk
This charming restaurant is full of Jacobean charm, with dark oak panels, a spiral staircase, wooden floors and a candle-filled fireplace. Staff are friendly, and the menus focus on fresh Scottish produce, with a slightly more sophisticated choice of dishes available at dinner.
Chef Andrew Moss **Seats** 32, Private dining 16 **Closed** 24 December to 3 January **Prices from** S £4.95, M £12.95, D £6.95 **Notes** Children welcome

Pig'Halle
◎ FRENCH
01738 248784 | 38 South Street, PH2 8PG
www.pighalle.co.uk
Pig'Halle has a Parisian look, with a map of the Metro embossed on a large mirror, wine memorabilia, brown banquette seating and red-upholstered chairs. It's atmospheric and buzzy, and pork is a theme on the France-inspired menu.
Chef Herve Tabourel **Seats** 40 **Closed** 25 December, 1 January **Notes** Vegetarian dishes, Children welcome

The Roost Restaurant
◎◎ BRITISH
01738 812111 | Forgandenny Road, Bridge of Earn, PH2 9AZ
www.theroostrestaurant.co.uk
Resembling a farmyard building, The Roost is smart as can be inside, with crisply clad tables and a plethora of pictures and mirrors. Thoroughbred Scottish ingredients include some from the Roost's own kitchen gardens.
Chef Tim Dover **Seats** 24 **Closed** 25 December, 1–18 January **Prices from** S £6, M £14, D £6.50 **Parking** 6 **Notes** Vegetarian dishes, Children welcome

63@Parklands
◎◎ MODERN EUROPEAN V
01738 622451 | Parklands Hotel, 2 St Leonards Bank, PH2 8EB
www.63atparklands.com
In a manor house in fine gardens overlooking South Inch Park, the format is a five-course fixed-price menu, with two or three choices at most stages. Cheeses precede the dessert alternatives, which could be poached rhubarb in pink peppercorn sabayon with white chocolate mousse.
Chef Graeme Pallister **Seats** 32, Private dining 22 **Closed** 25 December to 8 January **Parking** 25 **Notes** Children welcome

63 Tay Street Restaurant
◎◎ MODERN SCOTTISH ⬧ NOTABLE WINE LIST
01738 441451 | 63 Tay Street, PH2 8NN
www.63taystreet.com
Graeme Pallister's restaurant occupies part of the ground floor of an imposing stone building; there's a red and grey modern colour scheme with tartan carpet adding a touch of luxury. 'Local, honest, simple' is the aim.
Chef Graeme Pallister **Seats** 38 **Closed** Christmas, New Year, 1st week in July **Prices from** S £6, M £13.50, D £6 **Notes** Vegetarian dishes, Children welcome

Tabla

◉ INDIAN V
01738 444630 | 173 South Street, PH2 8NY
www.tablarestaurant.co.uk

At the Kumar family's central Perth eaterie the ambience has more personality than many a formula Indian restaurant, with exposed stone walls, full-drop windows and a glass panel looking into the kitchen. Indian music featuring the eponymous tabla drums plays softly.

Chef Praveen Kumar **Seats** 42 **Open** All year
Prices from S £5.95, M £10.95, D £4.95
Notes Children welcome

PITLOCHRY

Fonab Castle Hotel & Spa

◉◉◉ MODERN SCOTTISH V
01796 470140 | Foss Road, PH16 5ND
www.fonabcastlehotel.com

Built of red sandstone in 1892 in the Scots baronial style – and how – for a scion of the Sandeman port-shipping family, Fonab Castle stands on a wooded hillside opposite Pitlochry, overlooking Loch Faskally. It embarked on its career as a top-end hotel only in 2013, and its surviving panelled hall, exquisite plasterwork and magnificent stone fireplaces make an appealing contrast to the mod-cons spa facilities and contemporary Scottish cooking also on offer. That latter is enjoyed at its best in the Sandeman Fine Dining restaurant, where the six-course taster offers an exciting programme of cutting-edge dishes, with appetisers and a pre-dessert filling in the gaps between main items. These could take in foie gras with asparagus, ceps and parmesan, langoustine ravioli in its own bisque with crème fraîche, and tender, full-flavoured local Perthshire lamb shoulder with girolles and wild garlic. Dessert could be a gin-laced vanilla and rhubarb crumble, and there is the option of a sharing-plate selection of cheeses as an extra. An excellent slate of wines by the glass is an asset. Simpler food is served in the Brasserie.

Chef Paul Tyrrell **Seats** 60, Private dining 40
Open All year **Prices from** S £6.25, M £16.95, D £5.50
Parking 50 **Notes** Children welcome

Knockendarroch

◉◉ MODERN SCOTTISH
01796 473473 | Higher Oakfield, PH16 5HT
www.knockendarroch.co.uk

A handsome sandstone house in a wooded setting, Knockendarroch has country-house comforts and a diminutive restaurant delivering daily changing menus

Find amazing views and fabulous food in Perthshire at
The Meall Reamhar Restaurant ◉◉

The Four Seasons Hotel, Lochside, St Fillans, Perthshire PH6 2NF
T: 01764 685333   W: thefourseasonshotel.co.uk   E: info@thefourseasonshotel.co.uk

of classy modern Scottish food. It's very traditional within, with warming fires in the cooler months, ornate cornicing, chandeliers and the like, while hospitality is genuine.

Chef Graeme Stewart **Seats** 24 **Closed** mid December to mid February **Parking** 12 **Notes** Vegetarian dishes, No children under 10 years

ST FILLANS
Meall Reamhar
◉◉ MODERN INTERNATIONAL
01764 685333 | The Four Seasons Hotel, Loch Earn, PH6 2NF
www.thefourseasonshotel.co.uk

Perched right on the edge of Loch Earn, The Four Seasons has breathtaking views over the water and the wooded hills. In the waterside Meall Reamhar restaurant, those stunning views complement the modern menu, built on Scottish ingredients from local suppliers.

Chef Carlos Ragone **Seats** 40, Private dining 20 **Closed** Tuesday to Wednesday in March to April and October to December **Prices from** S £5.95, M £18.50, D £6.95 **Parking** 30 **Notes** Vegetarian dishes

See advertisement on page 405

SPITTAL OF GLENSHEE
Dalmunzie Castle Hotel
◉ MODERN CLASSIC FRENCH, INTERNATIONAL **V**
01250 885224 | PH10 7QG
www.dalmunzie.com

The castle was built in the 1920s in the Scottish Baronial style, turrets et al, while the Dalmunzie Estate itself dates from the early 1500s. Today's country-house hotel has a restaurant that reflects the traditional setting and offers a menu with contemporary touches.

Chef Lilian Thieron **Seats** 36, Private dining 16 **Closed** 1–23 December **Prices from** S £8.50, M £22, D £8 **Parking** 20 **Notes** Children welcome

▶ SCOTTISH BORDERS
KELSO
The Cobbles Freehouse & Dining
◉ MODERN BRITISH
01573 223548 | 7 Bowmont Street, TD5 7JH
www.thecobbleskelso.co.uk

Tucked just off the town's main square, this old inn has successfully negotiated the pub/restaurant dynamic. There are bar snacks such as wraps and burgers on offer, but in the dapper restaurant you'll find Scottish-inspired dishes that really impress. Steaks are sourced from Scottish herds.

Chef Daniel Norcliffe **Seats** 35, Private dining 30 **Closed** 25 December **Notes** Vegetarian dishes, Children welcome

Ednam House Hotel
◉ MODERN EUROPEAN
01573 224168 | Bridge Street, TD5 7HT
www.ednamhouse.com

Located in the peaceful Borders town of Kelso, with idyllic views of the Tweed, this country-house hotel is full of character. The elegant triple-aspect restaurant looks over the river to Floors Castle.

Chef Peter Carr **Seats** 60, Private dining 20 **Open** All year **Prices from** S £6.95, M £12.95, D £6.50 **Parking** 40 **Notes** Vegetarian dishes, Children welcome

MELROSE
Burts Hotel
◉◉ MODERN SCOTTISH
01896 822285 | Market Square, TD6 9PL
www.burtshotel.co.uk

Owned and run by the Henderson family for more than 40 years, this handsome 18th-century inn is rooted into Melrose life. The kitchen turns out modern Scottish dishes prepared from quality local produce.

Chef Craig Gibb **Seats** 50, Private dining 25 **Closed** 25–26 December **Prices from** S £5.95, M £14.95, D £7.95 **Parking** 40 **Notes** Vegetarian dishes, No children under 10 years

WALKERBURN
Windlestraw
◉◉ MODERN SCOTTISH, BRITISH **V**
01896 870636 | Galashiels Road, EH43 6AA
www.windlestraw.co.uk

Located only 40 minutes from Edinburgh and set in the rolling hills of the Scottish Border country, this beautiful venue is situated in 2 acres of grounds and lovingly restored by its present owners. Service is both personal and attentive in the oak panelled restaurant.

Chef Stu Waterston **Seats** 20, Private dining 20 **Closed** mid December to mid February **Notes** No children under 11 years

STIRLING

ABERFOYLE
Macdonald Forest Hills Hotel & Resort
MODERN SCOTTISH
01877 389500 | Kinlochard, FK8 3TL
www.macdonald-hotels.co.uk/foresthills

Twenty-five acres of mature gardens run down to Loch Ard at this white-painted mansion, where 'keep it simple' might be the kitchen's mantra and flavours are undiluted by an over-abundance of ingredients. You might finish with satsuma crème brûlée with decadent chocolate chip cookies.

Chef Kenny Sheeky **Seats** 78, Private dining 20 **Open** All year **Parking** 50 **Notes** Vegetarian dishes, Children welcome

CALLANDER
Roman Camp Country House Hotel
MODERN FRENCH V
01877 330003 | FK17 8BG
www.romancamphotel.co.uk

Dating back to the 17th century, when it was built for the Dukes of Perth, this stately old house with its pale pink walls is wonderfully located in the Loch Lomond and the Trossachs National Park. A hotel since the 1930s, it has 20 acres of gardens and a truly beautiful interior, with fine period details, from the secret chapel to the panelled library, and an antique grand piano and more than 40 malt whiskies in the bar. The two dining rooms are as sumptuous and splendid as you could wish for, with attentive, well-trained staff, and the food is focused and contemporary. The short carte and set-price menus are attentive to the seasons, so roast turbot might appear with carrot purée, coppa ham, and shellfish jus, followed by a curried sweet potato soup with cumin yogurt, before moving on to roast grouse with pear and celeriac remoulade, hibiscus gel and sauce poivrade. Three-chocolate mousse with passionfruit sorbet is the ideal conclusion, before withdrawing to the lounge for your coffee and petits fours.

Chef Ian McNaught **Seats** 120, Private dining 36 **Open** All year **Prices from** S £12.80, M £28.50, D £11.50 **Parking** 80 **Notes** Children welcome

DUNBLANE
Cromlix and Chez Roux
MODERN V NOTABLE WINE LIST
01786 822125 | Kinbuck, FK15 9JT
www.cromlix.com

Built for one Captain Arthur Drummond in the 1870s, when it was known with becoming modesty as Cromlix Cottage, then promptly rebuilt the same decade when it burned down, the turreted manor house is now owned by local boy Sir Andy Murray. Its public rooms are done in the height of country-house elegance, the dining room a glassed-in conservatory that looks over the sumptuous grounds. Named in honour of its executive presence, the much-garlanded Albert Roux, Darin Campbell's kitchen aims high, blending elements of French gastronomic classicism – the cheese-laden soufflé suissesse in its cream bath has been translated unscathed from its origins at Le Gavroche – with vivacious cooking in the modern global style. Home-cured Ardgay venison is given the bresaola treatment and served alongside salt-baked beetroot, quince purée and smoked ricotta, as a prelude to steamed Skrei cod with king prawn, Chinese vegetables and shiitakes in coconut broth, or powerfully rich braised Wagyu with snails and lardons in port. The culinary paths continue to diverge at dessert, between classic apple frangipane tart made with Braeburns, and chocolate and pistachio pavé with lychee sorbet.

Chef Darin Campbell **Seats** 60, Private dining 50 **Open** All year **Prices from** S £9, M £21.50, D £9 **Parking** 30 **Notes** Children welcome

FINTRY
Culcreuch Castle Hotel & Estate
TRADITIONAL SCOTTISH V
01360 860555 | Kippen Road, G63 0LW
www.culcreuch.com

Standing in 1,600 acres of grounds, including a picturesque loch, Culcreuch Castle has all the medieval accoutrements that could be desired. Country-house cooking with some imaginative touches is the approach. A deceptively complex Culcreuch lamb with peas, mint and sheeps' milk showcases the estate's produce.

Chef Paul O'Malley **Seats** 22, Private dining 30 **Closed** 25–26 December, 1st 2 weeks January **Parking** 60

STIRLING
The Stirling Highland Hotel
BRITISH, EUROPEAN
01786 272727 | Spittal Street, FK8 1DU
www.thehotelcollection.co.uk

A grand Victorian property just down the hill from Stirling's historic castle, The Stirling Highland Hotel was built in the 1850s as a school. The eating takes place in three dining rooms of generous Victorian proportions. The menu takes a modern approach to familiar ideas.

Chef Mark Bain **Seats** 96, Private dining 100 **Open** All year **Parking** 106 **Notes** Vegetarian dishes, Children welcome

SCOTTISH ISLANDS

SCOTTISH ISLANDS

ISLE OF HARRIS

TARBERT (TAIRBEART)
Hotel Hebrides
◉ MODERN SCOTTISH, SEAFOOD
01859 502364 | Pier Road, HS3 3DG
www.hotel-hebrides.com

The modern boutique hotel is the focal point of a village of some 500 souls on the Isle of Harris. In the Pierhouse seafood restaurant, a bare boarded look keeps things simple. Fish and shellfish are strong suits, ranging from chowder to seared megrim sole.

Chef Graham Smith **Seats** 35 **Closed** November to March **Parking** 30 **Notes** Vegetarian dishes, Children welcome

ISLE OF MULL

FIONNPHORT
Ninth Wave Restaurant
◉ MODERN PACIFIC RIM V
01681 700757 | PA66 6BL
www.ninthwaverestaurant.co.uk

On the southern tip of Mull where ferries leave for Iona, John and Carla Lamont's pocket-sized restaurant is about as remote as they come. The dinner-only affair seats just 18 lucky diners, who can expect skilfully cooked menus full of inventive ideas.

Chef Carla Lamont **Seats** 18 **Parking** 10
Notes No children under 12 years

TOBERMORY
Highland Cottage
◉◉ MODERN SCOTTISH, INTERNATIONAL
01688 302030 | 24 Breadalbane Street, PA75 6PD
www.highlandcottage.co.uk

Enjoying a stunning elevated location overlooking Tobermory harbour, this salmon-hued hotel close to the fishing pier is a jewel. The interiors are a delight and the place is cleverly laid out to lead you from the bar and conservatory into the suavely furnished dining room. It does a fine job of showcasing Mull produce.

Chef Josephine Currie **Seats** 24 **Closed** November to March **Notes** Vegetarian dishes, No children under 10 years

SHETLAND

SCALLOWAY
Scalloway Hotel
◉◉ SCOTTISH SEAFOOD V
01595 880444 | Main Street, ZE1 0TR
www.scallowayhotel.com

An unpretentious place that opens its arms to all-comers, from oil-rig workers to passing ships' crews, making the bar a convivial haunt for casual dishes. The restaurant has linen tablecloths, quality glasses and a seasonal, globally inspired menu that showcases the island's produce.

Chef David Errington **Seats** 36 **Closed** Christmas, New Year **Parking** 10 **Notes** Children welcome

ISLE OF SKYE

COLBOST
The Three Chimneys & The House Over-By
◉◉◉ SCOTTISH WITH NORDIC INFLUENCE ♦ NOTABLE WINE LIST
See pages 410–11

ISLEORNSAY
Duisdale House Hotel
◉◉ MODERN SCOTTISH
01471 833202 | Sleat, IV43 8QW
www.duisdale.com

With bags of boutique style and a dreamy location, Duisdale House has a lot going for it. The garden is a treat, especially if you're a fan of rhododendrons, and the conservatory restaurant boasts stylish looks. Expect modern cooking based on seasonal and regional ingredients.

Chef Brian Ross **Seats** 50 **Open** All year **Parking** 30
Notes Vegetarian dishes, Children welcome

Hotel Eilean Iarmain
◉ MODERN AND TRADITIONAL SCOTTISH
01471 833332 | Sleat, IV43 8QR
www.eileaniarmain.co.uk

The hotel is very much a part of this small community, with Gaelic spoken and regular ceilidh nights, while the owners also run a small distillery and art gallery next door. The restaurant has tables dressed in white linen and flickering candles, while the culinary output is rather more contemporary than you might imagine.

Chef Virgil Tiskus **Seats** 40, Private dining 22
Open All year **Parking** 10 **Notes** Vegetarian dishes, Children welcome

Kinloch Lodge

◉◉◉ FRENCH, SCOTTISH **V** ▲NOTABLE WINE LIST
01471 833214 | Sleat, IV43 8QY
www.kinloch-lodge.co.uk

Set off the main Armadale road, you follow a single-track lane until the Lodge comes into view, a grandly traditional country house with the Sound of Sleat as a glorious backdrop. Originally home to the chief of Clan Donald, this is a wild and remote location for a seriously comfortable hotel with a wonderfully relaxing atmosphere. The dark grey walls and antique paintings in the dining room make an elegant, refined setting for Marcello Tully's food, which makes the most of a remarkable choice of quality ingredients. A classically French approach broadens out to take in influences from Scotland and beyond. The five-course dinner menu might offer slow-roasted oxtail with langoustine and oriental sauce, followed by the Kinloch 'seafood collection' – perhaps including crab meat from Uig, home-cured salmon, and locally smoked mussels. Ballotine of roast quail is enclosed in cured ham, with vegetable and Perthshire honey mousse. A mango, lime and coconut espuma is a fresh, clean-tasting pre-dessert, before a very fine chocolate parfait with textures of hazelnut and coffee, and an excellent milk sorbet.

Chef Marcello Tully **Seats** 55, Private dining 12 **Open** All year **Parking** 40 **Notes** Children welcome

Toravaig House Hotel

◉◉ MODERN SCOTTISH
01471 820200 | Knock Bay, Sleat, IV44 8RE
www.toravaig.com

With enviable views over Knock Castle and the Sound of Sleat, the whitewashed Toravaig House serves up an enviable Skye vista. The cooking takes a modern Scottish path, in keeping with the majestic locale, and produces well-crafted plates of food.

Chef Finn Wood **Seats** 25 **Open** All year **Parking** 20 **Notes** Vegetarian dishes, No children under 10 years

PORTREE
Dulse & Brose

◉◉ MODERN
01478 612846 | Bosville Hotel, 9–11 Bosville Terrace, IV51 9DG
www.bosvillehotel.co.uk

Dulse & Brose takes its name from a type of seaweed and an oatmeal dish, symbolising the use of Scottish ingredients at this trendy boutique hotel and restaurant. There is a casual atmosphere here, with views of the Skye scenery, plus clever cookery.

Chef Peter Cullen **Seats** 60 **Open** All year **Prices from** S £7, M £16, D £7 **Notes** Vegetarian dishes, Children welcome

STEIN
Loch Bay Restaurant

◉ SEAFOOD, TRADITIONAL SCOTTISH, FRENCH
01470 592235 | Macleods Terrace, IV55 8GA
www.lochbay-restaurant.co.uk

With room only for a couple of dozen diners at a time, Loch Bay is a diminutive institution around these parts, a place of simplicity and integrity, and its position by the loch shore, in a row of 18th-century fishermen's cottages, is a magical one.

Chef Michael Smith **Seats** 22 **Closed** January to February, 1st week August and reduced winter hours **Parking** 6 **Notes** Vegetarian dishes, Children welcome

STRUAN
Ullinish Country Lodge

◉◉◉ MODERN SCOTTISH **V**
01470 572214 | IV56 8FD
www.theisleofskye.co.uk

If you're looking for a spectacular location and you like wild and lonely, you won't go far wrong here. This white-painted lodge, far out on a peninsula on the west coast of Skye, enjoys breathtaking views across the surrounding sea lochs to the flat-topped mountains known as MacLeod's Tables. Inside it's cosy and welcoming, with dark wood, tartan carpets, local artwork and friendly, helpful service. The formal, candlelit dining room, with its dark pink walls, is traditional, with a few contemporary touches, and the modern Scottish food is precise, with an emphasis, perhaps not surprisingly, given the location, on seafood. Start with a perfectly timed scallop, caramelised on the outside and sweet within, accompanied by a cylinder of lightly dressed crab meat in a slice of apple, with celeriac purée adding depth. Roasted sea bass with gnocchi, asparagus and Normandy sauce is a tightly focused dish – beautifully fresh fish with crisp skin and vibrant flavours, the soft, light gnocchi the ideal addition. Passionfruit cheesecake with coconut and mango ends on a more exotic note.

Chef David Smith **Seats** 22 **Closed** 24 December to 31 January **Parking** 10 **Notes** No children

COLBOST

The Three Chimneys & The House Over-By

◉◉◉ SCOTTISH WITH NORDIC INFLUENCE 🍷 NOTABLE WINE LIST

01470 511258 | IV55 8ZT

www.threechimneys.co.uk

Exceptional cooking in a wild, romantic setting

Don't be fooled into thinking as you traverse the Skye Bridge that you're nearly there. It's another good hour's drive, the last five miles or so by single-track road (or the B884, to give it its full dignity). Eddie and Shirley Spear's restaurant with rooms by Loch Dunvegan is one of the most remote addresses an AA inspector visits, and there's nary anything like a village around. Inside the whitewashed cottage, next door to which ('over by') is the accommodation building, a number of small, low-ceilinged rooms with exposed stone walls succeed each other, with polished dark wood floors matched by simply set tables with black slate place mats.

The service tone is surprisingly fairly formal, but in a way that adds to the specialness, indeed the romance, of the whole experience. As the years have passed, the culinary style has become noticeably more complex, still firmly rooted in its island environment naturally, but with the distinctly ambitious air that Scott Davies has brought to the production. It would be a major mistake not to take in some seafood, and it makes the perfect opener in

a dish such as Mallaig cod steamed in white miso, paired with seared Sconser scallops, with onion variations – caramelised, spring onions, rings, seeds – in light dashi broth. Alternatively, you might begin with local crab and scorched langoustines with pickled mussels, puffed wild rice, brown crab ketchup and apple. Main courses deliver impeccably sourced meats, such as the Orbost Soay lamb, incorporating portions of the loin, shoulder, belly and rib, together with a superlative haggis, offset with the sweetness of charcoal-roasted beetroot, good greens and a sweet-sour bramble wine sauce. Or there may be poached and roasted Gartmorn duck with rhubarb and spring onion in a classic orange sauce with coriander seeds. Autumn fruits are the building blocks of seasonal desserts like plum and orange cheesecake with plums (poached and a sorbet), chocolate sponge, chestnuts and oats, and heather honey is a matchless regional speciality, made into a parfait alongside its honeycomb, roasted figs and a black sesame tuile.

The eight-course taster will be a strong temptation, especially given that you may not be here again for a good while. It may proceed from langoustines with smoked cod's roe in carrot emulsion all the way to baked apple with a doughnut, cider cream and black-peppered crumble. The splendid wine list is under the care of an admirably well-versed sommelier.

Chef Scott Davies **Seats** 40 **Closed** 16 December to 18 January **Parking** 12
Notes Vegetarian dishes, No children under 5 years at lunch and under 8 years at dinner

WALES

▶ ISLE OF ANGLESEY

BEAUMARIS
Bishopsgate House Hotel
TRADITIONAL WELSH **V**
01248 810302 | 54 Castle Street, LL58 8BB
www.bishopsgatehotel.co.uk
The mint-green facade of Bishopsgate House stands out on its Georgian terrace overlooking Beaumaris Green and Snowdonia across the Menai waterfront, while the intimate, low-ceilinged restaurant is full of old-world charm. Straightforward menus finish with pecan tart and honeycomb ice cream.

Chef I Sankey **Seats** 40 **Open** All year **Parking** 10
Notes Children welcome

The Bull – Beaumaris
MODERN BRITISH
01248 810329 | Castle Street, LL58 8AP
www.bullsheadinn.co.uk
Hard by Edward I's castle and the attractive shoreline with its Victorian pier, the Loft is the fine dining restaurant at The Bull with its beamed sloping ceilings. Local materials are brought to the fore, including fine seafood. Look out for an ingeniously scented lemon tart.

Chef Andrew Tabberner **Seats** 45 **Closed** 25–26 December and 1 January **Notes** Vegetarian dishes, No children under 7 years

Château Rhianfa
MODERN FRENCH
01248 713656 | LL59 5NS
www.chateaurhianfa.com
Oak panels and a grand fireplace certainly make for an impressive dining room, but one would expect nothing less in this swanky 19th-century French chateau-style hotel surveying Snowdonia's peaks across the Menai Strait. The kitchen doesn't pull any left-field tricks, sticking to hearty country-house dishes.

Chef Jason Hughes **Seats** 30, Private dining 12
Open All year **Prices from** S £7.50, M £20, D £7
Parking 30 **Notes** Vegetarian dishes, Children welcome

MENAI BRIDGE
Sosban & The Old Butcher's Restaurant
MODERN **V**
01248 208131 | Trinity House, 1 High Street, LL59 5EE
www.sosbanandtheoldbutchers.com
Time can't pass fast enough from the moment the booking is secured to when you actually cross the threshold, for dining at Sosban is to be anticipated, dining at Sosban is a hot ticket, dining at Sosban is not your everyday restaurant experience. There is only enough room for 16 souls at any one time and it only happens three evenings and one lunch a week. But once you're inside you don't have to do much but give yourself over to the prodigiously talented Stephen

Stevens, who will serve up his no-choice menu at a fixed time. We're all in this together. Allow four hours from start to finish. The one-time butcher's shop on the high street has a rustic simplicity reflecting its former life (think natural wood, natural slate), and it perfectly suits the modern mood. The procession of dishes displays amazing creativity, compelling visuals, and mightily impressive flavours. Caribou moss is a stellar opening mouthful, rich with anchovy and malty flavours, and be prepared to use your fingers to pick up a divine lamb's cheek with pork crackling and dip it into the accompanying laverbread mayo. Next up, crisp cod skin with smoked roe and foraged leaves, and then a stunning cod number, with yeast purée, onion rings, crispy potato and ground heart. Rhubarb and custard gets a reappraisal when a crisp rhubarb sphere is filled with duck egg custard and hits of rhubarb from poached and freeze-dried fruit. The only decision to make is which of the well-chosen wines to go for alongside the complex, creative cuisine, and, of course, when you're able to return.

Chef Stephen Stevens **Seats** 16 **Closed** Christmas, New Year, January **Notes** No children

NEWBOROUGH
Marram Grass
◉◉ MODERN BRITISH
01248 440077 | White Lodge, LL61 6RS
www.themarramgrass.com

There's no escaping it, this restaurant is actually a shed on a campsite. But make no mistake, it's a pretty smart shed; it even has a slate-topped bar. Anglesey's island status provides the ingredients – crab risotto with roast celeriac, local apple, garlic and sea truffle for example.

Chef Ellis Barrie **Seats** 40 **Open** All year
Prices from S £6.95, M £18.50, D £7.50
Notes Vegetarian dishes, Children welcome

▶ CARDIFF

CARDIFF
Bully's
◉◉ FRENCH, EUROPEAN
029 2022 1905 | 5 Romilly Crescent, CF11 9NP
www.bullysrestaurant.co.uk

Bully's is a busy-looking restaurant, virtually every inch of its walls covered with pictures, mirrors and other paraphernalia. The kitchen relies on Welsh providers and devises menus that show a clear grounding in the French repertoire while pulling in ideas from near and far.

Chef Christie Matthews **Seats** 40 **Closed** 24–26 December, 1 January **Prices from** S £6.50, M £15, D £6.50 **Notes** Vegetarian dishes, Children welcome

Moksh
◉◉ INDIAN
029 2049 8120 | Ocean Building,
Bute Crescent, CF10 5AN
www.moksh.co.uk

Contemporary Indian fusion cooking is nothing new, but this kitchen throws elements of molecular wizardry into the mix. Dessert might be an innovative choice of a crisp tikka masala samosa alongside white chocolate and saffron mousse cake with coconut ice cream and applewood smoke.

Chef Stephen Gomes **Seats** 53 **Closed** 25 December **Prices from** S £8, M £14, D £5 **Notes** Vegetarian dishes, Children welcome

AA Wine Award for Wales and overall winner 2018–19

Park House Restaurant
◉◉ MODERN FRENCH V ◣ NOTABLE WINE LIST
029 2022 4343 | 20 Park Place, CF10 3DQ
www.parkhouserestaurant.co.uk

Housed in a Gothic architectural extravagance, the splendid panelled restaurant overlooks the gardens of the National Museum of Wales. Do try the chocolate platter involving a rich pavé and 'pulled' chocolate with a peppermint macaroon and spearmint sorbet. Features a stunning wine list that is both accessible and easy to navigate.

Chef Andrew Frost **Seats** 50, Private dining 40
Closed 26–28 December, 1–4 January
Prices from S £12, M £22, D £10 **Notes** No children

See pages 16–17 for details

▶ CARMARTHENSHIRE
LAUGHARNE
The Corran Resort & Spa
◉◉ MODERN BRITISH, WELSH
01994 427417 | East Marsh, SA33 4RS
www.thecorran.com

Amid the coastal marshland of Carmarthenshire, The Corran is a stylish spa hotel within three miles of Laugharne Castle. Salmon cured in black treacle with pickles and salad vies for attention with generously stuffed short-rib ravioli in mushrooms and Marsala to begin.

Chef Chris Lovell **Seats** 185, Private dining 30
Open All year **Parking** 30 **Notes** Vegetarian dishes, Children welcome

LLANELLI
Sosban Restaurant
®® MODERN BRITISH V
01554 270020 | The Pumphouse, North Dock,
SA15 2LF
www.sosban.wales

The Victorian pump-house building on Llanelli's North Docks has been reinvented as a powerhouse on the national culinary scene. Original exposed stone work, traditional wooden beams and commissioned oil paintings lead the way to the open-to-view kitchen. Modern dishes are carefully conceived and intriguing.

Chef Andrew Sheridan **Seats** 90, Private dining 20
Closed 1st 2 weeks of January, starting on 1st
Prices from S £7.50, M £18, D £6.50 **Parking** 50
Notes Children welcome

LLANSTEFFAN
Mansion House Llansteffan
®® MODERN BRITISH
01267 241515 | Pantyrathro, SA33 5AJ
www.mansionhousellansteffan.co.uk

The Mansion has five acres of windswept hilltop to itself, and a commanding position overlooking Carmarthen Bay, with the remains of a Norman castle for a near neighbour. In the Moryd Restaurant, which enjoys those views to the full, a straightforward but conscientiously rendered menu of modern brasserie food is offered.

Chef Paul Owen **Seats** 32, Private dining 24
Prices from S £4.95, M £16, D £4.95 **Parking** 50
Notes Vegetarian dishes, Children welcome
See advertisement below

NANTGAREDIG
Y Polyn
®® CLASSIC EUROPEAN ⬤ NOTABLE WINE LIST
01267 290000 | SA32 7LH
www.ypolyn.co.uk

A hospitable country pub where the owners deserve plaudits for their single-minded commitment to hard graft. The menu invites a lip-smacking start with crispy ham hock bonbons in a pool of vividly flavoursome parsley sauce with a poached egg and shards of Carmarthen ham.

Chef Susan Manson **Seats** 100, Private dining 40
Open All year **Prices from** S £7, M £16.50, D £8.50
Parking 35 **Notes** Vegetarian dishes, Children welcome

▶ CEREDIGION

CARDIGAN

Caemorgan Mansion

◉ MODERN EUROPEAN

01239 613297 | Caemorgan Road, SA43 1QU

www.caemorgan.com

Close to the beautiful Bay, Caemorgan Mansion occupies a peaceful location on the outskirts of Cardigan itself. Red walls dotted with local photographs and artwork gives the restaurant a contemporary look and it's an intimate platform to showcase carefully prepared Welsh produce.

Chef David Harrison-Wood, Abbie Jenkins **Seats** 30 **Open** All year **Prices from** S £5.90, M £14.95, D £6.95 **Parking** 20 **Notes** Vegetarian dishes, No children

EGLWYS FACH

Ynyshir

◉◉◉◉◉ MODERN BRITISH ☆ NOTABLE WINE LIST

01654 781209 | SY20 8TA

www.ynyshir.co.uk

Deep inside a 1,000-acre RSPB reserve, not far from the fringes of the Snowdonia National Park, Ynyshir may look like a modest enough white-fronted country house but is one of the Welsh nation's treasures. The pastoral tranquillity of the setting makes a stay in one of the 10 guest rooms a restorative treat, and the views over the gardens could hardly be more sumptuous. It should come as no surprise to learn that the house was once owned by Queen Victoria, who had a discerning eye for a country retreat. At the heart of the operation is a dining room in the unmistakable modern manner, done in subdued unpatterned tones, with the hive of activity in the kitchen opening off it. Gareth Ward offers tasting menus at both lunch and dinner, the latter extending to a bravura performance of 18 courses, mobilising the full range of present-day technique in presentations that see dishes turning up on lumps of stone or in knobbly earthenware bowls, among other vehicles. A nibble of bread is elevated into the first division when it arrives with cultured butter and Welsh Wagyu beef dripping (the meat itself will come later, as the centrepiece of the whole show). Along the winding way, the artful combinations of texture and taste take in mackerel, sharp with rhubarb and silky with pork back fat, pollock with shiitakes, and an Asian-style serving of black beans with shiso and garlic, before the principal meat, which, if not Wagyu, could well be premium Welsh lamb. Serving a single cheese in prime condition is always a good idea, as when Beauvale, a soft blue from Cropwell Bishop, is paired with ripe Comice pear, and then the dessert parade begins – Cox's apple with buttermilk and sorrel, miso treacle tart, and wild spins on favourites such as tiramisù, sticky toffee, and rhubarb and custard. Despite the multiplicity of dishes, it's all perfectly weighted. The shorter lunch menu, which might open with the famous Japanese-inspired onion soup made with dashi stock, tofu and miso, and take in a partnering of crab and turnip before the main meat, provides a good entrée to the repertoire.

Chef Gareth Ward **Seats** 18, Private dining 6 **Closed** 6 weeks during the year **Parking** 15 **Notes** Children welcome

LAMPETER

The Falcondale Hotel & Restaurant

◉◉ MODERN BRITISH

01570 422910 | Falcondale Drive, SA48 7RX

www.thefalcondale.co.uk

An Italianate mansion built in countryside, Falcondale has 14 acres all to itself. It's the kind of country-house hotel that delivers peace and that getting-away-from-it-all vibe. Cooking reveals classical roots, but this is gently modernised stuff, and good use is made of the regional bounty.

Chef Tony Shum **Seats** 36, Private dining 20 **Open** All year **Prices from** S £9, M £18.50, D £7 **Parking** 60 **Notes** Vegetarian dishes, Children welcome

LLECHRYD

Hammet @ Castell Malgwyn

◉◉ MODERN BRITISH V

01239 682382 | SA43 2QA

www.hammethouse.co.uk

The prim, creeper-swathed Georgian house opens into a new, designer-led contemporary-chic look, blending period plasterwork and high ceilings with an up-to-date palette of neutral greys and striking artworks. Neatly clothed tables continue the theme in the restaurant, where the cooking is as up-to-date as the surroundings.

Chef Matt Smith **Seats** 38, Private dining **Open** All year **Parking** 100 **Notes** No child age restriction at dinner until 7.30pm

TREGARON

Y Talbot

◉◉ MODERN BRITISH

01974 298208 | The Square, SY25 6JL

www.ytalbot.com

Drovers of old began their long treks to the markets of the Midlands and London from Tregaron, no doubt first fortifying themselves in this part-17th-century inn. Through the pillared front doorway there's a bar one side and a restaurant the other, with bilingual, wide-choice menus.

Chef Dafydd Watkin **Seats** 40, Private dining 8 **Open** All year **Prices from** S £6, M £9.50, D £6.50 **Parking** 8 **Notes** Vegetarian dishes, Children welcome

▶ CONWY

ABERGELE

Brasserie 1786

◉◉ MODERN BRITISH

01745 832014 | The Kinmel, St George's Road, LL22 9AS

www.thekinmel.co.uk

After a day in the Kinmel's spa, the hotel's bright, contemporary Brasserie 1786 is the place to head for some plain-speaking food. Despite the chic, minimalist looks, the place has been in the hands of the same family since, well, the clue's in the name.

Chef Adam Middleton, Mark Reilly **Seats** 48, Private dining 30 **Open** All year **Prices from** S £7.50, M £20, D £7.50 **Parking** 84 **Notes** Vegetarian dishes, No children under 12 years at dinner

The Kinmel Arms

◉◉ MODERN BRITISH, FRENCH

01745 832207 | The Village, St George, LL22 9BP

www.thekinmelarms.co.uk

A stone-built village inn at St George on the north Wales coast, The Kinmel is introducing a pantry and wine shop but already established is the elegant, award-winning dining room. You might decide to start with mushroom brûlée, toasted brioche and truffle butter.

Chef Chad Huges, Heddwen Wheeler **Seats** 70, Private dining 10 **Closed** 25 December, 1–2 January **Parking** 60 **Notes** Vegetarian dishes, Children welcome

BETWS-Y-COED

Craig-y-Dderwen Riverside Hotel

◉ TRADITIONAL, INTERNATIONAL

01690 710293 | LL24 0AS

www.snowdoniahotel.com

Built in the 1890s for an industrialist, the partly timbered house became a favourite bolt-hole for Sir Edward Elgar. A hotel since the 20s, it offers the full country-house package, complete with views of a riverside teeming with wildlife (including otters).

Chef Paul Goosey **Seats** 60, Private dining 40 **Closed** 2 January to 1 February **Prices from** S £7.25, M £13.95, D £7.45 **Parking** 50 **Notes** Vegetarian dishes, Children welcome

Llugwy River Restaurant@Royal Oak Hotel

◉ MODERN BRITISH, WELSH

01690 710219 | Holyhead Road, LL24 0AY

www.royaloakhotel.net

Cappuccino-coloured walls with yellow sconces and ceiling chandeliers characterise the restaurant at this Victorian coaching inn. The kitchen supports local suppliers and the menu buzzes with interest. Game shows up in season, perhaps wild mallard with root vegetable gâteau, sticky red cabbage and damson jus.

Chef Samantha Plester **Seats** 60, Private dining 20 **Closed** 25–26 December **Parking** 100 **Notes** Vegetarian dishes, Children welcome

CAPEL CURIG

Bryn Tyrch Inn

◉ MODERN WELSH

01690 720223 | LL24 0EL

www.bryntyrchinn.co.uk

The old whitewashed roadside inn with a stunning Snowdonia backdrop offers sanctuary to walkers, climbers and families. The interior has plenty of charm and you can eat in the bar or the terrace dining room and expect simple, homely stuff based on regional produce.

Chef Paul Ryan, Daniel Demetriou **Seats** 100, Private dining 20 **Closed** 15–27 December **Parking** 40 **Notes** Vegetarian dishes, Children welcome

COLWYN BAY

Bryn Williams at Porth Eirias

◉◉ BRITISH, SEAFOOD

01492 577525 | The Promenade, LL29 8HH

www.portheirias.com

The modern steel-and-glass building stands out on the seafront, with floor-to-ceiling windows offering sweeping views of Colwyn Bay, and exposed steelwork, pendant lights and industrial-chic looks that smack of a hip, big-city eatery. Expect sharp modern British bistro ideas built on prime materials.

Chef Bryn Williams, Christopher Jones **Seats** 66 **Open** All year **Prices from** S £6, M £12, D £6 **Parking** 25 **Notes** Vegetarian dishes, Children welcome

CONWY

Castle Hotel Conwy

◉ MODERN BRITISH

01492 582800 | High Street, LL32 8DB

www.castlewales.co.uk

Conwy is a UNESCO World Heritage Site and, when it comes to matters of history, the town's Castle Hotel can hold its own. Dawsons Restaurant & Bar, with its courtyard and stylish decor, offers modern British menus that deliver brasserie-style dishes and classic comfort options.

Chef Leigh Marshall **Seats** 70 **Open** All year **Prices from** S £5.95, M £13.95, D £7 **Parking** 36 **Notes** Vegetarian dishes, Children welcome

Signatures Restaurant

⑳⑳ MODERN BRITISH V

01492 583513 | Aberconwy Resort & Spa, Aberconwy Park, LL32 8GA

www.lovesignatures.co.uk

Located in a seaside holiday park, Signatures is well worth tracking down for its inspired modern cooking. The setting is smartly contemporary – an open kitchen adds to the buzz and there's a great attention to detail.

Chef Jimmy Williams, Sonny Walker **Seats** 58
Open All year **Parking** 40 **Notes** Children welcome

DEGANWY
Quay Hotel & Spa

⑳ MODERN EUROPEAN V

01492 564100 | Deganwy Quay, LL31 9DJ

www.quayhotel.com

Beautifully located on the Conwy estuary, with views across the marina to the castle, this is a stylish, modern boutique hotel. The smart Grill Room offers a relatively informal setting for straightforward European cooking. Locally landed fish and seafood feature on the menu.

Chef Jack Davison **Seats** 120, Private dining 60
Open All year **Parking** 110 **Notes** Children welcome

LLANDUDNO
Bodysgallen Hall and Spa

⑳⑳⑳ MODERN TRADITIONAL V 🍷NOTABLE WINE LIST

01492 584466 | The Royal Welsh Way, LL30 1RS

www.bodysgallen.com

A couple of miles south of Llandudno, Bodysgallen is a supremely elegant stone-built Stuart mansion in 200 acres of parkland. In the immediate environs of the house, a box-hedged parterre laid out in the 17th century is redolent of herbs to this day. Inside, the sober oak panelling is softened by garden views through mullioned windows framed by gathered drapes, and by sympathetic, personable service. Balancing traditional and modern British modes has become an essential skill of today's aspirant chefs, and John Williams possesses it in abundance, garnishing crab cocktail to start with a cod cheek fritter and saffron-scented cucumber jelly, and then brioche-crusting thoroughbred Welsh lamb for slow-roasting and serving in thyme jus with smoked sweet potato purée. For an aromatic sensation, Creedy Carver chicken is poached and grilled, and partnered with a truffled crush of Mayan Gold potato and matching truffle cream. The marine option might be monkfish, royally treated with aubergine variations, wine-glazed artichoke and butter-braised baby gem, and scarcely anything impresses like a soufflé to conclude, flavoured with pear and ginger, served with fennel ice cream.

Chef John Williams **Seats** 60, Private dining 40
Closed 24–26 December **Parking** 40
Notes No children under 6 years

Dunoon Hotel

⑳⑳ CLASSIC BRITISH

01492 860787 | Gloddaeth Street, LL30 2DW

www.dunoonhotel.co.uk

The restaurant here is full of old-world charm, with oak-panelled walls, brass fittings and chandeliers, flowers and linen napery on the tables and a cooking style that's more likely to reassure than to startle with modernism, and the kitchen quite rightly keeping its customers happy.

Chef Rob Kennish **Seats** 80, Private dining 12
Closed mid December to 1 March **Notes** Vegetarian dishes, Children welcome

Imperial Hotel

⑳⑳ MODERN, TRADITIONAL BRITISH

01492 877466 | The Promenade, Vaughan Street, LL30 1AP

www.theimperial.co.uk

The wedding-cake stucco facade of the Imperial is a landmark on Llandudno's seafront. Alfresco dining on the terrace offers a splendid backdrop of the bay. The kitchen turns out menus of classically inflected modern cooking featuring a sound showing of fine Welsh produce.

Chef Leighton Thomas, Andreas Leisinger **Seats** 150, Private dining 30 **Open** All year **Prices from** S £7.75, M £19.50, D £7.75 **Parking** 20 **Notes** Vegetarian dishes, Children welcome

The Lilly Restaurant with Rooms

⑳ MODERN WELSH

01492 876513 | West Parade, West Shore, LL30 2BD

Located in the sedate West Shore part of the town, and with unrestricted views over the coastline and restless sea, The Lilly can offer snacks and grills in its Madhatters Brasserie, or the Full Monty in the flamboyantly decorated restaurant.

Chef Phillip Ashe, Jonathon Goodman **Seats** 35 **Open** All year **Notes** Vegetarian dishes, Children welcome

St George's Hotel

⑳ MODERN, TRADITIONAL, WELSH

01492 877544 | The Promenade, LL30 2LG

www.stgeorgeswales.co.uk

Llandudno's prom is the place to be for splendid sunsets and sweeping views across the bay, and St George's Hotel sits centre stage. The place is a timeless slice of Victorian wedding-cake grandeur, with an irresistible terrace and floor-to-ceiling windows in the restaurant.

Chef Gwyn Roberts **Seats** 110, Private dining 12
Open All year **Prices from** S £7, M £15, D £7
Parking 36 **Notes** Vegetarian dishes, Children welcome

DENBIGHSHIRE–GWYNEDD

▶ DENBIGHSHIRE

RUTHIN
Ruthin Castle Hotel
◉ MODERN BRITISH
01824 702664 | Castle Street, LL15 2NU
www.ruthincastle.co.uk

In its 750-year existence, Ruthin Castle has been many things including a clinic for treating obscure internal diseases. Enjoy a drink in the Library Bar, then aim for Bertie's restaurant. The menu lists only four dishes for each course but still permits plenty of permutations.

Chef Ryan Hession **Seats** 70, Private dining 120 **Open** All year **Parking** 30 **Notes** Vegetarian dishes, No children permitted after 7pm

▶ GWYNEDD

ABERDYFI
Penhelig Arms
◉ BRITISH
01654 767215 | Terrace Road, LL35 0LT
www.sabrain.com/pubs-and-hotels/north-wales/gwynedd/penhelig-arms-hotel

Originally a collection of fishermen's cottages on the Dyfi estuary, the Penhelig Arms overlooks what centuries ago was a shipbuilding harbour. Its two blue-themed dining areas – the Fisherman's Bar and the restaurant – share a menu, backed up by specials.

Chef Gabriel Badescu **Open** All year **Parking** 5 **Notes** Vegetarian dishes, Children welcome

ABERSOCH
The Dining Room
◉ WELSH BISTRO
01758 740709 | 4 High Street, LL53 7DY
www.thediningroomabersoch.co.uk

In pole position among the buzzy bars and hip surfie shops of trendy Abersoch's main drag, this low-key bistro with a tea-shop frontage and mismatched chairs and tables is building a loyal fan base for its warm hospitality and confidently executed food.

Chef Si Toft **Seats** 24 **Open** All year **Notes** Vegetarian dishes, No children under 12 years

Porth Tocyn Hotel
◉◉ MODERN BRITISH ▲ NOTABLE WINE LIST
01758 713303 | Bwlchtocyn, LL53 7BU
www.porthtocynhotel.co.uk

The Fletcher-Brewer family converted a terrace of lead miners' cottages into the comfortable, relaxed and unstuffy place we see today. Inside are antique-filled lounges and a smart restaurant, with spectacular views over Cardigan Bay to Snowdonia. Louise's repertoire combines traditional values and more modern sensibilities.

Chef L Fletcher-Brewer, Darren Shenton Morris **Seats** 50 **Closed** November, 2 weeks before Easter **Parking** 50 **Notes** Vegetarian dishes, No children under 5 years at dinner

BALA
Palé Hall Hotel & Restaurant
◉◉◉ BRITISH, EUROPEAN **V** ▲ NOTABLE WINE LIST
01678 530285 | Llandderfel, LL23 7PS
www.palehall.co.uk

In the lush Dee Valley, with all Snowdonia laid out before it, Palé Hall (note the accent – there is nothing pale about Palé) is a plutocratic Victorian industrialist's idea of a bijou residence, built to the dimensions of a medieval castle. Its interiors are beautifully decorated in pastel tones and light wood panelling, with a bolder amber hue in the dining room, where still-lifes of fruit crowd the walls. Gareth Stevenson's menus are informed by the grandeur of the surroundings, but with today's ingenuity of approach adding interest throughout. Roast scallops in curry velouté with butternut squash purée, pickled onions and crunchy toasted seeds is the perfect appetite-honing device for mains such as Welsh black beef fillet sauced in red wine with puréed celeriac and roasted shallots, or a duo of stone bass and langoustine with pink grapefruit in vanilla and ginger jus. The lightest way to finish is with coconut pannacotta and mango sorbet with a tropical fruit salad, but devotees of the salting of caramel are not neglected. It comes in a baked custard with bitter chocolate ganache and yeast crémeux.

Chef Gareth Stevenson **Seats** 40, Private dining 40 **Open** All year **Parking** 40 **Notes** Children welcome

CRICCIETH
Bron Eifion Country House Hotel
◉ MODERN BRITISH, WELSH
01766 522385 | LL52 0SA
www.broneifion.co.uk

Built in 1883, the creeper-clad house has the dual charm of ravishing gardens and stone's-throw proximity to Criccieth's beach. A majestic staircase, oak panelling and comfortable country-house furniture give the right impression, though the Garden Room restaurant offers a more contemporary experience.

Chef Marius Curelea **Seats** 150, Private dining 24 **Open** All year **Parking** 50 **Notes** Vegetarian dishes, Children welcome

DOLGELLAU
Bwyty Mawddach Restaurant
⊚ EUROPEAN

01341 421752 | Pen Y Garnedd, Llanelltyd, LL40 2TA
www.mawddach.com

As barn conversions go, this one is rather impressive.
Ifan Dunn turned the old granite building on the family
farm into a snazzy modern restaurant with views over
the Mawddach Estuary and the slopes of Cader Idris
through a glass wall.

Chef Ifan Dunn **Seats** 40 **Closed** 26 December, 1
week January and April, 2 weeks November
Prices from S £7, M £14.50, D £7 **Parking** 20
Notes Vegetarian dishes, No children under 5 years

Penmaenuchaf Hall Hotel
⊚ MODERN BRITISH ▮NOTABLE WINE LIST

01341 422129 | Penmaenpool, LL40 1YB
www.penhall.co.uk

The greystone Victorian hall gives spectacular views to
Cader Idris and the Mawddach Estuary. Within, oak
floors, panels, artwork and fresh flowers give a real
sense of age and quality. The menu pays homage to
indigenous produce, and there's no lack of
contemporary creative flair.

Chef Daniel Peale, Tim Reeve **Seats** 36, Private
dining 20 **Open** All year **Prices from** S £7, M £21, D £8
Parking 36 **Notes** Vegetarian dishes, No children
under 6 years

PORTMEIRION
The Hotel Portmeirion
⊚⊚ MODERN WELSH

01766 770000 | Minffordd, LL48 6ET
www.portmeirion-village.com

The fantasy Italianate village, created by Sir Clough
Williams-Ellis, was conceived around the ruin of what
is now the hotel. When the whole place began to
materialise in 1926, the hotel became its focal point.
Fresh, lively, modern Welsh cooking enhances the
whole experience.

Chef Mark Threadgill **Seats** 100, Private dining 36
Closed 2 weeks November **Parking** 130
Notes Vegetarian dishes, Children welcome

PWLLHELI
Plas Bodegroes
⊚⊚ MODERN BRITISH ▮NOTABLE WINE LIST

01758 612363 | Nefyn Road, LL53 5TH
www.bodegroes.co.uk

The Chowns' restaurant with rooms has been a fixture
of the northwest Wales dining scene since the 1980s.
The dining room is a fresh, airy space with mint-green

walls hung with artworks, a barewood floor and very
elegant high-backed chairs.

Chef Chris Chown, Hugh Bracegirdle **Seats** 40,
Private dining 24 **Closed** December to February
Parking 20 **Notes** Vegetarian dishes, Children
welcome

► MONMOUTHSHIRE
ABERGAVENNY
Angel Hotel
⊚ BRITISH, INTERNATIONAL

01873 857121 | 15 Cross Street, NP7 5EN
www.angelabergavenny.com

This hotel in the heart of the town was a posting inn in
the first half of the 19th century, and its Georgian
facade and spacious interiors are in fine fettle today.
The brasserie-style menu is offered in the Foxhunter
Bar or Oak Room restaurant.

Chef Wesley Hammond, Paul Brown **Seats** 80, Private
dining 120 **Closed** 25 December **Prices from** S £6,
M £14, D £6 **Parking** 30 **Notes** Vegetarian
dishes, Children welcome

The Hardwick
⊚⊚ MODERN BRITISH

01873 854220 | Old Raglan Road, NP7 9AA
www.thehardwick.co.uk

Hard at work in a revamped old inn just outside
Abergavenny is Stephen Terry, a chef with a wealth
of experience at the sharp end of the restaurant biz.
Food is unpretentious, mood-enhancing stuff. Set
lunches and Sunday lunch are a cut above the norm.

Chef Stephen Terry **Seats** 100, Private dining 50
Closed 25 December **Parking** 50 **Notes** Vegetarian
dishes, Children welcome

Llansantffraed Court Hotel
⊚⊚ MODERN BRITISH, WELSH **V** ▮NOTABLE WINE LIST

01873 840678 | Old Raglan Road, Llanvihangel Gobion,
Clytha, NP7 9BA
www.thecourtdiningroom.co.uk

A handsome brick-built William and Mary house in
rural Monmouthshire, LLCH stands in 20 acres of
trimly kept lawns with mature trees and a walled
kitchen garden, within sight of the Tudor church of
St Bridget's. A page of proudly attributed local
suppliers inspires confidence.

Chef Tim McDougall **Seats** 50, Private dining 35
Open All year **Prices from** S £6.50, M £14.50, D £8
Parking 300 **Notes** Children welcome

Restaurant 1861

◎◎ MODERN BRITISH, EUROPEAN V

01873 821297 | Cross Ash, NP7 8PB

www.18-61.co.uk

After beginning his career with the Roux brothers, Simon King has gone native in Wales, and 1861 celebrates what the region has to offer, including fine vegetables grown by Kate King's dad. The culinary style applies classic techniques in unmistakably appealing modern combinations.

Chef Simon King **Seats** 40 **Closed** 1st 2 weeks in January **Prices from** S £8.50, M £22, D £7.50 **Parking** 20 **Notes** Children welcome

The Walnut Tree Inn

◎◎◎ TRADITIONAL BRITISH 🍷 NOTABLE WINE LIST

See pages 422–423

See advertisement opposite

ROCKFIELD
The Stonemill & Steppes Farm Cottages

◎◎ MODERN BRITISH

01600 716273 | NP25 5SW

www.thestonemill.co.uk

A beautifully converted barn in a 16th-century mill complex provides an impressive setting for

accomplished cooking. It's a riot of beams and vaulted ceilings, with chunky rustic tables around an ancient stone cider press. The kitchen uses regional produce to deliver simply presented modern dishes.

Chef Ben Mathias **Seats** 56, Private dining 12 **Closed** 25–26 December, 2 weeks in January **Parking** 40 **Notes** Vegetarian dishes, Children welcome

USK
Newbridge on Usk

◎◎ TRADITIONAL BRITISH

01633 451000 | Tredunnock, NP15 1LY

www.celtic-manor.com

On a bend in the Usk, with river views, this restaurant with rooms is surrounded by well-tended gardens. The property dates back 200 years, so you can expect the usual beams and fireplaces, while the two-level restaurant has a rustic charm.

Chef Adam Whittle **Seats** 90, Private dining 16 **Open** All year **Parking** 60 **Notes** Vegetarian dishes, Children welcome

See advertisement below

Usk continues on page 424

The Walnut Tree

offers proper dining and good wine for not too frightening amounts of money. The setting is informal with the emphasis shared between the produce, its handling and cooking, and of course south Wales's fine countryside. There are no chandeliers, bells or whistles and no dress codes or similar pomposities to contend with. Come if this appeals and keep on going if it doesn't.

ABERGAVENNY
The Walnut Tree Inn
◉◉◉ TRADITIONAL BRITISH ▮ NOTABLE WINE LIST
01873 852797 | Llanddewi Skirrid, NP7 8AW
www.thewalnuttreeinn.com

Blissfully unfussy and focused cooking by a culinary mastermind

The Walnut Tree Inn has been on the gastronomic map one way or another since the 1960s. Ensconced amid rolling fields in rural Monmouthshire, a couple of miles to the northeast of Abergavenny, the Walnut Tree is today the preserve of Shaun Hill, one of Britain's principal movers and shakers of the last 30 years. With productive stints at Devon's Gidleigh Park and the Merchant House in Ludlow on his CV, Hill has also been one of the country's great culinary thinkers, a regular contributor to the Oxford Symposium on Food and Cookery, and author of some of the more thoughtful chef's cookbooks of recent years. With its whitewashed frontage and potted topiary, the inn looks every inch the rural retreat, its cluster of cottages for guests a covetable addition to the overall appeal. The dining area is done in unpretentious country style, with bare tables simply laid up, sprays of foliage, and some striking artworks for sale.

Shaun Hill has always taken an eclectic approach, anticipating the current global tendency in British cooking by a generation. He cooks what he himself likes to eat,

in a resourceful style that is unified by the core of excellent ingredients on which the kitchen calls.

Menus are composed in best bistro style, neither overwritten nor determined to leave you guessing in the modern manner. A twice-baked Lancashire cheese soufflé with beetroot will be just that, its airy richness cut by the rooty sweetness of the vegetable, or you may opt to start with a perfectly timed serving of veal sweetbreads, gently seared, with sharper notes from sauerkraut and capers, in a deeply flavoured jus. A bracing taste of the distant sea is offered by a main course of Cornish sole topped with mussels and samphire for a truly salty hit, the whole sauced silkily with vermouth, the accompaniments of creamy mash and green beans is all the dish needs to complete it.

Main meat courses have taken in a robust partnership of Middle White pork loin, goose charlotte and morteau sausage, as well as venison loin and hash with lingonberries. For vegetarians, there could be roast hispi cabbage with mushrooms, pine nuts and parmesan. At the close, there's textbook biscuit-based vanilla cheesecake with segments of blood-orange and toffee popcorn to enjoy, as well as the all but irresistible house speciality, somloi, a carefully researched Hungarian trifle of apricots, walnuts and rum, not to mention a clutch of glorious French cheeses.

Chef Shaun Hill **Seats** 70, Private dining 26 **Closed** 1 week at Christmas
Prices from S £9, M £18, D £9 **Parking** 30 **Notes** Vegetarian dishes, Children welcome

USK continued

The Raglan Arms
◉ MODERN BRITISH
01291 690800 | Llandenny, NP15 1DL
www.raglanarms.co.uk

This unassuming property looking more like a private house is home to bistro-style cooking and a friendly atmosphere. Log burners and scrubbed tables bring home the inn-like feel, and a decked terrace allows diners to sit and enjoy the rural location.

Chef James Miller **Seats** 64 **Open** All year
Prices from S £5.95, M £14.50, D £6 **Parking** 20
Notes Vegetarian dishes, Children welcome

WHITEBROOK
The Whitebrook
◉◉◉◉ MODERN BRITISH, FRENCH V 🔖 NOTABLE WINE LIST
01600 860254 | NP25 4TX
www.thewhitebrook.co.uk

The lush Wye Valley that surrounds this whitewashed former drovers' inn is also the source of a good deal of the menu, such is chef-patron Chris Harrod's passion for the food on his doorstep. It's even possible to join in on a foraging trip. Chris and wife Kirsty run a restaurant with rooms that seems to fit organically into its environment, with stylish neutrally attired bedrooms and a restaurant that is done out in soothingly light and natural shades. It's an unpretentious and relaxing setting for dynamic cooking. Long neglected herbs find their way onto the tasting menus (and three-course lunch option), so look out for bittercress, lesser celandine, pennywort, and such like; the former, for example, brings its peppery flavour to an opening dish of creamed barley, roast Jerusalem artichokes and goats' curd. Duck liver parfait arrives with an accompanying duck croquette, with quince to cut through the glorious richness of the meat, while line-caught sea bass is paired with Swiss chard, blue leg mushrooms and young fennel. There is freshness and vitality to each course, including a wild fallow venison number, with smoked beets and celeriac, all the way to sweet courses like poached pear with buttermilk and yogurt crumble, with the scent of maritime pine. The vegetarian menu shows no less creativity and compelling flavour combinations, roasted cauliflower, say with romanesco, pickled pine and wild chervil. The wine list includes a goodly number of bottles from organic and biodynamic growers, including Welsh and English options, and is organised by style.

Chef Chris Harrod **Seats** 26 **Closed** 1st 2 weeks in January **Parking** 20 **Notes** No children under 12 years at dinner

▶ NEWPORT

NEWPORT
Gemelli Restaurant
◉◉ ITALIAN, INTERNATIONAL V
01633 270210 | G1, Tesco Store, Newport Retail Park, NP19 4TX
www.gemellinewport.co.uk

Located beneath a supermarket in a retail park, this family-run restaurant has recreated their own piece of Italy with a restaurant, deli and ice cream parlour. Banquette seating and white linen add a formal touch. Italian classics with a twist is the motto here.

Chef Sergio Cinotti **Seats** 60, Private dining 15
Closed Easter and Christmas **Prices from** S £9.95, M £14.50, D £6.20 **Parking** 80 **Notes** Children welcome

Rafters
◉ WELSH
01633 413000 | The Celtic Manor Resort, Coldra Woods, NP18 1HQ
www.celtic-manor.com

There are views over the Ryder Cup course from Rafters, a classy grill restaurant on the Celtic Manor Resort. It's within the Twenty Ten Clubhouse, and with its high cedar-beamed ceiling, smart, modern look and those views, there's much to like.

Chef Mike Bates, Simon Crockford **Seats** 80 **Open** All year **Prices from** S £7.50, M £21.50, D £6.50
Parking 115 **Notes** Vegetarian dishes, Children welcome
See advertisement opposite

Steak on Six
◉◉ MODERN BRITISH
01633 413000 | The Celtic Manor Resort, Coldra Woods, NP18 1HQ
www.celtic-manor.com

The 'Six' in question is the sixth floor of the upmarket, golf-centric Celtic Manor Resort. When the culinary proposition is this straightforward, the quality of the raw materials is key, and the pedigree meat here proudly flies the flag for prime British protein.

Chef Michael Bates, Simon Crockford **Seats** 60
Open All year **Prices from** S £9.25, M £24.50, D £7.95 **Notes** Vegetarian dishes, No children
See advertisement opposite

Set within Celtic Manor's Twenty Ten Clubhouse, offering spectacular views and the finest locally reared meats, seafood and grills.

DISCOVER MORE AND BOOK ONLINE AT
CELTIC-MANOR.COM OR CALL 01633 410262

Experience our Signature sixth floor restaurant showcasing succulent steaks from around the British Isles and beyond.

DISCOVER MORE AND BOOK ONLINE AT
CELTIC-MANOR.COM OR CALL 01633 410262

▶ PEMBROKESHIRE

HAVERFORDWEST
Slebech Park Estate
◉◉ MODERN, CLASSIC **V**
01437 752000 | SA62 4AX
www.slebech.co.uk

The castellated, 18th-century manor house of Slebech Park is surrounded by 600 acres of parkland bordering the 'hidden waterway' of the Eastern Cleddau River. The restaurant, a naturally lit, modern addition with a river view, draws people from all over Pembrokeshire for local fish, shellfish, lamb and beef on a daily changing dinner menu.

Chef David Bleay **Seats** 40, Private dining 20 **Open** All year **Prices from** S £7, M £16, D £7 **Parking** 40 **Notes** Children welcome

NARBERTH
The Fernery
◉◉◉ MODERN BRITISH **V** ⚘NOTABLE WINE LIST
01834 860915 | Grove, Molleston, SA67 8BX
See pages 428–429

See advertisement opposite

NEWPORT
Llys Meddyg
◉◉ CLASSIC
01239 820008 | East Street, SA42 0SY
www.llysmeddyg.com

The handsome Georgian townhouse is in the centre of Newport village: converted from a coaching inn, it is now a smartly-done-out restaurant with rooms. There's a cosy stone-walled cellar bar, a lovely kitchen garden for pre-dinner drinks, and an elegant restaurant hung with art. The kitchen champions local produce, and goes foraging to boost the repertoire.

Chef Matt Waldron **Seats** 30, Private dining 14 **Open** All year **Parking** 8 **Notes** Vegetarian dishes, Children welcome

PORTHGAIN
The Shed
◉ FISH, TRADITIONAL BRITISH, MEDITERRANEAN
01348 831518 | SA62 5BN
www.theshedporthgain.co.uk

Seafood is king at this simple beach hut-style 'fish and chip bistro' right on the quayside in the dinky fishing village of Porthgain. The place sells its own-caught and local sustainable fresh fish and seafood from a counter during the warmer months.

Chef Rob and Caroline Jones **Seats** 50 **Open** All year **Prices from** S £7.50, M £17.50, D £5.95 **Notes** Vegetarian dishes, Children welcome

ST DAVIDS
Cwtch
◉ MODERN BRITISH
01437 720491 | 22 High Street, SA62 6SD
www.cwtchrestaurant.co.uk

The name is pronounced 'cutsh' and it has all the cosseting connotations of hug, snug and cosy. Three small dining rooms spread over two floors are done out with the simplicity of whitewashed stone walls and sturdy beams. The cooking takes a similarly restrained approach.

Chef Richard Guy **Seats** 50, Private dining 18 **Closed** 25–26 December and January **Notes** Vegetarian dishes, Children welcome

Twr Y Felin Hotel
◉◉ MODERN BRITISH
01437 725555 | Caerfai Road, SA62 6QT
www.twryfelinhotel.com

Starting life as a windmill in 1806, the Twr lays claim to being Wales's first hotel dedicated to showcasing contemporary art. And there it is, striking modern paintings and prints taking centre-stage in the low-lit Blas (Taste) dining room. The cooking is equally aesthetically conceived, with bold assemblages delighting eye and palate.

Chef Simon Coe **Seats** 54 **Open** All year **Prices from** S £7, M £18, D £8 **Parking** 26 **Notes** Vegetarian dishes, Children welcome

SAUNDERSFOOT
Coast Restaurant
◉◉ MODERN BRITISH, SEAFOOD **V**
01834 810800 | Coppet Hall Beach, SA69 9AJ
www.coastsaundersfoot.co.uk

On the shoreline of lovely Coppet Hall Beach, this contemporary wooden structure provides diners with unrivalled bay views. Simple furnishings with a sea and sand colour scheme are complemented by a menu with a strong seafood theme. The sticky toffee pudding makes for a good finish.

Chef Tom Hine **Seats** 52 **Closed** 7–19 January **Prices from** S £10, M £16, D £9 **Parking** 200 **Notes** Children welcome

See advertisement on page 431

GROVE

NARBERTH
The Fernery

◉◉◉ MODERN BRITISH **V** 🍷 NOTABLE WINE LIST

01834 860915 | Grove, Molleston SA67 8BX

www.thegrove-narberth.co.uk

Stunningly restored manor with creative culinary edge

Arriving at the 17th-century manor it is hard to imagine that when Neil and Zoe Kedward got their hands on the place back in 2007 it was derelict, unloved, and long forgotten. Following a stunning restoration job of the main house and outbuildings, including a Plantangenet Longhouse which dates back to the 15th century, today's boutique hotel is an idyllic getaway. The setting is also part of its appeal, with the 26-acre estate including four acres of pretty gardens to explore, where soaring trees, colourful rhododendrons and walled gardens make it easy to lose track of time. There is also a kitchen garden, the fruits of which you will meet later (70 or so varieties of vegetables, fruits and herbs as it happens).

It you can tear yourself away from the place, there's the Preseli Hills, the fabulous beaches, and the Pembrokeshire Coastal National Park within easy striking distance. The interior of the house feels like no less of a haven, with its elegant blend of traditional comforts and contemporary touches, with bedrooms in the main house and various

cottages. The cocktail bar is the spot to head for before you eat, and maybe after, with four lounges on hand if sinking into a comfy settee fits the bill.

The restaurant – intimate, understated – is the domain of executive chef Allister Barsby. His kitchen makes use of the home-grown produce, the rest sourced with care from the region, to turn out dynamic contemporary food via a fixed-price carte and tasting menu. An opening course of pan-fried duck liver, for example, with poached rhubarb to hold the glorious richness of the liver in check, a luscious hazelnut cream and sherry vinegar sauce. Cured mackerel is another opener, with marinated daikon and Exmoor caviar, once again an essay in balance of taste and texture. Among main courses, saddle of Preseli lamb keeps company with the traditional flavour of mint, but also caper jam, and the leeks are charred in the modern manner. There's an Asian influence in a poached lemon sole main course, with its accompanying soy and shiitake purée and lemongrass foam. There's no less creativity in desserts; warm pear fritter, say, with hochija (a Japanese green tea) ice cream and spiced poached pear, or muscovado set custard with spiced fig jam, candied pecans and coffee ice cream. The wine list is a smart and varied collection, with good options by the glass.

Chef Allister Barsby **Seats** 34, Private dining 25 **Open** All year **Parking** 42
Notes No children under 8 years after 7pm

See advertisement on page 427

PEMBROKESHIRE

SAUNDERSFOOT continued

St Brides Spa Hotel
◉ MODERN BRITISH
01834 812304 | St Brides Hill, SA69 9NH
www.stbridesspahotel.com
Views of Saundersfoot harbour and Carmarthen Bay from its clifftop perch are reason enough to pay this laid-back spa hotel a visit, and the kitchen provides a brace of wide-ranging menus. Perhaps head for the outdoor terrace, or there's the Gallery bar and the Cliff Restaurant.
Chef Daniel Andrade **Seats** 100, Private dining 50 **Open** All year **Prices from** S £8, M £17, D £7 **Parking** 60 **Notes** Vegetarian dishes, Children welcome

SOLVA
Crug Glâs Country House
◉◉ MODERN BRITISH
01348 831302 | Abereiddy, SA62 6XX
www.crug-glas.co.uk
Owners Janet and Perkin Evans have renovated 12th-century Crug Glâs using local materials to achieve smart modernity without trampling on the house's history. At the end of the day, kick off the walking boots and settle into the formal Georgian dining room for country-house cooking.
Chef Janet Evans **Seats** 35, Private dining 16 **Closed** 25–26 December **Prices from** S £6, M £17, D £6 **Notes** Vegetarian dishes, Children welcome

TENBY
Penally Abbey Hotel
◉◉ MODERN **V**
01834 843033 | Penally, SA70 7PY
www.penally-abbey.com
Overlooking Carmarthen Bay, not far from Tenby, with the 12th-century ruins of the original chapel still seen in the grounds, the fully restored 18th-century Penally Abbey has soothingly elegant interiors, where the pale colour scheme and delightful period details lend an air of quiet luxury.
Chef Jerry Adam **Seats** Private dining **Closed** January **Parking** 15 **Notes** Children welcome

The Salt Cellar
◉◉ MODERN BRITISH **V**
01834 844005 | The Esplanade, SA70 7DU
www.thesaltcellartenby.co.uk
Occupying an enviable spot in a Victorian seafront hotel, the Salt Cellar is run by an independent team with a passion for prime Pembrokeshire produce. The setting is appropriately modern and the kitchen doesn't try to reinvent the culinary wheel.
Chef Duncan Barham, Matthew Flowers **Seats** 32 **Closed** 24–26 December, 2–6 January **Prices from** S £9, M £18, D £8 **Notes** Children welcome

Trefloyne Manor
◉ CLASSIC BRITISH
01834 842165 | Trefloyne Lane, Penally, SA70 7RG
www.trefloyne.com
This elegant manor house provides a relaxed country club setting in the heart of bustling Tenby. Accessed through a cosy bar area, the restaurant occupies a large glass-fronted orangery. The menu is supplemented with blackboard specials and a fish board, with classic British dishes.
Chef Pip Christopher **Closed** 25 December **Notes** Vegetarian dishes, Children welcome

WOLF'S CASTLE
Wolfscastle Country Hotel
◉◉ MODERN, TRADITIONAL
01437 741225 | SA62 5LZ
www.wolfscastle.com
Welsh rebel leader Owain Glyndwr may be buried in the field alongside this old stone country hotel where the principal restaurant offers unclothed tables and a menu of modern classics. Save room for chocolate fondant, served with salted caramel ice cream and orange jelly.
Chef Steve Brown **Seats** 55, Private dining 40 **Closed** 24–26 December **Prices from** S £5.50, M £11.50, D £5.95 **Parking** 75 **Notes** Vegetarian dishes, Children welcome

coast

SAUNDERSFOOT

▶ POWYS

BRECON
Peterstone Court
@ MODERN BRITISH, EUROPEAN
01874 665387 | Llanhamlach, LD3 7YB
www.peterstone-court.com

Georgian proportions and its position in the Brecon Beacons make Peterstone Court an ideal base for exploring the landscape. There's a contemporary feel and the classy finish includes a swish bar and a spa. Best of all, there's nifty modern food in the Conservatory Restaurant.

Chef Glyn Bridgeman **Seats** 30 **Open** All year **Prices from** S £6, M £11, D £6 **Parking** 40 **Notes** Vegetarian dishes, Children welcome

Three Horseshoes Inn
@ BRITISH
01874665672 | Groesffordd, LD3 7SN
www.threehorseshoesgroesffordd.co.uk

Just what you need to fuel a day in the great outdoors, this cosy pub is justifiably popular with hikers and bikers. The interior looks up to snuff with its slate floors, heritage paint palette and modern sheen, while food is buttressed by local suppliers.

Chef Adam Penfold **Seats** 46 **Open** All year **Prices from** S £5.95, M £11.95, D £5.50 **Notes** Vegetarian dishes, Children welcome

BUILTH WELLS
Caer Beris Manor
@@ MODERN EUROPEAN
01982 552601 | LD2 3NP
www.caerberis.com

This timber-framed country-house hotel sits in 27 acres of parkland. Dining takes place in the conservatory or the panelled dining room, where a large stone fireplace is a focal point. The kitchen gives a contemporary European spin on country-house cooking, confidently handling some beguiling combinations.

Chef Christian Naylor **Seats** 40, Private dining 100 **Open** All year **Parking** 50 **Notes** Vegetarian dishes, Children welcome

CRICKHOWELL
The Bear
@ MODERN BRITISH, INTERNATIONAL
01873 810408 | High Street, NP8 1BW
www.bearhotel.co.uk

The old stagecoach doesn't run past here any more, but a Victorian timetable in the bar remains. The Bear goes back further than that, to the 1430s. Its traditional interiors and ancient arched cellar where the beers are kept are all part of the deal.

Chef Stephan Trinci **Seats** 60, Private dining 30 **Closed** 25 December **Prices from** S £5.45, M £11.95, D £6.70 **Parking** 40 **Notes** Vegetarian dishes, No children under 7 years

Manor Hotel
@ BRITISH
01873 810212 | Brecon Road, NP8 1SE
www.manorhotel.co.uk

The sparkling-white hotel stands on an enthralling spot under Table Mountain. The relaxing dining room with tall plants and elegant furniture has views out towards the hills, and its bistro-style menu hauls in most of its prime materials from the family farm seven miles away.

Chef Glyn Bridgeman **Seats** 54, Private dining 26 **Open** All year **Prices from** S £6, M £18, D £6 **Parking** 200 **Notes** Vegetarian dishes, Children welcome

HAY-ON-WYE
Old Black Lion Inn
@ MODERN BRITISH, ITALIAN
01497 820841 | 26 Lion Street, HR3 5AD
www.oldblacklion.co.uk

Dating from the 17th century, the whitewashed inn has bags of character, with beams and stone fireplaces. You can eat in the bar or in the dining room. The kitchen proudly sources all their meats from organic farms in the foothills of Hay Bluff.

Chef Maximillion Evilio **Seats** 40, Private dining 20 **Closed** 3–13 January **Parking** 12 **Notes** Vegetarian dishes, Children welcome

KNIGHTON
Milebrook House Hotel
@ MODERN, TRADITIONAL **V**
01547 528632 | Milebrook, LD7 1LT
www.milebrookhouse.co.uk

This idyllic Georgian mansion in the Marches hills is much loved by shooting parties, with a kitchen garden to provide seasonal fruit and veg, and a skilled hand in the kitchen to track down the best local suppliers and deliver country-house classics cooked with flair and imagination.

Chef Katie Marsden **Seats** 40, Private dining 16 **Open** All year **Prices from** S £4.75, M £18.25 **Parking** 24 **Notes** No children under 8 years

LLANFYLLIN
Seeds
◎ MODERN BRITISH
01691 648604 | 5–6 Penybryn Cottages, High Street, SY22 5AP

When you don't require your food to push culinary boundaries or feature froths and gels, try Seeds, a little bistro with just 20 seats, run by an amiable husband-and-wife team. Mellow jazz floats around the artworks and curios decorating the low-beamed, slate-floored dining room.

Chef Mark Seager **Seats** 20 **Closed** 24–25 December, 1 week October, limited winter opening – phone in advance **Prices from** S £5.50, M £9.95, D £5.95 **Notes** Vegetarian dishes, Children welcome

LLANWDDYN
Lake Vyrnwy Hotel & Spa
◎ MODERN BRITISH
01691 870692 | Lake Vyrnwy, SY10 0LY
www.lakevyrnwy.com

Bird-watching, fishing and hill-walking are all possibilities at this stylish Victorian hotel with lovely views over the lake. Local produce is the backbone of the kitchen's output, some from the estate. Fish is handled deftly, perhaps roast halibut with samphire, pink grapefruit and basil sauce.

Chef Tyler Monroe **Seats** 85, Private dining 220 **Open** All year **Parking** 80 **Notes** Vegetarian dishes, Children welcome

LLANWRTYD WELLS
Carlton Riverside
◎◎ MODERN BRITISH
01591 610248 | Irfon Crescent, LD5 4SP
www.carltonriverside.co.uk

Wonderful views over the River Irfon enhance the dining room of this restaurant with rooms where the long-running chef-patron sources the best local produce. The technical proficiency of the kitchen is confirmed by a banana soufflé into which white chocolate sauce is poured.

Chef Luke Roberts **Seats** 18 **Closed** 18–31 December **Prices from** S £7, M £18, D £7 **Notes** Vegetarian dishes, No children under 6 years

Lasswade Country House
◎◎ MODERN BRITISH
01591 610515 | Station Road, LD5 4RW
www.lasswadehotel.co.uk

Run with great charm by owners Roger and Emma Stevens, this Edwardian house offers 360-degree views of the Cambrian Mountains and Brecon Beacons. In the kitchen, Roger keeps combinations straightforward, timings accurate, and interweaves flavours intelligently in daily changing dinner menus.

Chef Roger Stevens **Seats** 20, Private dining 20 **Closed** 25–26 December **Parking** 6 **Notes** Vegetarian dishes, No children under 8 years

LLYSWEN
Llangoed Hall
◎◎◎ MODERN BRITISH V ▮ NOTABLE WINE LIST
01874 754525 | LD3 0YP
www.llangoedhall.co.uk

An extensive kitchen garden and a smokehouse in the 17-acre grounds of this handsome Edwardian mansion in the Wye Valley attest to the culinary focus at Llangoed. Originally Jacobean, Clough Williams-Ellis (of Portmeirion fame) rebuilt the place in the early 20th century, so old-school elegance abounds, with luxurious lounges full of original features, fine furniture, and original artworks by Whistler and Augustus John. Nick Brodie and his team in the kitchen put organic pickings from the garden into 3-course à la carte menus of polished modern British cooking in a dreamy Wedgwood-blue-and-white setting. What arrives is savvy, sophisticated and complex stuff, including fashionably foraged and fermented ingredients and a whiff of the Orient – perhaps beef tartare updated with bone marrow, crisp tendon, anchovy cream and cured yolk, then a main course matching Welsh lamb with soft polenta, milk skin, samphire, anchovy and wood sorrel. The presentation of each plate is a visual treat, and there's no lack of invention among desserts either; a dish starring dark chocolate, say, supported by smoked walnut, caramel, aero and frozen yogurt.

Chef Nick Brodie **Seats** 40, Private dining 80 **Open** All year **Parking** 150 **Notes** Children welcome

MONTGOMERY
The Nags Head Inn
TRADITIONAL BRITISH
01686 640600 | Garthmyl, SY15 6RS
www.nagsheadgarthmyl.co.uk

The Grade II listed coaching inn on the A483 stands only a few yards from the Severn and the Montgomery Canal, a pleasant spot for an intelligently renovated country pub. The dining area is an expansive space opening on to a patio.

Chef Jacob Sampson **Open** All year

▶ RHONDDA CYNON TAF
PONTYCLUN
La Luna
MODERN INTERNATIONAL
01443 239600 | 79–81 Talbot Road,
Talbot Green, CF72 8AE
www.la-lunarestaurant.com

The family-run La Luna has an easy-going atmosphere and a contemporary finish, which fits the kitchen's sunny Med-style, brasserie-inspired output. There's an early evening menu, too, and some fair-weather outside tables.

Chef Craig Brookes **Seats** 91, Private dining 50
Closed 24 December, 1 January and Bank holidays
Notes Vegetarian dishes, Children welcome

PONTYPRIDD
Llechwen Hall Hotel
MODERN WELSH
01443 742050 | Llanfabon, CF37 4HP
www.llechwen.co.uk

The low-ceilinged, heavily beamed restaurant has plenty of atmosphere with its whitewashed walls hung with oils and candles flickering on bare wooden tables. The kitchen is ahead of the game when it partners pan-fried and sautéed scallops with confit chorizo cassoulet and aïoli.

Chef Paul Trask **Seats** 60, Private dining 300
Open All year **Prices from** S £5.50, M £14.95, D £5.50
Parking 100 **Notes** Vegetarian dishes, Children welcome

▶ SWANSEA
BISHOPSTON
The Plough & Harrow
MODERN EUROPEAN
01792 234459 | 88 Oldway, Murton, SA3 3DJ
www.ploughandharrow.eu

This unassuming gastro pub is in a quaint village near to Swansea on the Gower peninsula. Inside the old building, it's modern with a colour palette of cream, chalky blue and grey, a wood-burner, stacked logs and bare stone walls.

Chef Nick Jones **Seats** 40 **Prices from** S £6.50, M £14, D £7 **Parking** 16 **Notes** Vegetarian dishes, No children under 12 years

OXWICH
Beach House Restaurant at Oxwich Beach
MODERN BRITISH V ♦ NOTABLE WINE LIST
01792 390965 | SA3 1LS
www.beachhouseoxwich.co.uk

Occupying a fabulous seaside spot on the Gower peninsula, overlooking the sandy beach of Oxwich Bay, here's a place to blow the cobwebs away. Its spacious, light-filled interior is done in New England style, creating a supremely relaxing feel, and there are tables outdoors. The Beach House was the AA's Restaurant of the Year for Wales 2017–18.

Chef Hywel Griffith **Seats** 46 **Closed** 2nd and 3rd week January **Prices from** S £11, M £22, D £9
Notes Children welcome

See advertisement opposite

SWANSEA
Hanson at the Chelsea Restaurant
MODERN WELSH, FRENCH
01792 464068 | 17 St Mary Street, SA1 3LH
www.hansonatthechelsearestaurant.co.uk

Andrew Hanson's unassuming-looking restaurant resembles a classic modern bistro inside with clothed tables pressed in cheek by jowl, blackboard menus and small framed pictures against a delicate yellow colour scheme. The cooking is an appealing mix of local produce and French influences.

Chef Andrew Hanson, Nathan Kirby, Lucy Jenkins
Seats 50, Private dining 20 **Closed** 25–26 December
Prices from S £5.50, M £14.95, D £5.50
Notes Vegetarian dishes, Children welcome

BEACH HOUSE
OXWICH

BEACH HOUSE RESTAURANT, OXWICH BAY

reservations@beachhouseoxwich.co.uk
www.beachhouseoxwich.co.uk
01792 390965

TORFAEN–VALE OF GLAMORGAN

▶ TORFAEN

CWMBRAN
The Parkway Hotel & Spa
◉◉ MODERN EUROPEAN
01633 871199 | Cwmbran Drive, NP44 3UW
www.parkwayhotelandspa.com

Over seven acres of gardens surround the Parkway, making for a relaxing ambience. Ravellos Restaurant is at the heart of it all, with large geometric modern artworks to break up the white-walled space, and a fountain to distract you. Modern menus are sensibly balanced and confident.

Chef Clive Williams **Seats** 85, Private dining 20 **Open** All year **Prices from** S £6, M £15, D £6.50 **Parking** 250 **Notes** Vegetarian dishes, Children welcome

See advertisement opposite

▶ VALE OF GLAMORGAN

HENSOL
Llanerch Vineyard
◉ MODERN BRITISH
01443 222716 | CF72 8GG
www.llanerch-vineyard.co.uk

Around 22 acres of south-facing slopes of the Ely Valley have been planted with vines since 1986, and you can raise a glass to the industrious owners while dining in their restaurant or bistro, both of which offer the same menu. To wash it down – what else? – Welsh wine.

Chef Michael Hudson **Seats** 40 **Closed** 25–26 December **Prices from** S £7, M £14, D £7 **Parking** 400 **Notes** Vegetarian dishes, Children welcome

The Red Lion at Pendoylan
◉ MODERN, CLASSIC BRITISH
01446 760690 | Pendoylan, CF71 7UJ
www.theredlionatpendoylan.co.uk

A russet-coloured village inn in the Vale countryside, The Red Lion offers a pleasingly traditional bar area, with a multitude of hand-pumped ales and old-school furniture, and a more modern restaurant extension with plenty of natural light and well-spaced tables.

Chef (David) Mark Edwards **Seats** 40, Private dining 50 **Closed** 1st week January **Prices from** S £6, M £11, D £4.50 **Parking** 25 **Notes** Vegetarian dishes, Children welcome

The Vale Resort
◉ MODERN BRITISH
01443 667800 | Hensol Park, CF72 8JY
www.vale-hotel.com

The Resort luxuriates in 650 acres of the Vale of Glamorgan, but is only 15 minutes' drive from Cardiff. A bright airy room, the Vale Grill is one dining option, or there's a linen-clad restaurant, La Cucina, as well as a champagne bar.

Chef Justin Llewellyn **Seats** 120, Private dining 50 **Open** All year **Parking** 500 **Notes** Vegetarian dishes, Children welcome

LLANCARFAN
The Fox & Hounds
◉ MODERN CLASSIC BRITISH
01446 781287 | CF62 3AD
www.fandhllancarfan.co.uk

Next to a stream in the heart of the pretty village of Llancarfan in the Vale of Glamorgan, The Fox and Hounds occupies a peaceful location next to 15th-century St Cadoc's Church, but it's only 15 minutes from the M4. The restaurant offers pub classics.

Chef Jim Dobson **Seats** 80 **Open** All year **Prices from** S £6, M £11, D £6 **Parking** 15 **Notes** Vegetarian dishes, Children welcome

PENARTH
Restaurant James Sommerin
◉◉◉◉ MODERN BRITISH V ⓢ NOTABLE WINE LIST
029 2070 6559 | The Esplanade, CF64 3AU
www.jamessommerinrestaurant.co.uk

Reach the Severn Estuary and head for Penarth pier and just across the esplanade you'll find Restaurant James Sommerin (RJS) in a handsome Victorian terrace. The view is lovely and if the weather is not always calm and soothing, head indoors where you'll be greeted warmly and seated in the charmingly civilised dining room. It's a contemporary space, smartly so, with linen tablecloths and velour seats to sink into. RJS also has deliciously designed rooms if you've a mind to stop over, with sea views from the best of them. The eponymous chef-patron's menus don't give a lot away, with simple descriptions belying the complexity and creativity of each course from the carte or two tasting menus (six or nine courses). The seasons lead the way and a good deal of the produce comes from around these parts, with more than a whiff of European détente. Creamy burrata stars in an opening course with heritage carrots and seed granola, while pea ravioli is a dish that took James all the way to the BBC *Great British Menu* final. Main course delivers Welsh lamb, naturally, but with

Continues on page 438

PARKWAY
HOTEL AND SPA

★★★★

Cwmbran Drive
Cwmbran
NP44 3UW

Tel: 01633 871199

www.parkwayhotelandspa.com

Food . . . Just the way you like it

Located at the heart of the hotel, Ravellos is popular with both hotel residents and guests who live in the surrounding area.

We have been awarded our second AA Rosette, which reflects the passion that our Kitchen Brigade put into their food. There is an extensive A La Carte menu that reflects the use of Fresh Local Produce.

We pride ourselves on the best Sunday Lunch for miles, using only the best cuts of local meats.

Opening Hours
Breakfast from 7am – 9.30am
Dinner 6.30pm – last orders 9.30pm
Open for Sunday Lunch 12pm – last orders 2.30pm

coconut, cumin and mint, or go for monkfish with the well-judged flavour of curry spices. Like everything else, desserts look stunning on the plate; an inventive apple number, for example, with tarte Tatin flavours. The wine list includes interesting options by the glass, and also features Welsh organic and biodynamic wines from the Ancre Hill Estates.

Chef James Sommerin **Seats** 65, Private dining 12 **Closed** 26 December, 1 January **Prices from** S £8.50, M £18, D £9 **Notes** Children welcome

▶ WREXHAM

LLANARMON DYFFRYN CEIRIOG
The Hand at Llanarmon
◉◉ MODERN CLASSIC
01691 600666 | Ceiriog Valley, LL20 7LD
www.thehandhotel.co.uk

A whitewashed country inn buried in the sumptuous Ceiriog Valley, The Hand makes a concerted effort to come up to rustic expectations inside, with dozing dogs warming themselves before the open fires, plenty of chunky furniture and brass ornaments. Expect impressive renditions of classic and modern pub food.

Chef Grant Mulholland **Seats** 40 **Open** All year **Prices from** S £6, M £14.50, D £6.50 **Parking** 15 **Notes** Vegetarian dishes, Children welcome

ROSSETT

AA Restaurant of the Year for Wales 2018–19

Machine House Restaurant
◉◉ **V** MODERN BRITISH
01244 571678 | Chester Road, LL12 0HW
www.machinehouse.co.uk

With its sturdy oak beams, bare stone and whitewashed walls, the setting may speak of another era, but the modern British cooking in this intimate restaurant is bang up to date. The kitchen has strong supply lines to outstanding local producers, then dials the flavours up to 11 in lively, sharply executed dishes. Scorched mackerel with beetroot purée and powder, compressed apple and apple gel is a strong opener, followed by melt-in-the-mouth pork belly highlighted by crunchy crackling, cauliflower purée, crisp kale and rich, sticky jus. To finish, a cleverly crafted dessert of poached pear comes with butterscotch and buttermilk ice cream.

Chef Kevin Lynn **Seats** 30, Private dining 8 **Closed** 1st 2 weeks January and last 2 weeks August **Prices from** S £7.50, M £18.95, D £7.75 **Parking** 20 **Notes** Children welcome

NORTHERN IRELAND

▶ COUNTY ANTRIM

BALLYMENA
Galgorm Resort & Spa
◉◉◉ MODERN IRISH V ⚑ NOTABLE WINE LIST
See pages 440–441

See advertisement on page 442

BUSHMILLS
Bushmills Inn Hotel
◉ MODERN, TRADITIONAL V
028 2073 3000 | 9 Dunluce Road, BT57 8QG
www.bushmillsinn.com

For centuries a coaching inn at the heart of this world-famous whiskey village, this is now an upmarket boutique hotel. The peat fires may remain from the days when guests arrived by horse but modern-day visitors are more likely to arrive via helipad.

Chef Donna Thompson **Seats** 120 **Open** All year **Prices from** S £6, M £16, D £6 **Parking** 70 **Notes** Children welcome

NEWTOWNABBEY
Sleepy Hollow
◉ MODERN IRISH
028 9083 8672 | 15 Kiln Road, BT36 4SU
www.sleepyhollowrestaurant.com

It would take a jaded palate not to be thrilled by the hearty modern Irish cooking in this rustic restaurant.

Locally sourced artisan produce is at the heart of things, with meat and game supplied by neighbouring farms and estates, butchered in-house, and handled without fuss.

Chef Paul Dalrymple **Seats** 60 **Closed** 24–26 December **Parking** 22 **Notes** Vegetarian dishes, Children welcome

▶ BELFAST

BELFAST
Deanes at Queens
◉◉ MODERN BRITISH V
028 9038 2111 | 1 College Gardens, BT9 6BQ
www.michaeldeane.co.uk

In a stylish, contemporary space of chrome and glass, the cooking matches the modernity of the setting, delivering a genuine Irish flavour and some creative combinations. To finish, choose from a range of desserts, or go savoury with the French and Irish cheeses.

Chef Chris Fearon **Seats** 120, Private dining 44 **Closed** 25–26 December, 1 January, 12–13 July **Prices from** S £7.50, M £13.50, D £6 **Notes** Children welcome

Belfast continues on page 443

COUNTY ANTRIM

BALLYMENA
Galgorm Resort & Spa
◉◉◉ MODERN IRISH **V** 🍷NOTABLE WINE LIST

028 2588 1001 | 136 Fenaghy Road, Galgorm, BT42 1EA
www.galgorm.com

Ambitious contemporary cooking and river views

If all Galgorm had to shout about were its lavish rooms, cabins and cottages spread through 163 acres of parkland with the River Maine flowing through, it would be a seductive enough proposition. Add in the glossy spa, treatment areas and riverside hot tubs in the Thermal Village, extensive meetings, conference and wedding facilities, a champagne and gin bar, a pub and live entertainment, and you can see why an escape here is on many people's bucket lists. On the food front, there's a brasserie and grill in former stables, a relaxed Italian venue, and the enticing prospect of an afternoon tea blowout in the elegant conservatory lounge. But gastronomy here gets serious in the aptly named River Room Restaurant, where the floodlit river creates a magical atmosphere after dark, and its floor-to-ceiling windows mean everyone gets the watery views.

This is chef Chris Rees's domain and he sets out his stall with a five-course tasting menu and a thoughtfully composed à la carte designed to showcase his impressive skills, as well

as the splendid produce from trusty local suppliers (and as you'd hope with all those acres out there, a kitchen garden chips in with freshly plucked seasonal goodies). Things might get off the blocks with a well-crafted starter of scallops helped along by roast cauliflower, black trompette mushrooms and crispy chicken, or you might take a more robust route in with a cleverly deconstructed 'pie' of partridge and foie gras balanced by the sharp notes of quince, pickled turnip and rosemary.

Clarity of flavour is key, and while Rees is happy to use clever technical ideas when appropriate, the base of it all is solidly grounded in modern European thought, so main courses might see halibut in a pretty-as-a-picture medley with shellfish bisque, carrots and mussels, all pointed up with caramelised fennel. Meat courses, too, show real skill and confidence – perhaps salt-aged beef of fantastic mineral depth combined with frivole mini-cabbage, malt, braised onion and celeriac. As dessert beckons, there's yet more to admire in the likes of baked caramel tart with roast pear, hazelnut, and buttermilk ice cream, or you might bow out on a pungent note with artisan Irish cheeses ripened to prime condition. Everything, from the excellent home-made bread and inventive canapés to the superb petits fours is crafted with impressive attention to detail. A superlative wine list promises class and desirable drinking from top to bottom.

Chef Israel Robb, Chris Rees **Seats** 50 **Open** All year **Prices from** S £9, M £24, D £8.50 **Parking** 200 **Notes** No children under 12 years

See advertisement on page 442

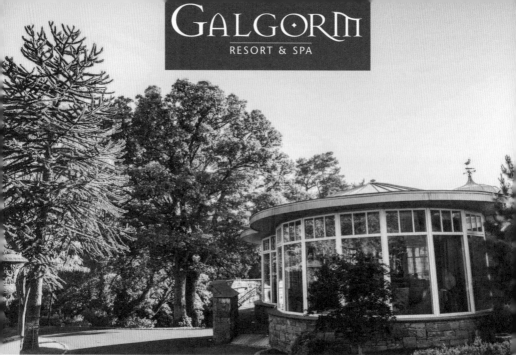

Deanes EIPIC

◉◉◉ MODERN EUROPEAN **V** 🍷NOTABLE WINE LIST

028 9033 1134 | 36–40 Howard Street, BT1 6PF

www.deaneseipic.com

It may be a little confusing for first-timers, but Deanes is a tripartite set-up, with dedicated meat and fish restaurants, through which bustly environs you pass to reach the more softly accented EIPIC dining room, which despite its shouty capitals, adopts a more sotto voce tone. The bar area is padded in white leather, while the restaurant itself is dimly lit and adorned with a trio of stylised full moons. Alex Greene worked his way from Dundrum to London and back to Belfast, and brings a cosmopolitan modernist sensibility to the kitchens, sending out a six-course taster that speaks of confidence and innovative energy at every turn. Highlights might be plump langoustine with leeks, shiitakes and smoked bacon, followed by a flawlessly timed serving of brill with salsify and lardo, before the main business of tenderly pink duck breast with chicory, carrot and mustard seeds. Chocolate desserts are a standout, perhaps a silky ganache with yuzu, coconut and coffee sauce. Accompanying wines are served either by small glass or shot measure, a helpful touch of flexibility that allows you to pace yourself from course to course.

Chef Michael Deane, Alex Greene **Seats** 26 **Closed** 26 December to 3 January, 28 March to 3 April, 11–24 July **Notes** Children welcome

Fitzwilliam Hotel Belfast

◉ MODERN **V**

028 90442080 | 1–3 Victoria Street, BT2 7BQ

www.fitzwilliamhotelbelfast.com

Next door to the Grand Opera House, the sleek Fitzwilliam Hotel makes a splendid upscale Belfast base for business or pleasure. The restaurant takes its style cues from Scandi minimalism, using blond wood tables and space-age, cherry-red seating as a backdrop to some well-conceived modern dishes.

Chef Ryan McFarland **Open** All year

James Street South Restaurant

◉◉ MODERN, CLASSIC

028 9043 4310 | 21 James Street South, BT2 7GA

www.jamesstreetsouth.co.uk

Tucked away behind City Hall, this capacious red-brick former linen mill makes a serene and understated setting for refined, French-accented food. Bargain lunch and pre- and post-theatre options keep things affordable, and there are tasting menus with matching wines if you're going for broke.

Chef David Gillmore **Seats** 60, Private dining 40 **Closed** 1 January, Easter Monday, 12–15 July, 25–26 December **Prices from** S £8.50, M £15.50, D £5 **Notes** Vegetarian dishes, Children welcome

The Merchant Hotel

◉◉ MODERN CLASSIC **V** 🍷NOTABLE WINE LIST

028 9023 4888 | 16 Skipper Street, Cathedral Quarter, BT1 2DZ

www.themerchanthotel.com

The former headquarters of Ulster Bank is a grand building and these days the beneficiaries are those who rock up for lunch or dinner. The kitchen delivers a classical-meets-modern repertoire where tip-top regional produce, such as lobster and scallops, is treated with respect.

Chef John Paul Leake **Seats** 85, Private dining 18 **Open** All year **Prices from** S £6.50, M £19.50, D £8.50 **Notes** Children welcome

OX

◉◉◉ MODERN IRISH

028 9031 4121 | 1 Oxford Street, BT1 3LA

www.oxbelfast.com

Stephen Toman and Alain Kerloc'h met while working in Paris restaurants and combined their talents (the former as chef, the latter as manager and sommelier) to open OX by the River Lagan. The simple, minimalist interior may be a little disarming for some, but this is the new order, where a lack of fuss and frills does not mean a lack of quality. The service is informed and charming, the cooking is out of this world. Fabulous Irish produce from land and sea star alongside local fruits and veg, so it goes without saying that this is a seasonal journey. Superb sourdough gets the ball rolling before scallops with a luscious bisque, salsify and squid ink, followed by salt-cured halibut with buttermilk and almonds. Presentation is somehow simple yet stunning. Baked celeriac stands centre stage with chanterelles and crapaudine beetroots, while a game offering could be wild Wicklow venison with bone marrow and chestnuts. Among sweet courses, rhubarb keeps company with thyme, honey and crème fraîche parfait. An Irish drinks list includes beers, whiskies and gins, while the wine list has enticing options by the glass and carafe.

Chef Stephen Toman **Seats** 40 **Closed** 2 weeks July, Christmas, 1 week April **Notes** Vegetarian dishes, Children welcome

Shu

◎◎ MODERN IRISH

028 9038 1655 | 253–255 Lisburn Road, BT9 7EN

www.shu-restaurant.com

Situated in a Victorian terrace, the airy space with an open-to-view kitchen is served by a smartly turned-out team. One or two dishes on the menu have an Asian flavour – witness a starter of salt-and-chilli squid served with classic dipping sauces.

Chef Brian McCann **Seats** 100, Private dining 24 **Closed** 25–26 December, 1 January, 12–13 July **Prices from** S £5, M £18, D £6.50 **Parking** 4 **Notes** Vegetarian dishes, Children welcome

▶ COUNTY DOWN

CRAWFORDSBURN

The Old Inn

◎◎ MODERN EUROPEAN **V**

028 9185 3255 | 15 Main Street, BT19 1JH

www.theoldinn.com

A busy dining venue, drawing people with its decor and its modern European-style cooking built on prime local produce. Canapés and breads are of a high standard, as are puddings along the lines of chocolate delice with salted caramel ice cream.

Chef Mateusz Ostradeki **Seats** 134, Private dining 50 **Closed** 25 December **Prices from** S £4.95, M £10.95, D £4.95 **Parking** 80 **Notes** Children welcome

DUNDRUM

Mourne Seafood Bar

◎ SEAFOOD

028 4375 1377 | 10 Main Street, BT33 0LU

www.mourneseafood.com

With a sister establishment in Belfast, the Dundrum branch of Mourne Seafood is in a refreshingly peaceful location. At the foot of the Mourne mountains, with a nature reserve nearby, it's dedicated to fish and shellfish, much of which comes from their own shellfish beds.

Chef Brendan O' Kane, Wayne Carville **Seats** 100, Private dining 80 **Closed** 25 December **Notes** Vegetarian dishes, Children welcome

NEWTOWNARDS

Balloo House

◎ MODERN BRITISH

028 9754 1210 | 1 Comber Road, Killinchy, BT23 6PA

www.balloohouse.com

A refurbishment a few years ago accentuated Balloo House's original historical features, while the additions of darkwood panelling and peacock-blue and tan leather booth seating helped to create an intimate atmosphere. When it comes to the menu, roast Kilmore pigeon with apple and celeriac remoulade gets the ball rolling.

Chef Danny Millar, Grainne Donnelly **Seats** 80, Private dining 30 **Closed** 25 December **Parking** 60 **Notes** Vegetarian dishes, Children welcome

▶ COUNTY FERMANAGH

ENNISKILLEN

Lough Erne Resort

◎◎◎ MODERN, TRADITIONAL **V**

028 6632 3230 | Belleek Road, BT93 7ED

www.lougherneresort.com

Piling on the style with Thai spa treatments, up-to-the-minute golf facilities and restorative views of the Fermanagh Lakelands, Lough Erne is one of the joys of northwest Ireland. Among the dining options, the pick is the Catalina restaurant, named after the Second World War seaplanes that were once stationed on the lough. Views over the 18th hole are a boon to anybody who can't tear themselves away from the putting action, but for those with their minds on dining, the charming service approach is all in keeping with the mood of relaxed civility. Noel McMeel maintains his highly burnished style of locally supplied, traditionally rooted cooking, opening perhaps with a hefty raviolo of mushrooms coated in matching sauce, offset with broad beans and tarragon oil, an earthy prelude to a dish of eloquent venison loin in anise and juniper jus with baked apple, pickled girolles and cauliflower purée, while fish might be Glenarm salmon with creamed leeks in herb velouté. Incomparable technique makes a blackcurrant soufflé with vanilla custard, ice cream and shortbread something special.

Chef Noel McMeel **Seats** 75, Private dining 30 **Open** All year **Parking** 200 **Notes** Children welcome

Manor House Country Hotel

🌸 IRISH, EUROPEAN

028 6862 2200 | Killadeas, BT94 1NY

www.manorhousecountryhotel.com

The colonel who rebuilt this old manor in the 1860s brought craftsmen over from Italy to spruce up the interior. The fine-dining action takes place in the Belleek Restaurant, housed in a conservatory extension that gets the very best of the view of the lough.

Chef David Irvine **Seats** 90, Private dining 350 **Open** All year **Notes** Vegetarian dishes, Children welcome

▶ COUNTY LONDONDERRY DERRY

LIMAVADY

The Lime Tree

🌸 CLASSIC MEDITERRANEAN

028 7776 4300 | 60 Catherine Street, BT49 9DB

www.limetreerest.com

The Lime Tree is a pint-sized neighbourhood restaurant in the town centre, its simply painted walls hung with vibrant artwork. Themed evenings, such as Spanish, are successes, and puddings can be as decadent as gooey chocolate brownie with creamy vanilla ice cream and chocolate sauce.

Chef Stanley Matthews **Seats** 30 **Closed** 25–26 December, 12 July **Prices from** S £4.75, M £17, D £5.50 **Notes** Vegetarian dishes, Children welcome

LONDONDERRY DERRY

Browns Bonds Hill

🌸 MODERN IRISH V

028 7134 5180 | 1 Bonds Hill, Waterside, BT47 6DW

www.brownsrestaurant.com

Situated on the edge of the city centre by Lough Foyle, Browns has built a local following since 2009. Get in the mood with some bubbly in the champagne lounge, then head for one of the white linen-swathed tables in the sleek, contemporary dining room.

Chef Ian Orr, Phelim O' Hagan **Seats** 60, Private dining **Closed** 3 days at Christmas **Prices from** S £7.95, M £18.95, D £6.25 **Notes** Children welcome

The Gown Restaurant

🌸 MODERN IRISH V

028 71 140300 | Bishop's Gate Hotel, 24 Bishop Street, BT48 6PP

www.bishopsgatehotelderry.com

In the heart of Cathedral Quarter, The Gown is the focal point of the late 19th-century Bishop's Gate Hotel. Original wall panelling and wooden flooring make an attractive setting for dining from the modern Irish menu's signature dishes, among them chargrills and fresh seafood. International influences are evident, too.

Chef Paul Sharkey **Seats** 64, Private dining 120 **Closed** 25 December **Notes** Children welcome

MAGHERA

Ardtara Country House

🌸🌸 MODERN IRISH V

028 7964 4490 | 8 Gorteade Road, BT46 5SA

www.ardtara.com

Built in the 19th century by a linen magnate, Ardtara is a country-house hotel in glorious grounds. It's an engaging spot for afternoon tea, and the restaurant, with its real fireplaces and oak panels, is a smart backdrop for the bright, contemporary cooking.

Chef Ian Orr **Seats** 50, Private dining 25 **Closed** 25–26 December **Parking** 50 **Notes** Children welcome

REPUBLIC OF IRELAND

▶ COUNTY CARLOW

LEIGHLINBRIDGE
Lord Bagenal Inn
◉ MODERN IRISH 🍷 NOTABLE WINE LIST
059 9774000 | Main Street
www.lordbagenal.com

In 1979, the original roadside restaurant was almost killed off by the advent of a new motorway, but the enterprising owners built a hotel on the site. It's distinctly contemporary these days, with its Signature Restaurant revamped to create an open-plan space.

Chef Shein Than, George Kehoe **Seats** 85, Private dining 60 **Closed** 25–26 December **Prices from** S €11, M €22, D €6 **Parking** 100 **Notes** Vegetarian dishes, Children welcome

TULLOW
Mount Wolseley Hotel, Spa & Country Club
◉ MODERN IRISH V
059 9180100
www.mountwolseley.ie

The restaurant here encompasses a stylish split-level dining room overlooking a garden courtyard, where smartly attired staff attend at well turned-out tables. Seafood is a forte. There's also the Aaron Lounge for casual all day dining.

Chef David Cuddihy **Seats** 150, Private dining 40 **Closed** 24–26 December **Parking** 500

▶ COUNTY CAVAN

CAVAN
Cavan Crystal Hotel
◉ MODERN IRISH
049 4360600 | Dublin Road
www.cavancrystalhotel.com

Sharing the same site as its factory, Ireland's second oldest crystal manufacturer also has a smart contemporary hotel, a leisure club and the clean-lined Opus One restaurant. It's a relaxed spot and food chimes in tune with the setting: confident, modern and uncomplicated.

Chef Dolores Reilly

Farnham Estate Spa & Golf Resort
◉ EUROPEAN, MODERN INTERNATIONAL V
049 4377700 | Farnham Estate
www.farnhamestate.ie

With lakes, rivers and ancient oak forests all over the 1,300-acre, 16th-century estate, it's easy to work up an appetite at this historic stately home that is now an upmarket country hotel. Clever use of plush drapes and screens softens the capacious space.

Chef Daniel Willimont **Seats** 130, Private dining 35 **Open** All year **Parking** 600 **Notes** Children welcome

▶ COUNTY CLARE

BALLYVAUGHAN

Gregans Castle

◉◉◉ MODERN IRISH, EUROPEAN

065 7077005

www.gregans.ie

It may not be an actual castle, but the 18th-century manor house is undeniably a luxurious hideaway filled with antiques and period Georgian elegance that is unlikely to disappoint. The location is a dream, set in the photogenic south-western wilderness that is the Burren, with sweeping views towards Galway Bay. The restaurant is a romantic and traditional room where picture windows open on to the views, candlelight flickers in the evening and the family-run hospitality is warm and welcoming. Head chef Robbie McCauley's menus are packed with modern ideas, where flavour, seasonality and ingredients from the local landscape point the way. The superb natural flavour of roasted scallops shines through in a starter that combines them with baked celeriac, apple, grape and hazelnuts to form a hugely satisfying whole. Next up, local lamb stars in a workout involving roast loin, sweetbreads and shoulder alongside wild garlic purée, morels, asparagus and a potent Madeira jus. For dessert, a lush dark chocolate and peanut pavé is further intensified by its accompanying caramelised banana, banana ice cream and malt.

Chef Robbie McCauley **Seats** 50, Private dining 30 **Closed** November to mid February **Parking** 20 **Notes** Vegetarian dishes

ENNIS

Legends Restaurant

◉ MODERN INTERNATIONAL V

065 6823300 | Temple Gate Hotel, The Square

www.templegatehotel.com

Set in a former convent, the fine dining restaurant of the Temple Gate Hotel is an impressive space with its soaring hammerbeam roof and striking contemporary decor. There's a capable hand in the kitchen, and daily specials mean seasonal produce is well represented.

Chef Reinhard Sprengard **Seats** 100, Private dining 60 **Closed** 25–26 December **Parking** 50 **Notes** Children welcome

LAHINCH

Moy House

◉◉ MODERN FRENCH V

065 7082800 |

www.moyhouse.com

Standing proud in 15 acres of grounds overlooking the bay at Lahinch, Moy House is full of period character, though the dining room with its minimalist chandeliers

and panoramic views is more contemporary. As is the food, which draws on unimpeachable local supply lines.

Chef Matthew Strefford **Seats** 35, Private dining 22 **Closed** November to March **Parking** 50 **Notes** Children welcome

VL Restaurant

◉◉ MODERN FRENCH, IRISH V

065 7081111 | Vaughan Lodge, Ennistymon Road

www.vaughanlodge.ie

Overlooking beautiful Liscannor Bay, this modern townhouse hotel is located right next to the world-famous Lahinch Golf Course. Vaughan Lodge's stunning coastal position means the kitchen is blessed with a bountiful supply of excellent fish and seafood including daily landings of langoustine, lobster and scallops.

Chef Pawel Gasiorowski **Seats** 50 **Closed** November to April **Prices from** S €12, M €24, D €10 **Notes** Children welcome

LISDOONVARNA

Sheedy's Country House Hotel

◉◉ CLASSIC FRENCH

065 7074026

www.sheedys.com

This small-scale country-house hotel exudes the sort of family-run, unpretentious tradition that keeps fans returning. John Sheedy has long-established local supply lines, and the kitchen garden provides fresh herbs and vegetables to supplement local organic meat and fish landed at nearby Doolin.

Chef John Sheedy **Seats** 28 **Closed** mid October to mid March **Parking** 25 **Notes** Vegetarian dishes, No children under 8 years

NEWMARKET-ON-FERGUS

Dromoland Castle Hotel

◉◉ TRADITIONAL IRISH, EUROPEAN V

061 368144

www.dromoland.ie

As well as a golf course and spa, you'll find turrets and ramparts at this fabulous country-house hotel. Formal dining takes place in the Earl of Thomond restaurant, a spectacular room filled with antiques, oak-panelled period character and a resident harpist.

Chef David McCann **Seats** 80, Private dining 70 **Open** All year **Prices from** S €16, M €32, D €12 **Parking** 140 **Notes** Children welcome

SHANNON
The Old Lodge Gastro Pub
◉ MODERN IRISH

061 364047 | Shannon Springs Hotel,
Ballycasey, V14A336
www.shannonspringshotel.com

Handy for Shannon airport, the restaurant is in one of three sections. The lunch menu is largely familiar old favourites, while in the evening expect more substantial dishes, classics included.

Chef Anthony Walsh **Seats** 60, Private dining 45
Closed 25 December **Prices from** S €4.50, M €13.95,
D €5.95 **Parking** 105 **Notes** Vegetarian dishes, Children welcome

▶ COUNTY CORK
BALLINGEARY
Gougane Barra Hotel
◉ CLASSIC, TRADITIONAL

026 47069 | Gougane Barra
www.gouganebarrahotel.com

The Cronin family has owned property in hauntingly beautiful Gougane Barra since Victorian times, when its potential as an idyllic retreat was first fully realised. Views over the lake towards the mountains of Cork look especially magnificent from the ample windows of the dining room.

Chef Katy Lucey **Seats** 70

BALLYLICKEY
Seaview House Hotel
◉◉ TRADITIONAL IRISH V

027 50073
www.seaviewhousehotel.com

The grand white-painted Seaview has the promised vista over Bantry Bay, glimpsed through the trees in the pretty gardens, while the restaurant comprises three rooms including a conservatory. There's much local produce on the menu and everything is handled with care.

Chef Damian O'Sullivan **Seats** 50 **Closed** November to March **Prices from** S €8, M €20, D €8 **Parking** 32 **Notes** Children welcome

BALTIMORE
Rolfs Country House
◉ FRENCH, EUROPEAN

028 20289
www.rolfscountryhouse.com

Set in beautiful sub-tropical gardens overlooking Baltimore Harbour to Roaringwater Bay and Carbery's 100 islands, it is hardly surprising that the Haffner family have put down roots here since 1979. The kitchen uses produce that is locally grown, reared and caught, organic whenever possible.

Chef Johannes Haffner **Seats** 50, Private dining 14
Closed Christmas **Prices from** S €6.50, M €22, D €7.50
Parking 45 **Notes** Vegetarian dishes, Children welcome

CORK
Bellini's Restaurant
◉◉ MODERN INTERNATIONAL V

021 4365555 | Maryborough Hill, Douglas
www.maryborough.com

There's a whiff of glamour at this Georgian country-house hotel, with later additions tacked on, surrounded by 14 acres of well-maintained gardens and woodland. The bar and restaurant, Bellini's, provide a modern glossy sheen. Fresh, locally sourced produce is the kitchen's stock in trade.

Chef Gemma Murphy **Seats** 170, Private dining 60
Closed 24–26 December **Prices from** S €7.50, M €23,
D €7.50 **Parking** 300 **Notes** Children welcome

Perrotts Garden Bistro
◉◉ MODERN IRISH, MEDITERRANEAN

021 4845900 | Hayfield Manor Hotel,
Perrott Avenue, College Road
www.hayfieldmanor.ie

Early 19th-century iron baron Richard Perrott lived here in what is today's Hayfield Manor Hotel, where the bistro occupies the contemporary conservatory. Glass-topped metal or timber tables, sofas and wine cabinets create a relaxing environment for international-style dining; eat alfresco, if you prefer. Frequently changing lunch and dinner menus.

Chef Mark Staples **Seats** 75, Private dining 22 **Open** All year **Prices from** S €8.50, M €26, D €10 **Parking** 110 **Notes** Vegetarian dishes, Children welcome

The Springboard Restaurant
◉ MODERN TRADITIONAL

021 4800500 | Victoria Cross
www.thekingsley.ie/springboard-restaurant

The Kingsley Hotel was built on the site of the city's public baths, resulting in a restaurant named after a diving-board. It's a split-level space with views into the kitchen, and full-drop windows on two sides looking over the River Lee and Cork's architectural heritage. Contemporary bistro food is the style.

Chef Tim Daly **Seats** 120 **Closed** Christmas
Prices from S €5, M €14, D €7 **Parking** 150
Notes Vegetarian dishes, Children welcome

DURRUS
Blairscove House & Restaurant
◉◉ MODERN EUROPEAN
027 61127
www.blairscove.ie

Blairscove brims with charm, on a promontory overlooking peaceful Dunmanus Bay. The main house is Georgian, and the accommodation and restaurant occupy a pretty development facing a pond, in what were the piggery, stables and barn. The dining room is full of character.

Chef Ronald Klotzer **Seats** 75, Private dining 48 **Closed** November to 15 March **Parking** 30 **Notes** Vegetarian dishes, Children welcome

GOLEEN
The Heron's Cove
◉ TRADITIONAL IRISH
028 35225 | The Harbour
www.heronscove.com

This delightful restaurant sits in an idyllic spot on Goleen harbour near to Mizen Head, where the lonely Fastnet Rock lighthouse beams out across the Atlantic. This is an exceptionally easy-going, friendly place, where you can enjoy sublime sea views on the balcony.

Chef Irene Coughlan **Seats** 30 **Closed** mid November to mid February **Prices from** S €7.25, M €19.50, D €7.25 **Parking** 10 **Notes** Vegetarian dishes, Children welcome

KINSALE
The White House
◉ MODERN IRISH
021 4772125 | Pearse Street, The Glen
www.whitehouse-kinsale.ie

The White House occupies a prime site in the centre of a town that holds a Gourmet Festival every autumn, so there's plenty to live up to in the gastronomic stakes. The kitchen triumphs with a resourceful repertoire of modern Irish dishes.

Chef Jonny Hartnett **Seats** 45 **Closed** 25 December **Prices from** S €8.50, M €16, D €6.50 **Notes** Vegetarian dishes, Children welcome

MALLOW
Springfort Hall Country House Hotel
◉ MODERN, IRISH
022 21278
www.springfort-hall.com

This is an immaculately preserved Georgian country house where the enthusiastic kitchen team don't cut corners – meat and fish is smoked in-house and everything is made from scratch. In the palatial Lime Tree Restaurant a crystal chandelier hangs above pristine white linen-clothed tables.

Chef Viktor Bosz **Seats** 60, Private dining 40 **Closed** 24–26 December **Prices from** S €7.50, M €14.50, D €7.50 **Parking** 250 **Notes** Vegetarian dishes, Children welcome

ROSSCARBERY
Kingfisher Bistro
◉ SEAFOOD **V**
023 8848722 | The Celtic Ross Hotel
www.celticrosshotel.com

Part of the wonderfully situated Celtic Ross Hotel, a contemporary building right on the waterfront, with fabulous views, the Kingfisher is ideally placed to take advantage of the great local produce available in the region. Signature dishes include 'the finest seafood chowder in West Cork'.

Chef Alex Petit **Seats** Private dining **Open** All year **Parking** 150 **Notes** Children welcome

SHANAGARRY
Ballymaloe House
◉◉ MODERN, TRADITIONAL
021 4652531
www.ballymaloe.com

The Allens were ahead of the curve 50 years ago when they opened a restaurant in their farmhouse. Now there's a cookery school and hotel, and the idea of fresh produce brought to the table in double-quick time seems the happy norm.

Chef Jason Fahy, JR Ryall **Seats** 110, Private dining 50 **Closed** Christmas, 6 January to 6 February **Parking** 100 **Notes** Vegetarian dishes, No children under 7 years at dinner

SKIBBEREEN
Kennedy Restaurant
◉ CLASSIC, TRADITIONAL
028 21277 | West Cork Hotel, Ilen Street
www.westcorkhotel.com

This riverside hotel's restaurant offers a carvery at lunchtime with a dessert buffet, while in the evening the à la carte focuses on locally sourced ingredients to ensure a sense of place. It all takes place in a simply stylish room with a buzzy atmosphere.

Chef Linda O'Brien **Seats** 60, Private dining 300 **Closed** 25–27 December **Prices from** S €5, M €13.95, D €6.50 **Parking** 50 **Notes** Vegetarian dishes, Children welcome

▶ COUNTY DONEGAL

BALLYLIFFIN
Jacks Restaurant
◎ MODERN EUROPEAN
074 9378146 | Ballyliffin Lodge & Spa, Shore Road
www.ballyliffinlodge.com

Ballyliffin Lodge has ditched the 'faine daining' approach in Jacks Restaurant, and the new look – brown leather seats and banquettes, bare tables and dark wood floors – backed by a pubby bar and an unbuttoned menu are a hit with the guests.

Chef Breid McDermott **Seats** 64, Private dining 400 **Closed** 24–25 December **Parking** 100 **Notes** Vegetarian dishes, Children welcome

DONEGAL
Harvey's Point Hotel
◎◎ MODERN, IRISH
074 9722208 | Lough Eske
www.harveyspoint.com

It was the heavenly setting that brought the Swiss family Gysling here to the shore of Lough Eske in order to build their luxurious hotel complex in the late 1980s. The kitchen uses pedigree Irish produce in imaginative contemporary dishes.

Chef Chris McMenamin **Seats** 120 **Open** All year **Parking** 200 **Notes** Vegetarian dishes, Children welcome

The Red Door Country House
◎ MODERN, TRADITIONAL EUROPEAN
074 9360289 | Fahan, Inishowen
www.thereddoor.ie

With views over Lough Swilly, this country house has a restaurant run by a hands-on team. The menu shows a passion for local produce, along with sound classical training and bright modern thinking.

Chef Sean Clifford **Seats** 120 **Notes** Vegetarian dishes, Children welcome

DUNFANAGHY
Arnolds Hotel
◎ TRADITIONAL
074 9136208 | Main Street
www.arnoldshotel.com

Overlooking Sheephaven Bay, a stroll away from Killahoey Beach, this is a friendly, comfortable place, with open fires and lots of windows in Seascapes Restaurant to capitalise on the coastal views. The kitchen takes a fuss-free approach.

Chef John Corcoran **Seats** 60 **Closed** November to April (excluding New Year) **Parking** 40 **Notes** Vegetarian dishes, Children welcome

LETTERKENNY
Port Grill & Bar
◎ MODERN IRISH
074 9194444 | Paddy Harte Road
www.radissonblu.ie/hotel-letterkenny

The smart TriBeCa Restaurant in this modern hotel sports a large screen showing kitchen action, which whets the appetite for the likes of duck confit with braised red cabbage and apple and cinnamon purée. The menu embraces modern brasserie cooking.

Chef Collette Langan **Seats** 120, Private dining 320 **Open** All year **Parking** 150 **Notes** Vegetarian dishes, Children welcome

MOVILLE
Redcastle Hotel, Golf & Spa Resort
◎◎ MODERN, INTERNATIONAL
074 9385555 | Inishowen Peninsula
www.redcastlehotel.com

The Redcastle estate can trace its lineage all the way back to a 16th-century proprietor called Cathal O'Doherty. At one point, it was owned by a Pennsylvania farming family, but today it makes a superbly located northwestern seafront hotel in the modern boutique style.

Chef Gordon Smyth **Seats** 140 **Closed** 25 December **Parking** 232 **Notes** Vegetarian dishes, Children welcome

▶ DUBLIN

DUBLIN
Balfes at The Westbury
◎ CONTEMPORARY IRISH
01 6463353 | Grafton Street
www.balfes.ie

With its own street entrance, and pavement tables, Balfes is an affable place with white walls, dark leather seats and a long bar-counter down one end. Kick off in the morning with an omelette or blueberry pancakes or come for lunch of roast sea trout.

Chef Jorge Ballester, Austin Byrne **Seats** 140 **Closed** 25 December **Prices from** S €7.50, M €18, D €8 **Notes** Vegetarian dishes, Children welcome

Castleknock Hotel
◎ TRADITIONAL IRISH
01 6406300 | Porterstown Road, Castleknock
www.castleknockhotel.com

Just 15 minutes from Dublin, Castleknock has plenty of pizazz. The pick of its eating and drinking choices is the elegantly finished Earth and Vine Restaurant. There are floor-to-ceiling windows with swagged

curtains, richly coloured walls and large artworks.
Steak is the mainstay of the kitchen's output.

Chef Neil Kearns **Seats** 80, Private dining 400
Closed 24–26 December **Prices from** S €6.95,
M €17.50, D €8 **Parking** 500 **Notes** Vegetarian dishes

Cliff Townhouse
◉◉ CLASSIC, TRADITIONAL
01 6383939 | 22 St Stephens Green
www.clifftownhouse.ie

Dubliners love this intimate seafood-focused
restaurant, whether it's for lunch after shopping in
classy Grafton Street, or for a pre-theatre dinner in the
Oyster & Champagne Bar. Afternoon tea features Yawl
Bay crabs and Irish smoked salmon open sandwiches.
Thoughtful sourcing of ingredients is, naturally, behind
everything.

Chef Sean Smith **Seats** 100, Private dining 44
Closed 25 and 27 December, St Stephens Day
Prices from S €9.75, M €17.95, D €8 **Notes** Vegetarian
dishes, Children welcome

Crowne Plaza Dublin Northwood
◉ ASIAN FUSION
01 8628888 | Northwood Park, Santry Demesne,
Santry
www.cpdublin.crowneplaza.com

The Crowne Plaza sits amid 85 acres of mature
woodland in Northwood Park. The whole place is done
in swish contemporary style, including the Touzai
restaurant, where east-meets-west for a menu of
creative fusion cooking. Wok dishes come as starters
or mains, as well as more western options.

Chef Logan Irwin **Seats** 156, Private dining 15
Closed 25 December **Parking** 350 **Notes** Vegetarian
dishes, Children welcome

Crowne Plaza Hotel Dublin – Blanchardstown
◉◉ ITALIAN, EUROPEAN, INTERNATIONAL
01 8977777 | The Blanchardstown Centre
www.cpireland.ie

The Blanchardstown branch of the Crowne Plaza
empire is a short hop from the district's glitzy shopping
centre. Its Forchetta restaurant works a loud and
proud contemporary look with bold floral wallpaper
and bare wooden tables, a buzzy, breezy setting that
suits the Italian menu.

Chef Iulian Suciu **Seats** 100, Private dining 45
Closed 24–25 December **Prices from** S €9.95,
M €17.50, D €7 **Parking** 200 **Notes** Vegetarian
dishes, Children welcome

Fahrenheit Restaurant
◉◉ MODERN IRISH
01 8332321 | Clontarf Castle Hotel, Castle Avenue,
Clontarf
www.clontarfcastle.ie

Fahrenheit is the destination restaurant of Dublin's
Clontarf Castle Hotel, a beguiling mix of the ancient
(12th-century roots) and a modern boutique, and it's a
dramatic showcase for some striking modern Irish
cooking. Try beetroot-cured wild salmon with smoked
salmon mousse, beetroot gel and horseradish.

Chef Stuart Heeney **Seats** 90, Private dining 20
Open All year **Parking** 200 **Notes** Vegetarian
dishes, Children welcome

The Iveagh Bar
◉ IRISH, EUROPEAN
01 6772324 | Parkgate Street
www.ashlinghotel.ie

The Ashling is a large, modern and glitzy hotel near
Phoenix Park and Dublin Zoo, where Chesterfields
Restaurant occupies a spacious, softly lit room with
plushly upholstered dining chairs and a busily
patterned carpet. The kitchen takes a modern tack
with its combinations of flavours.

Chef Gary Costello **Seats** 180 **Closed** 24–26 December
Parking 80 **Notes** Vegetarian dishes, Children
welcome

The Marker
◉◉ MODERN INTERNATIONAL
01 6875100 | Grand Canal Square
www.themarkerhoteldublin.com

Set in a cool, contemporary canalside hotel in the
rejuvenated Docklands zone, this sleek brasserie is
making quite a splash on the local dining scene, and
celebrates the pick of Irish produce in its ambitious
modernist food. Global accents abound.

Chef Gareth Mullins **Seats** 130, Private dining 250
Closed 24–25 December and January **Parking** 40
Notes Vegetarian dishes, Children welcome

Radisson Blu St Helens Hotel
◉ ITALIAN
01 2186000 | Stillorgan Road
www.radissonblu.ie/sthelenshotel-dublin

This grand old house dates from the mid-17th century
but has all the expected mod cons. The Talavera
restaurant serves up smart Italian food – especially from
Lombardy – in a series of rooms with either traditional
country-house decor or more contemporary chic.

Chef Giancarlo Anselmi **Seats** 150, Private dining 126
Open All year **Parking** 220 **Notes** Vegetarian dishes

Restaurant Patrick Guilbaud
◎◎◎◎ MODERN FRENCH
See pages 454–455

Roganstown Hotel and Country Club
◎ EUROPEAN
01 8433118 | Naul Road, Sword
www.roganstown.com

Golf, spa and conference facilities all feature at this large resort, but for dinner you'll be wanting the impressive, wood-panelled McLoughlins Restaurant. There's plenty of room between the well-dressed tables, and the kitchen seeks out first-class ingredients and delivers an ambitious, contemporary menu.
Chef Gareth Skelton **Seats** 100, Private dining 30 **Closed** 24–25 December and St Stephens Day **Prices from** S €6.50, M €19, D €6.50 **Notes** Vegetarian dishes, Children welcome

The Shelbourne Dublin, a Renaissance Hotel
◎◎ TRADITIONAL IRISH, EUROPEAN V ♦NOTABLE WINE LIST
01 6634500 | 27 St Stephen's Green
www.theshelbourne.ie

This grand modern hotel is in a prime location on St Stephen's Green, and offers a range of eating and drinking options culminating in the tip-top Saddle Room. The menu consists of modern brasserie dishes and specialises in seafood (including generously loaded platters).
Chef Garry Hughes **Seats** 120, Private dining 20 **Open** All year **Prices from** S €9, M €24, D €9 **Notes** Children welcome

Talbot Hotel Stillorgan
◎ MODERN FUSION
01 2001800 | Stillorgan Road
www.talbothotelstillorgan.com

A hotel with wedding packages among its attractions, The Talbot Hotel Stillorgan is also home to the Purple Sage restaurant, with its breezy air and contemporary finish. The menu has a gently conceived modern fusion tack. For dessert, expect bread-and-butter pudding made with croissants.
Chef Alan Shakespeare **Seats** 140, Private dining 60 **Closed** 25 December **Parking** 300 **Notes** Vegetarian dishes, Children welcome

Tom's Table
◎ IRISH
01 4593650 | Red Cow Complex, Naas Road
www.redcowmoranhotel.com

The modern Red Cow Moran Hotel is amply equipped with drinking and dining opportunities, the top choice being Tom's Table, an expansive space done out in contemporary city-slicker style. Lit by soaring floor-to-ceiling windows, its toffee-brown banquettes and clean-lined brasserie-style looks make a suitable setting for uncomplicated modern cooking.
Chef Brian McCarthy **Open** All year

Wilde
◎◎ MODERN IRISH V
01 6463311 | The Westbury, Grafton Street
www.wilde.ie

This prestigious city-centre hotel has a fine-dining restaurant dedicated to Oscar Wilde. The kitchen showcases the cream of Ireland's produce. Puddings are a strong suit when they include an authentic rendition of classic crema Catalana, or vanilla pannacotta with poached rhubarb.
Chef Sandeep Singh **Seats** 95 **Open** All year **Prices from** S €10, M €22, D €9 **Notes** Children welcome

▶ COUNTY DUBLIN

KILLINEY
Fitzpatrick Castle Hotel
◎ MODERN EUROPEAN
01 2305400
www.fitzpatrickcastle.com

The castellated house was built in the 18th century, and now offers a range of hospitable dining venues including the bar, housed in the former dungeon, and the Mapas Restaurant where you'll find a menu of well-wrought modern brasserie cooking.
Chef Sean Dempsey **Seats** 90 **Closed** 25 December **Prices from** S €6, M €15.50, D €5 **Parking** 200 **Notes** Vegetarian dishes, Children welcome

PORTMARNOCK
The 1780
◎◎ MODERN IRISH
01 846 0611 | Portmarnock Hotel and Golf Links
www.portmarnock.com

The Portmarnock Hotel stands on the estate that was once home to the Jameson Irish Whiskey family and is a fitting venue for a pint or a dram before a meal. The coastal location means there are close links between the kitchen and local fishermen.
Chef Thomas Haughton **Seats** 100 **Open** All year **Parking** 100 **Notes** Vegetarian dishes, Children welcome

▶ COUNTY GALWAY

BARNA

The Pins Gastro Bar
◉ INTERNATIONAL, MODERN IRISH
091 597000 | Barna Village
www.thetwelvehotel.ie

Part of the boutique-style Twelve Hotel, The Pins is an unusual amalgam of bar, bakery, bistro and pizzeria, the latter being authentic Neapolitan-style thin and crispy pizzas made in a Vesuvian stone oven. There's also a modern gastro pub menu of championing regional suppliers.

Chef Martin O'Donnell **Seats** 140, Private dining 20 **Open** All year **Parking** 120 **Notes** Vegetarian dishes, Children welcome

Upstairs@West, The Twelve
◉◉ MODERN IRISH ▮ NOTABLE WINE LIST
091 597000 | Barna Village
www.westrestaurant.ie

A boutique hotel with bags of swagger, The Twelve is in a coastal area a short distance from the town centre. There's a lot going on: a cool bar, a bakery, and a pizza place, but the main action takes place in the Upstairs restaurant.

Chef Martin O'Donnell **Seats** 94, Private dining 100 **Open** All year **Parking** 120 **Notes** Vegetarian dishes, Children welcome

CASHEL

Cashel House Hotel
◉◉ TRADITIONAL IRISH
095 31001
www.cashelhouse.ie

Standing at the head of Cashel Bay, Cashel House is a gracious 19th-century country pile that has belonged to the McEvilly family since 1968. The restaurant offers French-accented classics, served in either an airy conservatory extension, or a polished traditional setting amid antiques and artworks.

Chef Arturo Tillo **Seats** 70, Private dining 20 **Closed** 2 January to 1 March **Parking** 30 **Notes** Vegetarian dishes, Children welcome

GALWAY

Ardilaun Bistro
◉ MODERN IRISH
091 521433 | Taylor's Hill
www.theardilaunhotel.ie

Formerly Glenarde House, the Ardilaun was built in 1840 for the Persse family, Galway landowners of some grandeur. It was launched as a modern hotel in 1962, and the Bistro is its venue for dynamic modern Irish cooking of vaulting ambition.

Chef Ultan Cooke **Seats** 90 **Closed** 25–26 December **Prices from** S €5.95, M €9.95, D €4.95 **Parking** 250 **Notes** Vegetarian dishes, Children welcome

Dillisk on the Docks
◉ MODERN, TRADITIONAL
091 894800 | New Dock Road
www.harbour.ie

After a makeover, the main restaurant of the waterfront Harbour Hotel now sports a sharp contemporary brasserie-style look. It's a buzzy spot with royal blue seats, banquettes and high-level tables providing a variety of settings to suit the mood. Food-wise, the kitchen takes an uncomplicated, please-all approach.

Chef Patrick Anslow **Open** All year

Gaslight Bar & Brasserie
◉ MODERN IRISH
091 564041 | Eyre Square
www.hotelmeyrick.ie

One of several dining options in the Meyrick, the Gaslight looks out over Eyre Square. Lofty and bright, its seasonal daytime and evening menus usually feature international dishes, including Malaysian and Vietnamese. End on a high with spiced apple and rhubarb crumble with vanilla ice cream and crème anglaise.

Chef Roy Notu Atindra **Seats** 120 **Open** All year **Prices from** S €6.95, M €13.95, D €5.95 **Notes** Vegetarian dishes, Children welcome

Galway continues on page 456

DUBLIN
Restaurant Patrick Guilbaud
◎◎◎◎ MODERN FRENCH
01 6764192 | Merrion Hotel, 21 Upper Merrion Street
www.restaurantpatrickguilbaud.ie

Bold contemporary cooking with a French soul and Irish heart

The setting amid the elegant Georgian splendour of the five-star Merrion Hotel hints at the supremely civilised experience that is dining chez Guilbaud. The restaurant has its own separate entrance and an identity all of its own; the name Patrick Guilbaud has been the touchstone of fine dining in Ireland since first opening its doors back in 1981. Remarkably, the Paris-born patron has had the same chef, Guillaume Lebrun (now executive chef), running the kitchen since opening its doors all those decades ago, and the same manager, Stéphane Robin for nearly as long. This unprecedented level of consistency has not gone unnoticed, and is a steadfast platform for head chef Kieran Glennon to build upon.

The dining room, with its barrel-vaulted ceiling, is a soothing contemporary space, with warm tones and striking artworks from Irish artists on the walls, the room watched over by a professional and knowledgeable service team. The brigade in the kitchen gets to work with outstanding produce, sourced with passion and care, and a good amount of these

first-class ingredients come from the local area. The seasons are followed with due diligence. The à la carte menu is joined by a four-course dégustation menu (Tuesday to Thursday) and a full-works eight-course tasting menu that has to be taken by the whole table.

The cooking shows genuine ambition and creativity. An journey might take you from a red king crab and cucumber maki with lemon croquant, via Wicklow Hills lamb fillet with piquillo peppers and wet garlic, to combawa lime soufflé with lime leaf ice cream. Those exotic flavours are handled perfectly. A combination of French classical thinking and Asian flavours is very much to the fore in a starter of pan-roasted duck foie gras, with pineapple and dark rum caramel, and in a main course poached blue lobster, with a hint of cardamom running through the rich roasted lobster essence. Everything looks beautiful on the plate, not least desserts such as a contemporary dark chocolate tart with bourbon vanilla ice cream.

The wine list is a tour de force especially when dealing with the best French producers, but the rest of the world is far from excluded; the cellar contains some 30,000 bottles in total, so it is worth making use of the passionate sommelier to guide you to what you're looking for, or indeed what you didn't know you were looking for.

Chef Guillaume Lebrun **Seats** 80, Private dining 25 **Closed** 25–31 December, 1st week in January **Notes** Vegetarian dishes, Children welcome

COUNTY GALWAY

GALWAY continued

Marina Grill
MODERN IRISH, SEAFOOD
091 538300 | Galmont Hotel & Spa, Galway,
Lough Atalia Road
www.thegalmont.com

Part of the Galmont Hotel & Spa on the banks of Lough
Atalia, Marina's Grill overlooks Galway Bay which
supplies much of the seafood on the menu. The kitchen
lets the raw materials do the talking and the stylish
modern dishes are unpretentious and produce-driven.

Chef Adrian Bane **Seats** 220, Private dining 80
Open All year

No 15 Restaurant
MODERN IRISH
091 564041 | Hotel Meyrick, Eyre Square
www.hotelmeyrick.ie

Dating from 1852, Hotel Meyrick has been overlooking
Eyre Square in the heart of Galway for over 160 years
and it's ideally located for the city's theatres and
buzzing bars. The hotel may be packed with Victorian
character but there's nothing dated about the food.

Chef Phillip Dunleavy **Seats** 120, Private dining 50
Open All year **Prices from** S €8.95, M €16.95, D €6.95
Notes Vegetarian dishes, Children welcome

Park House Hotel & Restaurant
MODERN IRISH, INTERNATIONAL
091 564924 | Forster Street, Eyre Square
www.parkhousehotel.ie

Standing just off Eyre Square and built of striking pink
granite, Park House has offered high standards of food
and accommodation for over 35 years. Park Restaurant,
where paintings of old Galway help keep the past
alive, bustles at lunchtime and mellows in the evening.

Chef Robert O'Keefe, Martin Keane **Seats** 145, Private
dining 45 **Prices from** S €5.65, M €12.75, D €7.50
Parking 40 **Notes** Vegetarian dishes, Children welcome

Pullman Restaurant
MODERN FRENCH
091 519600 | Kentfield, Bushypark
www.glenloabbeyhotel.ie

As if this grandiose country house built in the early
Georgian era didn't have diversion enough, its dining
room has been fashioned from a pair of railway
carriages from the Orient Express. It's a splendid
design concept, and makes an elegant setting.

Chef Michael Safarik **Seats** 66, Private dining 30
Open All year **Parking** 150 **Notes** Vegetarian
dishes, Children welcome

Restaurant gigi's at the g Hotel & Spa
MODERN IRISH
091 865200 | Wellpark, Dublin Road
www.theghotel.ie

Looking a little like a modern office building, the g is
a fashionista's magnet, with an eye-popping dining
room in pulsating violet and many another hue. Artful
presentations of dishes are the norm, but the food
itself is more intuitive than you might expect.

Chef Jason O'Neill **Seats** 90, Private dining 30
Closed 23–26 December **Prices from** S €9.95,
M €19.95, D €7.95 **Parking** 200 **Notes** Vegetarian
dishes, Children welcome

See advertisement opposite

ORANMORE
Basilico Restaurant
ITALIAN
091 788367 | Main Street
www.basilicorestaurant.ie

Now into its tenth year, Basilico brings an authentic
slice of Italy to the heart of Oranmore, just 20 minutes
from Galway. A contemporary restaurant decorated
with artwork by owner Fabiano Mulas, there is a
genuine buzz. Crowd-pleasing pizzas are made in a
partly open kitchen.

Chef Paolo Sabatini **Seats** 70 **Closed** 25 December
Prices from S €5, M €11.50, D €6 **Parking** 16
Notes Vegetarian dishes, Children welcome

RECESS
Lough Inagh Lodge Hotel
IRISH, FRENCH
095 34706 | Inagh Valley
www.loughinaghlodgehotel.ie

This boutique hotel in a lovely spot on the Lough shore
has an oak-panelled bar, a library with a log fire, and a
restaurant where silver and glassware reflect
candlelight and an oval window gives wonderful
views. Chatty and attentive staff help you choose.

Chef J O'Flaherty, M Linne **Seats** 30 **Closed** mid
December to mid March **Notes** Vegetarian
dishes, Children welcome

The Owenmore Restaurant
MODERN IRISH
095 31006 | Ballynahinch Castle Hotel
www.ballynahinchcastle.com

Set in 700 acres of woodland, rivers and walks in the
heart of Connemara, Ballynahinch is one of Ireland's
most celebrated castle hotels. The work of many great
Irish painters hangs on the walls of the elegant
Owenmore Restaurant, which overlooks a salmon river.

Chef Pete Durkan **Open** All year

▶ COUNTY KERRY

DINGLE (AN DAINGEAN)
Coastguard Restaurant
◉ MODERN IRISH
066 9150200 | Dingle Skellig Hotel
www.dingleskellig.com/restaurant

It isn't possible to get much further west on the European continent than here. The Dingle Skellig is a sprawling establishment right on the coast with glorious views all round, best enjoyed from the Coastguard restaurant with its capacious picture windows.

Chef John Ryan **Seats** 120 **Closed** January **Parking** 150 **Notes** Vegetarian dishes, Children welcome

Gormans Clifftop House & Restaurant
◉ MODERN AND TRADITIONAL IRISH, SEAFOOD
066 9155162 | Glaise Bheag, Ballydavid (Baile na nGall)
www.gormans-clifftophouse.com

The stone-built house perching on the clifftops above Smerwick harbour has been owned by the Gorman family since the 18th century. Simplicity is the key: there's nothing to get in the way of the dining room's sweeping views across the Atlantic.

Chef Sheelagh Smyth Gorman **Seats** 30 **Closed** October to March **Parking** 25 **Notes** Vegetarian dishes, Children welcome

KENMARE
Park Hotel Kenmare
◉◉ CLASSIC IRISH V ▲ NOTABLE WINE LIST
064 6641200
www.parkkenmare.com

Set against a backdrop of the Cork and Kerry Mountains, with stunning views over Kenmare Bay, this landmark Victorian hotel dates from 1897. Top-notch ingredients sourced from the surrounding area dominate the menu. A carefully chosen and comprehensive wine list offers some notable bottles.

Chef James Coffey **Seats** 70 **Closed** 10–22 December, 2 January to 16 February **Prices from** S €8.10, M €14.50, D €9 **Parking** 60 **Notes** Children welcome

Sheen Falls Lodge
◉◉ MODERN EUROPEAN V
064 6641600 | Sheen Falls Lodge
www.sheenfallslodge.ie

Not far from the Rings of both Kerry and Beara, Sheen Falls maintains a refined tone in its La Cascade restaurant, enhanced by informed staff. Home-smoked salmon, superb seafood and organic produce

distinguish the output. Dishes on the menu take a classical French line.

Chef Cormac McCreary **Seats** 120, Private dining 100 **Closed** 2 January to 9 February **Prices from** S €8, M €18, D €10.50 **Parking** 75 **Notes** Children welcome

KILLARNEY
Bacchus Restaurant
◉ TRADITIONAL, FRENCH
064 6639200 | Killarney Riverside Hotel, Muckross Road
www.riversidehotelkillarney.com

Next to the Flesk River, the Killarney Riverside Hotel is just a 10-minute walk from the bustling town centre in Killarney. Irish ingredients are given a modern European spin, with first-rate fish and game getting a strong showing on the menu.

Chef Cyrille Durand **Seats** 88 **Closed** 22–28 December **Prices from** S €5.50, M €16.95, D €6.25 **Parking** 66 **Notes** Vegetarian dishes, Children welcome

Cahernane House Hotel
◉◉ CLASSIC, TRADITIONAL
064 6631895 | Muckross Road
www.cahernane.com

Guests can take a meal in the original dining room of this 19th-century manor house while enjoying views across parkland which dips down to the lake. Interesting desserts on the menu might include choux pastry with blackberry curd, wild berry crème fraiche.

Chef Eric Kavanagh **Seats** 60 **Closed** November to December midweek, January to February **Prices from** S €10, M €25, D €10 **Notes** Vegetarian dishes, Children welcome

Danu at The Brehon
◉◉ MODERN EUROPEAN V
064 6630700 | The Brehon Hotel, Muckross Road
www.thebrehon.com

Brehon was the name for the ancient body of law that governed Ireland. It gave its subjects an obligation of hospitality, so is a logical name for a hotel. The kitchen fast-forwards us to the present day with contemporary Irish cooking of impressive depth.

Chef Chad Byrne **Seats** 100, Private dining 100 **Open** All year **Parking** 250 **Notes** Children welcome

The Lake Hotel
◉◉ MODERN IRISH V
064 6631035 | On the Shore, Muckross Road
www.lakehotelkillarney.com

On the shore of Killarney's lower lake, Lough Lein, the hotel has been in the Huggard family for over a century. The windows reveal one of those splendid views in which Ireland specialises. Expect local place names on the menu, as in Dingle Bay crab.

Chef Noel Enright **Seats** 100, Private dining 65 **Closed** December to January **Prices from** S €10, M €20, D €9 **Parking** 150 **Notes** Children welcome

The Lake Room
◉◉ MODERN

064 6631766 | Aghadoe Heights Hotel & Spa, Lakes of Killarney
www.aghadoeheights.com

In a perfect setting on the shore of the lake, amidst some of Kerry's most beautiful landscapes, the restaurant is part of the impossibly luxurious Aghadoe Heights Hotel. You can expect a fine wine list, a cosmopolitan atmosphere and stunning views and amazing sunsets.

Chef Alan McCardle **Open** All year **Notes** Children under 8 years must dine before 7pm

The Park Restaurant
◉◉ IRISH **V**

064 6635555 | The Killarney Park Hotel, Kenmare Place
www.killarneyparkhotel.ie

Dining at The Park Restaurant is a luxurious experience. The linen-clad tables overlooking gardens, the red upholstery, decorative plasterwork ceiling and grand piano make a fine setting. Passion fruit crémaux with a champagne and yogurt sorbet is a real winner.

Chef Heiko Riebandt **Seats** 70, Private dining 40 **Closed** 23–26 December **Parking** 90 **Notes** Children welcome

The Yew Tree Restaurant
◉◉ IRISH, INTERNATIONAL **V**

064 6623400 | Muckross Park Hotel, Killegy Lower
www.muckrosspark.com

Set in the Victorian lounge of The Muckross Park Hotel, a former coaching inn, The Yew Tree Restaurant enjoys an ornate setting with linen-clad tables, high ceilings and luxurious drapes. A wine trolley holds recommended wines to accompany the dishes, which are seasonal and uncomplicated.

Chef John O'Leary **Seats** 45, Private dining 30 **Closed** 25–25 December **Prices from** S €10, M €26, D €12 **Parking** 144 **Notes** Children welcome

KILLORGLIN
Carrig House Country House & Restaurant
◉◉ MODERN IRISH, EUROPEAN

066 9769100 | Caragh Lake
www.carrighouse.com

Carrig is a lovingly restored Victorian country manor in acres of colourful woodland gardens with views across

Caragh Lake to the Kerry Mountains. Inside, the dining room is the image of 19th-century chic, with William Morris wallpapers, swagged curtains, polished floorboards, and formally laid tables.

Chef Patricia Teahan

TRALEE
Ballyseede Castle
◉◉ TRADITIONAL EUROPEAN

066 7125799
www.ballyseedecastle.com

This 16th-century castle surrounded by 30 acres of woodland is now a deluxe hotel. Its O'Connell Restaurant is a gracefully curved room with luxurious drapes at the windows, and columns, oil paintings and a chandelier. Top-quality native produce is used throughout, evident in well-conceived, unfussy main courses.

Chef Aidan McGurkin **Seats** 40, Private dining 70 **Closed** January to 3 March **Parking** 180 **Notes** Vegetarian dishes, Children welcome

▶ COUNTY KILDARE
STRAFFAN
The K Club
◉◉ TRADITIONAL FRENCH

01 6017200 | River Room
www.kclub.ie

Once home to the Barton wine family, this luxurious hotel has the look of a French château and there are dining options aplenty, not least of which is the River Restaurant, with its impressive views of the Liffey. The cooking is built around classic technique.

Chef Kevin McGrattan **Seats** 110, Private dining 30 **Open** All year **Parking** 300 **Notes** Vegetarian dishes, Children welcome

▶ COUNTY KILKENNY
KILKENNY
The Yew Restaurant
◉◉ MODERN IRISH, EUROPEAN **V**

056 7760088 | Paulstown Road
www.lyrath.com

The hotel and spa occupies an imposing 17th-century property set in 170 acres of parkland that includes lakes and ornamental gardens. The Yew Restaurant, a large room overlooking the rose garden, is the gem among the dining options. The kitchen works around a modern Irish repertoire.

Chef Gary Rogers **Seats** 120, Private dining 30 **Closed** 21–26 December **Prices from** S €9, M €24, D €11 **Parking** 420 **Notes** No children after 8pm

COUNTY KILKENNY–COUNTY LOUTH

THOMASTOWN
The Lady Helen Restaurant
◉◉◉ MODERN IRISH V
056 7773000 | Mount Juliet Hotel
www.mountjuliet.com

It isn't just golfing and spa treatments at the Mount Juliet Hotel – archers and falconers are looked after too. It all seems a fitting role for a grand Georgian country house, once owned by the late Lady Helen McCalmont, in whose honour the fine dining restaurant has been named. Windows give on to the grounds in a gentle arc in a room done in restrained taupe tones, where produce from the estate finds its way into modern Irish cooking of impressive reach. A seductive starter could be silky-textured truffled potato ravioli with a duck egg yolk and hazelnuts, or there could be sea-fresh king crab and mussels with rouille in rockfish sauce. Main-course meats are top-drawer, with local rose veal or venison from Wicklow among the options, the latter accompanied by beetroot, black trompettes and the scent of juniper, while brill fillet might be teamed with baby gem, Jerusalem artichoke and Alsace smoked bacon. Technical wizardry at dessert stage produces a combination of 70% chocolate ganache with compressed streusel crumbs and raspberry sorbet, or poached rhubarb with lovage ice cream and olive oil sablé.

Chef Ken Harker, John Kelly Seats 60, Private dining 80 Open All year Parking 200 Notes Children welcome

► COUNTY LAOIS
BALLYFIN
Ballyfin Demesne
◉◉ EUROPEAN V ❧NOTABLE WINE LIST
057 8755866
www.ballyfin.com

In possibly Ireland's most opulent Regency house, the high-ceilinged dining room gazes out towards a temple where a water feature cascades. A walled garden supplies plenty of produce, as do the resident bees, and lucky humans are regaled with French-inspired contemporary cooking of considerable dazzle.

Chef Sam Moody Seats 39, Private dining 39 Closed January to 14 February Notes No children under 9 years

► COUNTY LIMERICK
LIMERICK
Limerick Strand Hotel
◉ IRISH CONTEMPORARY
061 421800 | Ennis Street,
www.strandlimerick.ie

A new-build riverside hotel with all mod cons, including a bright, airy dining room. Sourcing from within the county supplies a menu of populist brasserie dishes, with an Irish contemporary gloss on international ideas. Good breads come with intensely anchovied tapenade.

Chef Tom Flavin Seats 120, Private dining 450 Open All year Parking 200 Notes Vegetarian dishes, Children welcome

► COUNTY LOUTH
CARLINGFORD
Ghan House
◉◉ MODERN IRISH
042 9373682 |
www.ghanhouse.com

Perched on the water's edge within a pretty walled garden complete with veg patch to fuel the kitchen, Ghan House has views over the Mourne Mountains. Just about everything is made in-house. Local sea scallops might turn up accompanied by white beans and chorizo.

Chef Stephane Le Sourne Seats 50, Private dining 50 Closed 24–26 and 31 December, 1–2 January Parking 24 Notes Vegetarian dishes, Children welcome

DROGHEDA
Scholars Townhouse Hotel
◉◉ MODERN IRISH V
041 9835410 | King Street,
www.scholarshotel.com

Built as a Christian Brothers monastery in 1867, ceiling frescoes of the Battle of the Boyne in the interlinked dining rooms furnish a historical note that's a contrast to the modern Irish cooking. Praline soufflé with pumpkin ice cream is an interesting way to finish.

Chef Matthias Ecker Seats 75, Private dining 36 Closed 25–26 December Parking 30 Notes Children welcome

▶ COUNTY MAYO

BALLINA

Belleek Castle

◉◉ INTERNATIONAL **V**

096 22400 | Belleek,

www.belleekcastle.eu

Built in the 1820s on the site of a medieval abbey, Belleek is more manor house than castle, but altogether splendid. The style is sophisticated, but retains a foothold in tradition, offering a house pie of pork in pork-fat pastry with orange and ginger marmalade.

Chef David O'Donnell **Seats** 55, Private dining 30 **Closed** Christmas, January **Parking** 90 **Notes** Children welcome

Mount Falcon Estate

◉◉ TRADITIONAL

096 74472 | Foxford Road

www.mountfalcon.com

The restaurant at this grand baronial-style hotel on the River Moy is the Kitchen Restaurant, which occupies the original kitchen and pantry area, looking good with its linen-clad tables and food-related prints on the walls. There's a definite French classicism to the kitchen's output.

Chef Daniel Willimont **Seats** 70, Private dining 30 **Closed** 25 December **Parking** 100 **Notes** Vegetarian dishes, Children welcome

CONG

The George V Dining Room

◉◉ TRADITIONAL EUROPEAN, INTERNATIONAL **V** 🍾 NOTABLE WINE LIST

094 9546003 | Ashford Castle

www.ashfordcastle.com

Once home to the Guinness family, Ashford Castle dates from the 13th century and sits grandly on the shores of Lough Corrib, amid 350 acres of parkland. The dining room was built to host a reception for the Prince of Wales in 1906.

Chef Philippe Farineau **Seats** 120, Private dining 40 **Open** All year **Prices from** S €19, M €29.50, D €16 **Parking** 115 **Notes** Children welcome

The Lodge at Ashford Castle

◉◉ CONTEMPORARY IRISH **V**

094 9545400 | Ashford Estate

www.thelodgeatashfordcastle.com

Wilde's restaurant is named after Sir William Wilde, a local surgeon who founded the first eye and ear hospital in Dublin, and, from its first-floor setting in the

original Victorian building, offers fabulous views over Lough Corrib. The kitchen impresses with an ambitious, contemporary output.

Chef Jonathan Keane **Seats** 60, Private dining 50 **Closed** 24–26 December **Parking** 50 **Notes** Children welcome

MULRANNY

Mulranny Park Hotel

◉◉ MODERN IRISH

098 36000

www.mulrannyparkhotel.ie

Once the station hotel for Mulranny, opened in the 1890s, this is now a sumptuous country-house with sweeping views over the Atlantic. A duo of Keem Bay smoked salmon and barbecued fresh salmon with honey-mustard aïoli, pickled cucumber and red onion dressing might start proceedings.

Chef Chamila Manawatta **Seats** 100, Private dining 50 **Closed** Christmas, January **Prices from** S €7.50, M €17, D €9 **Parking** 200 **Notes** Vegetarian dishes, Children welcome

WESTPORT

Hotel Westport Leisure, Spa & Conference

◉ MODERN IRISH, BRITISH, EUROPEAN

098 25122 | Newport Road

www.hotelwestport.ie

Heavenly scenery frames this expansive family-run hotel and spa set in seven acres of mature woodland. Miles of walking and cycling on the Great Western Greenway close by are more reasons to bring a keen appetite with you to the restaurant.

Chef Stephen Fitzmaurice **Seats** 120, Private dining 45 **Open** All year **Parking** 220 **Notes** Vegetarian dishes, Children welcome

Knockranny House Hotel

◉◉ MODERN IRISH

098 28600

www.knockrannyhousehotel.ie

This tranquil spa hotel makes the most of its Mayo situation, with stunning views every which way. Inside comes with all the accoutrements of an upscale hotel, including a full-dress dining room, La Fougère, which eschews modern minimalism in favour of immaculate linen and glassware.

Chef Seamus Commons **Seats** 90, Private dining 120 **Closed** 23–26 December **Prices from** S €7.50, M €23.50, D €9.50 **Parking** 150 **Notes** Vegetarian dishes, Children welcome

▶ COUNTY MEATH

DUNBOYNE
Dunboyne Castle Hotel & Spa
◉◉ MODERN EUROPEAN
01 8013500
www.dunboynecastlehotel.com

A Georgian rebuild following Cromwell's calamitous intervention in Ireland, Dunboyne, ancestral home of the Butler family, has fine plasterwork and ceiling frescoes to look out for as you head for the Ivy Restaurant, a contemporary space with smart linen and enticing, up-to-date country-house cooking.

Chef Ian Daly **Seats** 120 **Open** All year
Prices from S €7, M €19, D €8 **Parking** 360
Notes Vegetarian dishes, Children welcome

See advertisement opposite

ENFIELD
Fire & Salt
◉ MODERN IRISH
046 9540000 | The Johnstown Estate
www.thejohnstownestate.com

The main restaurant at the sporty Johnstown Estate Hotel & Spa, in this bright and airy steakhouse offers a variety of seating options. Although grass-fed, Irish-bred beef steaks cooked over charcoal on the grill are the main draw here, there are plenty of other options on the à la carte including local seafood.

Chef Val O'Kelly **Seats** 180, Private dining 30
Open All year **Prices from** S €9.95, M €22.95, D €7.50
Notes Vegetarian dishes, Children welcome

KILMESSAN
The Signal Restaurant
◉ MODERN IRISH
046 9025239 | The Station House Hotel
www.stationhousehotel.ie

In the heart of the stunning Boyne Valley Drive in County Meath, The Station House Hotel is set in its own attractive gardens and surrounded by beautiful countryside. Its rural location is reflected in the accomplished food served in the charming and elegant Signal Restaurant.

Chef Keith Hutton **Seats** 90, Private dining
Notes Children welcome

NAVAN
Bellinter House
◉◉ MODERN EUROPEAN V
046 9030900
www.bellinterhouse.com

A country-house hotel that is popular on the wedding scene, its interior combining period charm with 21st-century boutique glamour. Down in the vaulted basement there's a slick contemporary finish to the space and a menu to match. The kitchen's output is focused on regional produce.

Chef Francoise Herpin **Seats** 120, Private dining 20
Closed 24–25 December **Notes** Children welcome

SLANE
Conyngham Arms Hotel
◉ MODERN INTERNATIONAL
041 9884444 | Main Street
www.conynghamarms.ie

This 18th-century coaching inn is home to a smart brasserie-style restaurant offering straightforward food from breakfast through to dinner. There's a decent amount of Irish produce on the menu, including goods from the owners' bakery and coffee shop in the village.

Chef David Doyle **Seats** 35, Private dining 30 **Open** All year **Prices from** S €5.50, M €13, D €6 **Parking** 8
Notes Vegetarian dishes, Children welcome

Tankardstown – Brabazon Restaurant
◉◉ CLASSIC INTERNATIONAL
041 9824621
www.tankardstown.ie

In the restaurant situated in the one-time cow shed, expect a smart rustic finish with exposed stonework, a central fireplace and pretty terrace. The kitchen calls on the walled organic garden for supplies, and a smoker brings a potent aroma to proceedings.

Chef Jonas Sarkozy, Eoin Gilchrist **Seats** 70
Closed 3 days at Christmas **Prices from** S €7.50, M €19.50, D €7.50 **Notes** Vegetarian dishes, Children welcome

▶ COUNTY MONAGHAN

CARRICKMACROSS
Shirley Arms Hotel
◉ MODERN IRISH V
042 9673100 | Main Street
www.shirleyarmshotel.ie

The market town of Carrickmacross is home to this handsome stone-built hotel, once called White's, a name that lives on in its principal dining room, which is kitted out in checkered upholstery with wood dividers and big floral pictures. The style is modern Irish brasserie.

Chef Micheál Muldoon **Seats** 90, Private dining 150
Closed Good Friday, 25–26 December
Prices from S €5, M €15.50, D €6 **Parking** 150
Notes Children welcome

THE IVY RESTAURANT
AT DUNBOYNE CASTLE HOTEL & SPA
2 AA ROSETTE AWARD WINNING RESTAURANT

The IVY is about showcasing the best of modern cuisine through innovation and creativity. Our menus only feature ingredients from the finest local suppliers and are strongly influenced by our culinary team's shared passion for using first class produce. The IVY team dedicate their deep felt passion to ensure that you take away the best possible memories of your visit from start to finish, thanks to a perfect dining experience and the exquisite ritual of the service that goes with it. The IVY never fails to impress.

To make a reservation, contact +353 1 801 3500

Dunboyne Castle Hotel & Spa, Dunboyne, Co. Meath, A86 PW63.
T: +353 1 801 3500 | E: info@dunboynecastlehotel.com
www.dunboynecastlehotel.com

DUNBOYNE CASTLE
HOTEL & SPA

GLASLOUGH

Snaffles Restaurant

◎◎ TRADITIONAL IRISH, INTERNATIONAL

047 88100 | The Lodge, Castle Leslie Estate

www.castleleslie.com

The Castle Leslie Estate extends over 1,000 acres and boasts two plush bolt-holes – the Castle and the Lodge – operating as separate country-house hotels. The boutique-style Lodge comes with Snaffles, a stylish contemporary restaurant. The kitchen keeps its finger on the pulse.

Chef Andrew Bradley **Seats** 110, Private dining 50
Closed 24–27 December **Parking** 200
Notes Vegetarian dishes, Children welcome

▶ COUNTY ROSCOMMON

ROSCOMMON

Douglas Hyde Restaurant

◎◎ MODERN EUROPEAN V

071 9618000 | Ballyfarnon

www.kilronancastle.ie

Kilronan Castle lies at the top of a long driveway that wanders through an ancient forest, behind a set of medieval gates. Modern Irish country-house dishes make the most of superlative produce, served in the jewel of a dining room, named after Ireland's first president.

Chef David Porter **Seats** 80, Private dining 80
Open All year **Prices from** S €8.50, M €24.50, D €8.50
Parking 200 **Notes** Children welcome

See advertisement below

▶ COUNTY SLIGO

SLIGO

Radisson Blu Hotel & Spa Sligo

◎ MODERN IRISH

071 9140008 | Rosses Point Road, Ballincar

www.radissonblu.ie/sligo

A classy modern hotel designed with plenty of vivid colour, notably reds and purples in the Classiebawn dining room. Here, the bill of fare is contemporary Irish cooking of notable technical ambition. Why not try a deconstructed egg for starters?

Chef Joe Shannon **Seats** 120, Private dining 60
Open All year **Prices from** S €6, M €15, D €6.75
Parking 600 **Notes** Vegetarian dishes, Children welcome

Sligo Park Hotel & Leisure Club

MODERN IRISH

071 9190400 | Pearse Road
www.sligopark.com

Covering all the bases, Sligo Park's full-on leisure facilities and surrounding verdant countryside means there's plenty of opportunity to build up an appetite. The dining option is the Hazelwood Restaurant, which has a warm contemporary finish. The kitchen stays true to Irish produce.

Chef Chris Friel **Seats** 120 **Open** All year **Prices from** S €6.50, M €16, D €6.95 **Parking** 200 **Notes** Vegetarian dishes, Children welcome

COUNTY TIPPERARY

CLONMEL
Hotel Minella

TRADITIONAL **V**

052 6122388
www.hotelminella.com

The garden runs down to the banks of the River Suir and the Comeragh Mountains loom in the background – it's a charming spot. The restaurant is in the original Georgian house, so has plenty of character and a traditional, period feel.

Chef Christopher Bray **Seats** 120, Private dining 60 **Open** All year **Notes** Children welcome

COUNTY WATERFORD

ARDMORE
The House Restaurant

MODERN IRISH **V**

See page 466

WATERFORD
Bianconi Restaurant

TRADITIONAL IRISH

051 305555 | Granville Hotel, The Quay
www.granvillehotel.ie

Occupying pole position on Waterford's river quay, the Georgian Granville Hotel's genteel Bianconi Restaurant makes the most of those views over the River Suir and the marina from linen-clad tables beneath a coffered ceiling. The kitchen displays a feel for what's right on the plate.

Chef Stephen Hooper **Seats** 140, Private dining 36 **Closed** 25–26 December **Prices from** S €7.95, M €21.95, D €6.95 **Notes** Vegetarian dishes, Children welcome

Faithlegg House Hotel & Golf Resort

MODERN IRISH, FRENCH

051 382000 | Faithlegg,
www.faithlegg.com

The original mansion was built in the 1780s and is immaculately restored, while the high-ceilinged restaurant overlooks the garden from what was a pair of drawing rooms. The cooking is based on native produce and a range of neat ideas really make an impact.

Chef Jenny Flynn **Seats** 86, Private dining 50 **Closed** 25 December **Prices from** S €4.65, M €30, D €6.55 **Parking** 120 **Notes** Vegetarian dishes, Children welcome

The Munster Room Restaurant

IRISH, INTERNATIONAL **V**

051 878203 | Waterford Castle Hotel, The Island
www.waterfordcastleresort.com

With its dark oak panelling, intricate plasterwork ceiling and ancestral portraits, The Munster Room is exactly what you'd expect from the dining room of a luxe hotel set on its own private 300-acre island. It's a jacket-and-tie affair with a pianist adding to the ambience.

Chef Stan Cicon **Seats** 60, Private dining 24 **Closed** some days in winter

COUNTY WEXFORD

GOREY
Amber Springs Hotel

IRISH

053 9484000 | Wexford Road
www.amberspringshotel.ie

A modern hotel with a spa and host of dining opportunities, the Farm Steakhouse makes perfect sense given that the owners keep several hundred head of Angus cattle on their nearby farm. It's a smart dining room done out in dark, moody shades.

Chef William Miller **Seats** Private dining 80

Ashdown Park Hotel

IRISH, INTERNATIONAL

053 9480500 | Station Road
www.ashdownparkhotel.com

This modern hotel on a grand scale, within walking distance of Gorey, has 22 acres of grounds to explore before a trip to its Rowan Tree Restaurant. Here tables are dressed up in crisp white linen, and the kitchen turns out pleasingly straightforward dishes.

Chef Val Murphy **Seats** 120, Private dining 120 **Closed** 24–26 December, Winter and Spring open weekends only **Prices from** S €6.95, M €18.95, D €7.50 **Parking** 150 **Notes** Vegetarian dishes

ARDMORE
The House Restaurant
◉◉◉◉ MODERN IRISH **V**
024 87800 | Cliff House Hotel
www.cliffhousehotel.ie

Bayside seats for contemporary Irish cooking

Full-drop picture windows and a marine blue carpet are intuitive features of The House Restaurant, where executive chef Martijn Kajuiter uses Irish produce with a comprehensive range of modern technique, backed up the kitchen garden. A five-course tasting menu, drawn from the carte, is bookended by trios of canapés and desserts for the complete performance. Textural counterpoints are the hallmark of a contemporary classic starter of west Cork scallop with ham, black garlic, Avruga caviar, and spiky, briny codium seaweed. Equally impressive is a main course of crisp-skinned guinea fowl with three-cornered leek and its flowers, earthy morels, and a smoky barbecue jus. Fish could be sea bass with brown shrimp ravioli in a vivid saffron butter sauce, and the tripartite sweet finale comprises glossy organic chocolate with apricot and olive oil, sea buckthorn cream and rice with meringue shards, and a popcorn-garnished nougatine parfait with rhubarb.

Chef Martijn Kajuiter, Stephen Hayes **Seats** 64, Private dining 20 **Closed** 24–26 December **Parking** 30 **Notes** Children welcome

GOREY *continued*

Clonganny House

◎◎ CONTEMPORARY IRISH, FRENCH

053 9482111 | Ballygarrett

www.clonganny.com

A handsome creeper-covered Georgian house at the end of a tree-lined drive, Cloganny has a refined, traditional interior. The highly experienced French chef-patron cooks with confidence and delivers a classically inspired repertoire via a bilingual carte. Kick off with drinks and canapés in the drawing room.

Chef Phillipe Brillant **Seats** 20 **Open** All year **Parking** 12 **Notes** Vegetarian dishes, No children

Marlfield House Hotel

◎◎ CLASSIC

053 9421124 | Courtown Road

www.marlfieldhouse.com

This opulent Regency home is now a smart and luxurious hotel whose dining room consists of several handsomely decorated spaces, leading into an impressive conservatory. Huge windows open onto the immaculate garden. The kitchen garden delivers first-rate seasonal produce.

Chef Ruadhan Furlong **Seats** 80, Private dining 50 **Closed** Christmas **Parking** 100 **Notes** Vegetarian dishes, No children under 8 years at dinner

Seafield Hotel & Spa Resort

◎◎ MODERN IRISH, FRENCH

053 9424000 | Ballymoney

www.seafieldhotel.com

We've Italian designers to thank for the super-cool finish within this luxe spa and golf hotel on the cliffs. The high-end finish extends to the restaurant, where a huge bronze female centaur keeps watch, lighting and music are soft, and the decor is cool black.

Chef Susan Leacy (Executive Head Chef), Raman Kumar (Head Chef) **Seats** 90, Private dining 40 **Closed** Christmas **Parking** 100 **Notes** Vegetarian dishes, Children welcome

ROSSLARE
Beaches Restaurant at Kelly's Resort Hotel

◎◎ TRADITIONAL EUROPEAN

053 9132114

www.kellys.ie

Beaches restaurant sits on the golden sands in Rosslare, and is set up to capitalise on the views, bathed in light through good-sized windows, and with restful pastel hues, white linen on the tables, and a mini gallery of original artworks on the walls. The kitchen lets the quality of local produce do the talking in simple contemporary dishes.

Chef Eugene Callaglan **Seats** 200, Private dining 40 **Closed** mid December to mid February **Parking** 150 **Notes** Vegetarian dishes, Children welcome

La Marine Bistro

◎ MODERN FRENCH **V**

053 9132114 | Kelly's Resort Hotel & Spa

www.kellys.ie

The more casual stand-alone restaurant of Kelly's Resort Hotel is an easy-going venue with an open kitchen. The shipshape French bistro theme suits the beachside setting, as does its menu. Top-class fish and seafood comes a short way from Kilmore Quay.

Chef Ronan Dunne **Seats** 70, Private dining 40 **Closed** mid December to February **Parking** 150 **Notes** Children welcome

WEXFORD
Aldridge Lodge Restaurant and Guest Accommodation

◎◎ MODERN IRISH **V**

051 389116 | Duncannon

www.aldridgelodge.com

With its fashionably pared-back looks – wood floors, bare tables and black high-backed seats – chef-patron Billy Whitty's restaurant with rooms achieves a stylish informality. It has also become something of a hot spot on the local foodie scene thanks to its sharply executed dishes.

Chef Billy Whitty **Seats** 37 **Closed** 1st week January and 1st week May **Parking** 30 **Notes** Children welcome

Reeds Restaurant at Ferrycarrig Hotel

◎◎ MODERN IRISH

053 9120999 | Ferrycarrig

www.ferrycarrighotel.ie

In an absolutely stunning location overlooking the River Slaney as it meanders towards Wexford town, Reeds Restaurant makes the most of the views from its huge picture windows. The atmosphere in the stylish, contemporary dining room is laid back and relaxed.

Chef Tony Carty **Seats** 100 **Open** All year **Parking** 200 **Notes** Vegetarian dishes, Children welcome

COUNTY WICKLOW

COUNTY WICKLOW

BLESSINGTON
Lime Tree Restaurant
◉ MODERN IRISH
045 867 600
www.tulfarrishotel.com

Part of the Tulfarris Hotel and Golf Resort, the first-floor restaurant offers panoramic views towards the Blessington Lakes. The cooking uses intelligent combinations of quality ingredients, whether it's delicious pork belly from Tipperary or fresh fish off the boats in Howth.

Chef Eddie McDermott, Igor Buturla **Seats** 80, Private dining 50 **Open** All year **Parking** 150 **Notes** Vegetarian dishes, Children welcome

DELGANY
Glenview Hotel
◉◉ MODERN IRISH, EUROPEAN V
01 2873399 | Glen o' the Downs
www.glenviewhotel.ie

The Woodlands Restaurant at this hotel is on the first floor to maximise the view over the Glen o' the Downs, with arched windows looking down the valley. Inside, all is soothing pastels and sparkling glassware. The style is what is loosely termed modern Irish.

Chef Sandeep Pandy **Seats** 80, Private dining 36 **Open** All year **Prices from** S €6.95, M €27.50, D €7.95 **Parking** 150 **Notes** Children welcome

ENNISKERRY
Powerscourt Hotel
◉◉ MODERN EUROPEAN V
01 2748888 | Powerscourt Estate
www.powerscourthotel.com

With a sweeping Palladian mansion at its heart, the Powerscourt resort has two golf courses, a luxurious spa and an Irish pub, but the main event food-wise is the glamorous Sika Restaurant. There are glorious mountain views from its third-floor dining room.

Chef Peter Byrne **Seats** 140, Private dining 24 **Open** All year **Parking** 214 **Notes** Children welcome

MACREDDIN
BrookLodge & Macreddin Village
◉◉ MODERN IRISH, ORGANIC
0402 36444
www.brooklodge.com

This luxurious country-house hotel is the heart of purpose-built Macreddin Village. The Strawberry Tree is its blue-riband dinner option in an opulent setting. Being Ireland's first certified organic restaurant, provenance of seasonal ingredients is king, with herbs and fruit grown in the Village's walled garden.

Chef Evan Doyle, James Kavanagh **Seats** 120, Private dining 50 **Closed** 24–26 December **Prices from** S €12, M €36, D €10 **Parking** 200 **Notes** Vegetarian dishes, Children welcome

See advertisement opposite

NEWTOWNMOUNTKENNEDY
Druids Glen Hotel & Golf Resort
◉◉ MODERN EUROPEAN V
01 2870800 |
www.druidsglenresort.com

Druids Glen boasts the full package of spa, golf and leisure facilities with the Wicklow hills thrown in as a backdrop. Stylishly decorated in muted hues, with a feature fire set in a huge granite hearth, the main dining room is Hugo's Restaurant.

Chef Anthony Duggan **Seats** 170, Private dining 22 **Open** All year **Prices from** S €11.50, M €25, D €8.50 **Parking** 400 **Notes** Children welcome

RATHNEW
Hunter's Hotel
◉ TRADITIONAL IRISH, FRENCH
0404 40106 | Newrath Bridge,
www.hunters.ie

Barely half an hour from the Dun Laoghaire ferry, Ireland's oldest coaching inn sits in riotously colourful gardens, its dining room a vision of crisp linen, mahogany and fine living. Expect daily changing menus; you might be tempted by a selection of Ireland's latest artisan cheeses.

Chef Mark Barry **Seats** 54, Private dining 30 **Closed** 3 days Christmas **Parking** 30 **Notes** Children welcome

Tinakilly Country House
◉◉ MODERN IRISH
0404 69274
www.tinakilly.ie

A distinguished Italianate Victorian mansion is the diverting setting for the modernised country-house cooking. The timing and seasoning of dishes does them justice, as does an opening pairing of scallops and the famous Clonakilty black pudding from County Cork, with butternut purée and pea shoots.

Chef Pete Murphy **Seats** 80 **Closed** 24–26 and 31 December, 1–2 January **Notes** Children welcome

GIBRALTAR

GIBRALTAR
Nunos
◉◉ ITALIAN, MEDITERRANEAN
00 350 200 76501 | Caleta Hotel, Sir Herbert Miles Road, GX11 1AA
www.caletahotel.com

Nunos Restaurant at the Caleta has a fine-dining air and a stand-alone restaurant vibe, thanks to slick London-style service and Italian cooking. An open-to-view kitchen offers all the theatre of chefs on show. The menu is typically extensive, the colourful, modern-European approach intelligently uncomplicated.

Chef Martin Tomas **Seats** 72 **Open** All year
Prices from S £6, M £13.50, D £6.50 **Parking** 17
Notes Vegetarian dishes, Children welcome

The Rock
◉ MODERN MEDITERRANEAN
00 350 200 73000 | Europa Road, GX11 1AA
www.rockhotelgibraltar.com

Since it opened in 1932 this iconic hotel has attracted notable guests, including Winston Churchill, and John Lennon and Yoko Ono who stayed here when they married in Gibraltar. The restaurant's wisteria-clad terrace is a draw in itself, while the modern Mediterranean food is classy and interesting.

Chef Adam Soto-Robles **Open** All year

Sunborn Yacht Hotel
◉◉ MEDITERRANEAN
00 350 2001 6000 | Ocean Village, GX11 1AA
www.sunbornyacht.com/gibraltar

Located on a luxurious floating hotel moored in Gibraltar's Ocean Village Marina, this is a rooftop restaurant that offers a contemporary dining experience with views out to sea or overlooking Gibraltar itself. A wrap-around deck offers pleasant alfresco dining.

Chef Mirko Scarabello **Open** All year

INDEX

INDEX

INDEX

INDEX

INDEX

INDEX

INDEX